Legal Practice Companion

בס"ד

'A woman of valour - who can find one?
Her value is far beyond pearls'

Book of Proverbs (Mishlei), Ch.31, v.10

I thank G'd every day that He has given me the merit to find one.
This book is for my amazing wife. Dani - for you.

'There are three partners in man -
The L'rd (Blessed be He), his [the man's] father and his mother.'

Babylonian Talmud, Tractate Niddah 31a

I thank them all. I owe all that has been achieved to them.

M.W.

Legal Practice Companion

Gerald Montagu
BA (Hons), MA, Solicitor

Mark Weston
LLB (Hons), Solicitor

Foreword to the
Legal Practice Companion and the
Companion series

The Right Honourable Lord Woolf
Lord Chief Justice

Foreword to the
Legal Practice Companion

The Honourable Mr Justice Lightman

Published by
Blackstone Press Limited
Aldine Place
London
W12 8AA
United Kingdom

Sales enquiries and orders
Telephone +44-(0)-20-8740-2277
Facsimile +44-(0)-20-8743-2292
e-mail: sales@blackstone.demon.co.uk
website: www.blackstonepress.com

ISBN 1-84174-239-2

Fourth edition 1998
Fifth edition 1999
Sixth edition 2000
Seventh edition 2001

Previous editions of this work were published by CLT Professional Publishing

British Library Catologuing in Publication Data.
A catalogue record for this book is available from the British Library

Printed and bound in Great Britain by Ashford Colour Press Ltd, Gosport, Hampshire

Foreword to the *Legal Practice Companion*

The *Legal Practice Companion* is intended as a companion, friend and guide to the student and newly qualified practitioner. Its purpose is achieved with distinction. This work sets out the principles of substantive law in the areas where the reader will need to tread; and civil procedure can no longer be a mystery to those who have this book at hand. The quality of the contents and the clarity of thought and presentation combine to enable the authors, in one volume, to provide a map and a guided tour of legal practice today. Seasoned practitioners will find it valuable to have at their elbows such an up-to-date and reliable summary, and most certainly the *Legal Practice Companion* will occupy a place on my bookshelf.

The Honourable Mr Justice Lightman

Foreword to the *Companions*

I am wholly in favour of the *Companions*. Legal text books are not often to the fore when it comes to presenting legal information in an attractive, readily understandable and digestible form. However, this is exactly what the *Companions* achieve. The law is becoming ever more complex and there is undoubtedly a need to find new methods of communicating it to those who need to know, whether they be members of the public, law students, practitioners or for that matter judges. They will all find that it is a great advantage to have access to a *Companion*.

This is why the first volume in the series, *The Legal Practice Companion* (LPC) has proved to be a success. It is now in its seventh edition, having been first published in 1995. The *Intellectual Property and Media Law Companion,* the *Corporate Finance Companion* and the *Banking and Capital Markets Companion* are worthy successors to the first volume, LPC.

Some of the subjects which are now dealt with by the *Companions* are not ones with which I am particularly familiar and so I was able to find out for myself in practice whether they work. I can assure the potential reader that they do work as far as I am concerned and that they are very user friendly. The very clear method of presentation both provided an overview of the subject and a step by step guide. I am not surprised to learn that it is intended in due course to provide the text of the *Companions* on a CD -ROM. I feel confident that they will translate well to this format since their present style will be very familiar to regular users of information technology.

My enthusiasm for the *Companions* is in part because they complement the reforms I have recommended for civil procedure and which I hope will make our Civil Justice System an appropriate one for this new millennium. I am very conscious that a weakness of the reforms is that in general they were confined to procedural law and left substantive law intact and in a state which means that in the majority of areas it is impenetrable to those to whom it is unfamiliar. This creates a real impediment to access to justice. The virtue of the *Companions* is that they provide a clear path through what is so often a jungle. While the *Companions* will usually provide all that the reader requires, when this is not the case they will be a solid base from which to embark on a more detailed investigation of the tangled undergrowth of the law.

That I find the *Companions* refreshing is no doubt due to the fact that the authors are (by judicial standards) younger and obviously very bright. Having been schooled in the law and practice in more recent times, they know the needs of others in their position and how the existing texts do not always meet those needs. They have decided that something can and should be done to provide a solution. LPC was the start and there now follow the *Companions*. They deserve to succeed and I believe that they will succeed in meeting that need. I congratulate the team on their initiative and on what they are achieving and I look forward to the growth of the *Companions* into a complete series.

The Right Honourable, Lord Woolf

Lord Chief Justice

Introduction

Welcome to the *Legal Practice Companion*!

To the Practitioner

This book aims to help provide a guide to law and practice beyond your areas of specialisation. It sets out the context, general 'feel' and basic concepts of an area of law. Its purpose is to serve as a prelude to detailed research. The numerous references aid 'mapping out' research, before clients are given more considered advice based on that research.

The book is intended to provide an *overview* for the practitioner. It is *not* comprehensive - there are numerous specialist works on particular topics that are intended for that purpose. For example, the demands of converting highly complex statutes into digestible points have forced us to focus on those points that seem most relevant. When giving advice, original sources should *always* be checked. For example, we set out in the criminal sections the law applying to adults only and without taking into account the special provisions for sexual offences.

Meeting the needs of practitioners has required an original approach. After discussions with solicitors and trainees, we have evolved a novel format that represents something of a departure for legal publishing. This is reflected in both the choice of material and its presentation.

In this book:

1. procedures are often broken down into steps or flowcharts, so that they can easily be followed.
2. the law is set out schematically and areas are linked together as appropriate. For example, the *Business* section gives an integrated overview of the legal framework within which businesses operate, dealing with corporate governance, employment, and commercial agreements.
3. all this is packaged in one convenient volume. Therefore, for example, the conveyancer will find an outline of the possible tax treatment of the transaction a few pages away - the importance of which has been highlighted by Lightman J.'s judgment in *Hurlingham Estates Ltd v. Wilde & Partners* [1997] STC 627).
4. this book also flags statutes which have received Royal Assent (or will shortly receive it), which are not yet in force but are awaiting orders to bring them into force. This should help maintain an awareness of how the law *will* work (as well as how it *does* work).

We believe that this book will become a valued tool - a trusty companion for the practitioner who will, we hope, keep a copy within reach of his or her desk.

Introduction

Welcome to the *Legal Practice Companion*!

To the Student

With the advent of the **Legal Practice Course,** the worlds of work and law school have moved closer together than ever before. This volume is intended to help in both.

The information required for the compulsory topics and the pervasive topics on the LPC (under the Law Society's *Legal Practice Course Board's Written Standards*) is presented here in one volume. After you complete the course, the source references to lay the basis for your research in practice are included in a format which will quickly become familiar.

Other books and materials usually contain unwieldy blocks of text, which are often split over numerous pages and volumes. This often hinders grasping masses of information which appears unconnected and unclear. The *Legal Practice Companion* breaks new ground by presenting the relevant law and practice in a step by step format - it is all in one volume, and frequently one topic is presented per page. Charts, flow charts and summaries provide an accessible, clear and straightforward overview of modern legal practice. Please note that the book does assume some prior knowledge and comprehension of basic concepts - it is aimed at students undertaking a Legal Practice Course, or equivalent professional examinations. The *Legal Practice Companion,* for example, will not define a shelf company or an either way offence, but it will tell you what to do with respect to them and the procedures that apply to them.

This book is intended:

1. to explain complex parts of the course that you have already covered.
2. to provide a breakdown (aiding comprehension) for parts of the course that you are about to tackle.
3. to present an area of law coherently in one place (for example, taxation and conduct are grouped in their own sections).
4. to split topics up so that they appear where they fit best (such as EU law in *Business*).

For you, the student, this book is intended to cover all that you need for your courses, and to help you beyond into the world of work. No doubt your annotations will soon cover the pages and this is entirely suitable and to be encouraged. For those of you who can take books into examinations, this presentation of the course, together with your annotations, will be invaluable in helping you pass your exams.

Acknowledgements

Access to ... the law ... and to justice

In 1995, the *Legal Practice Companion* was launched into the stormy debate over legal education. Since then, some 20,000 copies have been sold. With Lord Woolf's civil justice reforms now well entrenched we hope that regular users of this book have found the civil litigation section useful. With ever more rapid change in the law and with the increasing demands of clients, we suspect that more rough seas are ahead. We hope to continue to tackle those seas and this has been possible so far due to the many who deserve our thanks. We start by thanking our readers, the Lord Chief Justice and Mr Justice Lightman for their whole-hearted support and encouragement.

More new *Companions* on the way...

The *Corporate Finance Companion* and the *Intellectual Property and Media Law Companion* have already achieved success in their own right. A second edition of the *Banking and Capital Markets Companion* and the *Employment Law Companion* are in preparation. The *Companions* continue to meet what, judging from the response, is a very real need both in the legal profession and further afield. Our thanks go to all at Blackstone and in particular to Alistair MacQueen, David Stott, Ruth Phillips and Moira Greenhalgh. They have have never let us forget that publishing should be, and can be, fun.

Behind the scenes ...

We would like to thank those in the Tax Group at Clifford Chance's London office including Michelle Burns (for practical, efficient, and always cheerful sanity), Peter Elliott (for much else), Mark Persoff and Clare McMath (for, respectively, a sharp journalistic eye and some accounting lore), to Vanessa Marsland a Partner in Clifford Chance's Intellectual Property Department (for kind advice as to where a hephalump trap might have lain) and also to summer students Jenny McIvor and Sara McLeish. Thanks go to Eugenia Dunn at Baker & McKenzie for developments in employment law. Many thanks also go to Mark's wife, Daniella, for her proof reading, RSI-busting typing and her continual support and madness at putting up with it all.

No *Legal Practice Companion* would be complete without mentioning Gill Zeiner who developed the original typeset for our approach many moons and editions ago.

We hope that readers will continue to write to us at our firms with suggestions on how the *Legal Practice Companion* can become even more helpful.

Without which ...

And of course, many thanks to our families and friends who put up with us during the writing process and to anyone inadvertantly missing ...

The law ...

We have tried to reflect changes until going to press, but the law is generally as stated at 15 June 2001.

Gerald Montagu and Mark Weston,

London and Chicago, 8 July 2001.

Preface

In the legal profession, as in most careers, there is no substitute for experience. However, the Legal Practice Course helps bridge the gap between the academic study of law and the cut and thrust of practice as a solicitor. The ever-growing number of *Legal Practice Companions* we see on the shelves of junior lawyers reflects the popularity of this work as a useful tool for students and practitioners.

The *Legal Practice Companion* is written by two authors who share their own expertise in law and teaching, and who have aggregated the experiences of others who have recently successfully tackled the demands and pitfalls of the Legal Practice Course. In addition, they are able to apply their experience as solicitors in the London offices of the two largest international law firms in the world.

The combination of knowledge of the Legal Practice Course and the demands of actual practice have been distilled into a well-presented, concise, and user-friendly work. It should prove an invaluable aid to those on the Legal Practice Course and a useful reference guide when starting the practice of law.

On behalf of the partners of *Baker & McKenzie* and *Clifford Chance,* we, together with Lord Woolf and Mister Justice Lightman, are sure that the *Legal Practice Companion* and the whole *Companion* series will continue to build on their already long-established success and will aid you in your career in the law.

Paul Rawlinson
Graduate Recruitment Partner
Baker & McKenzie

Julia Clarke
Graduate Recruitment Partner
Clifford Chance LLP

'Many rough and cragged by-ways have been ... trodden towards the intricate problems of the Law's mysteries, but no foot-path ... [has been] plainley beaten, so that anyone could ... find the way without being subject to any Aberrations [and which] should safely conduct the Zealous Pilgrim through the sullen deserts, and over the craggy precipicies of this Herculean voyage.'

Compleat Solicitor (London, 1668)

Contents

Conduct

Accounts

Taxation

Wills, probate and administration

Conveyancing

Business

Civil Litigation

Criminal Litigation

Appendix and Index

Boxes, conventions and update

I Boxes

Legal points and principles

- ➤ Square boxes contain information relating to a specific area of law or legal principle.

Practice points and principles

- ➤ Round boxes contain information relating to information that is useful in practice.

II Legislative citations and update

➤ At the time of going to press, certain legislation covered in this book awaits an order from a Minister before it comes into force (this is dependent on the drafting and approval of secondary legislation and/or regulatory codes).

- The *Financial Services and Markets Act 2000* comes into force on days to be appointed.
  - We understand from the Treasury that the *FSA 1986* will be repealed and the Financial Services Authority will assume its regulatory powers under the *FSMA 2000* at midnight on 30 November 2001.
  - The draft *Solicitors Financial Services (Scope) Rules 2001* published in the Law Society Gazette on 1 June 2001 has been used in the preparation of this book, the final rules are expected to be approved by the Master of the Rolls during July 2001 when this book is in press and will come into force at midnight on 30 November 2001.
- Provisions of various Acts relating to criminal justice which are referred to in the Criminal Litigation section will come into force on days to be appointed.
- The text in this book was prepared using the 24th amendment to the *CPR.* Elements of *CPR*, as amended by that amendment, do not come into force until 15 October 2001; the text states the rules set out in the 24th amendment as the rules will be in force on 15 October 2001.
- The *Homes Bill* and the *Commonhold and Leasehold Reform Bill* failed to complete their parliamentary passage before the General Election was called (for the position at the time of going to press, see p.225).

➤ For an overview of the Queen's Speech on 20 June 2001 and the *Land Registration Bill*, see pp.xvi-xvii.

The Queen's Speech, 20 June 2001

➤ The legislative programme for the 2001/2002 session of Parliament was outlined in the Queen's speech delivered on 20 June 2001. In relation to the topics covered in this book, the likely significance of the measures announced by the Queen included:

- ◆ *Land Registration Bill*
  - to repeal the *LRA 1925* and introduce faster, simpler and clearer arrangements.
  - to introduce all-electronic system for dealing with registered land.
  - to improve the security of property rights in and over registered land.
  - to establish a more accurate register offering more certainty and information as to the of an owner of registered land's rights and responsibilities .
  - NB: no reference was made to the reintroduction of the *Homes Bill.*
- ◆ *Commonhold and Leasehold Reform Bill*

  this Bill would be reintroduced (the reintroduced Bill received its 2nd reading in July 2001).
- ◆ *Enterprise Bill*

  Insolvency
  - to reduce the period of personal bankruptcy and abolish certain stigmatising features of personal bankruptcy.
  - to abolish Crown preference.
  - to restrict, or abolish, the ability of a creditor to appoint an administrative receiver.
  - to strengthen provisions relating to irresponsible or dishonest bankruptcy.

  Competition
  - to strengthen the independance and influence of the Office of Fair trading (and remove ministerial involvement from almost all merger decisions).`
  - to assess mergers by reference to a competition based test (rather than the current 'public interest' test'.
  - to strengthen penalities for anti-competitive behaviour (possibly imposing criminal penalities upon directors involved in cartels.
- ◆ *Criminal Justice Bill*
  - to implement aspects of the Sentencing Review (announced by the Home Secretary in May 2000 to review the legal framework for sentencing and its impact on reoffending).
  - to revise the 'double jeopardy' rule (so that a retrial for murder is possible, after an acquital, if there is compelling new evidence).
  - to modernise and reform aspects of criminal law (including the law of evidence).
  - to strengthen registration requirements under the *Sex Offenders Act.*
  - to create a single offence of corruption and reform the law to comply with the OECD Convention on Combating Bribery of Foreign Public Officials in Business Transactions.
- ◆ There will also be a draft *Criminal Justice (Reform) Bill* to address Lord Justice Auld's review of the criminal court system.

Land Registration Bill

➤ The *Land Registration Bill*, amongst other things:

- continues to provide for a register of title to estates in land and explain what interests can be the subject of registration (*Part 1*).
- specifies who is entitled to apply voluntarily for first registration of title (*Part 2*).
  - A lease with more than 7 years (rather than 21 years) unexpired may be registered (*cl.3(3)*).
- defines when an application for registration must be made, on whom the duty lies and the consequences of failing to apply for registration (*Part 2*).
- defines the classes of registered title which may be registered and the effects of registration (*Part 2*).
  - The Bill sets out unregistered interests which override first registration (*Sch.1*) and unregistered interests which override registered dispositions (*Sch.3*). According to the Explanatory Notes to the Bill, the list of such interests will be reduced in scope: categories will be narrowed, abolished and phased out over a 10 year period.
- provides for cautions against first registration (*Part 2*).
- defines the powers of an owner of registered land, and who can exercise these powers (*Part 3*).
  - Charge certificates are abolished and the importance of land certificates reduced; the registered owner is presumed to have unrestricted powers of disposition in the absence of any register entry.
- protects disponees from the effect of limits on powers which are not the subject of an entry in the register (*Part 3*).
- defines which dispositions of registered land must be registered (*Part 3*).
- lays down rules for the effect of dispositions on the priorty of interests effecting registered land (*Part 3*).
  - The priority of an interest affecting a registered estate or charge is not affected by a disposition (even if a disposition is registered): priority is determined by the date of creation (NB: under electronic conveyancing creation and registration will be simultaneous) (*cls.28-30*).
- provides for third party rights against registered titles by means of notices and restrictions (*Part 4*) ('Cautions' are to be abolished, subject to transitional rules in *Sch.12*).
- provides for the priority of charges on registered land and the powers and duties of chargees (*Part 5*).
- deals generally with the register, its alteration, public access to it, priorty periods during which the rights of intending buyers can be protected (*Part 6*).
- enables dispostions with connection to a land registration to be made by means of documents in electronic form (*Part 8*).
  - A document which makes provision for the time and date when it takes effect, has a certified electronic signature of each person by who it purports to be authenticated and satisfies any other conditions which rules provide for is regarded as a deed (*cl.91*).
- enables registration to be a made a pre-condition to effect dispositions of registered land or other interests which are the subject of a notice on the register (*Part 8*).
- to provide circumstances in which conveyancers may be required to use electronic means to complete and register transactions simultaneously (*Part 8*).
  - It is envisaged that completion and registration will take place simultaneously by electronic entry on the register. The Land Registry will control electronic access to the register.
- introduces a new regime dealing with adverse possession (*Part 9*).

Table of abbreviations

Statutes

A

AA 1870	Apportionment Act 1870.
AA 1976	Adoption Act 1976.
AA 1996	Arbitration Act 1996.
AEA 1925	Administration of Estates Act 1925.
AEA 1971	Administration of Estates Act 1971.
AE(SP)A 1965	Administration of Estates (Small Payments) Act 1965.
AIA 1996	Asylum and Immigration Act 1996.
AJA 1920	Administration of Justice Act 1920.
AJA 1952	Administration of Justice Act 1952.
AJA 1969	Administratiion of Justice Act 1969.
AJA 1982	Administration of Justice Act 1982.
AJA 1985	Administratiion of Justice Act 1985.
AJA 1999	Access to Justice Act 1999.
AtEA 1971	Attachment of Earnings Act 1971.

B

BA 1976	Bail Act 1976.
BA 1987	Banking Act 1987.
B(A)A 1993	Bail (Amendment) Act 1993.
BEA 1998	Bank of England Act 1998.
BNA 1985	Business Names Act 1985.
BSA 1986	Building Societies Act 1986.

C

CA	Companies Act 1985.
CA 1989	Companies Act 1989.
ChA 1989	Children Act 1989.
CA 1992	Charities Act 1992.
CA 1998	Competition Act 1998.
CAA 1968	Criminal Appeal Act 1968.
CAA 1995	Criminal Appeal Act 1995.
CAA 2001	Capital Allowances Act 2001.
CBN(CC) A 1999	Company and Business Names (Chamber of Commerce Etc.) Act 1999.
CCA 1974	Consumer Credit Act 1974.
CCA 1984	County Courts Act 1984.
CrDA 1971	Criminal Damage Act 1971.
CDA 1998	Crime and Disorder Act 1998.
CDDA 1986	Company Directors Disqualification Act 1986.
CEA 1898	Criminal Evidence Act 1898.
CEA 1968	Civil Evidence Act 1968.
CEA 1972	Civil Evidence Act 1972.
CEA 1995	Civil Evidence Act 1995.
CE(A)A 1997	Criminal Evidence (Amendment) Act 1997.
CHLRB	Commonhold and Leasehold Reform Bill.
CICA 1995	Criminal Injuries Compensation Act 1995.
CJA 1967	Criminal Justice Act 1967.
CJA 1987	Criminal Justice Act 1987.
CJA 1988	Criminal Justice Act 1988.
CJA 1991	Criminal Justice Act 1991.
CJCSA 2000	Criminal Justice and Courts Services Act 2000.
CJJA 1982	Civil Jurisdiction and Judgments Act 1982.
CJJA 1991	Civil Jurisdiction and Judgments Act 1991.
CJPA 2001	Criminal Justice and Police Act 2001.
CJPO 1994	Criminal Justice Public Order Act 1994.
CL(C)A 1978	Civil Liability (Contribution) Act 1978.
CLSA 1990	Courts and Legal Services Act 1990.
COA 1979	Charging Orders Act 1979.
CPA 1865	Criminal Procedure Act 1865.
CPA 1987	Consumer Protection Act 1987.
CPA 1997	Civil Procedure Act 1997.
CP(AW)A 1965	Criminal Procedure (Attendance of Witnesses) Act 1965.

CPIA 1996	Criminal Procedure and Investigations Act 1996.
C(S)A 1997	Crime (Sentences) Act 1997.
C(ROTP)A 1999	Contracts (Rights of Third Parties) Act 1999.

D

DDA 1995	Disability Discrimination Act 1995.

E

EA 1851	Evidence Act 1851.
EA 1989	Electricity Act 1989.
EEA 1979	Estate Agents Act 1979.
EPA 1970	Equal Pay Act 1970.
EPA 1990	Enviromental Protection Act 1990.
EPAA 1985	Enduring Powers of Attorney Act 1985.
ERA 1996	Employment Rights Act 1996.
ERA 1999	Employment Relations Act 1999.

F

FAA 1976	Fatal Accidents Act 1976.
FA 1930	Finance Act 1930.
FA 1931	Finance Act 1931.
FA 1942	Finance Act 1942.
FA 1971	Finance Act 1971.
FA 1985	Finance Act 1985.
FA 1986	Finance Act 1986.
FA 1989	Finance Act 1989.
FA 1990	Finance Act 1990.
FA 1993	Finance Act 1993.
FA 1994	Finance Act 1994.
FA 1995	Finance Act 1995.
FA 1996	Finance Act 1996.
FA 1997	Finance Act 1997.
FA 1998	Finance Act 1998.
FA 1999	Finance Act 1999.
FA 2000	Finance Act 2000.
FA 2001	Finance Act 2001.
F(No.2)A 1992	Finance (No.2)A 1992.
F(No.2)A 1997	Finance (No.2)A 1997.
FJ(RE)A 1933	Foreign Judgments (Reciprocal Enforcement) Act 1933.
FLA 1996	Family Law Act 1996.
FLRA 1969	Family Law Reform Act 1969.
FLRA 1987	Family Law Reform Act 1987.
FSA 1986	Financial Services Act 1986.
FSMA 2000	Financial Services and Markets Act 2000.

G

H

HA 1957	Homicide Act 1957.
HA 1980	Highways Act 1980.
HA 1985	Housing Act 1985.
HA 1988	Housing Act 1988.
HA 1996	Housing Act 1996.
HB	Homes Bill.
HPA 1964	Hire Purchase Act 1964.
HRA 1998	Human Rights Act 1998.
HSSA 1983	Health and Social Security Administration Act 1983.
HSWA 1974	Health and Safety at Work Act 1974.

I

IA 1978	Interpretation Act 1978.
IA	Insolvency Act 1986.
IA 1994	Insolvency Act 1994.
I(No2)A 1994	Insolvency (No2) Act 1994.
IEA 1952	Intestates' Estates Act 1952.
IHTA 1984	Inheritance Tax Act 1984.
IOA 1968	International Organisations Act 1968.
IOA 1981	International Organisations Act 1981.
I(PFD)A 1975	Inheritance (Provision for Family and Dependants) Act 1975.

J

JA 1838	Judgments Act 1838.
JA 1974	Juries Act 1974.

K

L

LA 1976	Legitimacy Act 1976.
LA 1980	Limitation Act 1980.
LD(A)A 1888	Law of Distress (Amendment) Act 1888.
LLCA 1975	Local Land Charges Act 1975.
LPA	Law of Property Act 1925.
LPA 1969	Law of Property Act 1969.
LPA 2000	Limited Partnership Act 2000.
LPCD(I)A 1998	Late Payment of Commercial Debts (Interest) Act 1998.
LP(JT)A 1964	Law of Property (Joint Tenants) Act 1964.
LP(MP)A 1989	Law of Property (Miscellaneous Provisions) Act 1989.
LP(MP)A 1994	Law of Property (Miscellaneous Provisions) Act 1994.
LP(R)A 1938	Leasehold Property (Repairs) Act 1938.

LRA	Land Registration Act 1925.
LRA 1967	Leasehold Reform Act 1967.
LRA 1997	Land Registration Act 1997.
LRB	Land Registration Bill.
LR(CN)A 1945	Law Reform (Contributory Negligence) Act 1945.
LRHUDA 1993	Leasehold Reform Housing and Urban Development Act 1993.
LR(MP)A 1934	Law Reform (Miscellaneous Provisions) Act 1934.
LR(PI)A 1948	Law Reform (Personal Injuries) Act 1948.
LR(S)A 1995	Law Reform (Succession) Act 1995.
LTA 1927	Landlord and Tenant Act 1927.
LTA 1954	Landlord and Tenant Act 1954.
LTA 1985	Landlord and Tenant Act 1985.
LTA 1987	Landlord and Tenant act 1987.
LTA 1988	Landlord and Tenant act 1988.
LT(C)A 1995	Landlord and Tenants (Covenants) Act 1995.

M

MA 1967	Misrepresentation Act 1967.
MCA 1980	Magistrates' Courts Act 1980.
MCA 1987	Minors' Contracts Act 1987.
MHA 1983	Matrimonial Homes Act 1983.
MntHA 1983	Mental Health Act 1983.

N

NAA 1948	National Assistance Act 1948.

O

OA 1978	Oaths Act 1978.
OAPA 1861	Offences Against the Person Act 1861.
OLA 1984	Occupiers' Liability Act 1984.

P

PA	Partnership Act 1890.
PA 1911	Perjury Act 1911.
PAA 1971	Powers of Attorney Act 1971.
PCA 1994	Proceeds of Crime Act 1994.
PACE	Police and Criminal Evidence Act 1984.
PCCA 1973	Powers of the Criminal Courts Act 1973.
PCC(S)A 2000	Powers of Criminal Courts (Sentencing) Act 2000.
PEA 1977	Protection from Eviction Act 1977.
PHA 1997	Protection from Harassment Act 1997.
PIL(MP)A 1995	Private International Law (Miscellaneous Provisions) Act 1995.
P(LBCA)A 1990	Planning (Listed Buildings and Conservation Areas) Act 1990.
POA 1985	Prosecution of Offences Act 1985.
POA 1986	Public Order Act 1986.

Q

R

ROA 1974	Rehabilitation of Offenders Act 1974.
RRA 1976	Race Relations Act 1976.
RPA 1976	Resale Prices Act 1976.
RTA 1988	Road Traffic Act 1988.
RTA 1991	Road Traffic Act 1991.
RT(C)A 1999	Road Traffic (NHS Charges) Act 1999.
RTOA 1988	Road Traffic Offenders Act 1988.

S

SA 1891	Stamp Act 1891.
SA 1974	Solicitors' Act 1974.
SLA 1925	Settled Land Act 1925.
SCA 1981	Supreme Court Act 1981.
SDA 1975	Sex Discrimination Act 1975.
SDA 1986	Sex Discrimination Act 1986.
SGA 1979	Sales of Goods Act 1979.
SG(A)A 1995	Sale of Goods (Amendment) Act 1995.
SGSA 1982	Supply of Goods and Services Act 1982.
SG(IT)A 1973	Supply of Goods(Implied Terms) Act 1973.
SG(A)A 1995	Sale of Goods (Amendment) Act 1995.
SSGA 1994	Sale and Supply of Goods Act 1994.
SS(RB)A 1997	Social Security (Recovery of Benefits) Act 1997

T

TA 1795	Treason Act 1795.
TA 1925	Trustee Act 1925.
TA 1968	Theft Act 1968.
TA 2000	Trustee Act 2000.
TCGA 1992	Taxation of Chargeable Gains Act 1992.
TCPA 1990	Town and Country Planning Act 1990.
TDA 1999	Trustee Delegation Act 1999.
TIA 1961	Trustee Investments Act 1961.
TLATA 1996	Trusts of Land and Appointment of Trustees Act 1996.
TMA 1970	Taxes Managment Act 1970.
TULR(C)A 1992	Trade Union and Labour Relations (Consolidation) Act 1992.

U

UCTA 1977 Unfair Contract Terms Act 1977.

V

VATA Value Added Tax Act 1994.

W

WA 1837 Wills Act 1837.

WA 1968 Wills Act 1968.

WIA 1991 Water Industry Act 1991.

WRPA 1999 Welfare Reform and Pensions Act 1999.

X

Y

YJCEA 1999 Youth Justice and Criminal Evidence Act 1999.

Z

Table of abbreviations

Statutory Instruments / Law Society codes

A

AIEDPO 1986 — Administration of Insolvent Estates of Deceased Persons Order 1986.

AJA(DA)O 2000 — Access to Justice Act 1999 (Destination of Appeals) Order 2000.

AJ(MO)R 2000 — Access to Justice (Membership Organisations) Regulations 2000.

ATAO(F)R 1988 — Assured Tenancies and Agricultural Occupational (Forms) Regulations 1988.

B

C

CA(ASMCMAA)R 1997 — Companies Act 1985 (Accounts of Small and Medium-Sized Companies and Minor Accounting Amendment) Regulations 1997.

CA(MAA)R 1996 — Companies Act (Miscellaneous Accounting Amendments) Regulations 1996.

CA(CD)R 1993 — Commercial Agents (Council Directive) Regulations 1993.

CA(DDE)R 1997 — Company Accounts (Disclosure of Directors' Emoluments) Regulations 1997.

CA(DR)(SPP)R 1997 — Companies Act (Directors' Report) (Statement of Payment Practice) Regulations 1997.

CA(EC)O 2000 — Companies Act (Electronic Communications) Order 2000.

CA(LVAE)O 2000 — Competition Act (Land and Vertical Agreements Exclusion) Order 2000.

CA(SACMS)R 2000 — Competition Act (Small Agreements and Conduct of Minor Significance) Regulations 2000.

CBNR 1981 — Company and Business Names Regulations 1981.

CC(ANEE)R 1987 — Crown Court (Advance Notice of Expert Evidence) Rules 1987.

CCFAR 2000 — Collective Conditional Fee Agreements Regulations 2000.

CCR — County Court Rules (CPR Sch. 2).

CDA(SOPE)R 2000 — Crime and Disorder Act (Scope of Prosecution Evidence) Regulations 2000.

CDS(F)O 2001 — Criminal Defence Service (Funding) Order 2001.

CDS(G2)R 2001 — Criminal Defence Service (General)(No.2) Regulations 2001.

CDS(RDCO)R 2001 — Criminal Defence Service (Recovery of Defence Costs Orders) Regulations 2001.

CDS(ROA)R 2001 — Criminal Defence Service (Representation Order Appeals) Regulations 2001.

CFAO 2000 — Conditional Fee Agreements Order 2000.

CFAR 2000 — Conditional Fee Agreements Regulations 2000.

CL(E)R 2000 — Contaminated Land (England) Regulations 2000.

CLRB — Commonhold and Leasehold Reform Bill.

CLS(CP)R 2000 — Community Legal Service (Cost Protection) Regulations 2000.

CLS(F)R 2000 — Community Legal Service (Financial) Regulations 2000.

CLS(C)R 2000 — Community Legal Service (Costs) Regulations 2000.

CP(DS)R 2000 — Consumer Protection (Distance Selling) Regulations 2000.

CPIA(DDTL)R 1997

	Criminal Procedure and Investigations Act (Defence Disclosure Time Limits) Regulations 1997.
CPR	Civil Procedure Rules 1998.
CT(IP)R 1998	Corporation Tax (Instalment Payments) Regulations 1998.

D

D(RPC)O 1996	Deregulation (Resolutions of Private Companies) Order 1996.
DLLPR 1999	Draft Limited Liability Partnership Regulations 1999.

E

F

FSMA(CRAWB)O 2001	Financial Services and Markets Act 2000 (Carrying on Regulated Actvities by Way of Business) Order 2001.
FSMA(FP)O 2001	Financial Services and Markets Act 2000 (Financial Promotion) Order 2001.
FSMA(RA)O 2001	Financial Services and Markets Act 2000 (Regulated Activities) Order 2001.

G

GR 1998	Groundwater Regulations 1998.
GS(IU)R 1998	Gas Safety (Installation and Use) Regulations 1998.

H

HB	Homes Bill.
HCCCJO 1991	High Court and County Courts Jurisdiction Order 1991.
HCCCJ(A)O 1996	High Court and County Courts Jurisdiction (Amendment) Order 1996.

I

IHT(DA)R 1998	Inheritance Tax (Delivery of Accounts) Regulations 1998.
IPO 1994	Insolvent Partnerships Order 1994.
I(P)R 1971	Indictments (Procedure) Rules 1971.
IR 1971	Indictment Rules 1971.
IS(IC)O 1977	Intestate Succession (Interest and Capitalisation) Order 1977.
ISR 1998	Individual Savings Accounts Regulations 1998.
IHT(DA)R 2000	Inheritance Tax (Delivery of Accounts) Regulations 2000.
IT(E)R 1993	Income Tax (Employments) Regulations 1993.
IT(NP)R 1994	Income Tax (Notional Payments) Regulations 1994.
IT(PA)R 1996	Income Tax (Payments on Account) Regulations 1996.

J

JD(RI)) 1993	Judgment Debt (Rate of Interest) Order 1993.

K

L

LRB	Land Registration Bill.
LRR 1925	Land Registration Rules 1925.
LR(RA)O 1999	Lay Representatives (Right of Audience) Order 1999.
LT(C)(N)R 1995	Landlord and Tenant (Covenants) Act (Notices) Regulations 1995.

M

MC(AI)R 1985	Magistrates' Courts (Advance Information) Rules 1985.
MC(ANEE)R 1997	Magistrates' Courts (Advance Notice of Expert Evidence) Rules 1997.
MCR 1981	Magistrates' Courts Rules 1981.
MLR	Money Laundering Regulations.

N

NA(AR)R 1992	National Assistance (Assessment of Resources) Regulations 1992.
NCPR 1987	Non-Contentious Probate Rules 1987.

O

P

PO(CTL)R 1987	Prosecution of Offences (Custody Time Limits) Regulations 1987.
PPC(EW)R 2000	Pollution Prevention and Control (England and Wales) Regulations 2000.
PTWDR	Part Time Worker Discrimination Regulations.
P(US)N16R 2001	Partnership (Unrestricted Size) No.16 Regulations 2001.

Q

R

RSC	Rules of the Supreme Court (in CPR Sch. 1) .

S

SAR 1998	Solicitors' Accounts Rules 1998.
SCICCC 1999	Solicitors' Costs Information and Client Care Code 1999.
SDC 1995	Solicitors' Discrimination Code 1995.

SFS(S)R 2001	Solicitors' Financial Services (Scope) Rules 2001 (draft).
SIBR 1995	Solicitors' Investment Business Rules 1995.
SIRC 1990	Solicitors' Introduction and Referral Code 1990.
SPC 1990	Solicitors' Publicity Code 1990.
SPR 1990	Solicitors' Practice Rules 1990.
SD(EI)R 1987	Stamp Duty (Exempt Instruments) Regulations 1987.
SRO 1994	Solicitors' Remuneration Order 1994.
SSC(I)R 2000	Social Security Contributions (Intermediaries) Regulations 2000.
SS(RB)R 1997	Social Security (Recovery of Benefit) Regulations 1997.
SS(RB)(A)R 1998	Social Security (Recovery of Benefits) (Appeals) Regulations 1997.

T

TCP(GPD)O 1995	Town and Country Planning (General Permitted Development) Order 1995.
TCP(UC)O 1987	Town and Country Planning (Use Classes) Order 1987.
TU(PE)R 1981	Transfer of Undertakings (Protection of Employment) Regulations 1981.

U

UTCCR 1999	Unfair Terms in Consumer Contracts Regulations 1999.

V

VATR 1995	Value Added Tax Regulations 1995.

W-Z

Table of authorities

Statutes

J-K

L

Statute	Page
s.4	137
Leasehold Reform Act 1967	217
Leasehold Reform, Housing and Urban Development Act 1993	217, 226
Legitimacy Act 1976	
s.5	
(3)-(4)	155
s.7	155
Limitation Act 1980	202, 310, 315
s.2	310
s.5	310
s.11	310, 322
s.12	322
s.14	310
s.14A	310
s.33	310
Limited Partnership Act 2000	76, 80, 89, 234, 271, 272, 273
s.1	
(1)	234
(3)	234
s.2	235
(1)(a)-(c)	235
(2)-(4)	235
s.3(1)-(4)	235
s.5	
(1)(a)-(b)	235
(2)	236
s.6	
(1)	237
(4)	237
s.7	236
s.9	236
s.12	122, 271
s.15(c)	235
Sch.1	
Part 1	235
Limited Partnerships Act 1907	234
Local Land Charges Act 1975	
s.10	204

M

Statute	Page
Magistrates' Courts Act 1980	
s.4	431
s.5	421
s.5A(6)	432
s.6	430
(1)-(2)	430, 431
(3)	420, 433
s.8	433
(2A)	433
s.10	421
(3)	420
s.17	424
(6)	428
s.18	418, 421, 424
s.19	424
(3)	424
s.20	424
(2)-(3)	424
s.21-s.24	424
s.25	424, 425
s.26-s.28	424
s.32	407
s.76	443
s.80(1)	443
s.83	443
s.88	443
s.97	427
s.97A	427, 432
(9)	432
s.108	451, 452
s.109-s.111	451
s.123	428
s.127	418
s.128	420
s.128A	420
s.132	441
s.133(2)	441, 442
s.136-s.137	443
s.142	452
Sch.1	
para.28(c)	425
Married Women's Property Act 1882	145
Matrimonial Homes Act 1983	277, 325, 328, 329, 334
Mental Health Act 1983	
Part VII	183
s.96(1)(g)	232
s.99	183
Minors' Contracts Act 1987	179
Misrepresentation Act 1967	
s.2(1)	224

N

Statute	Page
National Assistance Act 1948	
s.56	129

O

Statute	Page
Occupiers Liability Act 1957	298
Occupiers' Liability Act 1984	182
Offences Against the Person Act 1861	1861
s.20	425, 441
s.47	407, 425, 441

P-Q

Statute	Page
Partnership Act 1890	229
s.1	228, 229
s.5-s.8	230, 300
s.9	230, 231
s.10	230
s.14	231
s.17	230, 231
s.23	232
s.24	
(1)	229
(3)-(8)	229
s.25	229, 232
s.26	229, 232
(2)	232
s.28-s.30	230

European primary legislation

International primary legislation

Table of authorities

Statutory Instruments / Codes of Practice

European Legislation	***Page***

European Directives

European Regulations

Conduct

This chapter examines:

Solicitors' Practice Rules 1990 r.1

- This rule is the cornerstone of good conduct.

  'A solicitor shall not do anything in the course of practising as a solicitor, or permit another person to do anything on his or her behalf, which compromises or impairs or is likely to compromise or impair any of the following:

  a) the solicitor's independence or integrity.

  b) a person's freedom to instruct a solicitor of his or her choice.

  c) the solicitor's duty to act in the best interests of the client.

  d) the good repute of the solicitor or the solicitors' profession.

  e) the solicitor's proper standard of work.

  f) the solicitor's duty to the court.'
- Individual solicitors are liable for any breach of these rules.
- All partners of a law firm are jointly and severally liable for any breach of these rules by any fee earner.

A Taking instructions

I Advertising

➤ Advertisements must comply with the *SPC 1990,* which forbids:

- comparisons with other firms, *or*
- unsolicited intrusion upon members of the public (eg: tele-sales).

➤ Advertisements must comply with *SPR r.2* and:

- not be in bad taste, *and*
- contain accurate information and nothing which is misleading, *and*
- comply with the general law.

II Introductions and referrals

➤ Introductions by third parties are permitted (*SPR r.3*), provided the *SIRC 1990* and *SPR r.1* are complied with.

- The solicitor may *not* pay a third party for the introduction.
- The firm must keep a written record of any agreements for the introduction of clients, showing:

  a) that the clients concerned have been advised impartially, *and*

  b) the income which the firm derives from each agreement with an 'introducer', *and*

  c) that the *SIRC 1990* has been complied with.

➤ A solicitor may refer a client to a third party, provided he:

a) acts in the client's best interests, *and*

b) accounts to a client for commissions over £20, or retains the money with the client's prior consent (*SPR r.10*).

➤ A solicitor engaged in investment business must also comply with the *SIBR 1995*, disclosing in writing to the client *before* the client signs any proposal form or application:

a) the *total* amount of commission due to the solicitor *and* a permitted third party in cash terms, *and*

b) any subsequent change to the commission reflecting a change in the transaction.

III Accepting instructions

Money Laundering Regulations

- If a solicitor has a new client *and* 'will carry out relevant financial business in the UK', he must ensure compliance with the *Money Laundering Regulations* by making enquiries of the new client, to check his identity (eg: by asking to see a passport) and if the money is in cash, asking where the money has come from.
- There are criminal penalties for non-compliance.

Fees - quotations and estimates

- If a solicitor gives a quotation instead of an estimate of fees, he must do the job for that price.
- An estimate of fees should make clear how costs will be calculated; the solicitor must inform the client if it appears likely that costs will exceed the estimate.
- If VAT is not mentioned, the client is entitled to assume the price is inclusive of VAT.
- For conditional fee agreements, see pp.15-16.

1 A solicitor must always:

- take instructions directly from the client (ie: a request for advice on behalf of a potential client should be confirmed personally by the client).
- ensure a client is free to instruct whomever he wishes, and is aware of this right (*SPR r. 1*).

2 A solicitor should *not*:

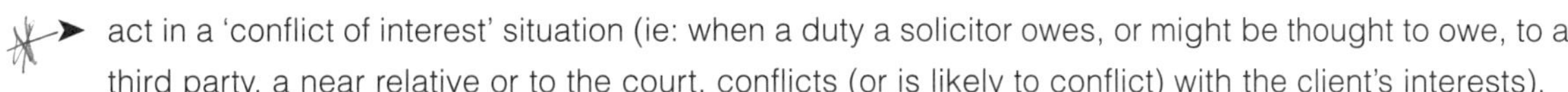

- act in a 'conflict of interest' situation (ie: when a duty a solicitor owes, or might be thought to owe, to a third party, a near relative or to the court, conflicts (or is likely to conflict) with the client's interests).
- accept instructions on a basis which excludes the jurisdiction of the Law Society.
- act for a client where the action is malicious.
- accept instructions during conveyancing, where *SPR rr.6-6A* are not complied with (see next page).
- act for a buyer and a seller in a 'contract race' (even if *SPR r.6* would otherwise permit the solicitor to act), nor may he act for more than one buyer (*SPR r.6A*).
  - A 'contract race' occurs when a seller of freehold or leasehold land *either:*

    a) instructs a solicitor to deal with more than one prospective buyer, *or*

    b) is known by the solicitor to be dealing with more than one prospective buyer (*SPR r.6A*).

Solicitors' Anti-Discrimination Code 1995

- A solicitor should not discriminate on grounds of race, sex or sexual orientation.
- A solicitor should not discriminate unreasonably or unfairly on grounds of disability.
- A solicitor may not refuse instructions on the above grounds, or discriminate against his staff on these grounds. If a client asks a solicitor to instruct a barrister of a particular race or sex, the solicitor should try to persuade him otherwise, and if this fails, he should refuse to act.

SPR r.6 generally

➤ *SPR r.6* applies where a solicitor is asked to act for a party in conveyancing, property selling or mortgage related services in connection with:

a) the transfer of land for value at arm's length, *or*

b) the grant or assignment of a lease, or some other interest in land, for value at arm's length, *or*

c) the grant of a mortgage over land.

- 'Arm's length' is not necessarily a market value transaction. It depends on the precise facts; usually a transaction will not be a transaction at arm's length if the parties are:
    - related by blood, adoption or marriage, *or*
    - the trustees of a trust and the settlor of that trust, *or*
    - a beneficiary of a trust (or a relative of a beneficiary) and the trustees of a trust, *or*
    - a beneficiary and PRs, *or*
    - trustees of separate trusts for the same family, *or*
    - a sole trader, partners, or a limited company established to incorporate their business, *or*
    - associated companies (ie: there is a subsidiary/holding company relationship for the purposes of *CA 1985*).

Acting for the Seller and the Buyer (*SPR r.6(2)*)

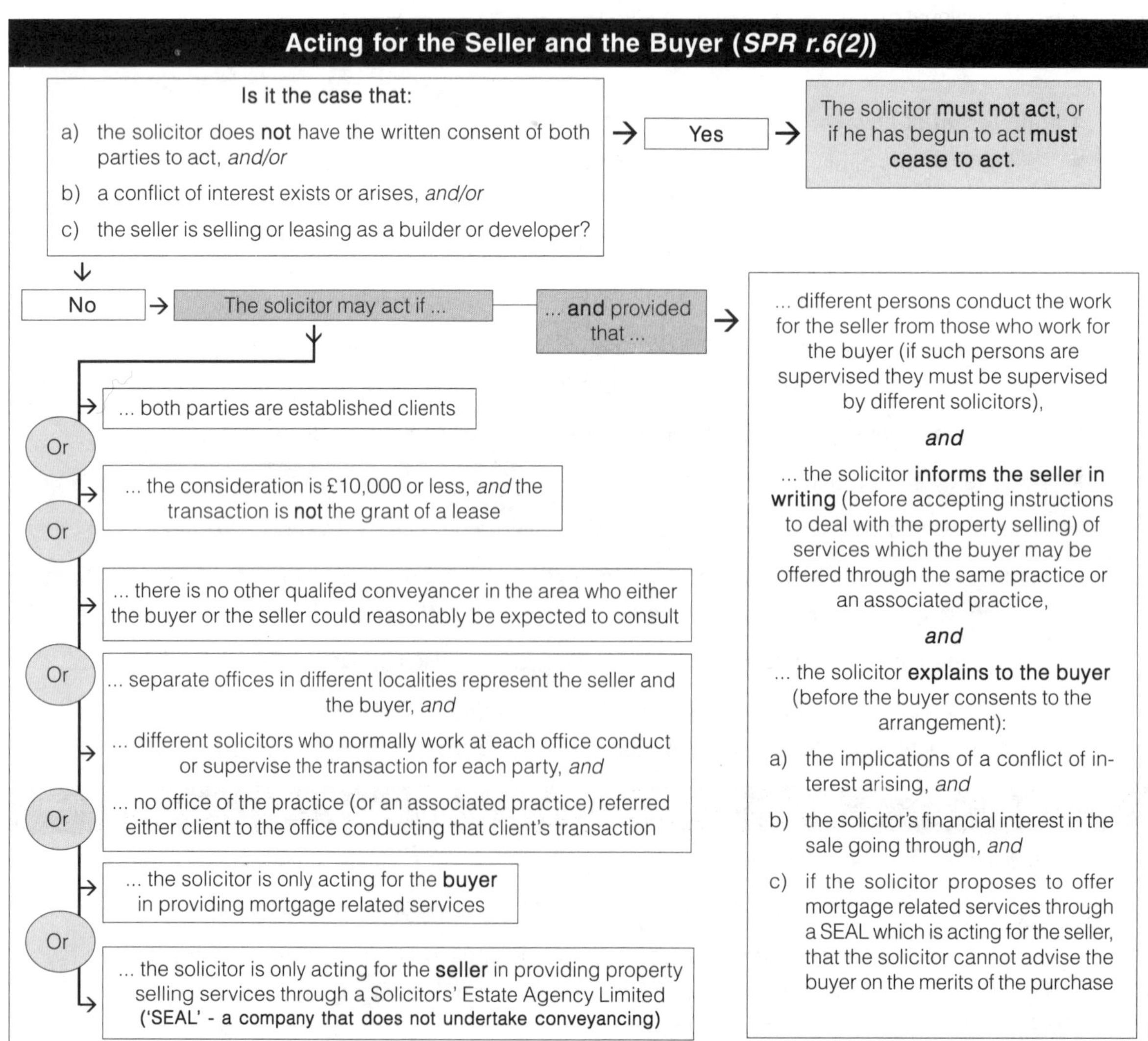

Is it the case that:
a) the solicitor does **not** have the written consent of both parties to act, *and/or*
b) a conflict of interest exists or arises, *and/or*
c) the seller is selling or leasing as a builder or developer?
Yes
The solicitor **must not act**, or if he has begun to act **must cease to act.**
No
The solicitor may act if ...
... both parties are established clients
Or
... the consideration is £10,000 or less, *and* the transaction is **not** the grant of a lease
Or
... there is no other qualifed conveyancer in the area who either the buyer or the seller could reasonably be expected to consult
Or
... separate offices in different localities represent the seller and the buyer, *and*
... different solicitors who normally work at each office conduct or supervise the transaction for each party, *and*
... no office of the practice (or an associated practice) referred either client to the office conducting that client's transaction
Or
... the solicitor is only acting for the **buyer** in providing mortgage related services
Or
... the solicitor is only acting for the **seller** in providing property selling services through a Solicitors' Estate Agency Limited ('SEAL' - a company that does not undertake conveyancing)
... **and** provided that ...
... different persons conduct the work for the seller from those who work for the buyer (if such persons are supervised they must be supervised by different solicitors),
and
... the solicitor **informs the seller in writing** (before accepting instructions to deal with the property selling) of services which the buyer may be offered through the same practice or an associated practice,
and
... the solicitor **explains to the buyer** (before the buyer consents to the arrangement):
a) the implications of a conflict of interest arising, *and*
b) the solicitor's financial interest in the sale going through, *and*
c) if the solicitor proposes to offer mortgage related services through a SEAL which is acting for the seller, that the solicitor cannot advise the buyer on the merits of the purchase

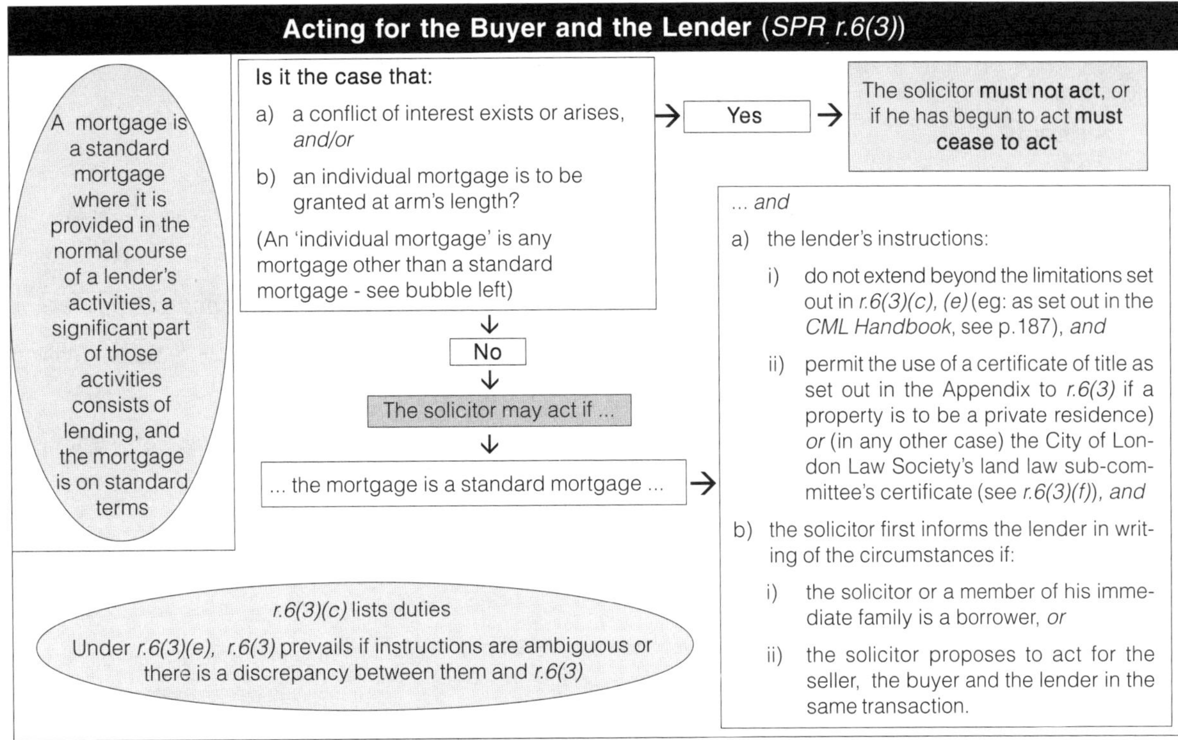

Acting for the Buyer and the Lender (*SPR r.6(3)*)
A mortgage is a standard mortgage where it is provided in the normal course of a lender's activities, a significant part of those activities consists of lending, and the mortgage is on standard terms
Is it the case that:
a) a conflict of interest exists or arises, *and/or*
b) an individual mortgage is to be granted at arm's length?
(An 'individual mortgage' is any mortgage other than a standard mortgage - see bubble left)
Yes
The solicitor **must not act**, or if he has begun to act **must cease to act**
No
The solicitor may act if ...
... the mortgage is a standard mortgage ...
... *and*
a) the lender's instructions:
i) do not extend beyond the limitations set out in *r.6(3)(c), (e)* (eg: as set out in the *CML Handbook*, see p.187), *and*
ii) permit the use of a certificate of title as set out in the Appendix to *r.6(3)* if a property is to be a private residence) *or* (in any other case) the City of London Law Society's land law sub-committee's certificate (see *r.6(3)(f)*), *and*
b) the solicitor first informs the lender in writing of the circumstances if:
i) the solicitor or a member of his immediate family is a borrower, *or*
ii) the solicitor proposes to act for the seller, the buyer and the lender in the same transaction.
r.6(3)(c) lists duties
Under *r.6(3)(e)*, *r.6(3)* prevails if instructions are ambiguous or there is a discrepancy between them and *r.6(3)*

3 **On accepting instructions, a solicitor should***:*

- in a 'contract race' for conveyancing clients, immediately inform each buyer's solicitor of the race by telephone or fax, and confirm this in writing (*SPR r.6A*).
- if acting for a buyer and a lender in respect of an institutional mortgage, where the property is to be used as a private residence and the lender has not certified that the lender's instructions, comply with *SPR rr.6(3)(c), (e)*, notify that lender that the certificate of title will be in the form approved under *SPR r.6* and that the solicitor's duties are limited to those duties set out in *SPR r.6(3)* (*SPR r.6(3)(d)*).
- comply with the Law Society's Client Care *SPR r.15* and *SCICCC 1999*. The solicitor must:
  - give the client the best information possible about the likely overall costs and keep the client informed as to the costs which have been, and are likely to be incurred (otherwise he may commit an offence under *CPA 1987 s.20*), *and*
  - give the client a breakdown between fees, VAT and disbursements, *and*
  - explain to a privately paying client that he can set an upper limit on fees, *and*
  - explain to the client how the firm's fees are calculated and whether the firm's charging rates may be increased (and if so, how), *and*
  - discuss with the client how, when and by whom costs are to be met, *and*
  - discuss with the client whether likely outcomes will justify the expense or risk of instructions, *and*
  - tell the client about his potential liability for his own costs and that of any other party, *and*
  - keep the client properly informed about costs at regular intervals (at least every 6 months), *and*
  - give the client a clear explanation of the issues raised in a matter, who is dealing with the matter, who is ultimately responsible and who the client may complain to, *and*
  - have a written complaints procedure and ensure that the client is given a copy on request.

NB: A serious breach or persistent material breaches of the *Code* may in addition to breach of *r.15* (leading to professional conduct implications and disciplinary sanctions) also be evidence of inadequate professional service. Material breaches which are not serious or persistent will not be a breach of *r.15* but may be evidence of inadequate professional service (see pp.19-20).

IV Authority and responsibilities during a retainer

1 Authority

- **Non-contentious business** (ie: before litigation is commenced): a solicitor has 'ostensible authority' to act on the client's behalf (see p.300).
- **Contentious business**: a solicitor has 'actual authority' to act on a client's behalf *and to bind a client.*
  - The solicitor should always obtain a client's express authority, preferably in writing, before making any commitment on their behalf, unless the matter is urgent.
  - A solicitor acting without a client's consent may be liable to a third party for breach of warranty of authority.

2 Responsibilities

- A solicitor should act in the client's best interests (*SPR r. 1*).
- A solicitor must not mislead the court (*SPR r. 1*).
  - In a criminal case, a solicitor can put the prosecution to proof even if the client admits guilt to the solicitor. However, assisting a client to give perjured evidence would breach the solicitor's duty to the court, and the solicitor should refuse to act if a client attempts this.
  - A solicitor is not obliged to inform the court if it is mistaken about a defendant's criminal record, provided the court does not request any positive representation. If a court requests information, the solicitor must advise the client to tell the truth, and must refuse to act if the client declines.
- A solicitor must maintain confidentiality during the retainer *and* after it ceases (*SPR r. 1*).
  - The duty is relaxed if:

    a) the client authorises it, *or*
    b) the solicitor believes his advice is being sought in preparation for a non-trivial crime, *or*
    c) a court order requires disclosure, *or*
    d) the police have a search warrant (and documents are not covered by legal privilege), *or*
    e) national security demands it, *or*
    f) the information concerns authorities on which a party intends to rely during a hearing, *or*
    g) the defence calls **expert** evidence (it must be disclosed before a hearing (*PACE s.84(1)*)), *or*
    h) an LSC funded client behaves unreasonably.
- A solicitor must write regularly to the client keeping him informed of what is (or is not!) happening, the costs incurred, and any action which the client ought to take (*SPR r. 15*).
- A solicitor must comply with the *FSA 1986/FSMA 2000* when advising the client (see pp.21-23).
  - Whether advice is classified as non-discrete investment business, *or* discrete investment business, a firm must abide by various requirements of *SIBR 1995* with regard to record keeping.
    - Eg: *r. 16(3)* mandates a solicitor to maintain records of client complaints, and any action taken in response to these over the last 6 years.
- A solicitor must comply with the *Solicitors' Accounts Rules 1998* (see p.52).

V Terminating a retainer

➤ The retainer may be terminated:

1 **by the client at any time, for any reason.**

2 **by the solicitor if there is 'good reason' and reasonable notice is given.**

- ◆ When stating the 'good reason', a solicitor must take care not to breach his duty of confidentiality.
  - Eg: if a solicitor is acting both for an insured person and that insured person's insurance company, and the solicitor becomes aware that the insured person is defrauding the insurers, the solicitor should refuse to act for both parties. The solicitor must maintain confidentiality to both clients, and must therefore not disclose any details to the insurer.
  - Eg: if a solicitor is acting for both a mortgage company and a house buyer, where the house buyer wishes to obtain a mortgage for more than the property is worth. The solicitor should refuse to act for both parties. The solicitor must maintain confidentiality to both clients, and must therefore not disclose any details to the mortgage company.
  - Circumstances which may entitle, or compel, a solicitor to end a retainer include:

    a) a conflict of interest arises

    - ▪ eg: a solicitor for 2 co-accused (with contradictory defences) should decline to act for both, *or*

    Note: where a conflict of interest does not threaten the administration of justice, and both parties consent, then a solicitor may continue acting for one of the parties.

    b) the client instructs a solicitor to break the law, *or*

    c) when confidence between the solicitor and the client breaks down, *or*

    d) when the client does not meet an interim bill during contentious proceedings.

3 **by operation of law.**

- ◆ Eg: the solicitor is declared bankrupt or is of unsound mind.

Actions on termination

➤ A solicitor should return the client's papers, unless the solicitor:

a) holds the papers as the client's agent, *and*

b) has a lien over them (eg: for unpaid work).

➤ If the client instructs another solicitor, the second solicitor must secure the documents by giving an undertaking as to the costs incurred by the first solicitor.

- ◆ When the client is LSC funded, there is no need for such an undertaking.

B Costs, help in funding a case and bills

I Types of costs

➤ A client will have to bear costs. These costs fall into 2 classes:

1 **Solicitor-own-client costs:** these are all the expenses which the solicitor incurs on the client's behalf, eg: the solicitor's own fees, fees for expert opinions, applications for police accident reports, counsel's advice, etc. The solicitor usually asks for payment on account, for expenses that he expects to incur.

2 ***Inter partes* costs:** in a civil action, these are expenses which other parties to an action incur and are usually the responsibility of whichever party loses litigation (subject to the court's ruling on costs - pp.390-395).

Contentious matters (civil) - solicitors must explain:	
Private clients	Community Legal Service funded clients
◆ the client's potential liability for his own costs and those of any other party ◆ the fact that the client will be responsible for paying the firm's bill in full regardless of any order for costs made against the opponent ◆ the probability that the client will have to pay the opponent's costs as well as the client's own costs if the case is lost ◆ the fact that even if the client wins, the opponent may not be ordered to pay or be capable of paying the full amount of the client's costs ◆ the fact that if the opponent is LSC funded, the client may not recover costs even if successful	◆ the client's potential liability for his own costs and those of any other party ◆ **the effect of the statutory charge and its likely amount** ◆ **the client's liability to pay the statutory charge and consequences of failure to do so** ◆ the fact that the client may still be ordered by the court to contribute to the opponent's costs if the case is lost even though the client's own costs are covered by the CLS ◆ the fact that even if the client wins, the opponent may not be ordered to pay or be capable of paying the full amount of the client's costs

➤ For further information on civil costs see pp.390-395.

II LSC funding

➤ The Legal Services Commission (LSC) replaced the Legal Aid Board in April 2000 to provide legal funding help - ie: the LSC pays set rates to solicitors who do legal work for people who need government help to fund legal cases/advice. The LSC has 11 regional offices and a number of Head Office departments.

➤ The Legal Services Commission is responsible for running 2 schemes (*AJA 1999*):

- for civil matters: **the Community Legal Service (CLS)**, *and*
- for criminal matters: **the Criminal Defence Service (CDS)**.

III Civil: CLS help

➤ Solicitors can only provide advice or representation funded by the LSC (via the CLS) if they have a 'General Civil Contract' with the LSC. For family cases and specialist areas like immigration and clinical negligence, only specialist firms are funded to do the work.

- Claims for personal injury (except clinical negligence) are not funded by the LSC. Such cases can instead be pursued under conditional fee agreements between solicitors and clients (see pp.15-16).
- Firms are audited against the Contract to ensure they continue to meet quality assurance standards.

➤ The CLS cannot be used to fund services (beyond the provision of general information about the law and the legal system and the availability of legal services) in relation to (*AJA 1999 Sch.2*):

- allegations of negligently caused injury, death or damage to property, apart from allegations relating to clinical negligence,
- conveyancing, *or*
- boundary disputes, *or*
- the making of wills, *or*
- matters of trust law, *or*
- defamation or malicious falsehood, *or*
- matters of company or partnership law, *or*
- other matters arising out of the carrying on of a business.

➤ The LSC funds a range of legal services. There are 5 main forms of civil legal help (*CLS(F)R 2000*):

1 **Legal Help**

2 **Legal Representation** (2 types):
   Type 1: **Initial Legal Help**
   Type 2: **Help at Court**

3 **Support Funding** (2 types):
   Type 1: **Investigative Support**
   Type 2: **Litigation Support**

4 **Approved Family Help**

5 **Family Mediation**

1 **Legal Help** (2 types)

Type 1: Initial Legal Help

- **Purpose:** initial advice/assistance with any legal problem. It covers general advice, writing letters, negotiating, getting a barrister's opinion, preparing a written case if going before a court or tribunal.

Type 2: Help at Court

- **Purpose:** allows for a solicitor or adviser to speak at court hearings, without acting for the client in the whole proceedings.

In either case:

- Financial Restrictions:
  - capital and income must be within certain prescribed financial limits.
  - No contribution is payable.
  - A maximum level of work only (set by standard rate) is allowed to be performed under this.
- **Age:** for anyone over 16. For minors, a parent's/guardian's capital and income are assessed.

2 **Legal Representation** (2 types):

Type 1: Investigative Help

- **Purpose:** investigation of the strength of a proposed claim where the prospects of success are not clear and the investigation is likely to be expensive.

Type 2: Full Representation

- **Purpose:** for representation in legal proceedings - to trial and beyond.

In either case:

- **Procedure:** the application is assessed by the LSC regional office, which decides (usually within 2 weeks) whether it meets the funding criteria. The regional office can either grant or refuse the application. If the application is refused, there is a right of review by the LSC's Regional Director and ultimately by the LSC's funding review committee.

  NB:It is also possible for both Investigative Help and Full Representation to be granted on an emergency basis where the matter is urgent and meets the criteria.
- Certificate:
  - copies are sent to the applicant and the solicitor and notice of issue is served on any other parties.

    NB: No notice of any limitation or restrictions on the legal help must be given to other parties.
  - if the certificate needs to be amended, an amended certificate is issued and notice must be served on all parties to the dispute.
- Financial Restrictions:
  - The calculation is based on the applicant's disposable capital and disposable income (together with a spouse's/unmarried partner's, provided that there is no conflict of interest between them).
  - An applicant gets legal help if his disposable income and capital are below certain limits.
  - Reassessments of income/capital may happen any time while the legal help certificate is in force.
  - The statutory charge will apply to any money or property recovered or preserved.
- **Merits Restriction:** the funding criteria must be satisfied: they are set out in the Funding Code.

3 **Support Funding** (2 types):

- Purpose: partial funding of very expensive cases which are otherwise funded privately, under a conditional fee agreement (CFA) (usually personal injury).
- There are two forms:

Type 1: Investigative Support:

- Purpose: provides limited funding for the investigation of the strength of a proposed claim with a view to proceeding under a CFA. Only work done investigating the strength of the claim is covered, not other work investigating eg: the size of the claim in detail. As soon as sufficient investigative work has been carried out to estimate prospects of success and to decide whether to proceed under a CFA, this must be reported to the LSC and no further work will be funded. Investigative Support is only available where the reasonable costs of investigation are exceptionally high, i.e. disbursements (such as expert's reports) are likely to exceed £1,000 or the solicitor's fees to investigate the case are likely to exceed £3,000. Other merits criteria apply to this level of funding, including a requirement that likely damages exceed £5,000.

Type 2: Litigation Support:

- Purpose: provides partial funding of high cost litigation already proceeding under a CFA. Litigation Support is only available where the reasonable costs of the litigation are exceptionally high, ie: disbursements (such as expert's reports) are likely to exceed £5,000 or the costs of the case excluding disbursements are likely to exceed £15,000. Other merits criteria apply to this level of funding, including a requirement that damages must exceed costs by set ratios, except where the claim has a significant wider public interest.

In either case:

- Solicitor Restrictions: Only solicitors contracted by the LSC to undertake personal injury cases may apply.
- Procedure: Applications for Investigative Support should be made to the LSC regional office. Applications for Litigation Support must be made to the LSC Special Cases Unit with a costed case plan.
- Financial Restrictions:
  - must meet the financial criteria.
  - The statutory charge will apply to any money or property recovered or preserved.
- Merits Restriction: the funding criteria must be satisfied: they are set out in the Funding Code.

4 **Approved Family Help** (not covered in detail)

- Purpose: provides help in relation to a family dispute.

5 **Family Mediation** (not covered in detail)

- Purpose: covers mediation for a family dispute.

IV Criminal: CDS help

- Solicitors can only carry out criminal defence work funded by the LSC (via the CDS) if they have a 'General Criminal Contract' with the LSC or some other franchised arrangement with the LSC.
  - Firms are audited against the Contract to ensure they continue to meet quality assurance standards.
- The LSC also directly employs some criminal defence lawyers (known as public defenders), initially at six pilot sites in England and Wales who can provide any CDS criminal services.
  - Employees of the CDS are subject to a strict code of conduct.
- There are 3 forms of CDS-provided help (*CDS(F)O 2001*):
  1. **Advice and Assistance (this covers advice and assistance on criminal matters)**
     Subcategory: Advice and Assistance if questioned by police
  2. **Advocacy Assistance (this covers some advice and representation at court)**
  3. **Representation for criminal offences**
     Subcategory: The court duty solicitor scheme

1 Advice and Assistance

- **Purpose:** this covers help from a solicitor including giving general advice, writing letters, negotiating, getting a barrister's opinion and preparing a written case. It enables people of small or moderate means to get help from a solicitor but does not cover representation in court.
- **Procedure:** The solicitor decides, based on the tests below, whether LSC funded help can be given. He can refuse to give advice without a reason but he may be asked to explain the reasons for his refusal by the LSC regional office.
- **Financial restrictions:** To qualify, disposable capital and disposable income of the applicant must be within the current financial limits (*CDS(G2)R 2001*).
  - If qualified to receive advice and assistance, no contribution is payable by the applicant.
  - If married (or living as a couple), the partner's capital and income will be included unless the parties live apart or there is a conflict of interest between them.
- **Merit restrictions:** the test is whether there is 'sufficient benefit' to the client (having regard to the circumstances of the matter, including the personal circumstances of the client) to justify work being carried out.
- **Age:** Children are eligible for Advice and Assistance, but in most cases where a child is under 17, a parent or guardian should apply on his behalf. A solicitor can sometimes advise a child directly.

Subcategory: Advice and Assistance if questioned by police

- **Purpose:** If the police question an alleged offender about an offence (whether or not he has been arrested and whether or not at a police station) there a right to free legal advice from a contracted solicitor. The police must contact a duty solicitor or the alleged offender's own solicitor or a solicitor on a police-kept list of local solicitors.
- **Restrictions:** None (*CDS(G2)R 2001*).

2 Advocacy Assistance

➤ **Purpose:** this covers the cost of a solicitor preparing a case and *initial* representation in certain proceedings in both the Magistrates' Court and the Crown Court.

- ◆ It covers representation for prisoners facing disciplinary charges before the prison governor/ controller, and for discretionary and automatic lifers and those detained at Her Majesty's Pleasure whose cases are referred to the Parole Board. It also covers representation for those who have failed to pay a fine or obey a court order of the magistrates' court and are at risk of imprisonment.

➤ **Procedure:** The solicitor decides whether this will be available based on the restrictions below (it is a devolved power from the LSC). The LSC pays the solicitor's bill if the merits restrictions test is met.

➤ **Financial restrictions:** There is no financial test (unless the advice and assistance is to be provided in the prison law class of work) (*CDS(G2)R 2001*).

- ◆ If qualified to receive advocacy assistance, no contribution is payable by the applicant.

➤ **Merit restrictions:** Advocacy assistance may not be granted if it appears unreasonable that approval should be granted in the particular circumstances of the case or if the case does not involve one of the *AJA 1999 Sch.3* criteria (listed overleaf).

3 Representation for criminal offences

➤ **Purpose:** Anyone charged with a criminal offence can apply for Representation. This covers the cost of a solicitor preparing a defence before going to court and representing the applicant there. It may also be available to apply for bail.

- ◆ If the case requires a barrister (particularly if in the Crown Court) that is also covered. Representation can also cover advice on appeal against a verdict or sentence of the Magistrates' Court or the Crown Court (or a decision of the Court of Appeal) and preparing the notice of appeal itself.

➤ **Procedure:** The solicitor assigns a Unique File Number (UFN) to the matter. The solicitor fills in the application form and sends it to the court where the case will be heard. **Details may need to be given of income and savings.** The court decides whether to grant Representation based on a financial and merits test ((*CDS(G2)R 2001*), *CDS(ROA)R 2001*).

- ◆ If the application is refused, the court will write giving the reason for refusing Representation.
  - • If the court has decided to refuse Representation because it is not in the interests of justice, the applicant may more applications (unlimited times up to the trial) to the court to review the case.
- ◆ If the application is refused by the Magistrates' Court and the applicant has to go to the Crown Court, the applicant can apply to the Crown Court for Representation.
- ◆ In any case, if Representation is refused, a solicitor may be able to give some help in case preparation for court under Advice and Assistance.

➤ **Financial restrictions:**

- ◆ No contribution is payable if represented in a Magistrates' Court. In any other court, the judge may make a 'Recovery of Defence Costs Order' (RDCO) for the accused to pay of some or all of the cost of any representation if it is reasonable in all the circumstances of the case (including the means of the applicant any any partner) ((*CDS(G2)R 2001*), *CDS(RDCO)R 2001*).

- **Merit restrictions:** The court will grant Representation **if it decides it is in the 'interests of justice'** that the applicant should be represented at the LSC's expense. The court's decision is based on the information given in the application form. Some circumstances when it is appropriate to give LSC funding are when (*AJA 1999 Sch.3*):
  - there is a likelihood of a) a custodial sentence, *or* b) loss of livelihood, *or* c) serious damage to reputation. There is no clear authority as to whether a community sentence under the *PCC(S)A 2000* qualifies.
  - there is a substantial question of law involved (eg: evidential difficulties).
  - a disability/linguistic barrier prevents the defendant from understanding the proceedings.
  - tracing *and* interviewing of witnesses is necessary.
  - the case involves expert cross-examination of a prosecution witness.
  - it is in the interests of someone other than the accused that the accused is represented.
- **Age:** Children are eligible for Representation but, in most cases where a child is under 17, a parent or guardian should apply on his behalf.

Subcategory: The court duty solicitor scheme

- **Purpose:** If an alleged offender has to go to a Magistrates' Court and does not have his own solicitor there will usually be a duty solicitor available either at the court or on call to give free advice and representation on his first appearance.
- **Restrictions:** None (*CDS(G2)R 2001*).

V Conditional fee agreements

A. Generally

Conditional fee agreements (*CLSA 1990 s.58, CFAR 2000, CFAO 2000, AJ(MO)R 2000*)

- A conditional fee agreement is an agreement where certain fees are payable only in specified circumstances. They allow clients to agree with their lawyers that the lawyer will not receive all or part of the usual fees or expenses if the case is lost; but that, if it is won, the client will pay an uplift to the solicitor in addition to the usual fee.
- *CLSA 1990 s.58* allows the use of conditional fee agreements in such types of case as the Lord Chancellor specifies by order (and subject to any requirements made by him in regulations).
  - *CLSA 1990 s.58(10)* excludes from conditional fees all criminal and family proceedings.
- The maximum uplift that can be charged if a lawyer is successful is 100% of the normal fees.
- The Vice Chancellor held that it was also lawful for a conditional fee agreement to apply in a case which is to be resolved by arbitration, even though these are not court proceedings, provided all the requirements specified by regulations as to the form and content of the agreement are complied with - *Bevan Ashford v Geoff Yeandle (Contractors) Ltd* [1998] 3 All ER 238 ChD.
- Insurance policies are available to cover the costs of the other party and the client's own costs (including, if not a conditional fee case, the client's solicitor's fees) if the case is lost. The *AJA 1999* makes a success fee under a conditional fee agreement recoverable and also makes any premium paid for protective insurance recoverable too (*AJA 1999 s.29*).
- The arrangements must be in writing and must contain a statement specifying (*AJ(MO)R 2000*):
  - when the member or other party may be liable to pay costs of the proceedings, *and*
  - whether such a liability arises:
    - if those circumstances only partly occur, *and*
    - irrespective of whether those circumstances occur, *and*
    - on the termination of the arrangements for any reason, *and*
  - the basis on which the amount of the liability is calculated, *and*
  - the procedure for seeking assessment of costs.

B. Requirements for non-collective conditional fee agreements

- Before a conditional fee agreement is made the solicitor must fully explain what is happening to the client and tell him orally and in writing the effect of the agreement. He must also in any event tell him:
  - when the client may be liable to pay the costs of the legal representative under the agreement, *and*
  - when the client may seek assessment of the fees and expenses of the legal representative and the procedure for doing so, *and*
  - whether the solicitor considers that the client's risk of incurring liability for costs is insured against under an existing contract of insurance, *and*
  - whether other methods of financing those costs are available, and, if so, how they apply, *and*
  - whether the solicitor considers that any particular method or methods of financing any or all of those costs is appropriate and, if he considers that a contract of insurance is appropriate, or recommends a particular such contract:
    - his reasons for doing so, *and*
    - whether he has an interest in doing so.

(this must be told orally and in writing)

Rules for non-collective conditional fee agreements (*CLSA 1990 s.58, CFAR 2000*)

- A non-collective conditional fee agreement must specify:
  - the particular proceedings or parts of them to which it relates (including whether it relates to any appeal, counterclaim or proceedings to enforce a judgement or order), *and*
  - when the legal representative's fees and expenses, or part of them, are payable, *and*
  - what payment, if any, is due:
    - if those circumstances only partly occur, *and*
    - irrespective of whether those circumstances occur, *and*
    - on the termination of the agreement for any reason, *and*
  - the amounts which are payable in all the circumstances and cases specified or the method to be used to calculate them and, in particular, whether the amounts are limited by reference to the damages which may be recovered on behalf of the client.
- A non-collective conditional fee agreement which provides for a success fee must specify:
  - briefly the reasons for setting the percentage increase at the level stated in the agreement, *and*
  - how much of the percentage increase, if any, relates to the cost to the legal representative of the postponement of the payment of his fees and expenses, *and*
  - (if the agreement relates to court proceedings), that where the percentage increase becomes payable as a result of those court proceedings, then:
    - if any fees subject to the increase are assessed *and* the solicitor/client is required by the court to disclose to the court or any other person the reasons for setting the percentage increase at the level stated in the agreement, that the solicitor/client may disclose this, *and*
    - if any fees are assessed *and* any amount in respect of the percentage increase is disallowed on the assessment (because the level at which the increase was set was unreasonable), that that amount ceases to be payable under the agreement (unless the court is satisfied that it should continue to be payable), *and*
    - if the preceding • bullet does not apply *and* the solicitor agrees with anyone liable to pay fees subject to the percentage increase, that a lower amount than the amount payable under the conditional fee agreement is to be paid instead, then the amount payable under the conditional fee agreement for those fees shall be reduced accordingly (unless the court is satisfied that the full amount should continue to be payable).

C. Requirements for collective conditional fee agreements

- A 'collective conditional fee agreement' is a conditional fee agreement which does not refer to specific proceedings, but provides for fees to be payable on a common basis in relation to a class of proceedings, whether or not the person liable for fees under the agreement is the client of the legal representative.

Collective conditional fee agreements (*CCFAR 2000*)

- A collective conditional fee agreement must specify:
  - when the legal representative's fees and expenses, or part of them, are payable, *and*
  - that when accepting instructions for any specific proceedings the legal representative must:
    - inform the client when he may be liable to pay the costs of the legal representative, *and*
    - if the client requires further explanation, advice or other information about this, provide as much of it as the client may reasonably require, *and*
    - after accepting instructions in relation to any specific proceedings, that the legal representative must confirm his acceptance of instructions in writing to the client.
- A collective conditional fee agreement which provides for a success fee must specify:
  - when accepting instructions in relation to any specific proceedings that the legal representative must prepare and retain a written statement containing his assessment or reasons:
    - of the probability of the circumstances arising in which the percentage increase will become payable in relation to those proceedings ("risk assessment"), *and*
    - of the amount of the percentage increase for those proceedings, having regard to the risk assessment, *and*
    - (referring to the risk assessment), for setting the percentage increase at that level.
  - if the agreement relates to court proceedings that where the success fee becomes payable as a result, the same rules as for non-collective conditional fee agreements.

VI Bills

➤ A bill must:

- be signed by a partner, and state enough to identify the matter and the period to which it relates, *and*
- state whether VAT is included (NB: if it does not mention VAT, then it is taken to be included), *and*
- bill disbursements (eg: experts' fees) separately.

1 Client's remedies

➤ For non-contentious business, a client who is dissatisfied with a bill can ask the Law Society's Remuneration Certificate Department to issue a remuneration certificate *unless*:

a) the bill has already been paid, *or*

b) at least 1 month has passed since the client was told of his right to seek a certificate, *or*

c) the bill is due for a detailed assessment under a High Court order, *or*

d) the bill is over £50,000 (not including VAT and disbursements).

- A remuneration certificate is free, and if it sets a lower figure, that lower figure only is payable.

➤ Whether the matter is contentious or non-contentious, a client is also entitled to apply to the High Court for a detailed assessment (see p.394).

- If a client asks for a detailed assessment first, he cannot then ask for a remuneration certificate.
- In a detailed assessment, if the client is not LSC funded, costs are assessed on an indemnity basis (see p.390) but are presumed (*CPR r.48.8*):
  - to have been reasonably incurred if incurred with the express or implied approval of the client,
  - to be reasonable in amount if their amount was expressly or impliedly approved by the client,
  - to have been unreasonably incurred if:
    - they are of an unusual nature or amount, *and*
    - the solicitor did not tell his client that he might not recover all costs from the other party.

➤ **If a conditional fee arrangement,** where the court is considering a percentage increase, the court will have regard to all the relevant factors as they reasonably appeared to the solicitor or counsel when the conditional fee agreement was entered into or varied (*CPR r.48.8(3)*).

2 Solicitor's remedies

➤ A solicitor can sue on a bill (or threaten to do so), if:

a) the bill has been signed by a partner, *and*

b) the client has been notified in writing of the right to request a remuneration certificate, *or* if the bill is for a contentious matter, of his right to a detailed assessment at the High Court, *and*

c) 1 month has passed since the bill was delivered to the client (unless the court grants leave to sue earlier than this under *SA 1974 s.69*).

➤ A solicitor can charge interest on an unpaid bill, at the rate for judgment debts (see p.398) if:

a) 1 month has passed since the bill was delivered to the client, *and*

b) the client has been informed in writing of his right to challenge the bill, *and*

c) for non-contentious business, notice has been given of the right to charge interest, *and*

d) for contentious business, this has been agreed beforehand.

C Undertakings

I Undertakings generally

II Enforcement

I Undertakings generally

- An undertaking is '... any unequivocal declaration of intention addressed to somebody who reasonably places reliance on it.'
- An undertaking can be given by a solicitor *or* any member of his staff.
- An undertaking can be written or oral in form, and it need not use the word 'undertake'.
- An undertaking binds the firm, and all the partners are personally liable to ensure its performance (even if it was made by a member of staff without a partner's authority).

Undertakings

- To avoid incurring liability, a solicitor should follow these 5 steps before giving an undertaking.

Steps	
1	Ensure that it will be possible to fulfil the undertaking.
2	Obtain a client's authority before giving the undertaking.
3	Put the undertaking in writing.
4	Mark the client's file *on the outside* to warn everyone dealing with it of the undertaking.
5	Ask the recipient for a written discharge, and keep it on the client's file.

- It might be a good idea to observe a 'house rule' that only partners can give undertakings.
- Note:

  a) ambiguities are construed against the person who gives the undertaking.

  b) a solicitor is not released from his obligations if his default is due to circumstances beyond his control.

  c) the Law Society has drafted 'model' undertakings for use in certain situations (eg: conveyancing).

II Enforcement

- The court has jurisdiction over solicitors as they are officers of the court. The court may therefore deal with breaches of undertakings.
- Breach of an undertaking is a breach of the professional conduct rules and the Law Society may take disciplinary action. If a client suffers loss as a result, then the solicitor may be liable for damages.
- The client also has a right to complain to the Legal Services Ombudsman under the *CLSA 1990*.

D Discipline

I Inadequate professional services/negligence

II Disciplinary bodies

I Inadequate professional services/negligence

➤ There is a distinction between inadequate professional services, negligence and work of low quality.

Inadequate professional services	Negligence	Low quality work
◆ These may include: • breach of the conduct rules • failure to follow instructions • unreasonable delays ◆ There is no need to show damage ◆ The Law Society may take disciplinary action ◆ Complaints are dealt with by: • the Solicitors' Disciplinary Tribunal for misconduct • the Office for the Supervision of Solicitors for other inadequate professional services	◆ Breach of 'duty of care' to a client or a third party ◆ Work is performed without 'reasonable skill and care' (*SGSA 1982 s.13*) ◆ The complainant must show damage • The test for this depends on whether the action is in contract or tort ◆ A civil remedy lies in contract for the client, or in tort for a third party ◆ The Law Society *may* take disciplinary proceedings	◆ This is to be avoided, but if it falls short of negligence and does not amount to inadequate professional services, it is not actionable

➤ A solicitor should take the following actions on discovering that there are grounds for a claim.

Steps

1. Inform the firm's insurers, and ask for their advice.
2. Advise the party concerned to seek independent legal advice.
3. Ensure all communications concerning this matter are confirmed in writing.
4. He must not admit liability without the insurer's consent.

II Disciplinary bodies

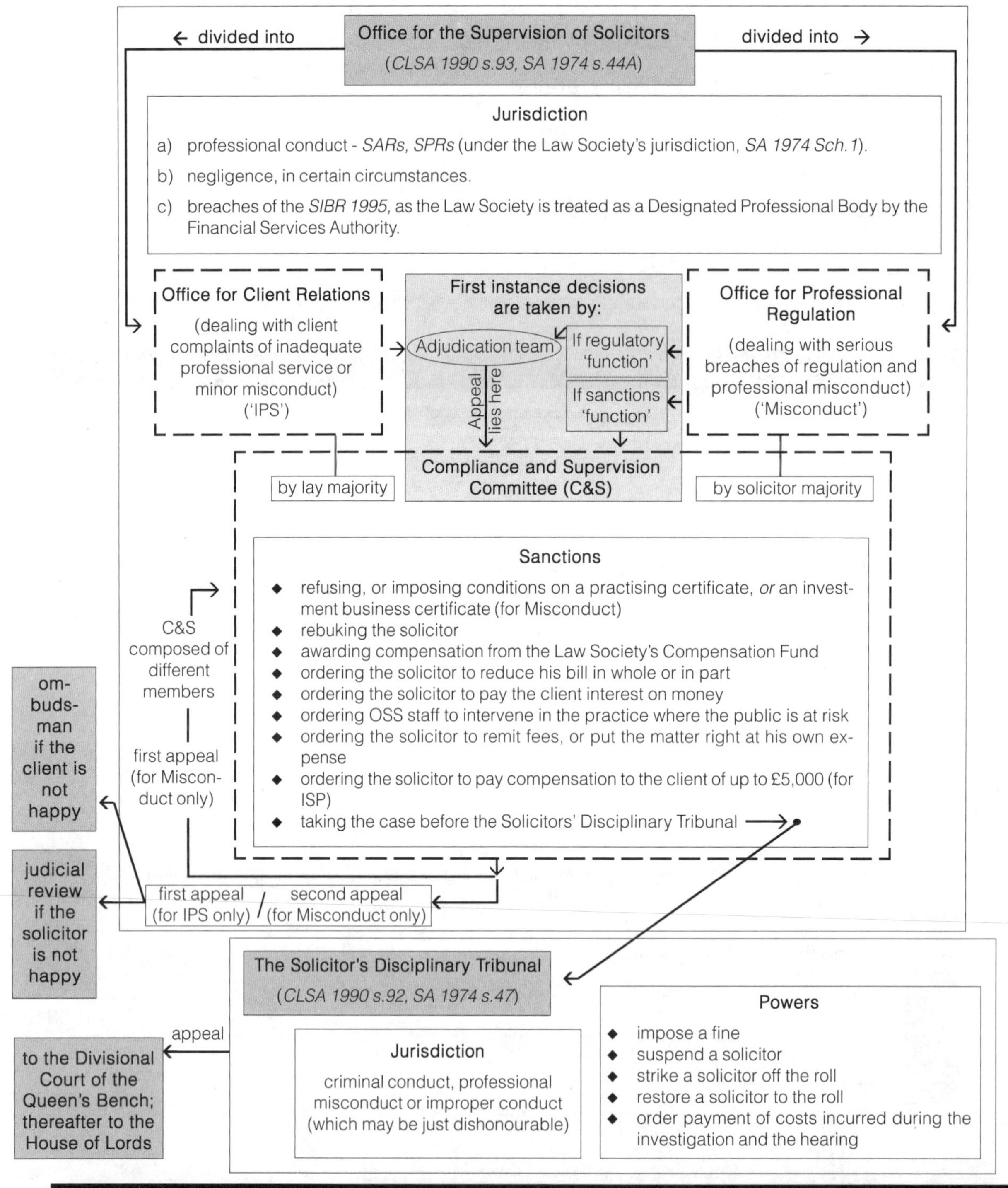
divided into
Office for the Supervision of Solicitors
(CLSA 1990 s.93, SA 1974 s.44A)
divided into
Jurisdiction
a) professional conduct - SARs, SPRs (under the Law Society's jurisdiction, SA 1974 Sch. 1).
b) negligence, in certain circumstances.
c) breaches of the SIBR 1995, as the Law Society is treated as a Designated Professional Body by the Financial Services Authority.
Office for Client Relations
(dealing with client complaints of inadequate professional service or minor misconduct)
('IPS')
First instance decisions are taken by:
Adjudication team
If regulatory 'function'
If sanctions 'function'
Appeal lies here
Office for Professional Regulation
(dealing with serious breaches of regulation and professional misconduct)
('Misconduct')
by lay majority
Compliance and Supervision Committee (C&S)
by solicitor majority
C&S composed of different members
first appeal (for Misconduct only)
Sanctions
refusing, or imposing conditions on a practising certificate, or an investment business certificate (for Misconduct)
rebuking the solicitor
awarding compensation from the Law Society's Compensation Fund
ordering the solicitor to reduce his bill in whole or in part
ordering the solicitor to pay the client interest on money
ordering OSS staff to intervene in the practice where the public is at risk
ordering the solicitor to remit fees, or put the matter right at his own expense
ordering the solicitor to pay compensation to the client of up to £5,000 (for ISP)
taking the case before the Solicitors' Disciplinary Tribunal
ombudsman if the client is not happy
judicial review if the solicitor is not happy
first appeal (for IPS only) / second appeal (for Misconduct only)
The Solicitor's Disciplinary Tribunal
(CLSA 1990 s.92, SA 1974 s.47)
appeal
to the Divisional Court of the Queen's Bench; thereafter to the House of Lords
Jurisdiction
criminal conduct, professional misconduct or improper conduct (which may be just dishonourable)
Powers
impose a fine
suspend a solicitor
strike a solicitor off the roll
restore a solicitor to the roll
order payment of costs incurred during the investigation and the hearing

Legal Services Ombudsman (*CLSA 1990 ss.21-26*)

- **Jurisdiction:** when a client is dissatisfied with the OSS's investigation of a complaint.
- **Powers:** to make a report recommending the Law Society to discipline the offender, *or* to reconsider the complaint, *or* to compensate the injured party or ensure the offender does so.
  - The Ombudsman has no powers of enforcement, but the recipient of a report must respond within 3 months.

E Financial Services

Steps

1 **Is an 'investment' involved?** (If so, go to **Step 2**)

'Investments' Part I Schedule 1	NOT 'Investments'
◆ Insurance policies with an investment element ◆ Unit trusts ◆ Company shares ◆ Debentures ◆ Government and public securities	◆ Insurance policies against risk (ie: no investment element) ◆ Building society shares ◆ Building society deposit and share accounts ◆ Bank deposits ◆ National savings (NS certificates, premium bonds) ◆ Mortgages over land and land ◆ Chattels

2 **Is the activity listed?** (If so, go to **Step 3**)

Activity	Description
◆ Dealing	Buying or selling
◆ Arranging	Fixing through a third party (but not referral)
◆ Managing	Control rather than just safekeeping
◆ Advising	About a specific investment (includes advising on others' advice)
◆ Establishing or operating collective investment schemes	

3 **Is it an excluded activity?** (If not, go to **Step 4**)

Excluded activity	Description
◆ Dealing as a principal	Acting privately on one's own behalf
◆ Sale of a company	Sale of 75% or more of the voting shares
◆ Necessary advice or arranging	Essential to the legal advice *and* no element of 'separate remuneration'
◆ Acting as (*not* for) a personal representative (PR) or trustee	No element of separate remuneration

4 **The solicitor must be authorised to conduct investment business by the Law Society, else he is in breach of the *FSA 1986*.** (Go to **Step 5**)

5 **Is the activity 'discrete investment business'?**

If so, the *SIBR 1995* apply in full. If not, the *SIBR 1995* apply in part.

Avoiding 'discrete'	Activity description
◆ Incidental business	The investment is subordinate to legal advice. (NB: However, unit trusts and life policies *are* discrete)
◆ Permitted third parties ('PTPs')	A solicitor with an investment business certificate who acts as a disclosed agent for a named client is a PTP A person may also be authorised *in his own* right to conduct investment business, eg: a stockbroker. If a member of IMRO is involved as a PTP for the client, the solicitor should set up a procedure for 'full disclosure', to ensure transparency

➤ Even for non-discrete activity, some *SIBR* requirements governing record-keeping must be followed.

➤ A non-exempt person who carries out investment business without authorisation commits an indictable criminal offence which carries a prison sentence of up to 2 years (*FSA 1986 s.4(1)*).

➤ An agreement made by, or through, an unauthorised person is unenforceable unless a court consents (*FSA 1986 s.4(2)*).

➤ Breaches of the *SIBRs* carry liability to compensate for resultant losses, and invite disciplinary action.

The Financial Services Authority ('FSA') and the *FSMA 2000*

- ➤ *The FSMA 2000 constitutes the FSA to regulate financial services in the UK by pursuing the following regulatory objectives (FSMA 2000 s.2(2)):*

  a) market confidence objective (FSMA 2000 s.3)

  - *Maintaining confidence in the financial system (eg: financial markets and exchanges and regulated activities)*

  b) public awareness objective (FSMA 2000 s.4)

  - *Promoting awareness of the benefits and risks associated with different kinds of investment and financial dealing and providing appropriate information and advice.*

  c) protection of consumers objective (FSMA 2000 s.5)

  d) reduction of financial crime (FSMA 2000 s.6)

- ➤ *In discharging its functions, the FSA must have regard to various considerations, including (FSMA 2000 s.2(3)):*

  - *the desirability of achieving innovation in connection with regulated activities, and*
  - *the international character of financial services and markets and the desirability of maintaining the competitive position of the UK, and*
  - *the need to minimise the adverse effects on competition that may arise from anything done in discharge of its functions, and*
  - *the desirability of facilitating competition between those who are subject to regulation by the FSA.*
    - *The FSA must also consider representations from a Practitioner Panel and a Consumer Panel (FSMA 2000 s.11).*

- ➤ *The FSMA 2000 will come into force at midnight on 30 November 2001; it will replace FSA 1986.*
- ➤ *The FSMA 2000 provides that:*

  - *no person may carry on a regulated activity 'in the UK' (FSMA 2000 s.418) unless he is an authorised person or an exempt person (known as the 'general prohibition') (FSMA 2000 s.19).*
    - *Certain 'regulated activities' are set out in FSMA 2000 Sch. 2 Part I (these are broadly equivalent to the activities set out in FSA 1986 Sch. 1 Part II, see also FSMA(RA)O 2001, FSMA(CRAWB)O 2001). Regulated activities relate to 'investments' set out in FSMA 2000 Sch 2. Part II (these are broadly equivalent to investments set out in FSA 1986 Sch 1 Part I).*
    - *The FSA may grant authorisation under FSMA 2000 Part IV.*
  - *a person must not, in the course of business, communicate an invitation or inducement to engage in investment activity (unless that person is an authorised person or the content of the communication is approved by an authorised person) (FSMA 2000 s.21, FSMA(FP)O 2001).*
    - *Contravention of either the general prohibition in s.19 or of s.21 is a criminal offence punishable by a fine and up to 2 years imprisonment (FSMA 2000 ss.23/25).*
    - *FSMA 2000 Part XX provides for the FSA to oversee the performance by members of the professions (eg: solicitors) of activities which are exempt from the general prohibition (FSMA 2000 s.327).*
    - *An agreement made by (or through) a person in the course of carrying out a regulated activity in contravention of the general prohibition is unenforceable, unless a court permits enforcement (FSMA 2000 ss.26-28).*

FSMA 2000, the Law Society and Solicitors

- *At midnight on 30 November 2001 the SIBR 1995 will cease to have effect.*
- *The Law Society is a designated professional body ('DPB') for the purposes of FSMA 2000 Part 20.*
  - *A DPB is required to have rules 'designed to secure that in providing a particular service to a particular client, the member carries on only regulated activities which arise out of, or are complementary to, the provision by him of that service to that client' (FSMA 2000 s.332(4)).*
  - *The Law Society has agreed with the FSA draft Solicitors' Financial Services (Scope) Rules 2001 that define 'mainstream investment advice' which solicitors may give within the DPB regime.*
    - *Non-mainstream investment advice is broadly analogous to discrete investment business under the SIBR 1995.*
  - *Following the policy of the FSMA 2000 that the FSA is to be the sole regulator of financial services, the FSA is empowered to disapply the exemption under the DPB regime with respect to particular firms, activities or the entire profession (FSMA 2000 ss.328-329).*
- *The draft SFS(S)R 2001 provide that a firm must not carry out 'prohibited activities' (without FSA regulation), eg (SFS(S)R 2001 r.3):*

  a) *market make in investments, or*

  b) *buy, sell, subscribe for or underwrite investments as principal where a firm holds itself out as engaging in the business of buying such investments with a view to sale, or*

  c) *buy or sell investments to stabilise or maintain the market price, or*

  d) *act as stakeholder pension scheme manager, establish, operate, or wind-up a stakeholder pension scheme, or*

  e) *enter into a broker fund arrangement, or*

  f) *effect or carry out a contract of insurance as a principal, or*

  g) *establish, operate, or wind-up a collective investment scheme, or*

  h) *manage the underwriting capacity of a Lloyds syndicate as a managing agent, or advise a person to become a member of a particular Lloyds syndicate, or*

  i) *enter as a provider into a funeral plan contract, or*

  j) *enter into a regulated mortgage contract as a lender, or administer a regulated mortgage contract.*
- *A firm which carries on an activity within the FSMA(RA)O 2001 must ensure that (SFS(S)R 2001 rr.4-5):*

  a) *activities arise out of, or are complementary to, the provision of a particular professional service to a particular client, and*

  b) *the provision of any service in the course of carrying out any regulated activities is incidental to the provision by the firm of professional services, and*

  c) *the firm accounts to the client for any pecuniary reward, or other advantage, the firm receives from a third party,*

  d) *neither the activities, nor the investments are within an order under FSMA 2000 s.327(6) and the FSA has not made a direction or order under FSMA 2000 ss.328-329, and*

  e) *the activity is not otherwise prohibited by the SFS(S)R 2001 (eg: recommending a packaged product or a securities and contractually based investment (other than in certain restricted circumstances), discretionary management (unless in a capacity such as a trustee and advised by an authorised person or an exempt person), or certain corporate finance activities (eg: sponsor for securities to be admitted to trading on the LSE)).*
- *Breach of the SFS(S)R 2001 is a criminal offence under FSMA 2000 s.23.*

F Professional ethics

I Conveyancing with non-solicitors

➤ When dealing with a buyer or seller who is not represented by a solicitor or a licensed conveyancer, a solicitor should:

- ensure he does not inadvertently commit an offence under *SA 1974 s.22* (eg: transferring title to land, or contracting to do so for profit without authorisation from the Law Society).
- tell his client he is dealing with an unrepresented party.
- consult the Law Society's published guidelines and write to the other party warning them (tactfully!) of the law, and asking them to confirm that they are not in danger of breaching it.
- not accept undertakings as these will not be enforceable.
  - He may be negligent in his duty to his client if he does so.
- advise the other party to seek proper legal advice. (The solicitor does not owe a duty to the other side to explain anything to them himself.)

II Criminal law - the prosecution's duties

The prosecution's duties

The duty of the prosecution is to ensure all material evidence is put before the court in a dispassionate and fair manner. *All* relevant facts should be put before the court, including, after conviction, facts relevant to mitigation.

➤ There is a duty to give evidence to the defence that the prosecution does not intend to use, eg: if the prosecution has in its possession the statement of a material witness showing the innocence of the defendant, it is its duty to disclose it to the defence. (See the 'Disclosure' provisions in 'Criminal Litigation' section - see p.453).

➤ There is a duty to tell the defence if a prosecution witness gives evidence which is inconsistent with an earlier statement.

III Criminal law - the defence's duties

The defence's duties

The defence has a duty to the court and a duty to the client.

- **When the client admits his guilt to the solicitor**, the solicitor is unable to act by positively misleading the court. However, on a plea of 'not guilty', he can still put the prosecution to proof.
- **When the client pleads 'guilty', but has a defence**, the solicitor can act. He can put the client's defence, but must advise the client that in mitigation it may not be possible to rely on the facts constituting the defence.
- **When the client gives inconsistent instructions**, the solicitor can act (if there is no false evidence).
- **The solicitor must never disclose the defence case without the client's consent.**
- **The solicitor has a positive duty to assist the court on points of law.**
- **The solicitor has a negative duty not to mislead the court on points of fact.**
- **If the client wishes to give a false name or address to the court,** the solicitor must try to persuade the client to be truthful. If he does not succeed, the solicitor cannot act.
- **If the court has an incorrect list of the client's previous convictions**, the solicitor may not correct the list without the consent of the client. If there is no such consent, the solicitor must refuse to act.
- **If for *any* reason, the solicitor is unable to act, he may not be able to say why without breaching a client confidence.** He should just say that it is impossible for him to act, without saying why.
- **If the prosecution does not realise that its detention limits are about to run out,** the defence owes a duty to the client not to remind the prosecution of this (see p.420).

IV Civil litigation

- **The overriding duty:** the solicitor has an overriding duty to the court when appearing before it or when conducting litigation, to act with independence in the interests of justice (*CLSA s.27 and 28* and see also p.316).
- There is a statutory duty to comply with the *SPR*s and other professional rules of conduct.
- **Disclosure:** the solicitor should make his client aware that it is important to:
  - preserve carefully all documents for disclosure whether they:
    - help the client's case, *or*
    - harm the client's case.
  - be truthful when dealing with such documents because:
    - the solicitor has a duty not to mislead the court, *and*
    - from the client's point of view, if it later arises at trial that documents have been withheld, lost, or 'destroyed', it may critically prejudice the client's case.

G Human rights

- ➤ Every solicitor should be aware of the impact of human rights law on all other areas of law.
- ➤ The European Convention on the Protection of Human Rights and Fundamental Freedoms (known as the European Convention on Human Rights or ECHR) was signed in Rome on 4 November 1950.
  - ◆ The ECHR establishes a European Court of Human Rights (in Strasbourg).
- ➤ The ECHR established international protection for human rights and entitled individuals to apply to the European Court of Human Rights for enforcement. This still applies even after the *HRA 1998*.
- ➤ The ECHR is now part of English law.

European Convention for the Protection of Human Rights and Fundamental Freedoms

Article	Content	Article	Content
2	right to life	8	right to respect for family and private life
3	prohibition of torture	9	freedom of thought, conscience and religion
4	prohibition of slavery and forced labour	10	freedom of expression
5	right to liberty and security ◆ includes right to be brought before a judge promptly if arrested or detained) ◆ includes compensation right if a victim of arrest / detention in held in contravention of this article	11	freedom of assembly and association
		12	right to marry
		14	prohibition of discrimination
		First Protocol	
6	right to a fair trial (includes the presumption of innocence until proven guilty)	1-3	rights to protection of property, education and free elections
7	no punishment without law (ie: victim must contravene a law in force at the time)	Sixth Protocol	abolition of death penalty except in time of war

Human Rights Act 1998

- ➤ The *HRA 1998* incorporates the Articles in the above table into English law.
  - ◆ The *HRA 1998* tries to balance protection of human rights with Parliamentary sovereignty.
- ➤ **New legislation:** all new legislation must comply with the convention rights above.
  - ◆ There must be a 'Declaration of Compatibility' before a second reading of a proposed Bill (*s.19*).
- ➤ **Existing legislation**
  - a) All legislation must (as far as possible) be interpreted by the courts to be compatible with the ECHR (*s.3*).
  - b) Courts and tribunals will have jurisdiction to hear human rights arguments.
  - c) The higher courts (eg: High Court, the Court of Appeal and the House of Lords and some others) may make a 'Declaration of Incompatibility' that a law does not accord with ECHR rights (*s.4*).
    - ◆ This does not affect the validity of the law.
    - ◆ The Crown is put on notice by the court. The Crown may make a counter-argument (*s.5*).
    - ◆ A Minister may draft a remedial order amending such legislation which must be approved by Parliament within 60 days in order to be effective (*s.10 and Schedule 2*).
      - • In cases of particular urgency, an order may be effective immediately but lapses if not approved by Parliament within 120 days.
- ➤ It is unlawful for public authorities to act in way incompatible with ECHR (*s.6*).
  - ◆ Proceedings must be brought within a year or such other period as a Court finds equitable (*s.7(5)*).
- ➤ It is unclear if ECHR rights have horizontal effect between private parties, but LJ Sedley in *Douglas & others v Hello! Ltd* [2000] All ER (D) 2435 says that for Art.10 rights at least, there is horizontal effect.

Accounts

This chapter examines:

Conventions in the presentation of accounts

- If a figure is underlined, this means it is being added or subtracted along with those ***above*** it.
- The answer may be placed in the column to the right of the underlined figure if there is one, or if there is no such column, directly below.
- The purpose of this is to help in the addition or subtraction of totals and subtotals.
- Final answers are usually double-underlined.

A Basic bookkeeping

Step 1 Produce 'T' accounts

➤ In a double entry accounting system, every transaction is recorded twice in order to produce an ongoing error check in the figures.

- 'T' accounts are used, named after the shape of the lines drawn.
  - These are 'fictional' devices which set out what is happening to particular items in a business.
    - Items can be assets, liabilities, receipts in or payments out eg: cash, a vehicle, debtors, etc.

    NB: 'T' accounts are *not* real accounts in the sense of a bank account.

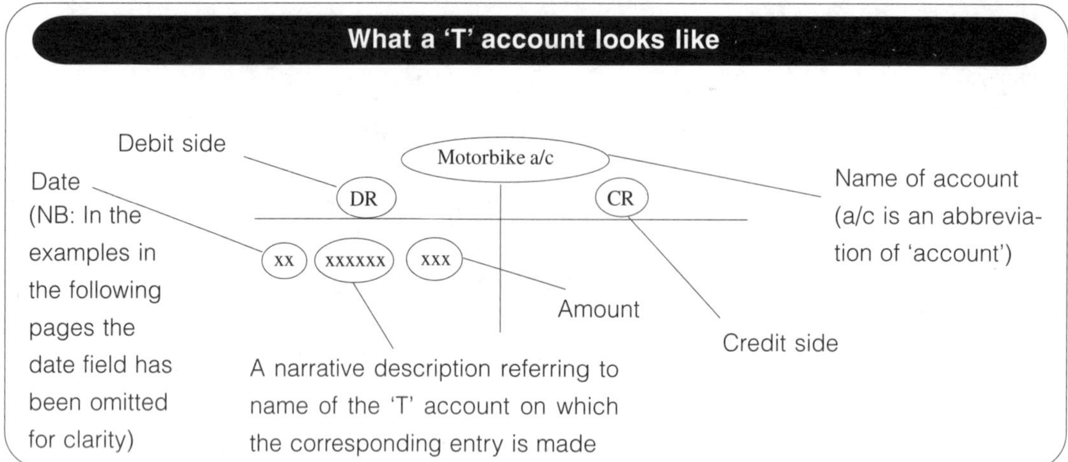

➤ A debit on 1 side of a 'T' account = a credit on 1 side of another 'T' account.

- Total debits *must* equal total credits.

➤ As many 'T' accounts as necessary are used. **It is easiest to start with the cash account entry.**

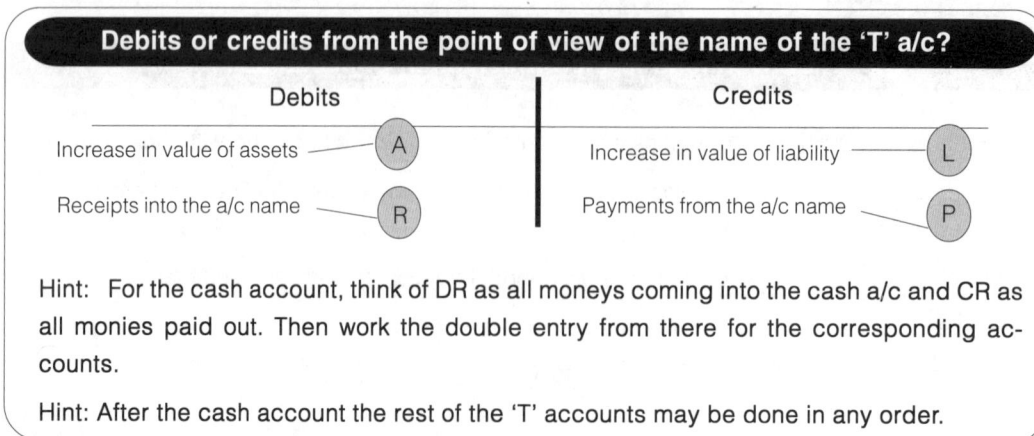

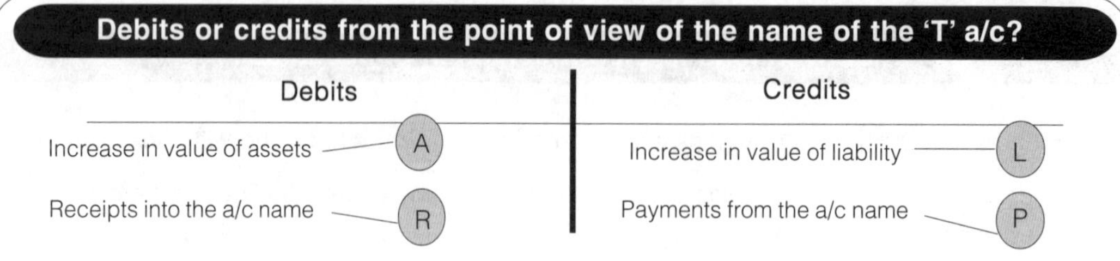

Hint: For the cash account, think of DR as all moneys coming into the cash a/c and CR as all monies paid out. Then work the double entry from there for the corresponding accounts.

Hint: After the cash account the rest of the 'T' accounts may be done in any order.

➤ The collection of 'T' accounts taken together' is known as:

- the general ledger, *or*
- the nominal ledger.

Step 1 — Example

Facts: Alpha and Beta start together as solicitors on 1 January, 2001. Each puts £15,000 into the new partnership. In the first year the following events occur:

	DR	CR
Staff salaries	27,000	
Rent	10,000	
Company motorbike	4,000	
Office equipment bought on credit	6,500	
Misc. and general expenses	1,500	
Bills delivered		90,000

They have only collected £62,000 of bills delivered and you will see that they still owe £6,500 for the office equipment.

Hint: Start with the cash account and work through the other accounts.

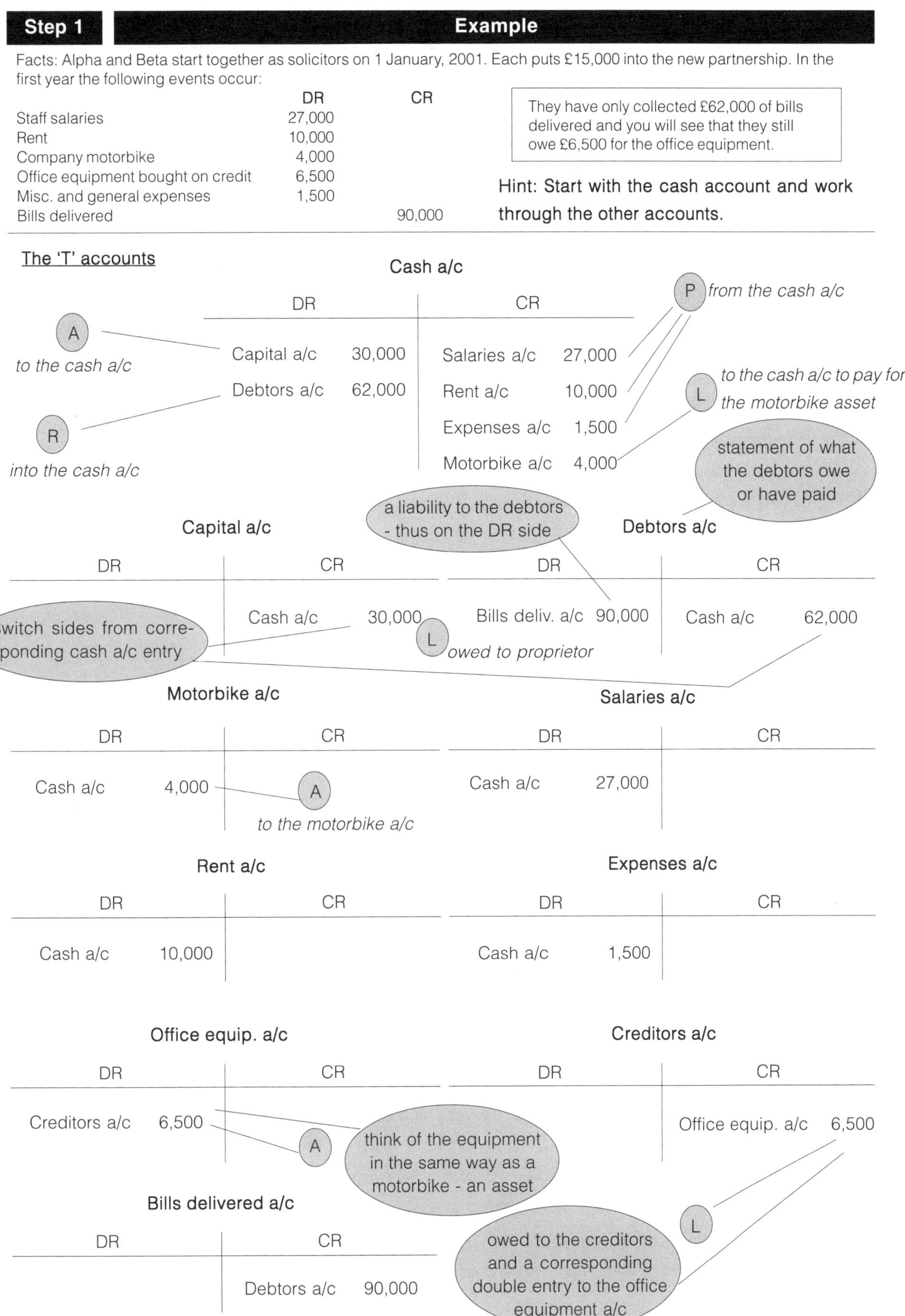

Step 2 **Balance the 'T' accounts and produce a trial balance**

A. Balancing the 'T' accounts

- The aim of balancing accounts is to draw the line under everything that has occured so far in each 'T' account and carry on into the next period with just one figure - so starting the process for each 'T' account all over again.
- Balancing off the 'T' accounts is the process of adding all the entries on each side of a 'T' account and working out what the difference is and on which side that difference falls.
- The balance is carried forward to the next period.
- There are 5 steps in this procedure which are set out (❶ to ❺) in the example opposite.

B. Producing the trial balance

- The purpose of producing a trial balance is to check the arithmetic in all of the 'T' accounts.
- A trial balance is produced as follows:
    - take each of the DR 'balance brought forward' entries (from the 'T' accounts with a balance brought forward on the DR side) and add them together to reach a total, *and*
    - take each of the CR 'balance brought forward' entries (from the 'T' accounts with a balance forward on the CR side) and add them together to reach a total, *and*
    - if the arithmetic is correct, the totals should be the same because of the double entry system whereby every time a CR is made, a corresponding DR is made, so total CR = total DR.
- The method of setting this out is illustrated in the example opposite.

Step 2 — Example

Facts: Continued from step 1.

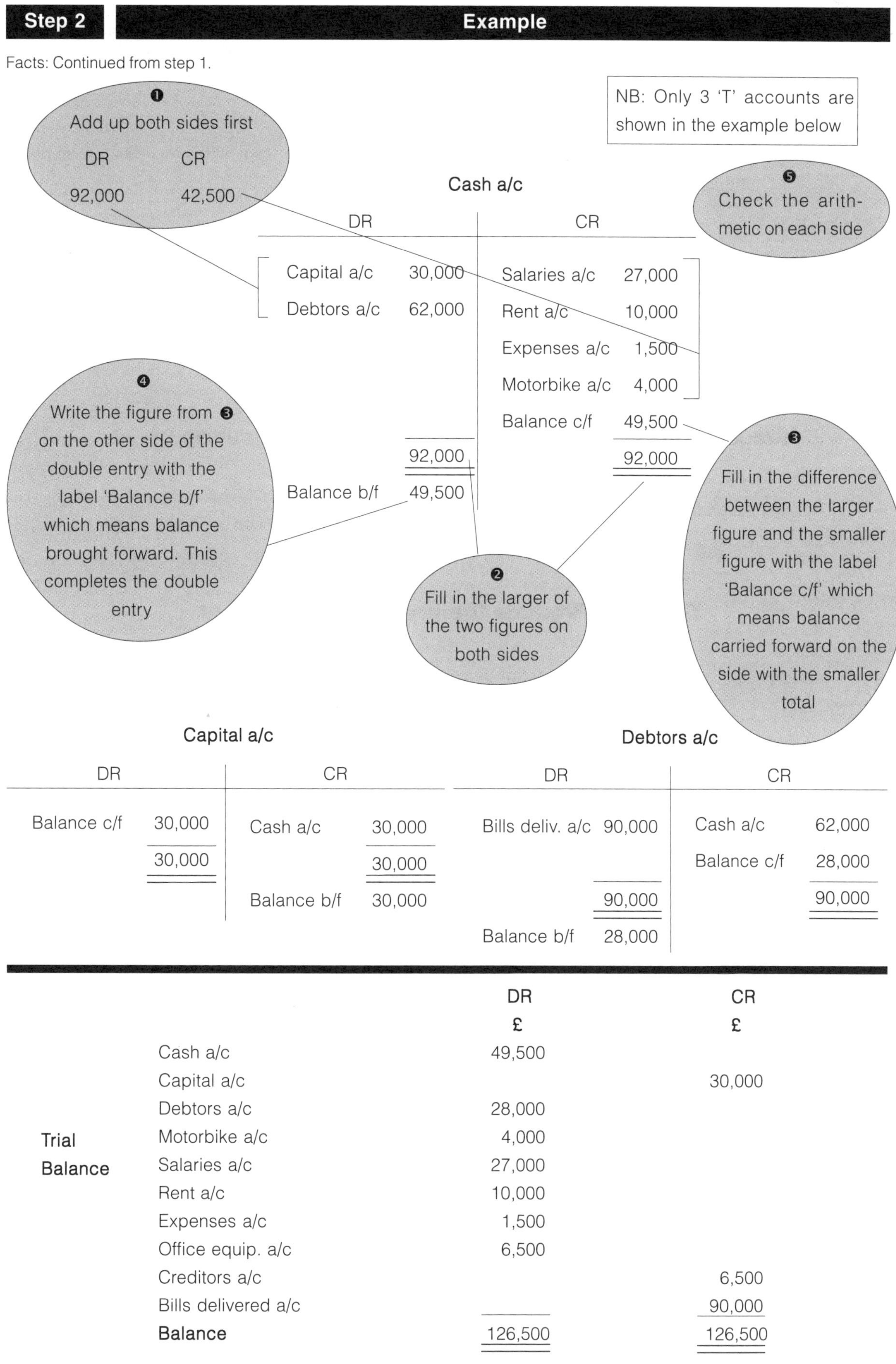
NB: Only 3 'T' accounts are shown in the example below
❶ Add up both sides first
DR CR
92,000 42,500
Cash a/c
DR
CR
Capital a/c 30,000
Debtors a/c 62,000
Salaries a/c 27,000
Rent a/c 10,000
Expenses a/c 1,500
Motorbike a/c 4,000
Balance c/f 49,500
92,000
92,000
Balance b/f 49,500
❺ Check the arithmetic on each side
❹ Write the figure from ❸ on the other side of the double entry with the label 'Balance b/f' which means balance brought forward. This completes the double entry
❷ Fill in the larger of the two figures on both sides
❸ Fill in the difference between the larger figure and the smaller figure with the label 'Balance c/f' which means balance carried forward on the side with the smaller total
Capital a/c
DR
CR
Balance c/f 30,000
30,000
Cash a/c 30,000
30,000
Balance b/f 30,000
Debtors a/c
DR
CR
Bills deliv. a/c 90,000
90,000
Balance b/f 28,000
Cash a/c 62,000
Balance c/f 28,000
90,000

		DR £	CR £
Trial Balance	Cash a/c	49,500	
	Capital a/c		30,000
	Debtors a/c	28,000	
	Motorbike a/c	4,000	
	Salaries a/c	27,000	
	Rent a/c	10,000	
	Expenses a/c	1,500	
	Office equip. a/c	6,500	
	Creditors a/c		6,500
	Bills delivered a/c		90,000
	Balance	126,500	126,500

Step 3 — Produce final accounts (Profit & loss account and balance sheet)

Stage 1 - Mark up the trial balance

- In order to produce the 2 final accounts, it is necessary to mark every item on the trial balance as being destined for the profit & loss account or the balance sheet.
  - Receipts and payments will go on the profit and loss account.
    - Receipts and payments have the nature of being ephemeral - coming and going.
  - Assets and liabilities will go on the balance sheet.
    - Assets and liabilties have a more permanent nature.
- An example of this marking is shown in the example opposite.

Stage 2 - Make any necessary adjustments as per pp.36-39.

- The example on the right has no necessary adjustments to make.

Stage 3 - Produce the profit & loss account

- The profit & loss account shows the profits or losses that the business has made during a particular period.
- The profit & loss account is part of the double entry system.
  - This means that to put entries into the profit & loss account, it is necessary to close off the relevant 'T' account.

    NB: Relevant 'T' accounts are those which are relevant to the profit & loss account from the marking up of the trial balance.
    - This means writing an entry labelled 'P&L a/c' on the opposite side to the 'balance b/f' entry with the same figure.
    - Then complete the double entry in the profit & loss 'T' a/c.
  - The relevant 'T' accounts for which this has been done are at zero and are said to be closed for the period in question. The new period will start from a zero balance again.
- There are 2 'styles' of presenting a profit and loss account.
  - Style 'A' is technical and is a presentation of the profit & loss 'T' account itself.
  - Style 'B' is more user-friendly and is a re-writing of the profit & loss 'T' account.

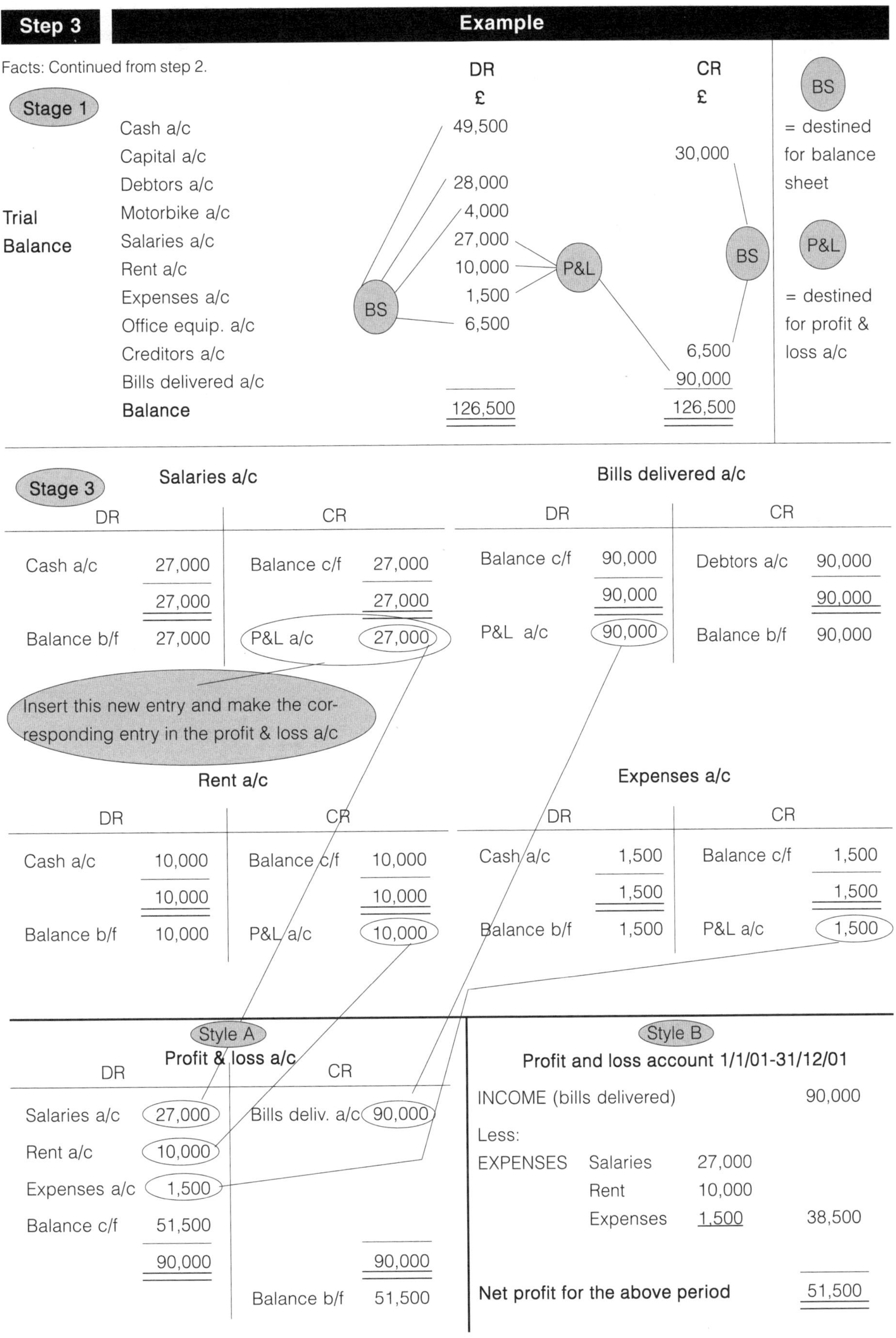

Step 3 | **Example**

Facts: Continued from step 2.

Stage 1

Trial Balance

	DR £	CR £	
Cash a/c	49,500		BS
Capital a/c		30,000	BS
Debtors a/c	28,000		BS
Motorbike a/c	4,000		BS
Salaries a/c	27,000		P&L
Rent a/c	10,000		P&L
Expenses a/c	1,500		P&L
Office equip. a/c	6,500		BS
Creditors a/c		6,500	BS
Bills delivered a/c		90,000	P&L
Balance	126,500	126,500	

BS = destined for balance sheet

P&L = destined for profit & loss a/c

Stage 3

Salaries a/c

DR		CR	
Cash a/c	27,000	Balance c/f	27,000
	27,000		27,000
Balance b/f	27,000	P&L a/c	27,000

Insert this new entry and make the corresponding entry in the profit & loss a/c

Bills delivered a/c

DR		CR	
Balance c/f	90,000	Debtors a/c	90,000
	90,000		90,000
P&L a/c	90,000	Balance b/f	90,000

Rent a/c

DR		CR	
Cash a/c	10,000	Balance c/f	10,000
	10,000		10,000
Balance b/f	10,000	P&L a/c	10,000

Expenses a/c

DR		CR	
Cash a/c	1,500	Balance c/f	1,500
	1,500		1,500
Balance b/f	1,500	P&L a/c	1,500

Style A

Profit & loss a/c

DR		CR	
Salaries a/c	27,000	Bills deliv. a/c	90,000
Rent a/c	10,000		
Expenses a/c	1,500		
Balance c/f	51,500		
	90,000		90,000
		Balance b/f	51,500

Style B

Profit and loss account 1/1/01-31/12/01

INCOME (bills delivered)			90,000
Less:			
EXPENSES	Salaries	27,000	
	Rent	10,000	
	Expenses	1,500	38,500
Net profit for the above period			51,500

Step 3... **Produce final accounts (Profit & loss account and balance sheet)**

Stage 4 - Produce the balance sheet

➤ The balance sheet performs 2 functions:

a) it is a snapshot of the business's assets and liabilities at a particular date, *and*

b) it is a check that 'Assets of the business = Liabilities of the business (ie: capital employed)'.

- The form of the balance sheet is derived from the equation as follows:

  Assets = Liabilities

  Assets = Inside liabilities (owed to the proprietor ie: capital and profit) + Outside Liabilities

  Assets = (Opening capital and profit) + Outside liabilities

  Assets - Outside liabilities = Opening capital and profit

➤ The balance sheet is *not* part of the double entry system.

- This means there is no adjustment to the 'T' accounts.

➤ The balance sheet is made up by taking the items from the marked up trial balance *and* taking the final figure from the profit and loss account and putting them into the balance sheet form. There is a pro forma balance sheet set out on p.42.

➤ The net assets [ie: (fixed + current assets) less (fixed + current liabilities)] should match the opening capital and profit. This is because it shows how the company capital is employed and tied up in assets and liabilities.

Step 3... Example (cont.)

Stage 4

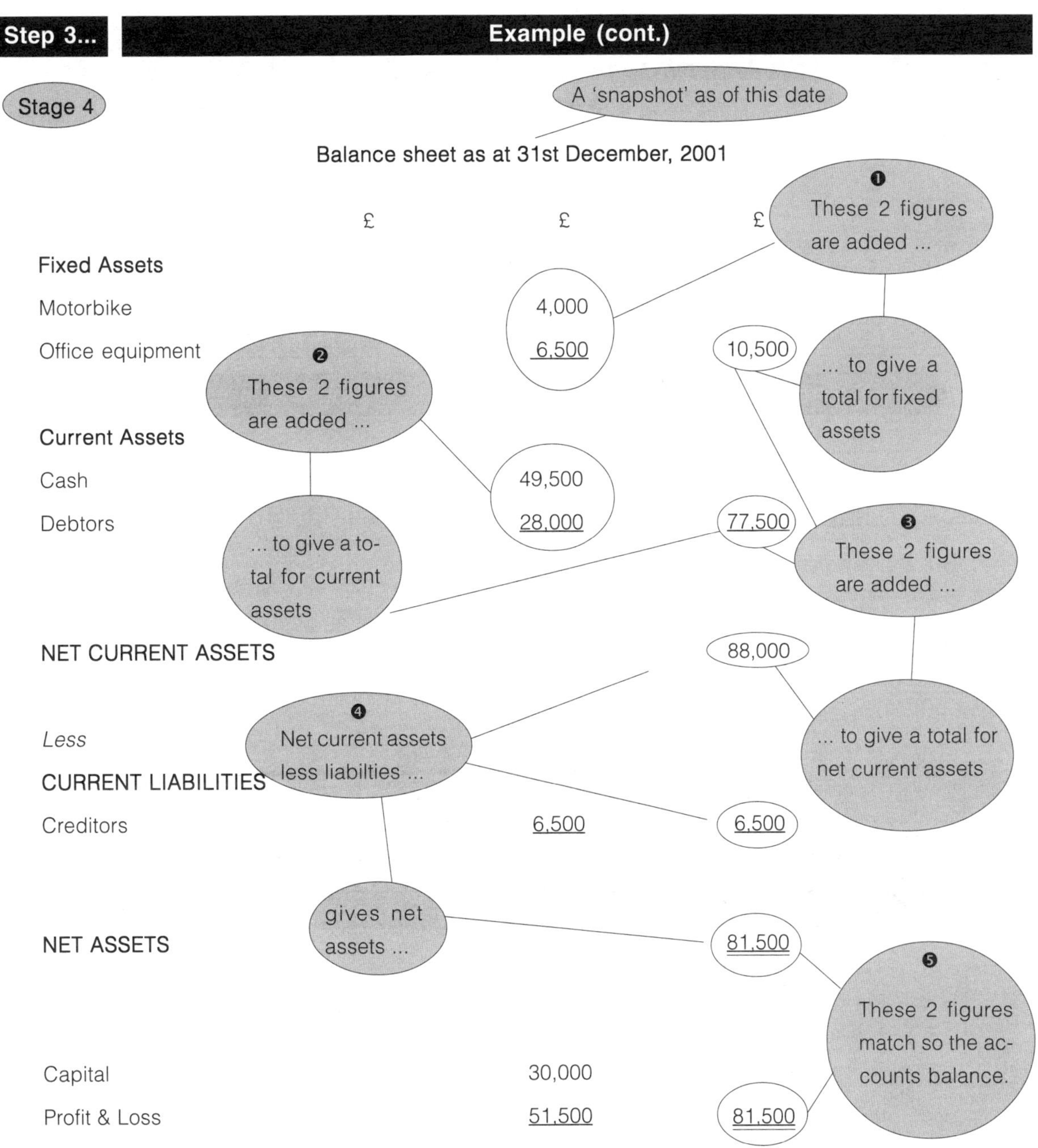

All figures used on this balance sheet are from the marked up trial balance

B Advanced bookkeeping

All advanced bookeeping in this section (A - G) necessitates changes to the profit & loss account (and other relevant 'T' accounts) and to the balance sheet. There is a fully worked example on pp.40-41.

A. Work in progress

➤ Work in progress is work that is being undertaken by the firm but which has not yet been been billed.

➤ It has value and this value must be shown in the same period as the expenses spent to produce it.

End of period 1 - taking period 1 work in progress into account

Profit & loss account

- The work in progress 'T' a/c should be debited with the period 1 work in progress figure (see p.28 because it is an asset).
- The profit & loss a/c should be credited with the period 1 work in progress figure (completing the double entry).
- If presenting the account in style B (see p.32), add the work in progress for period 1 to bills delivered.

Balance sheet

- Add work in progress under CURRENT ASSETS as per the pro forma on p.42.

Bills delivered

Start

Period 1

End

Work in progress

End of period 2 - taking period 2 work in progress into account and taking out period 1 work in progress from account

Profit & loss account

- The work in progress 'T' a/c should be debited with the period 2 work in progress figure (see p.28 because it is an asset).
- The profit & loss a/c should be credited with the period 2 work in progress figure (completing the double entry).
    - The 'T' a/cs will now be accurate as the period 1 work in progress was billed and gradually paid, the necessary entries will have been made in the work in progress a/c to bring the period 1 work in progress a/c to zero.
- If presenting the account in style B (see p.32), add the work in progress from period 2 to bills delivered and subtract the work in progress from period 1 from bills delivered.

Balance sheet

- Add work in progress under CURRENT ASSETS as per the pro forma on p.42.

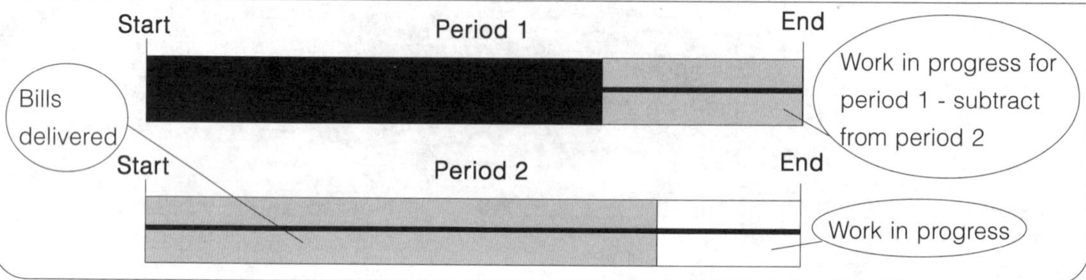

B. Bad debts

➤ Sometimes it is obvious that specific debts will not be paid by specific debtors and it is necessary to write off those debts.

➤ Adjustments:

- the balance sheet, by amending the profit & loss figure (see below) and the current assets, *and*
- the profit & loss account and other 'T' accounts:
  - The debtors a/c is credited with an entry labelled 'bad debts a/c' and the amount.
  - The bad debts a/c is debited with an entry labelled 'debtors a/c' and the amount. This is then closed off to the profit & loss account.
    - In Style 'B' presentations, bad debts is an expense of the business.

Eg: (showing the amendments to 'T' accounts only).

The facts are as on pp.29, 31 and 33 but it becomes obvious that £1,500 will never be paid:

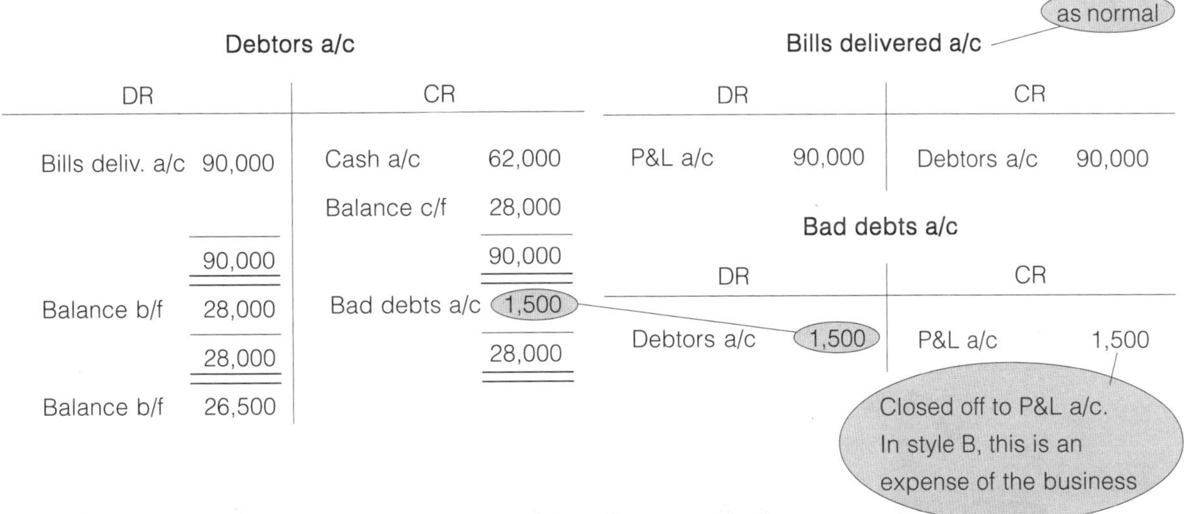

Debtors a/c
DR
CR
Bills deliv. a/c 90,000
Cash a/c 62,000
Balance c/f 28,000
90,000
90,000
Balance b/f 28,000
Bad debts a/c 1,500
28,000
28,000
Balance b/f 26,500
Bills delivered a/c
as normal
DR
CR
P&L a/c 90,000
Debtors a/c 90,000
Bad debts a/c
DR
CR
Debtors a/c 1,500
P&L a/c 1,500
Closed off to P&L a/c.
In style B, this is an
expense of the business

C. Doubtful debts

➤ It is careful accounting to make a provision for doubtful debts (unlike bad debts which is knowledge that a *specific* debtor will not pay).

- The figure chosen is based on experience of debts that as a fact have not been paid in the past and is usually a percentage of total debtors.

➤ Adjustments:

- the balance sheet, by amending the profit & loss figure (see below) and the current assets (by subtracting the figure from debtors), *and*
- the profit & loss account and other 'T' accounts:
  - The doubtful debts a/c is credited with an entry labelled 'profit & loss a/c' and the amount.
  - The profit & loss a/c is debited with an entry labelled 'doubtful debts a/c' and the amount.
    - In Style 'B' presentations, the doubtful debts are an expense of the business.

D. Payments in advance (prepayments)

➤ These are payments made in the current accounting period for goods/services in the following period.

➤ Adjustments:

- the balance sheet, by adding the prepayment as a current asset and amending the profit & loss figure (see below), *and*
- the profit & loss account and other 'T' accounts:
  - if the account with the prepayment is for example, rent, close off from the rent a/c to the profit & loss account the amount **actually paid out** for the period less the prepayment. The prepayment goes in in the CR column (of the rent a/c) (under the profit and loss a/c entry) as the "balance c/f" figure with the corresponding double entry figure being in the DR column as the balance b/f. This is the amount brought forward into the next accounting period.

NB: the cash a/c should always reflect the sums **actually paid** during the account period.

- In Style B presentations, subtract the prepayment from the rent figure.

E. Payments in arrears (accruals)

➤ These are payments that will be made in the next accounting period for goods/services used in the current accounting period.

➤ Adjustments:

- the balance sheet, by subtracting the accrual by putting it in as a current liability and amending the profit & loss figure (see below), *and*
- the profit & loss account and other 'T' accounts:
  - if the account with the accrual is for example, water, only close off from the water account to the profit & loss a/c an amount equal to the cash paid out less the prepayment. Carry forward the prepayment into the next account period.
    - In Style B presentations, add the accrual to the water figure for the period.

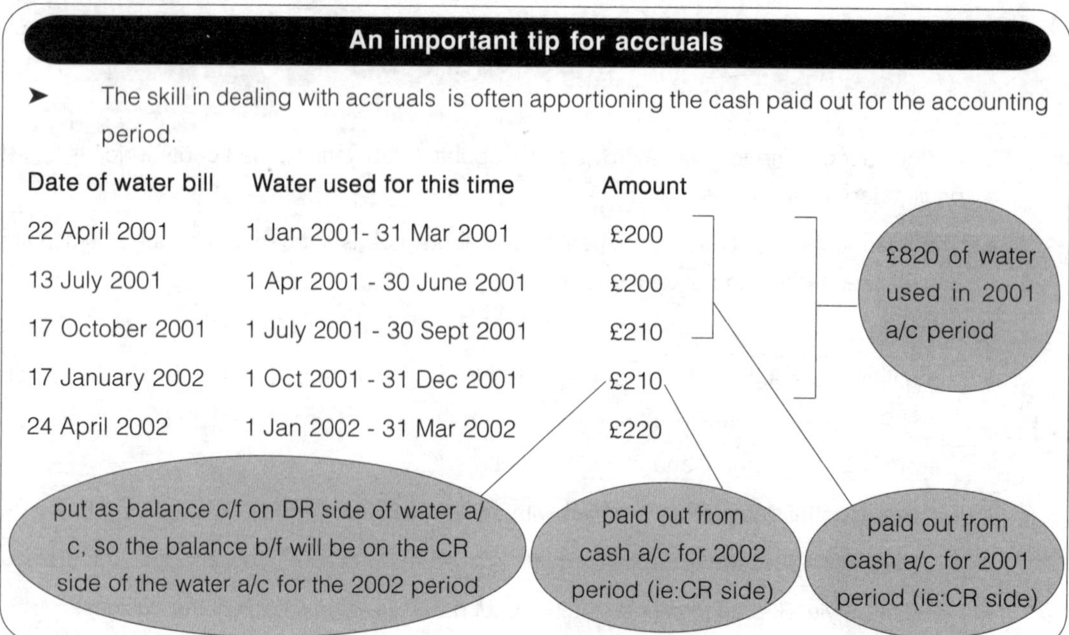

An important tip for accruals

➤ The skill in dealing with accruals is often apportioning the cash paid out for the accounting period.

Date of water bill	Water used for this time	Amount
22 April 2001	1 Jan 2001- 31 Mar 2001	£200
13 July 2001	1 Apr 2001 - 30 June 2001	£200
17 October 2001	1 July 2001 - 30 Sept 2001	£210
17 January 2002	1 Oct 2001 - 31 Dec 2001	£210
24 April 2002	1 Jan 2002 - 31 Mar 2002	£220

F. Depreciation

- Depreciation is a charge made to the business each year to reflect the loss in value of an asset, eg: if a £5,000 motorbike is expected to last the business for 5 years, we will charge a cost of £1,000 per year to the business.
  - The actual figure charged per year, although a 'guesstimate' is usually based on the experience of accountants.
- Adjustments:
  - using the motorbike example above, each year on the balance sheet under the fixed asset 'motorbike' there should be an entry labelled 'accumulated depreciation'. This will be listed as £1,000 in the first year, £2,000 in the next year until it reads £5,000 in the fifth year giving an asset value of nil.
  - 'T' accounts:
    - the motorbike a/c will have already have £5,000 listed on the DR side (as it is an asset - see p.28).
    - the accumulated depreciation a/c will already have the accumulated depreciation (for previous accounting years) listed on the CR side. Add to the CR side the depreciation for this year's accounting period and perform the 'balance c/f' and 'balance b/f' procedure to give a total figure for accumulated depreciation (for previous accounting periods and this accounting period) on the CR side.
    - the depreciation a/c should have this year's (and only this year's) motorbike depreciation put on the DR side and the account should be closed off to the profit & loss account.
      - In Style B presentations, this year's depreciation is an expense of the business.

G. Disposal of fixed assets

- When a business sells assets, it will make a profit or loss on the sale.
- This profit is reported at the end of the profit & loss account as a separate figure from the main profit figure of the business. (Since the mainstream income of the business is not derived from the buying and selling of assets, the figure from this is listed as separate, otherwise this would confuse the true proifit and loss figures.)
- When asset A is sold:
  - put in the CR column of the asset A a/c, the label 'transfer to disposal a/c' and the cost price - this clears the asset A 'T' account, *and*
  - put in the DR column of the accumulation depreciation a/c the accumulated depreciation for asset A and update the accumulation a/c by doing the balance c/f - balance b/f procedure, *and*
  - put in the DR column of the fixed asset disposal a/c the label 'Asset A a/c' and the cost figure (thus completing the double entry for (a) above), *and*
  - put in the CR column of the fixed asset a/c the label 'accumulated depreciation a/c' and the final accumulated depreciation figure for asset A (thus completing the double entry for (b) above), *and*

So far this has cleared off asset A from the main accounts into a special asset disposal account.

  - put in the DR column of the cash account the sale price, *and*
  - put in the CR column of the fixed asset disposal a/c, the sale price. Balance off the fixed asset disposal a/c and take the profit to the profit & loss a/c.
    - Style B presentations and adjustments to the balance sheet are self-explanatory.

Fully worked example

Sue, Grabbit & Run, a firm of successful solicitors in Erehwon, set up business on 1 January 1994. The accountants draw up a trial balance as at 31 December 2001 for the 2001 year of business. Produce a balance sheet and profit & loss account based on the following trial balance and extra facts:

Trial balance:	£	£
Opening capital in the business		50,000
Bank loan		80,000
Loan interest	9,000	
Balance in office account - cash	110,000	
Office equipment and computers - cost	20,000	
Office equipment and computers - accumulated depreciation		10,000
Messengers motorbikes - cost	14,000	
Messengers motorbikes - accumulated depreciation		4,000
Bills delivered		170,000
Work in progress as at 31 December 2000	80,000	
Debtors	13,500	
Creditors		8,500
Salaries	60,000	
Office rent	13,500	
Electricity	2,000	
Water	500	
	322,500	322,500

❶

Mark all items on the trial balance as destined for the BS or the P&L a/c

[white box] BS

[shaded box] P&L

Unmarked BS and P&L

- The office owes party contractors (ie: creditors) £1,000 (not yet in the account) for the 2001 office Xmas party.
- The office rent paid in advance at 31 Dec. 2001 is £2,000.
- The electricity accrued as at 31 Dec. 2001 is £400.
- The water accrued as at 31 Dec. 2001 is £100.
- It has been decided that a provision for doubtful debts of £8,500 should be made.
- Depreciation for the year is 20% of cost on office computers and equipment.
- Depreciation for the year is 15% of cost on messengers motorbikes.
- Work in progress at 31 December 2001 is £40,000.

❷

BS and P&L

Profit & Loss account for Sue Grabbit & Run for 2001 a/c period

INCOME			
Bills delivered			170,000
Less: last year's work in progress			80,000
			90,000
Add: this year's work in progress			40,000
			130,000
LESS:			
EXPENSES			
Salaries		60,000	
Loan interest		9,000	
Xmas party expense		1,000	
Office rent	13,500		
Less: rent advance	2,000	11,500	
Electricity	2,000		
Add: electricity accrual	400	2,400	
Water	500		
Add: water accrual	100	600	
Provision for doubtful debts		8,500	
Depreciation			
2001 office/computers (20% of £20,000)	4,000		
2001 motorbikes (15% of £14,000)	2,100	6,100	99,100
NET 2001 PROFIT			30,900

Total income for this year

See the box on 'conventions in the presentation of accounts' on p.27 to understand how the underlining of numbers works

Total expenses for this year

Fully worked example (continued)

Balance sheet of Sue, Grabbit & Run as of 31st December, 2001

pre 2001 office equip. depreciation

2001 office equip. depreciation

FIXED ASSETS			
Office equipment and computers - cost	20,000		
Less accumulated depreciation (10,000+4,000)	14,000	6,000	
Messengers motorbikes - cost	14,000		
Less accumulated depreciation (4,000+2,100)	6,100	7,900	13,900

pre 2001 motorbike depreciation

2001 motorbike deprecia-tion

ADD: CURRENT ASSETS			
Work in progress 2001		40,000	
Debtors	13,500		
Less provision for doubtful debts	8,500	5,000	
Prepayments		2,000	
Cash		110,000	157,000
LESS: CURRENT LIABILITIES			
Creditors	8,500		
Add creditors not yet in accounts	1,000	9,500	
Accruals			
Electricity	400		
Water	100	500	10,000
NET CURRENT ASSETS			**160,900**
LESS: LONG TERM LIABILITIES			
Bank loan			80,000
NET ASSETS			**80,900**
Capital and profit			
Capital		50,000	
Net 2001 profit		30,900	**80,900**

Pro-forma balance sheet

Balance sheet of [ ] as of [.]

V-W should equal AA+BB

FIXED ASSETS			
Asset 1 - cost	A		
Less accumulated depreciation for asset 1	B	C (A+B)	
Asset 2 - cost	D		
Less accumulated depreciation for asset 2	E	F (D+E)	G (C+F)
ADD: CURRENT ASSETS			
Work in progress current period		H	
Debtors	I		
Less provision for doubtful debts	J		
Less provision for bad debts	K	L(I+J+K)	
Prepayments (X+X+X+X+X+X+X etc.)		M	
Cash at bank		N	
Petty cash		O	P(H+L+M+N+P)
LESS: CURRENT LIABILITIES			
Creditors	Q		
Add creditors not yet in accounts	R	S(Q+R)	
Accruals (X+X+X+X+X+X+X+X etc.)		T	U(S+T)
CLIENT BALANCES			
Client bank account	Y		
Less client ledgers (owed to clients)	Y	NIL(Y-Y)	NIL
NET CURRENT ASSETS			**V(G+P-U)**
LESS: LONG TERM LIABILITIES			
Bank loan			W
NET ASSETS			V-W
Capital employed			
Capital		AA	
Net [year] profit		BB	AA+BB

Capital and Net [year] profit: if partnership accounts, this is the partners' capital and current accounts (see p.44)

C Bank reconciliations

➤ It is often necessary to 'reconcile' the bank statements of the business with the cash ledger (ie: the cash 'T' account) as a cheque on the double entry accounting. They may not match up because of:

- bank charges/bank interest on the statement but not in the cash book, *and/or*
- cheques received by the business but not yet paid into/credited to the bank account, *and/or*
- cheques paid out by the business but not yet cashed by those to whom they have been given, *and/or*
- error on the bank statement (quite common!) or in the cash book.

❶ Make sure the starting balances on the cash ledger and the bank statement are the same by bringing the previous month's transactions up to date. Then, cross off all similar items that appear in both the bank statement and the cash ledger and circle those that are different.

❷ write into the cash ledger all outstanding items (see grey boxes below)

❸ draw up a reconciliation statement to match the bank statement to the cash ledger - the end figures should be the same!

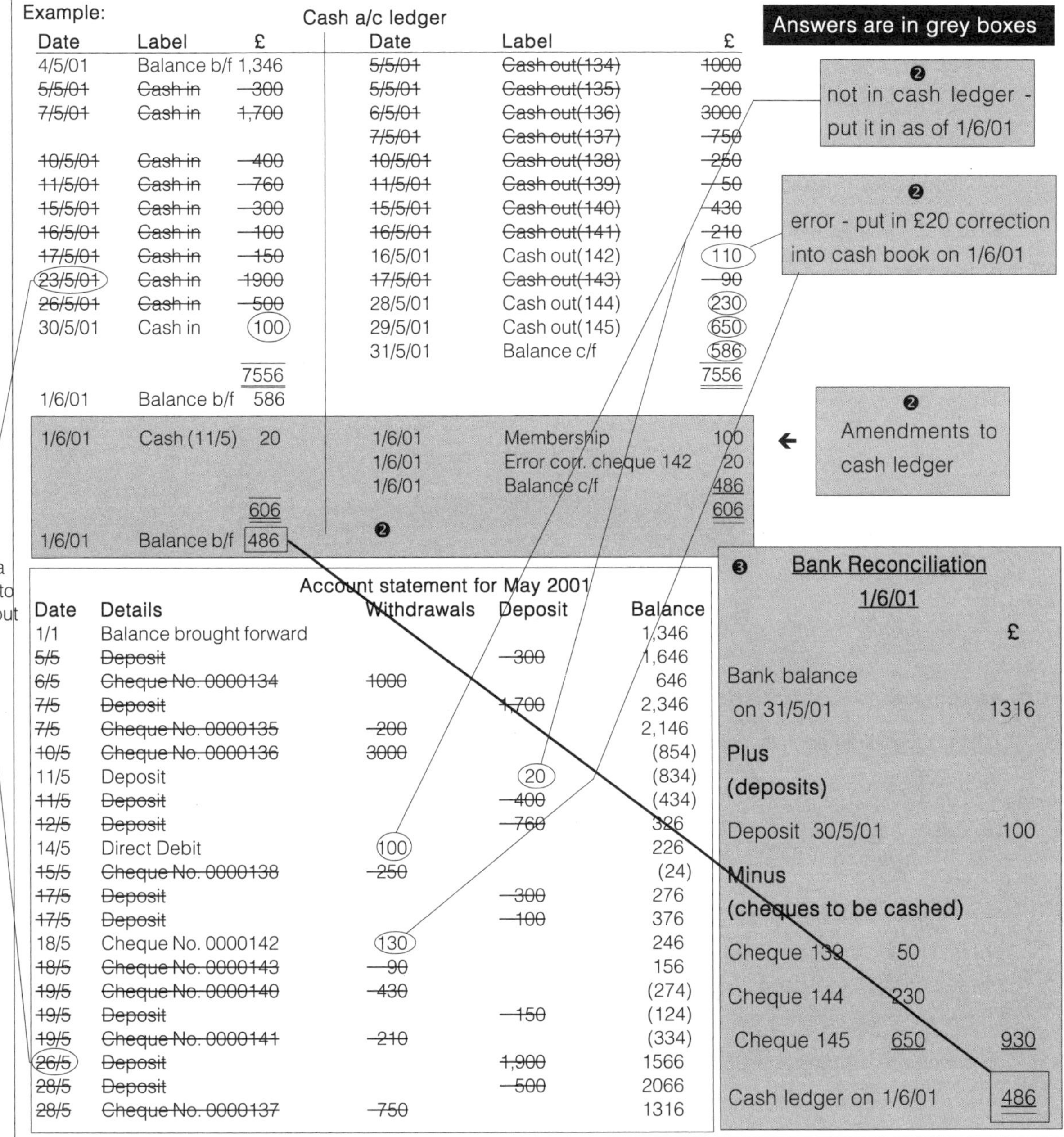

Example:

Answers are in grey boxes

Cash a/c ledger

Date	Label	£	Date	Label	£
4/5/01	Balance b/f	1,346	~~5/5/01~~	~~Cash out(134)~~	~~1000~~
~~5/5/01~~	~~Cash in~~	~~300~~	~~5/5/01~~	~~Cash out(135)~~	~~200~~
~~7/5/01~~	~~Cash in~~	~~1,700~~	~~6/5/01~~	~~Cash out(136)~~	~~3000~~
			~~7/5/01~~	~~Cash out(137)~~	~~750~~
~~10/5/01~~	~~Cash in~~	~~400~~	~~10/5/01~~	~~Cash out(138)~~	~~250~~
~~11/5/01~~	~~Cash in~~	~~760~~	~~11/5/01~~	~~Cash out(139)~~	~~50~~
~~15/5/01~~	~~Cash in~~	~~300~~	~~15/5/01~~	~~Cash out(140)~~	~~430~~
~~16/5/01~~	~~Cash in~~	~~100~~	~~16/5/01~~	~~Cash out(141)~~	~~210~~
~~17/5/01~~	~~Cash in~~	~~150~~	16/5/01	Cash out(142)	(110)
~~(23/5/01)~~	~~Cash in~~	~~1900~~	~~17/5/01~~	~~Cash out(143)~~	~~90~~
~~26/5/01~~	~~Cash in~~	~~500~~	28/5/01	Cash out(144)	(230)
30/5/01	Cash in	(100)	29/5/01	Cash out(145)	(650)
			31/5/01	Balance c/f	(586)
		7556			7556
1/6/01	Balance b/f	586			
1/6/01	Cash (11/5)	20	1/6/01	Membership	100
			1/6/01	Error corr. cheque 142	20
			1/6/01	Balance c/f	486
		606			606
1/6/01	Balance b/f	486			

❷ not in cash ledger - put it in as of 1/6/01

❷ error - put in £20 correction into cash book on 1/6/01

❷ Amendments to cash ledger

❶ eg: of a match to cross out

Account statement for May 2001

Date	Details	Withdrawals	Deposit	Balance
1/1	Balance brought forward			1,346
~~5/5~~	~~Deposit~~		~~300~~	1,646
~~6/5~~	~~Cheque No. 0000134~~	~~1000~~		646
~~7/5~~	~~Deposit~~		~~1,700~~	2,346
~~7/5~~	~~Cheque No. 0000135~~	~~200~~		2,146
~~10/5~~	~~Cheque No. 0000136~~	~~3000~~		(854)
11/5	Deposit		(20)	(834)
~~11/5~~	~~Deposit~~		~~400~~	(434)
~~12/5~~	~~Deposit~~		~~760~~	326
14/5	Direct Debit	(100)		226
~~15/5~~	~~Cheque No. 0000138~~	~~250~~		(24)
~~17/5~~	~~Deposit~~		~~300~~	276
~~17/5~~	~~Deposit~~		~~100~~	376
18/5	Cheque No. 0000142	(130)		246
~~18/5~~	~~Cheque No. 0000143~~	~~90~~		156
~~19/5~~	~~Cheque No. 0000140~~	~~430~~		(274)
~~19/5~~	~~Deposit~~		~~150~~	(124)
~~19/5~~	~~Cheque No. 0000141~~	~~210~~		(334)
~~(26/5)~~	~~Deposit~~		~~1,900~~	1566
~~28/5~~	~~Deposit~~		~~500~~	2066
~~28/5~~	~~Cheque No. 0000137~~	~~750~~		1316

❸ Bank Reconciliation 1/6/01

		£
Bank balance on 31/5/01		1316
Plus (deposits)		
Deposit 30/5/01		100
Minus (cheques to be cashed)		
Cheque 139	50	
Cheque 144	230	
Cheque 145	650	930
Cash ledger on 1/6/01		486

D Partnership accounts

- With partnership accounts, certain changes are made to the different areas of the accounts.
- The differences when dealing with partnerships are 4:

  a) partners may take interest on their capital contributions to the partnership, *and/or*

  b) partners may draw a salary for themselves, *and/or*

  c) partners will share profits according to a set formula (usually based on an agreed %age), *and/or*

  d) partners may take drawings from the business for themselves.

A. The trial balance

- Remember - a trial balance is a listing of all the balances of the 'T' accounts. Although the changes below are listed from the trial balance stage, they in fact occur much earlier when the individual 'T' accounts are worked on.
- In addition to the usual trial balance (p.30), the following changes should be made:
  - any net profit listed on the trial balance is usually, by convention, a figure taken before any of (a)-(d) above have been taken out.
  - the capital account entry is split into an entry per partner:

    eg: trial balance excerpt:

Non-partnership accounts

	DR	CR
capital		X

➔

Partnership accounts

	DR	CR
Partner's 1 capital		A
Partner's 2 capital		B
Partner's 3 capital		C

B. The appropriation accounts

- An appropriation account is a breakdown of how profit is distributed to each partner. It is not a 'T' account.
- The appropriation account lists the profit for the relevant period broken down into 3 elements:

  a) interest on capital, *and*

  b) salary, *and*

  c) profit division.

- The appropriation account is usually broken down into as many time segments as is necessary for the accounting period. Each segment represents a fixed group of partners *and* fixed levels of the list of (a)-(c) at the top of this page. If any of these change (eg: new partners are taken on, partners retire, profit share ratio changes etc.) it is necessary to start a new appropriation account for the new segment of time.
- The worked example opposite sets out how to set out the appropriation account.

Fully worked example

Alpha runs his garage business but due to pressure of work he decides to take on a new partner. On 1 August 2001 he takes on Beta who in exchange for a 35% partnership and a yearly salary of £2,000, agrees to put £10,000 in to the partnership. Alpha decides to take £1,000 p.a. salary from the time Beta joins. Both partners agree to take 5% p.a. interest on capital from the time Beta joins. Below is a trial balance for the 2001 period. Draw up the appropriation account and the partners current accounts (for current a/cs, see section C overleaf).

Trial Balance for period ending 31 December 2001

	DR £	CR £
Cash a/c	49,500	
Recovery van a/c	4,000	
Mechanical equip. a/c	6,500	
Staff salaries a/c	17,000	
Expenses a/c	12,500	
Rent a/c	10,000	
Debtors a/c	28,000	
Creditors a/c		7,500
Bills paid		139,500
Partners' capital accounts:		
Alpha		20,000
Beta		10,000
Partners' drawings:		
Alpha	45,500	
Beta	4,000	
Balance	177,000	177,000

NB: Profit for the period is bills paid (£139,500) less staff salaries (£17,000), expenses (£12,500) and rent (£10,000) = £100,000

Alpha & Beta
Appropriation account
1 January 2001 - 31 July 2001

	£	£	£
Net profit (7 out of 12 months = 7/12 of total profit) ie 100,000 x (7/12)			58333.33
Alpha (the owner)			58333.33

Alpha & Beta
Appropriation account
1 August 2001 - 31 December 2001

	£	£	£
Net profit (5 out of 12 months = 5/12 of total profit) ie 100,000 x (5/12)			41666.67 ❶
Interest on capital			
Alpha (5/12 x £20,000 x 5%)	416.67		
Beta (5/12 x £10,000 x 5%)	208.33	625.00 ❷	
Partners' salaries			
Alpha (5/12 x £1000)	416.67		
Beta (5/12 x£2000)	833.33	1,250.00 ❸	
Profit division			
Alpha (65%)	25864.59		
Beta (35%)	13927.08 ❺	39791.67 ❹	
			41666.67 ❶

First - write these

Second - calculate interest on capital and total

Third - calculate partners' salaries and total

Fourth - write in profit division [❶ - (❷ + ❸)]

Fifth - split ❹ into individual partners

C. The current accounts

- Each partner will have a current account, showing how much the business owes him (or how much he owes the business!).
- Each current account will be in a 'T' a/c format.
  - The example below is based on the facts on the previous page:

Current a/c - Alpha

DR		CR	
		31.12.01	
		profit div no.1	58,333.33
		31.12.01	
		int. on capital	416.67
31.7.01		31.12.01	
Drawings	45,500.00	partner salary	416.67
31.7.01		31.12.01	
balance c/f	39,531.26	profit div no.2	25,864.59
	85,031.26		85,031.26
		31.7.01	
		balance b/f	39,531.26

Current a/c - Beta

DR		CR	
		31.12.01	
		int. on capital	208.33
31.7.01		31.12.01	
Drawings	4,000.00	partner salary	833.33
31.7.01		31.12.01	
balance c/f	10,968.74	profit div	13,927.08
	14,968.74		14,968.74
		31.7.01	
		balance b/f	10968.74

- The current accounts are also presented in a certain format as notes to the balance sheet (see D below).

D. The balance sheet

- The 'capital employed' section of the pro forma balance sheet (p.42) is made up of:
  - the partners' capital accounts, *and*
  - the partners' current accounts.
- A note to the balance sheet lists the make-up of the current accounts.
- ALWAYS do the capital account first, followed by the balance sheet, even though they are displayed the other way round.
- An example based on the facts from the previous example is on the facing page.

E. Revaluations of assets

- A revaluation of each asset is usually carried out on a change in the partnership or a change in the profit-sharing ratio between them.
- A revaluation 'T' a/c is opened and the following ajustments are made:

	Revaluation a/c	Asset a/c	Partner capital a/c
Increase in asset value	CREDIT	DEBIT	
Decrease in asset value	DEBIT	CREDIT	
Profit on revaluation (close revaluation a/c)	DEBIT		CREDIT
Loss on revaluation (close revaluation a/c)	CREDIT		DEBIT

any credits/debits are in the agreed partner ratio of sharing profits and losses

Fully worked example (continued)

Balance sheet of Alpha and Beta as of 31st December 2001

	£	£	£
FIXED ASSETS			
Recovery van - cost		4,000	
Mechanical equipment - cost		6,500	10,500
ADD: CURRENT ASSETS			
Debtors		28,000	
Cash at bank		49,500	77,500
LESS: CURRENT LIABILITIES			
Creditors		7,500	7,500
NET CURRENT ASSETS			80,500
NET ASSETS			80,500
Capital employed			
Capital accounts			
Alpha	20,000		
Beta	10,000	30,000	
Current accounts (see note 1)			
Alpha	39,531.26		
Beta	10968.74	50,500	80,500

Do the balance sheet after the current accounts

Do this first

Notes to the balance sheet

Note (1)

Current accounts	Alpha	Beta
Interest on capital	416.67	208.33
Partners' salaries	416.67	803.33
Profit division no. 1	58,333.33	0.00
Profit division no.2	25,864.59	13,927.08
	85,031.26	14,938.74
Less drawings	45,500.00	4000.00
Balance	39,531.26	10,938.74

Put these figures into the balance sheet

E Interpreting accounts

I Generally

➤ When compiling accounts, accountants make use of guidance which the accountancy profession produces (under the auspices of the Accounting Standards Board). This guidance sets out UK generally accepted accounting practice (UK GAAP).

➤ This guidance is published in 'Statements of Standard Accounting Practice' (SSAP) and 'Financial Reporting Standards' (FRS); gradually the FRSs are replacing SSAPs.

➤ Where a feature of the accounts is unusual, or requires explanation, it should be explained in the 'Notes' found at the back of the accounts. These 'Notes' are an important aid to understanding accounts.

➤ In addition to information to be found in the 'Notes' the use of ratios provides a rough and ready way to:

- identify trends in a business (by comparing ratios in successive sets of accounts), *and/or*
- compare a business with other businesses in the same sector, or of a similar size.

➤ Some frequently used ratios, which are examined below, are designed to measure:

a) profitability.

b) financial risk.

c) cashflow.

- Ratios should be used with extreme caution - like all statistics they are misleading if looked at in isolation. Ratios are best used as a stimulus to ask questions about an enterprise (eg: why is 'dividend cover' so low?) rather than as a source of objective information.

II Ratios

A. Profitability

➤ The ratios which are used to assess a business' profitability, including the following:

1 Return on capital employed ('ROCE')

➤ This ratio relates 'profit before interest and tax' ('PBIT') to the working capital invested in a business.

➤ ROCE can be expressed as:

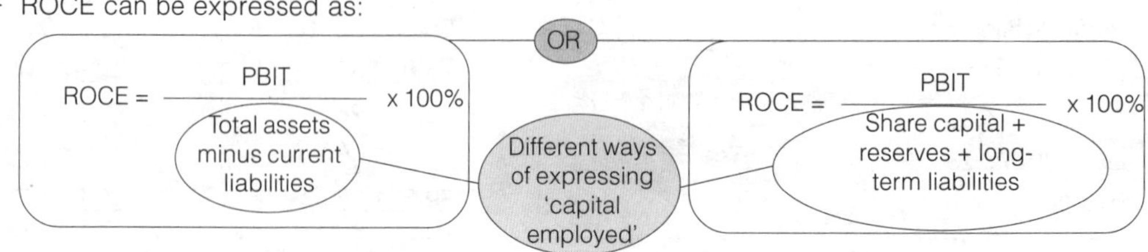

2 Asset turnover

- This ratio indicates the volume of sales the enterprise is generating using its assets/capital.
- The formula is:

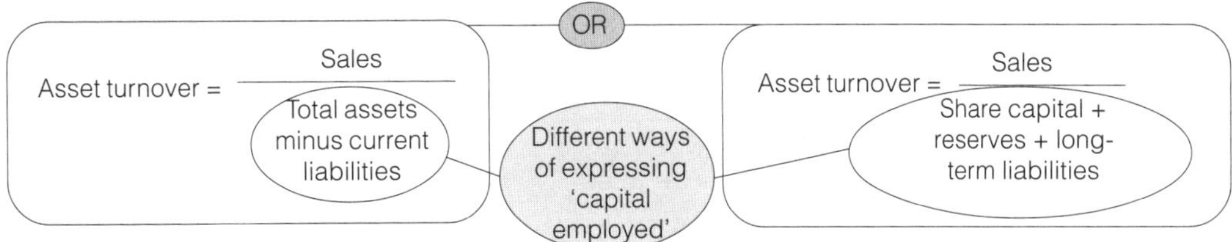

3 Profit margin

- This ratio can be used to measure an enterprise's gross profit margin (before general expenses are deducted) or net profit margin (after general expenses are deducted).

$$\text{Gross margin} = \frac{\text{Gross profit (sales less cost of sales)}}{\text{Sales turnover}} \times 100\%$$

$$\text{Net margin} = \frac{\text{Net profit (sales less all costs)}}{\text{Sales turnover}} \times 100\%$$

4 Ratios for companies with share capital

- **Earnings per share ('EPS'):** this shows how much profit is earned on each share.

$$\text{Earnings per share} = \frac{\text{Profit}}{\text{Number of issued shares}}$$

  - EPS has in the past frequently been used (indeed over used) as an indicator of whether shares are under or over priced. It is open to abuse, as the calculation of 'profit' or the use of complex capital structures mean that it can be manipulated. Note also the importance of cultural/economic influences when interpreting EPS as, for instance, the EPS is traditionally lower in the UK and the USA (eg: 10x-15x) than stock markets than on the Japanese market (eg: 20x-25x) while an internet ('.com') stock may have a large market capitalisation running into billions of dollars but generate no profit (or even incur a loss).

- **Dividend cover:** this relates the dividends a company pays to the profits the company earns.

$$\text{Dividend cover} = \frac{\text{Earnings per share}}{\text{Dividend per share}}$$

  - Note that a dividend cover of less than 1 means that the company is paying dividends out of retained profits earned in previous years, a cover of 1 or more indicates dividends are being paid out of current earnings. Public companies often maintain a dividend cover of 1.5 to 3 (eg: in the latter case £1 paid out for every £3 of profits).

B. Financial risk

➤ The following ratios are used to assess whether a company is likely to be unable to meet its obligations to its creditors.

1 Gearing

➤ Gearing relates debt finance to equity finance.

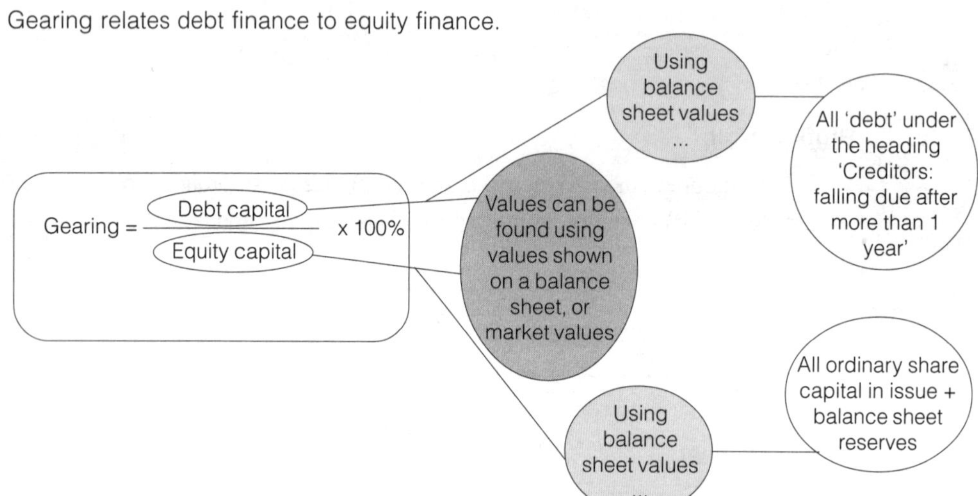

- Gearing can be measured in a number of different ways. For example, 'Total capital' can be used instead of equity capital.

➤ Whether 'gearing' (also known as 'leverage') is too high, or too low, depends on market conditions and the business sector in which the enterprise is operating. The higher the gearing, the more the equity capital may be perceived to be at risk.

2 Interest cover

➤ This ratio is a measure of credit risk - it shows how comfortably an enterprise can meet its interest obligations to creditors.

$$\text{Interest cover} = \frac{\text{PBIT}}{\text{Interest charges}}$$

3 Working capital

➤ This ratio reflects the amount of capital which is used to finance the enterprise from day-to-day.

Working capital = 'Current Assets' - 'Current Liabilities'

- Put another way, 'working capital' equals 'net current assets'.

C. Cashflow

- ➤ Cashflow is essential to any enterprise. Without sufficient liquidity to pay its liabilities as they fall due even an enterprise which on paper is extremely profitable will go bust.
- ➤ The following ratios offer a measure of how liquid an enterprise is:

1 Stock turnover ratio

➤ This ratio shows the average number of days it takes an enterprise to turn its stock over.

2 Debtor days

➤ This ratio reveals the average number of days' credit which the enterprise's customers are allowed.

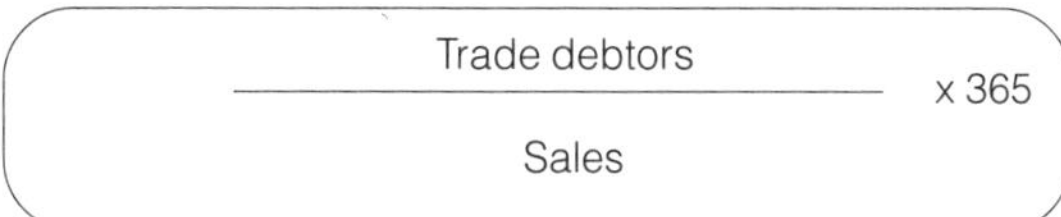

3 'Acid test' ratio

➤ This ratio can be useful if an enterprise necessarily has a slow stock turnover and it should normally exceed 1:1.

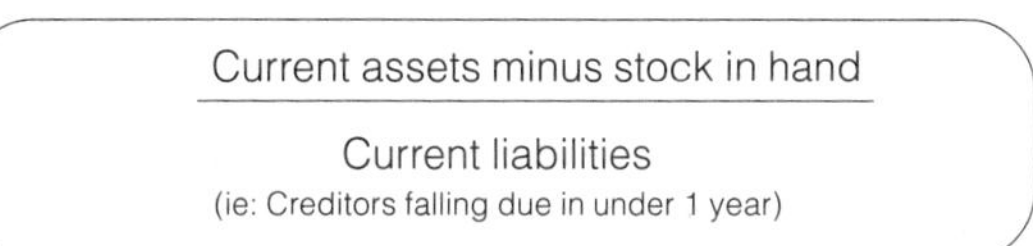

Current assets minus stock in hand
Current liabilities
(ie: Creditors falling due in under 1 year)

4 Current ratio

➤ This ratio demonstrates whether an enterprise can meet its current liabilities.

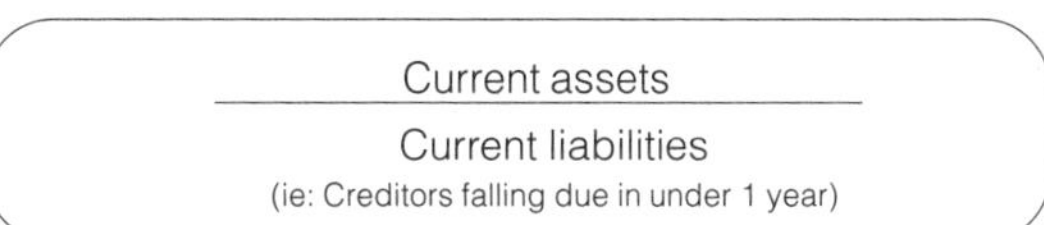

F Solicitors' Accounts Rules 1998

I Generally

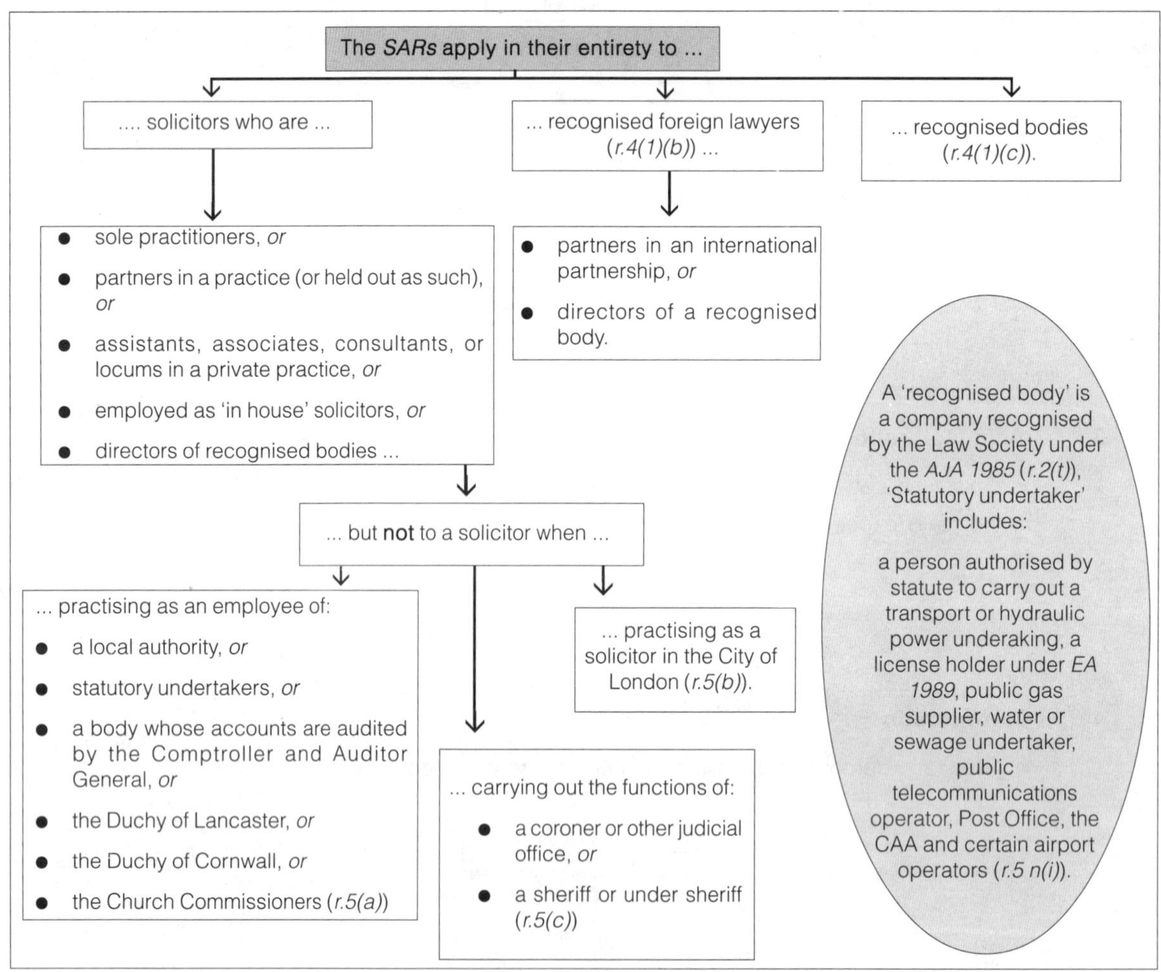

The *SARs* apply in their entirety to ...
.... solicitors who are ...
... recognised foreign lawyers (*r.4(1)(b)*) ...
... recognised bodies (*r.4(1)(c)*).
sole practitioners, *or*
partners in a practice (or held out as such), *or*
assistants, associates, consultants, or locums in a private practice, *or*
employed as 'in house' solicitors, *or*
directors of recognised bodies ...
partners in an international partnership, *or*
directors of a recognised body.
A 'recognised body' is a company recognised by the Law Society under the *AJA 1985* (*r.2(t)*), 'Statutory undertaker' includes:
a person authorised by statute to carry out a transport or hydraulic power underaking, a license holder under *EA 1989*, public gas supplier, water or sewage undertaker, public telecommunications operator, Post Office, the CAA and certain airport operators (*r.5 n(i)*).
... but **not** to a solicitor when ...
... practising as an employee of:
a local authority, *or*
statutory undertakers, *or*
a body whose accounts are audited by the Comptroller and Auditor General, *or*
the Duchy of Lancaster, *or*
the Duchy of Cornwall, *or*
the Church Commissioners (*r.5(a)*)
... practising as a solicitor in the City of London (*r.5(b)*).
... carrying out the functions of:
a coroner or other judicial office, *or*
a sheriff or under sheriff (*r.5(c)*)

'Solicitor', for the remainder of this section, refers to anyone subject to the SARs in their entirety

1 Responsibility for compliance (*r.6*)

➤ A principal (and a director of a recognised body) must ensure compliance by him or herself and everyone employed in a practice (and, in the case of a director, by the recognised body).

2 Duty to remedy breaches (*r.7*)

➤ Any breach must be remedied promptly upon discovery.

- This includes the replacement of money improperly withheld or withdrawn from client account - if necessary by the principals in the practice using their own resources.

General Principles (*r.1*)

➤ A solicitor must:

a) comply with the requirements of *SPR r.1, and*

b) keep other people's money separate from money belonging to the solicitor or the practice, *and*

c) keep other people's money safely in a 'bank' or 'building society' account identifiable as a client account except where the rules specifically provide otherwise, *and*

- A 'bank' is an institution authorised under the *Banking Act 1987*, the Post Office, or the Bank of England (*r.2(2)(c)*).
- A 'building society' is a society within the meaning of the *Building Societies Act 1986* (*r.2(2)(d)*).

d) use each client's money for each client's matters only, *and*

e) use controlled trust money for the purposes of that trust only, *and*

f) establish and maintain proper accounting systems, and proper internal controls over those systems, to ensure compliance with the *SARs*, *and*

g) keep proper accounting records to show accurately the position with regard to the money held for each client and each controlled trust, *and*

h) account for interest on other people's money in accordance with the rules, *and*

i) deliver annual accountant's reports as required by the rules.

Money a solicitor holds or receives in the course of practise is either (*r.13*):

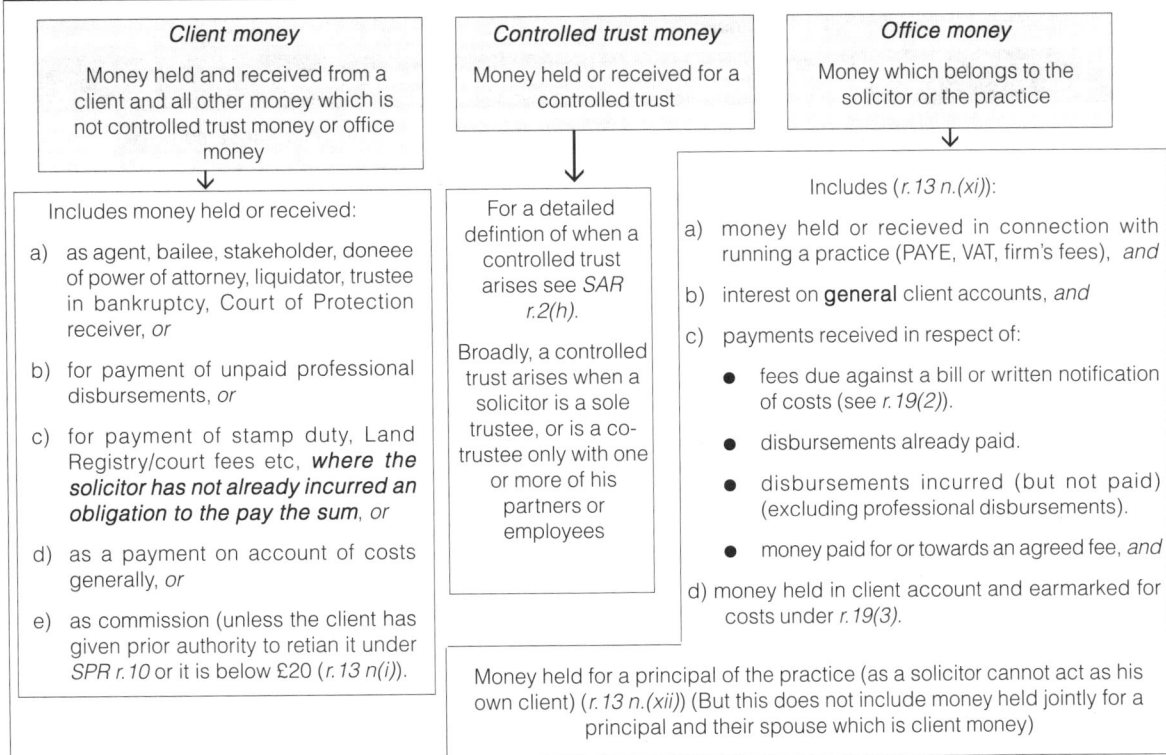

Client money

Money held and received from a client and all other money which is not controlled trust money or office money

Includes money held or received:

a) as agent, bailee, stakeholder, doneee of power of attorney, liquidator, trustee in bankruptcy, Court of Protection receiver, *or*

b) for payment of unpaid professional disbursements, *or*

c) for payment of stamp duty, Land Registry/court fees etc, ***where the solicitor has not already incurred an obligation to the pay the sum***, *or*

d) as a payment on account of costs generally, *or*

e) as commission (unless the client has given prior authority to retian it under *SPR r.10* or it is below £20 (*r.13 n(i)*).

Controlled trust money

Money held or received for a controlled trust

For a detailed defintion of when a controlled trust arises see *SAR r.2(h)*.

Broadly, a controlled trust arises when a solicitor is a sole trustee, or is a co-trustee only with one or more of his partners or employees

Office money

Money which belongs to the solicitor or the practice

Includes (*r.13 n.(xi)*):

a) money held or recieved in connection with running a practice (PAYE, VAT, firm's fees), *and*

b) interest on **general** client accounts, *and*

c) payments received in respect of:

- fees due against a bill or written notification of costs (see *r.19(2)*).
- disbursements already paid.
- disbursements incurred (but not paid) (excluding professional disbursements).
- money paid for or towards an agreed fee, *and*

d) money held in client account and earmarked for costs under *r.19(3)*.

Money held for a principal of the practice (as a solicitor cannot act as his own client) (*r.13 n.(xii)*) (But this does not include money held jointly for a principal and their spouse which is client money)

➤ Controlled trust money is treated as client money, except where the rules require otherwise (*r.8*).

➤ The *SARs* do not affect a solicitor's rights by way of lien, set off, counterclaim or otherwise against money standing to the credit of client account (*r.12*).

Categories of money *paid into* client account

May be paid into client account	a) the solicitor's own money to open or maintain the account, *or* b) an advance from the solicitor to fund a payment on behalf of a client or controlled trust (being in excess of money held for that client or controlled trust), *or* c) money paid in to replace money that has been withdrawn in breach of the *r.22, or* d) a sum *in lieu* of interest which is paid into client account instead of directly to the client (*r. 15(2)*).
Must be paid into client account	Client money (*r. 15(1)*) ◆ This must be done 'without delay', ie: in normal circumstances, the day of receipt or, if that is not possible, the next working day (*r.2(2)(z)*).
May be withheld from client account	**Client money** which is (*r. 17*): a) cash received and without delay paid in cash in the ordinary course of business to the client, or on the client's behalf to a third party, *or* b) a cheque or draft received and endorsed over in the ordinary course of business to the client or, on the client's behalf to a third party, *or* c) it is money which the client instructs the solicitor not to pay into client account, for the client's own convenience and instructions are given in writing or are given by other means and confirmed by the solicitor to the client in writing (*SAR r. 16(1)*), *or* d) unpaid professional disbursements included in a payment of costs under *r. 19(1)(b)* or *r.21, or* e) withheld on the written authorisation of the Law Society.

Controlled trust money which is (*SAR r. 18*):

a) cash received and without delay paid in cash in the execution of the trust to a beneficiary or to a third party, *or*

b) a cheque or draft received and endorsed without delay in the execution of the trust to a beneficiary or to a third party, *or*

c) money which in accordance with the trustee's powers is paid into or retained in the account of trustee (which is not client account) or properly retained cash in the performance of the trustee's duties,

d) on the written authorisation of the Law Society.

Categories of money *withdrawn* from client account

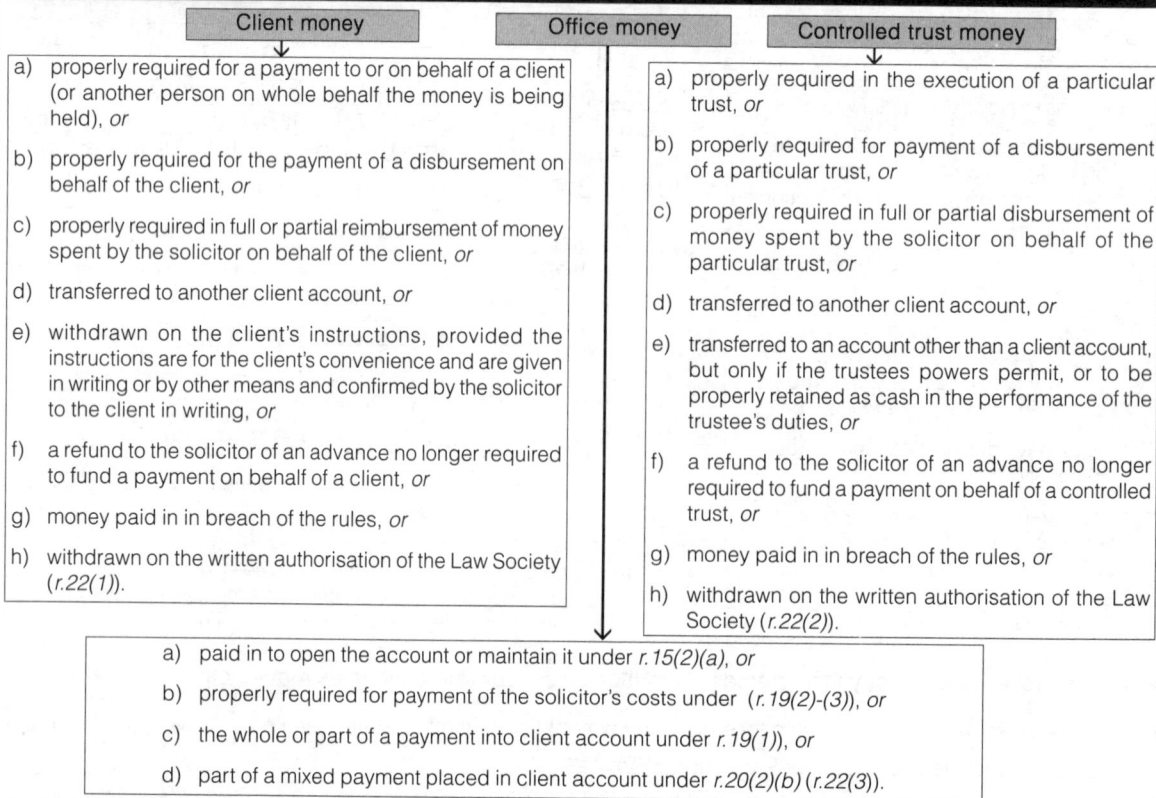

Client money

a) properly required for a payment to or on behalf of a client (or another person on whole behalf the money is being held), *or*

b) properly required for the payment of a disbursement on behalf of the client, *or*

c) properly required in full or partial reimbursement of money spent by the solicitor on behalf of the client, *or*

d) transferred to another client account, *or*

e) withdrawn on the client's instructions, provided the instructions are for the client's convenience and are given in writing or by other means and confirmed by the solicitor to the client in writing, *or*

f) a refund to the solicitor of an advance no longer required to fund a payment on behalf of a client, *or*

g) money paid in in breach of the rules, *or*

h) withdrawn on the written authorisation of the Law Society (*r.22(1)*).

Office money

a) paid in to open the account or maintain it under *r. 15(2)(a), or*

b) properly required for payment of the solicitor's costs under (*r. 19(2)-(3)*), *or*

c) the whole or part of a payment into client account under *r. 19(1)*), *or*

d) part of a mixed payment placed in client account under *r.20(2)(b)* (*r.22(3)*).

Controlled trust money

a) properly required in the execution of a particular trust, *or*

b) properly required for payment of a disbursement of a particular trust, *or*

c) properly required in full or partial disbursement of money spent by the solicitor on behalf of the particular trust, *or*

d) transferred to another client account, *or*

e) transferred to an account other than a client account, but only if the trustees powers permit, or to be properly retained as cash in the performance of the trustee's duties, *or*

f) a refund to the solicitor of an advance no longer required to fund a payment on behalf of a controlled trust, *or*

g) money paid in in breach of the rules, *or*

h) withdrawn on the written authorisation of the Law Society (*r.22(2)*).

A. Types of client account

- A solicitor who holds or receives client or controlled trust money must generally keep a client account at a bank, or a building society and the naming of the account must comply with certain formal requirements (*r. 14(1)-(3)*).
  - A bank account or building society account must be at a branch or head office in England and Wales (*r. 14(4)*).
  - A building sociey account must be a deposit or share account (*r. 14(4)*).
    - A bank means an institutions authorised under the *BA 1987* (including a European authorised institution), the Post Office, or the Bank of England. A building society means a building society for the purposes of the *BSA 1986* (*r.2(2)(c)-(d)*).
- A client account may be either (*r. 14(5)*):

  a) a separate designated client account - a deposit or share account relating to a single client, or a current, deposit or share account relating to a single controlled trust, *or*

  b) a general client account.

B. Mixed payments into client account

- A mixed payment includes both client money or controlled trust money and office money..
- A mixed payment must *either* be (*r.20(2)*):

  a) split as appropriate, *or*

  b) placed without delay in client account (in which case all office money must be transferred out of client account within 14 days of receipt (*r.20(3)*).

C. Withdrawing money from client account

- Money paid into client account in breach of the rules must be withdrawn promptly on discovery (*r.22(4)*)
- Money withdrawn from a general client account must not exceed the money held on behalf of the particular client or controlled trust in all the solcitor's general client accounts *unless*:

  a) sufficient money is held for that client or controlled trust in a separate designated client account, *and*

  b) the appropriate transfer from the separate designated client account to a general client account is made immediately (*r.22(5)-(6)*).
- Money held for a particular client or controlled trust must not be used for payments for another client or controlled trust (*r.22(7)*).
- A client account must not be overdrawn except in the following circumstances (*r.22(8)*:

  a) a separate designated client account for a controlled trust, if the controlled trustee makes payments on behalf of the truste (eg: for IHT) before realising sufficient assets to cover the payments, *or*

  b) a sole practitioner dies and his or client accounts are frozen, in which case the solicitor-manager can operate client accounts which are overdrawn to the extent of money held in the frozen accounts.

D. Receipt and transfer of costs

- A solicitor must first give or send a bill of costs, or other notification of costs, to the client or paying party (*r. 19(2)*).
  - When this has ben done, money earmarked for costs becomes office money and must be transferred out of client account within 14 days (*r. 19(3)*).
- Where a fee is fixed (this does not include a fee that can be varied upwards or that is dependant on a transaction being completed) it must be paid into office account (and the fee must be evidenced in writing) (*r. 19(5)*).

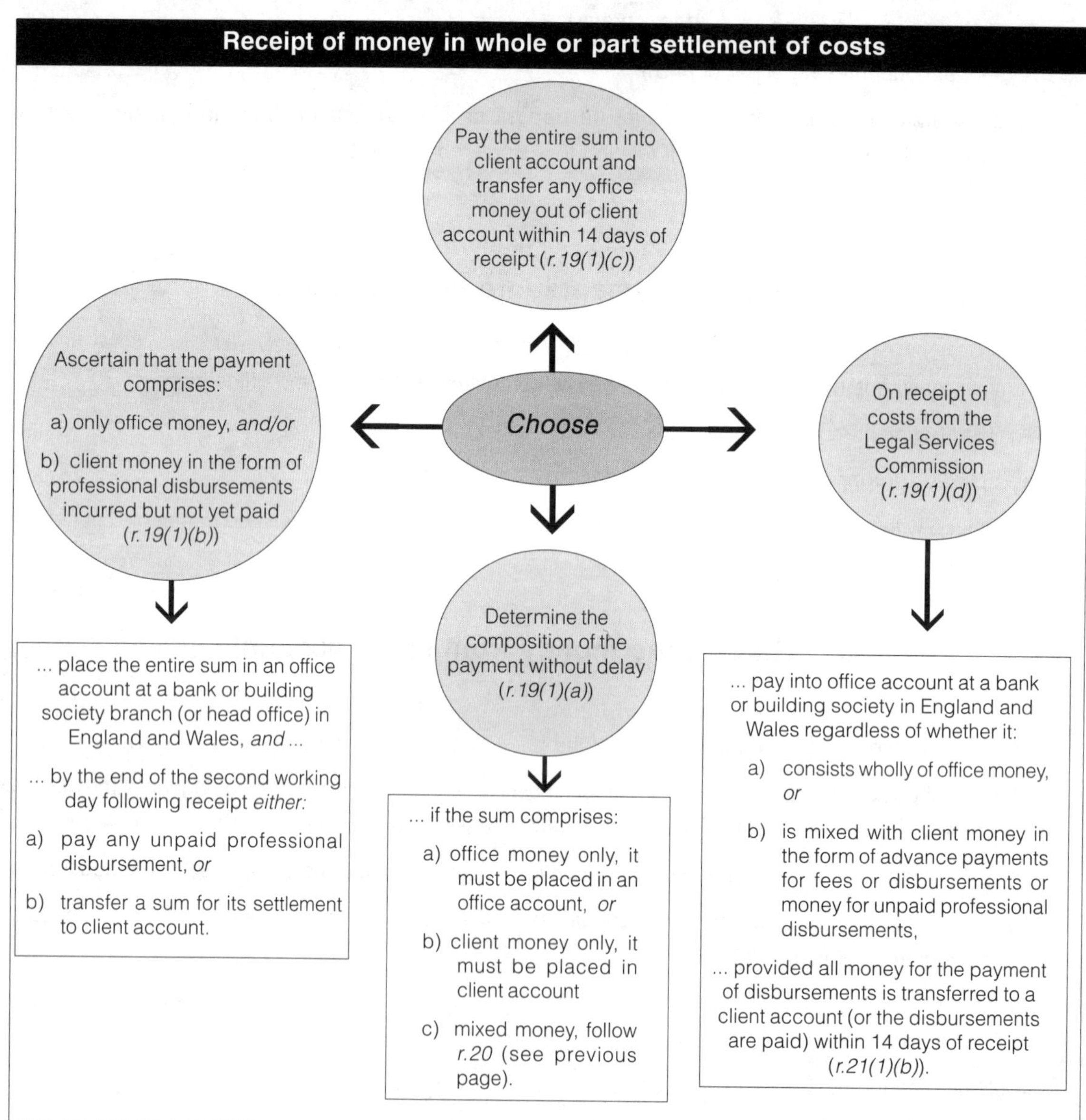

Receipt of money in whole or part settlement of costs
Pay the entire sum into client account and transfer any office money out of client account within 14 days of receipt (r. 19(1)(c))
Choose
Ascertain that the payment comprises:
a) only office money, and/or
b) client money in the form of professional disbursements incurred but not yet paid (r. 19(1)(b))
... place the entire sum in an office account at a bank or building society branch (or head office) in England and Wales, and ...
... by the end of the second working day following receipt either:
a) pay any unpaid professional disbursement, or
b) transfer a sum for its settlement to client account.
Determine the composition of the payment without delay (r. 19(1)(a))
... if the sum comprises:
a) office money only, it must be placed in an office account, or
b) client money only, it must be placed in client account
c) mixed money, follow r.20 (see previous page).
On receipt of costs from the Legal Services Commission (r. 19(1)(d))
... pay into office account at a bank or building society in England and Wales regardless of whether it:
a) consists wholly of office money, or
b) is mixed with client money in the form of advance payments for fees or disbursements or money for unpaid professional disbursements,
... provided all money for the payment of disbursements is transferred to a client account (or the disbursements are paid) within 14 days of receipt (r.21(1)(b)).

E. Payments to Legal Help practitioners

1 Payments from the Legal Services Commission

➤ An advance in anticipation of work to be carried out (although client money) may be placed in office account (*r.21(1)(a)*).

- ◆ This may only be done if the Legal Services Commission instruct in writing that it may be done.

➤ A payment for costs may be paid into office account (*r.21(1)(b)*) (see previous page).

2 Payments from a third party

➤ If the Legal Services Commission has *either* (*r.21(2)*):

a) paid costs to a solicitor *or* to a previously nominated solicitor ('green form' costs, advance payments or interim costs), *or*

b) paid professional disbursements direct and costs, *and* ....

... costs are subsequently settled by a third party:

- the entire third party payment must be paid into client account, *and*
- a sum representing payments made by the Commission must be retained in client account, *and*
- any balance belonging to the solicitor must be transferred to an office account within 14 days of the solicitor sending a report to the Commission containing details of the third party payment, *and*
- the sum retained in client account (as respresenting payments made by the Commission) must be *either*:

  i) recorded in the individual client's ledger account and identified as the Commission 's money, *or*

  ii) recorded in a ledger account in the Commission's name and identified by reference to the client or matter, *and*

  ... kept in the client account until notification from the Commission that it has recouped an equivalent sum from subsequent legal help payments due to the solicitor (The retained sum must be transferred to office account within 14 days of notification).

Some defintions in the *SARs*

'without delay'	in normal circumstances, either the day of receipt or the next day (*r.2(2)(z)*)
'costs'	fees and disbursements (*r.2(2)(j)*)
'disbursement'	any sum spent or to be spent by a solicitor on behalf of a client or controlled trust (incl. VAT) (*r.2(2)(k)*)
'professional disbursement'	the fees of counsel, lawyer, or of a professional or agent instructed by a solicitor (*r.2(2)(s)*)
'fees'	a solicitor's own charges or profit costs (incl. VAT) (*r.2(2)(l)*)

Record keeping

- A solicitor must keep a properly written up record of all dealings with client money (ie: client money received, held or paid by the solicitor) (*r.32(1)*).
    - The record (ie: a client ledger) must also distinguish a particular client's money from other money held in client account.
    - Each client ledger must show a current balance (but there is no requirement to keep a historic record of previous balances) (*r.32(5)*).
    - Transfers between client ledgers must be recorded through the cash account, or a separate record (often known as a transfer journal, or 'TJ') (*r.32(2)*).
    - A solicitor must keep a record of all bills of costs (distinguishing between profit costs and disbursements), and must record all bills and intimations of costs delivered to clients (*r.32(8)*).
- There is no obligation to keep a separate client ledger for a borrower and lender in a conveyancing transaction provided that (*r.32(6)*):
    a) the funds belonging to each client are 'clearly identifiable' (eg: the fact that an amount represents a mortgage advance from a particular lender must be clearly stated in the borrower's ledger), *and*
    b) the lender is an institutional lender providing mortgages in the normal course of its activities. (Consequently, this relaxation of the general rule does not apply if the lender is a private individual).
- At least once every 5 weeks (at least once every 14 weeks for controlled trust money held in pass-book operated designated client accounts), a solicitor must (*r.32(7)*):
    a) compare the balances in client ledgers with the cash account balance, *and*
    b) prepare a reconciliation showing the cause of any difference between the two balances and reconcile the cash account with balances shown on client account pass books or statements and money held elsewhere.
- A withdrawal from client account must not be made unless there is specific authority signed by (*r.23(1)*):
    a) a solicitor with a current practising certificate, *or*
    b) a person employed by the solicitor, being ...
        i) a solicitor,
        ii) a fellow of the Institute of Legal Executives (of not less than 3 years standing), *or*
        iii) a licensed conveyancer if an office deals solely with conveyancing.
    c) a registered foreign lawyer who is a partner or (in the case of a recognised body) a director of the practice.
        - This rule does not apply to tranfers from one general client account to another general client account at the same bank or building society (*r.23(2)*).
    - A solicitor must keep all cheques and copies of authorities (other than cheques) signed under *SAR r.23(1)* for at least 2 years, or must seek written confirmation from a bank or building society that it will retain them for at least 2 years (*r.32(10)*).
- A solicitor must keep all accounts, books, ledgers, records, and bank statements as printed and issued by a bank or building society, for at least 6 years from the date of last entry in each document (*r.32(9)*).

II Interest

A. When interest must be paid

1 **Money in a separate designated client account (*r.24(1)*)**

➤ A solicitor must account for all interest on a designated deposit account to:

- a client, if a solicitor holds money in such an account for a client.
- a person funding all or part of the solicitor's fees, if the solicitor holds money for such a person.

2 **Money held in general client account (*r.24(2)*)**

➤ A solicitor must account for a sum *in lieu* of interest (even if money should have been held in client account but was not):

- to a client, or
- to a person funding all or part of the solicitor's fees, ...

... *unless any of the following 6 exemptions applies*:

a) the amount calculated is £20 or less, *or*

b) the solicitor holds an amount for a period set out below, *or*

Amount	Period
Not exceeding £1,000	Not exceeding 8 weeks
Not exceeding £2,000	Not exceeding 4 weeks
Not exceeding £10,000	Not exceeding 2 weeks
Not exceeding £20,000	Not exceeding 1 week
Exceeding £20,000	For under 1 week or less if this is 'fair and reasonable' having regard to all the circumstances

c) money is held for payment of counsel's fees, after counsel has requested a delay in settlement, *or*

d) money held for the Legal Services Commission, *or*

e) an advance from the solicitor (under *r.15(2)(b)*) to fund a payment on behalf of the client in excess of funds held for that client, *or*

f) there is agreement to contract out of this rule under *r.27*.

3 **Money held outside client account on the client's instructions, or which a solicitor has been instructed to hold outside client account (but has not done so), under *r.16(1)(a)* (see p.54) (*r.24(6)*)**

➤ A solicitor must account:

- for all the interest earned on the account, or
- if the solicitor has failed to comply with instrustions under *r.16(1)(a)*, for a sum in lieu of an net loss of interest suffered by the client (or a person funding all or part of the solicitor's fees).

4 **Stakeholder money (*r.26*)**

➤ A solicitor must pay interest, or a sum in lieu of interest, in accordance with *r.24* to the person to whom the stake is paid.

Contracting out (*r.27*)

➤ A solicitor may come to a different arrangement from that set out in *r.24* if the solicitor enters into a written agreement:

a) with a client (and there are appropriate circumstances), *or*

b) with a client and the other party to the transaction, if the solicitor acts as stakeholder.

B. Amount of interest / *in lieu* of interest

A sum is '*in lieu*' of interest if it is not interest, but paid in respect of interest

1 **Separate designated deposit account**

➤ A solicitor must obtain a reasonable rate of interest (*r.25(1)*).

2 **General client account**

➤ A solicitor must account for a fair sum *in lieu* of interest (*r.25(1)*).

- ◆ This need not necessarily reflect the highest rate of interest obtainable, but it is unacceptable to look only at the lowest rate of interest obtainable.
- ◆ The sum must be calculated (*r.25(2)*):
  - on the balance[s] held over the whole period for which cleared funds are held, *and*
  - at a rate not less than the higher of:

    a) the rate of interest payable on a separate designated client account for the amount[s] held, *or*

    b) the rate of interest payable on the relevant amount[s] if placed on deposit on similar terms by a member of the business community, *and*
  - at the bank or building society where the money is held.

➤ If sums are held intermittently, and the sum *in lieu* of interest is £20 or less, a sum *in lieu* of interest should be paid if it is fair and reasonable in the circumstances to aggregate the sums in respect of the various periods (*r.24(4)*).

➤ If, for part of a continuous period during which money is held:

- ◆ money is held in a designated deposit account, *and*
- ◆ the sum *in lieu* of interest for the period during which it was held in general client account is £20 or less, ...

  ... a sum *in lieu* of interest should be paid if it is fair and reasonable to do so (*r.24(5)*).

G Keeping accounts as a solicitor

I Generally

- In order to comply with *SAR r.1*, a solicitor must use separate bank accounts for client money and office money. Separate cash account ledgers must be kept for each bank (or building society) account (these show amounts paid into / withdrawn from each account).
- A solicitor must keep a separate ledger for each client (*SAR r.32*) (these show amounts received from/ paid out for each client).
    - Since there are two separate cash accounts (one for office money and the other for client money), each client effectively has two ledgers - one dealing with that client's 'client money' and the other with that client's 'office money'.
- The diagram below shows how the 2 sets of ledgers relate to each other.
    - The Cash Account shows two separate accounts kept with a bank or building society (client account and office account). The Client Ledger shows the money which the firm is liable to the client for (client money) and which the client owes to the firm (office money).
    - Note that double entries are **never** made between the 'office' and 'client' ledgers, but between the those ledgers and the related ledgers in the Cash Account (for instance, when money is paid out of one account and into the other, eg: when a bill of costs is settled).

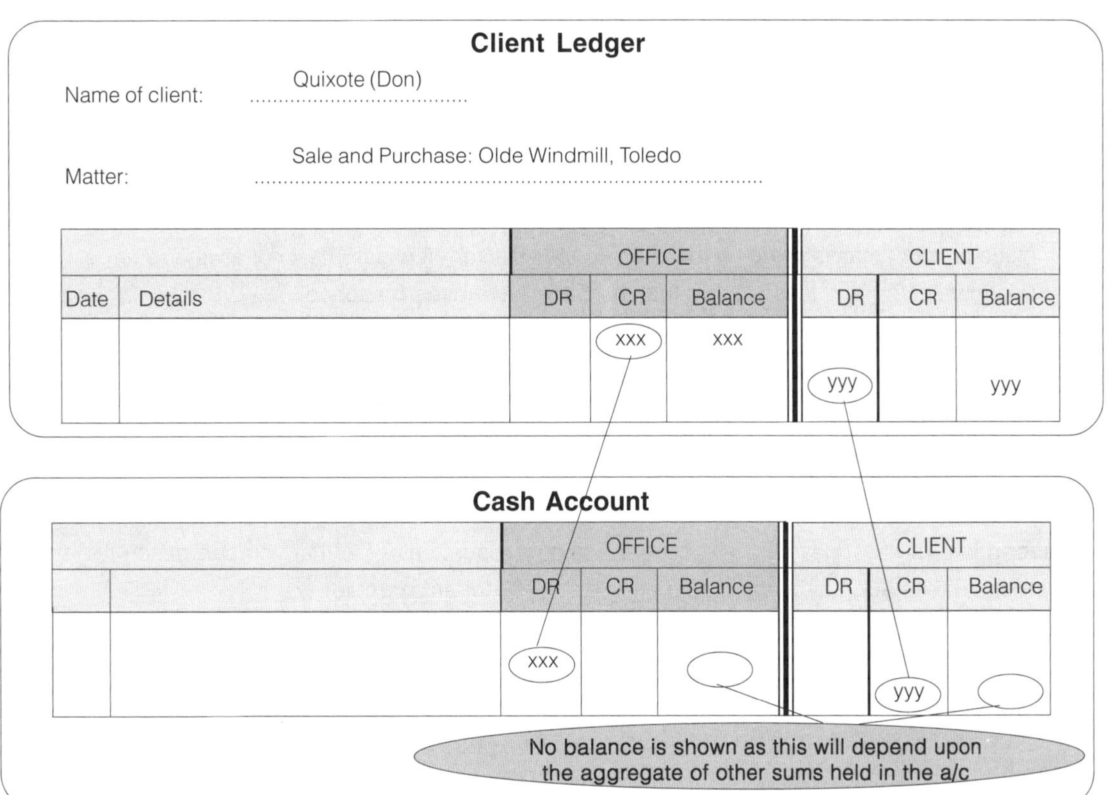

Client Ledger
Name of client: Quixote (Don)
Matter: Sale and Purchase: Olde Windmill, Toledo
OFFICE
CLIENT
Date
Details
DR
CR
Balance
DR
CR
Balance
xxx
xxx
yyy
yyy
Cash Account
OFFICE
CLIENT
DR
CR
Balance
DR
CR
Balance
xxx
yyy
No balance is shown as this will depend upon the aggregate of other sums held in the a/c

➤ Various formats can be used for ledgers, but the example below illustrates some important features of a Client Ledger comprising two separate sets of 'T' accounts (known as 'ledgers'), one showing office money and the other client money:

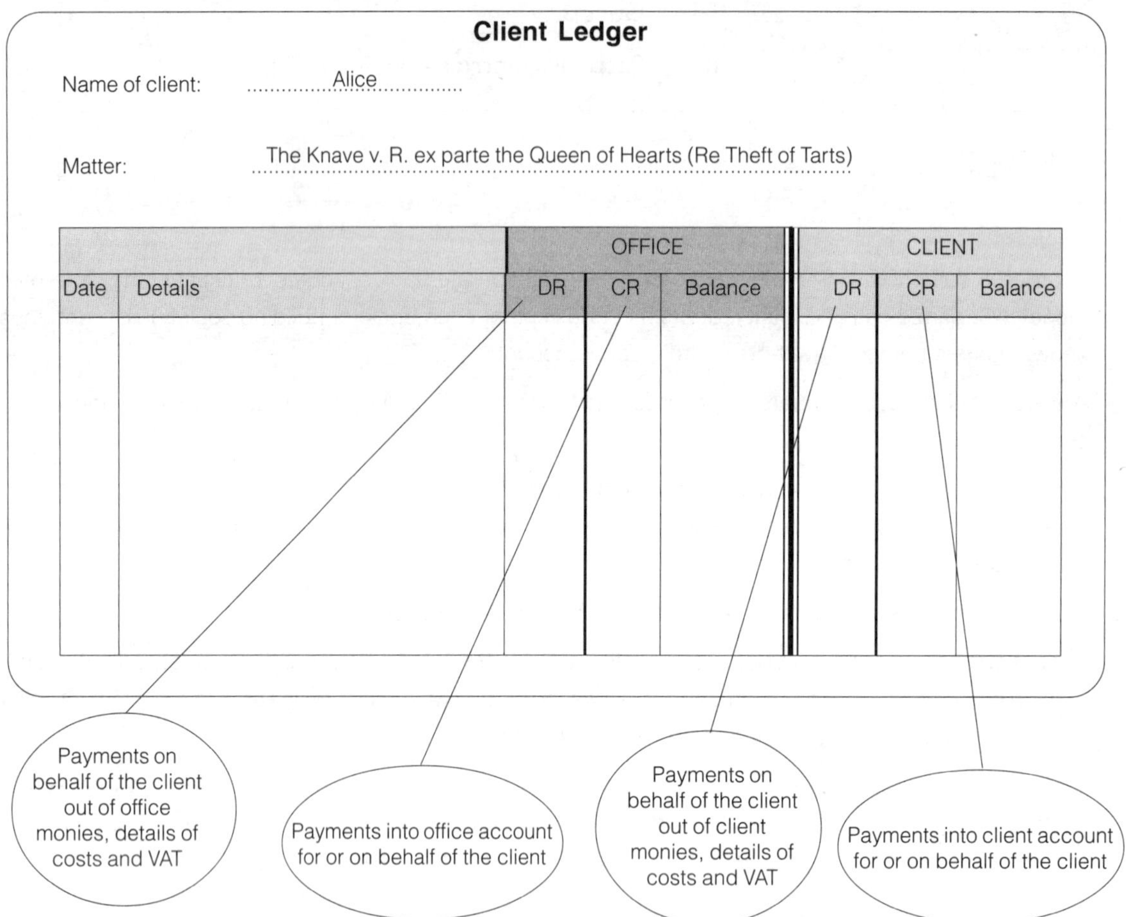

➤ **The balance in the office ledger should be a debit balance** - it indicates how much the client owes the firm for costs, disbursement etc.

- A credit balance (shown by putting 'CR' after the balance) indicates that more has been paid into the office account than is owed by the client to the solicitor - it usually (but not always, see below for the treatment of 'agreed fees') shows that the *SARs* have been breached.

➤ **The balance in the client ledger should be a credit balance** - it indicates how much money the solicitor holds on the client's behalf.

- A debit balance (shown by putting 'DR' after the balance) indicates that money has been withdrawn which does not belong to the client - the *SARs* have been breached and remedial action should be taken immediately (ie: by making good the deficiency with office money).

➤ **Description** - always 'describe' the corresponding account entry (so that you can match the entries to each other) then add any further information (see p.63 for an example).

A note on terminology

In the following pages the word 'Ledger' ('L' in caps) is used to refer to the Client Ledger recording office and client money associated with a particular client. It is also used to refer to Cash Account and other ledgers recording client or office monies (eg: Profit Costs a/c).

A 'ledger' ('l' in lowercase) dealing with 'client money' or 'office money' is called a 'column'. This is purely to avoid the confusion sometimes occasioned by accounting terminology which uses the term 'ledger' in more than one context. Thus, the 'columns' are themselves 'ledgers' (ie: separate 'T' accounts) relating respectively to 'office money' and 'client money' which are written up, for the sake of convenience, in the same 'Ledger'.

Terminology - an illustration

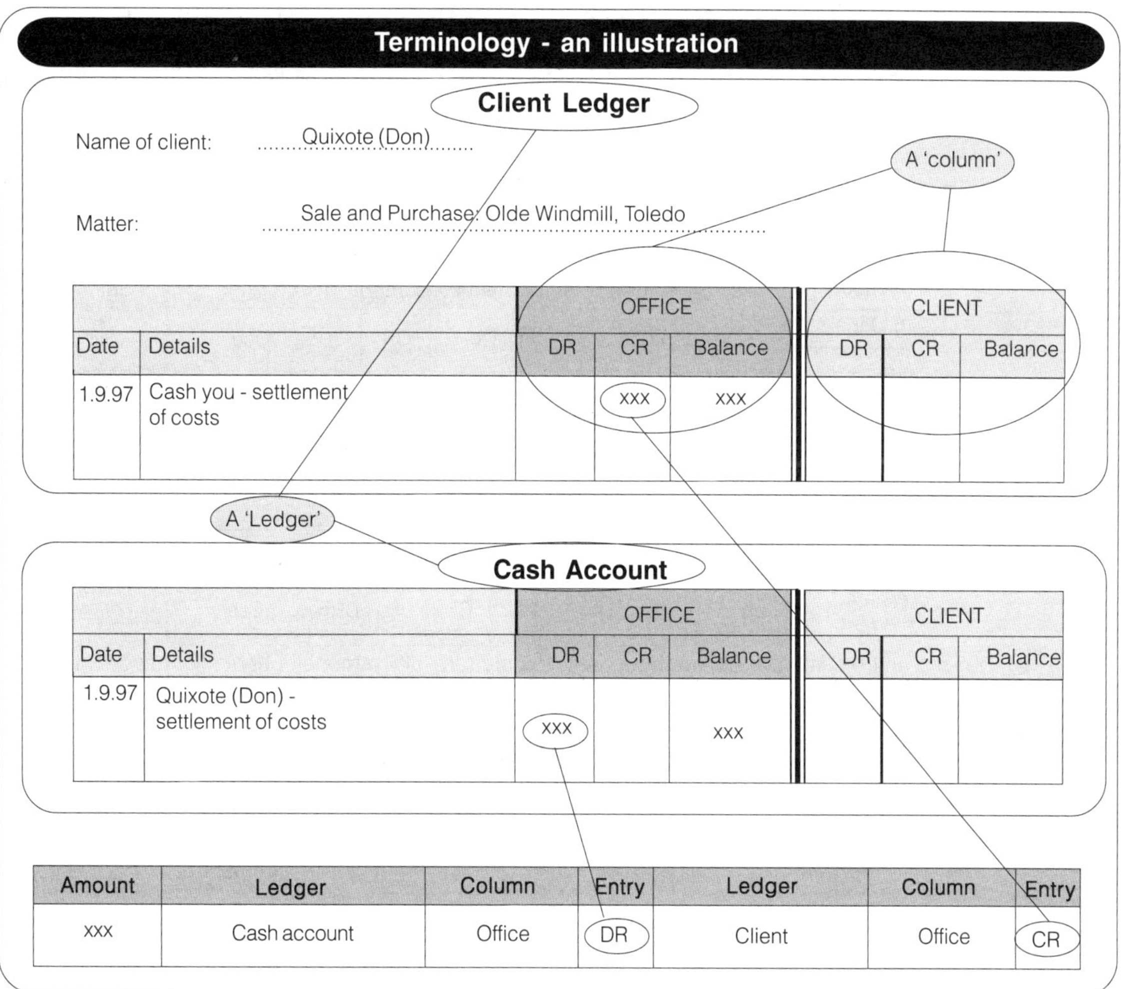

Amount	Ledger	Column	Entry	Ledger	Column	Entry
xxx	Cash account	Office	DR	Client	Office	CR

Problem solving hints

➤ Get into the habit of thinking of entries in a particular order with its own logic, eg: (following the cash)

a) is it client money or office money? (This dictates which 'column' is correct)

b) is it a receipt into Cash Account (always DR) or a payment out of Cash Account (always a CR)?

c) which Ledger should the corresponding CR entry (or DR entry) go in?

... does the column 'balance' as it should, or would the proposed entries breach the *SARs*?

I Particular entries

1 Costs and disbursements

➤ When a bill of costs is delivered to a client the following entries are made (see p.66 for VAT):

Amount	Ledger	Column	Entry	Ledger	Column	Entry
Costs	Client	Office	DR	Profit costs account	Office	CR

➤ When the bill is paid *either*:

a) the payment should be paid into office account as office money (*SAR rr.19(1)(a)-(b)*), *or*

Amount	Ledger	Column	Entry	Ledger	Column	Entry
Costs	Cash account	Office	DR	Office	Office	CR

- By the end of the 2nd working day following receipt, *either* (*SAR r.19(1)(b)*):
  - unpaid professional disbursements must be paid, *or*

Amount	Ledger	Column	Entry	Ledger	Column	Entry
Unpaid disbursement	Cash account	Office	CR	Office	Office	DR

  - a sum must have been transferred for the settlement of those disbursments to client account.

Out of office a/c

Amount	Ledger	Column	Entry	Ledger	Column	Entry
Unpaid disbursement	Cash account	Office	CR	Office	Office	DR

In to client a/c

Amount	Ledger	Column	Entry	Ledger	Column	Entry
Unpaid disbursement	Cash account	Client	DR	Client	Client	CR

b) pay the entire sum into client account and transfer any office money out of client account within 14 days (*SAR r.19(1)(c)*).

Into client a/c

Amount	Ledger	Column	Entry	Ledger	Column	Entry
Payment	Cash account	Client	DR	Client	Client	CR

Out of client a/c

Amount	Ledger	Column	Entry	Ledger	Column	Entry
Costs	Cash account	Client	CR	Client	Client	DR

Into office a/c

Amount	Ledger	Column	Entry	Ledger	Column	Entry
Costs	Cash account	Office	DR	Client	Office	CR

c) if the payment is mixed with other monies which are client money, and the solicitor does not split the cheque, the cheque should be paid into client account and the relevant amount subsequently transferred to office account (*SAR rr.19(1)(a), 20*). (The entries are as in b) above)

- Note that it is very unusual to 'split' a cheque as cheques are nowadays often crossed 'a/c payee' and so cannot be split. If a cheque is 'split', both portions are accounted for as separate payments into office and client account.

➤ Disbursements and sums paid on the client's behalf may be paid from client account if there is a sufficient balance and the solicitor has express or implied authority to make the payment. If there is not enough money in client account, then office money must be used.

2 Sums received on account of costs

➤ These are client money and should be entered on the client account.

Amount	Ledger	Column	Entry	Ledger	Column	Entry
Costs	Cash account	Client	DR	Client	Client	CR

3 VAT

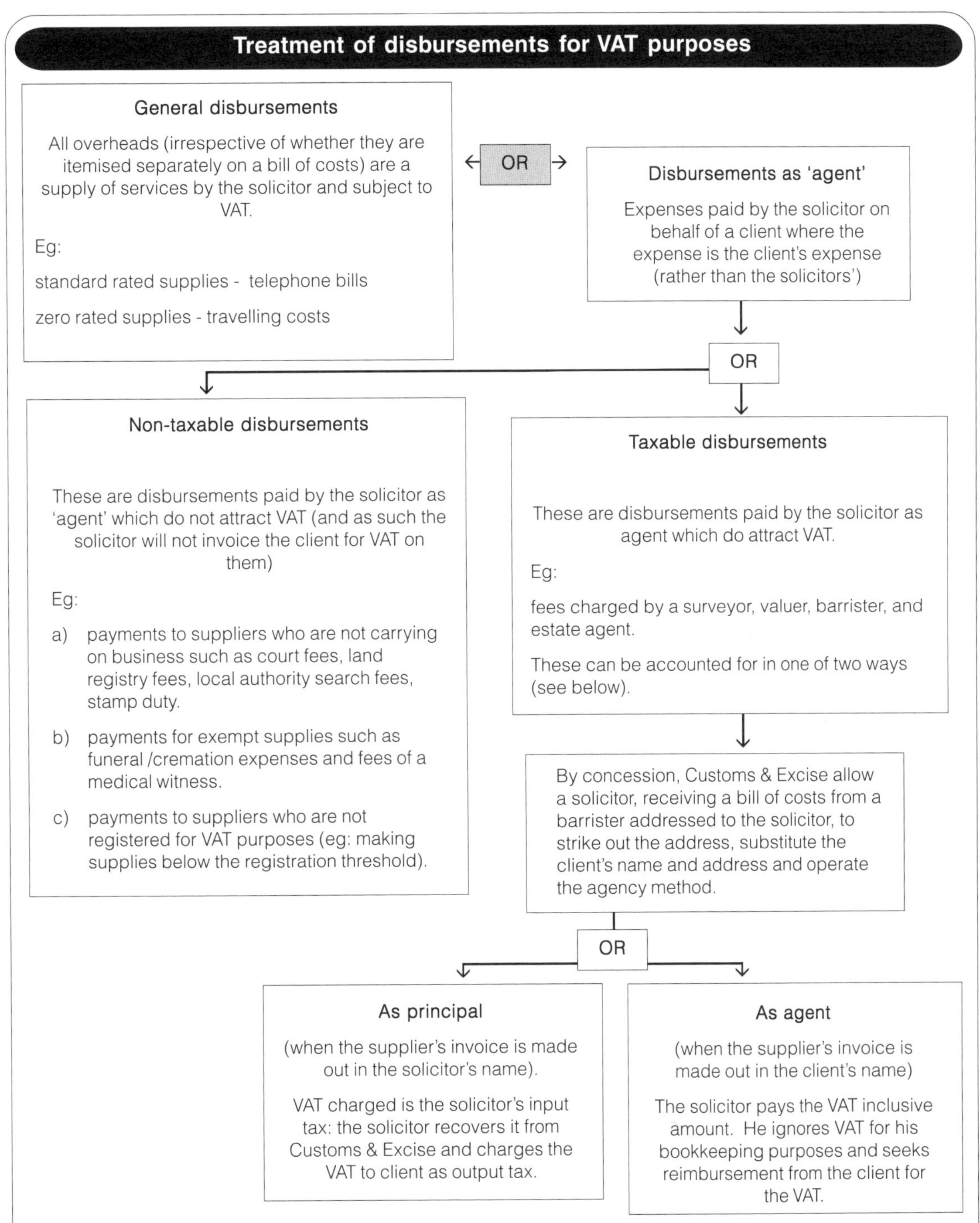

Treatment of disbursements for VAT purposes
General disbursements
All overheads (irrespective of whether they are itemised separately on a bill of costs) are a supply of services by the solicitor and subject to VAT.
Eg:
standard rated supplies - telephone bills
zero rated supplies - travelling costs
OR
Disbursements as 'agent'
Expenses paid by the solicitor on behalf of a client where the expense is the client's expense (rather than the solicitors')
OR
Non-taxable disbursements
These are disbursements paid by the solicitor as 'agent' which do not attract VAT (and as such the solicitor will not invoice the client for VAT on them)
Eg:
a) payments to suppliers who are not carrying on business such as court fees, land registry fees, local authority search fees, stamp duty.
b) payments for exempt supplies such as funeral /cremation expenses and fees of a medical witness.
c) payments to suppliers who are not registered for VAT purposes (eg: making supplies below the registration threshold).
Taxable disbursements
These are disbursements paid by the solicitor as agent which do attract VAT.
Eg:
fees charged by a surveyor, valuer, barrister, and estate agent.
These can be accounted for in one of two ways (see below).
By concession, Customs & Excise allow a solicitor, receiving a bill of costs from a barrister addressed to the solicitor, to strike out the address, substitute the client's name and address and operate the agency method.
OR
As principal
(when the supplier's invoice is made out in the solicitor's name).
VAT charged is the solicitor's input tax: the solicitor recovers it from Customs & Excise and charges the VAT to client as output tax.
As agent
(when the supplier's invoice is made out in the client's name)
The solicitor pays the VAT inclusive amount. He ignores VAT for his bookkeeping purposes and seeks reimbursement from the client for the VAT.

- A solicitor, like any taxable person, is obliged to charge VAT ('output tax') on supplies of services and may recover VAT ('input tax') on supplies attributable to taxable supplies which he or she makes. For a fuller explanation of how VAT works see p.114.
- A taxable person's liability to HM Customs & Excise is recorded in a Customs & Excise account.
- When a bill of costs is delivered to a client the following double entries must be made:

Amount	Ledger	Column	Entry	Ledger	Column	Entry
Costs (ex VAT)	Client	Office	DR	Profit costs account	Office	CR

Amount	Ledger	Column	Entry	Ledger	Column	Entry
VAT	Client	Office	DR	Customs & Excise a/c	Office	CR

- When an expense is paid (including VAT) the following double entries must be made:

Ledger	Column	Entry	Amount	Ledger	Column	Entry
Cash account	Office	CR	Expense including VAT → Expense	Nominal expenses	Office	DR
			→ VAT	Customs & Excise		

- In order to ease a subsequent bank reconciliation the apportionment between the expense and the VAT is recorded as in the following example:

Cash Account

		OFFICE			CLIENT		
Date	Details	DR	CR	Balance	DR	CR	Balance
1.1.1998	Mousetraps 240 VAT 42		282	282			

- When net VAT is paid to Customs & Excise (ie: output tax exceeds input tax for the accounting period) the following double entries must be made:

Amount	Ledger	Column	Entry	Ledger	Column	Entry
Net VAT	Cash account	Office	CR	Customs & Excise a/c	Office	DR

4 Agreed fees

- A payment from a client in respect of agreed fees is office money and should not be paid into client account (*SAR r.13*). (This may create a credit ('CR') balance in the office account - but this will be cancelled by a corresponding debit ('DR') in the office account when the solicitor issues his bill).

5 Deposits (Conveyancing transactions)

- A deposit can be held as agent for the seller, or as stakeholder. In both cases a deposit is 'client money' (*SAR r.13*).
- The accounting treatment differs depending on how deposit monies are held.
  - **As agent:** the solicitor may account immediately to the client for the deposit.

Amount	Ledger	Column	Entry	Ledger	Column	Entry
Deposit	Cash account	Client	DR	Client	Client	CR

  - **As stakeholder:**

a) The solicitor should not account immediately to the client for the deposit - the deposit is recorded in a separate ledger, the 'stakeholder account'.

Amount	Ledger	Column	Entry	Ledger	Column	Entry
Deposit	Cash account	Client	DR	Stakeholder a/c	Client	CR

b) On completion, a transfer is made from the 'stakeholder account' to the client's ledger account. This transfer between the 'stakeholder account' and the client's ledger is a transfer between client ledgers and although there is therefore no need to record the transfer in the cash account (as no money is being withdrawn from client account), the transfer must be noted in both client accounts (*SAR r.32*), stating in both cases 'transfer of deposit TJ' (for 'transfer journal')

Amount	Ledger	Column	Entry	Ledger	Column	Entry
Deposit	Stakeholder a/c	Client	DR	Client	Client	CR

- One 'stakeholder account' ledger will suffice for all stakeholder monies held by a solicitor (as it is all 'client money'), there is no need to have a separate ledger for each client in relation to whom the solicitor is a stakeholder.

6 Mortgages

- A solicitor may either treat an institutional lender as a separate client, or may take advantage of *SAR r.32(6)* and simply record a mortgage advance in the buyer's ledger noting the lender's interest.

7 Insurance premiums

- When a solicitor receives an insurance premium from a client, prior to accounting to an insurance company for the net premium (ie: the gross premium less the solicitors' commission), the insurance company is treated as the solicitors' client for the purposes of the *SARs*.
- A commission of less than £20 may be paid into office account if the solicitor has the client's permission to retain it (*SPR r. 10*), otherwise it is 'client money'.
- If the solicitor receives commission **without accounting to policyholder** for it the double entries are:

a) On payment by the policyholder:

Amount	Ledger	Column	Entry	Ledger	Column	Entry
Commission	Client (Insurance Co)	Office	DR	Commission account	Office	CR

Amount	Ledger	Column	Entry	Ledger	Column	Entry
Gross premium	Cash account	Client	DR	Client (Insurance Co)	Client	CR

- Note that there is no entry in the ledger account of the policyholder (assuming the policyholder is a client of the solicitor) as the payment is received as 'client money' held on behalf of the insurance company.

b) On payment by the solicitor to the insurance company.

Out of client a/c

Amount	Ledger	Column	Entry	Ledger	Column	Entry
Net	Cash account	Client	CR	Client (Insurance Co)	Client	DR

Out of client a/c

Amount	Ledger	Column	Entry	Ledger	Column	Entry
Commission	Cash account	Client	CR	Client (Insurance Co)	Client	DR

Into office a/c

Amount	Ledger	Column	Entry	Ledger	Column	Entry
Commission	Cash a/c	Office	DR	Client (Insurance Co)	Office	CR

- The commission account is an office ledger - at the end of the year the balance will be closed off to the solicitor's profit and loss account as income.

- If the solicitor receives commission **for which he is obliged to account to policyholder**.

Amount	Ledger	Column	Entry	Ledger	Column	Entry
Gross premium	Cash account	Client	DR	Client (Insurance Co)	Client	CR

- There is an entry in the ledger account of the policyholder as the payment is received as 'client money' for which the solicitor must account to the policyholder.

Amount	Ledger	Column	Entry	Ledger	Column	Entry
Commission	Client ledger (Insurance	Client	DR	Client (Policyholder)	Client	CR

  - Mark the entry as being 'a transfer of commission TJ' as a transfer between client ledgers (*SAR r.32*).

- No entries are made in the Commission account as the commission is accounted for to the policyholder as 'client money'. An internal transfer between client ledgers is made (which does not therefore go through the cash account as no money is drawn out of client account).

Amount	Ledger	Column	Entry	Ledger	Column	Entry
Net premium	Cash account	Client	CR	Client (Insurance Co)	Client	DR

8 Returned cheques

➤ A solicitor must record a cheque received from a client in that client's ledger without delay (*SAR r.15(1)*). Consequently, a client ledger may show uncleared funds as well as cleared funds.

Amount	Ledger	Column	Entry	Ledger	Column	Entry
Cheque	Cash account	Client	DR	Client	Client	CR

➤ If a client's cheque bounces the solicitor must make entries in the client's ledger and cash account showing that the cheque has been returned (ie: these reverse the entries made when the money was received).

Amount	Ledger	Column	Entry	Ledger	Column	Entry
Returned cheque	Cash account	Client	CR	Client	Office	DR

➤ If the solicitor has drawn on uncleared funds there will have been a breach of the *SARs* as the money drawn from client account will effectively belong to other clients of the solicitor. The solicitor must immediately make good this breach by making a compensating transfer from office account into client account.

- Note that drawing on uncleared funds is not itself a breach of the *SARs*.

9 Deposit interest

➤ The accounting treatment depends upon whether interest is held on a separate designated deposit account (ie: an account in the client's name, solely for holding money belonging to the named client), or the solicitor accounts to the client for interest.

➤ If a designated deposit account is used:

a) the solicitor must record the transfer of money to the designated deposit cash account.

Amount	Ledger	Column	Entry	Ledger	Column	Entry
Payment in	Cash account	Client	DR	Design. deposit a/c	Client	CR

b) on an interest payment by the bank:

Amount	Ledger	Column	Entry	Ledger	Column	Entry
Interest	Desig. deposit a/c	Client	DR	Client	Client	CR

c) in order to draw money from the designated deposit account the solicitor will have to transfer monies from the designated deposit account to general client account (ie: an account containing mixed client monies) as there will not generally be a cheque book facility on a designated deposit account. This involves reversing the entries in a) above.

Amount	Ledger	Column	Entry	Ledger	Column	Entry
Payment out	Cash account	Client	CR	Design. deposit a/c	Client	DR

- If money is transferred to a designated deposit account no entry need be actually made in the client ledger (as the credit balance indicating the funds owed to the client does not change), but it is good practice to record on the ledger that money has been placed in a designated deposit account.

➤ **If a solicitor pays money *in lieu* of interest:**

a) the solicitor must make a payment out of his own funds *in lieu* of interest. This can be done *either*:

- by a transfer from office account to client account, *or*

Amount	Ledger	Column	Entry	Ledger	Column	Entry
Interest	Cash account	Office	CR	Interest paid a/c	Office	DR

Amount	Ledger	Column	Entry	Ledger	Column	Entry
Interest	Cash account	Client	DR	Client	Client	CR

- by an office account cheque paid to the client.

Amount	Ledger	Column	Entry	Ledger	Column	Entry
Interest	Cash account	Office	CR	Interest paid a/c	Office	DR

10 Abatements and bad debts

➤ When a solicitor reduces a bill (known as 'abatement'), the client ledger must record the abatement and corresponding entries must be made in respect of VAT relating to the amount written off. The double entries are as follows:

Amount	Ledger	Column	Entry	Ledger	Column	Entry
Write-off	Client	Office	CR	Costs abatement a/c	Office	DR

Amount	Ledger	Column	Entry	Ledger	Column	Entry
VAT on write-off	Client	Office	CR	Customs & Excise a/c	Office	DR

➤ If client debt which has been outstanding for more than 6 months is written-off, a solicitor may generally claim VAT relief in respect of the 'output tax' that the solicitor will have paid to Customs & Excise one month after the end of the accounting period during which the supply to which the debt relates was made (VATA *1994 s.36*, see also *VATR 1995 rr.165-172* and *FA 1997 s.39*). A successful claim will be recorded by the following double entries:

Amount	Ledger	Column	Entry	Ledger	Column	Entry
VAT relief	Client	Office	CR	Customs & Excise a/c	Office	DR

➤ Any bad debt is treated on the same principles as an abatement.

Taxation

This chapter examines:

Income or capital?

Income is usually a receipt or expense which recurs, eg: rent money or buying paperclips.

Capital is usually a once-off payment for an asset, eg: paying for office furniture.

Individuals are presumed to be domiciled, resident and ordinarily resident in the UK.

Companies are presumed to be resident solely in the UK and trading in the UK

A Income tax (IT)

References in this section are to the TA 1988, unless otherwise stated.

I Calculation

A. Individuals as private persons

Steps	
1	**Calculate 'statutory income' under Schedules A-F**
2	**Calculate 'total income' (ie: subtract 'charges on income')**
3	**Calculate 'taxable income' (ie: subtract 'personal reliefs')**
4	**Calculate tax payable on the 'taxable income'**

Step 1 **Calculate 'statutory income'**

➤ Income is taxed under Schedules in the *Taxes Act 1988*. Different rules govern assessment under each Schedule. A loss under a Schedule gives a nil assessment for that Schedule.

Schedule	Type of income
A	Rents and receipts from land in the UK (*s.15(1)*)
D Case I Case II	Profits of a trade in the UK (*s.18(3)*) Profits of a profession or vocation (*s.18(3)*)
D Case III	Interest, annuities, trust income and other annual payments (*s.18(3)*)
D Case IV Case V	Income from foreign securities (*s.18(3)*) Income from foreign possessions (ie: other than securities) (*s.18(3)*)
D Case VI	Income not caught elsewhere (*s.18(3)*)
E Case I, II and III	Income deriving from an office, employment and pensions (*s.19(1)*)
F	Dividends and other company distributions (*s.20*)

Schedules B and C have been repealed

Exemptions
- Interest on National Savings certificates (*s.46*) and a TESSA account opened pior to 6 April 1999 (*s.326A*)
- The first £70 of interest earned on National Savings Bank deposits (*s.325*)
- Interest on personal injury damages or death damages (*s.329*)
- Qualifying loan or loan on ordinary commercial terms from an employer (*ss.161A-B, Sch. 7A*)
- Certain social security benefits (eg: child benefit) (*s.617(2)*)
- Scholarship income (*s.331*), provided it is not chargeable under *s.165(1)*
- Gross income up to £4,250 from letting a furnished room in a 'main residence' (*FA(No2)1992 Sch 10*)
- Maintenance from a former spouse under a court order or written agreement in the hands of the recipient (*s.347A(1)*)

➤ Where tax is deducted at source, 'gross up' the income to its value *before* tax was deducted to arrive at the 'statutory income' (eg: multiply by 100/80 for a 20% deduction).

Schedule A

➤ Rents and income from United Kingdom property - this is known as income from a 'Schedule A business'.

➤ Part of a premium received on the grant of a lease with a term not exceeding 50 years, or on the surrender or variation / waiver of a lease (even if the original term exceeded 50 years), may be treated as an income receipt and as a part disposal for CGT purposes - for the apportionment see *s.34* (see also *TCGA 1992 Sch. 8* for CGT treatment).

➤ **Deductible expenditure and capital allowances:** calculated on Schedule D Case I principles.

➤ **Capital allowances:** see p.81.

Schedule D Case I and II, 'income profit' = 'chargeable receipts less deductible expenditure'

- A chargeable receipt a) derives from income not capital, *and* b) derives from the taxpayer's trade.
- **Deductible expenditure:** expenses of an income nature that are 'wholly and exclusively' incurred for the purposes of a trade, profession, or vocation are deductible (*s.74(1), Mallalieu v. Drummond* [1983] 2 AC 861).
- For the purposes of Schedule D Cases I and II, accounts must (subject to any adjustment required or authorised by law) be computed on an accounting basis which gives a 'true and fair view' of profits (*FA 1998 ss.42-46*).
  - There is a limited exemption for barristers of not more than 7 years call (*FA 1998 s.43*).
  - Creative artists may make an 'averaging claim' if their profits fluctuate (*Sch. 4A* inserted by *FA 2001*).
- **Capital allowances:** see p.81.

Schedule D Case III, interest, annuities, trust income and other annual payments

- Whether an individual claims a rebate, need pay nothing more, or owes tax, depends on the rate at which he pays tax (*s.1A*).
- Sources of income arising on or after 6 April 1994 are assessed on the current year basis (ie: the year in which income accrues), although for a partnership with Case III income its basis period (see p.78) serves as the period of assessment if this differs from its accounting period (*s.111(4)*).
  - An individual receives interest from a UK bank or UK building society (*s.480A*) and annual interest from a UK company (*s.349(2)*) net of lower rate tax (currently, 20%) (ie: for £100 of interest, the individual receives £20 and the payer accounts to the Inland Revenue for £80).

Non-taxpayer ↓ Full rebate (20%)	10% and 22% taxpayer ↓ No more tax to pay	40% taxpayer ↓ 20% more tax to pay

  - **Bank/Bulding Society interest:** a non-taxpayer can receive the gross amount, without a deduction at source, if he or she sends the correct form to the bank/building society.
  - **National Savings certificates and accounts:** tax is not deducted at source; interest is paid gross.
  - Annual payments are subject to a deduction at source at the basic rate of tax (currently, 22%) (*s.349(1)*).
  - Deduction at source (also known as a 'withholding tax') makes tax collection easier/more reliable and gives the Government a cashflow advantage as institutions account for tax quarterly (*viz*: before payment of tax falls due under self assesment).
- **Deductible expenditure:** none. However, if a debenture holder borrows to lend money to a company then the interest may be a 'charge on income'.

Schedule D Case IV, income from foreign securities

Schedule D Case V, income from foreign possessions (other than securities)

- **Deductible expenditure:** none (unless income is from a trade, profession or vocation which is computed on Schedule D Case I and II principles). Consider whether relief is availiable (eg: under a double tax treaty) for tax paid, or deducted, abroad.

Schedule D Case VI, other income

- The 'full amount' of any income not caught by another Schedule. This is assessed in a similar fashion to Schedule D Case III, so income arising during a current tax year is assessed, although a partnership's basis period serves as the period of assessment if this differs from its accounting period (*s.111(4)*).
- **Deductible expenditure:** on Case I principles (*s.69*).

Schedule E, 'emoluments of office or employment', Case I

(Cases II & III, which may apply if the taxpayer is not both resident and ordinarily resident in the UK during the tax year, are not covered here)

➤ These are benefits which derive from an office or employment. They can come *either* from an employer *or* from a third party. In addition to cash sums (eg: a monthly salary), Schedule E catches payments in the form of goods or services (known as 'benefits in kind').

Assessment of benefits in kind depends upon the amount of remuneration the individual receives for the purpose of this Schedule. Apply category ***'A'*** *then* **either** *option* ***'B'*** **or** *option* ***'C'****.*

Category 'A'

➤ For all employees, benefits in kind include:

a) a gain on the exercise of share options (*s.135*) (options granted under approved schemes involving shares with a value of £30,000 or less are exempt (*s.185*)).

b) non-cash vouchers (*s.141*) and credit tokens (*s.142*), which are taxed on the cost to the voucher provider of providing the goods or services which the employee enjoys via the voucher or token.

c) low rent and rent-free accommodation which bear tax on the value of the benefit to the employee (*s.145*) unless the accommodation falls within limited exceptions in *s.145(4)* (eg: necessary for the 'proper performance of his duties'). If the cost of providing the accommodation exceeds £75,000, there is an additional charge assessed on the cost to the employer of providing this benefit (*s.146*).

d) training on a 'qualifying course' (*ss.588-589*) and certain other training (*s.200C*), but not in relation to work related training (*TA ss.200B, 200D*).

e) education/training by an individual learning account holder if the education/training qualifies for a Department for Education and Employment grant or discount (*ss.200E-200G*).

f) counselling on the termination of an employment (*ss.589A-589B*).

g) relocation expenses, unless these qualify for exemption under *Schedule 11A* and do not exceed £8,000.

h) sport and recreation facilities (*s.197G*).

i) sick pay (*s.149*), maternity pay (*s.150*) and income support (*s.151*).

j) pensions (*s.133*).

k) a lump sum at the start *or* end of employment. A sum paid on injury or death is exempt from tax, as is a sum not exceeding £30,000 if it is not paid under an employment contract (*ss.148, 188, Schedule 11*).

l) cycle/motor cycle parking spaces (*FA 1999 s.49*).

Option 'B'

Employees earning less than £8,500 a year

Non-taxable items	Taxable items
◆ Private use of a car. ◆ Interest free loan. ◆ Medical insurance.	Any goods or services (other than those subject to the specific statutory provisions outlined above) which are convertible into cash (*Tennant v. Smith [1892] AC 150*). Tax is calculated on the cash equivalent value of the benefit in the employee's hands.

Option 'C' (*ss.153-168*)

i) Directors (unless working part-time *and* owning under 5% of the company's shares).

ii) Employees with emoluments £8,500 or more a year.

Benefit	Taxable value	Exemptions or exceptions
Loan (*s.160*)	Interest saved by comparison with an official rate which is set periodically	**Exception**: loan under £5,000 (*s.161*) **Exemption:** qualifying loan, or loan on ordinary commercial terms (*ss.161A-B, Sch. 7A*)
Company car (*s.157*)	Tables in *Sch. 6* relate to a car's original value, its cubic capacity and age* The resulting figure is modified to reflect the proportion of business use	**From 6 April 2002 there will be a charge on a percentage of a car's price graduated according to the car's carbon dioxide emissions (FA 2000 Sch. 11)*
Pension scheme (*s.597*)	Cost to the employer in providing the benefit	Contributions which the employer and the employee make to approved pension schemes are not chargeable (*ss.639, 643*)
Child care facilities		When the care is provided on premises made available by the employer, and the employer wholly or partly finances the care (*s.155*)
Computer equipment (*s.156A*)		Cash equivalent up to £500 (eg: no tax on computer costing up to £2,500)
'Green travel' to work or between workplaces		A cycle/cycle safety equipment (*s.197AC*), 'qualifying journeys' on an employer's 'work bus service' or financial or other support for such journeys on a 'public transport bus service' (*s.197AA-AB*)
Other benefits (*s.154*)		Expense 'made good' by the employee (*s.156*), or accommodation, supplies & services used in performing duties of employment (*s.155ZA*)

Deductible expenditure (this is very restrictively defined)

The burden of proof rests upon the employee to show that expenditure is:

a) 'wholly, exclusively and necessarily' on behalf of the business, *and*

b) 'incurred in performance of his duties' (*s.198(1)(c)*).

There are different rules for:

- **Pension contributions:** contributions to a personal (*s.639)* or occupational pension scheme (*s.592(7)*) are deductible up to certain limits. An employee's national insurance contributions are not deductible (*s.617(3)*).
- **Travelling expenses:** the expense has to be 'necessarily expended' in the performance of duties (*ss.193-195, s.198, Schedule 12A*), unless it is an 'incidental overnight' expense (*FA 1995 s.93*).
- **Capital expenditure on machinery and plant:** if it is 'necessary' for the performance of duties, this is treated as an 'allowance' and set off in the same manner as a 'capital allowance' under Schedule D Case I (*s.198(2)*).
    - Expenditure on a 'mechanically propelled road vehicle' or a 'cycle' need not be 'necessary' (*CAA 2001 s.80*).

Tax due under Schedule E (together with national insurance contributions) is collected under the PAYE scheme (*ss.143-144A, ss.203-211, IT(E)R 1993, IT(NP)R 1994*) which generally obliges employers to pay tax directly to the Inland Revenue within 14 days of the fifth of the month following the month in which either the payment takes place or the benefit in kind is conferred.

Schedule F

➤ **Distributions** (*s.231*): for a fuller explanation see p.101:

Non-taxpayer ↓ No more tax to pay - no rebate	10% and 22% taxpayer ↓ No more tax to pay	40% taxpayer ↓ 32.5% more tax to pay

➤ **A close company writes off a loan to a participator** (*ss.419-421*): the amount written off is 'grossed up', so the sum which the company laid out to finance the loan (including tax at the rate of 20%) is assessed as the shareholder's income. Since the company has already, with the payment to the Revenue, satisfied the shareholder's liability for basic rate tax, the shareholder has effectively postponed liability for higher rate tax (see p.105).

Non-taxpayer, 10% and 22% taxpayer ↓ No more tax to pay	40% taxpayer ↓ 32.5% more tax to pay

➤ **A company repurchases its own shares** (*s.20*): the difference between the original issue price of the shares and their value on sale may be taxed as if it were a dividend. Alternatively, the gain may be subject to CGT if conditions set out on p.266 are fulfilled.

➤ **Deductible expenditure:** none (*s.20(1)*).

Step 2 'Total income' = 'statutory income' - 'charges on income'

➤ Charges on income

a) Interest on qualifying loans which the taxpayer takes out (*s.353*):

- as a PR to pay inheritance tax (*s.364*).
- to invest in a partnership (*s.362*): buy a share in, lend or contribute capital to a partnership or LLP formed under *LPA 2000* (subject to restrictions in *s.363* and provided a LLP is not as member of an investment LLP the activities of which consist wholly or mainly in making investments).
- to invest in a close company (not a close investment holding company) (*ss.360-360A*) (subject to restrictions in *s.363*).
- to invest in an employee controlled company (ie: 50%+ of the voting rights or ordinary shares are held by employees) which is not quoted on the Financial Services Authority's Official list within 12 months of the company becoming an employee controlled company (*s.361*) (subject to restrictions in *s.363*). The taxpayer works full time for the company (or a 51% subsidiary) and *either*:

  i) lends money to a trading company or the holding company of a trading group, *or*

  ii) acquires ordinary shares in such a company or pays off a loan financing such an acquisition.

b) Payments to fund a qualifying vocational training course where the individual rather than an employer pays for a course. Tax at up to 22% is deducted at source, so fees are lower (*FA 1991 s.32*)✂.

c) A 'qualifying donation' to charity and the donor makes a Gift Aid Declaration (*FA 1990 s.25* as amended by *FA 2000*).

d) A disposal of a qualifying investment to charity (*s.83B*).

e) A loss on the sale of shares in a qualifying unquoted trading company (eg: for shares issued on or after 6 April 1998, EIS shares) for which the individual was the original subscriber (*s.574*).

Step 3 — 'Taxable income' = 'total income' - 'personal reliefs'

➤ These reliefs depend on the individual's personal circumstances.

Personal relief (*s.257*): dependent on age		
Under 65	£4,535	
Over 65, but under 75*	£5,990	
Over 75*	£6,260	
***Additional* relief for some married couples (*s.257A*)✣**		
Either spouse over 65 and under 75*†	£5,365	The couple live together for part of the year By default this relief goes to the husband, unless the couple elect before the beginning of the tax year to share it differently
Either spouse over 75*†	£5,435	The spouse can claim any allowance unused by the other spouse at the end of the year
* Relief is *only* available on income up to £17,600 (*s.257A(5)*)		
Other *additional* relief		
Blind person (*s.265*)	£1,450	If the taxpayer is registered blind A husbands and a wife can both claim this relief
† Relief is restricted to 10% (*s.256*)		
✣ Abolished on 6 April 2000 (but may be retained if born before 6 April 1935 (*FA 1999 ss.30-35*)) Children's Tax Credit introduced on 6 April 2001 at 10% to £5,420 (*s.257AA-BA*)		

The complex provisions relating to the Working Family Tax Credit (worth £225 a week for a family with one child) and the Disabled Person's Tax Credit (worth £257 a week for a couple with one child on the DPTC) (assuming one earner working a 35 hour week for the national minimum wage) (*REV/C&E 3 7 March 2001*) are beyond the range of this book.

Step 4 — Calculate tax payable on the 'taxable income'

➤ Taxable income £0 - £1,880: taxed at the 'starting rate' of 10% (*s. 1(2)(aa)*).

➤ Taxable income £1,881 -28,400: taxed at the 'basic rate' of 22% (*s. 1(2)(a)*).

➤ Taxable income over £28,400: taxed at the 'higher rate' of 40% (*s. 1(2)(b)*).

Trustees

➤ UK resident trustees of discretionary trusts and accumulation and maintenance trusts, pay income tax at 34% (*ss.686-687*).

- Distributions made on or after 6 April 1999 are taxable at 25% (*TA s.686(1AA)*).

➤ Trustees of fixed interest trusts have tax at 20% deducted at source on investments and savings, and are subject to basic rate tax at 22% on other income.

➤ Trustees have no personal allowances, but may claim capital allowances and loss relief in respect of any trade they carry on as trustees.

B. Individuals as sole traders/partners

Follow the 4 steps in '*A. Individuals as private persons*',

BUT use these additional rules.

Step 1 Set the 'accounting date'

- Profits are taxed by reference to an 'accounting date' (*s.60(3)(b)*), unless special circumstances give rise to a 'basis period'. A 'basis period' arises when *either*:
  - the business ceases for good (*s.63*), *or*
  - an accounting date is other than 5 April (*s.62(2)(1)*), or is changed for certain reasons (*s.62A(1)*).
- There is some flexibility in the Inland Revenue's approach to 'accounting dates'.
  - An accounting date fixed for a particular day which falls on different dates (eg: the Last Night of the Proms), will be treated as the same accounting date provided the date does not alter by more than 4 mean days in any year (*Inland Revenue Publication, SAT1*).
  - An accounting date on 31 March will be treated as if it were 5 April (*SAT1).*
- Special rules set the basis period during the first 3 years of a business. During the first year, the basis period runs from commencement to the following 5 April (*s.61(1)*). Thereafter, the rules align the basis period with the accounting period as quickly as possible.
  - Alignment happens in year 2 if *either*:

    a) there are 12 months or more between commencement and the accounting date (*s.60(3)(a)*), *or*

    b) there is a change of accounting date between years 1 and 2 (*s.62(2)(a)*), ...

    ... in which case the basis period is the 12 months to the new accounting date.
  - Alignment happens in year 3 if *either*:

    a) there are 12 months or less between commencement and the accounting date (*s.61(2)(a)*), *or*

    b) the accounting date is changed in years 1 or 2 so that the new date is less than 12 months after the business began (*s.61(2)(b)*), *or*

    c) the basis period for year 2 actually ends in year 3 (*s.60(1), s.60(4)(b)*), ...

    ... in the case of a) and b) the basis period in year 2 is the first 12 months, but for c) the basis period is the tax year itself.

Step 2 Claim any 'overlap relief'

- When basis periods overlap, 'overlap relief' is available. The profit from the preceding year attributable to the overlapping days is apportioned, and used as a relief to prevent a double liability (*s.63A*).
- A loss cannot be used more than once, so overlap relief cannot be used to recycle any other form of loss relief such as relief under *s.380* (*s.382(4)*).

Step 3 Claim any loss relief

	Period	Loss can be claimed ...	Use on ...
Start-up relief *s.381*	First 4 tax years	... over the 3 tax years before the year in which the loss incurred	... any income
Terminal loss relief *s.388*	Final year	... the final tax year and the 3 years preceding it	... trading income
Schedule A relief *s.379A*	Any accounting year	... the next tax year of taxable income, any excess in future years	... Schedule A income
Carry across relief *s.380*, subject to restrictions, *s.384*		... the tax year in which the accounting year of the loss ends, and the preceding year	... any income
Carry forward relief *s.385*		... the next tax year with taxable profit; any excess in future years	... trading income

- ➤ Using *s.380* wastes personal reliefs as this relief must be used on the whole of income
- ➤ Using *s.385* allows personal reliefs to be set off against other income
- ➤ *s.385* can be claimed whether *s.380* is used or not
- ➤ If *s.385* is used with a *s.380* loss, then *s.385* can only be claimed to the extent that a loss remains unused after *s.380* has been claimed

Relief on incorporation of a business *s.386*

If a trading loss is unrelieved when the business is transferred to a company 'wholly or mainly in return for the issue of shares' (ie: shares form at least 80% of the consideration), this loss can be carried forward and provide relief against dividends *or* salary which the former trader or partner gains from the company in future years

- ➤ Relief which an individual who is a partner (*s.117*), or an individual who is a member of a LLP (*ss.118ZC-D*), can claim for interest and trading losses against other income is restricted to that partner's/member's capital contribution to the partnership/LLP.
- ➤ For R & D tax credits, see p.100.

The detailed rules relating to tax efficient investments such as venture capital trusts (*TA s.842AA, TCGA 1992 s.100*), the Enterprise Investment Scheme (*TA ss.289-312, TCGA 1992 ss.150-150D, Sch. 5B-BA*) and ISAs, are beyond the scope of this book, however, for an outline see pp.126-127

C. Partnerships

Steps
1 Send in the partnership return
2 Split the profit or loss amongst the individual partners

Step 1 Send in the partnership return

- The partnership must send in a return giving details of the firm's business for an accounting period (eg: partnership income, profit allocation and any capital allowances claimed) (*TMA 1970 s.9*).
- Claims for expenditure and capital allowances etc which affect profits and losses of the partnership are made when the partnership return is completed (*TMA 1970 s.42*).
  - Expenditure incurred by a partner must be included on the partnership return; a claim as an individual will be disallowed.
  - Claims for allowances for plant and machinery owned by a partner, but used by the partnership, must generally be made on the partnership return (*CAA 2001 s.264*).

Step 2 Split the profit or loss amongst the individual partners

- Profit and loss are calculated for the partnership as a whole (*s.111(2)*).
- Partners complete individual self assessments, each being liable for their own share of the profits under the profit sharing ratio during the period of assessment concerned (net of any deductions successfully claimed by the partnership).
  - Partners are generally not jointly and severally liable for taxation arising on the profit earned by each other (*ss.111(3)-111(4)*).

Continuance of partnerships

- Under the old rules, before the introduction of self assessment on 6 April 1994, a partnership was deemed to discontinue if its membership changed, unless the partners elected for it to continue.
- If the membership of a partnership changes on or after 6 April 1994, then it is deemed to continue unless none of the partners continues in the business (*s.113*).

D. LLPs incorporated under the *LPA 2000*

- A trade, profession or business carried on by a LLP with a view to profit is treated as a partnership carried on by its members (and not the LLP itself) (*s.118ZA* as substituted by *FA 2001 s.75(1)*).
  - The property and income of a LLP are treated as the property or income of the members of the LLP.

B Capital allowances

I What allowances are and how they may be used

A. What allowances are

➤ Capital allowances allow the depreciation of capital assets to be brought into account for taxation purposes and offset against income profit (earned by traders, partners and companies).

➤ Different methods of depreciation are used for different types of asset:

4% straight line		25% reducing balance			
Period	Straight line depreciation	Period	Reducing balance	Depreciation	
1	£4	1	£100	£25 (25% of £100)	and so on ... until allowances reach £100. The majority of the value of a 25% allowance is extracted over 7 years, thereafter the allowance becomes less significant
2	£4	2	£56.25	£18.75 (25% of £75)	
3	£4	3	£42.19	£14.06 (25% of £56.25)	

B. How allowances may be used

➤ A capital allowance may be set against 'income profits' and used to create a loss for Schedule A or D.

- ◆ If there is more than one item of plant /machinery, an allowance is granted on a 'pool'.
  - Separate single asset pools may exist, eg: for 'short life' assets (*CAA 2001 ss.83-89*), cars expenditure on which exceeds £12,000 (*CAA 2001 ss.74-82*), ships (*CAA 2001 ss.127-128*), contribution allowances (*CAA 2001 s.538*).
  - Expenditure on assets leased outside the UK (*CAA 2001 s.107*) and 'long life' assets (*CAA 2001 s.101*) is allocated to a class pool (ie: a pool which may contain expenditure relating to more than asset).

➤ When a 'disposal event' occurs in respect of a capital asset, the sum written down against the 'capital allowance' is compared with the disposal value to determine whether a balancing charge or allowance arises (*CAA 2001 ss.55-56*).

- ◆ If the sale proceeds (or original cost if less) exceed the sum written down (in respect of the asset, or the pool if there is a pool), a balancing charge arises on the excess taxed as a chargeable receipt of the trade.
- ◆ If the proceeds are less than the sum written down, the shortfall is deductible as a balancing allowance from the chargeable receipts of the trade.
  - A 'disposal event' includes where a person ceases to own plant or machinery, a qualifying activity is permanently discontinued, or equipment is destroyed (*CAA 2001 s.61*).

II Who can claim allowances

➤ For plant and machinery, the general rule is that a person may claim capital allowances if that person carries on a 'qualifying activity' and incurs 'qualifying expenditure' (*CAA 2001 s.11(1)*).

- A 'qualifying activity' includes a trade, an ordinary Schedule A business, a profession or vocation, or special leasing of plant or machinery (*CAA 2001 s.15(1)*).
- 'Qualifying expenditure' exists where there is:

  a) i) capital expenditure on the provision of plant or machinery wholly or partly for the purposes of a qualifying activity carried on by the person incurring the expenditure, *and*

  ii) the person owns the plant or machinery as a result of incurring the expenditure (*CAA 2001 s.11(4)*), *and*

  b) expenditure which is not excluded, see eg: *CAA 2001 ss.21-23* (expenditure on buildings, etc is excluded).

➤ Special rules govern how allowances may be claimed in respect of expenditure incurred on plant or machinery which becomes a fixture to land (*CAA 2001 ss.172-204*).

➤ Anti-avoidance rules can restrict, or lead to a denial of, allowances. These can apply, for example, in relation to finance leases or sale and leaseback transactions (eg: *CAA 2001 ss.213-233*).

➤ For industrial buildings, the general rule is that a person can claim a writing down allowance if (*CAA 2001 s.309*):

a) qualifying expenditure is incurred on a building, *and*

- 'Qualifying expenditure' is defined in *CAA 2001 s.292*.

b) at the end of a chargeable period that person is entitled to a relevant interest in a building in relation to that expenditure, *and*

c) at the end of that chargeable period, the building is an industrial building.

- An 'industrial building' is a building or structure which is, or is to be (*CAA 2001 s.271*):

  i) in use for the purposes of a qualifying trade (*CAA 2001 ss.274-278*), *or*

  ii) a qualifying hotel (*CAA 2001 s.279*), *or*

  iii) a qualifying sports pavillion (*CAA 2001 s.280*), *or*

  iv) in relation to qualifying enterprise zone expenditure, a commercial building or structure (*CAA 2001 s.281*).

III What capital allowances can be claimed

➤ A capital allowance can be claimed:

a) **25% on a reducing balance basis** for plant and machinery (*CAA 2001 s.56*).

b) **6% on a reducing balance basis** for certain plant and machinery which constitute 'long life assets' that can reasonably be expected to have a useful economic life of at least 25 years (*CAA 2001 ss.91, 102*). This treatment does **not** apply to:

i) a person (other than a lessor) who incurs expenditure during a chargeable period of 12 months not exceeding £100,000 (*CAA 2001 ss.98-100*).

ii) expenditure on any of the following:

- machinery or plant which is a fixture in, or provided for use in, any building which is wholly or mainly for use as a dwelling house, retail shop, showroom, hotel or office (*CAA 2001 s.93*).
- a car (*CAA 2001 s.96*).
- prior to 1 January 2011 certain types of ship (basically seagoing vessels) (*CAA 2001 s.94*).
- prior to 1 January 2011 the provision of a railway asset wholly and exclusively for the purposes of a railway business (*CAA 2001 s.95*).

c) **4% on a straight line basis** for industrial buildings (*CAA 2001 s.310*).

d) in certain cases allowances are accelerated and/or offered on special terms, eg: in enterprise zones (*CAA 2001 Part 3*), agriculture and forestry (*CAA 2001 Part 4*), conversion or renovation of flats over shops or commercial premises for rental (*CAA 2001 Part 4A*), mineral extraction (*CAA 2001 Part 5*), research and development (*CAA 2001 Part 6*), know-how (*CAA 2001 Part 7*), patents (*CAA 2001 Part 8*), dredging (*CAA 2001 Part 9*) and assured tenancies (*CAA 2001 Part 10*).

➤ A small or medium sized enterprise may claim:

a) a 40% first year allowance for expenditure incurred on plant or machinery (*CAA 2001 ss.44, 52*), *and/or*

- This first year allowance is not available for expenditure on machinery and plant for leasing or letting on hire, cars, long-life assets, sea-going ships or railway assets (*CAA 2001 s.46).*

b) a 100% allowance for ICT expenditure incurred on or before 31 March 2003 on certain information and communications technology (eg: computers, software, 3rd generation mobile phones, WAP telephones, TV data feeds) (*CAA 2001 ss.45, 52)*), *and/or*

c) a 100% allowance for expenditure on energy-saving plant or machinery (*CAA 2001 ss.45A-C, 52)*).

Definition of a 'small or medium-sized enterprise'	
Company	Business
➤ A company which is: a) 'small or medium sized' for the purposes of *CA s.247* during the financial year of the company in which the expenditure is incurred, *and* b) is not a member of a large group when the expenditure is incurred (*CAA 2001 ss.47, 49*)	➤ A business which, were one to take all its trades together and prepare its accounts as if it were a hypothetical company, would qualify as a 'small or medium sized' for the purposes of *CA s.247* (*CAA 2001 s.48*)
'Small or medium sized' for the purposes of *CA s.247*	
➤ A company is 'small or medium' sized for the purposes of *CA s.247* if, broadly speaking, it satisfies at least 2 of the following conditions: a) turnover of not more than £11.2 million, *or* b) assets of not more than £5.6 million, *or* c) not more than 250 employees	

C Capital gains tax (CGT)

References in this section are to the Taxation of Chargeable Gains Act 1992, unless stated otherwise.

I Calculation

Steps	
1	**Identify the disposal**
2	**Calculate the 'chargeable gain' or 'allowable loss' on *a* disposal**
3	**Calculate the 'taxable gain' for the tax year on *all* disposals of chargeable assets, taking due account of exemptions and reliefs**
4	**Calculate the tax due**

Step 1 — Identify the disposal (*ss.22-28*)

➤ A sale *or* gift of a 'chargeable asset' (*s.15(2)*). Note that a disposal to a spouse (*s.58*), or charity (*s.257*), does not give rise to a 'chargeable gain' or an 'allowable loss' for CGT.

Step 2 — Calculate the 'chargeable gain' or 'allowable loss' on *a* disposal

Steps

1 Take *either* the market value of the asset on its 'disposal' (*s.17*) *or* the consideration on its sale.

2 Subtract the 'allowable expenditure'.

Allowable expenditure

➤ Allowable expenditure is calculated by adding up the following:

- the initial cost of the asset. If the asset was acquired before 31 March 1982, then use *either*:

  a) its value on that date, *or*

  b) the cost of acquisition, whichever produces a smaller loss or gain (*s.35*).

- any expense 'wholly and exclusively' incurred in enhancing the asset's value (not routine maintenance) (*s.38*).
- the cost of establishing title to the asset, and any costs incurred in disposing of it (*s.38*).

3 Apply indexation (if appropriate. Note that taper relief may also be available):

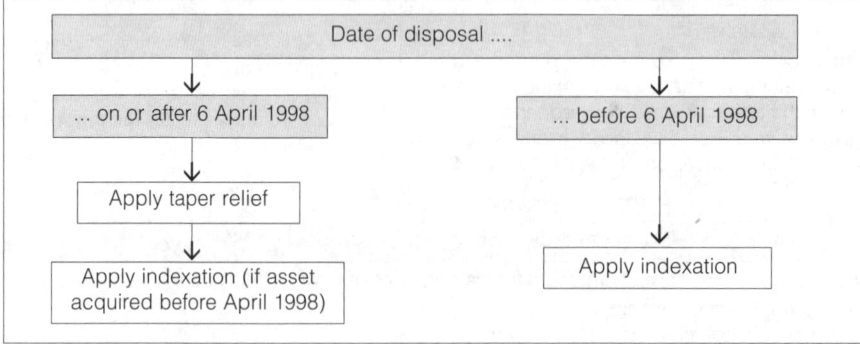

Indexation allowance

➤ The 'indexation allowance' accounts for the impact of inflation on a gain (prior to April 1998).

- Where an asset was owned on 31 March 1982, the indexation allowance can be taken *either*:

  a) from the asset's value on 31 March 1982, *or*

  b) from the 'actual expenditure' on the asset (ie: acquisition, maintenance, etc), whichever carries a higher indexation (*s.54*).

Note: since 30 November 1993, this allowance has only reduced or extinguished a gain, it may not be used to increase the size of a loss, nor to convert a gain into a loss.

Step 3 Calculate the 'taxable gain' for the tax year

➤ Add up the total 'chargeable gains' for the tax year and deduct:

- any 'allowable losses' from that tax year (*s.2(2)(a)*), *and*
- any 'allowable losses' from previous tax years not previously brought into account for CGT (*s.2(2)(b)*).

➤ Ensure that relevant exemptions and reliefs are left out of account:

Exemptions

➤ Annual exemption of £7,500 for the tax year 2001/2002 (*s.3(2)*) (£3,750 for trustees).

➤ 'Wasting assets' which have a life of under 50 years (*ss.44-45*).

➤ Tangible moveables if the consideration is less than £6,000 (*s.262*).

➤ A private dwelling house which is used as a 'main residence' (or which has been used as such during the period of ownership) and land up to half a hectare (*s.222*). The following periods of absence are permitted:

- the first year of ownership (*Extra Statutory Concession D49*).
- up to 3 years' absence for any reason, split over as many periods as the owner's absence (*s.223(3)(a)*)
- for as long as the owner is employed outside the UK (not self-employed) (*s.223(3)(b)*).
- up to 4 years of absence within the UK at the reasonable behest of an employer (*s.223(3)(c)*).
- the last 3 years of ownership (*s.223(1)*).
  - Married couples can only use this exemption for one house - if they own more than one, they must choose which qualifies for the exemption (*s.222(5)*).
  - The exemption will be reduced proportionately to the extent the property is used for business purposes (*s.223(2)*).
  - Trustees can claim exemption from CGT so long as the occupier was entitled to occupy the house *either*:

    a) as tenant for life, *or*

    b) under the terms of the trust (*s.225*).
  - Land over half a hectare will not come within the exemption unless the owner can show it is for the 'reasonable enjoyment' of the house (*ss.222(2)-222(3)*).
  - If land of up to half a hectare is sold off, but the house is retained, the exemption will apply to the land sold (*s.222(4)*).

Reliefs (other than taper relief)

Retirement relief (*ss.163-164, Schedule 6*) (gains realised prior to 6 April 2003)

Person a) 50 or over *or* ill *and* b) disposes of a 'business interest' *and* c) owned the 'interest' for at least 1 year.

i) **An individual** carrying on a business may claim relief when:

a) the asset is used for the business *and* b) an 'interest' in business as well as the asset itself is disposed of.

ii) **A shareholder** may claim relief when:

a) the asset is in a personal trading company *and* b) he is a full-time officer/employee of the company.

NB: Relief is reduced if rent is charged by an amount which the Inland Revenue deem 'just and equitable'.

Relief

Year in which gain realised	100% relief on gains up to:	50% relief on gains between:
2001-2002	£100,000	£100,001 and £400,000
2002-2003	£50,000	£50,001 and £200,000

Amount of relief: this depends on how long the 'interest' being disposed of has been owned:

- 10 years or more: full relief.
- 1-10 years: the years of ownership divided by 10.

Roll-over relief on the replacement of 'qualifying assets' (*ss.152-157*)

Qualifying assets: a) goodwill *and* b) land *and* c) fixed plant and machinery.

- A replacement is acquired *either* within 1 year prior to the disposal *or* within 3 years after the disposal.
- The replacement asset does not have to be of the same kind as the asset disposed of.

NB: For a shareholder the assets must be used by a personal trading company.

NB: Relief is restricted if the asset is not used in the seller's trade throughout the period of ownership *or* if the whole proceeds are not reinvested in a new qualifying asset.

Roll-over relief on EIS investments (*ss.150-150D, Schedules 5B-BA*)

- Any gain on the disposal of assets sold on or after 6 April 1998 to subscribe for shares issued by an EIS company.
- A company may be a 'qualifying company' for the EIS if:

a) it has gross assets of less than £15 million before an investment and no more than £16 million after the investment, *and*

b) it is not an excluded company. It should not be excluded if it carries on a 'qualifying trade' or is the parent company of a trading group.

Note that certain activities such as property backed activities are excluded, eg: farming, operating or managing nursing or residential care homes, property development and forestry.

- The replacement shares are acquired within 1 year prior to the disposal *or* within 3 years after it.

Roll-over relief on the incorporation of a business (*s.162*)

- The business is transferred to a corporate body as a going concern.
  - The business is transferred with all its assets (ignore cash).
  - The relief only applies to the proportion of the gain for which the consideration is in shares.

Hold-over relief on gifts of business assets (*s.165, Schedule 7*)

Qualifying assets: a) used by the business, *or* b) shares in a personal trading company, *or* c) unquoted shares.

- The disposal was a gift, *or* at below market value.
- There must be a joint election for relief by the donor and the donee.

NB: any IHT due is deductible from CGT as an 'expense' (*s.260(7), s.165(11)*).

Taper relief (*s.2A*) (disposals on or after 6 April 2000)

➤ Calculate the 'qualifying holding period' (*ss.2A(8)-(9)*).

- If an acquisition took place **before 5 April 1998**, this is *either*:

  a) the period after 5 April 1998 for which an asset is held on its disposal, *or*

  b) where an asset was acquired before 17 March 1998, the period after 5 April 1998 for which a **non-business** asset is held on its disposal **plus one year** (there is no 'extra' year for a business asset).

- If an acqusition took place **after 5 April 1998**, it is the period between acquisition and disposal.

➤ Ascertain whether an asset is a business asset. The following are business assets:

Shares, or an interest in shares (*Sch A1 para 4, 6*)	Other assets (*Sch A1 para 5*)
➤ Shares, or an interest in shares, in a company which is a 'qualifying company' in relation to an individual ➤ A company is a 'qualifying company' if it is *either:* a) a non-tradi ng company and an employee does not have a material interest of more than 10% in the company, *or* b) a trading company or the holding company of a trading group *and either:* i) the company is unlisted (AIM is not 'listing' for these purposes), *and/or* ii) the individual is an officer or employee of the company, or a company having a relevant connection with it, *and/or* iii) not less than 5% of the voting rights are exercisable by the individual.	➤ An asset used wholly or partly for the purposes of: a) a trade carried on by an individual or by a partnership of which he is a member, *and/or* b) a trade carried on by a company which is a 'qualifying company', or a company the holding company of which is a 'qualifying company' in relation to an individual, *and/or* c) an office or employment held by that individual with a person carrying on a trade, *and/or* d) an office or employment held by an eligible beneficiary with a person carrying on a trade.
NB: special rules apply in certain circumstances, eg: an asset is held by a PR or trustee, *or* is used as a business and a non business asset at the same time or at different times	

➤ If an asset was not a business asset prior to 6 April 2000, an apportionment is made to reflect the proportion of the qualifying holding period during which the asset is a business asset.

➤ Apply the taper to arrive at the percentage of a gain which is chargeable to tax.

Taper - % of gain chargeable to tax

Number of whole years in the qualifying holding period	Business assets	Non-business assets
1	87.5	100
2	75	100
3	50	95
4	25	90
5	25	85
6	25	80
7	25	75
8	25	70
9	25	65
10 or more	25	60

On 18 June 2001, the Chancellor announced that the Finance Bill 2002 will, for disposals on or after 6 April 2002, reduce the effective rates of CGT for business assets to 20% after 1 year and thereafter 10 %.

Application of taper relief

- The taper is applied to 'adjusted net gains' (*s.3(5)*).
  - This means that the taper is applied *then*:
    a) any losses for the tax year in which the gain is realised are deducted from the gain, *and*
    b) any losses carried forward from previous tax years are deducted from the gain (but not so as to displace the annual exemption), *and*
    c) the annual exemption (£7,500 in 2001/2002) is deducted.
- The following special rules govern the interaction of taper relief with other reliefs (*Sch. A1*):

Transfer between spouses

- If an asset is transferred between spouses, the taper relief on a subsequent disposal is based on the period of combined ownership by both spouses (*para.15*).

No-gain No-loss transfer / Hold over relief on gifts

- The taper takes into account the period of ownership of the owner after the no-gain no-loss transfer / the gift (*para.16*).

Relief reducing the cost of a replacement asset (eg: roll over relief on 'qualifying assets')

- The taper operates by reference to the period for which the new asset is held (*para.16*).

Relief defers a gain on a disposal (eg: re-investment in a VCT, or EIS shares)

- The taper is governed by the holding period of the asset on which the deferred gain arose, if EIS shares disposed of after 5 April 1999 are rolled over into more EIS shares the holding period over which the EIS shares are held is cumulated (*para.16, Sch. 5BA*).

- The taper requires each acquisition on or after 6 April 1998 to be recorded and segregated (rather than pooled, as previously). When a disposal is made after 5 April 1998, it will be identified with acquisitions in this order (*s.106A*):
  a) same day acquisitions, *then*
  b) acquisitions within the following 30 days, *then*
  c) other acquisitions after 5 April 1998. The most recent acquisition is identified first (ie: a 'last in first out basis applies), *then*
  d) shares in the pool on 5 April 1998, *then*
  e) shares held on 5 April 1982, *then*
  f) shares acquired prior to 6 April 1965, *then*
  g) subsequent acquisitions.

Interaction of other roll-over and hold over reliefs

- If **hold-over** relief or **roll-over** relief is used, the annual exemption may not be used with respect to the asset concerned. Retirement relief and taper relief can be used with any other exemption, but retirement relief is applied before taper relief.
- **Roll-over** relief treats the disposal as representing neither a gain nor a loss; it reduces the value of the consideration for the new asset by the amount of the gain realised on the disposal of the old asset.
- **Hold-over** relief holds any gain over so as to reduce the consideration which the transferor would have received on a sale at market value, and reduces the consideration for which the transferee acquires the asset by the same amount.

Step 4 Calculate the tax due

Individuals: tax is paid on the 'chargeable gains' for the year of assessment at 20% (if income tax is paid at the 'starting rate' or 'basic rate') or 40% (if income tax is paid at the 'higher rate') (see p.77) (*s.4* as amended by *FA 1999 s.26*).

Trustees / PRs: trustees of settled property and (in respect of gains arising on or after 6 April 1998) and PRs tax at the rate of 34% (*s.1AA*).

Partnerships: calculate the 'chargeable gain' by subtracting a partner's share of an asset's acquisition cost from that partner's share of the asset's disposal value. It is the individual responsibility of each partner to ensure that his CGT is paid (*s.59*).

LLPs: Where a LLP **carries on a trade or business with a view to profit**, assets held by a LLP are treated for CGT purposes as being held by its partners and tax on a disposal of such assets is assessed and charged on the partners separately (and not on the LLP) (*s.59A(1)*).

If a LLP **ceases to carry on a trade or business with a view to profit** (eg: it goes into liquidation) tax is assessed and charged on (*s.59A(5)* as substituted by *FA 2001 s.75(2)*):

- the LLP in respect of any chargeable gains accruing on the disposal of its assets, *and*
- on the LLP's members in respect of chargeable gains accruing on the disposal of their capital interests in the LLP (see also *s.169A* inserted by *FA 2001 s.75(3)*).

Equivalent tax rates (%) (for disposals on or after 6 April 2000)

Number of complete years after 5 April 1998 for which asset held	Business assets		Non-business assets	
	Higher rate taxpayer	Lower rate taxpayer	Higher rate taxpayer	Lower rate taxpayer
0	40	20	40	20
1	35	17.5	40	20
2	30	15	40	20
3	20	10	38	19
4	10	5	36	18
5	10	5	34	17
6	10	5	32	16
7	10	5	30	15
8	10	5	28	14
9	10	5	26	12
10 or more	10	5	24	11

Instalment option

➤ The instalment option enables tax to be paid in 10 annual instalments, where:

a) the disposal was a gift (*s.281(1)(a)*), *and*

b) hold-over relief is not available, as opposed to not claimed (*s.281(1)(b)*), *and*

- Normally, the 'instalment option' is not available for sole traders/partners/members of a LLP incorporated under the *LPA 2000* as there is 'hold over' relief.

c) the property disposed of was (*s.281(3)*):

- land, *or*
- a controlling shareholding in a quoted or unquoted company, *or*
- a minority holding in an unquoted company.

D Inheritance tax (IHT)

References in this section are to the Inheritance Tax Act 1984, unless otherwise stated.

I Liability
II Calculation

I Liability

<table>
<tr><th>Property</th><th colspan="2">Liability for IHT</th><th>Burden (if a will is silent)</th></tr>
<tr><td>Vesting in the PRs</td><td colspan="2" rowspan="2">PRs: are liable to the extent that resources fall into their hands or would do so but for their default (ss.200, 204)</td><td>Residuary beneficiary</td></tr>
<tr><td>Jointly and nominated</td><td>Beneficiary</td></tr>
<tr><td>LCTs, PETs</td><td rowspan="2">Donor and donee (s.199)</td><td rowspan="3">PRs for IHT is unpaid after 1 year after the end of the month of death (s.204(8))</td><td rowspan="2">Donee</td></tr>
<tr><td>GBRs</td></tr>
<tr><td>Life interest in possession</td><td>Donee and trustees (s.199)</td><td>Donee and trust fund</td></tr>
</table>

II Calculation

During life (L)

Steps	
L1	**Identify a 'transfer of value' which reduces the estate's value**
L2	**Value the transfer**
L3	**Deduct any exemptions or reliefs**
L4	**Cumulate transfers over 7 years and calculate the tax due**

On death (D)

Steps	
D1	**Identify property deemed to pass on death: 'the free estate'**
D2	**Value the 'free estate'**
D3	**Deduct any exemptions, reliefs or deductible property**
D4	**Calculate IHT on death, on pre-death chargeable transfers (LCTs, PETs, GBRs) and on the 'free estate'**

'PET' - Potentially Exempt Transfer
'LCT' - Lifetime Chargeable Transfer
'GBR' - Gift in respect of a which a donor Reserves a Benefit under *FA 1986 ss.102-102C*

Steps L1 and L4 — Identify the lifetime transfer and calculate the tax due

Lifetime transfers which are potentially chargeable				
Transfer	Definition	Tax on transfer	Cumulation on death	Tax on death
Lifetime chargeable (*s.2*)	a) To a NIP[†] trust (gross up transfer) b) To a company	Up to £242,000 at 0% Over £242,000 at 20% Cumulate LCTs over 7 years prior to the LCT	LCTs and chargeable PETs over 7 years prior to death	Tapering relief: year 6-7: 8% year 5-6: 16% year 4-5: 24% year 3-4: 32% Otherwise death rate at 40% Credit is given for tax already paid
Potentially exempt (*s.3A*)	a) To an individual b) To an accumulation and maintenance trust c) To a disabled trust	Nil, unless the donor dies within 7 years, then cumulate LCTs over 7 years prior to the PET	If a PET becomes chargeable, add it to the cumulative total	Tapering relief applies (as above)

[†] A 'NIP' trust is a 'non interest in possession' trust (eg: a discretionary trust), *s.59.*

Steps L2 and D2 — Value the transfer and/or the 'free estate'

➤ The value of a lifetime transfer is the value of the asset transferred at the time of the transfer (*s.160*).

➤ The probate value of the free estate is the value of the death estate minus any lifetime transfers of value.

Valuation	
Bank, building society a/c	The balance of the account and interest which has accrued to the date of death
Debts	Sums owed to the deceased. Overpaid income tax is reclaimed and accounted for on *CAP D3* (*s.174*)
Life interest in trust	The capital value of the beneficial interest which the deceased enjoyed *and* income accrued but unpaid at death (*s.49*)
Insurance	If a policy matures on the deceased's death and the estate is beneficially entitled, the sum it produces on maturity. If it matures on another event, the value of premiums paid less any sum paid to surrender rights under the policy before death (*s.167*)
Quoted shares	In accordance with the Stock Exchange's *Daily Official List* on the day of death. The value is the 'sell' price plus one quarter of the difference between the 'sell' and the 'buy' price. Prices are usually quoted 'cum div.' (ie: with the right to the next dividend). If the dividend has been declared but not paid, the price is quoted 'ex div.' as only those registered on the company's Register of Members when the dividend is declared are entitled to receive the dividend. If the testator dies before payment of the dividend, his estate is entitled to any declared dividend. The dividend is treated as a separate asset in the estate, and the estate's gross value is calculated by adding the dividend to the 'ex div.' price of the shares
Unquoted shares	The open market value. The firm's accountants and the firm itself will advise on a valuation. The latest annual accounts should be consulted as a guide (*s.168*)
Land	The open market value. Estate agents will advise on this. The figure must be agreed with the local district valuer before the estate is wound up (*s.160*)

Loss relief on death

For some assets, the sale price may replace the probate value *if* it is less than their aggregate probate value.

➤ Sale within 1 year of shares and securities quoted on a recognised stock exchange at death, or of units in an authorised unit trust (*ss.178-189*).

Note: if qualifying investments are cancelled (and not replaced by the institution which issued them), they are treated as having been sold.

➤ Sale within 4 years of land (*ss.190-198*).

Steps L3 and D3 — Deduct any exemptions, reliefs and (on death) deductible property

Exemptions *available on lifetime transfers only* per tax year

- £3,000 per annum, which can be carried forward for 1 year so that £6,000 becomes available in a given year.
- Normal expenditure (*s.21*).
  - Regular payments + the transfer is from income + the transferror retains sufficient income to maintain his standard of living.
- PETs which are not yet chargeable *or* have become extinct as they occurred more than 7 years before death.
- £250 small gift exemption for gifts up to this sum to any particular individual (*s.20*).
- Marriage: a) up to £5,000 from a parent, b) up to £2,500 from a remoter relation, c) up to £1,000 from a non-relation (*s.22*).

Exemptions and reliefs *on lifetime transfers and on death*

Exemptions	➤ Gift to spouse (*s.18*) ◆ The transfer of a lifetime interest in possession is treated as capital within this exemption ◆ On death, a gift qualifies for exemption if it is immediate *or* conditional on survivorship for up to 1 year ➤ Gift to charity (*ss.23-26*) ➤ Gift for the public benefit (*ss.30-35*). Providing that: a) the Treasury classes the asset as being as of national, artistic, historic or scientific interest, *and* b) an undertaking is given that the asset will i) remain in the UK, *and* ii) be preserved, *and* iii) be open to public access	
Business property relief (*s.105*)	Relief is at 100%	➤ A business *or* an interest in a business property ➤ Any shares in an unquoted company
	Relief is at 50%	➤ Quoted shares if the transferror had control of the company immediately before the transfer ➤ The transferror is a partner *or* controls a company *and* transfers land, buildings, machinery or plant which were wholly or mainly used for the business
	Property must be owned for 2 or more years before the transfer takes place (*s.106*)	
Agricultural property relief (*ss.115-24*)	Relief is at 100%	➤ The transferor used the property for agriculture for 2 years prior to the transfer, *or* ➤ The transferor owned land used for agricultural purposes during the last 7 years and is entitled to occupy it within 1 year (or the land is let under an agricultural tenancy granted on or after 1 September 1995)
	Relief is at 50%	➤ The transferor owned land used for agricultural purposes during the last 7 years and the land is subject to a tenancy granted before 1 September 1995

Exemptions, reliefs and deductible items *available on death only*

Quick succession (*s.141*)	Relief is a fraction of the tax already paid on a previous transfer: 1-2 years before death: 80% 2-3 years before death: 60% 3-4 years before death: 40% 4-5 years before death: 20%	➤ Tax was paid on a chargeable transfer to the deceased within the last 5 years ➤ Tax is payable on the deceased's estate
Woodlands (*ss.125-130*)	Timber is exempt	➤ Timbered land not qualifying for agricultural property relief ➤ Timber itself (not the land) is exempt provided the land was bought at least 5 years before death
Funerals (*s.162*)	Fully deductible	➤ Reasonable burial expenses are deductible
Debts (*s.505*)		➤ Debts incurred for money or money's worth are deductible
Liabilities are deductible (*s.5(3)*) unless the deduction is excluded (*s.162*) (More complex liabilities are not dealt with here)		

Step D1 — Identify property deemed to pass on death

Identifying the 'free estate' on death (*IHTA 1984 ss.5, 200*)

- Assets to which the testator is beneficially entitled and which pass under the will or on intestacy, eg: a life assurance policy in the deceased's name and in his favour.

- Assets passing outside the will or intestacy:
  - to which the deceased is beneficially entitled under property law: joint tenancies, nominated property (Friendly societies, Industrial and Provident societies, some TSB accounts, with deposits up to £5,000)
  - to which the deceased is deemed to be beneficially entitled to for IHT purposes: GBRs, life interest under a trust

Step D4 — Calculate IHT on death and on pre-death chargeable transfers

Calculation of IHT on the death estate

LCTs and PETs	Any of these occurring within 7 years prior to the death represent additional liability	(See *Step L1*, p.91)
Tax rate on 'free estate'	Not exceeding £242,000 at 0% Exceeding £242,000 at 40%	

Note
In calculating these bands, cumulate LCTs and PETs which occurred in the 7 years prior to death

Apportionment of IHT over the estate

Subject to instructions to the contrary in the will, the IHT burden is 'apportioned' over the whole estate by the formula:

$$\text{Estate rate} = \frac{\text{Tax payable}}{\text{Taxable estate}}$$

The tax due on each asset is calculated by multiplying the value of the asset by the 'estate rate'.

E Corporation tax (CT)

References in this section are to the Income and Corporation Taxes Act 1988, unless otherwise stated.

I Calculation

Steps	
1	**Calculate 'income profit'**
2	**Calculate 'capital profit'**
3	**Calculate 'total profit'**
4	**Deduct 'charges on income'**
5	**Calculate the corporation tax due on profits**

Step 1 Calculate the 'income profit'

(Profit under Schedules A, D and F) plus (Profit on 'loan relationships', foreign exchange and financial instruments) less (any available losses (see p.99)).

Schedule A income (from the exploitation of land in the United Kingdom)

➤ Income received on or after 1 April 1998 is calculated on Schedule D Case I principles (*FA 1998 s.38, Sch. 5*).

- Remediation relief (at the rate of 150% of the actual expenditure incurred) may be claimed for expenditure incurred in cleaning-up contaminated land (*FA 2001 Sch.22*).

➤ Part of a premium received on the grant of a lease with a term not exceeding 50 years, or on the surrender or variation / waiver of a lease (even if the original term exceeded 50 years), may be treated as an income receipt and as a part disposal for CGT purposes - for the apportionment see *s.34* (see also *TCGA 1992 Sch. 8* for CGT treatment).

➤ Subtract any **capital allowances**, or add any **balancing charges** see p.81.

Schedule D Case I and Case II trading income ('chargeable receipts' minus 'deductible expenditure')

➤ **Chargeable receipts** a) derive from income not capital, *and* b) derive from the company's trade.

➤ **Deductible expenditure:** expenses of an income nature that are 'wholly and exclusively' incurred for the purposes of a trade, profession, or vocation are deductible (*s.74(1)*). Case law governs whether expenses are deductible (see eg: *Mallalieu v. Drummond* [1983] 2 AC 861).

➤ Subtract any **capital allowances**, or add any **balancing charges** see p.81.

Schedule D Case III, income from loan relationships, annuities, annual payments and discounts

Schedule D Case V, income from foreign possessions (other than loan relationships)

Schedule D Case VI, other income

Schedule F income

➤ Qualifying distributions received from UK companies are FII which is not taxable (provided the company is not a dealer in securities in which case the net distribution is taxable (*s.95*).

Profits on 'loan relationships' (and FX and FI in outline)

➤ A company has a 'loan relationship' when:

a) it stands in the position of a creditor or a debtor as respects a money debt, *and*

b) the debt arises from a transaction for the lending of money (*FA 1996 s.81*) (eg: not a trade debt).

- A 'money debt' is a debt in any currency which is to be settled by the payment of money, *or* the transfer of a right to settlement of a debt which is a money debt (*FA 1996 s.81*).

➤ Profits and losses are calculated using one of the 'authorised accounting methods' (*FA 1996 s.85*):

- **the accruals basis:** allocates income and expenditure to the period to which it relates, irrespective of when payment is made or received, *or*
- **the mark-to-market basis:** the fair market value at the accounts date.
  - Broadly speaking, the accounting method used is that followed in a company's statutory accounts (*FA 1996 s.86*). There are rules in the legislation governing how accounting methods may be used and what happens when different methods are used at different times with respect to a particular loan relationship (*FA 1996 ss.89-90*).
  - In certain situations, an accruals basis must be used (eg: *FA 1996 s.87* (parties to a relationship are 'connected'), *s.92* (the 'creditor' relationship in respect of a convertible security), *s.93* (asset-linked debt)).

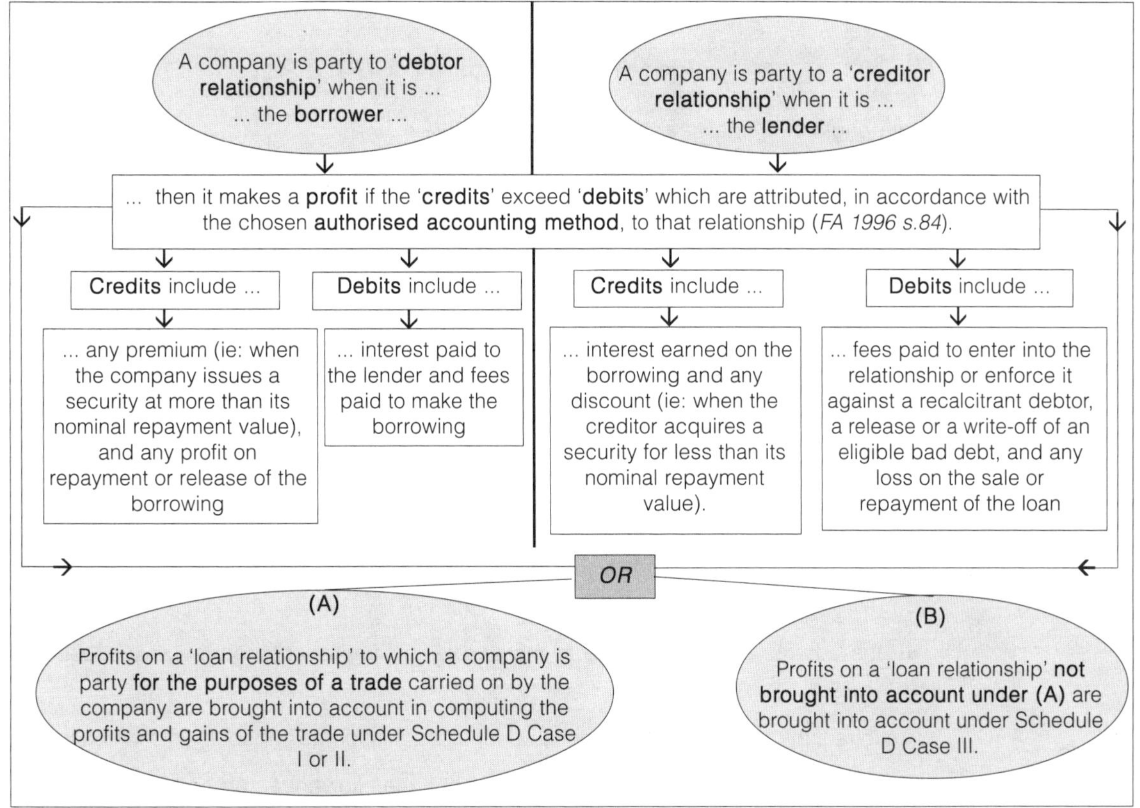

➤ Various anti-avoidance provisions may prevent a company gaining deductions in respect of interest or other 'debits'. Details are beyond the scope of this book (see the *Banking & Capital Markets Comopanion*).

- Provisions of general application include *TA ss.209(2)(d)-(e), TA s.787* and *FA 1996 Schedule 9 para.13.*
- There are also rules which apply in particular circumstances, eg: *FA 1996 Schedule 9 para.6(1)* which restricts the availability of 'debits' for a creditor when a debt between connected parties becomes a bad debt.

➤ The general intention of this regime is that 'capital' gains and losses (as well as 'income' profits and losses) on money debts should be taxed and relieved as income (*FA 1996 s.80(1), 84(1)(a)*). There are however exceptions when only 'income' is in the regime, eg:

- a creditor relationship, if a 'loan relationship' is a convertible security (*FA 1996 s.92*).
- a relationship linked to the value of chargeable assets (unless the disposal of the asset would take place as an integral part of a trade carried on by the company) (*FA 1996 s.93*).

➤ Foreign exchange (Forex) gains and losses, and gains and losses on financial instruments (FI) (eg: options, swaps and derivatives) are brought into account under complex legislation which in principle aims, like the 'loan relationship' rules, to follow accountancy treatment.

- The primary legislation relating to Forex is in the *FA 1993* (*ss.92-95, 125-170*) and that relating to FI in *FA 1994* (*ss.147-177*).

Step 2 Calculate 'capital profit'

Steps	
I	**Identify the disposal**
II	**Calculate the 'taxable gain' or loss on *a* disposal**
III	**Calculate the 'taxable gain' on all disposals for the accounting period, taking account of exemptions and reliefs**

Step I Identify the disposal (*TCGA 1992 ss.22-28*)

➤ A sale *or* gift of a 'chargeable asset' (*TCGA 1992 s.15(2)*).

Step II Calculate the 'taxable gain' or 'allowable loss' on *a* disposal

➤ Take *either* the market value of the asset on its 'disposal' (*s.17*) *or* the consideration on its sale, and subtract the 'allowable expenditure'.

- The allowable expenditure is calculated by adding up the following:
  - the initial cost of the asset. If the asset was acquired before 31 March 1982, use *either*:

    a) its value on that date, *or*

    b) the cost of acquisition, whichever produces a smaller loss or gain (*s.35*).
  - any expense 'wholly and exclusively' incurred in enhancing the asset's value (not routine maintenance) (*s.38*).
  - the cost of establishing title to the asset, and any costs incurred in disposing of it (*s.38*).

➤ Then subtract the 'indexation allowance', which accounts for the impact of inflation on the gain.

- Where an asset was owned on 31 March 1982, the allowance can be taken *either*

  a) from the asset's value on 31 March 1982, *or*

  b) from the 'actual expenditure' on the asset (ie: acquisition, maintenance, etc), whichever carries a higher indexation (*s.54*).

  Note: since 30 November 1993, this allowance only serves to reduce or extinguish a gain, it cannot be used to increase the size of a loss, nor to convert a gain into a loss.

Step III — Calculate the 'taxable gain' for the accounting period

➤ Add up the total 'chargeable gains' for the accounting period.

➤ Then deduct:

- any 'allowable losses' from that accounting period (*TCGA 1992 s.2(2)(a)*), *and*
- any 'allowable losses' from previous accounting periods not brought into account to corporation tax (*TCGA 1992 s.2(2)(b)*), *and*

➤ Ensure relevant exemptions and reliefs are left out of account:

Exemptions
'Wasting assets' which have a life of under 50 years (*TCGA 1992 ss.44-45*)
Tangible moveables if the consideration is less than £6,000 (*TCGA 1992 s.262*)

Reliefs
Roll-over relief on the replacement of 'qualifying assets' (*TCGA 1992 ss.152-157*)
Qualifying assets: a) goodwill *and* b) land *and* c) fixed plant and machinery (*ss.155-156*) ➤ A replacement is acquired *either* within 1 year prior to the disposal *or* within 3 years after the disposal ➤ The replacement asset does not have to be of the same kind as the asset disposed of NB: Relief is restricted if the asset is not used in the seller's trade throughout the period of ownership *or* if the whole proceeds are not reinvested in a new qualifying asset
Roll-over relief on paper for paper transactions (*TCGA 1992 ss.127-137A*)
➤ See the *Banking & Capital Markets Companion*
Corporate venturing scheme (*FA 2000 Sch.15*)
➤ See the *Banking & Capital Markets Companion*

Step 3 — 'Total profits' = 'income profit' + 'capital profit'

Step 4 — Deduct any 'charges on income'

➤ Since the introduction on 1 April 1996 of 'loan relationships' by *FA 1996* the 'charges on income' in respect of which deductions can be claimed against a company's 'total profits' have been reduced to (*s.338*):

a) certain annuities and annual payments (not being payments in respect of loan relationships), *and*

b) certain charitable donations (ie: those falling within *s.339*), *and*

c) patent royalties, mining rents/royalties and payments for easements.

- Note that certain detailed conditions (which are beyond the scope of this book) must be satisfied for charges on income to be deducted.

Step 5 Calculate the corporation tax due on profits (*TA ss.13,13AA*)

➤ The rates are fixed for a financial year (1 April to 31 March): if the rate changes during the accounting period, the taxable profit is apportioned across the applicable tax rates.

Full rate of 'mainstream corporation tax':	30%	on profits over £1,500,000.
Tax on profits between £300,000 and £1,500,000:	32.5%	relief is effectively given at this marginal rate
Tax on profits over £50,000 and not exceeding £300,000:	20%	the 'small companies rate' of corporation tax
Tax on profits between £10,000 and £50,000	22.5%	relief is effectively given at this marginal rate
Tax on profits not exceeding £10,000	10%	the 'starting rate' of corporation tax

On 18 June 2001 the Chancellor announcedhis intention in the Finance Bill 2002 to extend the starting rate band to reduce the tax bills of more businesses.

➤ Franked investment income is ignored when paying tax, but it is included when calculating the rate of tax applicable.

Private service providers

➤ An individual is treated as receiving a deemed Schedule E payment (*FA 2000 Sch.12 paras 1-2*) ...:

a) if an individual (the '**worker**') personally performs, or is under an obligation personally to perform, services for the purposes of a business carried on by a client, *and*

b) the services are provided not under a contract directly between the client and the worker but under arrangements involving an intermediary, *and*

c) if the services were provided under a contract directly between the client and the worker, the worker would be regarded for tax purposes as the employee of the client, *then if either the intermediary is*:

i) **a company** in which the worker has a material interest (eg: more than 5% of the company's ordinary share capital, a right to more than 5% of the company's distributions, *or* more than 5% of the company's assets on a winding-up) (*FA 2000 Sch 12 para 3*), *or*

ii) **a partnership** and the worker (and his relatives) are *either* entitled to 60% or more of partnership profits, *or* most of the partnership profits derive from the client and its associates, *or* the profit share of any of the partners is based on the income generated by that partner by the provision of services within a)-c) above (*FA 2000 Sch 12 para 4*), *or*

iii) **an individual** and payment/benefit is received or receivable by the worker directly from the intermediary and can reasonably be taken to represent remuneration for services provided by the worker to the client (*FA 2000 Sch 12 para 5*).

➤ Theses provisions (known as 'IR 35' after the press release in which they were announced) were introduced to counter perceived avoidance of PAYE and National Insuranace Contributions by service providers (see also the *WRPA 1999 ss.75-76*, *SSC(I)R 2000*).

- Their legality was upheld in *R (On the application of Professional Contractors Group Ltd and others) v. IRC* [2001] STC 629, QBD).

II Loss relief / R&D tax credits

➤ Companies may use their losses in a number of ways.

	Loss can be claimed ...	Use on ...
Carry-across and carry-back relief *s.393A*	a) ... for the accounting period, *and* b) ... any unrelieved loss may be carried back against any profits from an accounting period in the previous 1 year, *provided*: i) the company is carrying on the same trade as it had been in the earlier year, *and* ii) the loss is set against later years first	... total profits
Losses (trading) other than terminal losses *s.393*	... following accounting periods, against losses of the trade, for as long as the company carries on the trade	... trading income
Losses from a Schedule A business *s.392A* (from 1 April 1998)	a) ... for the accounting period, *and* b) ... any unrelieved loss may be carried forward if the company continues to carry on the Schedule A business in that succeeding period	... total profits

NB: special rules apply for losses on a Schedule D Case V trade (*s.393(5)*) and Schedule D Case VI losses (*s.396*)

NB: a company which is a member of a group of companies can claim group relief (see the *Banking & Capital Markets Companion*)

Loan relationships, Forex and FI

➤ Special rules govern the use of losses on 'loan relationships'.

- 'Debits' on 'loan relationships' to which a company is a party **for the purposes of a trade carried on by it** are deductible in computing the profits of that trade (*FA 1996 s.82(2)*) and losses may be relieved under the normal rules for the set-off of losses on income (ie: *ss.393-396*).
- All the 'debits' and 'credits' on 'loan relationships' to which a company is party **otherwise than for the purposes of trade carried on by it** are aggregated respectively together. If the 'non-trading debits' exceed the 'non-trading credits', a company has a 'non-trading deficit' on its 'loan relationships'. A 'non-trading deficit' may be dealt with in one of 4 ways (*FA 1996 s.83(2)*):

  a) set-off against profits from the same accounting period (in the priority required by *FA 1996 Schedule 8 para 1*).

  b) relieved through group relief (see the *Banking & Capital Markets Companion*).

  c) carried back against profits which are attributable to loan relationships taxed under Schedule D Case III and earned over the previous 1 year (*FA 1996 Schedule 8 para 3*).

  d) carried forward against profits for the next accounting period (providing the profits are not classed as trading income within *s.393A*) - this option is used to the extent that the others are not claimed (*FA 1996 s.83(3)*).

➤ These rules also apply to Forex (*FA 1993 ss.128-130*) and FI (*FA 1994 ss.159-160*) losses.

R&D tax credits

- R&D is an activity that is treated as research and development under normal accountancy practice (effectively, UK GAAP) (*TA s.837A(2)-(6)*).
- If a company (*FA 2000 Sch.20 para. 1*):

  a) is a small or medium sized enterprise in an accounting period, *and*

  - A small or medium sized enterprise is as defined in Commission recommendation 96/20/EC (3 April 1996) - this is very similar to the test adopted for capital allowance purposes (see p.83) (*FA 2000 Sch.20 para. 2*).

  b) incurs qualifying R&D expenditure in that accounting period which is not less than £25,000 and is allowable as a deduction in computing the profits of a trade carried on by a company (or would have been so allowable if the company had been carrying on a trade at the time).

  - Qualifying expenditure is (*FA 2000 Sch.20 paras 3-12*):

    i) not of a capital nature, *and*

    ii) attributable to R&D carried on by the company or on its behalf, *and*

    iii) incurred on staff costs, consumable stores, or qualifying expenditure on subcontracted R&D, *and*

    iv) incurred on R&D related to a trade carried on by the company or which it is intended a trade to be carried on by the company will be derived.

- If a company is (*FA 2000 Sch.20 paras. 13-14*):

  a) **trading** and has qualifying R&D expenditure which is allowable as a deduction it may deduct an amount equal to 150% of its qualifying R&D expenditure in computing the profits of that trade, *or*

  b) **not trading**, but has qualifying R&D expenditure which would have been allowable if at that time it had been carrying on a trade consisting of the activities in respect of which the expenditure was incurred, it may elect to be treated as if it had incurred a trading loss in that period equal to 150% of the amount of its qualifying R&D expenditure.

  - Where a company under (a) has an unrelieved loss, or a company is treated as having an unrelieved loss under (b), it may claim a credit equal to 16% of that loss (*FA 2000 Sch.20 paras. 15-16*).

F Distributions

References in this section are to the Income and Corporation Taxes Act 1988, unless otherwise stated.

I Generally

➤ In 1972 corporation tax became an 'imputation system'. The aim was to restrict the extent to which profits made by companies and distributed to their shareholders were subject to double taxation: first as the company's profits and secondly as income in the hands of individuals who are its shareholders.

- The logic underpinning the imputation system was virtually abandoned in the Budget on 2 July 1997 (changes were enacted by *F(No2)A 1997* and are phased in between 2 July 1997 and 6 April 2004).
- In his Green Budget (November 1997) the Chancellor announced that advance corporation tax ('ACT'), the cornerstone of the imputation system, would be abolished in April 1999.
  - Companies used to pay ACT, at the rate of 20%, on a distribution (eg: ACT on £100 distribution was £20). The shareholder used to receive a matching credit (eg: £20) which could be reclaimed by a non-taxpayer or set against a taxpayer's liability to income tax.
    - The abolition of ACT was implimented by measures introduced in *FA 1998.*
- The taxation of companies and their shareholders is, therefore, in the midst of the most radical changes for over 25 years.

II Shareholders

➤ Reforms contained in *F(No2)A 1997* provide for the two stage withdrawal of the 'tax credit' which was the mechanism through which tax paid by a company was 'imputed' to its shareholders:

Stage 1 - for distributions made on or after 2 July 1997:

a) pension funds ceased to be entitled to repayment of a 'tax credit'.

- Pension funds suffered a reduction in their income. Corporate schemes may need topping up by employers if the scheme is to pay out a pension tied to the employee's final salary (ie: a 'defined benefit scheme'), holders of personal pensions may need to increase contributions to their pensions to make good the shortfall.

b) companies lost the entitlement to reclaim the tax credit element associated with FII.

Stage 2 - for distributions made on or after 6 April 1999:

a) individuals are only be entitled to a tax credit equal to $1/9^{th}$ of the distribution received by the shareholder (ie: 10% of the gross distribution including the tax credit).

b) charities cease to be entitled to repayment of the tax credit.

- Transitional rules which apply to distributions made on or after 6 April 1999 and before 6 April 2004 are intended to cushion charities from the resulting drop in their income.

- The term 'tax credit' suggests a 'credit' for which a taxpayer could claim a cash repayment.
  - From 6 April 1999 this became something of a misnomer as no UK resident shareholders will be entitled to a cash repayment (except in respect of distributions made by UK tax resident companies before 6 April 2004 on shares held in a PEP or ISA).
    - Shareholders who may be entitled to a (much reduced) repayment in respect of a 'tax credit' (unlikely to exceed 0.25%) are shareholders resident in foreign jurisdictions who are entitled to claim repayment under a 'double tax treaty' with the UK.
      - The whittling away of the tax credit has caused dissatisfaction abroad; the Government has entered into negotiations for a new 'double tax treaty' between the UK and the USA.

➤ In outline, the system works as follows:

- Shareholders receive a tax credit and are treated as having paid tax at the 'Schedule F ordinary rate'.
- Quite how the system operates depends on the tax status of the shareholder. The basic principle is that:

a) **an individual** receives a tax credit (*s.231(1),(3)*):

The tax credit
Distribution (of £100) on or after 6 April 1999
1/9th† (£8.89) of the net distribution (£80) received by the shareholder
† This is equivalent to 10% of the gross distribution (£88.89) which the shareholder receives

- **non-taxpayers** cannot claim a repayment of the credit (They could claim a credit for distributions made before 6 April 1999).
- **starting (10%)** and **basic rate (22%) taxpayers** have no further income tax liability in relation to the distribution (*s.231*). Their liability is at the 'Schedule F ordinary rate' - 10% of the gross distribution (*s.1A(1A)*). The tax credit satisfies this liability.
- **higher-rate (40%) taxpayers** owe an extra 32.5% more tax (*s.1A*). For distributions made on or after 6 April 1999, their liability is at the 'Schedule F upper rate' - 32.5% (*s.1B*).

b) **a company** receives 'franked investment income' (FII).

- The term FII refers to both the distribution *and* the tax credit.
- FII is taken into account in working out the rate of corporation tax applicable to a company for an accounting period, but is ignored when calculating the tax actually due (*s.208*).

c) **a pension** fund used to be able to reclaim a tax credit, but cannot do so in respect of distributions made on or after 2 July 1997 (*s.231A*).

d) **a charity** may reclaim a tax credit on distributions made before 6 April 1999, thereafter it may claim transitional relief for distributions made before 6 April 2004 (*F(No2)A 1997 s.35, Sch. 5*).

➤ Note that the Inland Revenue may restrict or deny a tax credit in certain circumstances, for instance if a distribution is abnormally large and not commercially justified (*ss.703-709*). A further anti-avoidance provision, *s.231B*, has been introduced to counteract arrangements designed to pass on the value of a tax credit to a person who would not (without such arrangements) be entitled to it.

Higher rate taxpayer's liability

		Distributions before 6 April 1999		Distributions on or after 6 April 1999
		£		£
Distribution (net of ACT)		80		80
Tax credit	(20%of income)	20	(10% of 88.89, or 1/9th of 80)	8.89
Gross income		100		88.89
Higher rate tax	(40%)	40	(32.5% of 88.89)	28.89
After tax income		60		60

➤ Individuals who hold shares through an ISA or PEP can reclaim the tax credit in respect of distributions made prior to 6 April 2004 (*FA 1998 s.76*).

G Close companies

I Generally

➤ For corporation tax purposes, a 'close company' is a company that is *either*:

a) 'controlled' by 5 or fewer 'participators', *or*

b) 'controlled' by its directors, *or*

c) has amongst its shareholders 5 or fewer 'participators', or directors who are 'participators' *and* on a winding-up of the company these 'participators' would be entitled to receive the greater part of the company's assets.

- 'Control' means control as defined in *TA s.416.*
  - For the definition of 'control' in *TA s.416,* and the also for the (different) definition of 'control' in *TA s.840,* see p.106. (Both definitions are used in the *Taxes Act* and it is important to make sure that the correct definition is used in the right context).
- A 'participator' is a person who has a share or interest in the capital or the income of a company and specifically someone entitled to acquire capital or voting rights, or to ensure income or assets will be deployed for his benefit, or entitled to distributions or the proceeds of a premium or redemption paid by the company, or certain loan creditors (*TA s.417(1)*).
- The definition of 'director' is a wide one, and focuses on substance rather than the title (*TA s.417(5)*).

➤ Companies which may not be close companies for corporation tax purposes include:

- companies not resident in the UK (*TA s.414*).
- quoted companies, if shares bearing not less than 35% of the votes at a general meeting have been unconditionally allotted or acquired so that members of the public enjoy them beneficially (*TA s.415*).
- companies controlled by one or more non-close companies and which could only be treated as a close company by including a non-close company as one of the 5 participators, or by including non-close loan creditors on a liquidation (*TA s.414(5)*).

➤ The definition of a 'close company' is different in repect of the taxation of individuals who hold shares in such companies.

- For IHT purposes, the definition of a 'close company' is the same as for corporation tax purposes except that:

  a) it includes non-resident companies, *and*

  b) the test for a 'participator' disregards the interests of loan creditors (*IHTA 1984 s.94*).

- For capital gains tax purposes, the definition includes non-resident companies (*TCGA 1992 s.13*).

II Taxation of a 'close company' and its participators

- The taxation treatment of a 'close company' depends on whether it is also a 'close investment holding company'.
- The rules in A. **'Close companies'** apply to all 'close companies', the additional rules in B. **'Close investment holding companies'** apply only to 'close investment holding companies'.

Definition of a 'close investment holding company'

- A close company is a 'close investment holding company' unless it exists during an accounting period 'wholly or mainly' for one of 6 purposes.
  - These purposes include carrying on a trade on a commercial basis, and investing in land provided the land is not intended to be let to connected persons (*TA s.13A(2)*).

A. 'Close companies'

1 **Loans to 'participators' (*TA ss.419-421*)**

- A company pays tax (at the rate of 20%), to the Inland Revenue in respect of a loan to a participator (eg: if the company wishes to lend £100 gross it pays £20 tax to the Revenue and the participator receives £80).
- This does not apply if *either*:

  a) the loan is in the usual course of business for a company whose business is moneylending, *or*

  b) the following conditions are fulfilled:

     i) the company's total loans to the 'participator' stand at less than £15,000, *and*

     ii) the 'participator' owns 5% or less of the shares in the company, *and*

     iii) the 'participator' works full time for the company (*s.420(2)*).
- If a claim for repayment of the tax is made within 6 years of the end of the accounting period in which the repayment of the loan is made, the Inland Revenue refund the tax to the company.

2 **Expenses of 'participators', and their 'associates', taxed as distributions (*TA s.418*)**

- An expense to benefit a 'participator' or their 'associate', is a 'qualifying distribution' on which the participator is taxed under Schedule F (*TA s.418(2)*).
- A charge to tax under this section is excluded if the 'participator' is taxed on the benefit under *TA s.154* (*TA s.418(3)*).

3 **Attribution of capital gains to a 'participator' (*TCGA 1992 s.13*)**

- Capital gains made by a non-resident company (which would be close if UK resident) are apportioned to 'participators' in that company in proportion to their beneficial interest in the company.

4 **Liability to IHT on a transfer of value by a 'close company' (*IHTA 1984 s.94(1)*)**

- A transfer at an undervalue by a close company is treated as a transfer out of a 'participator's' estate and is chargeable to IHT. Liability rests primarily on the company, although limited recovery is possible from each 'participator' or the transferee (*IHTA 1984 s.202(1)*).
  - Altering the rights of unquoted share or loan capital is treated as a transfer (*IHTA 1984 s.98(1)*).

5 **Relief on interest on loan to, or to buy ordinary shares in, a close company (*ss.360-360A, 363)***

➤ The individual:

a) has a 'material interest' (he or an associate control more than 5% of the ordinary shares or would be entitled to more than 5% of the assets of the company distributable amongst 'participators' in the company), *or* he (or his associate) already own shares in the close company, *and*

b) the taxpayer spends the majority of time working for the company when the interest is paid, *and*

- lends money to a close company, *or*
- borrows money for the close company to use in the course of its business, *or*
- borrows to purchase ordinary shares in a close company.

B. 'Close investment holding companies'

1 **Rate of corporation tax**

➤ Tax is paid at the full corporation tax rate of 30% (eg: not the smaller companies' rate of 20%).

2 **Abuse of tax credit**

➤ Anti-avoidance rules deny the benefit of a tax credit where arrangements are entered into under which a person obtains a payment representing a tax credit and those arrangements are entered into for an unallowable purpose (*TA s.231B*).

Principal definitions of 'control' in the *Taxes Act*

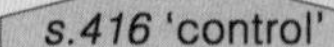

➤ The test is complex, but involves establishing that a person exercises, is able to exercise or entitled to acquire, direct or indirect control over a company's affairs.

- Examples of such control include the possession of, or entitlement to acquire:

  a) the greater part of a company's issued share capital or of the voting power in a company.

  b) enough of the company's issued share capital as would entitle that person to receive the greater part of the income of the company if that income were to be distributed amongst the 'participators' in the company.

  c) on a winding-up of the company, to receive the greater part of the assets of the company which would be available for distribution amongst the 'participators' in the company (*s.416(2)*).

s.840 'control'

➤ A person 'controls' a company (the 'relevant company') if that person has power to secure ...

a) by means of the holding of shares or the possession of voting power in or in relation to the relevant company or any other company, *or*

b) by virtue of any powers conferred by the articles of association or other document regulating the relevant company or any other company, ...

... that the affairs of the relevant company are conducted in accordance with the wishes of that person.

H Assessment and payment of tax (IT, CGT, IHT, CT)

I Assessment of income tax and capital gains tax

References in this section are to TMA 1970, unless otherwise stated.

1 Notification of chargeability

- An individual is under a duty to notify the Inland Revenue of any chargeable income or capital gain within 6 months of the taxable event in respect of which tax falls due, unless the individual is exempt as:
  - no chargeable income and gains arise in the year of assessment (above the exempt amount), *and*
  - his net income tax liability is nil *or* tax deducted at source covers any liability (*ss.7(3)-7(7)*).

2 Filing a tax return

- An individual must submit a tax return stating his liability to income tax and capital gains tax (*s.8(1)(a)*).
- The filing date depends on whether the individual completes a self assessment.
  - If he only wishes to supply information, without completing a self assessment, he must submit the return on or before 30 September following the end of the tax year or if a notice is issued after 31 July following the end of the tax year within 2 months of the notice being issued (*s.9(2)*).
  - If he is prepared to assess his own tax, then he must submit the return on or before 31 January following the end of the tax year, unless the return is issued to him late (after 31 October) in which case he has 3 months from when the return is issued (*ss.8(1)(a), 8(1A)*).
    - If a return is submitted, but the self assessment is not completed, the Inland Revenue are under a duty to complete it (*s.9(3)*).
- Penalties for failing to file a return on time are hefty.
  - £100 automatically if a return is not submitted on time, *and*
  - a further £100 if it is still outstanding 6 months later, *and*
  - then up to £60 a day (*ss.93(2)-93(4)*).
- If no return is submitted, the Inland Revenue may, within 5 years of the end of the year of assessment, estimate the tax and make a determination stating the tax due (*s.28C*).

3 Records

- Records relevant to calculating tax liability must be kept: there is a fine of up to £3,000 for non-compliance (*ss.12B(1)-12B(6)*).

	Individual	Sole trader/partner
Time the return is issued ...	... within 1 year of the **filing date**	... within 5 years of the **filing date**
Obligation to keep records expires	1 year after the **filing date**	5 years after the **filing date**, or when a formal Inland Revenue enquiry is finished or becomes impossible

Overview of income tax and CGT calculations

Income tax	CGT
Calculate **'statutory income'** *Income according to the rules of each Schedule.* Schedule A - Income from land Schedule D - Income from trade, etc Schedule E - Income from employement Schedule F - Income from UK shares NB: certain income is exempt.	**Identify a 'disposal' of a 'chargeable asset'**
↓	↓
Calculate **'total income'** *Deduct charges on income from statutory income.*	**Calculate 'chargeable gain'/'allowable loss'** *Market value or consideration on disposal ...* *... less allowable expenditure* (ie: cost (or 31 March 1982 value) + expenses of enhancement and establishing title) *... less indexation allowance.*
↓	↓
Calculate **'taxable income'** *Deduct personal reliefs from total income.*	**Calculate 'taxable gain' for tax year** *All chargeable gains ...* *... less allowable losses* *... less exemptions/reliefs* *... less taper relief* *... less annual exemption*
↓	↓
Calculate **tax liability** *Apply tax at the appropriate rate.* Sch. F lower rate (10%), Sch. F higher rate (32.5%) Lower rate (20%) for savings (other than Schedule F income) ↓ Starting (10%), basic (22%) and higher rate (40%)	**Calculate tax liability** Apply rate of top rate of income tax applicable to taxpayer (known as 'top slicing), ie: starting, basic or higher rate. NB: consider whether the instalment option applies
↓	
Calculate **tax to pay/reclaim** *Deduct tax already paid* Eg: lower rate tax (20%) withheld on interest PAYE *Add tax overpaid* Eg: in respect of pension contributions	

II Payment of income tax and capital gains tax

➤ Tax assessed under self assessment is payable 'on account' on 31 January during the year of assessment, and on 31 July following the end of the year. Any corrective 'balancing' payment is due on the next 31 January (*TMA 1970 s.59A(2)*).

- No payment need be made on account if the income tax due is *either:*

  a) less than £500, *or*

  b) less than 20% of the taxpayer's total income tax liability for the year (ie: including income from which tax has been deducted at source) (*TMA 1970 s.59A(1)(c)-(d), IT(PA)R 1996*), ...

  ... in which case tax is payable on the 31 January following the year of assessment.

- The taxpayer may opt for tax to be deducted under PAYE if the tax due is less than £1,000.

➤ Interest runs on tax due 'on account', or as a balancing payment (*TMA 1970 ss.59A-59B*) from the date the payment is due (*TMA 1970 s.86*). Interest on overpaid tax is paid to the taxpayer (*s.824, TCGA s.283*).

➤ A surcharge of 5% is levied on tax outstanding 28 days after it falls due, and there is a further 5% surcharge if the tax is still unpaid 6 months after it is due (*TMA 1970 s.59C*).

III Assessment of IHT

➤ If the estate is an 'excepted estate'

- An estate is an 'excepted estate' (for deaths on or after 1 May 2000) if (*IT(DA)R 2000*):

  a) the deceased was domiciled in the United Kingdom, *and*

  b) none of the estate's assets *either:*

     i) pass under the terms of a trust, *or*

     ii) constitute settled property, *or*

     iii) comprise a gift with a reservation of benefit, *and*

  c) the value of the estate outside the United Kingdom does not exceed £50,000, *and*

  d) any taxable lifetime gifts within 7 years of death were only cash, shares or quoted securities with a total value not exceeding £75,000, *and*

  e) the gross value of the estate does not exceed £210,000.

  - The 'gross estate' is calculated before debts, administrative expenses or IHT reliefs or exemptions are deducted.

➤ If an estate is not an excepted estate, complete *form IHT 200, then ...*

... **if there is no tax to pay *and* the deceased was domiciled in the United Kingdom** send:

- *form D18* (and other papers necessary to apply for a grant) to the probate registry, *and*
- *form IHT 200* (plus supplementary pages, but not *form D18*) to the Capital Taxes Office, *or*

... **if there is tax to pay *or* the deceased was not domiciled in the United Kingdom** send *form IHT 200* (plus supplementary pages), *form D18 and* payment to the Capital Taxes Office ('CTO'). The CTO complete *form D18* and return it. On receipt of the completed *form D18*, send *form D18* (and other papers necessary to apply for a grant) to the probate registry.

Filling in a reduced *form IHT 200*

➤ Leaflet *IHT 19* sets out when and how (ie: which pages need not be filled in) a reduced *form IHT 200* may be submitted.

➤ A reduced *form IHT 200* may be submitted, generally speaking, when:

a) the deceased was UK domiciled, *and*

b) assets passing by will or intestacy mostly go to exempt beneficiaries (spouse or charity), *and*

c) the gross value of:

   i) the estate passing to non-exempt beneficiaries, *and*

   ii) assets not passing by will or on intestacy but which are chargeable on death (eg: property passing on survivorship), *and*

   iii) the chargeable value of transfers made within 7 years of death ...

   ... does not exceed the nil rate band.

➤ Where a reduced *form IHT 200* is submitted, *form D18* may be sent straight to the probate registry (rather than initially to the CTO) to speed-up obtaining a grant.

➤ The Inland Revenue has published an explanatory leaflet, *IHT 210*, as a guide to *form IHT 200.*

- *IHT 200, IHT 210, IHT 19* and supplementary pages can be downloaded from the Inland Revenue's website at www.inlandrevenue.gov.uk/cto/forms1.htm.

IV Payment of IHT

References in this section are to IHTA 1984, unless otherwise stated.

- ➤ IHT is payable:

  a) 6 months from the end of the month of the chargeable transfer, *or*

  b) for lifetime transfers made between 5 April and 1 October, 30 April in the next following year (*s.226*).

- ➤ IHT on 'instalment property' is payable in 10 equal annual instalments, with the first due 6 months from the end of the month of death, rather than on delivery of the Inland Revenue account (*s.227*). It is available for:

  a) land, *and*

  b) an interest in a business, *and*

  c) shares (quoted and unquoted) which entailed control of a company immediately prior to death, *and*

  d) unquoted shares if *either*:

  - they form a large holding (10% of the nominal capital of a company worth £20,000 or more), *or*
  - the Inland Revenue accepts 'undue hardship' would follow if payment was due immediately, *or*
  - IHT on the instalment option exceeds 20% of the total IHT due on the estate as a whole.

  ◆ If instalment property is sold, tax and interest are both payable immediately (*s.227(4)*).

- ➤ Interest runs ...

  ... 6 months after a chargeable transfer: on non-instalment property vesting in PRs, land that is 'instalment property', GBRs, LCTs, PETs (on death) and life interests in possession (*s.233*).

  ... from the instalment date: sums unpaid on the date they are due under the instalment option (*s.234*)

Paying IHT on non-instalment option property

- ➤ Tax which falls due immediately can be funded:

  a) by assets for which a grant of representation is not needed, *and/or*

  b) by a building society/ bank holding a deceased's current account and willing to release funds, *and/ or*

  c) by loans from ...

  - ◆ ... **beneficiaries**: they may be in position to help, particularly if they are the assignees or nominees of an insurance policy maturing on the deceased's death.
  - ◆ ... **banks**: they demand a commercial rate of interest.

- ➤ Interest on a loan for personalty vesting in PRs may be offset against the estate's income tax.
- ➤ A bank may require an undertaking from PRs to repay a loan as soon as the property is available.

V Self assessment of corporation tax

References in this section are to FA 1998 Schedule 18, unless otherwise stated.

Self assessment for corporation tax applies to accounting periods ending on or after 1 July 1999 (the law relating to accounting periods ending before 1 July 1999 is not dealt with here).

1 Notification of chargeability

➤ A person within the charge to corporation tax must notify the Inland Revenue if it is chargeable to corporation tax for an accounting period and it has not received a notice requiring a company tax return (*para. 2*).

- ◆ A company must notify the Inland Revenue within 12 months of the end of the accounting period (or face a penalty not exceeding the tax payable in respect of that accounting period).

2 The company tax return

➤ The Inland Revenue may require a person to submit a 'company tax return' (*para.3(1)*) (*Form CT 603*).

- ◆ The term 'company tax return' (*Form CT 600*) includes such relevant information, accounts, reports, statements as may be reasonably required (*para.3(2)*).
  - ● Where *CA 1985* requires a company to produce accounts for a period, the power to require the delivery of accounts is limited to those accounts (*para.11*).
- ◆ A company tax return must include a self assessment of the amount of corporation tax payable by the company for an accounting period (*para.7*).
  - ● The corporation tax payable is calculated according to four steps (*para.8*):

Steps

1 **Calculate the tax due on the company's profits, then give effect to any other reliefs or set offs available against corporation tax chargeable on profits:**

2
a) any double taxation relief under *TA ss.788-790* (tax credits in respect of foreign tax), *and*

b) any set off in respect of shadow ACT.

3 **Add amounts assessable or chargeable as though they were corporation tax:**

a) any amount due in respect of a loan to a participator under *TA s.419*, *and*

b) any sum chargeable as the profits of a 'controlled foreign company' (CFC) under *TA s.747(4)(a)*.

- ▪ A CFC is a company which during an accounting period is controlled by a company within the charge to corporation tax and is subject to a lower level of taxation (less than 75% of tax payable in the UK) in the territory in which it is resident.
- ▪ Unless an exemption applies the company submitting the self assessment must pay tax on the CFC's income profit, in proportion to its interest in the CFC.

4 **Deduct any amounts to be set off against a company's overall tax liability for a period under *TA s.7(2)* or *s.11(3)* (income tax borne by deduction)**

3 Filing a company tax return

- The filing date for a company tax return is whichever of the following periods is last to end (*para.14*):
  a) 12 months from the end of the period for which the return is made, *or*
  b) if the relevant period of account is not longer than 18 months, 12 months from the end of that period, *or*
  c) if a company's period of account is longer than 18 months, 30 months from the beginning of that period, *or*
  d) three months from the date on which the notice requiring the return is served.
- If a company is required to deliver a company tax return and does not do so by the filing date, it is liable to a flat rate penalty of (*para.17*):
  a) £100 if the return is delivered within 3 months of the filing date, *and*
  b) £200 in any other case, *unless ...*

  ... it has an excuse for late filing (because it is not required to deliver accounts under *CA 1985* for that period and the return is delivered no later than the last date allowed by *CA 1985* for delivering accounts to Companies House) (*para.19*).

  - On the third successive failure, the figures in a) and b) are increased to £500 and £1,000 respectively.
- If a company is required to deliver a company tax return and fails to do so *either*:
  a) within 18 months of the end of the accounting period for which the return is required, *or*
  b) the filing date, if the filing date is later than the period in a) ...

  ... it is liable to a tax-related penalty (*para.18*).

  - A tax-related penalty is:
    - 10% of the unpaid tax if the company tax return is submitted within 2 years of the end of the period in respect of which the return is required, *or*
    - 20% of the unpaid tax, in any other case.
- If company does not deliver a company tax return, the Inland Revenue can determine (to the best of their information and belief) the tax due (*paras 36-49*).

4 Information and records

- A company must preserve such records (*para.21*), or information (*para.22*), as are needed to enable it to complete a correct and complete return for an accounting period.
- The duty to preserve records or information exists (*para.21*):
  a) for 6 years from the end of a period in respect of which a company may be required to submit a company tax return, *or*
  b) if a company is required to submit a company tax return before the end of the 6 year period in a) until *either*:
     i) any Inland Revenue enquiry into that return is completed, *or*
     ii) if there is no enquiry, the Inland Revenue no longer have power to enquire into the return (broadly, if a return is submitted on or before the filing date (and is not subsequently amended), within 12 months of the filing date (*para.24*)).
  - A company which fails to keep records required under *para 21* is liable to a penalty not exceeding £3,000 (*para.23*).

VI Payment of corporation tax

References in this section are to CT(IP)R 1998, unless otherwise stated.

➤ Corporation tax falls due 9 months after the end of each accounting period (*TMA 1970 s.59(D)*), unless a company is a 'large company'.

- A company is a 'large company' if (*r.3*):

  a) its profits in an accounting period exceed £1.5 million, *and*

  b) its total corporation tax liability for that accounting period exceeds £10,000 (or a proportion of £10,000 if the accounting period is less than 12 months) (£5,000 for accounting period beginning before 2 July 2000), *and*

  c) it was a large company in the 12 months preceeding that accounting period **or** its profits for that accounting period exceed £10 million.

➤ If a company is a 'large company' during an accounting period then the corporation tax for that period, broadly speaking, is due and payable:

a) where the length of the accounting period so allows, in instalments (not exceeding 4) at intervals of 3 months beginning on the date which is 6 months and 13 days from the start of the accounting period and ending on the date which is 3 months and 14 days from the end of the accounting period (*r.5(3)*), *or*

b) in other cases on a date 3 months and 14 days from the end of the accounting period (*r.5(2)*).

Eg: for an accounting period ending 31 December 2001, the payment dates are: 14 July 2001, 14 October 2001, 14 January 2002 and 14 April 2002.

➤ Where tax is payable in instalments, the amount due on each installment is (*rr.4,6*):

$$\frac{3}{\text{The number of whole calendar months falling with the accounting period PLUS the number of days falling outside the accounting period divided by 30}} \times \text{Total corporation tax liability (as defined in r.2(3))}$$

➤ Transitional rules apply to accounting periods ending on or after 1 July 1999 but before 1 July 2002 (*r.4*). The instalment regime applies to:

... 60% of the total liability (a/c period ending before 1 July 2000), *and*

... 72% of the total liability (a/c period ending before 1 July 2001), *and*

... 88% of the total liability (a/c period to 1 July 2002).

In April 1999 the Inland Revenue published a *Guide to Corporation Tax Self Assessment For Tax Practitioners and Inland Revenue Staff*

I Value added tax (VAT)

I Generally

- A registered person accounts periodically to HM Customs and Excise for VAT on 'output' (sales) of goods and services in the course of business, and any VAT on 'inputs' (*VATA s.1*).
- VAT is designed, in theory, to pass a tax charge on the value added by manufacturers and suppliers to the final customer (a non-taxable person, or one who makes exempt supplies).
- A taxable person who can attribute all his inputs to taxable supplies (ie: all supplies other than exempt supplies) pays no tax insofar as he reclaims 'input' tax he has paid to his suppliers against 'output' tax which he receives from his customers. The attribution of 'inputs' to 'outputs' is governed by *VATR 1995 rr.99-116.*
- A taxable person pays HM Customs and Excise the amount by which a business's 'output' exceeds its 'input', unless 'input' exceeds 'output' in which case he claims a rebate of the excess 'input' tax.

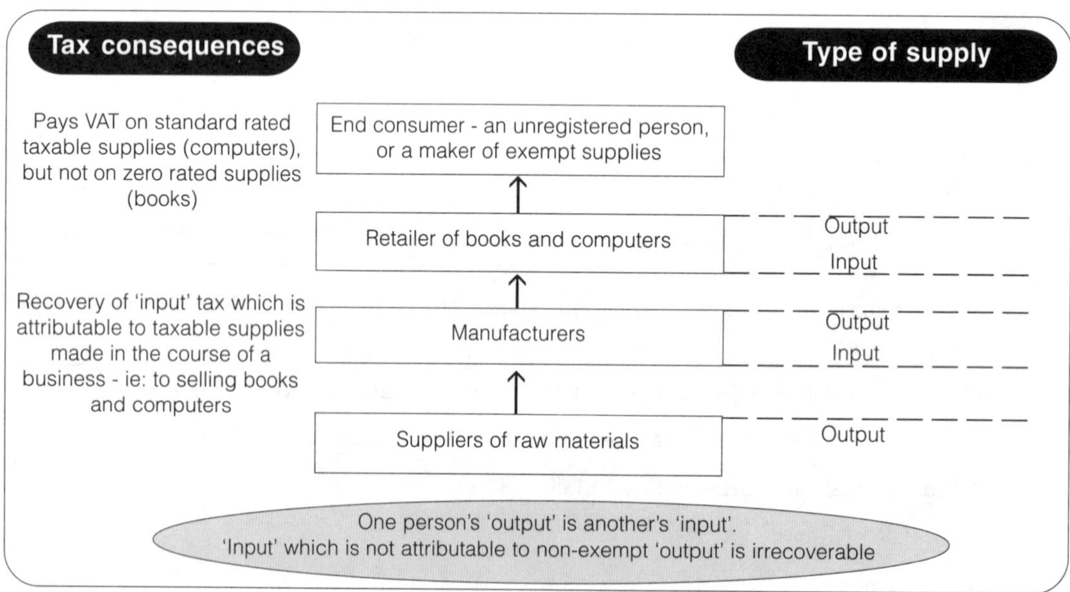
Tax consequences
Type of supply
Pays VAT on standard rated taxable supplies (computers), but not on zero rated supplies (books)
End consumer - an unregistered person, or a maker of exempt supplies
Retailer of books and computers
Output
Input
Recovery of 'input' tax which is attributable to taxable supplies made in the course of a business - ie: to selling books and computers
Manufacturers
Output
Input
Suppliers of raw materials
Output
One person's 'output' is another's 'input'.
'Input' which is not attributable to non-exempt 'output' is irrecoverable

- A sole trader, partnership, or company which makes 'taxable supplies' of 'goods or services' in the course of a business exceeding £54,000 a year must register for VAT with HM Customs and Excise as a 'taxable person' (*VATA 1994 s.2*). Partners and trustees must register jointly. For lower turnovers registration is optional; it is only advisable if reclaimable 'input' tax outweighs the extra cost to customers of the VAT which must be charged to them, and the administrative burden is not judged too inconvenient.

On 18 June 2001, HM Customs & Excise published proposals for a flat rate VAT scheme intended to reduce tax and compliance cost for smaller businesses.

➤ Supplies of goods and services are standard rated at 17.5% unless they fall within the categories set out in the boxes below.

Exempt supplies (*VATA 1994 s.31(1), Schedule 9*)

- Some grants (including assignments and surrenders) of interests in or over land (*Group 1*).
  - Supplies which do not fall within this exemption are listed in *Items1(a)-(n)* in *Group 1*. They include supplies which are zero rated and some which are standard rated.
  - If the option to tax is exercised, the exemption does not apply.
- Insurance and reinsurance services (*Group 2*).
- Postal services (*Group 3*).
- Betting, gaming and lotteries (*Group 4*).
- Finance (*Group 5*).
  - Supplies within this group include transactions in money, transactions in securities, underwriting security transactions, running current, deposit or savings accounts, and managing unit trust schemes.
- Education (*Group 6*).
  - This exemption embraces education services by 'eligible bodies', examination services, certain private tuition, services provided by youth clubs, research and vocational training.
- Health and welfare services (*Group 7*).
- Burial services (*Group 8*).
- Trade union subscriptions (*Group 9*).
- Sporting services (*Group 10*).
- Works of art (*Group 11*).
- Fund-raisng events (*Group 12*).

Zero rated (*VATA 1994 s.30(2), Schedule 8*)

- Food (*Group 1*).
  - Certain foods are, however, standard rated, eg: supplied in the course of a catering business, hot take aways, or food sold for consumption on the premises where the supply is made, pet food, luxury and 'frivolous' foods.
- Sewage and water services (*Group 2*).
- Books and newspapers (*Group 3*).
- Talking books and wireless sets (*Group 4*).
- Certain buildings and civil engineering works (*Group 5*).
  - This includes the first grant of a 'major interest' in land (ie: of a freehold or a lease with a term exceeding 21 years) by a person who:
    i) constructs a building designed as a dwelling, or converts a building or part of a building into one or more dwellings.
    ii) constructs a building, or converts a non-residential building or part of a building, for a 'relevant residential purpose'.
    ii) constructs a building for a 'relevant charitable purpose'.
- Supplies of and in relation to certain protected buildings that are listed buildings or scheduled monuments (*Group 6*).
- Certain international services (*Group 7*).
  - Services on goods obtained in, or imported into, EEC States and for export from the EEC:
    a) i) by or on behalf of the supplier, or ii) where the recipient of the services belongs in a place outside the EEC.
  - Making arrangements for i) the export of goods from the EEC, ii) a supply of services of the description in item a), or iii) any supply of services which is made outside the EEC.
- Transport (*Group 8*).
  - This includes supplies of ships and aircraft, passenger transport services and some freight transport.
- Caravans and houseboats (*Group 9*).
- Gold (*Group 10*).
- Bank notes (*Group 11*).
- Drugs medicine and aids for the disabled (*Group 12*).
- Certain imports/exports (*Group 13*) .
- Supplies to or by charities (*Group 15*).
- Clothing and footware including pedal cycle helmets (*Group 16*).
- Commodities traded on terminal markets such as futures transactions (*VAT(TM)O 1973*).
- Goods exported to third countries (*VATA 1994 s.30(6)*).

(*Group 14* has been repealed)

Supplies rated at 5% (*VATA 1994 s.29A, Schedule 7A*)

- Fuel and power (for domestic use, or use by a charity other than in the course of a business).
- Installation of energy saving materials
- Grant funded installation of heating equipment, security goods or connection of gas supply.
- Women's sanitary products.
- Children's car seats.
- Supplies in the course of a residential conversion or renovation.

II VAT and land - the option to tax

- A taxable person may waive the exemption from VAT in respect of a supply of land which he would otherwise make as an exempt supply under *VATA 1994 Schedule 9, Group 1.*
- This is known as the 'option to tax' and is governed by *VATA 1994 Schedule 10 paras 2-6.* It is subject to some restrictions in that it:
  - does not apply in relation to zero rated supplies within *VATA 1994 Schedule 8, and*
  - if made in respect of part of a building, it covers the whole building.
  - does not apply if at the time of the grant there is an intention or expectation that the land will become 'exempt land' and it is bought by a developer, financier or a connected person (broadly, land other than land used by a taxable person wholly or mainly for making supplies which are not exempt) (*VATA Schedule 10 para 3(AA)* inserted by *FA 1997 s.37*).
- An election must fulfil the following conditions (with effect from 1 March 1995):
  - it may be in any form, *but*
  - it must be notified in writing to HM Customs and Excise within 30 days of its being made (there is discretion to extend this period).
- If a taxable person wants to elect and he has already made exempt supplies in relation to the land, he should seek clearance by writing to their VAT office, unless the circumstances fall within *Customs & Excise's Notice 742 para 8.6* which lists when permission will be granted automatically.
- From 1 March 1995, an election can be revoked, with the written permission of the Commissioners, if it is done *either*:
  - within 3 months of the election becoming effective provided that no input tax has been recovered and the land has not been sold as part of a TOGC (Transfer Of a business as a Going Concern), *or*
  - 20 years or more after the election took effect.

Some advantages and disadvantages of opting to tax	
✓ VAT on developing or purchasing the land or building will be recoverable ✓ Input tax will be recoverable on the landlord's overheads attributable to the taxable supply ✓ A landlord will be able to recover VAT on continuing maintenance costs such as expenditure on service charges ✓ If a tenant is fully taxable, it will be able to recover VAT on service charges (this is impossible if the service charge is an exempt supply)	× Compliance costs associated with issuing VAT invoices etc × A future disposal of the building may be adversely affected as: a) the disposal may be standard rated, so stamp duty will be paid on a greater amount b) even if the disposal is part of a TOGC (so that VAT will not fall due) the buyer will also have to opt to tax × Some tenants, whose business activities are not fully taxable, will have to bear the cost of VAT which they will be unable to recover (eg: insurers or underwriters who carry out exempt business) × The capital value of the property may be affected if local market conditions discriminate for or against buildings which are taxable

III Capital goods scheme

- Under this scheme 'input tax' recovered in respect of a capital item is adjusted over a period of 5 (if under a) below) or 10 (if under b) below) years (Further adjustments are made if, during the period over which the adjustment is made, the item is sold, lost or stolen, the taxable person de-registers, or a lease in respect of the item expires) (*VATR 1995 rr.114-115*).
- A capital item qualifies for the scheme if it is:

  a) of a value not less than £50,000 and is computer equipment (*VATR 1995 r.113(a)*), *or*

  b) of a value not less than £250,000 and is:

     i) an interest in land, a building (or part of a building), a civil engineering work (or part of civil engineering work) acquired as a standard rate supply (*VATR 1995 r.113(b)*), *or*

     ii) an interest when the taxable person changes the use of a building (or part of a building) which was previously used for a residential or charitable purpose (*VATR 1995 r.113(c)*), *or*

     iii) an interest in a building (or part of a building) when the taxable person either makes an exempt supply or ceases to be completely taxable (*VATR 1995 r.113(d)*), *or*

     iv) a building (or part of a building) which the owner constructed and used for the first time on or after 1 April 1990 (*VATR 1995 r.113(e)*), *or*

     v) a building which has had its floor area increased by not less than 10% (*VATR 1995 rr.113(f)*).

  c) a building refurbished or fitted out by the owner if the expenditure on taxable supplies (other than zero rated supplies) of services and of goods fixed to the building is not less than £250,000 (*VATR 1995 r.113(h)*).

IV Penalties

Penalties for evading VAT			
Offence	Statute	Penalty	Punishment
Default surcharge	*VATA s.59*	Civil	Failure to send in the 3 monthly return within 1 month of the end of each quarter: the surcharge rises to as much as 20% of the tax due over this period
Dishonest conduct	*VATA s.60*	Civil	Fine equal to the tax evaded by dishonestly acting *or* omitting to act, so as to avoid paying tax
Misdeclaration or neglect	*VATA s.63*	Civil	Fine equal to 15% of the tax the offender attempts to avoid by *either* understating his liability, *or* overstating the rebate due to him, *or* not taking reasonable steps to draw an error to HM Customs and Excise's attention (subject to *de minimis* limits)
Failure to register	*VATA s.67*	Civil	Fine equal to 10%-30% of the tax due, on a rising scale relative to the length of time during which the offender was unregistered (for up to 18 months)
Breach of regulations	*VATA s.69*	Civil	Failure to keep certain records is punishable by a fine of up to £500 Other infringements carry a daily penalty
Fraudulent evasion	*VATA s.72*	Criminal	It is an indictable offence to knowingly or deceitfully avoid VAT. The penalty may be an unlimited fine and imprisonment for up to 7 years

J Stamp duty

I Calculation

Steps

1. **Is there a dutiable instrument?**
2. **What is the head of charge and what is the rate of charge?**
3. **Is there an exemption or relief?**
4. **Does duty have to be paid, or can it be deferred?**

(This section focuses on stamp duty on selected heads of charge, there are others which are not considered)

Step 1 Is there a dutiable instrument?

A. Is there an 'instrument'?

➤ Stamp duty is a charge upon 'instruments'.

- Note that because stamp duty is chargeable on 'instruments', stamp duty can be avoided altogether if an agreement is oral and transfer is by delivery.
  - However, in such cases care must be taken that the terms of the agreement are not subsequently recorded in a memorandum of agreement as such a memorandum will be stampable (this is known as the 'memorandum rule').
  - If the agreement relates to shares or securities consider whether there is a SDRT charge.

B. Does the 'instrument' relate to stampable property?

➤ A stamp duty charge only arises when an instrument relates to 'property' for which 'stampable consideration' is given.

- Certain things, such as know-how, are not 'property' for stamp duty purposes.

C. Is there 'stampable consideration'?

➤ Stampable consideration comprises money, stock/marketable securities (*SA 1891 s.55*) and debts (*SA 1891 s.57*), or if land is sold any consideration (*FA 1994 s.241*).

Step 2 What is the head of charge and what is the rate of charge?

A. Generally

➤ Depending on which head of charge applies, duty is either:

a) 'fixed' (£5), *or*

b) calculated by reference to the value of the stampable consideration passing under the instrument (known as 'ad valorem' duty).

B. Heads of charge

➤ An instrument liable to stamp duty under 2 heads of charge may be charged to the higher (*Speyer Brothers* v. *IRC* [1908] AC 92). But an instrument chargeable under a specific head of charge is not usually charged with greater duty under a more general head (*North of Scotland Bank* v. *IRC* 1 SC 149).

Heads of charge

Head of charge	Property	Rate of charge
Conveyance or transfer on sale (*FA 1999 Sch.13 Part I para 1*)	Stock or marketable securities	0.5% (*FA 1999 Sch.13 Part I para 3*)
	Property other than marketable securities	a) consideration is: • certified not to exceed £60,000: nil • otherwise: ▪ if the consideration does not exceed £500 - 0.5%, *or* ▪ if the consideration exceeds £500 but does not exceed £60,000 - 1% b) consideration is: • certified to exceed £60,000 but not to exceed £250,000 - 1% • otherwise - 4% c) consideration is: • certified to exceed £250,000 but not £500,000 - 3% • otherwise - 4% d) consideration is over £500,000: 4% 'Certification' means that an instrument contains a statment that the transaction effected by the instrument does not form part of a larger transaction or series of transactions in respect of which the amount or value, or aggregate amount or value, of the consideration exceeds that amount (*FA 1999 Sch.13 Part I para 6*) Duty under c)-d) was last increased on 28 March 2000, but not with respect to instruments executed after that date pursuant to a certain contracts made on or before 21 March 2000 (*FA 2000 s.114*))
Conveyance or transfer other than on sale (*FA 1999 Sch.13 Part III para 1*)		Fixed duty (£5) (*FA 1999 s.101(2)*)

Main heads of charge		
Head of charge	**Charge**	**Rate of charge**
Contracts or agreements for sale (*FA 1999 Sch. 13 Part I para 7*)	➤ Agreements relating to *either:* a) an **equitable interest** in any property, *or* b) **any interest** (ie: including a legal interest) an any property **except:** i) land, *or* ii) goods, wares and merchandise, *or* iii) stock or marketable securities (Note that agreements for the sale of securities fall outside the stamp duty net, but such agreements may be liable to SDRT), *or* iv) ships or vessels or any part of them, *or* v) property outside the UK.	As a 'conveyance or transfer on sale If such an agreement is stamped, and an instrument of transfer is subsequently executed in accordance with the agreement, there is no double charge to duty (but any excess consideration is chargeable to duty).
Repurchase of own shares by a company	When a company files a return at Companies House within 28 days of receiving the shares (*CA 1985 s.169*), the return is treated as an 'instrument'.	Duty is payable at the rate of 0.5% per £100 (*FA 1986 s.66*).
Lease (*FA 1999 Sch. 13 Part II para 1*)	Leases of land (ie: not licences) (also, not leases or licences of personal property)	Duty is charged on rent and any premium. **Rent** Furnished lettings: there is no duty on a term certain of under 1 year if the rent is under £5000, if rent is over £5000 duty is £5 Other leases bear duty depending on the rent shown in tables in *FA 1999 Sch. 13 Part II para 3* (Nil to 24% of rent if term more than 100 years). **Premium** Duty is as for a conveyance or transfer on sale (p.119) on the premium **Surrender** Fixed duty (£5), unless it is a 'transfer or conveyance on sale in which case it is chargeable as such (*FA 1999 Sch. 13 Part III para 8*) **Instrument increasing rent/partition or division** See *FA 1999 Sch. 13 Part II paras 5-6*
Release or renunciation		£5, unless on a transfer or conveyance on sale (*FA 1999 Sch. 13 Part III para 7*)
Bearer instruments (On issue or first transfer)	The details are beyond the range of this book - see the *Banking & Capital Markets Companion* (*FA 1999 Sch. 15*)	

When any property is conveyed:
a) in consideration of a debt due to that person, *or*
b) subject to the payment of money (whether secured or unsecured) (eg: a mortgage) ...

... the debt is treated as the consideration for the conveyance and is chargeable with *ad valorem* duty at the rate of 0.5% (*SA 1891 s.57*).

Step 3 Is there an exemption or relief?

1 **Exemptions under *SD(EI)R 1987* from the head 'conveyance or transfer on sale'**

➤ An instrument falling under one of the following categories is exempt if it provides for:

a) the vesting of property subject to a trust in the trustees of the trust on the appointment of a new trustee, or in the continuing trustees on the retirement of a trustee.

b) the conveyance or transfer of property the subject of a specific devise or legacy to the beneficiary named in the will (or his nominee).

c) the conveyance or transfer of property which forms part of an intestate's estate to the person entitled on intestacy (or his nominee).

d) the appropriation of property in satisfaction of a general legacy of money, or in satisfaction of any interest of surviving spouse and in Scotland also of any interest of issue within *FA 1985 s.85(4), (6), (7).*

e) the conveyance or transfer of property which forms part of the residuary estate of a testator to a beneficiary (or his nominee) entitled solely by virtue of his entitlement under the will.

f) the conveyance or transfer of property out of a settlement in or towards satisfaction of a beneficiary's interest, not being an interest acquired for money or money's worth, being a conveyance or transfer constituting a distribution of property in accordance with the provisions of the settlement.

g) the conveyance or transfer of property on and in consideration only of marriage.

h) the conveyance or transfer of property in connection with divorce (within *FA 1985 s.83 (1)*).

i) the conveyance or transfer by the liquidator of property which formed part of the assets of the company in liquidation to a shareholder of that company (or his nominee) in or towards satisfaction of the shareholder's rights on a winding-up.

j) the grant in fee simple of an easement in or over land for no consideration in money or money's worth.

k) the grant of a servitude for no consideration in money or money's worth.

l) the conveyance or transfer of property operating as a voluntary disposition inter vivos for no consideration in money or money's worth nor any consideration referred to in *SA 1891 s.57.*

m) the conveyance or transfer of property by an instrument varying a disposition on death within *FA 1985 s.84(1).*

- Note that these regulations only apply to instruments executed on or after 1 May 1987 and the nature of the instrument must be certified in accordance with *SD(EI)R 1987 r.3*. *r.3* requires a certificate stating that the donor / transferror or his solicitor, or someone authorised to do so (using their own knowledge), certifies that the instrument falls within category [A-M] in the Schedule to the *SD(EI)R 1987.*
- If there is no certificate of exemption, duty of £5 is due.

2 **Mortgages granted after 1 August 1971**

➤ Mortgages granted after 1 August 1971 are exempt (*FA 1971 s.64, FA 1999 Sch. 13 Part IV para. 2*).

3 **Corporate reorganisations - under the head 'conveyance or transfer on sale' (*FA 1986 ss.75-77*)**

➤ See the *Banking & Capital Markets Companion.*

4 **Intellectual property (*FA 2000 s.129*)**

➤ An instrument for the sale, transfer, or other disposition of intellectual property is exempt.

5 **Transfer/conveyance of, or lease of, property in a disadvantaged area (*FA 2001 s.92*)**

6 **Transfer to a LLP incorporated under the *LPA 2000* (*LPA 2000 s.12*)**

- A conveyance or transfer to a LPP in connection with its incorporation within 1 year of incorporation (if, broadly, there is no change in the partner's beneficial ownership in the assets) is exempt.

7 **Associated companies (*FA 1930 s.42* as amended by *FA 2000*)**

- See the *Banking & Capital Markets Companion.*

8 **Loan capital (*FA 1986 s.79, FA 1999 Sch. 13 Part IV para. 3*)**

- 'Loan capital' includes any debenture stock, corporation stock or funded debt, by whatever name known, issued by a body corporate or other body of persons (*FA 1986 s.78*).
- *FA s.1986 s.79* provides an exemption for an instrument on transfer of 'loan capital' from all stamp duties (*FA 1986 s.79(4)*) unless:

  a) at the time the instrument is executed, the instrument carries a right (exercisable then or later) of conversion into shares or other securities, or to the acquisition of shares or other securities, including loan capital of the same description (*FA 1986 s.79(5)*), *or*

  b) at the time the instrument is executed or any earlier time, it carries or has carried a right (*FA 1986 s.79(5)*):

     - to interest the amount of which exceeds a reasonable commercial return on the nominal amount of the capital, *or*
     - to interest the amount of which falls or has fallen to be determined to any extent by reference to the results of, or of any part of, a business or to the value of any property (see also *s.79(7A)*), *or*
     - on repayment to an amount which exceeds the nominal amount of the capital and is not reasonably comparable with what is generally repayable under the terms of issue of loan capital listed in the FSA's Official List.

9 **General exemptions (*FA 1999 Sch. 13 Part IV para. 1 (a)-(c), 2(b)*)**

- Transfers of shares in, or of, government stocks or funds or strips.
- Instruments making a disposition of a ship/vessel or any part, interest or property in a ship/ vessel.
- Testaments, testamentary dispositions and dispositions *mortis causa* in Scotland.
- Renounceable letters of allotment (if rights renounceable not later than 6 months after issue).
- Life insurance policies and superannunation annuities (*FA 1989 s.173*).

Step 4 Does duty have to be paid, or can it be deferred?

- An instrument must be correctly stamped if it relates to any property situated or any matter or thing done or to be done in the UK, otherwise it will be inadmissible in evidence before a civil court in the UK (*SA 1891 s.14(4)*) and may not be registered (*SA 1891 s.17*).
- If an instrument is executed outside the UK, the 30 day period (after which a penalty becomes due) only begins to run when the instrument is first received into the UK (*SA 1891 s.15B*).
- Consequently, if an instrument does not need to be received into the UK (eg: for production in evidence before a civil court, or enrolment in the UK (eg: on a share register)), the payment of duty can be deferred indefinitely or at least until it becomes necessary to bring the instrument into the UK. To this extent, stamp duty is sometimes referred to as a voluntary imposition.

  - Executing (and retaining) an instrument outside the UK is, therefore, sometimes an element in stamp duty planning, although care must be taken that execution does not take place in a jurisdiction with higher stamp duty than the UK (and that there is no memorandum of the agreement which is subsequently made in or brought into the UK).

    NB: interest runs from 30 days after the date on which an instrument is executed (irrespective of where execution takes place) (*SA 1891 s.15A*).

II Collection and penalties

- When stamp duty was introduced in 1691, it was intended that instruments should be written on pre-stamped paper; however if ordinary paper is used (invariably the case) duty may be paid *either* within:
  - 30 days of the instrument being executed (if an instrument is executed outside the UK, the 30 day period runs from when it is first received into the UK), *or*
  - 14 days of the Stamp Office issuing an assessment where adjudication is requested during the 30 day period.
- Late (or insufficient) stamping invites the following sanctions (in addition to the stamp duty due):
  - if an instrument is not stamped within 30 days of execution, **interest**: (at a rate set by the Treasury) from the end of that 30 period to the day on which the instrument is stamped (but interest is not payable if an amount less than £25 is due) (*SA 1891 s.15A* as introduced by *FA 1999 s.109*), *and*
  - a **penalty**; if there is no 'reasonable excuse' for late stamping. The maximum penalty is:
    - the lesser of £300 and the unpaid duty - if the instrument is stamped **within 1 year** after the 30 day period ends, *or*
    - the greater of £300 and the unpaid duty - if the instrument is stamped **1 year** after the end of the 30 day period (*SA 1891 s.15B* as introduced by *FA 1999 s.109*).
- The *Stamp Acts* do not provide any general statements of who is liable to pay duty. However, an unstamped document may not generally be produced in evidence before a court (*SA 1891 s.14(4), Parinv (Hatfield) Limited v. IRC* [1998] STC 305), or enrolled on a register (*SA 1891 s.17*) (eg: a share register) so the onus is usually on whoever wishes to prove title (usually the transferee / buyer) to pay duty.
  - Any arrangement or undertaking for assuming liability on account of the absence or insufficiency of stamp, or any indemnity against such liability, absence or insufficiently is void (*SA 1891 s.117*).
    - Attempts are sometimes made to circumvent this prohibition by covenanting to pay duty if and when an instrument executed outside the UK is received into the UK. Opinion is divided as to whether such a covenant is enforceable.
- Different heads of charge used to have various fines and penalties. *Schedule 17* of the *FA 1999* replaced fines with penalties which are recoverable by the Commissioners.

For instruments executed on or after 1 October 1999:

a) amounts of stamp duty on a 'conveyance or transfer on sale' are **rounded up** to the nearest £5 (*FA 1999 s.112*), *and*

b) interest is are **rounded down** to the nearest £5 (*s.15A(4)*).

K Stamp duty reserve tax ('SDRT')

Generally

➤ Stamp duty reserve tax ('SDRT') is *not* a stamp duty. It is a separate tax.

➤ SDRT is a tax on agreements relating to 'chargeable securities'.

- A 'chargeable security' includes:
  - stocks, shares or loan capital, *and*
  - interests in, or dividends, arising from stocks, shares, or loan capital, *and*
  - rights to allotments of, or to subscribe for, or options to acquire, stocks shares or loan capital, *and*
  - units under a unit trust scheme (*FA 1986 ss.93(3)-93(6)(a)*), ...

    ... *unless* the securities are issued by a body corporate not incorporated in the UK *and* the securities are:

    - not registered in a register kept in the United Kingdom by or on behalf of the body corporate by which the securities are issued, *or*
    - in the case of shares they are not paired with shares issued by a body corporate incorporated in the United Kingdom (*FA 1986 s.93(4)*).
- Loan capital which is exempt from all stamp duties under the loan capital exemption in *FA 1986 s.79(4)* (see p.122) is not a 'chargeable security' (*FA 1986 s.99(5)*).

➤ SDRT falls on an agreement, not the instrument of transfer. Where there is a SDRT charge and within 6 years of the SDRT charge arising:

a) a transfer is executed in relation to the securities to which the agreement related, *and*

b) stamp duty paid on the transfer ...

... the SDRT charge is cancelled (*FA 1986 s.92*).

➤ On an agreement to transfer 'chargeable securities' a SDRT charge arises irrespective of whether:

a) the agreement, transfer, issue or appropriation in question is made or effected in the UK or elsewhere, *and*

b) any party to the agreement is resident or situate in any part of the UK (*FA 1986 s.86(4)*).

- Note that an oral agreement can be within the charge to SDRT.

II The principal charge

- The 'principal charge' to SDRT is imposed when one person (A) agrees with another (B) to transfer (whether or not to B) 'chargeable securities' for money or money's worth (*s.87(1)*).
    - There is a SDRT charge:
        - a) if the agreement is conditional, on the day on which the condition is satisfied, *and*
        - b) if the agreement is unconditional on the day on which the agreement is made (*s.87(3)*).
    - Tax is charged at 0.5% (*s.87(6)*). Liability to the SDRT charge falls upon (B) (*s.91(1)*).

- The precise requirements for the various exemptions are beyond the scope of this book, but note that the following 2 exemptions in particular exist:

1 **Intermediaries (*FA 1986 ss.88A-88B*)**

- Agreements entered into by 'intermediaries' effected on an EEA exchange or a recognised foreign exchange are exempted from a *s.87* charge.
    - An 'intermediary' is, broadly speaking, a member of an EEA exchange or a recognised foreign exchange who is recognised as an intermediary by the exchange and who carries out a bona fide business of dealing in chargeable securities but does not carry on an 'excluded business'.
        - An 'excluded business' includes any business which consists wholly or mainly in the making or managing of investments or any business which consists of the insurance business or acting as trustee/managing investments on behalf of a pension fund.

2 **Public issues of securities (*FA 1986 s.89A*)**

- This exemption applies to various categories of issuing houses and intermediaries who enter into agreements, conditional on the admission of the securities concerned to the Stock Exchange's Official List, for the transfer of chargeable securities in order to facilitate the offer of the securities to the public.

- There are other SDRT charges, in addition to the 'principal charge', but these are beyond the scope of the book, as are the precise requirements for all the various exemptions to the 'principal charge' (see the *Banking & Capital Markets Companion*).

L Some planning ideas

➤ Often a transaction incurs liability for more than one tax - the transfer of an asset may incur CGT and IHT, and have income tax implications. Set out below are some approaches to tax-planning for individuals.

I During a client's lifetime

➤ Submit self assessment returns and make payments on account on time, to avoid large penalties.

➤ If a taxpayer is not resident in the UK (See *IR 20* and note the CGT provisions (*TCGA 1992 s.10A*) bringing chargeable gaings realised by certain temporary non residents into charge), or may be able to establish a non-UK domicile (eg: birth outside the UK, or regard another country as real home to which he intends to return), take specialist advice about possible tax savings.

➤ Make full use of income tax loss reliefs.

➤ Make full use of a married couple's personal allowances and their individual basic rate bands. If the marriage is stable, consider transferring assets from one spouse to the other so that they receive income more tax efficiently. (There will be no CGT to pay as transfers between spouses do not give rise to a 'chargeble gain' or an 'allowable loss'.)

➤ Consider investing in Enterprise Investment Scheme ('EIS') shares, a Venture Capital Trust (VCT), or an Individual Savings Account ('ISA') for various advantages with regard to both income tax and CGT.

The EIS (outline) (*TA ss.289-312, TCGA 1992 ss.150-150D, Schs. 5B-BA*)

➤ If a company raises money for a qualifying activity, and both the individual and the issuing company meet certain conditions for the relevant periods, then:

a) a chargeable gain can be rolled over into a subscription for eligible shares, *and*

b) any capital gain realised on a disposal of the eligible shares after 3 years is tax free, *and*

c) income tax relief (at 20%) is granted at the time of the subscription for the shares, *and*

d) if there is a loss on the disposal of EIS shares further income tax relief is available.

➤ An individual cannot invest more than £150,000 in a tax year under the EIS.

The VCT (outline) (*TA s.842AA, TCGA 1992 s.100*)

➤ Investment in a VCT may entitle the investor to:

a) income tax relief (at 20%) on subscription for *new* shares in a VCT (for subscriptions up to £100,000 in a tax year) if the shares are retained for at least 3 years, *and*

b) CGT exemption on the disposal of such shares (a loss on such a disposal will not be an allowable loss), *and*

c) exemption from income tax on dividends in respect of ordinary shares (either purchased or subscribed for, at up to £100,000 in a tax year), *and*

d) deferral of CGT on a disposal of any asset if the disposal can be matched against an investment in a VCT under a) and the investment is made within 1 year before or 1 year after the disposal concerned.

➤ A VCT does not pay tax on chargeable gains which it makes.

ISAs, PEPs and TESSAs (outline)

PEPs and TESSAs - what happened on 6 April 1999

- Investments in a PEP can continue to be held in a PEP, but subject to the (reduced) tax incentives available for securities held in an ISA.
- A TESSA holder is able to pay money into a TESSA for the full life of the TESSA and continues to enjoy the tax benefits offered by the TESSA.
- PEP and TESSA holdings do not prejudice an individual's rights under the ISA rules

ISAs - 2001/2002

- An individual can invest up to £7,000 a year in an ISA. No more than ...:

  ... £3,000 can go into cash (including National Savings).

  ... £1,000 can go into life assurance (*ISAR 1998 r.4*).
- An ISA account will run for at least 10 years from 6 April 1999.
- Investments in an ISA are described 'tax free'. In practice, this means that:

  a) interest is not subject to tax, *and*

  b) dividends paid by UK companies before 6 April 2004 qualify for a 10% tax credit (*FA 1998 s.76*), *and*

  c) any gains are not subject to CGT (but a loss is not an 'allowable loss').
- Withdrawal can be instant and will not lead to the forfeiture of tax benefits (although if the maximum subscription for a tax year has been made more cannot be subscribed in that year).
- 'Cat' marks demonstrate compliance with Treasury benchmarks (eg: interest rate no less than 2% above base rate, no inital fee, annual fee of 1% or less).
  - These benchmarks should be treated with caution. They are no substitute for researching an investment (eg: 1% annual fee may be expensive for an index tracker fund).
- An investor may choose, for a tax year, either a 'mini' ISA, a 'maxi' ISA, or a 'TESSA' ISA:

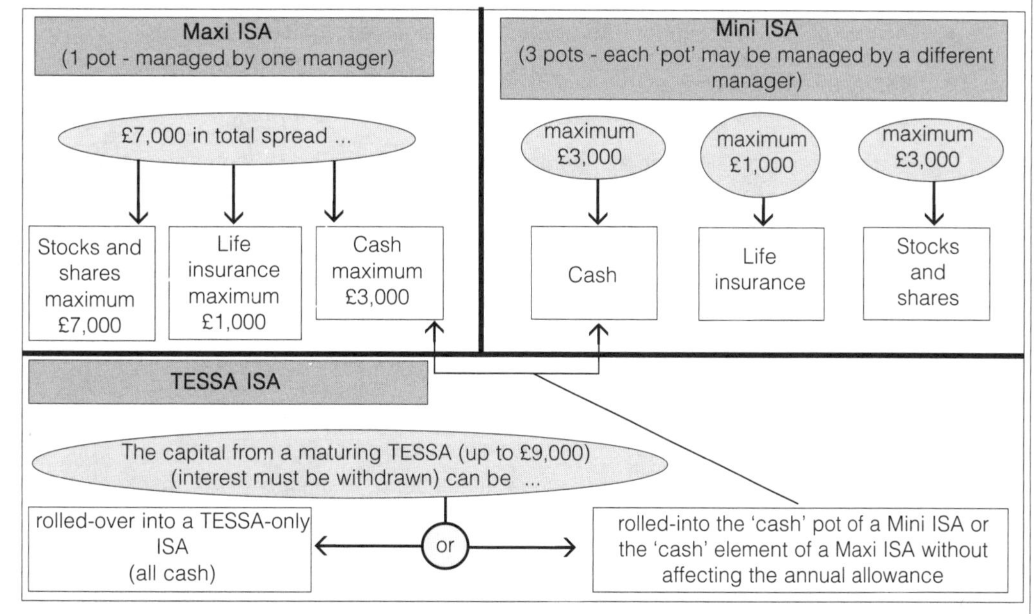

- Make full use of CGT 'allowable losses' and use exemptions or reliefs (roll-over or hold-over).
  - Complex identification rules (*TCGA 1992 s.106A*) have been introduced by *FA 1998* with the intention of frustrating 'bed and breakfasting' - the practice of selling shares and buying them back on the same or the following day to crystalise a chargeable gain while harvesting the annual CGT allowance. The new rules match disposals with acquisitions made within 30 days of a disposal.
    - These anti-avoidance rules may be sidestepped, for instance, by:

      a) 'bed and spousing' - shares are sold and bought on the same day by a spouse who subsequently transfers the repurchased shares back to their partner, *or*

      b) 'bed and ISAing' - shares are sold and repurchased through a ISA.
  - Chargeable gains with the least taper should be set against allowable losses so as to make best use of taper relief on gains where the relief will bring the most benefit.
- If retirement is being considered give careful thought to the interaction of retirement relief and taper relief. Retirement is being phased out rather quickly so that an individual who retires before sufficient taper relief has ratcheted-up will be adversely affected.
- Where 'related property' (property which is jointly owned) is valued for IHT, ensure it is discounted to reflect the unsaleability of the share concerned by itself - discounts of , eg: 10%-30% can be allowed.
- When making lifetime gifts, make full use of exemptions and reliefs.
  - Time gifts to gain the benefit of tapering relief for IHT (eg: plan gifts while still in good health, and do not wait until approaching 100).
  - On death, the value of the transfer is frozen at the value at the time of the *inter vivos* transfer.
    - PETs: if the donor survives 7 years they are exempt.
    - If a donor has plenty of disposable income, make regular gifts using the exemption under *IHTA 1984 s.21* - unlike a PET these gifts are completely exempt irrespective of whether the donor survives for 7 years.
- A LCT to a NIP (non interest in possession (*IHTA 1984 s.59*)) trust (eg: a discretionary trust) will invite a 10 year charge on the settlor or the trust fund on the tenth anniversary of the gift.
  - The rate of tax levied under a ten year charge does not exceed 6%.
  - Tax is calculated on a notional transfer, which the settlor is treated as having made on the anniversary, assessed under a special formula set out in *IHTA 1984 ss.64-69*).
- Unlike a transfer to a NIP trust, a transfer to an accumulation and maintenance trust ('A & M') is not a LCT and is not subject to a 10 year charge.
  - An A & M trust must last for under 25 years or be for beneficiaries descended from a common grandparent, vest in possession by a specified age (not over 25), and until the interest vests income must be accumulated or used on a discretionary basis for the beneficiaries (*IHTA 1984 s.71*).
- Use the IHT nil rate band fully.
  - One way of achieving this is through including in a will a flexible nil rate band gift. An amount equal to the unused nil rate band available on death is *either* left on discretionary trust to the executors to distribute within 2 years in accordance with a letter of wishes, *or* is left absolutely to named beneficiaries (ideally these should not be exempt beneficiaries such as a spouse or charity).
- Assign the benefit of a life assurance policy and any life interest in possession.
- Avoid making gifts and reserving the benefit (GBRs).

➤ Retain property necessary to maintain the donor's standard of living and security. If advising a client who is elderly, read the Law Society's guidelines 'Legal services for elderly people - gifts of property: implications for future liability to pay for long-term care' (*Professional Standards Bulletin No. 15, March 1996*).

➤ Advise elderly clients considering disposing of their home of the consequences if they subsequently need residential care.

- The local authority determines the level of fees which the resident must contribute by reference to means testing under *NA(AR)R 1992 (as amended).*
  - Means testing does not cover a minimum charge which is payable by the resident, and leaves the resident a personal allowance. The test relates to income and capital. Broadly, a resident is only entitled to have fees subsidised if their capital does not exceed £16,000, and they qualify for a tapering subsidy below that figure. A home is taken into account unless:
    - a) the property is occupied by a spouse, partner or relative who is *either*:
      - i) incapacitated, *or*
      - ii) aged 60 or over, *or*
      - iii) a child under 16 who the resident is obliged to maintain.
    - b) someone else occupies the property *and* the local authority uses its discretion.
    - c) the person's stay in care in only a temporary one.
- If the gift prevents the donor from funding care, the local authority may only fund a basic level of care. This may leave the donor dependent on others to supplement fees for better care.
- The anti-avoidance provisions are formidable:
  - if a 'significant' motivation for a gift is to prevent a local authority imposing a charge on the client's home to pay for care, the authority can:
    - a) place a charge on property transferred to a third party while the donor is in care, or within 6 months of the donor going into care (*HSSAA 1983 s.21*), *or*
    - b) place a charge on property owned by a resident in a care home (interest runs from the date of death) (*HSSAA 1983 ss.22, 24*), *or*
    - c) recover fees as a civil debt in the Magistrates' Court (*NAA 1948 s.56*).
  - When outstanding fees reach £750, a local authority can take insolvency proceedings and have the transaction set aside as a transaction at an undervalue, or as a transaction intended to defraud creditors (*IA 1986 ss.339-341, 423-425*).

➤ Do not resort to 'associated operations' (ie: a series of operations concerning a particular asset or a series of operations carried out by reference to each other which are designed to escape IHT). They will be ineffective as IHT is due under the anti-avoidance provisions (*IHTA 1984 s.268*).

II On a client's death

➤ Alter gifts in a will by a disclaimer or a variation.

Disclaimers

➤ A disclaimer is a refusal of a gift (*Townson v. Tickell* (1819) B & Ald 31). It:

- may relate to part of a gift provided the disclaimed part is severable and is not onerous (but it need not affect a separate gift under the same will).
- may not take effect if a beneficiary has benefited from property, but can be revocable.
- does not allow a disclaimor to determine property's destination unless a will permits this.

➤ The disclaimed property falls into residue (if residue is disclaimed, the property passes according to the intestacy rules) provided that there is no contrary intention in the will.

- Where an interest under the intestacy rules is disclaimed, the property is apportioned amongst the rest of the class who are entitled (or if there are none, to those next entitled).

Variations

➤ A variation enables a beneficiary to determine the destination of property.

➤ Written notice must be given to the Inland Revenue (whereas a disclaimer can be by conduct).

Some tax implications of disclaimers and variations

➤ The disclaimer or variation will not amount to a PET (*IHTA 1984 s.142*), nor will it be a chargeable transfer for CGT purposes (*TCGA 1992 s.62(6)*) if:

a) it is made within 2 years of the death, *and*

b) it is not for money or money's worth (except consideration for varying other dispositions), *and*

c) if a variation, an election is in writing *and* that election is made within 6 months of the variation.

➤ The IHT and CGT elections are entirely independent of each other. If an election is made, the property is treated as if the alteration had been made by the testator, or written into the statutory trusts governing an intestacy. If election(s) are not made, the transfer is treated as an ordinary *inter vivos* gift by the beneficiary, which qualifies as a PET/LCT and/or is subject to CGT on the gain realised by the donor on the disposal.

IHT elections

➤ A beneficiary making a variation must notify the Inland Revenue within 6 months of electing to vary the gift, and if the estate incurs additional IHT as a result the PRs must join the election.

➤ In the case of a disclaimer, no election need be made, and there is no requirement for PRs to join in the election (*IHTA 1984 s.142*).

CGT elections

➤ The PRs do not have to join in the election in the case of a variation, but the Inland Revenue must be told of the election within 6 months of its being made (*TCGA 1992 s.6(7)*).

- Make efficient use of IHT and CGT loss reliefs.
- Dispose of property so as to make full use of the three CGT annual exemptions which are available.

Anti-avoidance

- There is a fundamental distinction between:

  a) tax evasion (which is illegal and is not dealt with here), *and*

  b) tax avoidance (which is legal) (see, for example *IRC v. Willoughby* [1997] STC 995, HL, *Ingram v. IRC* [1999] STC 9).

- Counter-measures to restrict avoidance have traditionally taken two forms:

  a) specific statutory provisions designed to block perceived 'loopholes', *and*

  b) the 'recharacterisation' of 'artificial' transactions including steps inserted for tax reasons without a commercial purpose.

  - For the House of Lords rulings which have shaped this judical approach to a purposive interpretation of tax statutes, see *W T Ramsey v. IRC* [1981] STC 174, *Furniss v. Dawson* [1984] STC 153, *Craven v. White* [1985] STC 351, *Ensign Tankers (Leasing) Limited v. Stokes* [1992] STC 226, *IRC v. McGuckian* [1997] STC 908, *McNiven v. IRC* [2001] STC 237.

Tax and the *Human Rights Act 1998*

- The following provisions of the European Convention on Human Rights may be particularly relevant to tax.

  - Every ... person is entitled to the peaceful enjoyment of his possessions. No one shall be deprived of his possessions except in the public interest and subject .... to law. (*First Protocol, art. 1(1)*) (on the construction of this article see, *National Provincial Building Society and others v. UK [1997] STC 1466*).

    - This is subject to the proviso that this principle does not:

      'in any way impair the right of the State to enforce such law as it deems necessary to control the use of property in accordance with the general interest or to secure the payment of taxes or other contributions or penalties' (*First Protocol, art. 1(2)*).

      (On the breadth of a State's prerogative in relation to tax, see *Gasus Dosier und Fördertechnik GmbH v. Netherlands (1995) 20 EHRR 403.*)

  - In tax appeals, consider *art. 6*: 'in the determination of his civil rights and obligations or of any criminal charge against him, everyone is entitled to a fair and public hearing within a reasonable time by an independant and impartial tribunal established by law'.

Wills, Probate and Administration

This chapter examines:

A Valid wills

A. Generally

There are three requirements for a valid will.

1 The testator has testamentary '**Capacity**'.

2 The testator has general *and* specific '**Intention**' to make the will.

3 The testator's signature and the form of the will must comply with the required '**Formalities**'.

	Requirements	Presumed to be satisfied ...	Safeguards
1 Capacity (must have both a) and b))	a) 'Soundness of mind, memory and understanding' (*Marquess of Winchester's Case* (1598) 6 Co Rep 32a)	... if the testator comprehends: the nature of the act, *and* the general extent of his property, *and* the moral claims on the estate. ... the will appears to be rational *and* the testator generally has capacity. A mental state is presumed to persist, so if the testator generally lacks capacity, it must be shown that he possessed it when making the will	➤ Obtain a written medical opinion on the testator's capacity, and ask the person giving this opinion to witness the will ➤ Make a detailed file note of the circumstances
	b) over 18 years of age*		
2 Intention	a) General: intention to make *a* will *and* b) Specific: intention to make *this particular* will The testator must intend the will to be valid unconditionally on execution (*Corbett v. Newey* [1996] 2 All ER 914, CA)	... if the testator has capacity when he executes the will. However, this presumption does not arise if: ➤ the testator is blind or illiterate, *or* ➤ 'suspicious circumstances' exist: the testator did not give free approval due to force, fear, undue influence, or because he mistook the will's contents	➤ Explain the meaning of all the clauses ➤ Ensure the client reads the will, and that it is as he wishes. If necessary, read it aloud in the presence of the witnesses, and alter the attestation clause to record this act ➤ If a gift to the solicitor is 'significant' (over £2,000 *or* 10% of the estate), recommend the client takes independent legal advice
Intention and **Capacity** must be present *either*: a) when the will is executed (*Banks v. Goodfellow* [1870] LR 5 QB 549), *or* b) when the solicitor is instructed to prepare a will if a) these instructions are followed in the will, *and* b) when the testator executes the will, he comprehends that he previously gave instructions to draw it up (*Parker v. Felgate* [1883] 8 PD 171)			
3 Formalities*	➤ A will may be handwritten, typed or printed ➤ The will is properly executed if: ◆ a testator, or another at his direction, signs anywhere on the will, *and* ◆ the signature is intended to validate the will, *and* ◆ 2 people witness the signature by signing the will *or* acknowledging the testator's mark in his presence *(WA 1837 s.9)* Note: a) a witness must be physically and mentally present at execution, and able to give evidence of this, eg: a child must understand the significance of acting as a witness b) a witness does not have to see the testator sign, or know the document is a will c) both witnesses must be present at the same time d) the testator need not see the witnesses sign		➤ An attestation clause is evidence that these requirements have been met ➤ A witness who is blind, drunk, or mentally unsound is not suitable ➤ A witness should not be a beneficiary *or* married to a beneficiary at the time, as a gift to them lapses. A partner must not witness a will with a charging clause for his firm (*WA 1837 s. 15*). But if 2 capable witnesses sign, a signature by a beneficiary or their spouse will not cause a gift to lapse (*WA 1837 s. 1*)
Burden of proof: rests on the person relying on the will - the 'propounder' of the will (*Griffin & Amos v. Ferard* (1835) 1 Curt 97)			

* Not applicable to 'privileged' wills made by members of the armed forces on active service, or sailors at sea.

B. Alterations

Wills Act 1837 s.21	Presumptions
➤ Before execution alterations are valid ➤ After execution alterations are void unless *either:* a) the testator and the witnesses initial the alteration in the margin, *or* b) a subsequent codicil republishes the will and confirms the alteration	➤ Completed blanks predate execution (eg: date) ➤ Other alterations postdate execution

Problems
If the alteration is void and the original wording is: a) **legible**: the alteration is disregarded and the original is admitted to probate b) **illegible**: probate is granted as if there is a blank, unless *either*: i) there is evidence that the testator intended to revoke the wording if the substitution was valid ('conditional revocation'), *or* ii) the testator had no intention to revoke the original wording, in which case the original wording is effective if extrinsic evidence reveals it, or if the original script can be successfully revealed

C. Revocation

There are 6 ways to revoke the whole *or* part of a will.

1 **Express revocation** (*WA 1837 s.20*)

➤ The insertion of suitable words in a subsequent will or a codicil executed as a will.

2 **Implied revocation**

➤ When a disposition is inconsistent with an earlier will, the original disposition is revoked and superseded insofar as it is incompatible with the subsequent disposition.

3 **Dependant relative revocation** (*Re Irvine* [1929] 2 IR 485)

➤ When the replacement of a disposition is conditional on a specified event: if the event does not occur, the earlier disposition remains valid, otherwise the conditional disposition is substituted for it.

4 **Marriage** (*WA 1837 s.18* as amended *AJA 1982)*

➤ Marriage revokes a will, unless the will shows contrary intention.

➤ A will made on or after 1 January 1983 in anticipation of marriage, with a clause displaying the testator's intent that the will (or part of it) should remain valid after marriage, will be valid, *provided that*:

a) the will names a particular person as the intended spouse, and this person is married, *and*

b) the testator's intention 'appears from the will . . . at the time it was made'; extrinsic evidence is inadmissible.

➤ Marriage does not revoke a mutual will as a trust arises on the death of the first to die, and this trust is not revoked by a subsequent marriage (*Re Goodchild (deceased)* [1996] 1 All ER 670, Ch D).

5 **Divorce** (*WA 1837 s.18A as amended by LR(S)A 1995 s.3* for deaths on or after 1 January 1996)

➤ If a marriage ends in divorce or annulment, the appointment of an ex-spouse as executor *or* trustee, or a gift to the spouse, take effect as if the former spouse died on the day of the dissolution or annulment.

6 **Destruction** (*WA 1837 s.20*)

a) Burning, tearing *or* otherwise destroying the will, *and*

b) destruction by the testator *or* by some person in his presence and by his direction, *and*

c) destruction with the intention of revoking the will.

- Destruction must be physical - crossing a will out, or writing 'revoked' across it is insufficient.
- Symbolic destruction is not sufficient. Destruction of part may only revoke the part destroyed; this depends on the condition of any remains and quite which part of the will is destroyed.
  - Destruction of a signature revokes the whole will (*Hobbs v. Knight* (1838) 1 Curt 768).
  - If parts are cut out, only those parts are revoked (*Re Everest* [1975] Fam 44).
- The presumption is that a missing will is intentionally destroyed.

B Contents of a will

I Common clauses

1 Commencement

- States the testator's name and address.
- The words 'last will and testament' are evidence of an intention to make a will.

2 Revocation of previous wills

- Quite what is revoked depends on the wording of the clause.
  - 'Wills' refers to wills and codicils.
  - 'Testamentary dispositions' covers wills, codicils and privileged wills.

3 Disposal of remains

- This is a request, it does not bind the executors.
- If organ donation or medical research are envisaged, the testator should carry a donor card and inform his family. Details should be kept with the will of how to contact HM Inspector of Anatomy (organ donation) and/or the Department of Health (research).

4 Appointment of executors

- Individuals

  These should be suitable, willing and capable of taking a grant of representation (not a minor, a convicted criminal, or a bankrupt). Private individuals will not charge, but they may need to engage professionals who will bill the estate. It is advisable to appoint a minimum of 2 people.

- Trustees

  A maximum of 4 may apply for a grant of probate, so avoid appointing more than this.

- Banks and trust corporations

  For large complex estates, where the extra expense involved is justified, and the slightly more impersonal approach which may be taken is not a concern.

- Solicitors

  An individual partner may retire or cease to practice, so appoint the firm in the alternative.

  a) Ensure the will appoints partners acting at death, rather than those at the time of the will, *and*

  b) provide for the firm's amalgamation, change of name, or future incorporation.

- Public trustee

  This is expensive and inconvenient, but available if there is no alternative.

5 **Appointment of guardians** (*ChA 1989*)

➤ A parent with 'parental responsibility' may appoint a guardian for a minor under the age of 18.

- An unmarried father does not have 'parental responsibility' unless he is granted it by a court order.
- If both parents have 'parental responsibility', then an appointment is effective on the death of both parents; where both appoint different guardians, the responsibilities are shared between them.

➤ An appointment must be written, dated and signed; it can be revoked in the same fashion *even* if the original appointment was by will *s.5(3).* No codicil is needed to revoke an appointment, but divorce and annulment revoke the appointment unless the appointment shows a contrary intention (*ChA 1989 s.6(3A)* as amended by *LR(S)A 1995 s.4*).

- Ensure both parents appoint the same guardian and that the person consents.
- Financial provision for the care of the children should be made by appointing the guardian trustee of a fund, with power to spend income and capital for the child's benefit.

6 **Legacies**

➤ These are classified as 'General', 'Demonstrative', 'Specific', 'Pecuniary' or 'Residuary' (see p.138).

7 **Administrative powers**

➤ PRs and trustees have powers under the general law to administer trust funds.

➤ The will may extend powers granted under the general law (see pp.139-140).

8 **Attestation clause**

➤ This is not compulsory, but it is evidence that the will has been properly executed.

Note: a space for the date is left either in the 'Commencement', or in the 'Attestation' clause.

II Hints on drafting and interpretation

Class closing rules

Unless the will excludes the class closing rules, these will determine how a class gift is construed.

Vested gifts

a) 'To the children of X' - if there are members of the class alive at the time of the testator's death, the class closes then, otherwise it remains open until X dies.

b) 'To S for life, remainder to the children of X' - as in a), but the class *may* close from S's death.

Contingent gifts

c) 'To the children of X who attain the age of 21' - if the contingency has been fulfilled, the class closes at X's death, and it includes any children alive at the testator's death who have reached, or who may in the future reach 21. Otherwise the class closes as soon as one of X's children fulfils the contingency.

d) 'To S for life, remainder to the children of X who attain the age of 21' - as in c), but the class *may* close from S's death.

Gifts to individuals within a class: 'to *each* of the children of X' - the class closes on the testator's death.

Early closing: the class in b) and d) may close immediately the prior interest fails, then the gift operates like a) or c) respectively.

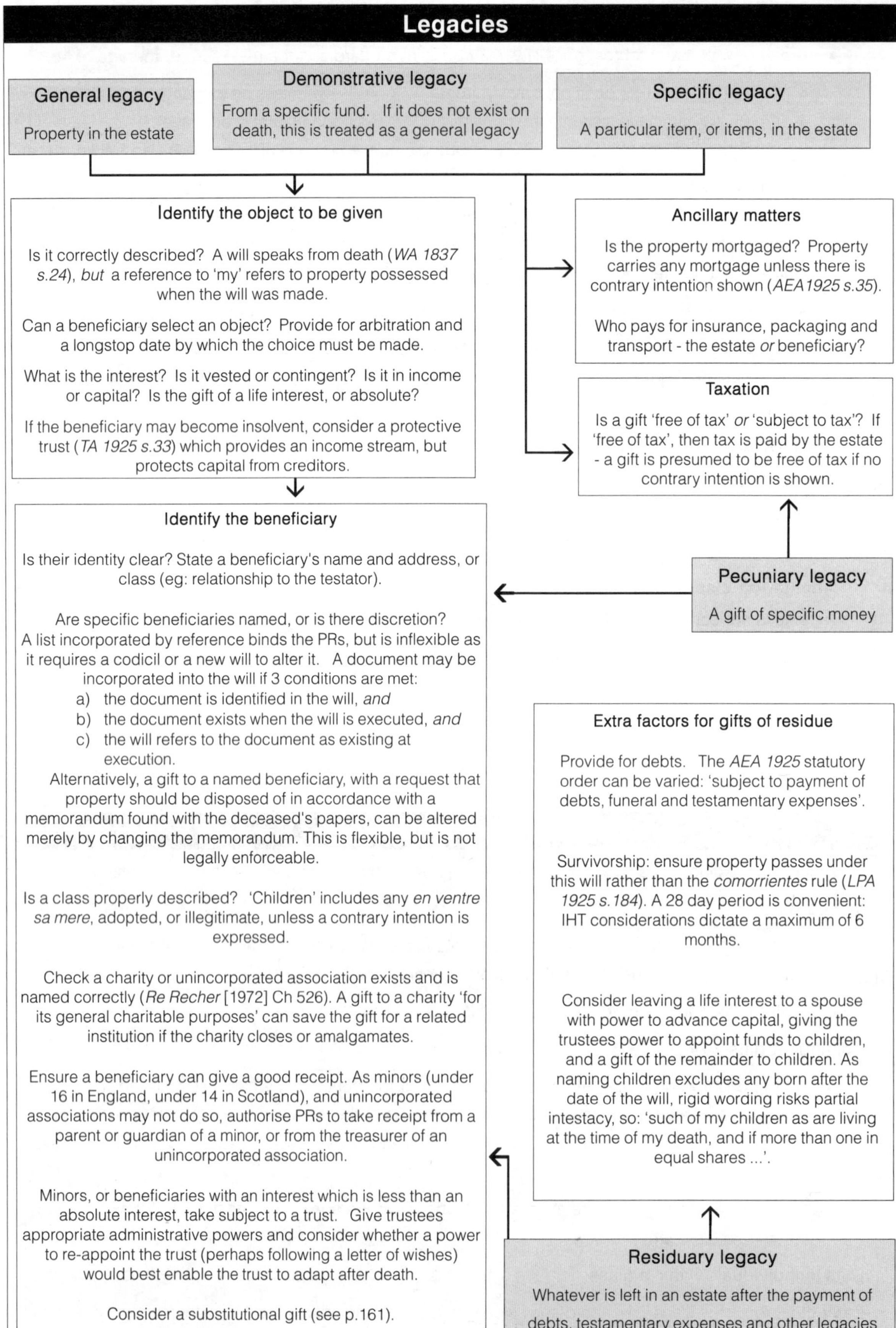
Legacies
General legacy
Property in the estate
Demonstrative legacy
From a specific fund. If it does not exist on death, this is treated as a general legacy
Specific legacy
A particular item, or items, in the estate
Identify the object to be given
Is it correctly described? A will speaks from death (*WA 1837 s.24*), *but* a reference to 'my' refers to property possessed when the will was made.
Can a beneficiary select an object? Provide for arbitration and a longstop date by which the choice must be made.
What is the interest? Is it vested or contingent? Is it in income or capital? Is the gift of a life interest, or absolute?
If the beneficiary may become insolvent, consider a protective trust (*TA 1925 s.33*) which provides an income stream, but protects capital from creditors.
Ancillary matters
Is the property mortgaged? Property carries any mortgage unless there is contrary intention shown (*AEA 1925 s.35*).
Who pays for insurance, packaging and transport - the estate *or* beneficiary?
Taxation
Is a gift 'free of tax' *or* 'subject to tax'? If 'free of tax', then tax is paid by the estate - a gift is presumed to be free of tax if no contrary intention is shown.
Identify the beneficiary
Is their identity clear? State a beneficiary's name and address, or class (eg: relationship to the testator).
Are specific beneficiaries named, or is there discretion? A list incorporated by reference binds the PRs, but is inflexible as it requires a codicil or a new will to alter it. A document may be incorporated into the will if 3 conditions are met:
a) the document is identified in the will, *and*
b) the document exists when the will is executed, *and*
c) the will refers to the document as existing at execution.
Alternatively, a gift to a named beneficiary, with a request that property should be disposed of in accordance with a memorandum found with the deceased's papers, can be altered merely by changing the memorandum. This is flexible, but is not legally enforceable.
Is a class properly described? 'Children' includes any *en ventre sa mere*, adopted, or illegitimate, unless a contrary intention is expressed.
Check a charity or unincorporated association exists and is named correctly (*Re Recher* [1972] Ch 526). A gift to a charity 'for its general charitable purposes' can save the gift for a related institution if the charity closes or amalgamates.
Ensure a beneficiary can give a good receipt. As minors (under 16 in England, under 14 in Scotland), and unincorporated associations may not do so, authorise PRs to take receipt from a parent or guardian of a minor, or from the treasurer of an unincorporated association.
Minors, or beneficiaries with an interest which is less than an absolute interest, take subject to a trust. Give trustees appropriate administrative powers and consider whether a power to re-appoint the trust (perhaps following a letter of wishes) would best enable the trust to adapt after death.
Consider a substitutional gift (see p.161).
Pecuniary legacy
A gift of specific money
Extra factors for gifts of residue
Provide for debts. The *AEA 1925* statutory order can be varied: 'subject to payment of debts, funeral and testamentary expenses'.
Survivorship: ensure property passes under this will rather than the *comorrientes* rule (*LPA 1925 s.184*). A 28 day period is convenient: IHT considerations dictate a maximum of 6 months.
Consider leaving a life interest to a spouse with power to advance capital, giving the trustees power to appoint funds to children, and a gift of the remainder to children. As naming children excludes any born after the date of the will, rigid wording risks partial intestacy, so: 'such of my children as are living at the time of my death, and if more than one in equal shares ...'.
Residuary legacy
Whatever is left in an estate after the payment of debts, testamentary expenses and other legacies

Administration

Insurance (*TA 2000 s.34* substituting *TA 1925 s.19*)

➤ Power to insure trust property against loss or damage and pay the premiums from income or capital

Investment

➤ A **general power of investment**: power to make any kind of investment as if the trustee were absolutely entitled to the trust assets (*TA 2000 ss.3(1)-(2)*).

- This power does not permit a trustee to make an investment in land, other than in loans secured on land (*TA 2000 ss.3(3)-(6)*).
- A trustee must have regard to the standard investment criteria, which are (*TA 2000 s.4*):
  - i) the suitability to the trust of investments of the same kind as any particular investment proposed to be made or retained and of that particular investment as an investment of that kind, *and*
  - ii) the need for diversification of investments, in so far as is appropriate to the trust's circumstances.
- Unless a trustee reasonably concludes that it is unncessary or inappropriate, he must obtain and consider proper advice before exercising the power of investment and when reviewing investments (*TA 2000 s.5*).

➤ A power to **acquire freehold or leasehold land in the UK:** as an investment, for occupation by a beneficiary, or for any other reason (*TA 2000 s.8*).

Land, etc

Powers under the general law	Drafting considerations
➤ Prior to 1 January 1997, land was held on a strict settlement under *SLA 1925* unless it is given to a trustee on an 'immediate binding trust for sale'. *TLATA 1996* prevents new strict settlements arising and creates a system of 'trusts of land'.	Consider how to achieve the testator's wishes under *TLATA 1996*, see further pp.181-182. *TLATA* only gives trustees of land a power to sell, so consider a power to sell personalty

Operate a business

Powers under the general law	Drafting considerations
➤ PRs can only run a business to preserve its sale value. They are restricted to using assets the business relied on at the testator's death (*Re Hodson, ex parte Richardson* (1818) 3 Madd 138)	PRs can be permitted to use assets from the general estate to run the business, or it may be left as a specific legacy

Delegation, agency, etc

➤ Power to **authorise any person to exercise delegable functions as their agent** (*TA 2000 s.11*).

- A beneficiary may not act as an agent (*TA 2000 s.12(3)*) (For 'delegable functions, see p.150).
- An agent's authorisation in relation to asset management functions must be evidenced in writing and be accompanied by guidance (known as a 'policy statement') (*TA 2000 s.15*).

➤ Power to **appoint a nominee** (*TA 2000 s.16*) or **custodian** (*TA 2000 s.17*) (*TA 2000 Part IV*).

- The appointment must be evidenced in writing.

➤ Professionally drafted wills may continue to include express powers and duties. The statutory framework provided by *TLATA 1996/TA 2000* offers a 'safety net' in cases where specific provision is not made.

Administration (cont.)

Remuneration / Reimbursement

- An entitlement to receive **payment in respect of services** (*TA 2000 s.28*).
  - This applies to a trust corporation or a trustee acting in a professional capacity if the trust instrument confers an entitlement to payment out of trust funds in respect of services provided by the trustee; it applies even if the services are capable of being provided by a lay trustee.
- An entitlement to receive **reasonable remuneration** for services to the trust (*TA 2000 s.29*)
  - This applies to a trust corporation, or a trustee acting in a professional capacity (but not the trustee of a charitable trust) where no provision for remuneration has been made in the trust instrument.
  - If a trustee acts in a professional capacity, each of the other trustees must agree in writing.
- An entitlement to **reimbursement of/payment for a trustee's expenses** (*TA 2000 s.31*).
- A power to **remunerate an agent/nominee/custodian** (*TA 2000 s.32*).

Distribution

Appropriation

Powers under the general law	Drafting considerations
➤ PRs can appropriate property to pay a pecuniary legacy provided that (*AEA 1925 s.41*): a) a beneficiary does not suffer, *and* b) that beneficiary consents	Relieve PRs of the duty to obtain a beneficiary's formal consent

Apportionment

Powers under the general law	Drafting considerations
➤ *Howe v. Dartmouth* (1802) 7 Ves 137: 'wasting, hazardous and unauthorised' assets, and those which produce no income are sold, so that a life tenant benefits from capital ➤ *Allhusen v. Whittell* (1867) LR 4 Eq 295: debts, administration and tax are apportioned between capital and income ➤ *AA 1870 s.2*: rent/dividends are income arising daily: they are treated as capital before death, and income thereafter	These **complex bureaucratic** rules can be expressly excluded to assist the administration of the trust If the will creates a trust of land under *TLATA 1996*, then the rule in *Howe v. Dartmouth* may be automatically excluded (*Re Pitcairn* [1896] 2 Ch 199). However, this will occur if a will trust contains land so exclude the rules expressly

Receipt

Powers under the general law	Drafting considerations
➤ A married minor can only give receipt for income (*LPA s.21*) ➤ PRs can accept receipt on behalf of minors with an absolute interest from trustees who may be appointed for this purpose (*AEA 1925 s.42*).	Authorise PRs to accept receipt from a parent, guardian of a minor under 16, to avoid appointing trustees Cater for receipt if a minor's interest is contingent, *or* if a married minor receives capital

Income / Capital

Powers under the general law	Drafting considerations
Income for 'maintenance, education or benefit', acting 'reasonably' and with regard to other resources (*TA 1925 s.31*) ➤ At 18 a beneficiary of an absolute or contingent interest is entitled to income ➤ Accumulated income is released if a beneficiary has a life interest in capital, otherwise accumulations and capital are retained until the gift vests absolutely **Capital** for 'advancement or benefit' whether an interest is absolute or contingent (*TA 1925 s.32*) ➤ Payments are subtracted when capital vests absolutely ➤ A holder of a prior life interest must consent in writing ➤ Only half a presumptive/ vested interest may be advanced	Give the trustees discretion to make payments as they think fit NB: the rule against cumulation imposes a long-stop of 21 years after the testator's death, after which the beneficiary must be allowed access to the capital Postpone a beneficiary's right to receive income, and/or capital, until after the statutory age of 18 Increase the capital which trustees can advance Give the trustees discretion to distribute capital without making deductions in respect of prior advancements

C Intestacy

Steps	
1	**Discover the extent of the estate passing on intestacy**
2	**Property passes to the PRs on statutory trusts (*AEA 1925 s.33*)**
3	**Deduct funeral, testamentary and administrative expenses *and* debts**
4	**Set aside a pecuniary legacy fund**
5	**Work out who is entitled to the property (apply the statutory order of entitlement)**
6	**Consider whether the spouse wishes to exercise his/her rights**

Step 1 Discover the extent of the estate passing on intestacy

➤ Only property capable of passing by will can pass on intestacy.

Step 2 Property passes to the PRs on the statutory trusts

➤ Property passes to PRs on the statutory trusts (*AEA 1925 s.47*).

➤ The terms of the trust dictate that the gift is construed as being:

- to those entitled within a class, in equal shares, *and*
- to all 'living' persons within the class, including any children *en ventre sa mere*, *and*
- on the death of a member of a class who was entitled on the intestate's death, to that beneficiary's issue in equal shares, *and*
- contingent on the beneficiary marrying *or* reaching the age of 18.

  Note: if a contingency is not met, the failed interest is disregarded, and the distribution of the estate is reassessed as if the failed interest had never existed.

➤ The trustees have:

- powers of maintenance and advancement given by the *TA 1925 ss.31-32*, *and*
- (from 1 January 1997), power to sell.
  - Prior to 1 January 1997 trustees were under a duty to sell with a power to postpone sale and a direction that the deceased's 'personal chattels' should not be sold without a 'special reason' such as the payment of debts and administration expenses (*AEA 1925 s.33*).
    - When *TLATA* came into force on 1 January 1997 the duty to sell and convert ceased to apply (*TLATA 1996 Sch. 2 para 5*).

Step 3 Deduct funeral, testamentary and administrative expenses

Step 4 Set aside a fund from which to pay pecuniary legacies

Step 5 — Work out who is entitled to property

A. The statutory order of entitlement

➤ A surviving spouse takes priority over anyone else. Depending on the size of the estate, the spouse may share an interest with one class of kinsmen (see the chart below); if one class exists those classes further down the line are excluded (*AEA 1925 s.46*).

➤ If there is no spouse, blood kin take in the statutory order:

a) issue, *then*

b) parents, *then*

c) brothers and sisters of whole blood, *then*

d) brothers and sisters of half-blood, *then*

e) grandparents, *then*

f) uncles and aunts of whole blood, *then*

g) uncles and aunts of half-blood, *then*

h) *bona vacantia* goes to the Crown, the Duchy of Lancaster, or the Duke of Cornwall; there is discretion to provide for those an intestate 'might reasonably have been expected to make provision' for,

➤ For deaths on or after 1 January 1996, the spouse is treated as not having survived the intestate if he or she dies within a period of 28 days beginning on the day of the intestate's death (*AEA 1925 s.46(2A)* as inserted by the *LR(S)A 1995 s.1*).

	Size of estate	Spouse's entitlement	Others' entitlement
Spouse alone		Everything passing on intestacy	Nothing
Spouse and issue	Estate under £125,000	Everything (including personal chattels)	
	Estate over £125,000	Personal chattels absolutely £125,000 statutory legacy* Life interest in half the residue	On the statutory trusts: ➤ half the residue, *and* ➤ interest in remainder of residue
Spouse, no issue† but other kin	Estate under £200,000	Everything (including chattels)	Nothing
	Estate over £200,000	Personal chattels absolutely £200,000 statutory legacy* Half the residue absolutely	On the statutory trusts: ➤ half the residue
No spouse			Everything on statutory trusts

† Issue: children and other descendants including adopted, legitimated and legitimised children

* Statutory legacy:
a) this is paid free of tax and costs. It also includes interest from the date of death until the legacy is paid to the spouse
b) the value of any personal chattels is not taken into account in establishing whether the estate is worth £125,000 or £200,000

Step 6 Consider whether the spouse wishes to exercise his/her rights

1 **A spouse's right to redeem a life interest**

- The spouse may choose to convert the life interest into a lump sum.
- The spouse must notify the PRs within 1 year of the date when the grant of representation is issued.
  a) All those entitled to the remainder may, if they are *sui juris*, agree the value of the life interest in writing with the spouse. Otherwise the sum is calculated according to *IS(IC)O 1977*.
  b) The entitlement of other beneficiaries is recalculated.
  c) IHT is recalculated and the spouse bears any resulting charge.

2 **A spouse's right to appropriate the matrimonial home (*IEA 1952 s.5* and *Schedule II*)**

- The spouse can demand that PRs transfer the house to him/her as part of the inheritance to which he/she is absolutely entitled.

Steps

1 The spouse must notify the PRs within 1 year of the date when the grant of representation is issued.

2 The house is valued at the time of appropriation, not death. If its value exceeds the spouse's entitlement, he or she can pay the difference to the estate as 'equality money'.

NB: if the spouse is the sole surviving PR, then the President of the Family Division must be notified of an intention to invoke either of these statutory rights. This is done by lodging the notification together with the original grant at the Probate Registry so that this intention can be recorded on the grant.

D Probate

I Overview of a solicitor's role

A solicitor's duty to PRs

1. Advise on succession and revenue law.
2. Prove the testator's will.
3. Administer the estate.
4. Prepare estate accounts.

How to carry out this duty

1. Take instructions directly from the PR.
2. Obtain the deceased's will (and ensure PRs each have a copy).
3. Attend to the deceased's wishes as regards cremation, organ donation, etc, in consultation with the PRs.
4. Secure property (ie: check an empty house is locked and insured, locate and safeguard documents of title to assets).
5. Attend to financial arrangements (ie: loans to support a family pending grant of probate or during the administration of the estate).
6. Obtain the death certificate.
7. Compile a list of the deceased's assets and liabilities. This list should be continuously updated during the administration of the estate, to show their state at any given time and what steps have been or are being taken with regard to them.
8. Discover details of all the beneficiaries (ie: ages and addresses).
9. Protect PRs from personal liability against unknown or missing creditors or beneficiaries (eg: place advertisments in good time for the purposes of *TA s.1925 s.27*, see p.159).
10. Prepare the oath and the Inland Revenue account.
11. Obtain a grant and make office copies of the grant.
12. Collect and realise assets.
13. Pay debts.
14. Pay legacies.
15. Ascertain and distribute residue.

I Administering property immediately after death

➤ The executor's first duty, after making suitable arrangements for a funeral, is to ascertain what assets and liabilities there are in the estate.

◆ Certain assets can be paid to someone who appears to be beneficially entitled to them without sight of a grant (which may take a little time to obtain) - this is a discretion to be exercised by whomever holds the assets, PRs cannot demand payment as of right.

<table>
<tr><th>Type of property</th><th>Comments</th></tr>
<tr><td>Salaries of public sector employees</td><td rowspan="5">The PRs can administer such property if (AE(SP)A 1965):
➤ payment is at the discretion of the trustees, and
➤ the asset is not worth more than £5,000, and
➤ the applicant appears to be beneficially entitled to the asset</td></tr>
<tr><td>Some pensions</td></tr>
<tr><td>National Savings bank accounts, TSB accounts</td></tr>
<tr><td>National Savings certificates and premium bonds</td></tr>
<tr><td>Building society and Friendly society accounts</td></tr>
<tr><td>Life assurance policy held on trust</td><td>A death certificate is needed to gain access to the proceeds of the policy
The proceeds are paid to whomever was assigned the benefit of the policy, or in the case of a MWPA policy in favour of children, to the trustees who were appointed under the terms of the policy</td></tr>
<tr><td>Property held under a joint tenancy</td><td>A death certificate establishes a tenant's right to take through survivorship
Only if a survivor murders another tenant will he not be entitled to the property</td></tr>
<tr><td>Chattels</td><td>Although a grant is theoretically necessary to prove title, in practice it is not usually necessary to produce one</td></tr>
</table>

- These assets can be used to meet debts and to pay for funeral expenses and IHT.

➤ The executors should write to institutions holding assets, quoting whatever details they possess about the assets and inquiring about:

a) the value of the asset(s) on the date of death (including accrued interest), *and*

b) the daily interest which is accruing on the asset(s), *and*

c) whether the institution holds any other assets on behalf of the deceased.

- It is usual to *either* request a cheque for the sum due *or* to ask for the relevant papers needed to close the account.
- The PRs should send appropriate evidence of their title, eg: to claim an insurance policy written into trust, send a certified copy of the trust instrument and any appointments/resignations of trustees plus a certified copy of the death certificate.

II Applying for a grant of representation

- A PR's duty is (*AEA 1925 s.25* as amended *AEA 1971 s.9)*: 'to collect and get in the real and personal estate of the deceased and administer it according to law'.
- A grant of representation is necessary to administer the rest of the deceased's estate as the executor(s) will need to be able to prove that he/they are entitled to sell or dispose of assets.
- The procedure for '**Swearing the oath**' and '**Applying for the grant**' is as follows:

Steps

1. **Decide what sort of grant is appropriate.**
2. **Ascertain who is entitled to take a grant.**
3. **Complete form *IHT 200* (unless the estate is 'excepted') (see p.109).**
4. **Fill in the oath.**

Swearing/affirming the oath

- Executors complete the jurat before an independent solicitor with a current practicing certificate or commissioner for oaths (*not* an executor or connected with a firm acting for the PRs).
    - If the oath is affirmed, rather than sworn, an executor does not need to hold a Bible/the New Testament and simply states 'I do solemly sincerely and truly declare and affirm ...'
- Executors and a solicitor, or a commissioner for oaths, initial the will and any codicils.

Applying for the grant

- Send to the Probate Registry (using a District Registry may minimise publicity):
    - the oath (*NCPR r.8*), *and*
    - the will, *and*
    - the court fee, *and*
        - The basic fee is calculated by reference to the value of the net estate. Add to this the photocopy for each office copy of the grant of representation requested. (Work out how many copies to ask for by reference to the number of assets for which the grant will need to be produced).
    - a fee sheet showing how the fee was calculated *and*
    - the Inland Revenue account (unless the estate is 'excepted').
- The Probate Registry usually issues the grant in 5 to 15 days.
- Where an estate is 'excepted', the Inland Revenue has 35 days after the grant is issued in which to demand the production of an account.
    - If the PRs discover other assets, making it necessary to submit an account, then they must tender an account to the Inland Revenue within 6 months of making this discovery.

Step 1 Decide what sort of grant is appropriate

➤ A straightforward grant of probate *or* letters of administration is usually sought:

Grant	Circumstances	Effect of grant	PRs identified
Grant of probate	The executor appointed in a valid will is willing *and* able to act (even if the estate actually passes under the intestacy rules)	➤ It confirms the appointment made in the will ➤ It is conclusive evidence that the PRs have title to the estate *and* that the will is valid	In the will
Letters of administration with will annexed	The appointment of executors in the will fails as *either* it is invalid *or* they are unwilling to act	➤ It confers authority on the PRs ➤ It vests title to the estate in PRs	Following *NCPR r.20*
Simple administration	Total intestacy		Following *NCPR r.22*

➤ However, in certain circumstances, a different form of grant of representation will be appropriate:

Type of grant	Circumstances: when ...
Grant for the use and benefit of a person who is mentally incapacitated *NCPR r.35*	... a sole executor or only potential administrator is mentally incapacitated. Grant to a capable adult in the following order: a) adult authorised by the Court of Protection to apply for a grant b) lawful attorney of the incapacitated person, with registered enduring power of attorney c) the deceased's residuary legatee or devisee
Administration for the use and benefit of a minor *NCPR r.32*	... a minor is the sole executor, or the only administrator in the category with highest priority. The grant is made to an adult, often the minor's guardian
Grants over specified property *NCPR r.53*	... a will appoints an executor in respect of particular property *or* the court exercises its discretion to make a grant over part of the estate (*SCA 1981 s.113*)
Grant *ad litem* *SCA 1981 s.116*	... an estate is a party to legal proceedings and there is no PR
Administration with litigation pending *SCA 1981 s.117*	... assets need safeguarding while a probate action takes place. This requires the consent of all parties to the action
Administration *ad colligenda bona* *NCPR s.52*	... a person with an interest in the estate seeks to ensure the collection and preservation of its property - this grant does not permit distribution, and ceases when a full grant is made
Attorney grants *NCPR r.31*	... a letter of administration is granted to the lawful attorney of someone who is entitled to a grant
Double grant of probate *	... power is reserved - it operates in tandem with the original grant
Cessate grant *	... a grant which was made for a limited time expires - it is a regrant to an executor of what remains of the estate
Grant *de bonis administrandum* *	... a sole surviving PR dies so that the chain of representation is broken
* With applications for such grants submit *Form A5-C* to the probate registry (no need to frist send *Form A5-C* to the Revenue)	

Step 2 — Ascertain who is entitled to take a grant

➤ Applicants for grants must satisfy the following criteria:

	Executors	Administrator
Mentally incapable	Not suitable (*NCPR r.35*)	
Renunciation (*NCPR r.37*)	If the executor has not 'intermeddled' with the estate (actively administered the estate) (*Re Stevens, Cooke v. Stevens* [1898] 1 Ch 162) he may renounce. When this is done he may not apply for a grant. A renunciation must be in writing, signed, witnessed *and* filed at the probate registry	
Minor	Not suitable, until majority is reached when a cessate grant can be sought. If an adult is appointed, power can be reserved to a minor. If only a minor is appointed, parents or a guardian take letters of administration with the will annexed	Not suitable, until majority is reached, when a cessate grant can be sought. A parent or guardian can apply for a minor's 'use and benefit' (*NCPR r.32*); anyone entitled in the same degree takes in preference to a guardian (*NCPR r.27(5)*)
Former spouse	Not suitable, *unless* the will indicates an intention that, despite the divorce, the appointment should stand (*WA 1837 s.15*)	Not suitable
Power reserved	Yes, if an appointee entitled in the same degree requests it. Notice must be given to all those entitled	No power may be reserved
Number needed	Up to 4 (reserve power if a future vacancy is likely)	At least 2 if there is a minority or life interest; unless the court permits one

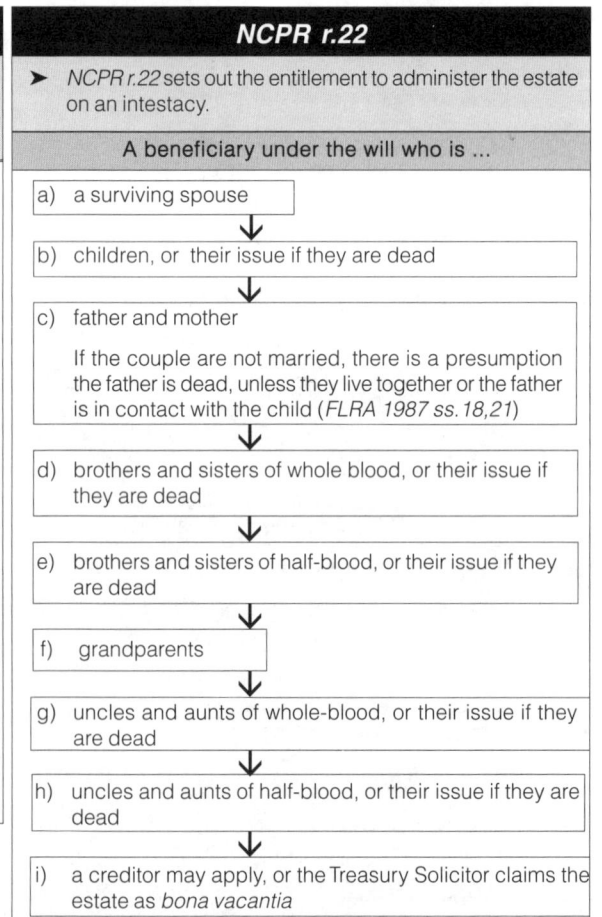

NCPR r.20

➤ *NCPR r.20* allows the appointment of administrators if:
- the appointment is void, *or*
- the appointee is incapable.

a) Any executor

↓

b) A residuary legatee holding in trust for any other person

↓

c) A residuary legatee: a vested interest takes in priority to a contingent one, and those entitled to residue take priority over any entitled under a partial intestacy

↓

d) A PR of any residuary legatee, or of one entitled to residue under the intestacy rules, provided the deceased beneficiary had an absolute interest (eg: not a life interest)

↓

e) Any legatee, or creditor. A legatee of a vested interest takes priority over one entitled to a contingent interest

↓

f) A PR of any legatee (with an absolute interest) or creditor

NCPR r.22

➤ *NCPR r.22* sets out the entitlement to administer the estate on an intestacy.

A beneficiary under the will who is ...

a) a surviving spouse

↓

b) children, or their issue if they are dead

↓

c) father and mother

If the couple are not married, there is a presumption the father is dead, unless they live together or the father is in contact with the child (*FLRA 1987 ss.18,21*)

↓

d) brothers and sisters of whole blood, or their issue if they are dead

↓

e) brothers and sisters of half-blood, or their issue if they are dead

↓

f) grandparents

↓

g) uncles and aunts of whole-blood, or their issue if they are dead

↓

h) uncles and aunts of half-blood, or their issue if they are dead

↓

i) a creditor may apply, or the Treasury Solicitor claims the estate as *bona vacantia*

➤ An applicant for a grant under *NCPR r.20* or *r.22* must swear why those with priority are unable or unwilling to apply for the grant - this is known as 'clearing off'.

Step 3 — Complete form *IHT 200* (unless the estate is 'excepted')

➤ See p.109.

Step 4 Filling in the oath

Consider (and fill in or delete as appropriate) ...

... when preparing an oath for an executor

- details (in the top left hand corner) of the solicitor's firm lodging the oath.
- the deceased's name, plus any alias (and the reason for such an alias).
- the deceased's date of death and age at death. If the date of death is uncertain, the time when the deceased was last seen alive and the date on which the body was found are sworn.
- the deceased's last address and the address of the deceased when the will was made if this differs.
- whether any settled land was vested in the deceased.
- whether power is reserved and, if so, to whom.
- the gross and net value of the estate and whether it is 'excepted'.
    - If an executor has renounced, ensure a Form of Renunciation is annexed to the oath.

... additionally when preparing an oath for an administrator with a will annexed

- if a minority arises under the estate, *or* the deceased at his death had an interest in land under a strict settlement, 2 administrators will be needed (one executor could have acted alone).
- details of the applicant's right under the *NCPR r.20* to seek a grant of representation:
    a) an explanation of why an executor is not applying, ie: none was appointed, renunciation, or death, *and*
    b) the applicant's capacity to take a grant - eg: 'residuary legatee and the devisee under the said will', 'specific legatee and devisee named in the said will'.

... additionally when preparing an oath for an administrator of an intestate

Marital status	Single	Married	Divorced	Judicially separated	Annulled
	Bachelor/spinster	Married man/woman, or widow/er			Status before annulment
Fill in			The court which implemented the divorce, date of the order (if the court was outside England and Wales, provide an office copy of the decree)		
			That the deceased did not remarry	That the separation continued until death	

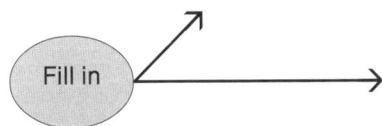

- Clear off those with a prior entitlement under *NCPR r.22* (but not those in the same category). Mention any renunciation and clear off using the following terms depending how the deceased died.
    - Spouse: a bachelor/spinster, widow(er), single man/woman
    - Children: without issue
    - Parents
    - Brothers, sisters/issue: (or) brother or sister of [whole/half] blood or issue thereof
    - Grandparents: (or) grandparent
    - Uncle, aunt/issue: (or) uncle or aunt of [whole/half] blood or issue thereof

  If a spouse survives, and there are no issue qualifying for a share in the estate, the words 'or any other person entitled in priority to share in [his/her] estate by virtue of any enactment' remain - otherwise delete them.

- State the applicant's relationship to the deceased.
    - Spouse: lawful husband/widow
    - Child: son/daughter (whether or not parents were married at birth)
    - Grandchild: grandson/daughter (state that the applicant's parents have died)
    - Brother/Sister: brother/sister of [whole/half] blood
    - Parent: father/mother
    - Grandparent: grandfather/grandmother
    - Cousin: cousin german of [whole/half] blood (state that the applicant's parents have died)
- State why the applicant is entitled to a share in the estate, eg: 'the only person entitled to the estate', 'one of the persons entitled to share in the estate'.

E Administration

I Collecting in all the deceased's assets
II Ensuring the estate meets its tax liability
III Paying debts
IV Paying legacies
V Obtaining a discharge

I Collecting in all the deceased's assets

- A PR's duty is (*AEA 1925 s.25* as amended *AEA 1971 s.9*): 'to collect and get in the real and personal estate of the deceased and administer it according to law'.
- PRs should write to institutions holding the deceased's assets, enclosing an office copy of the grant together with any other appropriate documents (eg: building society pass-book if the account is to be closed, insurance policy) and requesting details of the assets.
  - Ask for the office copies of the grant to be returned, to reduce costs.
- PRs and trustees have statutory powers, and may receive additional powers in the will.

PRs' statutory powers, rights and duties
Insure the estate's assets: *TA 1925 s.19* (see p.139).
Appropriate property in the estate amongst the beneficiaries (*AEA 1925 s.41*).
Pay an agent: *TA 2000 s.32* (see p140).
PRs (and trustees) can **delegate the exercise of powers or discretions for up to 1 year**. ◆ This is useful if renunciation is impossible but the PR is going abroad, etc) (*TA 1925 s.25* as substituted by *TDA 1999 s.5*). PRs can **employ agents to exercise 'delegable functions'** (*TA 2000 s.11*); these are any function other than: a) any function relating to whether or in what way any assets of the trust should be distributed, *or* b) any power to decide whether any fees or other payment due to be made out of trust funds should be made out of income or capital, *or* c) any power to appoint a person to act as trustee of the trust, *or* d) any power conferred by any other enactment or trust instrument which permits the trustees to delegate any of their functions or to appoint a person t act as a nominee or custodian.
Reimbursement of/payment of expenses: *TA 2000 s.31* (see p.140).
Charging: *TA 2000 ss.28 -29* (see p.140).
Apportionment: sell wasting assets (*Howe v. Dartmouth*), pay debts fairly (*Allhusen v. Whittell*), *AA 1870 s.2* (see p.140).
Running a business: duty to run the business to maintain its value as an asset for sale (see p.139).
Power and duties in respect of land forming part of the estate during the administration: In respect of estates arising due to deaths on or after 1 January 1997 when *TLATA 1996* came into force PRs have the same powers and duties as trustees of land (see p.181), except that they will not be bound to obtain the beneficiaries' consent before selling land.
Power to invest (see p.140)
Power to appoint trustees who will be able to give the PRs valid receipt on behalf of a minor who is absolutely entitled (*TA 1925 s.42*).
Power to postpone distribution even if the will specifies payments within a time-frame (*AEA 1925 s.44*). If payment is delayed beyond a year after death, interest is payable from that date. If the testator specifies a date or contingency upon which payment is to be made, interest runs from that point. The rate of interest is 6% per annum, *or* as laid down in the will.

II Ensuring the estate meets its tax liability

- PRs should complete a self assessment tax return for the deceased's income and capital expenditure from 6 April to his death. Any reliefs and allowances available for the full year may be claimed. Any liability or repayment forms part of the estate, and must be met or accounted for by the PRs during the administration.
- Throughout each tax year during the administration, the PRs must make tax returns on behalf of the estate.

1. Income tax

- This is chargeable on the deceased's income and is a debt due from the estate (*TA s.60(4)*).
- Interest on a loan for paying IHT is deductible as a 'charge on income' (*TA s.358*).
- Personal allowances are available for the tax year in which death occurs, but not for the remainder of the administration.
- The Schedule F ordinary rate (10%) applies to distributions from UK companies. Interest is taxed at the lower rate (20%) and other income is subject to tax at the basic rate (22%) (*TA s.686(6)*).
  - If a beneficiary is entitled to income, the PRs supply a certificate of deduction of tax (*Form 185E*).
    - When a beneficiary prepares his self assessment he uses *Form 185E*.
    - A beneficiary is liable for tax on the gross income.

2. Capital gains tax

- As death is not a disposal, no charge to CGT arises on death (*TCGA 1992 s.62(1)(b)*).
- The probate value becomes the base value (ie: rather than the original acquisition value) (*TCGA 1992 s.62(1)(a)*).
- Tax is due at a flat rate of 34% on chargeable gains realised during the administration.
  - Taper relief is available.
- The PRs are entitled to use an annual exemption (£7,500 for 2001/2002) (*TCGA 1992 s.3(7)*):
  - for the year of death (*in addition* to the deceased's exemption accruing before his death), *and*
  - for 2 subsequent years.
- Losses may be carried back 3 years and forward during the administration period, but not after it.

3. Loss relief for capital gains tax and inheritance tax

- PRs may opt either for:
  - IHT loss relief at up to 40% (preferable if an estate is in the nil rate band/exempt), *or*
  - CGT loss relief at 34% (advisable in most other circumstances).

Final adjustments

➤ PRs should retain sufficient assets to discharge any outstanding IHT liability, including provision for the payment of tax on instalment option property, and the need to meet any further liability from:

- LCTs or gifts with benefit reserved where the donee does not pay what he owes.
- newly discovered LCTs or PETs which the deceased made within 7 years of death, and which alter cumulation and tapering relief.
- valuations which are agreed with the Inland Revenue at a level different from the probate value.
- the discovery of assets or liabilities which were unknown on probate.
- any agreement with the Inland Revenue on the deceased's pre-death liability for income tax or CGT.
- sales which qualify for IHT 'loss relief' (see p.91).
- post-death variations or disclaimers.

Steps

1 **The PRs send a corrective account to the CTO.**

➤ For minor adjustments the PRs may write a letter to the CTO, otherwise they complete a *Form Cap D3,* and send it to the CTO, who prepare a final assessment.

2 **The PRs send the CTO 2 copies of *Form Cap 30,* requesting a certificate of discharge.**

3 **The CTO return the form with an endorsement.**

➤ The endorsement discharges the PRs of liability and extinguishes any charge over the estate for unpaid IHT.

➤ Where instalments are outstanding, the discharge is partial: on their fulfilment PRs should seek a full certificate.

➤ The certificate of discharge provides only limited protection, as the Inland Revenue may re-open the account if the PRs have supplied any incorrect or misleading factual information (*IHTA 1984 s.239*).

III Paying debts

The rules depend on whether an estate will be **A. Insolvent**, *or* **B. Solvent**, after the payment of:

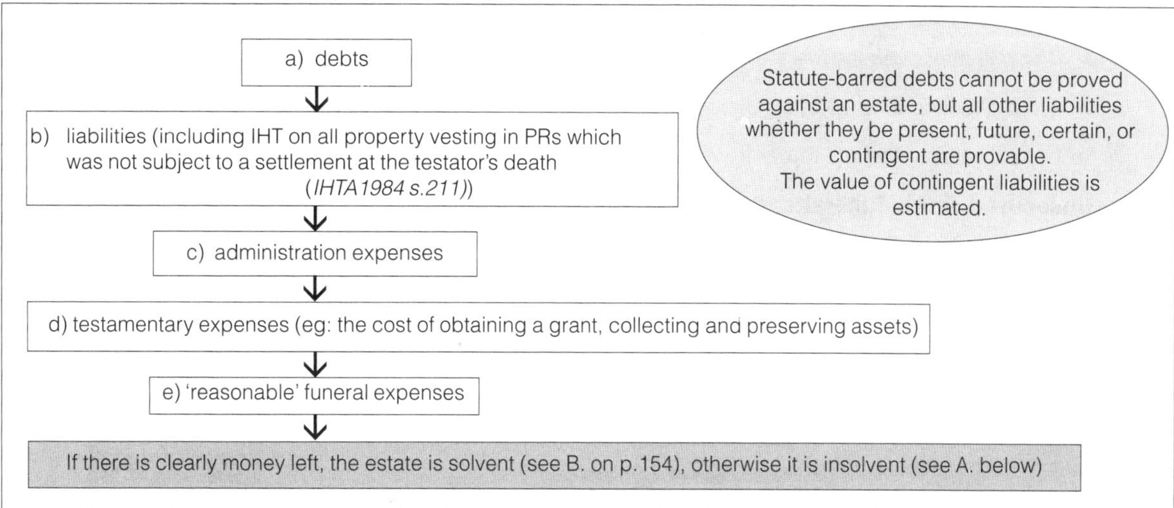

a) debts
b) liabilities (including IHT on all property vesting in PRs which was not subject to a settlement at the testator's death (*IHTA 1984 s.211*))
c) administration expenses
d) testamentary expenses (eg: the cost of obtaining a grant, collecting and preserving assets)
e) 'reasonable' funeral expenses
If there is clearly money left, the estate is solvent (see B. on p.154), otherwise it is insolvent (see A. below)
Statute-barred debts cannot be proved against an estate, but all other liabilities whether they be present, future, certain, or contingent are provable.
The value of contingent liabilities is estimated.

A. Insolvent estates (or where solvency is doubtful)

1 Secured creditors

➤ They have three options:

a) sell the secured asset and seek to recover outstanding liability as unsecured creditors, *or*

b) value the security and seek any outstanding balance as unsecured creditors, *or*

c) simply rely on the fixed charge and collect the debt whenever the estate sells the security.

2 Unsecured creditors (*AIEPDO 1986*)

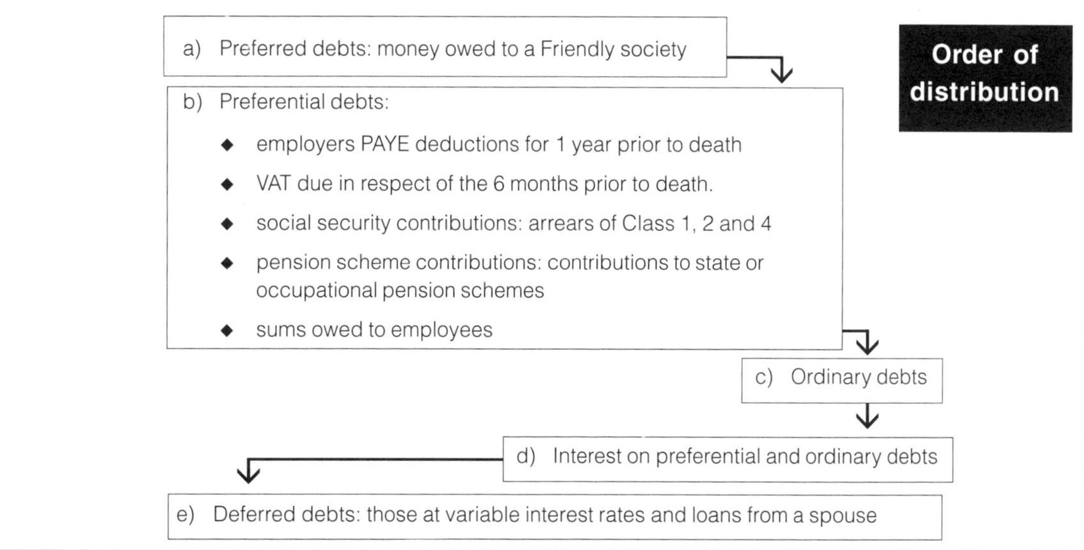

Order of distribution
a) Preferred debts: money owed to a Friendly society
b) Preferential debts:
employers PAYE deductions for 1 year prior to death
VAT due in respect of the 6 months prior to death.
social security contributions: arrears of Class 1, 2 and 4
pension scheme contributions: contributions to state or occupational pension schemes
sums owed to employees
c) Ordinary debts
d) Interest on preferential and ordinary debts
e) Deferred debts: those at variable interest rates and loans from a spouse

➤ Debts of equal priority rank equally, and abate proportionately, if there are insufficient funds available.

B. Solvent estates

1 **Property in the estate subject to any charge (*AEA 1925 s.35(1)*)**

- Mortgages, any charge imposed for unpaid IHT, or a debt in favour of a judgment creditor, is met by the property over which the charge is fixed.
- The will may override the statutory provisions by *either*:
  a) a direction to 'pay debts including any mortgage charge on Whiteacre out of residue', *or*
  b) expressing the gift to be 'free of mortgage'.

2 **Unsecured debts, funeral and testamentary expenses (*AEA 1925 s.34(1)*)**

- PRs first set aside a fund comprising undisposed of property from which they will later pay out pecuniary legacies. From this fund, they meet debts in the order dictated by the *AEA 1925 Sch. I Part II*.

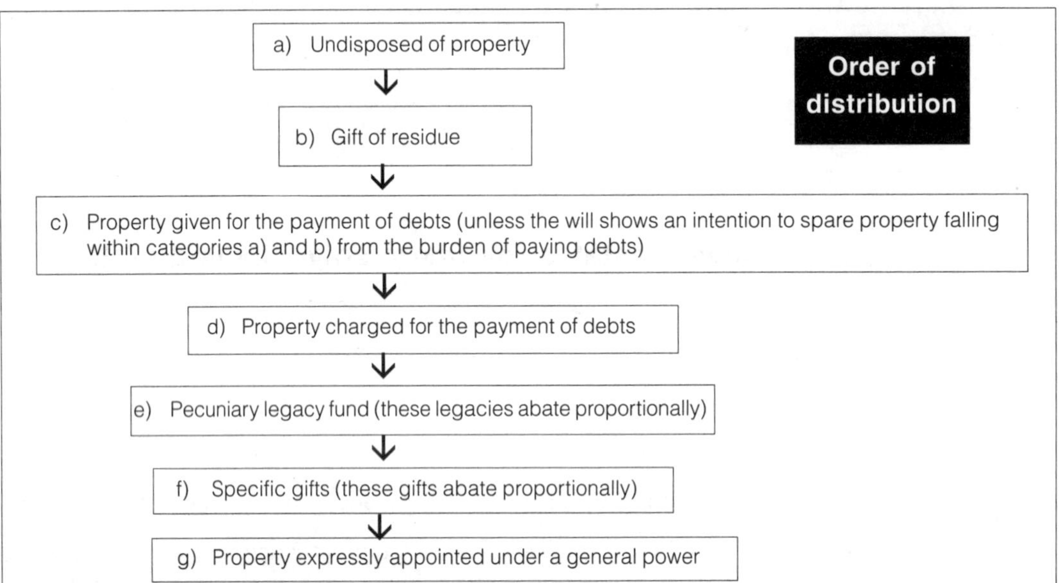

Order of distribution
a) Undisposed of property
b) Gift of residue
c) Property given for the payment of debts (unless the will shows an intention to spare property falling within categories a) and b) from the burden of paying debts)
d) Property charged for the payment of debts
e) Pecuniary legacy fund (these legacies abate proportionally)
f) Specific gifts (these gifts abate proportionally)
g) Property expressly appointed under a general power

- Property passing under a will or intestacy bears the burden of debt equally. If there is no provision in the will, property which is undisposed of (ie: on a partial intestacy) is available first.
- The will may displace the statutory order by making:
  a) a gift of residue 'subject to' the payment of debts, *or*
  b) by charging property for this purpose and stating that property in a) and b) should not bear the liability.

IV Paying legacies

Transferring property to beneficiaries

Property	Method of transfer
Personal chattels	An assent (written or oral) stating that the PRs have no further need of the items for the administration of the estate
National Savings certificates	Withdrawal or transfer forms
Shares	Stock transfer form; the grant will have to be produced
Premium bonds	These must be surrendered and the cash transferred to the beneficiary
Money in residuary estate	Cheque drawn on PRs' bank account
Land	A written assent signed by the PRs which names the person in whose favour it is made out (*AEA 1925 s.36(4)*). If the PRs are taking an indemnity covenant, the assent must be by deed. The assent should be endorsed on the original grant of representation; HM Land Registry has its own standard form of assent. *Either*: a) the PRs can register as proprietors, on producing the grant, and subsequently transfer the title to the beneficiary, *or* b) the PRs can supply the beneficiary with the assent and a certified copy of the grant so that he can apply for registration The Register is conclusive. Although it dispenses with the requirement for the grant to be endorsed, it is still good practice to obtain an endorsement

➤ The PRs should always obtain a valid receipt.

A. Identifying the beneficiaries

1 **Class gifts**

See p.137 for the rules governing the construction of these gifts.

2 ***Wills Act 1837 s.33***

➤ Where a beneficiary dies a substitutional gift is implied in favour of the deceased beneficiary's children if the beneficiary was the testator's 'issue'.

3 **Children**

➤ References to 'children' are interpreted as follows (unless contrary intention is shown).

Statute	Effect	Protection of PRs
FLRA 1987 s.19(1)	For wills or codicils executed after 3 April 1988, a reference to a relationship is construed without regard to whether the relationship existed as a marriage Wills or codicils executed between 31 December 1969 and 4 April 1988 are construed similarly (*FLRA 1969 s.15*)	This offers PRs no protection The PRs should comply with the requirements of the *TA 1925 s.27* (p.159)
AA 1976 s.39	An adopted child is treated as the child of his adopted, rather than his natural parents An adopted child is deemed to have been born on the date of adoption Where more than one child is adopted on a day, then the actual order of their births dictates the order in which they are held to have been 'born' on the day of their adoption, but this maxim does not affect any reference to their ages (*s.42(2)*)	PRs are not under a duty to enquire into adoptions. They are not liable if they distribute in ignorance of an adoption (*AA 1976 s.45*) An adopted child may seek any property to which he is entitled from other beneficiaries
LA 1976 s.5(3)	A legitimated child is treated as a legitimate one. *s.5(4)* duplicates *AA 1976 s.42(2)*	*LA 1976 s.7*: this is a similar provision to the *AA 1976 s.45*

B. Paying different types of legacy

Specific legacies

- These gifts vest from death, so beneficiaries are entitled to income accruing from death.
- If the testator disposed of the property between making the will and dying, then the gift 'adeems' (ie: it fails). If the property's form has altered but it remains substantially the same (eg: a gift of shares in a company which has been taken over in return for shares in the company, the gift will not adeem.
- The beneficiary is responsible for costs incurred in preserving the asset between the death and transfer, unless the will states otherwise.
- The PRs supply *Form 185E* stating the gross income received; this enables a beneficiary to account to the Inland Revenue and meet whatever tax liability is owed as an individual.
- Where an asset is transferred directly to the legatee (rather than sold), the probate value serves as the 'base cost' at which the legatee is deemed to have acquired the asset (*TCGA 1992 s.62(4)*).

Pecuniary legacies

- Where the will is silent, the choice of which property to pay pecuniary legacies from is determined by different sets of rules, depending upon the circumstances.

  a) **The gift of residue is valid** (ie: there is no partial intestacy)

  The legacy is paid from personalty, unless one of 3 common law rules apply:

  i) the will specifies a fund of realty and personalty from which pecuniary legacies should be paid - both types of property bear the burden of gifts proportionately (*Roberts v. Walker* [1830] 1 R & My 752).

  ii) where a gift of realty does not distinguish realty from personalty, residuary realty can be used if personalty is insufficient (*Greville v. Brown* [1859] 7 HLC 689).

  iii) the testator leaves realty specifically for the payment of pecuniary legacies.

  b) **Partial intestacy and *no* express trust in the will**

  A trust arises under the *AEA 1925 s.33(1)*. Pecuniary legacies are paid from undisposed of property (*s.33(2)* requires that *Schedule I Part I (i)-(ii)* of the Act should be followed).

  c) **Partial intestacy and an express trust in the will**

  The *AEA 1925 s.33* institutes a trust under which pecuniary legacies are paid from money realised on the sale of undisposed of property. However, under *s.33(7)* the statutory trust is supplanted by the express trust in the will. There is conflicting authority as to whether *either*:

  i) PRs should set aside a fund for the payment of pecuniary legacies in the order dictated by *AEA 1925 Sch. II Part I (i)-(ii)* (*Re Midgley* [1955] Ch 576), *or*

  ii) the common law rules (above) apply (*Re Taylor's Estate* [1969] Ch 245).

- If there are insufficient funds available, pecuniary legacies abate proportionately.
- Pecuniary legacies are payable 1 year after the testator's death. PRs are not under a duty to distribute before this period is up (*AEA 1925 s.4*).
- Interest is payable in the following circumstances:

  a) when a pecuniary legacy is unpaid after a year, or after the passing of a named contingency, whichever occurs first, *or*

  b) if the legacy is in satisfaction of a debt which the testator owed, *or*

  c) the beneficiary is a child of the testator and no other fund exists for that child's maintenance, *or*

  d) the beneficiary is a minor and the testator's intention was to provide for the child's maintenance.

F Problems which can arise

There are 5 areas in which difficulties are likely to arise (this list is not exhaustive!).

I Obtaining a grant and interpreting the will
II A claim under the *I(PFD)A 1975*
III Breach of duty by a PR
IV A PR's death
V Failure of a gift

I Obtaining a grant and interpreting the will

1 **Someone objects to the issue of a grant** (*NCPR r.44*)

➤ A caveat is lodged with the Probate Registry to prevent the issue of a grant.

2 **A person entitled to take an oath fails to do so *or* fails to renounce**

Citation to take or refuse a grant (*NCPR r.47*)

➤ When an executor has intermeddled, but not taken steps to acquire a grant within 6 months of the testator's death, then unless the executor can show good reason for his inaction, the citator can apply to court for an order allowing letters of administration to be issued under *NCPR r.20.*

➤ An applicant wishes to 'clear off' those with prior entitlement to a grant who have not applied for a grant.

3 **A person entitled to a grant wishes to prove his right when another contests it**

Citation to propound a will (*NCPR r.48*)

➤ To compel a named person with an interest in the estate (beneficiary or executor) to prove a will if they can.

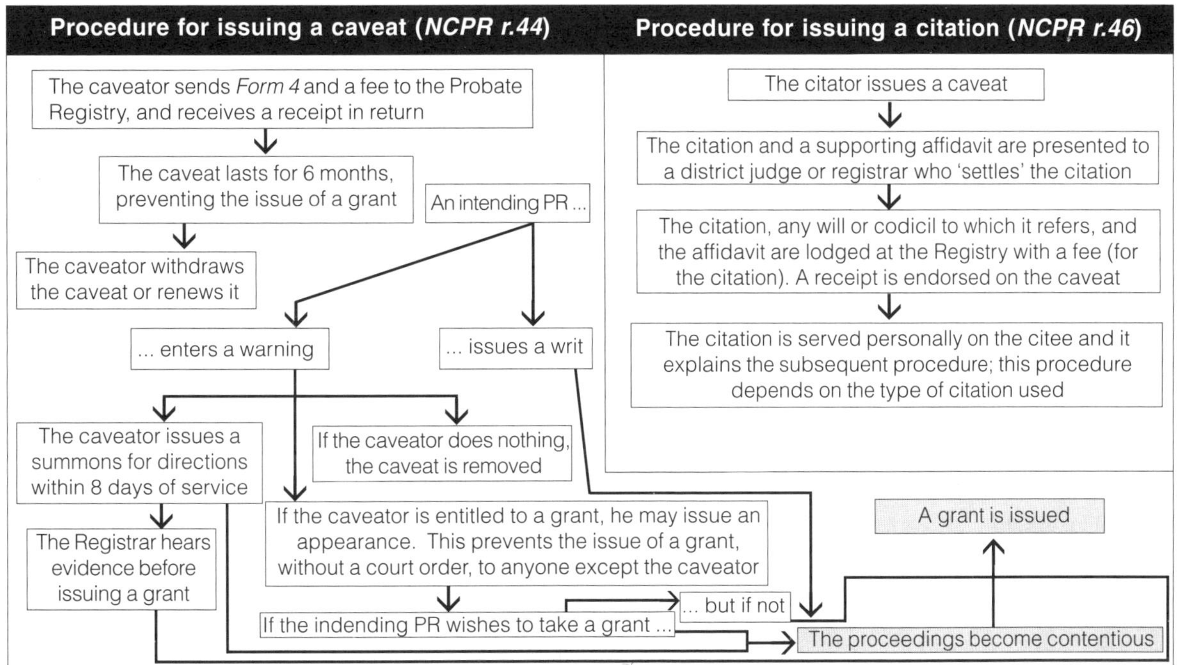
Procedure for issuing a caveat (NCPR r.44)
The caveator sends Form 4 and a fee to the Probate Registry, and receives a receipt in return
The caveat lasts for 6 months, preventing the issue of a grant
An intending PR ...
The caveator withdraws the caveat or renews it
... enters a warning
... issues a writ
The caveator issues a summons for directions within 8 days of service
If the caveator does nothing, the caveat is removed
The Registrar hears evidence before issuing a grant
If the caveator is entitled to a grant, he may issue an appearance. This prevents the issue of a grant, without a court order, to anyone except the caveator
If the indending PR wishes to take a grant ...
... but if not
The proceedings become contentious
A grant is issued
Procedure for issuing a citation (NCPR r.46)
The citator issues a caveat
The citation and a supporting affidavit are presented to a district judge or registrar who 'settles' the citation
The citation, any will or codicil to which it refers, and the affidavit are lodged at the Registry with a fee (for the citation). A receipt is endorsed on the caveat
The citation is served personally on the citee and it explains the subsequent procedure; this procedure depends on the type of citation used

4 **The Registrar requires additional evidence before issuing the grant**

Affidavit of due execution (*NCPR r.16*)

- This is necessary if *either* an attestation clause is not present *or* is corrupt, *or* there is some doubt about the execution due to uncertainty about the testator's capacity or intention.
- The affidavit is sworn by witnesses to the execution of the will.

Affidavit as to knowledge and approval (*NCPR rr.13,16*)

- This is necessary if the testator was blind, *or* illiterate, *or* frail, *or* there were suspicious circumstances.
- The affidavit is sworn by a witness, *or* anyone who went through the will with the testator and can give first-hand factual evidence.

Affidavit of plight and condition (*NCPR rr.14,16*)

- This is necessary if there are *either* alterations to the will after its execution, *or* a mark suggesting that other documents were originally attached to the will, *or* signs of an attempt to revoke the will.
- An affidavit is sworn by anyone with relevant first-hand factual knowledge.

Lost will (*NCPR rr.15,16*)

- Such a will is presumed to be destroyed with the intention to revoke it.
- If this presumption can be rebutted, or evidence can be produced to show *either* that the will existed after the testator's death *or* that a copy (or reconstruction) of it is accurate, then the Registrar may grant probate on the production of an affidavit testifying to these facts.

5 **The validity of a codicil is doubted**

- The executor(s) should commence a probate action under *NCPR r.45.*

6 **The interpretation of the will is uncertain**

- PRs may seek clarification from the court by issuing a claim for - usually this is done through an application to the Chancery Division of the High Court (see *RSC Ord.85*), but the County Court has jurisdiction for actions with a value up to £30,000.
    - The admission of extrinsic evidence is permitted if the will is a) meaningless, *or* b) *prima facie* ambiguous, *or* c) ambiguous in the light of evidence (other than evidence of the testator's intention) (*AJA 1982 s.21*).
    - The court can rectify the will so as to carry out the testator's intentions, if the will's failure to do this is due to a clerical error *or* the draftsman's failure to understand the testator's instructions (*AJA 1982 s.20, NCPR r.55, CPR r.57.12, Re Segelman (deceased)* [1995] 3 All ER 676, ChD).
    - The court can make an order authorising PRs to act as instructed by a barrister who has been practicing for at least 10 years. The barrister can resolve matters of construction which are *not* disputed. This absolves the PRs of liability and, since the court does not hear any argument, saves the estate expense (*AJA 1985 s.48*).

II A claim under the *I(PFD)A 1975*

- The *I(PFD)A 1975* allows close family, dependants and co-habitees to seek provision from an estate when none is made under a will or the intestacy rules.
- Unless the value of the claim is clearly within the County Court's jurisdiction (ie: under £30,000), an application is made to either the Chancery Division or the Family Division of the High Court.
- The High Court and County Court procedure is governed by *RSC Ord.99.*
- The costs of pursuing litigation are considerable, and the defence will often send a 'Calderbank' letter to the claimant so that the claimant is liable for costs incurred after the letter.

III Breach of duty by a PR

- The standard of duty is that of 'utmost good faith', except for professional trustees when it is higher.
  - Liability is personal and unlimited (*Kennewell v. Dye* [1949] Ch 517).
  - A breach of duty occurs if a PR fails to preserve the value of estate assets, *or* to distribute as required by the will and statute, *or* uses the estate's assets for the wrong purposes (eg: self-enrichment).
- Unless it is excluded by the trust instrument, a trustee is under a duty of care when exercising powers conferred under *TA 2000 ss.3, 8, 11, 16-7, 34* and in certain other situations (*TA 2000 s.1, Sch.1*).
  - The duty is to exercise such care and skill **as is reasonable in the circumstances, having regard in particular to any special knowledge that he has (or holds himself out as having) and (if he acts in the course of a business or profession) any special knowledge or experience that it is reasonable to expect of such a person.**
- Likely claimants include the following.
  - **Missing beneficiaries**
    - The PRs should advertise to locate them, but if this fails they should seek a 'Benjamin' order from the court (*Re Benjamin* [1902] 1 Ch 723) (see *RSC Ord.85*). This shields the PRs from liability, but it does not prejudice the claimant's (or his PRs') right to pursue assets from other beneficiaries of the estate.
  - **Creditors who are unknown to the PRs**
    - The PRs should protect themselves by:
      a) advertising in the *London Gazette,* and in a local newspaper in the vicinity of land the deceased owned, as well as placing a notice anywhere else which is appropriate (*TA 1925 s.27*).
         - An advertisment/notice must state a time period (of not less than 2 months from the date of the advertisment/notice) within which claimants may supply particulars of a claim; distribution should not begin until this period ends.

      b) searching HM Land Registry, the Central Land Charges Department and conducting local land searches to reveal any charges subsisting over land in the estate.
    - Creditors may pursue assets into the hands of the beneficiaries with a tracing action in equity.
  - **Claimants under the *I(PFD)A 1975***
    - A PR should not distribute until 6 months after the grant of representation has been issued, thereafter there will be no personal liability under the *I(PFD)A 1975*, although the estate will be subject to any order which the court makes under its discretion to waive the limitation period.
  - **Creditors who are unpaid after an 'unreasonable' delay**
    - PRs should pay pre-death debts with 'due diligence' (*Re Tankard* [1942]Ch. 69).
    - PRs owe this duty to beneficiaries *and* creditors alike; any attempt to alter this duty by will is void.
  - **Beneficiaries when debts are paid from the wrong property**
    - Where the interests of some beneficiaries are prejudiced, the doctrine of marshalling applies, so that their loss is made good from the rest of the estate.
  - **Landlords**
    - Leaseholds (except statutory tenancies under the *Rent Acts*) vest in a PR in his 'representative' capacity, and *may* do so in a 'personal capacity' as a result of actual or constructive entry into possession (see table overleaf).

Liability	Release for PRs
In 'representative' capacity (*Re Bowes* (1887) 37 Ch D128)	
Under privity of estate: rent and breaches of covenant prior to death (to the extent that property is in their hands)	On the assignment, expiry or surrender of the lease
Under privity of contract: where the deceased was the original lessee Note: abolished for new leases granted on or after 1 January 1996 (*LT(C)A 1995 ss.1-5*)	a) PRs satisfy existing claims arising under the lease, *and* b) set aside money against any fixed or ascertained sums which the deceased had agreed in respect of the property, *and* c) assign it to a beneficiary or a purchaser (*TA 1925 s.26*)
In 'personal capacity' (*Re Owers, Public Trustee v. Death* [1941] Ch 389)	
Liable as assignees of the deceased's interest for: **Covenants**: liability is unlimited for any breach **Rent**: liability is limited to rent which the PRs actually receive, or would have done if they had acted with diligence	On the assignment, expiry or surrender of the lease, PRs can seek to protect themselves in one of 3 ways: a) taking out insurance, *or* b) seeking an indemnity from the beneficiaries, *or* c) creating an indemnity fund which is distributed to the beneficiaries once the liability has ended
Note: a landlord's remedies against beneficiaries are unaffected by any of this	

Relieving PRs of liability	
Either	a) by the court if the PR 'acted honestly and reasonably and ought fairly to be excused' (*TA 1925 s.61*) (see *RSC Ord.85*),
or	b) in the form of an indemnity from a beneficiary's interest in the estate when the court is shown the written consent of a beneficiary who has been fully informed of the breach (*TA 1925 ss.62,68(1)*),
or	c) where the beneficiary (being *sui juris*) who has been fully informed of the breach of trust (known as '*devestavit*') consents to it (*Walker v. Symonds* (1818) 3 Swan 1 at 64).

IV A PR's death

- If a PR dies before a grant is issued, then his rights to the grant die with him.
- After a grant has been issued, one PR can administer the estate if the other PRs die: this is known as the chain of administration (*Flanders v. Clarke* (1747) 3 Atk 509).
- On the death of a sole surviving PR, the PR's executor steps into the deceased PR's shoes and shoulders all burdens and powers to administer the first testator's estate as well as the PR's estate (*AEA 1925 s.7*).
- Where a grant of probate or letters of administration are made to a deceased PR, and the chain of representation is broken, a grant *de bonis non administratis* is sought from the court in favour of whomever is entitled under *NCPR r.20* or *NCPR r.22* (Blackstone, *Commentaries,* (14th ed) *506*).

V Failure of a gift

A gift can fail through **Ademption**, **Lapse**, or **Abatement**.

1 Ademption

➤ As a will 'speaks from death', property given in the will may not still form part of the estate on death. If the substance of the gift, rather than its form has altered, then the gift fails.

2 Lapse

a) joint tenants:	if a tenant predeceases the testator, the remaining tenant(s) take the gift in full - the gift does not lapse unless they all predecease the testator.
b) tenants in common:	if one tenant predeceases the testator, the gift as a whole lapses.
c) class:	remains valid *unless* all members of a class have predeceased the testator.
d) witness:	this lapses *unless* the witness's signature merely supplemented those of 2 other valid witnesses.
e) divorced spouse:	this lapses unless the will shows a contrary intention (*WA 1837 s.18A*).

3 Abatement

➤ Where the estate is not able to meet all the legacies, and there is no contrary intention in the will, general legacies abate in equal proportions (*Re Whitehead* [1913] 2 Ch 56).

➤ Demonstrative legacies do not abate with general legacies, unless the fund out of which the demonstrative legacies are to be paid is insufficient to pay them all (*Roberts v. Pocock* (1748) 4 Ves 150).

➤ If the estate is unable to meet all its debts, specific legacies abate amongst themselves, otherwise they do not abate with general legacies.

Substitutional gifts

➤ A gift which adeems *or* lapses falls into residue, unless the will contains a valid gift over in favour of another beneficiary.

➤ *WA 1837 s.33* implies a substitutional gift to the testator's lineal descendants where the original gift was to the testator's children or remoter issue, and the intended donee predeceases the testator.

- There is no clear authority whether *WA 1837 s.33*:

  a) saves a contingent gift if the original donee has not satisfied the contingency before dying, *or*

  b) allows issue to take on satisfying the contingency specified for the original donee, *or*

  c) applies to class gifts 'to children living at my death'.

- A will should therefore always provide an express substitutional provision in case the named beneficiary predeceases the testator - this avoids uncertainty and ensures that the testator's wishes are followed.

Conveyancing

This chapter examines:

HM Land Registry plan colouring

- Red edging round a title.
- Green edging round land removed from the title.
- Blue shading over land subject to rights of way.
- Brown shading over land over which the registered title enjoys right of way.
- Green shading over areas of land within the title which do not form part of it.

It is not compulsory to adopt this scheme, but it is good practice to do so.

A A chronological conveyance

The conveyance is divided into nine separate steps, outlined below.

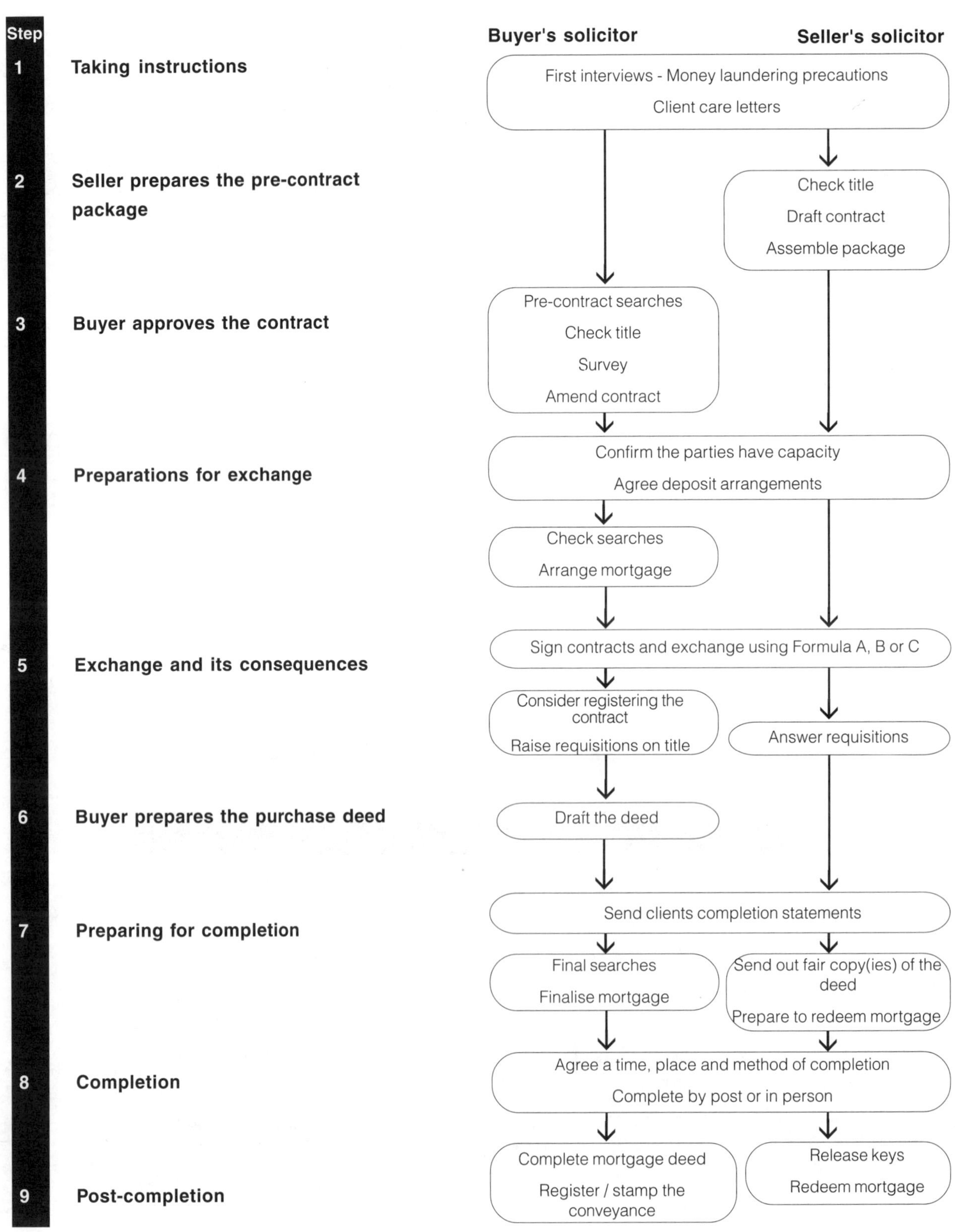
Step
1 Taking instructions
2 Seller prepares the pre-contract package
3 Buyer approves the contract
4 Preparations for exchange
5 Exchange and its consequences
6 Buyer prepares the purchase deed
7 Preparing for completion
8 Completion
9 Post-completion
Buyer's solicitor
Seller's solicitor
First interviews - Money laundering precautions
Client care letters
Check title
Draft contract
Assemble package
Pre-contract searches
Check title
Survey
Amend contract
Confirm the parties have capacity
Agree deposit arrangements
Check searches
Arrange mortgage
Sign contracts and exchange using Formula A, B or C
Consider registering the contract
Raise requisitions on title
Answer requisitions
Draft the deed
Send clients completion statements
Final searches
Finalise mortgage
Send out fair copy(ies) of the deed
Prepare to redeem mortgage
Agree a time, place and method of completion
Complete by post or in person
Complete mortgage deed
Register / stamp the conveyance
Release keys
Redeem mortgage

Step 1 Taking instructions

I First interviews

II Post-interview formalities

I First interviews

With the seller

Is there a conflict of interest? There are special provisions regarding this in *SPR r.6-6A*

Seller's name and address: ....
Seller's home and business telephone: ....
Buyer's name and address: ....
Estate agent's name and address: ....
Buyer's solicitor's name, address, telephone, fax, DX: ....
Property address: ....

Finance

- *Proceeds*:
  - will these cover the costs of sale, pay off any mortgage and/or fund another purchase?
  - where should money be paid (bank details, account number)? If the solicitor is to hold any client money comply with the *Money Laundering Regulations 1993*.
- *Deposit*:
  - has a preliminary deposit been paid? (Take a copy of the receipt for the file.)
  - has a deposit been agreed?
- *Taxation*: will CGT be payable?
- *Mortgage*: will this need to be redeemed? (Note the name(s) and address(es) of lender(s).)
- *Solicitor's fees*: explain what these will be (see p.3).

Property

- *Tenure*: freehold or leasehold? Will there be a full or limited title guarantee?
- *Deeds*: if a client does not hold them, obtain the address of whoever does (eg: building society).
- *Contents*: ask the client to fill out a fixtures and fittings form listing the property's contents.
- *Property*: are restrictive covenants breached? Have planning and use regulations been obeyed?
- *Residents:* are there any third parties with rights to occupy the property?

Transaction

- *Completion*: when convenient, synchronisation? (ie: is the seller co-ordinating a purchase?)
- *Terms*: have any particular terms been agreed?

With the buyer

As for the seller plus -

Finance

- *Money*: can the client afford the acquisition, including the associated costs (eg: stamp duty, legal fees - estimate the cost of the searches, land registry fees, etc)?
- *Deposit*: will bridging finance be needed while an existing property is sold?
- *Mortgage*: is this already arranged, or is advice needed?
    - Do not unwittingly give advice qualifying as DIB without authorisation (or, after N2, comply with the *SFA(S)R 2001* and do not give advice outside *SFA(S)R 2001 r.3* without FSA regulation).
    - Comply with *SIRC 1990* if your firm has a relationship with a mortgage provider.

Property

- *Intended use of the property?*
- *Survey*: the *caveat emptor* principle applies; the buyer chooses what sort of survey to have.
- *Location*: are plans, or special searches necessary?
- *Insurance:* how will the buyer protect himself from exchange to completion?

Transaction

- *Who is buying the property*: is advice about co-ownership needed?
    - For a joint tenancy the 'four unities' must be present - of 'possession', 'interest', 'title' and 'time' (known as 'PITT'). If a joint tenant dies, the property passes to the survivor(s).
    - A tenancy in common arises if the 'four unities' are not present, if severance is implied or stated in a conveyance or transfer *or* under an equitable presumption. Tenants' share(s) pass by will or under the intestacy rules.
- *Client's present residence*: will it be sold, or will notice have to be given to a landlord?

II Post-interview formalities

- Write the client a letter complying with the *SCICCC 1999* (see p.5) summarising what was agreed at the meeting, what will happen next, what if anything the client needs to do, and your likely fees.
    - Ask the seller to fill in a *Seller's Property Information Form* (*prop 1*) which should ideally have been supplied at the interview, but may otherwise be enclosed with this letter.
- Fill out an attendance note.
- Write to the other party, explaining who you are acting for and how you can be contacted.
    - Explain whether you intend to use the *Law Society's Standard Terms and Conditions* and whether you wish to follow the *Law Society's Protocol* (4th ed., May 2001).
    - The *Protocol* should only be used if the other party is represented by a solicitor or a licensed conveyancer.
- Write to the estate agents to inform them you have been instructed and to ask for a copy of their particulars. (These provide information about the property which it is useful to have on file.)

Step 2 Seller prepares the pre-contract package

I Check details of the seller's title

II Draft the contract

III Assemble the pre-contract package

I Check details of the seller's title

➤ Find and trace the root of title (see pp.197-202).

Unregistered land	Registered land
Obtain title deeds ◆ If a mortgagee holds the deeds as security, he will usually release them in return for an undertaking from the solicitor that he will be paid first out of any proceeds of sale	Obtain office copy entries of the Register

II Draft the contract

➤ All contracts take a similar form, and will generally include three sections:

a) parties to the sale.

b) conditions of the sale.

c) memorandum of agreement.

➤ For the sake of convenience, the *Law Society* has produced *Standard Terms and Conditions.* These provide the model around which the following guide is based.

➤ When drafting a contract there are three layers of terms.

- ◆ The first layer is the open contract rules: these are terms which common law implies into contracts in the absence of any contrary intention between the parties.
- ◆ The second layer is the 'Standard Terms and Conditions' (*StC*): these form the backbone of the *Law Society's Standard Terms and Conditions,* and are found in small print on the inside pages of the Law Society's contract.
- ◆ The third layer is the 'Special Conditions' (*SpC*): these override the *Standard Terms and Conditions,* and are found on the back page of the Law Society's contract.

➤ Check the accuracy of responses supplied by a seller against the title deeds or otherwise in the solicitor's possession (a failure to do this could be a breach of *SPR r. 1* as a failure to act in the client's best interests).

Complete the *Standard Terms and Conditions*

Agreement date	Leave this blank on the draft; fill it in on the engrossed contract on exchange
Seller	Seller's full name and address
Buyer	Buyer's full name and address

Property **Freehold / Leasehold**	Delete 'Freehold' or 'Leasehold' as applicable **Plan** The contract should state whether a plan is: a) 'for identification purposes only' - the verbal description of the property prevails, *or* b) 'as more particularly delineated on the plan'. The plan prevails if doubt arises A scale of 1:1,250 is sufficient, except for flats and units which need a smaller scale Do not rely on the Land Registry plan - it is only for 'general purposes of identification' (*LRR r.278*) The seller is not usually obliged to make a statutory declaration (*StC 4.3.1*), but where the physical extent of the property is uncertain the buyer should insist that he does so The plan is usually paid for by: a) the seller if it is reasonable of the buyer to require one (*StC 4.3.2*), *or* b) the buyer in other circumstances Include any appurtuances (easements and rights from which the title benefits)

Root of title/ Title number	*Unregistered land*: describe the root of title eg: 'the conveyance dated . . between . . (1) and . . . (2)' *Registered land*: the title number on the Property Register

Incumbrances on the property	The seller should disclose: a) latent defects affecting the title to the property, *and* b) anything the seller does, or should, know about (*StC 3.2.2.1(c)*), *and* c) overriding interests in the property held by a third party, *and* d) the existence of any occupiers The seller should disclose fully, as *SpC 2* prevents the buyer raising questions about incumbrances at a later date, provided they have been disclosed in the contract The seller need *not* disclose: a) his mortgage (*StC 3.1.2(d)* obliges the seller to remove this before the sale), *or* b) physical defects apparent on inspection (*StC 3.1.2(b)* puts the buyer on notice of these) Note that the buyer accepts the property in the physical state it is in on exchange (*StC 3.2.1*) and subject to any patent defects in title.

Title guarantee (full / limited)	Delete as appropriate and/or qualify by a *SpC* if appropriate. If this is left blank, the seller gives full title guarantee (*StC 4.5.2*) The *LP(MP)A 1994* implies covenants into a contract governing the disposition of land (whether or not for valuable consideration). The covenants affirm that in the purchase deed the disposer: 1 has the right to dispose of the property (*s.2(1)*), *and* 2 will at his own cost give the title he purports to give (ie: title which is sufficient to satisfy the Chief Land Registrar) (*s.2(2)*), *and* ***a) a beneficial freeholder may give a full title guarantee*** 3 that the title is free of all charges and incumbrances and third party rights (*s.3(1)*) ***b) a trustee, fiduciary, PR or mortgagee (s.12) may give a limited title guarantee*** 4 that no right or charge over the property has been granted to a third party since the last disposition for value (*s.3(3)*) NB: a trustee appointed to overreach an equitable interest will generally not give any title garantee ***c) a leaseholder (s.4) (in addition to 1-3, or 1,2 & 4) covenants that at the time of the disposition:*** 5 there is no breach of the tenant's obligations and nothing to render the lease liable to forfeiture, *and* 6 the lease is valid and subsisting ***d) a mortgagor covenants to perform all enforceable obligations under a rentcharge or lease (s.5)*** Note that these covenants may be modified by deleting *SpC 3* and drafting an appropriate *SpC*

Completion date	Under the open contract rules, this is in a 'reasonable time' *StC 6.1.1* specifies that completion will occur 20 working days after the contract date and that time is not of the essence unless a notice to complete is served If another date is envisaged fill it in here

Contract rate	This is the rate of interest at which compensation is paid for delayed completion (*StC 7.3.2*) The rate is 'The Law Society's interest rate from time to time in force' (*StC 1.1(g)*); this rate is currently 4% above Barclays base rate

Purchase price	Fill this in as agreed

Deposit	This is 10% of the purchase price (*StC 2.2.1*) If the sum agreed differs, then fill in the agreed value here If the deposit is held as 'agent' for the seller (rather than stakeholder), then draft a *Special Condition* to this effect; this may, for example, happen where the seller is buying another property and wishes to use the deposit monies for the purchase

Amount for chattels	Fill this in as agreed (details are found on the *Fixtures, Fittings and Contents Form*), or delete *SpC 4*

Balance	Add together the 'Purchase price' and the 'Amount of chattels', then subtract the 'Deposit' Stamp duty may be payable on the sale if the consideration exceeds £60,000; the value of chattels is disregarded in working out how much (if any) stamp duty is payable

Consider drafting *Special Conditions*:

Chattels	If the sale includes these, a *Fixtures, Fittings and Contents Form* should accompany the contract If chattels are not part of the sale, delete *SpC 2*
Vacant possession	Delete one of the alternative versions of *SpC 5* If the property is subject to leases or tenancies, then insert the details here
Liability on covenants	*StC 4.5.4* makes the buyer indemnify the seller against all future breaches of covenants. The buyer may seek a *SpC* that '*StC 4.5.4* shall not apply' The buyer's solicitor may try to include a *SpC* under which the seller indemnifies the buyer for any past breaches, *or* any which are current on the day of completion
Insurance	Common law passes risk to the buyer on exchange unless loss is due to the seller's lack of care *StC 5.1.1* places risk with the seller until completion. Unfortunately, under this *StC*: a) the seller is under no obligation to insure the property during this time (*StC 5.1.3*), *and* b) the buyer may rescind if damage prevents the seller completing with the property in substantially the same state as on exchange (*StC 5.1.2(a)*) There are various possible solutions via *Special Conditions* to the lack of certainty this creates: a) oblige the seller to insure to completion, ensure that the terms of the policy protect the buyer's interest in the property (and that the buyer receives written notice that his interest is noted on the policy) b) cover the property under a block policy maintained by the solicitor c) take out a special policy (this is expensive and may lead to 'double insurance' and disputes between insurance companies over liability) d) seek agreement from a buyer or potential lender (eg: building society) to cover the risk Note: lenders often prefer it if the buyer to whom they will lend the purchase price takes the risk rather than leaving it up to the seller
Occupation by the buyer prior to completion	*StC 5.2* sets out terms under which, with the seller's consent, the buyer may occupy the property prior to completion. If these terms are inappropriate, an alternative *SpC* should be drafted
Void conditions	Conditions will be void that: ➤ oblige a trustee to obtain consent from beneficiaries (*LPA s.42(1)*) ➤ restrict the buyer's choice of solicitor (*LPA s.48*) - this is also a breach of *SPR r.1* ➤ require the buyer to pay for the stamping of improperly stamped documents - this is the seller's responsibility (*SA 1891 ss.14(4), 117*)

Draft any other releases or documents which are necessary to accompany the contract.

➤ If a third party is in occupation that person may have an overriding interest or an interest under a trust of land, he or she should *either* be joined to the contract, *or* should sign a release:

> 'In consideration of the buyer entering this contract I, [..................]:
>
> a) [declare that I have no interest in or claim over the Property] / [give up any claim in or interest I may have over the Property];
>
> b) agree to the sale of the Property under this contract and will vacate the Property on or before completion of the contract; and
>
> b) will not register any rights over the Property, whether under the *FLA 1996* or otherwise, and I will ensure that any registrations made by me are removed before completion of the contract.'

- This should estop such a third party from entering a claim in equity.

◆ A child under the age of 18 should not have have an equitable interest, assuming that it has not paid anything towards the cost of the property and occupies the property because its parents live there.

➤ Alternatively, appoint the third party as a trustee over the land and join them as such to the contract. This:

a) ensures any equitable interest the third party may have is overreached, *and*

b) binds the third party to vacate the property (*SpC 5*), *and*

c) implies a term into the contract that the third party will, prior to completion, remove the registration of that person's rights under the *FLA 1996*.

III Assemble the pre-contract package

Unregistered land	Registered land
Certified copies of documents which must be included in the title: ➤ Evidence of devolutions on death - death certificates, assents, grants of representation ➤ Evidence of any change of name of an estate owner - marriage certificate, deed poll, etc ➤ Discharges of any legal mortgages ➤ Pre-root documents specifying restrictive covenants ➤ Memoranda endorsed on documents of title, eg: sale of part, assent to a beneficiary, severance of a joint tenancy ➤ Power of attorney (under which a document within the chain of title has been executed) Include an Index Map search (so the buyer can see that the land has not been registered)	*LRA s.110*: a) Copy of Register entries b) Copy of file plan ➤ Evidence or an abstract if registered title is inconclusive about anything ➤ A copy or an abstract of any document mentioned on the Register *StC 4.2.1* ➤ Requires Office Copy Entries (OCEs) rather than copies of the Register entries ➤ a) and b) may *not* be excluded by a *Special Condition*

- ➤ TWO copies of the draft contract
- ➤ Evidence of any discharged equitable interests
- ➤ Details of equitable interests which will be overreached in the transaction
- ➤ Expired leases if the tenant is still in possession
- ➤ Other documents referred to in the contract, or in the seller's possession which may prove helpful to the buyer:
    - copies of any relevant planning permission
    - NHBC certificates if the property is a new building
    - copies of any relevant insurance certificates or guarantees (eg: relating to roofing or dampcourse work)
    - any necessary consents (eg: building regulation consents)
    - any plans
    - *Seller's Property Information Form*
    - TWO copies of a *Fixture, Fittings and Contents Form*
    - copies of any searches which the seller has made (these should not be relied on by the buyer, but they can provide the buyer with some comfort if a Bankruptcy search has been done against the seller (*Form K16*) showing that the seller is not subject to insolvency proceedings)
- ➤ Notification of the seller's target completion date(s)

Step 3 Buyer approves the contract

I Make pre-contract searches

➤ For the searches necessary at this stage, see p.205.

II Check the title documents supplied

➤ The documents required are set out on pp.197-203.

➤ Questions to ask:

- is the root as described in the contract?
- is the chain unbroken since the root?
- are there any defects in title adverse to the buyer's interest?

III Investigate each document

A. Registered land

➤ Check that the OCEs are correct and that priority periods have not, or are not about to, expire.

➤ Check that any plans are accurate.

B. Unregistered land

➤ Start at the root, make written notes of omissions in the list of documents and of errors in the documents.

◆ Check

- **Compulsory registration:** do an Index Map search (if not supplied by the seller) to ensure there has been no conveyance or sale since the area became subject to compulsory registration. Any unregistered conveyance on sale since the area became subject to registration is likely to be void at law (*LRA s.123* as amended by *LRA 1997 s.1*).
- **Searches:** were these done against *all* previous owners under the correct names for the correct periods? Was completion for previous transfers within the priority period? Will completion be within the priority period (If the answer to this question is 'no', the buyer should do a fresh search.)?
- **Incumbrances:** what are they? Is there an unbroken chain of indemnity for covenants?
- **Easements and rights:** do they follow the title? Are there additions or subtractions?
- **Description of property:** is this accurate? Are plans provided where necessary?
- **Dates:** do these form an unbroken chain from the root?
- **Parties:** check the identities of the parties to conveyances (eg: their names may have altered due to marriage or divorce; if so ask for documentary evidence to verify this).
- **Receipt clause in a conveyance:** this is evidence that a seller's lien has been extinguished.
- **Acknowledgement for the production of earlier deeds:** if needed, are the deeds present?
- **Execution:** was this done by the correct parties in the correct form (ie: if positive covenants are present, did the buyers and the sellers both sign the conveyance)? Were any assents by deed (this imports consideration without which an assentee is not bound)?
- **Power of attorney:** if one was used, was it valid? A copy of the grant should be supplied.
- **Endorsements on deeds:** if needed, are these present? Are there adverse memoranda?

➤ Examine documents included in the abstract of title.

◆ Deeds must be in the correct form:

BEFORE 31 JULY 1990

- by an individual: signed, sealed, delivered as a deed. The seal must precede the signature. Delivery depends on intention; this is inferred from the signature and seal (*LPA s.73*).
- by a company: sealed before a company secretary and a director (*LPA s.74*).

AFTER 31 JULY 1990

Clear on its face that it is a deed and delivered as a deed (*LP(MP)A 1989 s.1(2)(2)*):

- by an individual: signed, signature witnessed and attested, or signed in his presence and at his command before 2 witnesses who attest the deed (*LP(MP)A 1989 s.1(2)(3)*).
- by a company: execution by affixing a seal, *or* by a director and a company secretary's signature if the document is expressed to be executed by the company. Execution and delivery are presumed if it is clear on its face that the document was intended as a deed (*CA s.36A(5)*).
- by a LLP (formed under *LPA 2000*): as for a company, except signature is by 2 members.

◆ There should be a 'Particulars Delivered' (PD) stamp from the Inland Revenue on:

a) freehold conveyances, *and*

b) grants or assignments of leases of 7 years or more (*FA 1931 s.28*).

◆ A conveyance should be stamped as evidence that duty has been paid at the correct rate unless it involved an instrument which is exempt from stamp duty and is certified as such.

IV Check the terms of any restrictive covenants

1 Inform the buyer that the covenant exists.

2 Find out whether it:

a) affects the buyer's plans for the property, *or*

b) has been breached in the past (eg: by building work), *or*

c) adversely alters the property's value (a covenant preserving the character of the neighbourhood may actually enhance the value of a property, eg: if it was imposed by a developer and is rigorously enforced).

Validity

3 Does wording effectively annex the covenant to the land? If it does not, the covenant may be unenforceable.

4 If the covenant is post-1925, is it noted on the Charges Register, or as a Class D(ii) land charge?

➤ An unregistered covenant will be unenforceable.

Options if valid

5 If the covenant is valid, consider three options:

a) Insurance: the insurance company will normally need:

- a copy of the document imposing the covenant, or its exact wording, *and*
- details of past breaches, and a copy of any planning permission for development, *and*
- the date of the covenant's imposition, *and*
- the date of the covenant's registration, *and*
- a description of the nature of the neighbourhood, *and*
- steps taken to trace whoever has the benefit of the covenant.

b) Consent of the person with the benefit of the covenant.

c) An application to the Lands Tribunal (*LPA s.24*): this is slow and expensive.

V Ensure there are no planning difficulties

Check ...

1 ... the date the property was originally built *and* the dates of subsequent additions or extensions.

2 ... that any alterations within the last 4 years *either* had planning permission *or* did not need it (and that any covenants in a lease have been complied with).

3 ... that any change of use over the last 10 years *either* did not need planning permission, *or* that it was granted (*and* that consent was granted by a landlord, if needed).

4 ... whether building regulation consent was gained *and* complied with for work done in the past year.

5 ... whether the property is a listed building *or* in a conservation area.

6 ... whether a Unitary Development Plan, or a Structural Development Plan affects the property.

Planning permission

1 **A 'development' requiring permission (*TCPA 1990 s.55*) involves *either*:**

a) 'building, engineering, mining, in, on, over or under the land', *or*

b) a 'material change' in use, (ie: not within same use class under *TCP(UC)O 1987*), *or*

c) an alteration of a listed building, or demolition in a conservation area (*P(LBCA)A 1990 s.74*).

2 **Limited permission to develop without permission is available (*TCP(GPD)O 1995*) for:**

a) maintenance work.

b) internal work not affecting the exterior.

c) use within the curtilage of a building for a purpose incidental to dwelling in the building.

d) change of use within a use class, *TCP(UC)O 1987*: Class A1, the majority of shops; Class A2, providing financial or professional services to the public; Class B1, use as an office outside A2.

e) development within a general development order, or under a local authority's *Article 4* direction.

3 **Applications for planning permission**

➤ An applicant need not own land, but must tell the owner (*TCPA 1990 s.66*); if a development order requires it, it will be necessary to advertise the application in the local press (*TCPA 1990 s.65*).

➤ There are two main types of permission.

a) Outline permission: matters which are 'reserved' must be approved within 3 years.

Work must usually start within 2 years from approval being granted for matters 'reserved', *or* 5 years from the original application, whichever is later (*TCPA 1990 s.91*).

b) Full permission: no matters 'reserved'; work must begin in 5 years (*TCPA 1990 s.92*).

➤ Listed building consent

This is required for altering listed buildings. It should only be granted after considering 'the building or its setting or any features of architectural or historic interest' (*P(LBCA)A 1990 s.72*).

➤ Conservation area consent

This is required to demolish a building in a conservation area. It should only be granted after considering 'preserving or enhancing the appearance of the area' (*P(LBCA)A 1990 s.66*).

4 **Penalties/enforcement**

➤ An enforcement notice may be served up to 4 years after a breach if there are unauthorised building operations, or an unauthorised change of use to a use as a single dwelling house. Otherwise, a notice may be served within 10 years of any other breach (*TCPA 1990 s.172*).

➤ The local authority may issue:

a) a stop notice (*TCPA 1990 s.183*): where an enforcement notice has been served, this compels builders to stop work or face criminal penalties.

b) a breach of condition notice (*TCPA 1990 s.187A*): to compel compliance with a condition.

c) a completion notice (*TCPA 1990 ss.94-96*): to compel the recipient to complete work.

d) a repair notice (*P(LBCA)A 1990 ss.47-48*): to protect a listed building; this can be a prelude to compulsory purchase.

e) a building preservation notice (*P(LBCA)A 1990 s.3*): to prevent demolition or alteration.

VI Commission a survey

➤ There are 3 common types of 'survey' which a buyer can commission:

1 **Valuation**

✓ Cheap and fast.

✗ Very superficial, it only provides a guide as to whether a price appears fair in the present market.

2 **Housebuyer's report and valuation**

✓ This is more thorough than a valuation.

✗ A surveyor's duty is owed primarily to the lender. (With very 'low' priced property there is a duty to the buyer as well (*Smith v. Eric S. Bush* [1990] 1 AC 831).

✗ A lender is primarily concerned with ascertaining the property's resale value, so the survey will not give the buyer a clear idea of any major works which will need doing in the future.

3 **Full structural survey**

✓ This is always relatively expensive.

✓ A full structural survey always provides the most detailed information.

✓ If the property is unusual (eg: has its own drains in a remote location), a buyer can request special checks.

✓ The surveyor owes the buyer a duty of care, and may be held liable in contract or tort.

- ◆ A survey is always advisable, but it should be considered particularly if:
  - the property's construction is unconventional, *or*
  - the property is in an unstable area, or is likely to be a source of structural problems (eg: mining area), *or*
  - the property is not detached, *or*
  - the property is of high value, *or*
  - the property is over 100 years old, *or*
  - a mortgage will provide only a small proportion (eg: under 75%) of the purchase price, *or*
  - alterations or extensions are planned,*or*
  - the property is not in good condition.

➤ Consider enviromental liabilities and what action to take if contamination may be an issue.

- ◆ Compliance with a remediation notice issued by a local authority or the Environment Agency under *EPA 1990 Part IIA* may be prohibitively expensive; other relevant legislation includes *CL(E)R 2000*, *GR 1998* and the *PPC(EW)R 2000*. See also DETR *Guidance on Contaminated Land* (April 2000) and the Law Society's warning card issued in June 2001.
- ◆ If a person who causes or knowingly permits (a class A person) contamination cannot be identified, liability falls on an owner/occupier of land (including a mortgagee in possession) (a class B person) and complex exclusion provisons deal with the transfer of liability.
  - Make full enquiries, seek a specialist site investigation and consider where liability rests (under contract and the statutory exclusion provisons). It may be appropriate to require a seller to remedy contamination before completion, or to advise withdrawal from a transaction.

VII Check and amend the contract

Amending the contract

- ➤ Use red ink (and then green ink) to make amendments.
- ➤ Date alterations.
- ➤ Note on the contract 'Approved as drawn/amended on . . . [date].'

➤ **Questions to ask**

- ◆ Does the contract fulfil a client's instructions?
- ◆ Does it reflect what the buyer actually wants?
- ◆ Is it concise and unambiguous?
- ◆ Does it cater for the resolution of disputes?
- ◆ Does it describe the property accurately?
- ◆ Is a plan needed, and if so is one supplied to an adequate scale?
- ◆ Is the seller offering full title guarantee and if not, why not?
    - ● If the answer to this final question is 'no', it is for the buyer to make a commercial judgment of the extent of any liability, the risk involved in the circumstances, and the likely impact on the property's resale value.

Competition Act 1998

➤ Certain agreements relating to land are excluded from *CA 1998 Part I (Agreements effecting UK trade having the effect of preventing, restricting or distorting competition)* under the *Competition Act 1998 (Land and Vertical Agreements Exclusion) Order 2000* (*SI 2000/310*).

- ◆ *CA 1998 Part I* came into force on 1 March 2000.

➤ The exclusions embrace (*CA(LVAE)O 2000 r.5*):

a) a 'land agreement' which creates, alters, transfers or terminates an interest in land, or an agreement to enter into such an agreement (*CA(LVAE)O 2000 r.2*), *and*

b) obligations or restrictions which are ancillary to a land agreement as they are imposed and accepted in the capacity of a holder of an interest in land (*CA(LVAE)O 2000 r.6*).

Eg: positive or restrictive covenants as to user, (in the case of a lease) covenants not to assign without obtaining a landlord's consent, to repair, or to insure.

➤ However the exclusions in the *CA(LA(VAE)O 2000* will not protect restrictions:

a) to the terms of trading activity (eg: by reference to a type of product, brand, quantity, cost etc).

b) which relate to any trading relationship between landlord and tenant (eg: requiring the tenant to buy only from the landlord).

Step 4 Preparations for exchange

I Precautions regarding the parties

1 Minors

➤ Provided that there is no restriction on the Register, the buyer may assume the seller is over 18.

➤ If land is held on trust *and* ...

... the trust instrument provides that a person should consent to any act of the trustees in relation to the land *and* that person is a minor, *then* ...

... a buyer is not prejudiced if this consent is not obtained.

- Trustees of land are under a duty to obtain consent from the minor's parent, or whoever has parental responsibility for him, or is his guardian (*TLATA 1996 s.10(3)*).

➤ A contract may be repudiated during a minority or in a reasonable time of majority (*MCA 1987*).

◆ A conveyance to a minor used to operate like a contract to convey (*SLA 1925 s.27(1)*), but from 1 January 1997 a conveyance has operated as a declaration of trust over land in favour of the minor (a contract under *SLA 1925 s.27* now also operates as a trust) (*TLATA 1996 Sch. 1, para 1*).

2 Married couples

➤ If the seller is married, a spouse may have 'matrimonial home rights' (*FLA 1996 ss.30-31*); these may be registered already *but* they can be registered at any time before completion.

◆ A spouse should either be:

a) asked to execute a release before exchange, or

b) appointed as a trustee and made party to the contract. This ensures:

i) any equitable interest the spouse may have is overreached, *and*

ii) binds the spouse to vacate the property (*SpC 5*), *and*

iii) implies a term into the contract that the spouse will remove any *FLA* notice prior to completion.

▪ Such a trustee would not usually give any title garantee.

◆ A right registered under the *FLA 1996* can be removed by submitting to the Registrar *either*

- an application from the spouse benefiting from it, *or*
- an official copy of a court decree stating that the marriage has been terminated,*or*
- an official copy of a court order ending the spouse's matrimonial home rights, *or*
- a death certificate (*FLA 1996 Sch. 4, paras 4(1)(a)-(c), 5(1)*).

➤ See also (3) overleaf for land held on trust for sale, or (after 1 January 1997) under a trust of land.

3 Land held on trust

- If land is held on trust, pay to all the trustees (being 2-4) or a trust corporation (*LPA ss.2, 27*).
  - If there is only one trustee (not being a trust corporation), a second trustee should be appointed *either*:

    a) before the contract is entered into, *or*

    b) after the contract is entered into (so that the seller can fulfill the covenants as to title).
  - A second trustee appointed to satisfy *LPA ss.2, 27* may not be prepared to give any covenant as to title, but the original owner who holds subject to the trust may give full or limited title guarantee.
- If a sole owner is named as the proprietor on the Register, comply with any restriction to take free of any equitable interest.
- There may be a restriction on the Register regarding a joint tenancy.
  - On the death of a tenant the legal estate vests in the survivor(s), *either*:

    i) execute a vesting assent in favour of a fully entitled survivor, *or*

    ii) insist on the appointment of another trustee and pay the purchase money to them both.
      - If a joint tenant murders his fellow tenant, the property does not pass on survivorship.
  - If there is no restriction, assume that joint tenants hold absolutely; so only a death certificate for the deceased tenant is usually needed (*LRR r.172*).
- From 1925, tenants-in-common and joint tenants held land under a trust for sale (under which they had a duty to sell land and a power to postpone sale). From 1 January 1997 land has been held by trustees under a trust of land (under which trustees have a power to sell land and a power to postpone sale).
  - Trustees of land are under a duty to 'as far as is practicable, consult the beneficiaries of full age and beneficially entitled to an interest in possession in the land' (*TLATA 1996 s.11(1)*).
    - This duty only applies to trusts created by irrevocable deed. It does not apply to trusts which exclude this provision, nor to will trusts made or arising before 1 January 1997 (*TLATA 1996 ss.11(2)-11(4)*).
  - A buyer of unregistered land who is not put on notice is not prejudiced by any limitation of the trustees' power to convey land, or their failure to consult beneficiaries (*TLATA 1996 s.16(1)*).
    - A buyer who is on notice may take subject to the trust.
  - A buyer of unregistered land is not (in any circumstances) prejudiced by any act of the trustees which contravenes any enactment or a rule of law or equity (*TLATA 1996 s.16(2)*).
  - Trustees of unregistered land must, if the beneficiares are absolutely entitled and of full age, execute a deed declaring that they are discharged from the trust. If they fail to do so, a court may order them to do so.
    - A buyer may rely on such a deed, provided he is not on notice that the trustees erred in making the conveyance to the beneficiaries (*TLATA 1996 ss.16(4)-(5)*).

Overview of the powers and duties of trustees of land

- Trustees have power to sell land and power to postpone sale (*TLATA 1996 s.4*).
  - For trustees' power to buy a legal estate in land (leasehold or freehold) anywhere in the United Kingdom, see *TA 2000 s.8*.
  - This power can be expressly excluded or modified in the trust instrument or will (*TLATA 1996 s.8*).
- Trustees of land, when exercising 'any function' relating to the land subject to the trust must:

  a) 'as far as practicable' consult beneficiaries who are of full age and beneficially entitled to an interest in possession, *and*

  b) give effect to the beneficiaries' wishes, so far as is consistent with the general interest of the trust. If the beneficiaries dispute among themselves, the trustees should have regard to the wishes of the majority (by reference to the value of their combined interests under the trust) (*TLATA 1996 s.11(1)*).

    - This does not apply either to trusts which expressly exclude this requirement *or* to will trusts which arose before 1 January 1997 (*TLATA 1996 s.11(2)*).
    - This only applies to trusts created before 1 January 1997, if such of the settlor(s) who are still alive and of full capacity execute(s) a deed making an irrevocable election that it shall apply (*TLATA 1996 ss.11(3)-(4)*).
- If the beneficiares are of full age and absolutely entitled the trustees may, having obtained their consent, partition land, convey it to them or mortgage it to pay the beneficiaries 'equality money' *(TLATA 1996 s.7*).
  - This power can be expressly excluded or modified in the trust instrument (*TLATA 1996 s.8*).
- If beneficiaries are of full age and absolutely entitled to an interest in possession, the trustees may delegate, by power of attorney, any of their functions as trustees which relate to the land (*TLATA 1996 s.9*).
- Trustees may not act so as to prevent *any* person occupying land from remaining in occupation, or so as to make it likely that *any* person might cease to occupy land, unless that person consents, or the trustees obtain a court order under *TLATA 1996 ss.14-15*.
- A beneficiary's interest under a trust is no longer subject to the 'doctrine of conversion' under which land given to a beneficiary under trust for sale was deemed to be a gift of the proceeds from the sale of the land, and a beneficiary of a trust of money to be invested in land had an interest in the land rather than the cash. Land is now be treated as land, and personal property as personal property (*TLATA 1996 s.3*).
  - This only applies to will trusts when the testator died on or after 1 January 1997 (*TLATA 1996 s.18(3)*).

The rights of beneficiaries under trusts of land

- A beneficiary of a trust of land, who is absolutely entitled to an interest in possession under the trust may occupy the land if occupation is among the purposes of the trust, or the trustees hold the land so that it is available for occupation, provided the land is not unsuitable for occupation by that beneficiary (*TLATA 1996 s.12*).
  - For a critique of this statutory scheme and an analysis of common law rights of co-owners, see D G Bansley, 'Co-Owners' Rights to Occupy Trust Land', *CLJ 57 [1998]*, pp.123-145.
- If 2 or more beneficiaries are entitled to occupy land held on trust, trustees may not:
  - unreasonably exclude a beneficiary's right to occupy land, or restrict it with regard to:
    - the purposes for which the land is held, *or*
    - the settlor's intentions, *or*
    - each beneficiary's circumstances, *but*
  - they may impose reasonable conditions on occupation, such as requiring a beneficiary to:
    - pay outgoings or expenses in respect of the land, *or*
    - assume any obligation in relation to the land or activities which take, or may take place on it (eg: comply with farming regulations, insure against a claim under the *OLA 1984*), *or*
    - pay compensation to other beneficiaries whose entitlement to occupy the land has been restricted or excluded, *and*
    - forgo another benefit under the trust to which the beneficiary would otherwise have been entitled (*TLATA 1996 s.13*).
- These provisions of *TLATA 1996* may *not* be excluded in the trust instrument and they apply to all trusts of land from 1 January 1997.

4 PRs

- PRs may become registered as proprietors of registered land by submitting the grant of probate (*LRA s.41, LRR r.170*).
  - PR is registered: the buyer should comply with any restriction on the Register.
  - PR is ***not*** registered: the buyer should request a certified copy of a grant of probate and submit it with his application for registration.
- From 1 July 1995, one PR ceased to be able to bind the estate by contract. All the PRs who take a grant must be party to both the contract and the purchase deed (*LP(MP)A 1994 s.16*).
  - Where there is a sole PR, the death certificate and the grant must be produced to show he acts alone.
- PRs do *not* need to seek consent from those interested in the administration of an estate before they sell land for the purposes of administration (*TLATA 1996 s.18*).

5 **Companies**

- ➤ Lenders may insist that the Memorandum and Articles are checked to confirm that the company is acting within its powers, but a buyer should not be prejudiced if this is not done (*CA s.35A*).
- ➤ Limitations on the power to purchase may be contained in a restriction on the Register.

6 **Charities**

- ➤ If there is no restriction, no precautions are needed. Otherwise check:
  - a) whether the transaction was authorised by statute or the deed governing the charity.
  - b) whether the charity has been granted an exemption certificate under the *Charities Act 1992*.
  - c) if there is no exemption certificate, whether consent has been gained. This needs evidence that:
    - the trustees are satisfied that the deal is a good one, *and*
    - the land was advertised for a period, and in the way a surveyor advised, *and*
    - there is a written report from a qualified surveyor approving the sale, *and*
    - prescribed words have been inserted stating that:
      - ▪ the charity is not exempt, *and*
      - ▪ the land is subject to *CA 1992 s.32*, *and*
      - ▪ the land is held on trust for the charity, *and*
      - ▪ the requirements of *s.32* have been complied with.

7 **Mental impairment**

- ➤ A contract or conveyance for value is binding unless one of the parties is unaware of the other's disability (*Hart v. O'Connor* [1985] 2 All ER 880), in which case it is voidable. A conveyance for no value involving someone of unsound mind is void.
- ➤ A receiver may deal with property with the court's consent (*MntHA 1983 s.99*); there will be no restriction on the Register unless the receiver is registered as the proprietor.
- ➤ If a trustee is mentally incapable of exercising his functions as a trustee, *and* ...

  ... all the beneficiaries are fully entitled *and* of full age, *and* ...

  ... nobody is willing and able to appoint a trustee to replace him under *TA 1925 s.36(1)*, *then*

  ... the beneficiaries may issue a written direction to the trustee's receiver, his attorney under an enduring power of attorney, or a person authorised under *MntHA 1983 Part VII,* requesting that person to appoint a replacement trustee (*TLATA 1996 s.20*).

  - ◆ A buyer should ask to see a certified copy of any such direction together with the deed of appointment.
    - Pre-contract enquiries should include a question as to whether a direction has been made and requisitions on title could include a request for confirmation that none of the beneficiaries withdrew the direction before it was complied with under *TLATA 1996 s.21(1)*.

Undue influence

- The solicitor should ensure that the parties are not subject to undue influence:
    - the price is fair, *and*
    - all the circumstances are known to any subordinate party (eg: an occupier), *and*
    - independent legal advice is available to all the parties and they are all aware of this.
- In order to establish 'undue influence' it will usually be necessary to show:
    a) a relationship suggesting that undue influence may be exercised, *and*
    b) *prima facie* a party would not benefit from a transaction (*CIBC Mortgages plc v. Pitt* [1994] 1 AC 200).

II Searches

- The buyer should check that these are all correct, and that exchange will occur before priority periods expire.

III Deposit

1 **Where is the deposit coming from?**

- ➤ Payment is by banker's draft or cheque drawn on cleared funds from client account (*StC 2.2.1*).
  - ◆ If a client account cheque is used the solicitor must be put in funds at least 5 working days in advance to ensure it clears (otherwise the *SARs 1998* may be breached).
- ➤ If payment is from a deposit account ensure that notice of withdrawal is given sufficiently early to avoid incurring an interest penalty *and* to make certain that the money is released for exchange.
- ➤ If bridging finance is required, arrange this in good time.
  - ✓ A loan may qualify for tax relief as a 'charge on income'.
  - ✗ A loan may be expensive.
  - ✗ If the sale does not proceed liability must be discharged fast to prevent exorbitant interest payments.

2 **How will the deposit be held?**

- ➤ As agent for the seller
  - ◆ This is the position under the general law unless the parties agree otherwise (or an auctioneer holds the deposit, in which case the auctioneer holds as stakeholder).
  - ◆ *StC 2.2.2* permits a seller to use the deposit, or part of it, as a deposit on the purchase of a property in England or Wales as his residence, if the related purchase contract is entered into before completion (ie: of the contract for the seller's sale) and that related contract contains similar provisions to *StC 2.2.2-2.2.3*.
  - ◆ A trustee is under a duty not to lose control of money held on trust, so if the seller is a trustee the seller's solicitor should hold the deposit as the seller's agent.
- ➤ As stakeholder (envisaged by *StC 2.2.3*).
  - ◆ Unless the sellers are trustees *or* the seller wishes to use the deposit to buy another property (in accordance with *StC 2.2.2*), the seller's solicitor holds the deposit as stakeholder and is obliged to pay it to the seller on completion, together with accrued interest.

3 **Where will the deposit be held?**

- ➤ In a deposit account? This depends on whether interest penalties are imposed for short-term deposits and the feasibility of transferring money so it is available at need.

4 **Interest on the deposit**

- ➤ The solicitor must pay the client interest in accordance with *SAR 1998 r.24*.
- ➤ Estate agents must account to their client for interest over £500 (*EA(A)R 1981 r.7*).
- ➤ If money is held as stakeholder, interest should be paid to the buyer on completion (*StC 2.2.3*).

5 **Troubleshooting**

- ➤ Deposit insurance: an insurance policy is advisable if it is feared the seller may run off with the deposit.
- ➤ Buyer's lien: this attaches to the house for the amount of any deposit.
  - ◆ The buyer can protect it with a caution/notice (Registered land) or a C(iii) charge (Unregistered land).
- ➤ Estate agents must carry insurance against insolvency while holding a deposit (*EAA 1979 s.16*).
- ➤ If the cheque bounces this breaches a condition of the contract: the seller can treat the breach as repudiatory (*StC 2.2.4*), or allow the contract to continue. In either case he may sue for damages.

IV Mortgage arrangements

<table>
<tr><th colspan="4">Types of mortgage</th></tr>
<tr><th colspan="2">Repayment</th><th rowspan="2">Endowment</th><th rowspan="2">Pension</th></tr>
<tr><th>Capital & Interest</th><th>Interest only</th></tr>
<tr><td>The borrower makes monthly repayments of interest and capital</td><td>The borrower makes monthly repayments of interest only
The borrower is responsible for repaying capital before the end of the mortgage term. It is vital for a borrower to make arrangements to fund the capital, but if this is done this type of mortgage can very flexible and simple</td><td rowspan="2">The borrower makes repayments of interest only
An insurance policy is taken out on the borrower's life when the mortgage is granted, and this repays the capital when it matures
✓ When the policy matures any surplus is paid to the borrower
✓ The insurance policy on the borrower's life gives the lender extra security on a borrower's death
✗ If the policy does not cover the loan, the borrower must make good the shortfall
✗ The mortgage cannot be transferred unless the whole sum is repaid
Note: this is an 'investment' under the FSA 1986</td><td rowspan="2">These are linked with pension arrangements
✓ May be tax efficient for the self- employed on high salaries
Court procedure for mortgage claims
CPR Part 55</td></tr>
<tr><td colspan="2">✗ On the borrower's death the debt falls due from the estate; if the estate is insolvent and property prices fall, the lender is left with a bad debt. A mortgage repayment policy insures against this occurring (a lender often insists on the borrower taking out such a policy)</td></tr>
<tr><td colspan="4">Interest rates can be, for a period or for the whole term of a mortgage, either:
◆ fixed - interest is payable at a set rate (eg: 8%), or
◆ capped - the interest rate may vary, but will not exceed the 'cap' (eg: will not exceed 9%, but unlike a with a fixed rate the borrower will take benefit if the rate is below the cap by paying the lower rate), or
◆ variable - the interest floats, usually in line with the rate set by the Bank of England under the BEA 1998.</td></tr>
</table>

➤ Ensure that:

- if there is more than one borrower, that both borrowers are named on the mortgage offer.
- none of the borrowers are subject to undue influence.
- if the mortgage is an 'investment' (ie: it is an endowment mortgage), that the firm has the necessary authorisation to provide advice and that the *FSA 1986/FSMA 2000* are complied with.
- the borrower is aware of the repayments and can afford them (even, if the mortgage carries interest at a variable rate, when interest rates rise).
- the borrower knows the overall cost of the mortgage (eg: the lender may insist the property is insured under its own block policy *and* that the borrower pays for this).
- the buyer has enough money in hand, after moving expenses, to proceed with the purchase.
- retentions for repair work are not such as to prevent the borrower meeting his financial obligations. If the lender retains some of the capital until specified repairs have been done, this may cause additional financing difficulties.
    - The seller may allow the buyer access before completion to carry out work the lender requires. The lender will then release the whole of the loan to enable the buyer to complete.

- any conditions attached to the mortgage are not too onerous. Explain the effect of any conditions to the client, eg the terms of the mortgage may:
    - prohibit the borrower letting part of the property without the lender's consent, *and/or*
    - require the borrower to repair or alter the property (can the borrower afford to comply?), *and/or*
    - impose penalites for early redemption (this is common if the lender offers the borrower favourable terms as an inducement to select a particular mortgage, eg: a low rate of interest for an initial period), *and/or*
    - oblige the borrower to give a full title guarantee to the lender in the mortgage deed (This may present difficulties if the borrower does not receive full title guarantee from the seller).
- any guarantee premium (also known as a 'mortgage indemnity') which the lender demands is satisfactory. Is this sufficient to protect the borrower if house prices fall below the purchase price (known as the 'negative equity' trap)? Is the premium expensive?
    - If acting for the lender, note that the lender will only be able to recover the difference between the correct valuation and the negligent one (ie: not the fall in market values), *South Australia Asset Management Corporation v. York Montague Limited* [1996] 3 All ER 365, HL.
- there is no conflict if the lender instructs the buyer's solicitor. (Comply with *SPR r.6*)
    - If acting for a lender check whether the lender's instructions follow the *CML Lender's Handbook for England and Wales*.
        - This handbook, first published in July 1999 by the Council of Mortgage Lenders, is intended for use under the revised *SPR r.6(3)* from 1 October 1999. *Part 1* contains general instructions. *Part 2* comprises instructions for Halifax, Abbey National, Cheltenham & Gloucester, Woolwich, Nationwide, Alliance & Leicester and Natwest Mortgages Services , other lenders send their *Part 2* directly to conveyancers (For a copy of the handbook go to *http://www.cml.org.uk*).
    - If a conflict of interest arises subsequently, the solicitor must cease acting, but he may not tell the other party the reason why as this would breach the duty of confidentiality.
- once a satisfactory offer has been made, the buyer accepts it within the time allowed.
- any arrangements with a mortgagee are co-ordinated with the rest of the transaction: with a repayment mortgage, mortgage insurance should be taken out so that the mortgage policy will be redeemed if the borrower dies.
- the borrower is aware of, and takes out, appropriate insurance policies (lenders may insist on some/all of these):

    a) **Endowment policy** - suitable only for an endowment mortgage, covers the borrower's life.

    b) **Mortgage indemnity policy** - provides protection when the loan is for a high percentage (eg: 80% or more) of the purchase price.

    c) **Mortgage repayment policy** - pays off the mortgage if the borrower dies prior to redemption.

    d) **Mortgage payment protection policy** - will pay amounts due under the mortgage while the borrower is unemployed.

    e) **Building insurance** - offers cover if the building is subject to subsidence, fire, flooding, storm damage, etc. If part of a property (eg: a flat) is subject to a policy taken out by the landlord for the whole building, a lender may be satisfied with the landlord's policy if that policy meets its requirements.

    - Risk moves to the borrower in accordance with common law or the provisions of the contract.

Step 5 Exchange and its consequences

I Exchange

II Consequences of exchange

I Exchange

➤ The contract is signed.

- *Either* both parties sign one contract *or* they each sign identical copies (*LP(MP)A 1989 s.2*). For a contract to be binding under *s.2,* documents containing the terms of the contract must actually be exchanged (*Commission for the New Towns v. Cooper (Great Britain) Limited* [1995] EG 26 129).
- The signatures need not be witnessed.
- A solicitor may sign, but should do so *either* under a power of attorney *or* with express written authority.
  - Failure to obtain the proper authority may be a breach of warranty of authority (*Suleman v. Shahisavari* [1989] 2 All ER 460).

➤ Do not exchange without a client's express written authority to do so.

➤ Exchange using either *Formula A, B, or C* (see box below) via:

- telephone (make a file note of the time of the exchange), *or*
- post (*StC 2*): a contract is made when the contract (or the last copy, if more than one) is posted, *or*
- personally (usually at the office of the seller's solicitors), *or*
- DX *(StC 2*): a contract is made when the contract (or the last copy, if more than one) is deposited at the DX, *or*
- fax (*StC 1.3.3*): for messages required under one of the Law Society's *Formulae* (ie: not to exchange the contract itself). A fax must be confirmed with hard copies as soon as possible.

Formula A	Formula B	Formula C
When one solicitor holds both contracts	When each solicitor holds their client's contract	For a 'chain' of transactions Each solicitor holds their client's contract and exchange is by telephone

➤ After exchange has taken place:

- make an attendance note.
- notify the insurer of the property (*StC 5.1* provides for the seller to bear the risk until completion).
- inform client/lender
- comply with undertakings given under the exchange *Formula* and deal with the deposit in accordance with the contract and the *SARs*.
- if acting for the seller, write to any mortgagee asking for the confirmation of the amount required to redeem the mortgage on completion.
- consider registering the contract.

II Consequences of exchange

- ➤ Any subsequent variation to the contract which is agreed between the parties must comply with the *LP(MP)A 1989 s.2* (see previous page) (*McCausland and Another v. Duncan Lawrie Limited*, The Times, 18 June 1996, CA).

1 Consider whether to register the contract

- ➤ This is advisable if:
  - a) the seller's good faith is doubted, *or*
  - b) a dispute arises, *or*
  - c) there are more than 2 months between exchange and completion, *or*
  - d) the seller delays completion beyond the contractual date, *or*
  - e) the transaction is a sub-sale.
    - ◆ Unregistered land: register the contract as a Class C(iv) land charge.
    - ◆ Registered land: enter a caution/notice on the Register as a minor interest in the land.

2 Death of a party

- ➤ PRs are bound to complete a contract which the deceased entered. This can cause difficulties for the estate as the buyer's death may lead to a revocation of the mortgage offer.

3 Seller's bankruptcy

- ➤ The seller's trustee in bankruptcy may complete with a redrafted purchase deed (the bankrupt is not party to the deed), or the trustee may disclaim the contract.

4 Requisitions on title

- ➤ *StC 4.1.1*: these are made in writing within 6 working days of exchange, *or* when evidence of the seller's title is delivered to the buyer, whichever is later. The seller replies within 4 working days.
- ➤ Common law: the buyer accepts the seller's title on delivery of the draft purchase deed to the seller. Often the draft deed is submitted with requisitions on title.
  - ◆ *StC 4.5.1.* preserves the buyer's right to raise requisitions.

Step 6 Buyer prepares the purchase deed

1 Procedure

➤ At least 12 working days before completion the buyer sends the seller a draft of the deed: 2 copies, one of which is engrossed (*StC 4.1.2*).

➤ The seller's solicitor replies with any queries within 4 working days of the draft being delivered to him (*StC 4.1.2*).

➤ The buyer must deliver an engrossment to the seller at least 5 days before completion (*StC 4.1.2*).

- *Protocol 7.1*: the draft deed and requisitions on title should be submitted as soon as possible after exchange, and within time limits set by the contract.

2 Form of the deed

➤ The deed should comply with the *LPA s.52* as amended by the *LP(MP)A 1989 s.1*.

➤ Unregistered land: there is no prescribed form. *Form TR1* may be used.

➤ Registered land: use *Form TR1* and ensure the execution clause complies with *LRR Sch.3*.

3 Drafting

➤ The deed should reflect the terms of the contract.

➤ Consideration (*SA 1891 s.5*): exclude chattels; a separate receipt for these is given to the buyer on completion.

- VAT (if due) is included in the figure for consideration.

4 Parties

➤ All those whose consent to the transaction is necessary:

- a receiver or liquidator.
- a sub-purchaser on a sub-sale.
- a lender with a charge over unregistered land may *either* join a conveyance *or* give the buyer a separate deed of release.
    - A lender with a charge over registered land will not do this as it will release the land using *Form DS1* or a deed of release/receipt.

5 Signature

➤ The seller always signs the deed. The buyer signs the deed if it contains a covenant or a declaration on his behalf.

➤ If an individual is incapable of signing, the deed is read to him, and it can be signed on his behalf in the presence of 2 witnesses who attest his signature (*LP(MP)A 1989 s.1(2)(3)*).

➤ An attorney signs *either* 'O by his attorney P' *or* 'P as attorney on behalf of O'.

➤ A company may affix a seal in the presence of 2 directors who sign the deed. The seal is not essential, but the document must be a deed on its face (*CA s.36A*).

6 **Plans**

- ➤ Attach these to the deed.
- ➤ HM Land Registry requires parties to sign the plan if it is to accept its inclusion.
  - ◆ Signing the plan is not compulsory for unregistered land, but it is advisable nonetheless.
  - ◆ If a company seals the deed, it should seal the plan as well (this need not be witnessed).

7 **Witnesses** (where necessary)

- ➤ For evidential reasons an independent party is preferable. A witness cannot be a party to the deed (*Seal v. Claridge* (1881) 7 QBD 516).
- ➤ 2 witnesses are required if a signature is by proxy.

8 **Delivery**

- ➤ A deed is usually held 'in escrow' (ie: conditional upon completion, signed but not dated).
- ➤ Delivery is presumed to be the date of execution unless the contrary is shown (*CA s.36A*).
- ➤ Receipt clause: this is sufficient discharge for the buyer (*LPA s.67*).
  - ◆ A receipt clause authorises the buyer to pay consideration to the seller's solicitor (*LPA s.69*).
  - ◆ A receipt is evidence, but not conclusive evidence, that the seller's lien over the property in respect of unpaid consideration is extinguished.

Step 7 Preparing for completion

1 **Send the seller (and the buyer if necessary) a letter with an engrossed purchase deed**

➤ Explain:

- the purpose and contents of the purchase deed.
- any instructions for executing the deed and the date by which the purchase deed should be returned to the solicitor.
- that the client should not date the purchase deed.

2 **Make final searches** (see p.205)

3 **Prepare and send completion statements to the clients**

➤ The seller's solicitor sends:

- the seller a statement of the sum due on completion, explaining how this was calculated, *and*
- the buyer 2 copies of the appropriate statement, together with any receipts if *either* the proceeds do not cover the price agreed *or* an apportionment is due (eg: in respect of a service charge), *or* for chattels.

➤ The buyer's solicitor sends the buyer a statement giving:

- the sum needed to complete, explaining how this was calculated, *and*
- a statement of the mortgage, mentioning how much will be advanced and retained, *and*
- the amount due in disbursements (eg: search fees, stamp duty, etc), *and*
- the solicitor's costs (plus VAT).

4 **Finalise arrangements with the lender** (if acting for a lender)

➤ Buyer's solicitor ...

... sends the lender a report on the title and requests a cheque to cover the advance. Ensure that the cheque is paid in to client account at least 5 days before completion.

... prepares an engrossment of the mortgage deed.

... checks that all outstanding requisitions and enquires have been satisfactorily answered, and advises the client of any remaining difficulties.

➤ Seller's solicitor ...

... gives an undertaking to the lender to secure redemption of the mortgage insofar as monies come into the solicitor's hands, and seeks authority to act as the lender's agent to redeem the mortgage just before completion.

... verifies that the completion statement is correct.

... prepares a form of discharge of the mortgage, and if acting for a lender, checks its instructions as to completion.

5 **Settle arrangements for completion**

➤ If completion is by post consider using the *Law Society's Code for Completion by Post* and (irrespective of whether the *Code* is adopted) make preparations appropriate to the method of completion chosen.

Step 8 Completion

➤ The contract and the purchase deed do *not* merge on completion (*StC 7.4*).

- This ensures that an action in contract is preserved after completion.

1 Time

➤ Completion takes place on the twentieth working day after exchange (*StC 6.1*), subject to any *SpC*.

➤ If completion takes place after 2 pm, it is deemed to occur on the following working day (*StC 6.1.2*).

- Late completion on a Friday afternoon involves the buyer paying 3 days' interest.

2 Place

➤ At the seller's office, or any place the seller may reasonably specify (*StC 6.2*).

3 Money

➤ Legal tender (*StC 6.7(a)*).

➤ Banker's draft: this is drawn on the bank's funds and is therefore secure (*StC 6.7(b)*).

➤ Telegraphic transfer: this is a direct credit to an account which the seller nominates (*StC 6.7(c)*).

Note: a) the deposit is released unconditionally by a stakeholder (*StC 6.7(d)*).

b) telegraphic transfer from client account is made after a cheque clears, otherwise the *SARs* may be breached.

Usual methods of completion

Postal	Personal
The buyer's solicitor and the seller's solicitor agree, preferably in writing, whether to use the Law Society's *Code for Completion by Post*. This is presumed to be adopted under the *Protocol 8.2* The buyer's solicitor usually sends the balance of the completion monies to the seller's solicitor by telegraphic transfer early on the morning of completion See next page for the *Code* (as revised with effect from from 1 July 1998)	The buyer's solicitor: ◆ brings the deed, other relevant documents (see below) and a banker's draft for the balance of the purchase price. (A cheque is not good enough as only cash or an equivalent to cash is permitted by *StC 6.7*) The seller's solicitor: ◆ checks and signs 2 copies of the schedule of deeds (and retains one, giving the other to the buyer)

In all cases:

- the seller obtains discharges for any mortgages, or gives an undertaking to discharge any mortgages.
- the buyer (on a personal completion) or the seller (on a postal completion) checks the purchase deed.
- the seller gives a receipt for chattels.

For unregistered land: documents of title are checked against the epitome of title which the seller has supplied.

- If the seller sells as a PR, *or* on a conveyance of part, endorse a memorandum on the grant of representation or original conveyance of the whole respectively.
- If the seller will retain any of the documents (eg: sale of part, or trust instrument (*LPA s.45(9)*), the buyer's solicitor marks the abstract 'Examined against the originals at the office of .... on ...', and signs the abstract.
- If any of the documents of title are missing, the seller (or a fiduciary with custody of the relevant document) gives a written acknowledgement and undertaking, both of which are fulfilled at the seller's expense (*StC 4.5.4*).

Law Society's Code for Completion by Post

- A solicitor must expressly agree to adopt the *Code*, preferably in writing (*para 1).*
  - Alterations must be agreed in advance and be in writing (*Preamble*).

1 Before completion

- The seller's solicitor **specifies in writing** to the buyer's solicitor the mortgages or charges which will be redeemed or discharged on or before completion to the extent that they relate to the property (*para 3*).
- The seller's solicitor **undertakes**:

  a) to have the seller's authority to receive the purchase money on completion, *and*

  b) on completion to have the authority of the proprietor of each mortgage or charge to receive the sum intended to repay it (*para 4(i)-(ii)*), *and*

  c) not to complete until he has the buyer's solicitor's instructions to do so (*para 4(iv)*).

  - The seller's solicitor **undertakes** that, notwithstanding a) and b), if he does not have the necessary authorities, he will advise the buyer's solicitor *either:*
    - no later 4pm on the working day before the completion date that he does not have the authorities referred to in a) and b) above,*or*
    - immediately if any authority is subsequently withdrawn (*para 4(iii)*).
- The buyer's solicitor sends the seller's solicitor instructions as to (*para 5*):

  i) documents to be examined and marked', *and*

  ii) memoranda to be endorsed, *and*

  iii) undertakings to be given, *and*

  iv) deeds and documents (eg: relating to rents, deposits, keys) to be sent after completion to the buyer ('*para 5(iv) documents*'), *and*

  v) any other relevant matters.

  - If no instructions are given the seller's solicitor is under no duty to examine, mark or endorse a document.
- The buyer's solicitor remits to the seller's solicitor the completion amount (notified in writing by the seller's solicitor, or else as stated on the contract), these funds are held to the buyer's solicitor's order.
  - If telegraphic transfer is used the seller's solicitor instructs the bank to telephone immediately on reciept.
- The seller's solicitor will notify the buyer's solicitor if at the time agreed for completion any of these requirements is outstanding.

2 Completion

- The seller's solicitor will complete (on receiving the completion monies, or later if so agreed with the buyer's solicitor) (*para 8*).
- The seller's solicitor **undertakes** when completing to comply with instructions as to the examination of documents etc under *para 5* and to redeem or discharge any mortgages specified in *para 3* which have not been redeemed or discharged (*para 9*).
- The seller's solicitor acts as the agent of the buyer's solicitor, without fee or disbursements (*para 2*).

3 After completion

- The seller's solicitor **undertakes:**

  a) to hold deeds and *para 5(iv)* documents referred to the buyer's solicitor's order, *and*

  b) as soon as possible, and in any event on the same day, to:

  i) confirm to the buyer's solicitor by telephone or fax that completion has occured, *and*

  ii) to send written confirmation and (at the risk of the buyer's solicitor) the *para 5(iv)* documents by first class post or DX.

Step 9 Post - completion

1 Seller's solicitor ...

... instructs the estate agents to release the keys. Under the *Protocol 8.3*, the solicitor should ensure the keys are released immediately and inform the buyer's solicitor when this has been done.

... deals with the proceeds of sale as instructed, and fulfils any undertakings (eg: to a mortgagee).

... redeems the mortgage and (once the mortgagee has redeemed the mortgage) sends the appropriate receipt to the buyer:

- Registered land: obtain *Form DS*.
- Unregistered land: obtain a receipted mortgage deed.

... sends the client a letter, report and bill (for the rules regarding bills, see pp.17). This letter should make it clear that the client is responsible for informing the water authority, suppliers of gas, electricity, telephone services and the local Council (Council Tax) of the change in ownership (*Protocol 8.4*).

2 Buyer's solicitor ...

... completes the mortgage deed (eg: add date of completion).

... fulfils any undertaking to repay bridging finance (eg: from a mortgage advance).

... ensures the purchase deed is stamped and *ad valorem* duty is paid at the correct rate (see p.119). (He submits the purchase deed to the Inland Revenue within 30 days for stamping if duty is payable.)

... obtains a Particulars Delivered stamp if a freehold interest (*FA 1930 s.28*) is being transferred. He applies to the District Land Registry if no stamp duty is payable, and if the land is registered or to be registered for the first time. Otherwise he submits *Form L(A)451* when paying stamp duty.

- It is a criminal offence, punishable by a fine on summary conviction, not to obtain a PD stamp within 30 days of execution (if execution takes place in the UK) or of first receipt in the UK (if execution is outside the UK).

... registers the title and the mortgage deed, if appropriate (see next page) (*LRA s.123*).

- From 1 April 2000 the purchase price must be indicated on the land registry form, if this is practicable (*LR(No.3)R 1999*).

... if the buyer is a company/LLP, any fixed charge must be registered at Companies House within 21 days.

... makes a diary entry for the date when HM Land Registry should return the land certificate or the charge certificate.

... discharges any entries which have been registered at HM Land Registry or the Central Land Charges Department to protect the contract.

... if HM Land Registry sends back a land certificate check it and *either*:

a) retain it (subject to the client's instructions), *or*

b) send the charge certificate (together with related documents and two copies of a schedule of related documents (the second copy is for the lender to receipt and return) to the lender (and obtain a receipt from the lender).

... if the buyer has bought unregistered land from an attorney with a non-enduring power, or a power of attorney granted under *TLATA 1996 s.9*, he should advise the buyer to make a statutory declaration. If the buyer dies without doing so there will be a defect in the title where statute does not offer protection.

Registration of a conveyance or transfer at HM Land Registry

1 **Time limits for registration application**

- **Compulsory first registration:** within 2 months of disposition (*LRA ss.123A(4)*).
  - Enter a caution against first registration on *Form CT1* (*LRA s.53, LRR r.64*) if:
    - a) the buyer is buying of a freehold estate, *or*
    - b) the tenant is taking a lease with more than 21 years to run, *or*
    - c) a person is responsible for applying for registration under *LRA s.123A(2)*.
- **Subsequent dealings:** register within 30 working days (by 9.30 am on the final day) (*LRR r.85*). Protection is under a pre-completion search, otherwise another application may gain priority.

2 **Method**

- Send the following to HM Land Registry.
  - *On first registration:*
    - an application (*Form FR1*), fee, documents, list of documents (*Form DL1*).
  - *On a transfer of registered land*:
    - an application (*Form AP1*), transfer (*Form TR1*), land or charge certificate and fee, *plus* (as appropriate):
      - a discharge of a registered charge (*Form DS1*).
      - if the disposition is in favour of a sole or last surviving trustee, an application for the registration of a restriction in *Form 62* (*LRR r.213(3)*).
      - if the transfer of legal title is in favour of trustees of land, or PRs, whose powers under the trust are limited by virtue of *TLATA 1996 s.8*, an application for a restriction in *Form 11A* or *11B* respectively (*LRR r.59A, 106A*).
      - the new mortgage deed (and a certified copy).
      - if the seller is a PR, a certified copy of the grant of representation.
      - if the transfer was executed under a special power of attorney limited to the disposal the original power, *or* a certified copy of any other type of attorney.
      - a PD form *LA(451P)*, if needed.
      - a stamped addressed card for the District Registry to acknowledge the application.
- The *LRR rr.308-308B* are prescriptive. If the space on a form is inadequate use *Form CS*.

Compulsory first registration - applies (from 1 April 1998) to ...

... a 'qualifying disposition' by way of ...

a) conveyance, *or*

b) grant (of term absolute of 21 or more years), *or*

c) assignment (of a term with 21 or more years to run on the date of the assignment) (*LRA s.123(1)(a)-(b)*).

- A 'qualifying disposition' is a disposition:
  - a) for consideration, *or*
  - b) by gift, *or*
  - c) by court order (*LRA s.123(6)*).

... a disposition by way of assent or vesting deed of a freehold estate or a term absolute which has 21 or more years to run (*LRA s.123(1)(c)*).

... a legal mortgage of a freehold estate or term of years absolute with 21 or more years to run (*LRA s.123(2)*).

B Checking title and making searches

I Unregistered title

A. Freehold title

Root of title

A valid title has a 'root' which may be (*LPA s.44*):

either a) a conveyance on sale, or legal mortgage at least 15 years old (this is preferable),

or b) a voluntary assent or conveyance made after 1925,

and it must be at the start of a chain which is uninterrupted up to the present day.

It is not necessary to look behind the root except for (*LPA s.45*):

- ➤ an abstract of a power of attorney under which an abstracted document was executed, *or*
- ➤ earlier documents referred to in an abstract, *or*
- ➤ a plan referred to in the abstract, *or*
- ➤ any limitation or trust over any part of property in an abstracted document, or any document creating a trust, or any limitation relating to a document forming part of the epitome.

Do an index map search to check there is no caution against first registration

Documents capable of forming title

1 Conveyance by trustees to themselves

➤ This may be a breach of trust, and is voidable unless ...

a) ... there is *either*:

i) a pre-existing contract to purchase land or an option or right of pre-emption in favour of a trustee or PR,

or

ii) a PR is a beneficiary under a will or intestacy.

b) ... the consent of the beneficiaries was obtained and all were *sui juris*.

c) ... the conveyance was sanctioned by the trust instrument.

d) ... the conveyance was executed under a court order.

2 Conveyance by trustees of land

➤ Prior to 1 January 1997 when *TLATA 1996* came into force land was held by PRs, trustees, tenants in common and joint tenants under a trust for sale. Subsequently, such land has been held under a trust of land by trustees who have a power to postpone sale and a power to sell land (*TLATA 1996 s.4*).

➤ A buyer takes free of any interests under a trust if he pays to 2 or more trustees, or a trust corporation (*LPA ss.2, 27*). A conveyance by an individual trustee needs further investigation.

- Valid receipt is not given if money is paid or receipt given by 1 person acting *either*:

  a) as trustee and attorney for 1 or more trustees, *or*

  b) as attorney for 2 or more trustees (*TDA 1999 s.7*; this came into force on 1 March 2000).

➤ From 1 January 1997, a buyer of unregistered land does not take free of the trust (even if he pays to 2 trustees) if he is put on notice of any limitation of the trustees' power to convey *or* of their failure to take proper account of the beneficiaries' interests (*TLATA 1996 s.16*).

➤ Tenants in common

If only one tenant survives, the buyer should ask to see the death certificate, the grant of representation and the assent in favour of the tenant's successor under the will or intestacy.

➤ Joint tenants

A buyer can assume severance has not occurred if (*LP(JT)A 1964 s.1*):

a) no memorandum of severance is endorsed on the conveyance under which the joint tenants bought the property, *and*

b) no bankruptcy proceedings are registered against either joint tenant, *and*

c) the conveyance *either*:

   i) contains a recital that the seller is solely and beneficially entitled, *or*

   ii) was executed pursuant to a contract for the sale of land dated before 1 July 1995, and the seller conveyed as 'beneficial owner'.

3 Conveyance by PRs

➤ If a grant is to 2 or more PRs, all must join the assent or conveyance.

➤ If only one PR survives, he can act alone.

- Check death certificates to ensure the other PRs were deceased at the time of the transfer.

➤ An assent passes the property to a beneficiary under a will. It should:

- be in writing, *and*
- be to the beneficiary named, *and*
- be signed by all the surviving PRs, *and*
- if covenants are contained, be by deed (*AEA 1925 s.36(4)*).

➤ An assentee (or buyer) should demand an endorsement on the grant of representation, otherwise the trustees may subsequently defeat the assent by making a statement under the *AEA 1925 s.36* so that a subsequent buyer for value takes in priority to the assentee.

- A donee is not protected by statute against trustees defeating the assent in this manner.

4 Voluntary dispositions below full market value

➤ These may be revocable under *IA 1986* (see also *I(No 2)A 1994* for the position of a buyer who gives value to a seller where the seller has acquired land for a disposition which was below market value).

5 Conveyance from an attorney

➤ The buyer's position depends on the type of power of attorney which the seller has: ...

- ... if the seller's attorney has a ***security power***, the buyer takes a clean title if he has no actual knowledge that the power has been revoked (*PAA 1971 s.4*).
- ... if the seller's attorney has a ***non-enduring power*** the buyer takes a clean title if he acts in good faith without knowledge of revocation (death amounts to revocation) (*PAA 1971 s.4*).
  - Examples of a non-enduring power are:
    a) a general power (over all donor's assets).
    b) a special power (over specified assets).
    c) a trustee power (over assets held on trust),
  - A buyer acquiring land from a seller under a non-enduring power, or an unregistered enduring power, is protected if (*PAA 1971 s.5(4), EPAA 1985 s.9(4)*) *either*:
    a) the dealing between the attorney with the non-enduring power and the buyer occurred within 1 year of the power being granted, *or*
    b) the buyer makes a statutory declaration within 3 months of completion that he is ignorant of the revocation of the power (usually sent to the Land Registry with *Form AP1*).
      - A purchaser is protected if, within 3 months of the exercise of a trusteee function, an attorney provides an 'appropriate statment' that at the time of exercise the donor had a beneficial interest in the property (*TDA 1999 s.2*).
- ... if the seller's attorney is a beneficiary of a trust and has a power of attorney granted by a trustee under *TLATA 1996 s.9(1)*, the buyer is protected if he deals in good faith, having no knowledge of the power's revocation (eg: by the beneficiary ceasing to be entitled to an interest in possession (*TLATA 1996 s.9(4)*), and swears a statutory declaration to this effect within 3 months of the completion of the purchase (*TLATA 1996 s.9(2)*).
- ... if the seller's attorney has an ***enduring power*** of attorney, check the Court of Protection to ensure that the power was correctly registered under *EPAA 1985 s.6*.

➤ *TA 2000 s.11* enables a trustee to delegate delegable functions, see p.140.

- Delegation may be permitted by the trust instrument, by all the beneficiaries being *sui iuris*, or *TA 1925 s.25* as substituted by *TDA 1999 s.5* which permits a trustee to delegate powers and discretions in relation to land, the capital proceeds of land or income arising from land (subject to any prohibition in the trust instrument).

➤ Powers granted before 1 October 1971 are governed by *LPA ss.126-128.*

6 Conveyance from a lender

➤ Legal mortgages: if the lender sold under a power of sale there will be no receipt on deed.

- For a building society mortgage receipted on or afte 1 January 1987, valid receipt may be assumed if prescribed wording is present, signed by an authorised person (*BSA 1986, Schedule 4 para 2(3)*) (the receipt need not name the person making the payment to redeem the mortgage).
- For a building society mortgage receipted before 1 January 1987, or for a bank mortgage, ensure the receipt names the holder of the legal and equitable title as the payer of the debt. Otherwise, the receipt operates to transfer the mortgage (*LPA s.115*); so if a PR or a trustee redeems a mortgage, the receipt should state that no transfer is intended.
  - If in doubt (or if the mortgage discharge post-dates the conveyance) make a land charge search against whoever bought from the borrower and ask for the title deeds from the lender/seller.
  - If a property is sold under a lender's power of sale, check that the power had arisen.

Documents retained by the seller

- If a seller has at any time retained documents of title (eg: the original conveyance on a sale of part, or a trust instrument on sale by trustees), a conveyance may include (*LPA s.64*):

  a) an 'acknowledgement' entitling the buyer and any successor in title (but not a tenant paying rent) to demand whoever possesses the documents to produce them at the cost, of the person making the request, *and*

  b) an 'undertaking' giving the buyer and any successor in title (but not a tenant paying rent) a remedy in damages if the documents are mislaid, or perish due to fire or undue care.

  Fiduciaries (eg: mortgagees, PRs, tenants for life, and trustees) are unlikely to have given an undertaking. If they have custody of documents, they may have given an acknowledgement.

Proving title

1 **Produce a sound root of title at least 15 years old**

- Include incumbrances not evidenced on the root, and which predate the root.
- A voluntary conveyance or assent will serve as a root provided it was made after 1925.

2 **Ensure that the root is sound**

- It should deal with *all* legal interests in the land.
- It should contain a recognisable description of the land.
- There are no elements which could cast doubt on the title.

3 **Produce an abstract, or an epitome of the title**

- List the documents comprising the root: these go to the buyer on completion *(StC 4.2.3)*.

If the root is not sound consider whether defective title indemnity insurance is affordable and offers adequate protection

B. Leasehold title

Proving title			
	Grant (lease)	Grant (sub lease)	Assignment
Open contract rules	No title is given if the lease is under 15 years	*LPA s.44*: a head lease and title root (eg: all assignments) going back at least 15 years	*LPA s.44*: the lease itself and all assignments going back at least 15 years
	No entitlement under *LPA s.44(2)* to call for deduction of freehold title		
StC 8.2.4.	The seller provides everything necessary to give absolute title (ie: an epitome going back at least 15 years)		*StC 8.2.4* does **not** apply to assignments
Effect of a *SpC*?		To exclude *StC 8.2.4* if the head tenant never asked to see the freehold	To enable the buyer to check that the lease was validly granted *if* it was granted under 15 years ago (ie: right to call for head lease or evidence of reversionary title)

II Registered title

A. The 'Register'

The Register comprises three different registers.

1 **Property Register** (*LRR r.3*)

- ➤ Describes the property. The description does not exclude extraneous evidence from deeds, etc, unless the boundaries are 'fixed' by HM Land Registry at the proprietor's request.
- ➤ It gives details of:
  - ◆ any mineral rights, *and*
  - ◆ any rights from which the land benefits, *and*
  - ◆ cross references to any related titles (eg: a lease, or head lease).

2 **Proprietorship Register** (*LRR r.9*)

- ➤ States the names and addresses of the proprietors, and gives the class of title. It notes:
  - ◆ restrictions on the right of a sole proprietor (*Form 62*), trustees (*Form 11A*), PRs (*Form 11B*), a limited company or a charity to deal with land. To enter a restriction submit *Form 75* or *Form 76* (*LRA s.58*, *LRR rr.235-236*).
  - ◆ inhibitions: if the proprietor is insolvent.
  - ◆ personal covenants: such as indemnity covenants which do not run with the land.

3 **Charges Register** (*LRR r.7*)

- ➤ Charges (eg mortgages): the Register states the date of the mortgage and the lender's address.
- ➤ Minor interests:
  - ◆ third party rights such as registrations under the *FLA 1996*.
  - ◆ estate contracts.
  - ◆ equitable easements.
  - ◆ restrictive covenants - the wording is usually in a schedule to the Charges Register.
  - ◆ rights of beneficiaries under *TLATA 1996 s.6* or *s.8*.
- ➤ Notices of minor interests: these are placed on the Register with the proprietor's consent.
  - ◆ Submit *Form AP1* with the land or charge certificate.
    - ● Registration under *FLA 1996* (*Forms MH1/MH2*) does not require the proprietor's consent, so the land certificate need not be submitted.
      - ■ From 28 May 2001, to comply with *HRA 1998*, the Land Registry automatically serves a notice informing a registered proprietor that an entry under the *FLA 1996* has been made: the proprietor may then challenge the entry.
- ➤ Cautions: these are entered without the proprietor's consent.
  - ◆ Submit *Form CT2* with a statutory declaration on the back, or (for a caution against first registration) *Form CT1*.
    - ● If a caution is entered on the Register, the Registrar can warn off an applicant.
    - ● After a limited period the right to prove the caution lapses.

Overriding interests

- These bind a buyer even if they are not entered on the Register (*LRA s.70(1)(a)-(k)*), eg:
  - legal easements and profits pre-dating first registration (*LRA s.70(1)(a)*) and rights excepted from first registration when the title is not absolute (*LRA s.70(1)(h)*).
  - squatters' rights to land through adverse possession which have been acquired or are being acquired under *LA 1980* (*LRA s.70(1)(f)*).
  - a right of anyone in occupation or receipt of rent except when there is no disclosure in response to enquiries by a buyer for value (*LRA s.70(1)(g)*).
  - local land charges (eg: planning permission) (*LRA s.70(1)(i)*).
  - legal leases of under 21 years (*LRA s.70(1)(k)*).

B. Freehold title

There are three classes of freehold title

1 **Absolute title** (*LRA s.5*)

- The State gives an indemnity if title is invalid, or is subject to incumbrances or minor interests (defined at *LRA s.3(xv)*) which the Register should show but omits (*LRA s.83(2)* as amended by *LRA 1997 s.2*).
- Absolute title is (despite it's name) still subject to overriding interests, Register entries, beneficial interests of which the proprietor has notice and lease covenants (if relevant).

2 **Possessory title** (*LRA s.6*)

- This title is subject to adverse interests subsisting, or capable of subsisting at the date of first (or subsequent) registration.

3 **Qualified title** (*LRA s.7*)

- The State indemnity excludes a specified defect in the title.
  - The Registrar may upgrade a title after 12 years or when he is satisfied a different class of title is merited (eg: possessory title can be upgraded to absolute title (*LRA s.82)*). He may also rectify the Register if it is erroneous, and pay appropriate compensation (*LRA s.83(8)* as amended by *LRA 1997 s.2*).

Proving title

LRA s.110

a) A copy of Register entries.

b) A copy of the filed plan.

- Evidence or abstract if the Register is inconclusive.
- Copy or abstract of any document mentioned on the Register (eg: a conveyance containing a restrictive covenant).
- Note that a) and b) may *not* be excluded by a *Special Condition.*

StC 4.2.1

- Requires OCEs rather than copies.

C. Leasehold title

There is a fourth class of title, 'Good leasehold' title (*LRA ss.8, 10*).

➤ The freehold reversion is unregistered, so the Registrar guarantees the lease only insofar as the grantor acted within his rights in granting the lease.

<table>
<tr><th colspan="4">Proving leasehold title</th></tr>
<tr><th></th><th>Grant (lease)</th><th>Grant (sub lease)</th><th>Assignment</th></tr>
<tr><td rowspan="2">Open contract rules</td><td colspan="2">LRA s.110 does not apply
As the Register is a public document it is possible to apply for OCEs</td><td rowspan="2">LRA s.110 applies
Under StC 4.2.1 the seller must supply OCEs rather than just copies</td></tr>
<tr><td></td><td>There is no right to see the head lease</td></tr>
<tr><td>StC 8.2.4.</td><td>Imposes an obligation to apply for OCEs
StC 4.2.1 applies so a copy of a OCE is insufficient</td><td>Imposes an obligation on the seller to produce OCEs and a copy of the head lease</td><td>StC 8.2.4 does not apply.
Insert a SpC requiring the assignee to produce OCEs which show absolute title
If the lease only carries good leasehold title, insert a SpC requiring the assignor to deduce satisfactory the superior title (ie: absolute reversionary title, or a good root of title at least 15 years before the grant of the lease)</td></tr>
</table>

III Searches

Checklist for making searches

1 Which searches are necessary? Is the form being used the correct one?

2 If a plan is needed, are 2 correctly coloured copies attached and is the scale sufficiently large?

3 Have any additional questions been correctly entered on the form? (eg: *CON29* Part II).

4 Is the correct fee included with the form (telephone first to confirm the rate)?

5 Are the addresses of the property and that for the answers to the search correct?

➤ Make a file note when the search request is despatched.

➤ Check the file and chase up any late responses with the relevant authorities.

Where arrangements approved by the Chief Land Registrar are in place, it is possible to search the Charges register electronically (*LRR 2000*).

Pre-contract searches			
Type of search	**Information**	**Protection**	**Application**
In all cases			
Enquiries of seller	The *Protocol* provides a standard form on which the seller lists fixtures, fittings and chattels included in the sale	The seller can refuse to answer questions. Misrepresentation is the buyer's only protection	*Form SPIF (+ FF & C)* There is a supplementary form for a tenant to fill in if a lease is being assigned
Local land charges	Information statute makes local authorities keep	Yes (*LLCA 1975 s. 10*)	*Form LLC1*
Local authority	Information *not* required by statute: ➤ adopted roads/sewers, *and* ➤ road schemes, *and* ➤ planning information, *and* ➤ smoke control orders, *and* ➤ imminent compulsory purchase orders	The authority is liable in negligence, subject to any exclusion clause on the search form	*Form CON29* **Part I:** for general queries **Part II and additional enquiries:** for specific matters, a charge is usually made for each item queried
Coal search	Details of past, present and anticipated mineral extraction Check the Law Society's *Coal Mining Directory* for areas likely to be affected		*Form CON29M* is submitted to the surveyor at the Coals Authorities' head office
Commons registration	A registered common, or rights of common may: a) restrict planning permission, *or* b) subject land to third party rights (eg: grazing)		*Form CR1*
Company search	a) The company exists, *and* b) it has power to buy or sell land, *and* c) it is not in receivership, administration or liquidation, *and* d) that the land is not subject to a charge	None	Companies House search
Unregistered land			
Index Map	➤ Cautions against first registration ➤ Pending applications for registration ➤ Date when registration became compulsory	15 day priority period	*Form 96*
Central Land Charges Department	Incumbrances existing over unregistered land: a) easements and covenants affecting the land b) mortgages c) estate contracts d) occupation rights under *FLA 1996*	15 day priority period	*Form K15* Search the names of all past and present title holders since 1926 (if known) for the period of their ownership of the estate Search against any owner who made a voluntary disposition in the last 5 years Search through pre-1973 counties as well as present day ones
Registered land			
OCEs	Details of title and incumbrances on HM Registry		*Form 94C* non-priority search *Form 109* OCE & filed plan *Form 110* additonal documents
Index Map	Unregistered interests in registered land	15 day priority period	*Form 96*
Law Society Search Validation Insurance Scheme ➤ For residential properties selling up to £500,000 (a premium is payable to take advantage of the scheme) ➤ The scheme covers the difference between the original market price of the property and its value with the adverse entry			

Pre-completion searches		
Type of search	**Information**	**Application**
Unregistered land		
Land Charges Department	See p.204	
Registered land		
HM Land Registry search	See p.204. There is a 30 day priority period	*Form 94A* for whole of property *Form 94B* for part of property
Land Charges Department	Details of *unregistered freehold* if a lease has good leasehold title	*Form K15* search against landlord's name
If acting in particular circumstances		
With a company involved in the transaction	Use this to check that: a) the company is not in receivership, administration or liquidation, *and* b) that the land is not subject to a charge	Companies House search
For a lender	Bankruptcy search against the buyer	*Forms K15* and *K16*
	If making a priority search against the Register, do so in the lender's name so the buyer is protected. Note that the lender is not protected if the search is done in the buyer's name	*Form 94A* for whole of property *Form 94B* for part of property There is a 30 day priority period
When a grant of probate (or a certified copy) are not available	Check that a grant has been issued to the party concerned and is still valid	Principal Probate Registry
When a party will complete using an enduring power of attorney	Check whether the power is registered, or whether registration is pending. a) If the power is registered *and* the grantor is still alive, the attorney may execute the deed b) If registration is pending, the attorney may only execute if the power falls within a limited categorydefined by *EPAA 1985*	Probate Registry *Form EP4*
If more than 3 months have passed since exchange	Repeat the Local Authority and Local Land Charges search	See p.204
If the contract is conditional on the results of subsequent searches		
House is under construction	Inspect the fabric to verify that it is satisfactory	Not applicable

Action if a pre-completion search shows an adverse entry

- Ascertain what the entry relates to.
- Contact the seller's solicitor and seek an undertaking that it will be removed prior to completion.
- If the search was at the Central Land Charges Department, apply for a copy of *Form 19* on which the entry was originally registered, to find out when (and by whom) it was registered.
- Keep client, lender and seller informed subject to the duty of confidentiality.
- Consider defective title indemnity insurance.

C Variations to the standard contract

I Conditional contracts

➤ The terms and conditions must be clear and certain.

- ◆ If planning permission is needed:
  - decide, if conditions are attached, what would entitle the buyer to rescind. In particular, consider whether the buyer may rescind if:
    - planning permission is not granted within a specified period, *or*
    - a planning application is never submitted.
  - settle who pays the fee for the application.
  - agree whether the application for planning permission should be for outline or for full consent, and the form of application.

➤ The contract should deal with all these issues and it must state unambiguously:

- ◆ the precise event on which the contract is conditional.
- ◆ by what time any conditions must be fulfilled.
- ◆ the exact terms on which the party with the benefit of the condition may rescind.

➤ Ensure there are no loopholes, except the single express condition enabling a party to rescind.

II Sale of part

The transaction proceeds as normal, with these differences.

Step 1: Taking instructions

➤ Obtain the consent of any lender with a charge over the land.

- ◆ Unregistered land: the lender executes a deed of release, or is joined to the conveyance.
- ◆ Registered land: the part to be sold is released from the mortgage by the lender completing *Form DS3,* to which a plan will be attached.

Step 2: Seller prepares the pre-contract package

- ➤ There must be a scale plan, and a definition of the land sold and retained.
  - ◆ Registered land: if the land is on a building site use *Form 102* in lieu of a filed plan.
- ➤ Adapt the contract: draft any appropriate *Special Conditions.*

Protect the retained land from implied rights in favour of the plot disposed of	Ensure that the sale does not include: any easement of way, light, or air which might interfere with, or restrict the free use of the retained land, for building or any other purpose The transfer to the buyer should expressly exclude any such rights

Impose new covenants	These should be stated expressly Covenants which are negative in substance are advantageous as they will run with the land If covenants are to be enforceable against future owners they must be: a) expressly taken for the benefit of the retained land, *and* b) registered at HM Land Registry or the Central Land Charges Department

Grant any easements in favour of the plot over the retained land	These may be needed to gain access to the plot, or connect services to it

Step 6: Buyer prepares the purchase deed

- ➤ Unregistered land: a plan is advisable, though not essential.
  - ◆ Include in the deed an acknowledgement that the seller has produced title deeds to the retained land and that they are in safe custody (*LPA s.64*, *StC 4.5.4*).
- ➤ Registered land: fill in the seller's title number on the purchase deed (*Form TP1)* and attach a plan.

Step 7: Preparing for completion

- ➤ Registered land: make a pre-completion search on *Form 94B* attached to a plan.
  - ◆ Before completion, deposit the land certificate at the Registry with *Form DP1,* giving 'sale of part' as the reason for the deposit of the certificate.

Step 8: Completion

- ➤ Unregistered land
  - ◆ The buyer marks the abstract or epitome as examined against the original. The seller also does this under the *Protocol.*
  - ◆ A memorandum of sale is endorsed on the seller's most recent title deed (*LPA s.200*).
  - ◆ The seller takes a note of any restrictive covenants which have been imposed, and keeps this with his documents of title.

III New buildings

This is the same as for a freehold, with these additions:

Step 3: Buyer approves the contract

- The contract is likely to be in a standard form which the developer wishes to use for the whole development. It may be that the seller is consequently reluctant to negotiate terms which differ from the standard model. Nonetheless, the buyer's solicitor must ensure that:
  - any restrictive covenants to which the land is subject do not unduly restrict the buyer's use of the property and any new covenants to be imposed in the transfer are not too onerous.
  - the seller undertakes to remedy any minor defects (known as 'snagging') which emerge after completion within a specified time (and/or that the buyer is protected by an NHBC 'Buildermark' insurance policy).
  - the seller undertakes to leave the property in 'ship-shape and Bristol fashion' and will:
    - landscape the development appropriately.
    - hand the property over in a neat state and remove all builder's rubble.
    - errect suitable boundary fences.
  - extra payments for fixtures and fittings (jacuzzis, washing machines, etc) are quantified.
  - a plan or *Form 102* is supplied with the contract and is accurate.
  - a 'long stop' completion date is incorporated in the contract. This should enable the buyer to rescind the contract if the work is unfinished after the time agreed. The seller may ask for completion to take place a certain number of days after work on the site is finished, in which case the buyer's solicitor should ensure that:
    - the period before completion is long enough for pre-completion searches and site inspections by the buyer and his lender.
    - the buyer has alternative accommodation while waiting for completion.
    - the buyer has access to bridging finance for this period of time, and that the buyer is given enough notice of the works being completed for the lender to put the buyer's solicitor in funds.
- If the seller offers a financing package, ensure that the buyer is properly (by a permitted third party, if appropriate) advised on whether it is suitable for his needs.
- The seller may offer comfort in the form of an NHBC 'Buildermark' insurance policy, or a similar product. A 'Buildermark' policy protects the buyer and his successors in title against structural defects for 10 years after completion. The buyer is insured against the builder's default, including its insolvency, for 2 years after completion.
  - A lender may insist on such insurance cover.
- Examine a copy of any agreement between the developer and the highway authority under which the developer will put in roads and street lighting, and the authority will adopt them at a later stage (these agreements are authorised under *HA 1980 s.38*). Ensure the agreement is backed by an adequate bond, in case the developer becomes insolvent before completing its obligations.

- Similar considerations apply to drains and sewers, and agreements with the water authority under *WIA 1991 s.104*.
- Ensure there are appropriate easements (eg: to use roads) so that the buyer will have a right of access prior to adoption.
- Note that if the bond is inadequate the buyer may have to pay for the works to be carried out or for adoption.

Step 9: Post-completion

➤ Ensure the buyer receives the following documentation, and that it is kept with the title deeds:

- an NHBC pack (if appropriate). Return the tear-off form to the NHBC.
- a 'final certificate' from the local authority confirming that planning consent and building regulations have been complied with.

➤ Before 2 year cover under a 'Buildermark' policy against the builder's default runs out, advise the buyer to carry out a full structural survey to reveal any latent defects.

D Leases

I Drafting a lease - outline points

1 Definitions section

2 Grant

- The premium, ie: the sum which the tenant pays the landlord for the grant of the lease.
- The term, ie: how long the lease lasts for.
- Starting date, ie: when the term runs from; this need *not* be the date of completion as the landlord may wish a batch of leases to start on the same day irrespective of when he finds tenants so as to ensure that the reversion dates are the same.
- Ground rent: this is often paid on the quarter days.
- Rent review: basis of calculation/frequency.

Quarter days

Lady Day: 25 March
Midsummer Day: 24 June
Michaelmas: 29 September
Christmas: 25 December

2 Easements and reservations

3 Common parts

- Identify these, provide for their maintenance and repair. This is usually done through a periodic service charge.

4 Tenant's covenants

- To pay rent, repair, not to make alterations or improvements, not to change user, or alienate the lease (eg: by subletting the property without the landlord's consent).

5 Landlord's covenants: to insure and keep common parts in repair

6 Insurance

- This can be achieved in several ways, but contributions to a block policy taken out by the landlord (or management company) ensure tenants are covered for the same risks.

7 Cesser of rent

- A tenant may cease to pay rent if a building is burnt down, or on specified events.

8 Forfeiture clause

- This states in what circumstances the landlord may regain possession. A court order is needed for an occupied dwelling (*PEA 1977 s.2*). On breach of covenant, a notice is usually served under the *LPA s.146*.

Flats: common law presumptions
a) If the tenant is not responsible for something, then the landlord is presumed to be so.
b) External walls are included in the demise, even if the landlord is responsible for repairing them.
c) A flat includes the ceiling, at least to the underside of the floor joists to which the ceiling is attached.
d) If the ownership of a roof is not expressly reserved by the landlord, the top floor tenant can occupy or alter it (eg: build extra stories).
e) There is *no* presumption that internal boundary walls divide flats from each other or from common parts; therefore an accurate plan marking the extent of the flat, common parts and rights of way is essential.

II Management schemes

These schemes govern how an estate is maintained; there are 3 types of scheme commonly used.

1 The landlord manages the estate either directly, or through an agent

✘ The landlord cannot walk away and wash his hands of day to day administration.

✘ Tenants are not given the freedom to organise things as they wish.

✘ Tenants do not have a contractual right to ensure their neighbours comply with their covenants. They rely on the landlord to police covenants which he has with each tenant.

2 Tenants covenant with each other by deed of covenant

✘ There is no co-ordination or general oversight - each tenant is on his own.

✘ Enforcement can be haphazard and difficult.

3 A management company is set up

✓ Enforcement by the company is practicable.

✓ The landlord is freed from the burden of administration.

✓ The landlord retains his investment in the reversion.

➤ There are two ways of setting up a private company (see p.239): in both cases the landlord grants the lease and covenants to provide services. Then *either*:

a) at a later date, the management company can join the lease and the landlord irrevocably instructs the tenant to pay the service charge to the company in consideration of the company undertaking the service obligations, *or*

b) the landlord grants the company a concurrent lease of the block (effectively leasing the reversion). During the lease, the company becomes the tenant's landlord and provides the services specified in the lease', *or*

c) transfer of reversion to a managment company (only if the reversion has no real value).

III Procedure for granting a lease

This is the same as for a freehold conveyance, with these additions:

Step 2: Seller prepares the pre-contract package

- The landlord drafts the lease and the contract. He sends the buyer:
  - proof of the freehold title (see pp.197, 202), *and*
  - evidence that any lender with a charge over the land consents (if such consent is required as a term of the mortgage) to:
    i) the grant of the lease, *and*
    ii) any alterations to the property, *and*
  - a draft contract and a draft lease.

Liability on covenants

- For leases granted on or after 1 January 1996 (other than under an agreement entered into, or a court order made before that date *and* assignments made by operation of law after that date) the tenant is released from covenants on any subsequent assignment (*LT(C)A 1995 s.5*).
- The landlord can protect his position by inserting a covenant that the tenant shall:
  a) secure adequate references from a future assignee and other requirements relating to financial standing.
  b) enter into an 'authorised guarantee agreement' under which the tenant agrees to guarantee the performance of any covenants by the assignee until the assignee makes another assignment (or the tenancy is assigned by operation of law) (*LT(C)A 1995 s.16*).

Step 3: Buyer approves the contract

- The buyer checks the freehold title.
- The buyer should also discover whether the lease is sufficiently marketable and whether it will remain so if the buyer envisages assigning the term before the lease expires to secure a mortgage.
  - Banks and building societies are reluctant to lend money for leases of under 60 years.

Step 6: Landlord prepares the 'deed'

- The landlord sends a fair copy to the buyer at least 5 working days before completion (*StC 8.2.6*).
  - A lease for less than 3 years does not need to be by deed (*LPA s.53*).

Step 9: Post-completion

- If the lease is granted for a term of more than 7 years, a PD stamp is needed.
- Stamp duty is payable, calculated by reference to the length of the term, the rent and the premium.

IV Procedure for assigning a lease

This is the same as for a freehold conveyance, with these additions:

Step 2: Seller (ie: assignor) prepares the pre-contract package

➤ The seller should ensure that the contract contains an indemnity for the covenants.

- **Prior to 1 January 1996 (at common law - but could be overridden by contract):**

  Unregistered lease: the burden of disclosure was on a seller *for value* (*LPA s.77*).

  Registered lease: *LPA 1969 s.24* placed the burden of disclosing incumbrances on a seller.

- **Leases granted on or after 1 January 1996:**

  An indemnity is effectively provided for (*LT(C)A 1995, StC 4.5.3-4*).

➤ The seller sends the buyer (ie: the assignee):

Pre-contract package

- the landlord's licence(s) permitting assignment (in the past and consent this time), *and*
- proof of leasehold title (unregistered title, see p.200; registered title, see p.203), *and*
- a copy of the original lease, *and*
- a *Seller's Leasehold Information Form* (*prop 4*) ('**SLIF'**) and a *Fixtures Fitting and Contents Form* (*prop 6*) ('**FFCF**'), *and*
- a copy of the insurance policy, and a receipt for the last premium payment, *and*
- a copy of the receipt for the last payment of rent and the service charge, *and*
- a lender's consent to the assignment (if required under the terms of a loan subject to which the property is charged).

Step 4: Preparations for exchange

➤ As well as checking the lease, the SLIF/FFCF, the contract, the consents and the seller's title, the buyer must ensure:

- any references the landlord requires are prepared, *and*
- a surety is found (if required by the lease).

Step 6: Buyer prepares the purchase deed

➤ Registered land: use *Form TR1*.

➤ Unregistered land: add a covenant for title.

Step 7: Preparing for completion

➤ The seller should take the necessary steps to obtain the landlord's consent.

- The apportionment of rent or service charge should be checked (this is governed by *StC 6.3.5*). The buyer should ask to see service charge accounts for recent years.

Step 9: Post-completion

➤ Stamp duty is payable on the transfer or assignment of lease (see p.119). A licence is not generally dutiable, provided that if it is by deed it has a certificate as required by the *SD(EI)R 1987*.

➤ A PD stamp is needed if the lease has more than 7 years to run (*FA 1930 s.28*).

➤ Send two copies of a notice of dealing to the landlord (and lender if appropriate) - the second copy to be receipted and returned.

V Obtaining a landlord's consent to an assignment or transfer

Transfer of part - leases granted after 1 January 1996

➤ The general rule is that the tenant ceases to be liable for the covenants given by the tenant, or to be entitled to the benefits of covenants given by the landlord, in respect of the part of the premises which he assigns (*LT(C)A 1995 s.5(3)*).

➤ If the performance of a covenant is not attributable to the tenant or the assignee, the parties can agree to apportion liability (*LT(C)A 1995 s.9*) provided that within 4 weeks of the assignment the parties serve a notice on the landlord detailing the assignment, their agreement and their request that he should be bound by the apportionment.

- ◆ If the landlord does not serve a notice objecting to the apportionment within 4 weeks of service on him, he is bound (if he does object, the parties may apply to the County Court for a declaration that it is reasonable for the apportionment to bind him) (*LT(C)A 1995 s.10*).
  - ● A notice should comply with the *LT(C)A(N)R 1995*.

1 **Qualified covenants** (ie: where the landlord covenants not to unreasonably withhold consent)

➤ Consent may not be unreasonably withheld (*LTA 1927 s.19*).

- ◆ For leases granted on or after 1 January 1996 (except those granted under an agreement or court order dated before that date) ...

  ... over property which is *not* let as a private residence, ...

  ... the landlord shall not be regarded as acting unreasonably if he refuses to grant consent, or agrees to grant it subject to conditions if the landlord cites a reason listed in an agreement with the tenant (eg: not to assign without securing for the landlord adequate references) (*LTA 1927 s.19A*).

➤ The landlord must respond within a 'reasonable' time, and must grant consent unless it is reasonable to withhold it (*International Drilling Fluids Ltd v. Louisville Investments (Uxbridge) Ltd* [1986] 1 EGLR 39).

- ◆ The landlord must send the tenant a notice giving any conditions attached to the consent or reasons for refusing it (*LTA 1988 s.1(3)*).

➤ The seller is responsible for seeking consent and using 'all reasonable endeavours' to obtain it. If he fails, the buyer's remedy is rescission (*StC 8.3.4*).

➤ The landlord does not usually charge a premium, but he may ask the tenant to pay a reasonable administrative charge to cover his expenses.

➤ The licence is written, but it is not by deed unless it contains a covenant by the buyer (assignee).

- ◆ The landlord sends the seller a licence and retains a copy with his deeds of title.

2 **Absolute covenants prohibiting assignment**

➤ Although the lease prevents assignment, a tenant who wishes to assign can persuade the landlord to:

a) grant a deed of release from the covenant against assignment, *or*

b) vary the lease, *or*

c) give consent.

VI Procedure for assigning a reversion

This is the same as for a freehold conveyance, with these additions:

Step 2: Assignor (ie: landlord) prepares the pre-contract package

- The seller discloses the leases which have been granted over the property, together with details of the service charge accounts.

Steps 4 to 9: Assignor and assignee comply with the requirements of *LT(C)A 1995*

- The landlord may apply to be released from his covenants under the tenancy (*LT(C)A 1995 s.6(2)*), and a former landlord who immediately before the assignment was bound by a covenant under that tenancy may also apply for release (*LT(C)A 1995 s.7(2)*).
  - The procedure involves service on the tenant of a notice, and an opposition procedure over 4 weeks from the date of service, similar to that set out in the box on p.214 (*LT(C)A 1995 s.8*).
- Any release of liability in respect of the landlord's covenants is accompanied by a loss of the benefit of the tenant's covenants.
- If the landlord only assigns the reversion in part and wishes to apportion liability in respect of non-attributable covenants which the landlord is obliged to perform, a procedure similar to that for tenants assigning part of the demised premises should be followed (*LT(C)A 1995 s.9(2)*).
  - For this procedure, see the box on p.214. The only difference is that the application for the apportionment to become binding is served on the tenant(s) of the premises.

Gas safety

- A landlord (including a local authority, housing association, hostel owner, a private sector landlord, or landlord renting out a room or bedsit) who permits people to live in his property must ensure that there is maintained in a safe condition:

  a) any relevant gas fitting, *and*

  b) any flue,

  ... so as to prevent the risk of injury to any person in lawful occupation of the premises (*GS(IU)R 1998 r.36(2)*).
- A landlord may not delegate his duty to a tenant, must use a CORGI registered gas installer for the safety check and must leave a copy of that check with the tennant.
- Non-compliance is a criminal offence punishable, if the Health and Safety Executive take enforcement action under *HSWA 1974 s.37*, by imprisonment and/or an unlimited fine as well (if the landlord is a company) as disqualification for directors.

E Security of tenure

There are 2 classes of tenancy which, on a new grant of a leasehold interest, may qualify for security of tenure by virtue of statute.

I Residential tenancies

II Commercial tenancies

I Residential tenancies

The main features of assured and assured shorthold tenancies

- The tenant has some security of tenure. When the fixed term expires, a statutory periodic tenancy automatically arises (*HA 1988 s.5(2)*). Unlike the situation for commercial property under *LTA 1954 Part II*, the tenant does not have to serve a notice to obtain a new tenancy.
- The statutory periodic tenancy may be ended by:
  a) a court order (*HA 1988 s.7*), *or*
  b) action taken by a tenant at common law to end the tenancy (surrender, etc) (*HA 1988 s.5(2)*).
- A landlord may regain possession of property let on an assured shorthold tenancy by serving a notice under *HA 1988 s.21*.

1 Is the tenancy an assured tenancy, or an assured shorthold tenancy?

Assured tenancy	Assured shorthold tenancy
Requirements (*HA 1988 s.1(1)*) ➤ dwelling house ➤ let (ie: lease not a licence) ➤ as a separate dwelling (ie: at the time of the grant), ➤ to a tenant who is an individual (ie: not a company) Note: a dwelling has been held to be somewhere where 'all the major activities of life, particularly sleeping, cooking and feeding ...' take place (*Wright v. Howell* (1947) 92 Sol Jo26, CA)	***As for an assured tenancy plus*** (*HA 1988 s.20*): ➤ fixed term, for a term certain, ➤ the term starts not less than 6 months from the grant of the lease, ➤ no landlord's break clause in the first 6 months, ➤ Before 28 February 1997 a shorthold notice was given to the tenant before the lease was granted. On or after 28 February 1997 the landlord serves a notice if the tenancy is *not* to be an assured shorthold (*HA 1988 s.19A*). A tenant who does not receive a notice under *s.19A* is entitled to request a written statement of the terms of the tenancy from the landlord (*HA 1988 s.20A*)
Exclusions (outline) ➤ Lease granted, or contract to grant a lease, dated before 15 January 1989 ➤ Student lettings ➤ Lettings to homeless persons under *HA 1985 Part II* ➤ Properties of a high rent or rateable value (eg: over £25,000 per annum if granted after 1 April 1990) ➤ Low rent properties (eg: under £1000 per annum in the Greater London area if granted after 1 April 1990) ➤ Tenancies within the scope of the *LTA 1954 Part II*, or (in respect of assured shorholds) *HA 1988 Schedule 2A*	

2 **Are there special terms which statute implies into the lease, or another statutory regulation?**

- ➤ There are controls on the calculation and payment of service charges (*LTA 1985 ss.18-30*).
  - ◆ These controls were extended when *HA 1996 s.83* (inserting *s.19(2A)-19(2C)* into *LTA 1985*) came into force.
    - Tenants and landlords may ask a leasehold valuation tribunal to assess whether a service charge is 'reasonable' and whether work paid for by a service charge has been done to a 'reasonable standard'.
      - ■ The tenant may challenge the landlord's choice of insurer or excessive premiums.
    - The right to apply to a tribunal under *HA 1996 s.83* does not apply if a tenant:

      a) agrees to or admits the service charge or insurance, *or*

      b) is a party to an arbitration agreement which covers the dispute.
  - ◆ If a property is let as a 'dwelling', a landlord may not be able to re-enter the property or forfeit the lease for non-payment of a service charge, unless:
    - the tenant agrees the amount of the service charge, *or*
    - the amount is determined by a court or tribunal under an arbitration agreement (as defined by *AA 1996*) (*HA 1996 s.81*).
      - ■ A notice served under *LPA 1925 s.146* is effective, provided it informs the tenant of his rights (in the form set out in the regulations) under *HA 1996 s.81*.
- ➤ Certain assured tenancies are subject to rent control provisions (*LTA 1988 s.22*).
- ➤ For *all* new residential leases of under 7 years granted to a new tenant (eg: not a former tenant or one in possession at the time of a grant), statute implies covenants that the landlord will:

  a) keep the exterior and structure in repair, *and*

  b) ensure installations for heating, water and space and those supplying water, gas, electricity and sanitation are kept in repair and proper working order (*LTA 1985 ss.11-14*).

3 **Can the landlord regain possession?**

- ➤ If the tenancy is an assured shorthold, the landlord will need to serve a notice under *s.21* of the *HA 1988* giving at least 2 months' clear notice of his intention to take possession.
- ➤ The landlord commences proceedings by serving a notice on the tenant stating the ground(s) upon which he intends to take possession of the property (*LTA 1988 s.8*). If *Ground 14A* (domestic violence) is relied on, the landlord's notice must meet additional requirements which are beyond the scope of this book (*LTA 1988 s.8A*).
  - ◆ A notice under *HA 1988 ss.8-8A* may specify an earlier date for the commencement of the proceedings if the landlord relies upon *Grounds 1,2,5,6,7,9,14* or *16*.

4 **Does the tenant have the right to buy the freehold, or to a lease extension?**

- ➤ The tenant may have the right to buy the freehold, or extend the lease by up to 90 years if the term of the lease exceeds 21 years (*LRA 1967, LRHUDA 1993* as amended by *HA 1996*).
- ➤ If, without 'reasonable excuse', a landlord fails to offer tenants first refusal on a disposal of his interest on or after 1 October 1996 he commits a criminal offence punishable by a fine of up to £5,000 (*HA 1996 Schedule 6*).
  - ◆ This applies if the premises contain 2 or more flats more than half of which are rented (*LTA 1987, Part I*).

Are there grounds for a court order for possession?

Assured tenancies			
Mandatory 1-8	Ground 1*:	a)	at some time before the tenancy began the property was the landlord's principal home, *or*
		b)	the landlord seeks possession for himself or his spouse as a principal home *and* the reversion was not acquired for money or money's worth
	Ground 2*:	a mortgagee under a pre-existing mortgage is exercising a power of sale	
	Grounds 3-5*:	out of season holiday lettings, vacation lettings to students, lettings to ministers of religion	
	Ground 6:	a)	the landlord 'intends to demolish or reconconstruct the whole or a substantial part of the dwelling, or carry out substantial building works ...', *and*
		b)	the landlord did not acquire the reversion for money or money's worth, *and*
		c)	possession is essential for the works (Varying the lease is unacceptable to the tenant or impractical)
	Ground 7:	death of a tenant. (A spouse's right to succession is unaffected bythis ground (*HA 1996 s.17*))	
	Ground 8:	rent arrears of 8 weeks if paid weekly, or 2 months if paid monthly, *when* notice is served *and* at the date of the hearing (plead Grounds 10 and 11 in the alternative) (amended by *HA 1996 s.101*)	
	*	The landlord must serve a notice stating that possession may be sought under the appropriate ground. This must be given 'not later than the beginning of the tenancy'	
Discretionary 9-17	Ground 9:	the landlord offers 'suitable' alternative accommodation as definedin *HA 1996 Sch. 2 Part III*	
	Ground 10:	less than 3 months' rent is in arrears	
	Ground 11:	persistent delay in paying rent	
	Ground 12:	breach of tenancy clause which does not relate to rent	
	Ground 13:	deterioration of the dwelling due to the tenant's neglect	
	Ground 14:	the tenant or a person residing in or visiting the dwelling:	
		a)	is a nuisance or annoyance to anyone engaged in lawful activity in the vicinity, *or*
		b)	is convicted for using the premises or allowing them to be used for illegal or immoral purposes, *or*
		c)	commits an arrestable offence in the locality (as amended by *HA 1996 s.147*)
	Ground 14A:	a)	the occupiers are a married couple or living together as man and wife, *and*
		b)	one of the partners has left because of violence to themself or a child and is unlikely to return, and
		c)	the landlord seeking possession is a 'registered social landlord' or a 'charitable housing trust' (inserted by *HA 1996 s.148*)
	Ground 15:	deterioration of furniture due to the tenant's conduct	
	Ground 16:	the tenant's employment ends when the letting was a consequence of that employment	
	Ground 17:	tenant's false statement, made knowingly or recklessly, induced the landlord to grant the lease (*HA 1996 s.102*)	

Assured shorthold tenancies

- The grounds are the same as those for assured tenancies
- In addition, a notice can be served under *s.21* of the *HA 1988* giving the tenant not less than 2 months' notice that the landlord requires possession of the dwelling

II Commercial tenancies

Commercial property leases in England & Wales - code of practice

- This code of good practice, endorsed by the Law Society and the British Property Federation, should be brought to the attention of landlords and tenants, especially if either are small businesses, before the grant of a lease.
- If the industry does not voluntarily implement the Code to make the market more transparent, the Government may legislate on the conduct of rent reviews and alternative dispute resolution.

The *LTA 1954 Part II* provides some security of tenure to tenants of commercial property by extending the term indefinitely after the date on which it would otherwise determine at common law (*LTA 1954 s.24(1)*).

1 Does the *LTA 1954* apply to the tenancy?

- If a lease to which the Act would otherwise apply is to be granted, the parties may wish to consider contracting out of the *LTA 1954*.
- If the parties wish to contract out, a copy of the lease and an originating application should be lodged at the County Court several weeks before the lease is granted.

Tenancies protected by the *LTA 1954 Part II*

- A tenancy is protected if it (*LTA 1954 s.23*):
  - a) is a tenancy (ie: not a licence), *and*
  - b) is of premises, *and*
  - c) is occupied at least in part by the tenant, *and*
  - d) is for the purposes of a business (*Grayism Holdings Ltd v. P & O Property Holdings Ltd* [1995] 3 WLR 854, HL),

  ... provided that it is not excluded for any reason, eg:

  - i) the tenancy is 'contracted out' under *LTA 1954 s.38(4)*. An application to the County Court in the name of both the landlord and the tenant must be made before a lease is granted and the lease must be for a term certain, *or*
  - ii) it is an agricultural holding (*LTA 1954 s.43(1)(a)*), *or*
  - iii) it is granted by reason of employment (*LTA 1954 s.43(2)*), *or*
  - iv) it is for a term certain not exceeding 6 months (*LTA 1954 s. 43(3)*) (a tenancy at will is not for a 'term certain' and is therefore excuded).

2 If the *LTA 1954* applies, how can the landlord regain possession, or a new lease be granted under the *LTA 1954*?

- The *LTA 1954* operates a bureaucratic system of notices, which must be served correctly and at the appropriate times.
- The procedural clock is set by reference to the 'termination date' of the lease. This date is set as follows:
  - for a fixed term tenancy: not earlier than the date on which the tenancy would have expired at common law.
  - for a periodic tenancy: not earlier than the earliest date on which the landlord could have served a notice to quit under *s.25(3)(a)*.

- A *s.25* notice is served by a landlord who wishes to regain possession. To be valid it must be:
  - served not less than 6 months and not more than 1 year before the termination date, *and*
  - given to the tenant, *and*
  - specify the termination date, *and*
  - demand action of the tenant (eg: vacate the premises, or enter negotiations for a new tenancy), *and*
  - explain whether the landlord will oppose the grant of a new tenancy - there are 8 grounds on which the landlord may seek to end the tenancy (it is impossible to rely on grounds not cited in the *s.25* notice):

    a) a breach of the tenant's repairing obligations.

    b) persistent delay in paying rent.

    c) other substantial breaches.

    d) the landlord can provide suitable alternative accommodation.

    e) the landlord needs possession for letting or disposing of the property as a whole.

    f) the landlord intends to demolish or reconstruct the property.

    g) the landlord intends to occupy the premises for his business or as his residence, *and*
  - be in the correct form set out in the *Landlord and Tenant Act 1954 Part II (Notices) Regulations 1983.*
- A *s.26* request is served by a tenant who wants a new tenancy. This can only be served if the tenant has not indicated that he will leave *or* if he has received a *s.25* notice from the landlord. It must:
  - specify a date for the new tenancy to begin which is not more than 1 year and not less than 6 months after the date specified in the notice (which cannot be earlier than the termination date), *and*
  - contain proposals for the new lease (the amount of detail depends on the tenant's negotiating tactics, eg: whether the tenant wishes to tell the landlord early on exactly what he wants), *and*
  - demand action from the landlord, *and*
  - be served by a tenant with an interest in the tenancy on a competent landlord, *and*
  - be in the form set out in the *Landlord and Tenant Act 1954 Part II (Notices) Regulations 1983.*

3 Is the tenant entitled to any compensation on termination?

- If the landlord terminates the tenancy under grounds in *ss.30(1)(e)-(g)*, then generally the tenant will be entitled to compensation (*s.37*).
- If the tenant has made improvements to the property, he may be entitled to compensation under *LTA 1927 Part I.*

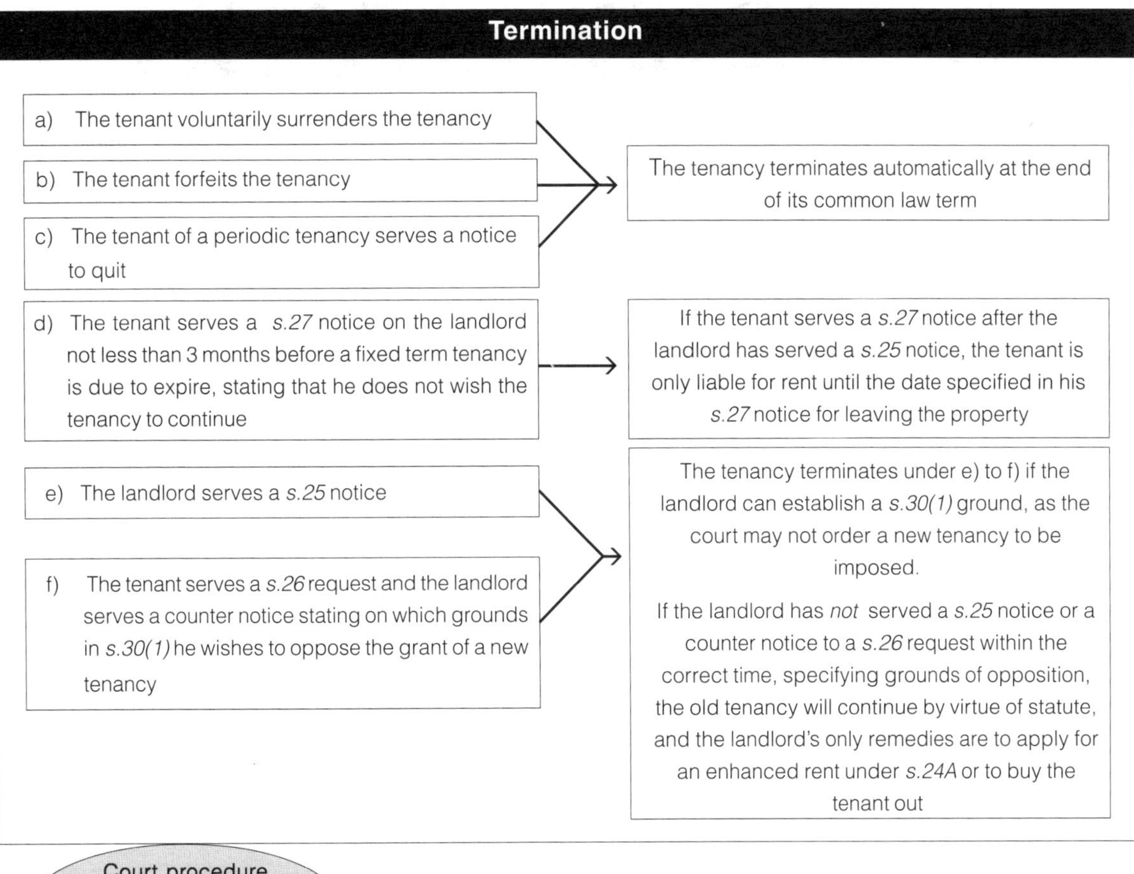
Termination
a) The tenant voluntarily surrenders the tenancy
b) The tenant forfeits the tenancy
c) The tenant of a periodic tenancy serves a notice to quit
The tenancy terminates automatically at the end of its common law term
d) The tenant serves a s.27 notice on the landlord not less than 3 months before a fixed term tenancy is due to expire, stating that he does not wish the tenancy to continue
If the tenant serves a s.27 notice after the landlord has served a s.25 notice, the tenant is only liable for rent until the date specified in his s.27 notice for leaving the property
e) The landlord serves a s.25 notice
f) The tenant serves a s.26 request and the landlord serves a counter notice stating on which grounds in s.30(1) he wishes to oppose the grant of a new tenancy
The tenancy terminates under e) to f) if the landlord can establish a s.30(1) ground, as the court may not order a new tenancy to be imposed.
If the landlord has not served a s.25 notice or a counter notice to a s.26 request within the correct time, specifying grounds of opposition, the old tenancy will continue by virtue of statute, and the landlord's only remedies are to apply for an enhanced rent under s.24A or to buy the tenant out

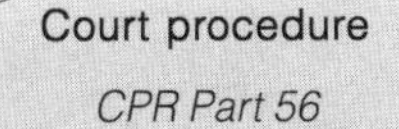
Court procedure
CPR Part 56

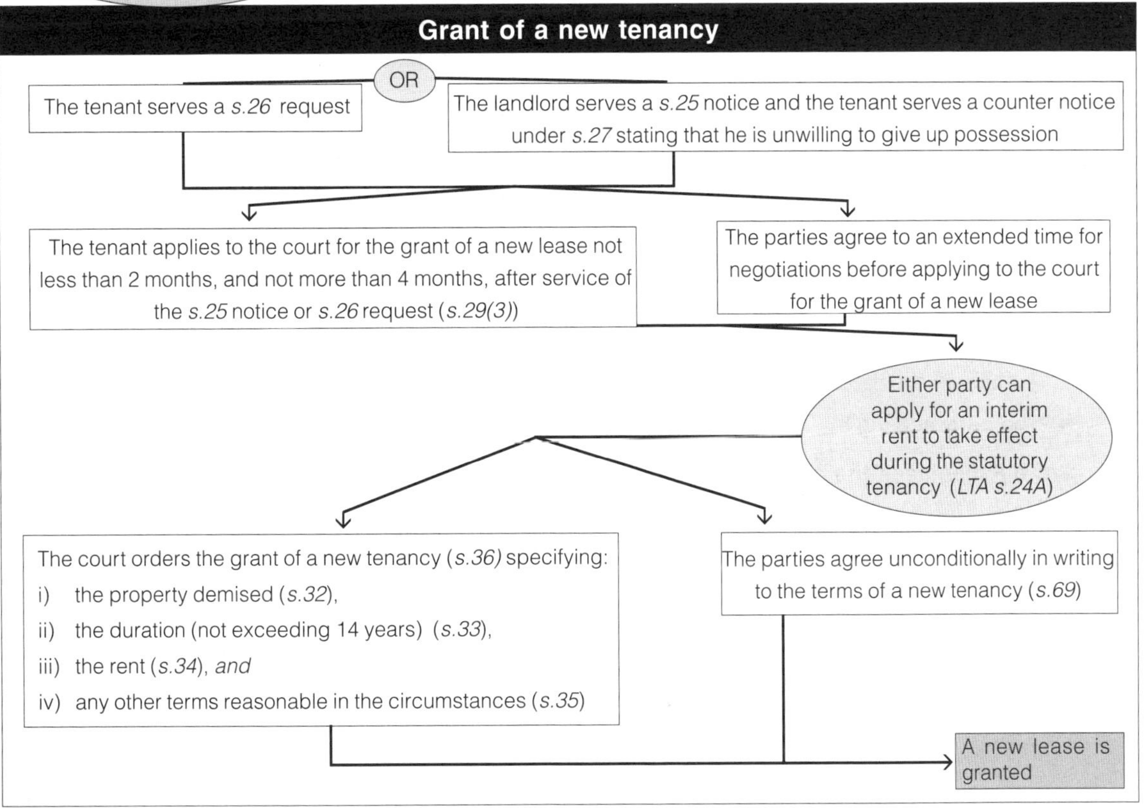
Grant of a new tenancy
The tenant serves a s.26 request
OR
The landlord serves a s.25 notice and the tenant serves a counter notice under s.27 stating that he is unwilling to give up possession
The tenant applies to the court for the grant of a new lease not less than 2 months, and not more than 4 months, after service of the s.25 notice or s.26 request (s.29(3))
The parties agree to an extended time for negotiations before applying to the court for the grant of a new lease
Either party can apply for an interim rent to take effect during the statutory tenancy (LTA s.24A)
The court orders the grant of a new tenancy (s.36) specifying:
i) the property demised (s.32),
ii) the duration (not exceeding 14 years) (s.33),
iii) the rent (s.34), and
iv) any other terms reasonable in the circumstances (s.35)
The parties agree unconditionally in writing to the terms of a new tenancy (s.69)
A new lease is granted

F Remedies

Vendor and purchaser application (*LPA s.49(1)*)

Under this section, either party may issue an application under *CPR 1998 Part 8* to resolve disputes connected with the transaction (but *not* one questioning the validity or existence of the contract itself).

The court has summary jurisdiction to resolve such matters as:

- ➤ the validity of a notice to complete.
- ➤ whether the buyer is taking a clean title as promised in the contract.
- ➤ whether a requisition on title is valid.

I Notice to complete

- ➤ Initially time is not of the essence (*StC 6.1*), unless the contract is conditional. It can be made of the essence if completion is delayed by serving a notice to complete.
- ➤ Time is 'of the essence' from the service of a notice to complete. Consequently, if completion does not occur when the notice specifies the party at fault commits a breach of contract.
  - ◆ The innocent party may choose to terminate the contract after this breach and/or sue for damages.
  - ◆ If the party who served the notice defaults, the recipient of the notice has an action for breach. Consequently, a notice should only be served if you are sure you can complete.

1 At common law

- ➤ The notice must specify a 'reasonable' time for the new completion date.
- ➤ The party serving the notice must be ready, willing, and able to complete if the notice is to be valid.

2 *StC 6.8* displaces the common law rules

- ➤ The notice should state that it is served under this contractual provision.
- ➤ If a notice is served, the new completion date is set 10 clear days from the day of service.
- ➤ If the buyer has paid a deposit of under 10%, he must pay the full 10% on receipt of the notice.
- ➤ If the notice is ignored, the seller may rescind if he served the notice (*StC 7.5*), *or* the buyer may rescind if he served the notice (*StC 7.6*).

II Compensation for delayed completion

1 **Delay due to the seller's fault** (at common law)

- The seller pays outgoings on the property during the period of delay.
- The seller retains *whichever is less of*:

  a) the interest on the purchase price which the buyer pays at the general equitable rate, *or*

  b) the net income on the property.

2 **Delay due to the buyer's fault** (at common law)

- The buyer pays outgoings on the property.
- The buyer retains any income from the property.
- The buyer pays the seller interest on the balance at the general equitable rate.

3 ***StC 7.3*** (this overrides the common law regime)

- Whichever party causes the greater period of delay pays the other compensation at the contract rate.
- The sum on which interest is paid depends on which party is liable to pay compensation.
  - The buyer's interest is calculated on the balance of the purchase price outstanding (ie: the deposit is deducted).
  - The seller's interest is calculated on the purchase price.
- Interest runs for whichever is the shorter of:

  a) the time between the contractual completion date and actual completion, *or*

  b) the length of time during which the party liable to pay compensation was in default.

Note: compensation under *StC 7.3* is deducted from any damages a court subsequently awards.

III Contractual remedies

Pre-completion	Post-completion

Action on the covenants for title

For a list of the covenants implied by statute on, or after 1 July 1995, see p.169

Before 1 July 1995, *LPA s.76(1)* implied into conveyances or transfers of land for value covenants which depended on the seller's capacity (as 'beneficial owner', 'fiduciary' or 'settlor'), and whether the interest concerned was freehold or leasehold

- This action is *only* available *after* completion if the contract incorporates a non-merger clause similar to *StC 7.4*, otherwise the contract and the deed 'merge', removing the right to a remedy under the contract alone

Rescission

- This restores the parties to their original position
- The claimant may seek an indemnity in the contract for any loss incurred
- The claimant may seek damages if:
  a) he is claiming rescission under *MA 1967 s.2(1), or*
  b) rescission is due to the defendant's breach, *or*
  c) the claimant is seeking a declaration from the court that the defendant has committed a repudiatory breach of contract
- The claimant may *not* seek damages where obtaining rescission is the purpose of the action

The *StC* expressly reserve the right to rescind if:

a) the seller makes a misrepresentation (an error of fact upon which the buyer relies in entering the contract) (*StC 7.1*), *or*
b) the landlord does not grant a licence to assign (*StC 8.3*), *or*
c) the condition of the property alters substantially before completion (*StC 5.1*)

StC 7.2 lists rights on rescission *under the contract*:

a) documents are returned to the seller, *and*
b) the buyer pays for cancelling any entry on the Register to protect the contract, and regains the deposit plus interest

Damages for breach of contract

- Calculated on the principle in *Hadley v. Baxendale* (1854) 9 Exch 341: all loss arising naturally from the breach which the parties could reasonably have foreseen on entering the contract would result from the breach

Specific performance

- An equitable remedy in the court's discretion
- The court may award damages instead of granting specific performance (*SCA 1981 s.51*)
- The court may award damages as well as specific performance (*Johnson v. Agnew* [1979] 1 All ER 883)

Rectification

- This is an equitable remedy: the document is altered to reflect the party's original intentions

Either the parties agree,

or the court grants the remedy at its discretion if:

- *both* parties were mistaken, *or*
- *one* party was mistaken *and* the party 'in the know' was ...
  a) aware of the error and so is estopped from resisting rectification, *or*
  b) fraudulent, *or*
- only one party is party to the document

Note: if both rescission and rectification are available, the court may let the plaintiff choose, *Solle v. Butcher* [1950] 1 KB 671

G Law reform

Both the *Homes Bill* and the *Commonhold and Leasehold Reform Bill* failed to complete their passage through Parliament before Parliament was dissolved by the Queen in May 2001.

The *CLRB* was re-introduced in the new session and received its second reading in July 2001; the *HB* was not mentioned in the Queen's Speech on 20 June 2001 and it is not known whether (and if so, when) it will be reintroduced.

The outline that follows does no more than highlight some of the important features of these Bills.

I *Homes Bill*

➤ *Part I* of the *HB* proposed:

- the imposition of new duties on those marketing residential property in England and Wales.
- a seller, or its agent, would have been required to prepare a seller's pack for prospective buyers before the property's availability or possible availability for sale was first advertised or otherwise made known to the public or a section of the public (*HB cls.3-4*).
  - The contents of a seller's pack were to have been specified by regulations, but included information about (*HB cl.7*):
    - the interest for sale and the terms on which sale is proposed, *and*
    - the title to the property, *and*
    - anything relating to or affecting the propoerty that is contained in a register required by statute to be kept or kept by a person who could reasonably be expected to give information to the seller, *and*
    - the physical condition of the property and the energy efficiency of the property (known as a 'home condition report'), *and*
    - any warranties or guarantees subsisting in relation to the property, *and*
    - any taxes (eg: council tax), service charges or other charges payable in relation to the property, *and*
    - a draft contract, *and*
    - replies the seller proposes to give to prescribed pre-contract enquiries, *and*
    - documents or particular information indexing or otherwise explaining the contents of the seller's pack.
- the *HB* excluded the marketing of non-residential property, mixed commercial (or industrial) and residential property, property sold with sitting tennants, certain property portfolios and leases of less than 21 years.
- a penalty, if a person failed without reasonable excuse to supply a seller's pack, on conviction to a fine of up to £5,000 (level 5 on the standard scale).

II *Commonhold and Leasehold Reform Bill*

References are to the version of this Bill passed by the House of Lords at 2nd reading in July 2001

➤ *Part I* of the *CLRB*:

- proposes the creation of a new form of tenure: commonhold.
- specifies that for a commonhold to exist there must be:
  - a) a registered freehold estate in land registered at the Land Registry as a freehold estate in commonhold, *and*
  - b) a commonhold association, *and*
    - This would be a company limited by guarantee (the liability of each member would be £1) and registered at Companies House with a standard memorandum and articles. Its business would be to own and manage the common parts of the development.
  - c) a commonhold community statement (rules and regulations governing the operation and management of the commonhold).
- proposes that individuals would own 'units' within a development and the commonhold association would hold the common parts of that development.
- allows for the conversion of leasehold tenure to commonhold tenure where 100% of all the leaseholders consented to conversion taking place.
- empowers the Lord Chancellor to approve an Ombudsman scheme for commonhold disputes.

➤ *Part II* of the *CLRB* proposes various reforms to leasehold tenure, including:

- giving leaseholders of flats the right to manage the building via a qualifying company (a RTM company).
- simplifying the eligibility criteria for tenants to collectively buy a freehold under the *LRHUDA 1993* by:
  - abolishing the requirement that:
    - a) at least 2/3rds of the leaseholders must participate, *and*
    - b) at least half of those participating must have lived in their flats for a minimum period (eg: the previous year) (Instead, leaseholders would be required to have held a lease for at least 2 years), *and*
  - dispensing with the low rent test for most leases of under 35 years, *and*
  - allowing 25% (rather than 10%) of a builing to be occupied for non-residential purposes.
- modifying the right of an individual leaseholder to buy a new lease.
- permitting PRs to exercise a deceased's rights of leasehold enfranchisement or extension within 6 months of probate or letters of administration being granted.
- obliging a landlord to provide an annual accounting statment certified by a qualified accountant and a summary of leaseholders' rights and obligations in relation to service charges.
- entitling tenants to withhold service charges in certain circumstances and improving their right to inspect documentation relating to accounting statements.
- consolidating/extending rules governing the procedure and jurisdiction of leasehold valuation tribunals.

III *Land Registration Bill*

➤ See p.xvii above.

Business

This chapter examines:

All taxation aspects are dealt with together in the 'Taxation' section of this book.

Treaty of Rome - *Article 43*

The right of an EU citizen to establish a business in any member state, provided that the requirements of national law regarding the running of that type of business are satisfied (ie: company, partnership, etc).

Treaty of Rome - *Article 49*

The right of an EU citizen to provide services into any member state

A Partnerships

I Formation of a partnership

- A partnership 'subsists between persons carrying on a *business in common* with a view to profit' (*PA s.1*) (our emphasis).
- A partnership can come into existence orally, *or* by an agreement, *or* through a course of conduct.
- 20 partners is the maximum permitted, except for partnerships consisting of members of certain professions (eg: solicitors, accountants, registered medical practitioners in general practice) or unless authorised under the *FSA 1986* (*CA s.716* and *P(US)N.16R 2001*).
- However the partnership comes into existence, the *Business Names Act 1985* should be complied with.

Business Names Act 1985	
Section	Content
1	➤ If the name is the partners' surnames, either alone or with their initials, forenames or an 's' to show that there is more than one partner with a given name, then no restrictions apply.
2-3	➤ Words listed in the *Company and Business Names Regulations 1981 (as amended)* (eg: names suggesting a connection with HM Government or the royal family or the words 'Chamber of Commerce') require the approval of the President of the Board of Trade.
4	➤ Unless a name approved under *s.1* is used, then the names of partners and the address for service of documents must appear both: a) on letters, orders, invoices, receipts and written demands for payment, *and* b) at the place of business to which suppliers and customers have access. These details must also be given to anyone who requests such information. If a firm has more than 20 partners, it is sufficient to give the address of the main place of business where the addresses and names can be found.
5	➤ Fines may be imposed for non-compliance with the *Act*, and a contract with a third party who is prejudiced by the infringement will be unenforceable.
7	➤ Breach of the *Act* is a crime.

II A written agreement for a partnership

- A written agreement is safest to effect a partnership. Various matters are highlighted below which the draftsman may wish to consider. References are to the *Partnership Act 1890*, unless otherwise stated, and the Act will apply if the partnership agreement is silent on a particular matter.

1 **Commencement date:** an objective test based on *s.1* - the date stated in the agreement is not conclusive.

2 **Name:** the firm's name (and its trading name if this is different). These must comply with *BNA 1985*.

3 **Financial input:** of each partner.

4 **Salaries:** if the agreement is silent, the partners will not be entitled to a salary (*s.24(6)*).

5 **Interest**
- Partners are entitled to interest at 5% on capital they advance in excess of their obligations under the terms of the partnership (*s.24(3)*).
- There is no entitlement to interest on capital until profits have been ascertained (*s.24(4)*).

6 **Capital profits or losses:** if the agreement is silent, these are shared equally (*s.24(1)*).

7 **Shares in profit derived from income:** if the agreement is silent, these are shared equally (*s.24(1)*).

8 **Drawings of money**

9 **Place and nature of business**

10 **Ownership of assets:** either i) by the partners privately, or ii) by partners on trust for all the partners.

11 **Work input**
- Full or part-time?
- Bar on the involvement of partners in other businesses during their membership of the partnership?

12 **Partners' roles**
- All the partners may manage the firm (*s.24(5)*), but this is inappropriate for 'sleeping' partners.

13 **Management**
- A simple majority prevails, unless otherwise stated (*s.24(8)*).
- Unanimity is required for i) changing the nature of the business (*s.24(8)*), ii) admitting new partners (*s.24(7)*), iii) changing the partnership agreement.
- If unanimity is required for anything else, put it in the contract.

14 **Duration of the partnership**
- i) At will, or ii) for a fixed term, or iii) for as long as a minimum of two partners remain.
- *PA s.26* provides that if no date is given, then if a notice of dissolution is given, it is effective immediately. To prevent this occurring inadvertently, a notice period should be specified.

15 **Death/bankruptcy/retirement:** if the agreement is silent, these dissolve a partnership (*PA s.33*).

16 **Expulsion of partners:** this is impossible without an express provision in the agreement (*PA s.25*).

17 **Paying for an outgoing partner's share.** Consider:
- either an *obligation* on (or an *option* for) the remaining partners to purchase the share.
- a method for valuing the share. Provide for professional valuation if the partners do not agree.
- a date on which payment falls due (a grace period allows those remaining to find new equity).
- whether an indemnity is included in the valuation.

18 **Restraint of trade on outgoing partners:** the clause must be 'reasonable' to be enforceable at common law (ie: with regard to time, geographical area, and whether the activity competes with the partnership).

19 **Income tax**
- An outgoing partner may be obliged to join the others in sending a tax election to the Inland Revenue.
- An outgoing partner should be indemnified against additional liability resulting from his election.

20 **Arbitration:** name an arbitrator in case of disputes between the partners (else recourse is to court).

III Obligations and liability of partners

A. Generally

➤ Partners are bound to each other:

1. **in contract:** in accordance with the terms of the partnership agreement, *and*
2. **under the *PA ss.28-30* and a century of case-law as follows:**
   - **Duty of utmost good faith:** partners are bound to each other by a set of duties that can collectively be called a duty of utmost good faith.
   - Duty to render to each other true accounts and full information on all matters affecting the partnership (*s.28*).
   - Duty to account for any benefit (eg: a transaction concerning the partnership made without the consent of the partnership) (*s.29*).
   - Duty to account for the profits derived from any competing business (*s.30*).

➤ See also the effect of *C(ROTP)A 1999* on p.299.

B. Firm's liability

Recovery from the firm

➤ The firm is a group of persons who were partners at the time the cause of action arose (*PA ss.9,17*).
➤ Recovery is possible from the partnership assets and also from partners personally.

➤ The firm may be liable:

1. **in tort:** for a partner's act or omission in the ordinary course of business, *or* an act with a partner's authority (*PA s.10).*
2. **in contract:** for agreements made by a partner with, or with the partners', 'actual' or 'ostensible' authority.
   - **Actual authority:** this can be expressly *or* impliedly given in the partnership agreement, or it may arise from a factual situation or a decision of the partners.
   - **Ostensible authority:** 4 conditions must be satisfied (*PA ss.5-8*):

subjective test:
a) the third party knows or believes he is dealing with a partner, *and*
b) the third party is unaware that the partner was not actually authorised, *and*

objective test:
c) the partner would usually be expected to be authorised to enter into such a transaction, *and*
d) the firm's type of business is consistent with the nature of the transaction.

C. Personal liability of a partner

1 **A partner to a third party**

➤ A partner is personally liable in contract (if he or the firm are party to the contract) and in tort.

- Liability is without limit for debts incurred while a partner (*PA s.9*).
- Liability does *not* cease on leaving the firm for obligations incurred while a partner (*PA s.17*).

2 **A partner to a partner**

➤ A partner acting outside his authority can be liable to the other partners for breach of warranty of authority.

3 **An ex-partner to a third party**

➤ Any partner is liable for obligations incurred *after* his departure from the partnership if there is:

a) 'holding out' that the ex-partner is a partner (*PA s.14*) by:

i) a representation (oral/written/conduct) *either* by the ex-partner, *or* with his knowledge, *and*
ii) reliance on this representation by a third party,

or b) failure to notify of leaving the partnership (*PA s.36*).

- An ex-partner is liable *unless* notice of the change:
  i) is given to all who have dealt with the firm recently. This protects against claims from previous customers.
  ii) appears in the *London Gazette*. This protects against claims from future customers.

  Note: i) and ii) do not apply on death or bankruptcy, so an estate is not liable for a firm's subsequent acts.

4 **A stranger to a third party**

➤ A stranger will be liable for an obligation if he has been 'holding out' that he is a partner (*PA s.14*):

i) by making a representation (oral/written/conduct) that he is a partner, *and*
ii) a third party relies on this representation.

D. Limitation of personal liability

1 **By indemnity**

a) No actual authority

Where a partner has acted without actual authority, the other partners are entitled to an indemnity for any loss they suffer as a result of the unauthorised act.

Note: i) an indemnity will only protect the other partners if the indemnifier is solvent.
ii) the other partners will only be entitled to any indemnity if they act to mitigate their loss.

b) Outgoing partner indemnity

An outgoing partner may negotiate an indemnity from the remaining partners to protect himself.

2 **By novation**

➤ A 3-way agreement between a new partner, creditor and continuing partners by which the new partner takes on the outgoing partner's liability.

3 **By suitable acts**

➤ A leaving partner may try to limit liability by certain practical acts (see section 3b in C above).

- Eg: change the notepaper and the list of partners at the place of business, put suitable notices in relevant newspapers etc.

IV Dissolution of a partnership

➤ The partnership agreement will usually make provisions for when a partnership may be dissolved. Where it does not (or there is no partnership agreement), the following list of 9 defaults will apply.

- **Always:** '5' below will apply even if a partnership agreement caters for the other situations.
- **Automatic termination:** '1', '3' and '6' will terminate the partnership automatically.

➤ A partnership may be dissolved by ...

1 **... expiry**

➤ A 'fixed term' partnership terminates at the end of its term (*PA s.32(a)*).

➤ A partnership intended to achieve a single undertaking ends when that undertaking is attained (*PA s.32(b)*).

- If the partners continue acting in concert the agreement continues, but as a 'partnership at will'.

2 **... notice**

➤ This is when any partner gives notice to the other(s) of his intention to dissolve the partnership.

- Notice may be effective immediately, or after a specified period (*PA s.32(c)*).
- Notice does not need to be written unless the partnership agreement is by deed (*PA s.26(2)*).

3 **... illegality**

➤ When an event occurs that makes it unlawful to continue in partnership (eg: loss of a licence which is required for running the business) (*PA s.34*).

4 **... court order under *PA s.35***

➤ Regardless of what a partnership agreement may provide, the court has discretion to dissolve a partnership on one of the following grounds:

Either when a partner, other than the partner applying to court ...

s.35(b)	is rendered 'permanently' incapable of carrying out obligations under the agreement, *or*
s.35(c)	engages in conduct prejudicial to the partnership's business, *or*
s.35(d)	wilfully breaches the partnership agreement, or behaves in such a way that it is not reasonably practical for the other partners to continue the business.
s.35(e)	Also, when the partnership can only be continued as a loss-making business, *or*
s.35(f)	when the court regards dissolution as 'just and equitable'.

5 **... court order under *Mental Health Act 1983* s.96(1)(g)**

➤ This happens if a partner is a 'patient' (ie: mentally incapable of managing his affairs).

6 **... death, bankruptcy (*PA s.33(1)*), retirement (*PA s.26*) or expulsion (*PA s.25*) of a partner**

➤ These events dissolve the partnership.

7 **... charging order**

➤ If a partner's share in the partnership assets is subject to an order for payment of a private debt (*PA s.23*), a creditor can seek a court order for the asset's sale; when this sale takes place, a purchaser gains a share in the asset without becoming party to the partnership.

➤ When an order is made, the other partners may give notice of dissolution to prevent a third party purchaser gaining title to the asset (*PA s.33(2)*).

8 **... disposal**

➤ A partner may insist on the sale of the business as a whole or in parts (*PA s.39*).

9 **... winding up**

➤ Any partner, except a bankrupt, can apply to the court for the appointment of a receiver (*PA s.38*).

V After dissolution - distribution of assets

- Partners all have continuing authority to act on behalf of the partnership after its dissolution (*PA s.38*).
- On dissolution, every partner has a right to insist that the partnership property is used to pay the firm's debts (*PA s.39*).
- If a dissolution occurs, the business may be sold:
  - as a going concern, *or*
  - by breaking up the business and selling off the assets.
- The assets (or proceeds from sale of the assets) are distributed in the following order (*PA s.44*):

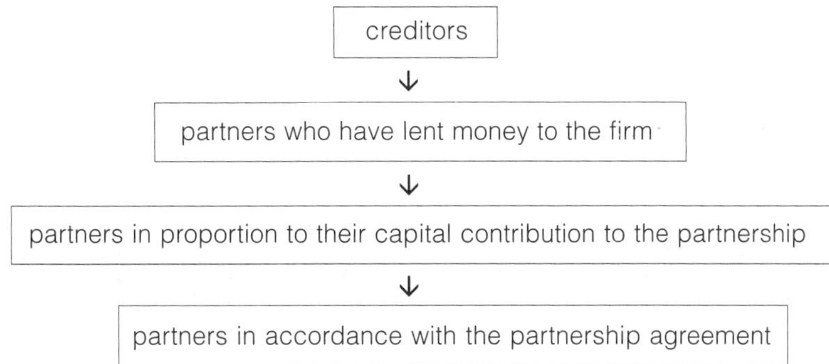

- When other partners continue the business, the outgoing partner is entitled to:
  a) interest at 5% on that partner's share of the assets, *or*
  b) whatever profit the court attributes to that partner's share of the partnership assets between the dissolution and the actual payment of his share (*PA s.42*).
- Where a partner dies, the entitlement under *s.42* to interest or ongoing profits is regarded as a debt owed to his estate from the date of his death (*PA s.43*).

VI Taxation

- See the Taxation chapter - Income tax, CGT and IHT.

B Limited liability partnerships (LLPs)

This section deals solely with an English law limited liabilty partnership (LLP) incorporated under the LPA 2000. It does not cover limited partnerships established under the Limited Partnerships Act 1907.

I Formation of a limited liability partnership (LLP)

A. What is an LLP?

What is a LLP?

➤ A LLP is a new form of legal entity (*LPA 2000 s.1(1)*). It is a legal person in its own right as a body corporate formed under the *LPA 2000*.

- ◆ A LLP is a body corporate with unlimited capacity to act (eg: it can buy and sell property, sue and be sued and do anything which a natural person can do) (*LPA 2000 s.1(3)*).

➤ LLPs have been introduced with the broad intention of offering:

a) limited liability to 'members' akin to that enjoyed by shareholders, *and*

- In a partnership, partners have unlimited liability. For partnership debts and obligations this liability is joint; for loss or damage from a wrongful act or omission (in the ordinary course of a partnership's business or with the authority of the partners) of partners in a partnership, it is joint and several.

b) the tax advantages of a partnership, as opposed to a company (ie: although the existence of the partnership may be important for computational purposes, a LLP or partnership is, unlike a company, transparent for tax purposes), *and*

- See further the Taxation chapter.
  - Note, in addition, that:

    ... the exemption from tax otherwise accorded to a pension funds and friendly societies, *and*

    ... the special treatment of the assets of an insurance company's long term insurance business

    ... do not apply if (and to the extent that) such an entity is a member of a property investment LLP whose business consists wholly or mainly of investing in land (*FA 2001 Sch.25*).

c) limited public disclosure to protect a LLP's creditors.

B. Formation of a LLP

Steps

1 2 or more persons associated for carrying on a lawful business with a view to profit subscribe their names to an incorporation document (*LPA 2000 s.2(1)(a)*).

2 Deliver to the Registrar (*LPA 2000 ss.2(1)(b)-(c)*) (*Form LLP2* suffices for both a) and b)):

a) the incorporation document (or an authenticated copy), *and*

Incorporation document
➤ The incorporation document must (*LPA 2000 s.2(2)*): ◆ be in a form approved by the Registrar (or as near to such form as the circumstances allow), *and* ◆ state the name of the LLP (which must comply with *LPA 2000 Sch 1 Part 1*), *and* ◆ state whether the LLP's registered office is to be situated in England and Wales, in Wales, or in Scotland, *and* ◆ state the address of the registered office, *and* ◆ state the name and address of each of the persons who are members of the LLP on incorporation, *and* ◆ *either* specify which of those persons are to be designated members *or* state that every person who from time to time is a member of the LLP is a designated member.

b) a statement made by a solicitor engaged in the formation of the LLP or a subscriber to the incorporation document, that Step 1 has been complied with.

- It is an offence, punishable by a fine and/or imprisonment for up to 2 years to make this statement is a person knows it to be false or does not believe it to be true (*LPA 2000 ss.2(3)-(4)*).

3 The Registrar retains the incorporation document (or copy), registers it and issues a certificate that the LLP is incorporated with the name specified in the incorporation document (*LPA 2000 ss.3(1)-(3)*).

◆ The certificate is conclusive evidence that the requirements of *LPA 2000 s.2* have been complied with and that the LLP is incorporated (*LPA 2000 s.3(4)*).

II A written agreement for a LLP

➤ The mutual rights and duties of a LLP and its members may be governed by agreement between the members, or between the LLP and its members (*LPA 2000 s.5(1)(a)*).

◆ If there are no agreement *LLPR 2001* resolve matters by applying (with suitable modifications) law relating to partnerships (*LPA 2000 s.5(1)(b)*). Partnership law does not apply generally, but only in accordance with default provisions set out in *LLPR 2001 rr.7-8*.

Default provisions for agreement between members (*LLPR 2001 rr.7-8*)

- All the members of a LLP are entitled to share equally in the capital and profits of the LLP (*r.7(1)*).
- The LLP must indemnify every member in respect of payments made and personal liabilities incurred by him:
  a) in the ordinary and proper conduct of the LLP's business, *or*
  b) in or about anything necessarily done for the preservation of the business or property of the LLP (*r.7(2)*).
- Every member may take part in the management of the LLP (*r.7(3)*).
- No member is entitled to remuneration for acting in the LLP's business or management (*r.7(4)*).
- No person may be introduced as a member or voluntarily assign an interest in a LLP without the consent of all existing members (*r.7(5)*).
- Any difference arising as to ordinary matters connected with the LLP's business may be decided by a majority of the members, but no change may be made in the nature of the LLP's business without consent of all members (*r.7(6)*).
- The LLP's books and records are to be available for inspection at the LLP's registered office or at such other place as the members think fit and every member of the LLP may when he thinks fit have access to and inspect and copy any of them (*r.7(7)*).
- Each member shall render true accounts and full information of all things affecting the LLP to any member or his legal representative (*r.7(8)*).
- If a member, without the LLP's consent, carries on any business of the same nature as and competing with the LLP, he must account for and pay over to the LLP all profits made by him from that business (*r.7(9)*).
- Every member must account to the LLP for any benefit derived by him without the consent of the LLP from any transaction concerning the LLP, or from his use of the LLP's property, name or business connection (*r.7(10)*).
- No majority of the members can expel any member unless a power to do so has been conferred by express agreement between the members (*r.8*).

- An agreement made before a LLP's incorporation between the subscribers may obligate a LLP (ie: it is not necessary to novate an agreement between the partners after incorporation) (*LPA 2000 s.5(2)*).

➤ If a member:
- ceases to be member, *or*
- dies, *or*
- becomes bankrupt, *or*
- has his estate sequestrated or wound-up, *or*
- has granted a trust deed for the benefit of his creditors, *or*
- has assigned the whole or part of his share in a LLP (absolutely or by way of charge or security) ...

... his PR/trustee in bankruptcy/liquidator/trustee/assignee may not interfere in the management or administration of any business or affairs of the LLP, but may receive from the LLP any amount to which the former member would have been entitled (*LPA 2000 s.7*).

➤ A LLP must ensure that where (*LPA 2000 s.9*):

a) a person becomes or ceases to be a member (or a designated member) notice is delivered to the Registrar within 14 days, *and*

b) there is a change in the name/address of a member, notice is delivered to the Registrar within 28 days.
- The notice must be signed by a designated member of the LLP.
- Non-compliance is an offence by the LLP and every designated member, punishable by a fine not exceeding level 5 on the standard scale (currently £5,000).

III Obligations and liability of a LLP and its members

1 Obligations and liability of a LLP to third parties

➤ Every member is the agent of the LLP (*LPA 2000 s.6(1)*). *But* a LLP is not bound by anything done by a member dealing with a person if:

a) the member in fact has no authority to act for the LLP, *and*

b) the person knows that the member has no authority or does not know or believe the member to a member of the LLP.

- A former member of a LLP is regarded (in relation to any person dealing with the LLP) as still being a member of a LLP *unless*:

  i) the person has notice that the former member has ceased to be a member of the LLP, *or*

  ii) notice that the former member has ceased to be a member has been delivered to the Registrar.

➤ A LLP is liable to the same extent as a member if that member is liable to any person (other than another member of the LLP) as result of that member's wrongful act or omission in the course of the LLP's business or with its authority (*LPA 2000 s.6(4)*).

➤ A document signed by 2 members of a LLP and expressed to be executed by the LLP has the same effect as if executed under the LLP's common seal (*CA 1985 s.36A, LLPR 2001 Sch 2 Pt. I*).

◆ A purchaser (in good faith for valuable consideration, including a lessee/mortgagee) may assume a document has been duly executed by a LLP if it purports to be signed by 2 members of the LLP.

2 Obligations of a LLP under *CA 1985* (as modified for LLPs by *LLPR 2001*)

➤ Certain *Companies Acts* obligations apply to LLPs (*LLPR 2001 Sch 1* applies *CA 1985 Part VII* to LLPs, and *Sch.2* applies the *CDDA 1986* and other provisions of the *CA 1985* to LLPs).

Eg: a LLP must: ...	*CA 1985*
... ensure the LLP's name appears outside its place of business	*s.348*
... ensure the LLP's place of registration, registered number and the address of its registered office appear on its on its correspondence	*s.349*
... keep accounting records	*s.221*
... prepare accounts (These are approved by the designated members and signed by designated members on behalf of the members)	*ss.224-233*
... deliver accounts and any auditor's report to every member of the LLP and holder of its debentures wihtin 1 month of signature and in any event not later than 10 months after the end of the relevant accounting reference period • The accounts must state the contributions of the partners to the LLP (*CA 1985 Sch.4 para 37A, Sch 8 para 37A, Sch.8A*) • Small and medium sized LLPs, like small companies, may submit less detailed accounts	*s.238*
... deliver accounts and auditor's report and annual returns to the Registrar of Companies	*s.242, s.363*
... register charges with the Registar of Companies	*s.399*

3 Obligations and liability of members ...

... to the LLP

➤ Members owe a LLP a duty of good faith (similar to the fiduciary duty directors owe a company).

- The DTI issued a consultation paper in February 2000 on the desirability of a statutory duty of good faith between partners. The DTI decided not to impose such a duty, but the default provisions in *LLPR 2001 rr.7(9)-(10)* are intended to address this issue in a targeted way.

... to third parties

➤ The DTI took the view in a consultation paper issued in relation to the LLPs that the law is uncertain as to whether a third party who has suffered economic loss could successfully sue a member of the LLP.

- *Williams & another v. National Life Health Foods Limited & Richard Mistlin* ([1998] 1 WLR 830),HC suggests that the courts would consider whether:
  - the member assumed personal responsibility, *and*
  - the third party relied on that assumption, *and*
  - such reliance was reasonable.

... compliance with *CA 1985/IA 1986* (as modified for LLPs by *LLPR 2001*)

➤ A designated member may commit an offence if a LLP is in default of its statutory obligations, eg: if annual accounts are not filed with 28 days of the return date (*CA 1985 s.363*)).

➤ The designated members must appoint auditors, otherwise the members may do so at a meeting convened for that purpose (*CA 1985 ss.384-385*).

➤ A member may be liable for wrongful trading (*IA 1986 s.214*), or fraudulent trading (*CA 1985 s.458*).

- The court may require a member to make a contribution if that member withdrew property within 2 years of the LLP being wound-up (*IA 1986 s.214A* as inserted by *LLPR 2001 Sch. 3*).

IV Taxation

➤ A LLP is essentially 'transparent', or 'look through', for tax purposes.

➤ See the Taxation chapter - Income tax, CGT (for IHT see *IHTA 1984 s.267A*) and p.234.

C Private companies

References in this section apply to the Companies Act 1985, unless stated otherwise.

I Establishment
II Shareholders
III Directors
IV Finance
V Taxation - see 'Corporation tax' section

Note: *CA(EC)O 2000* now permits documents/forms to be sent to and from the Registrar of Companies electronically

I Establishment

A. Checks before establishing a company

- **Check 1:** search the index at Companies House to see if a desired name already exists.
- **Check 2:** do a trade mark search to see if the desired name already exists.
- **Check 3:** search local directories (eg: Yellow Pages, Thomson Local) to see if the desired name is already in use (to avoid passing off).

B. Establishing a company

- There are 2 methods of establishing a company as a vehicle through which to run a business.

Method 1 - from scratch

Steps

1 Prepare:
1) Statutory books
2) *Form 10*
3) *Form 12*
4) Memorandum of Association
5) Articles of Association
6) Fee

File: items 2 to 6 with the Registrar of Companies.

2 The Registrar incorporates the company if the documentation is in order (eg: the name does not need approval under *BNA 1985*). Incorporation occurs on the same day if submission is to the Central Registry (Cardiff) before 3 pm. Regional branches (London, Birmingham, Leeds, Edinburgh) also offer same day service.

3 The Registrar issues the 'Certificate of Incorporation', bringing the company into existence as a legal person. Any pre-incorporation contract is voidable. The company can only participate in a pre-existing agreement through a contract of novation.

Method 2 - buy a shelf company

- A shelf company has already been incorporated and 'sits on the shelf'.
- The existing directors of the shelf company resign and members complete a stock transfer form.
- It costs around £200 and it is fast and immediate. It is usual to change:
  a) directors and secretary
  b) shareholders
  c) registered office
  d) name
  e) objects
  f) articles
  g) share capital.
- The purchased company comes with resignation letters from existing directors.

C. Company documentation

1 **Statutory books** (These must be updated throughout the company's life.)

a) Register of Members,
b) Register of Directors,
c) Register of Company Secretaries,
d) Register of Directors' Interests,
e) Register of Charges (this is necessary even if the company does not take out any loans),
f) Minute Books for board and general meetings,
g) Accounting records (only after incorporation), *and*
h) Copies of directors' service contracts (only after incorporation).

2 ***Form 10***

- This states the postal address of the company's registered office.
- It gives the details of the first directors and the company secretary who automatically take office on incorporation (see p.251 and p.257 for an explanation of what details of the officers are required).
- It is signed by the subscribers to the memorandum, or by a solicitor on their behalf.

Later alteration of a company's registered office		
The registered country must stay the same for this method:		
First: the board passes a resolution	→	**Second:** file *Form 287*

3 ***Form 12***

- This is a statutory declaration by a director, the company secretary, or a solicitor involved in the formation of the company that the *Companies Act*s have been complied with.
- It is sworn before a solicitor or commissioner for oaths.

4 **Memorandum of Association**

- The memorandum is printed and signed by at least one subscriber.
- It states the name, address, occupation of each subscriber, and the number of shares each will take on formation.
- It is dated and witnessed (one witness for both signatures is sufficient).
- It contains the following:

  a) Company name

  - This must end with 'Limited' or 'Ltd' (*s.25*) *unless* the company is limited 'by guarantee' and conditions in *s.30* apply (limiting the company to humanitarian non-profit making activities).
    - A 'business name' is a trading name which a company may use in addition to the name under which it is incorporated. It need not end with 'Limited', but should comply with *BNA 1985* (see p.228):

As well as the business name...

...give the corporate name, and an address in the UK for serving documents:

a) on all letters, orders, invoices, etc, *and*
b) at all places of business to which customers have access, *and*
c) to any member of the public who requests this information.

- Existing company names are not permitted (*s.26*). A search of the Trademarks Index and Companies House will check if a name is in use (NB: no protection period after a search).
- An offensive name, or one suggesting a criminal offence, is also forbidden (*s.26*).
- The following require the President of the Board of Trade's written approval (*s.29*): any name suggesting connection with HM Government, the royal family, local authorities, any word or expression contained in continually updated regulations, or use of the words - 'Chamber of Commerce' (*CBN(CC)A 1999)*).

Alteration of an existing company name

➤ A 'special resolution' alters the name (*s.28*). The change is advertised by the Registrar of Companies in the *London Gazette* (*s.711*); a third party is not fixed with notice until 15 days after the advertisement appears (*s.42*).

➤ The Registrar will issue a new certificate after payment of the fee.

➤ A change of name may become necessary if:
a) the Registrar orders it because the name may harm or mislead the public (*s.32*), *or*
b) a third party's injunction prevents its use (eg: for appropriating good will - 'passing off').

b) Country in which the registered office is situated *(s.2)*

◆ This cannot be altered.

c) Limitation of members' liability *(s.3)*

◆ This is frequently limited by 'share capital', unless stated otherwise.

◆ Alternatively, liability can be limited 'by guarantee', in which case the members are liable to the extent of the guarantee.

d) Nominal capital

◆ The maximum value of shares the company can issue. An ordinary shareholder resolution can alter this. (Such a resolution must be filed with the Registrar - see p.249.)

e) Objects of the company *(s.2)*

◆ The objects set out the purposes of the company and what it is allowed to do (ie: its powers).

◆ *CA 1989* permits a description as a 'general commercial company'. This wording gives the company full freedom to do whatever it likes commercially, but it is unclear whether the company may perform actions which do not advance its business (eg: gifts to political parties or charitable donations).

◆ Old-style objects clauses may have a *Bell Houses* formula. This is wording as follows: The company is permitted to 'carry on any other trade or business whatsoever which can, in the opinion of the board ..., be advantageously carried on by the company in connection with, or ancillary to, any of the above businesses or the general business of the company' (*Bell Houses Ltd v. City Properties Ltd* [1966] 2 QB 656).

◆ Old clauses may also end with an 'independent objects' clause. This is done to avoid restrictive case law which in some instances reads 'lesser' objects clauses as subordinate to a 'main' object (ie: as powers of the company rather than an object). An independent objects clause says that each object is an independent object.

Alteration of objects

➤ A special resolution alters the objects (*s.4*).
➤ Minority shareholders can appeal to court within 21 days (*s.5*).

5 **Articles of Association** (the 'constitution' governing a company's internal workings)

- This is a contract between the company and its members, *governing members' rights in their capacity as members of the company (s.14).*
- It is printed and signed by the subscribers to the memorandum, dated and witnessed.
- 'Table A' (see table below) is a model set of articles that will apply in the absence of other articles unless specifically excluded (*s.8*). However, it may need changes by including special articles, to:
  - **empower directors to allot shares** (*s.80*).
  - **empower directors to allot shares to whomever they wish:** lifting the statutory pre-emption rights of existing members to a pro rata allotment of newly issued shares (ie: in proportion to their existing holdings) without recourse to a general meeting (*s.89*).
  - **enable directors to vote on issues in which they have a personal interest:** *Art.96* permits this in particular conditions; otherwise with a small company it can be difficult to achieve a quorum.
  - **restrict members' right to transfer shares:** likely in a small family company where the members are anxious to retain control of membership. *Art.24* allows directors to refuse to transfer shares in certain limited circumstances.
  - **prevent removal of directors:** likely in small company. If a director holds shares, a *Bushell v. Faith* clause is sensible as it multiplies his votes if a resolution proposes his removal. This provides some job security, but shareholders retain the right to remove directors by ordinary resolution (*s.303*).

  Note: References in this chapter to Articles (Arts.) assume Table A applies.
- Articles can be altered by a special resolution if the change is *bona fide* and in the best interests of the company as a whole (*s.9*).

Summary of Table A

Articles	Subject matter	*Articles*	Subject matter
Shares		*72*	Delegation of directors' powers
2-5	Share capital	*73-80*	Directors' appointment and retirement
6-7	Share certificates	*81*	Directors' disqualification and removal
8-11	Lien over shares	*82*	Directors' remuneration
12-22	Calls on shares and their forfeiture	*83*	Directors' expenses
23-28	Transfer of shares	*84-86*	Directors' appointments and interests
29-31	Transmission of shares	*87*	Directors' gratuities and pensions
32-34	Alteration of share capital	*88-98*	Directors' proceedings
35	Purchase of own shares	General	
Meetings		*99*	Secretary
36-37	General meetings	*100*	Minutes
38-39	Notice of general meetings	*101*	Company seal
40-53	Proceedings at general meetings	*102-108*	Dividends
54-63	Members' votes at general meetings	*109*	Accounts
Directors		*110*	Capitalisation of profits
64	Number of directors	*111-116*	Notices
65-69	Alternate directors	*117*	Winding up
70-71	Directors' powers	*118*	Indemnity

First board meeting

Consideration may be given to the following:

1 Electing a chairman / managing director / any directors with special responsibility.

2 Approving the cost of formation: the company can reimburse the subscribers by a novation contract.

3 Adopting a business name.

4 Opening a bank account.

5 Ordering stationery complying with the requirements in *s.349*, to state:

a) the company name, its place of registration and registered number (*s.351*), *and*

b) the address of its registered office (*s.351*), *and*

c) *either* the names of *all* its directors *or* none of their names (*s.305*).

- If a business name is used, the company's name and an address in Great Britain for the service of documents must be given.
- The information given in a) and b) demanded by *s.351* for stationery should also be displayed at any place where the company conducts business (*s.348*).

6 VAT registration with HM Customs and Excise.

7 PAYE and National Insurance obligations: contact the local tax office.

8 Insurance.

- Ensure all the company's assets and necessary insurance policies are in its own name.

9 Appointing an auditor.

10 The accounting reference date is fixed by statute as the last day of the month of incorporation (*CA(MAA)R 1996*). This may be changed later by submitting *Form 225*.

11 Adopting a company seal (*s.350*).

12 Awarding directors' service contracts.

- If the contract is for over 5 years, the board must resolve to seek shareholders' approval.

13 Allotting shares.

14 Whether to call a general meeting to obtain authority from shareholders to:

- award directors service contracts of longer than 5 years.
- allot shares (ordinary resolution *s.80).* Ensure that any pre-emption rights (*s.89*) do not restrict this.
- adopt an elective regime - see box at the base of this page.

15 Issuing debentures.

Elective resolutions

➤ These simplify the management of private companies by:

a) giving the directors authority for any specified or indefinite period to allot shares (rather than being limited to 5 years) (*s.80A*).

b) dispensing with the obligation to lay accounts and reports before an AGM (*s.252*).

c) dispensing with the need to call AGMs automatically (but a member can still insist on one being called) (*s.366A*).

d) reducing consent required to hold an EGM at short notice from 95% to a minimum of 90% (*s.369(4) and s.378(3)*).

e) dispensing with the annual reappointment of auditors (*s.386*).

➤ These must be passed unanimously.

➤ Revocation of any of these is by ordinary resolution (*s.379A*).

II Shareholders

A. Joining a company (ie: becoming a member)

- The original subscribers to the memorandum are members automatically, regardless of whether they are entered on the Register of Members.
- Anyone can become a member of a company if he buys shares in that company.
  - However, the directors must agree to write a person into the Register of Members, otherwise there are consequences which are listed below.

Register of Members

- This must state: the name, address and the number of shares held by each member, plus consideration for the shares, and the dates on which the shareholder's membership of the company begins and ceases (*s.352*).
- The details of new members must be entered within 2 months of acquisition, however they acquire their shares. Directors cannot refuse to enter a name unless the articles permit this - wrongful refusal can be overcome by applying to a court for rectification of the register.
- Between acquisition and registration, the prospective member is beneficially entitled to the shares. Dividends and voting rights of the existing registered member must be 'used' at the acquirer's direction.
- If a company has only one member, the register must state when this state of affairs begins and ends (otherwise there is a fine for the company and the responsible officer, plus a daily default fine).
- The court can order the register to be rectified if *either*:

  a) a name is 'without sufficient cause' entered incorrectly, or there is 'default ... or unnecessary delay' in entering a member's details (*s.359*), *or*

  b) it is 'just and equitable' to do so (*Burns v. Siemens Brothers Dynamo Works Ltd* [1919] 1 Ch 225).

B. Shareholders' rights

- Obligations between shareholders and the company (or any combination of them) are governed by the memorandum and articles (*s.14*).
- For a summary of shareholders' rights, see the chart overleaf.
- If Table A is effective, shareholders may *not* reverse management decisions made by the board (*Art.75*).
- **Voting:** a shareholder can generally vote as he sees fit *unless*:

  a) individually, or together with other directors, he holds 50% or more of the shares: this prevents his voting to permit an abuse of power in his capacity as a director, *or*

  b) a majority shareholder ignores 'equitable considerations'. The court may overrule a special resolution passed which disregards these 'equitable considerations' (*Clemens v. Clemens Brothers Ltd* [1976] 2 All ER 268).
- All members have a right to attend and vote at an Annual General Meeting ('AGM') of the company.
- All members have a right to attend and speak at a general meeting called at any other time - an Extraordinary General Meeting ('EGM').

Rights	Notes	Statute
All shareholders' rights		
Restrain an *ultra vires* act	Only before the act is done (after the company is bound). Remedy is an injunction	*s.35(2)*
To a share certificate	Within 2 months of allotment/lodgement of share transfer. *Prima facie* evidence of title	*s.185*
To a copy of annual accounts	Applies even if an elective resolution dispensing with an AGM is in force	*s.240*
To have a say in removing or appointing a director		*s.303*
Name on Register of Members	Unless subject to a special article	*s.352*
To a dividend (if declared)	May not increase the sum recommended by directors, but may decrease it	*Arts. 102-8*
To an AGM	This applies even if an elective resolution dispensing with the need to call an AGM is in force. Ultimately, a member may apply to the DTI which may convene a meeting for the purposes of which that member alone will represent a quorum (*CA s.367*)	*s.366* *s.366A*
To prevent an AGM being held on short notice		*s.369*
To receive notice of general meetings		*s.370*
To attend and vote at general meetings		*s.370*
Ask a court to call an EGM	If a members' boycott prevents a quorum, a court can reduce the quorum required to 1	*s.371*
To prevent the adoption of the elective regime		*s.379A*
To block a written resolution		*s.381A*
Inspect AGM/EGM minutes	Available at the registered office for consultation	*s.383*
Not to be unfairly prejudiced	Prejudice to rights as a member may be past, present, or future	*s.459*
Have a company wound up	Available if 'just and equitable' and the member has a 'tangible interest'. Not available if it prejudices someone unfairly.	*IA 1986* *s.122(g)*
Members with a minimum of 5% of the voting rights		
Place item on the agenda for an AGM	Written request to a company 6 weeks before an AGM with money to cover the company's expenses. (This may be refunded at the meeting.) If directors call an AGM within the 6 weeks, adequate notice is deemed to have been given	*s.376*
Circulate written statement	Written requisition deposited with company at least 1 week before a GM	*s.376*
Members with a minimum of 10% of the voting rights		
Call an EGM	May *not* be excluded by articles Members deposit at the registered office a written requisition which is signed by them all and states the reason for calling the meeting. If within 21 days, the directors do not call a meeting, to be held within 28 days of notice being sent out (ie: the maximum delay is 7 weeks from request), then members can call a meeting within 3 months and recover the cost from the company, which may deduct it from the directors' fees. Where members call the meeting they have an implied right to set the agenda (*s.368(3)*)	*s.368*
	This section, like *s.368*, allows members to call an EGM, but it differs in 3 respects: a) it applies to members with 10% or more of the *issued* (not the *paid up*) shares, *and* b) it permits the members themselves to summon the meeting, *and* c) it may be excluded by the articles	*s.370*
Prevent an EGM being held on short notice (unless an elective resolution is in force, in which case they can only do this with *greater than 10%* of the voting rights)		*s.369(3)(b)*
Demand a poll vote		s.373 Art. 46

Shareholders' agreement

➤ This binds members in matters beyond the scope of the articles and is used in practice to impose extra obligations on those concerned.

- It is a private document, and unlike the articles is not open to public inspection.
- It cannot be altered without the *unanimous* consent of all those who are party to it.
- It cannot override obligations under the articles or statute.
- It provides a remedy in breach of contract - via an injunction or damages.
- Possible uses include:
    - to arrange for the sale of the business as a going concern to the company when a company is initially set up,
        - Eg: setting out the allotment of shares or the grant of debentures,
    - agreeing to appoint a particular managing director, chairman, director etc,
    - joining a director, who is not a shareholder, to the agreement to enhance his job security by obliging the other signatories not to vote for his dismissal,
    - agreeing to grant a particular member a services contract,
    - binding the signatories to pursue a particular management policy - such matters are usually left to the board by the articles, and an agreement gives shareholders a direct influence on how the company is managed,
    - agreeing to change the name of the company or to have some policy regarding this,
    - pre-emption rights, where enshrining this in the articles would be too public an act,
    - to allow a member to leave the company by obliging the other signatories to purchase the shares.

Methods to control the Board

➤ This shareholders may specifically want to control the board and may use the following methods:

- increasing the number required for a quorum at a GM,
- appointing proxies when a shareholder is not at a GM,
- preserving the balance of power (eg: by inserting special articles restricting the transfer of shares),
- specifying in a shareholders' agreement a valuation and buy-out mechanism,
- replacing or amending the statutory pre-emption rights,
- inserting a restrictive objects clause in the memorandum,
- amending *Article 70* (Table A) to limit the powers of the board,
- amending *Article 72* (Table A) (concerning delegation of board powers).

C. Safeguards for shareholders

➤ Members have a cause of action in contract to enforce rights as members of the company (*s.14*).
- ◆ Relevant rights include rights to:
  a) a share of surplus capital on winding up.
  b) a lawfully declared dividend.
  c) vote at meetings.
- ◆ The liability of shareholders is limited to the amount invested in their shares.

  Note: a company can use *s.14* to compel members to fulfil contractual obligations (eg: pay for shares).

1 Shareholders' common law actions

➤ General rule: members cannot sue in the company's name (*Foss v. Harbottle* (1843) 2 Hare 461).

➤ There are 4 exceptions to this rule (not dealt with in this book). If a member *does* succeed in bringing an action under these exceptions:
- ◆ the action is 'derivative' as the claimant is pursuing a right which belongs to the company itself. *The company* is the claimant. If successful, *the company* is granted a remedy, not the member.
  - There is a preliminary hearing to see whether the facts fall within one of the relevant exceptions. If so, this is followed by the main hearing, to determine liability.

2 Shareholders' statutory actions: 'unfair prejudice' (*s.459*)

➤ The member's rights as a shareholder include rights under statute, the memorandum, the articles and any shareholders' agreement.

➤ Whether or not there is unfair prejudice is an objective test, so prejudice is viewed from the perspective of the 'reasonable bystander' (*Re R. A. Noble (Clothing) Ltd* [1983] BCLC 273).
- ◆ A shareholder cannot ordinarily complain of unfairness unless there has been a breach of the terms by which he had agreed that the company would be run (but this is tempered by equitable considerations). *s.459* depends on 2 features (*O'Neill v Phillips* [1999] 1 WLR 1092):
  - the way in which a company is run is regulated by rules to which the shareholders agree, *and*
  - this 'contract' is treated by equity as a contract of good faith.

➤ The court can make 'any order it thinks fit' (*s.461(1)*) and a non-exhaustive list of powers is given (*s.461(2)*). These include:
- ◆ authorising a member to bring a civil action in a company's name.
- ◆ restraining a company from an act, or compelling it to act so as to avoid the 'unfair prejudice'.
- ◆ providing for a member's shares to be purchased by other members or a company at a fair price.

➤ An action brought under *s.459* is not derivative, as the claimant is suing in his own right. Consequently, *the claimant* will receive a remedy if his plea is successful.

3 Petition to wind up the company (only if 'just and equitable') (not covered in detail here)

Will the courts intervene?

➤ There is conflicting authority as to whether the courts will now intervene wherever it is equitable if there is no precedent for them to do so (*Heyting v. Dupont* [1964] 2 All ER 273, *Prudential Assurance Co. v. Newman Industries Ltd (No.2)* [1982] 1 All ER 354).

➤ Previous cases where the courts have granted a minority shareholder a remedy include where:
- ◆ the company acted illegally.
- ◆ the company passed an ordinary resolution when a special or extraordinary resolution is needed.
- ◆ the majority shareholders 'defrauded' a minority member (*Clemens v. Clemens Bros.* [1976] 2 All ER 268).

D. Shareholders' meetings

Extraordinary General Meetings ('EGMs')	Annual General Meetings ('AGMs')
➤ If Table A is applicable, then the board may call these at any time (*Art.37*), and in certain circumstances shareholders may do so (see p.245)	➤ No AGM need be held in the calendar year of incorporation or the following year, provided one is held within 18 months of incorporation (*s.366*) ➤ An AGM is called once every calendar year; the maximum gap between convening AGMs is 15 months (*s.366*) ➤ If an elective resolution is in force, then the need to call an AGM may be dispensed with (*s.366A*)

➤ There are **5** requirements for a meeting, discussed below:

1) a valid notice of the meeting must be sent out.
2) the correct form of resolution must be proposed.
3) the meeting must be quorate.
4) the correct formalities must be observed at the meeting itself.
5) the voting must be correctly carried out.

1 Notice of the meeting (*s.369, Art. 38*)

If by post: add 2 days to these numbers because a notice is deemed to be given 48 hours after it was posted (*Art.115*).

Meeting	Notice	Short notice	
AGM	21 clear days	If *all* the shareholders agree	An elective resolution is effective if less than 21 days notice is given, if all entitled to attend and vote at a meeting agree (*s.379A(2A)*)
EGM (generally, but see the box below)	14 clear days	If a majority holding 95% of the voting capital agrees NB: An elective resolution can reduce this to 90%	
EGM where: a) there are special or elective resolutions proposed, *or* b) there is a resolution to appoint a director, *or* c) (according to some interpretations of *s.379*, which is ambiguous), there is a resolution to remove a director (see p.252)	21 clear days		
	Invalid notice (the time given or the contents of the notice are incorrect)		
	General rule: in Table A, any resolution passed will be invalid (*Art.111*) *unless* the error in the notice is accidental (*Art.34*)		

a) Contents of the notice

➤ Name of company, date, time and place of meeting.

➤ State whether the meeting is an AGM or an EGM.

➤ The exact wording of special *or* extraordinary resolutions *or* resolutions requiring special notice.

➤ Ordinary resolutions *must* be given in sufficient detail for members to decide whether to attend.

➤ A proxy notice *must* be included (*s.372(3)*).

➤ Accidental errors may not invalidate the notice (see 'Invalid notice' in table above).

b) Recipients and service

➤ Notice is sent in writing to all members, directors, the auditor and all persons entitled to a share in consequence of death or bankruptcy of a member (*Art.38*), provided that:
   i) the member has a registered address in the UK (*Art.112*).
   ii) a PR or trustee in bankruptcy informs the company of their address, otherwise service is sufficient at the member's registered address (*Art.116*).

➤ Notice may be served personally, else it is deemed to be served 48 hours after posting (*Art.115*).

2 Resolutions to be proposed

➤ An ordinary resolution (more than 50%) is sufficient unless statute or the articles require otherwise. (For written resolutions, see below; for elective resolutions, see p.243.)

Note: directors (or members with minimum 5% voting rights) may, at the company's expense, prepare a statement for circulation before the meeting.

Resolution	Type of meeting	Majority needed
Special	AGM or EGM	75% of those present and voting **NB:** more than 25% blocks these
Extraordinary	AGM or EGM	
Ordinary	AGM or EGM	More than 50% of those present and voting **NB:** 50% blocks these - this is 'negative control'
Elective	AGM or EGM	Unanimous consent of all who are entitled to vote

Shareholders' written resolutions (*s.381A*)

➤ A less cumbersome alternative to holding a general meeting.

➤ Where statute requires documents such as a director's service contract to be open to inspection, copies must be sent to members with the resolution.

➤ Written resolutions must be signed by ***all*** the members entitled to attend and vote at a general meeting, or on their behalf.

➤ The resolution is passed on the signature of the final member (*s.381A(3)*).

- The resolution must be sent to the auditors for checking at the time, or before the resolution is supplied to a member for signature (*s.381B*).
- If a director/the secretary does not ensure that this is done, the party responsible will be liable for a fine (*s.381B(2)*) *unless*:
  - it is not practical to comply, *or*
  - he believed on reasonable grounds either that the copy had been sent or that the auditors had otherwise been informed of its contents.
- If the resolution is not shown to the auditor, this does not affect the validity of the resolution (*s.381B(4)*).

➤ This procedure may *not* be used (according to *Schedule 15A*) to dismiss *either*:

- a director (*s.303*), *or*
- an auditor (*s.390*).

➤ Records and filing are as for a normal resolution at a GM.

After a shareholders' resolution has been passed (*s.380*)

1 Resolutions should be filed with the Registrar at Companies House within 15 days if they are:

- special
- extraordinary
- ordinary, **but** only those that increase the authorised share capital, give or revoke *s.80* authority to allot shares, or revoke an elective resolution
- elective
- written

2 Write up the minutes.

3 The board must meet and resolve to carry out any act which the shareholders have authorised *if* they wish to use this authority, but they are not compelled to do so.

3 Quorum

- The necessary quorum is 2, unless the company has 1 member (*s.370*).
- The articles can increase the minimum required (*s.370).*
- A member present through a third party proxy counts, provided the proxy is not a member in his own right as well.
- A quorum must be maintained throughout the meeting, else resolutions passed are invalid (*Art.41*).

4 Formalities at the meeting (proxies, minutes, sole members, chairman)

- The rights of proxies must be respected:
  - a company may not require the deposit of a proxy more than 48 hours notice before a meeting (*s.372(5)*).
  - a proxy may speak at the meeting (*s.372).*
- Minutes of the meeting should be kept (*s.382*).
- A sole member must provide the company with written notice of his resolution, otherwise although its validity is unaffected, he will be liable for a fine (*s.382B).*
- A chairman runs the meeting. He is usually the same individual as the chairman in a board meeting.

5 Voting

- Voting is *either* on a show of hands *or* by poll.
  - **On a show of hands:** one vote per person, proxies are not counted.
    - This usually happens unless a poll vote is called.
  - **A poll vote:** one vote for each share, proxies count.
    - A poll vote can be demanded by (*Art.46*) *either*:

      a) the chairman, *or*

      b) two members or proxies, *or*

      c) members or proxies with 10% or more of the total voting rights or paid up capital.
    - The *CA 1985* provides a safeguard that articles may *not* be altered so as to raise the threshold above a top limit of *either* at most ...

      a) ... 5 members, *or*

      b) ... members with more than 10% of the total voting rights or paid up capital

      ... having the ability to request a poll (*s.373*).
- The chairman has a casting vote that can be used if votes are tied (*Art. 50*). It cannot be used to create a tie.
- If votes are equal, the negative view takes priority and a resolution is defeated (unless a chairman's casting vote is used).

III Directors

A. Appointment

- The first directors are named on *Form 10,* and they take office on incorporation.
- Thereafter they are appointed by the board's resolution confirmed by ordinary resolution, or directly by ordinary resolution (*Arts.38,76-79*).
    - A prospective director must sign a consent, *Form 288a*, which is filed at Companies House (and there is one form per director).
- A director will need to possess 'qualification shares' to join the board if a special article requires this.
- The director's name, occupation, and nationality must be entered on the Register of Directors.
- If necessary, the Register of Directors' Interests is also updated.

1 Number of directors

- There must be at least 2 directors (*Art.64*), but this can be altered by a special article.

2 Shadow director

- This is a person (ie: any legal person - this includes a parent company) who instructs the board or a governing majority of it and they are accustomed to follow that person's directions (*s.741* and *Re Unisoft Group Ltd (No.2)* [1994] BCC 766).
- This excludes a professional advisor.

3 Alternate director

- A director may appoint a fellow director as an alternate director, but the board must approve the appointment of a non-board member (*Art.65*).
- An alternate director is treated like the other directors and is given notice of board meetings (*Art.66*).

4 Remuneration of non-executive directors

- This is set by a general meeting (*Art.82*).

5 Service contracts

- When the board is about to discuss a director's contract, the director must declare his personal interest (*s.317*) (see p.254).
- The director concerned may not either vote *or* count in a quorum for this particular matter (*Arts.94-96*).
    - In a small company, a special resolution could reduce the quorum in this instance, or an ordinary resolution could be used to the same end.
- Members must consent by ordinary resolution for contracts over 5 years, otherwise the fixed-term clause is void and the agreement becomes terminable at 'reasonable notice' (*s.319*).
    - The contract must be available for inspection for 15 days before the members' meeting and at the meeting itself.
- All contracts with more than 1 year to run, and with a notice period of more than 1 year, must be permanently available for inspection by members at the registered office, the place where the Register of Members is kept, or the company's principal place of business *(s.318).*

B. Loss of office

1 **Events on loss of office**

- A director may, depending on his contract, simultaneously lose any executive office.
  - He may claim for wrongful or unfair dismissal, or redundancy.
  - He may be entitled to compensation under his contract.
- The board and officers:
  - file *Form 288b* at Companies House, *and*
  - delete the director's name from the Register of Directors and amend the Register of Directors' Interests, *and*
  - remove the director's service contract from the registered office.

2 **Automatic removal**

a) ***Articles 73-80***

- The directors (except the managing director) retire by rotation.
- All directors retire at the first AGM, but are automatically reappointed unless members pass a resolution to the contrary.
- Thereafter 1 in 3 directors must retire and be put forward for re-election. They must take turns to comprise this third. Those who retire are automatically re-elected unless members pass a resolution to the contrary.
- In a small company where membership and directorship go hand in hand, a special article can remove the requirement to retire every 3 years.

b) ***Companies Act 1985 s.303*** **- removal by members**

Steps

1 The members have the right to remove a director at any time by ordinary resolution.

2 Members contemplating seeking the dismissal of a director should check the director's service contract to ascertain what compensation may be due under it.

3 A member gives 'special notice', leaving a formal notice at the registered office at least 28 days before a general meeting. (If one is called in this period (ie: less than 28 days after this special notice), then notice is deemed to have been given) (*s.379*)

4 On receipt of the 'special notice', the company should immediately inform the director concerned (*s.304(1)*).

5 If the board does not call a meeting the member can *either*:

i) if he owns at least 5% of the shares, request an AGM and put a resolution on the agenda, *or*

ii) if he owns at least 10% of the shares, summon an EGM.

- Due to ambiguous drafting in *s.379*, it is better to give 21 days notice of the meeting (although depending on the clause's construction 14 days may be sufficient).

6 The director can make a written representation to members and circulate a statement to them, as well as speak at the meeting (even if he is not a member).

7 If there is a *Bushell v. Faith* clause (see next page) in the articles and the resolution concerns a director's employment, his votes will increase in proportion to the size of his shareholding.

- Where the director has enough shares to defeat an ordinary resolution removing him from the board, consider passing a special resolution to remove this article.

3 Disqualification

a) *Article 81*

➤ This article lists 5 circumstances in which a director will cease to be entitled to hold office:

a) the director ceases to be a director because of the *CA 1985* or otherwise by law.

b) the director is declared bankrupt.

c) the director becomes mentally ill.

d) the director resigns.

e) the director is absent from board meetings for more than 6 months without the board's permission, and the board resolves that he should cease to sit on the board.

b) *Company Directors' Disqualification Act 1986*

➤ Disqualification may last from 2 to 15 years, depending on the director's previous conduct and the nature of the offence (*CDDA 1986* and *Re Sevenoaks Printers Ltd.* [1991] Ch. 164).

➤ Disqualification is imposed for *either*:

- general misconduct in relation to the company, *or*
- a criminal offence, *or*
- persistent default over filing with the Registrar of Companies, *or*
- fraudulent trading, *or*
- for a company which has gone insolvent, and the director's conduct during the insolvency makes him unfit to hold office.

4 Protecting a director's position

➤ To protect his position, a director might try to:

- insert a *Bushell v. Faith* clause in the articles. Where the director is also a shareholder, this multiplies the director's voting power at a general meeting at which his dismissal is on the agenda.
- pass a special article restricting the transfer of shares.
- replace the statutory pre-emption rights under *s.89* with a special article covering shares issued for any consideration.
- hold 25% of the voting shares for some, or over 50% to control the board's composition.
- hold a debenture which is conditional on the lender remaining a director.
- ensure damages are due under a service contract if the director is removed.
- remove the chairman's casting vote (especially if there are only 2 directors on the board).
- set the necessary quorum at a higher number than 2.
- replace *Arts. 94 and 95* with a special article permitting directors to contribute to a quorum and to vote on resolutions which concern themselves.
- ensure the appointment of an alternate director to represent an absent director at board meetings.

C. Directors' duties and restrictions

Duty to declare personal interests
➤ Whenever the board is about to discuss a matter in which the director is personally interested, he must make a formal declaration of his interest (*s.317*). **Failure to do so is a criminal offence.**

1 **Fiduciary duty**

a) **A general duty of good faith owed to the company**

➤ Power must be used for the benefit of the company *and* for the reason it was conferred.

➤ A breach entitles the company to seek losses or an account of profits from a director.

Note: the articles, or service contract, may impose extra obligations.

b) **Not to make a secret profit**

➤ If a conflict of interest arises, a director must *either*:

i) fully disclose relevant facts and obtain the members' resolution to sanction it (impossible if the director is a majority shareholder, as this endorses a fraud on the minority), *or*

ii) account to the company for any profits which accrue from the secondary venture.

➤ *Art.85* permits personal interests if they are disclosed to the board and the director is not defrauding the company.

c) **Not to exceed power under articles or abuse powers**

➤ The director should not use powers for a purpose other than that for which they were given.

➤ An ordinary resolution can absolve a director of liability for a particular act, so long as there is no fraud on the minority.

d) **Duty to disclose information**

➤ Service contracts: right for shareholders to inspect, unless under 12 months (see p.251).

2 **Duty of skill and care**

➤ **Skill** is a subjective test - ie: the competence reasonably expected of someone with a particular director's knowledge and experience.

➤ **Care** is an objective test - ie: the care a reasonable person would exercise on his own behalf.

➤ Unless extra duties are owed under a service contract, a director only owes a duty to attend board meetings and vote when he reasonably can.

3 **Administrative duties**

A director must comply with the following administrative duties in respect of company records:

a) **Annual accounts** (*s.226*)

➤ Duty to ensure these are compiled annually and sent to members and the Registrar within 10 months of the accounting reference date (*s.244*).

➤ These contain Profit and Loss account, Balance Sheet, Auditor's report, Directors' report (*s.248*), details of directors' emoluments and other benefits (*CA(DDE)R 1997*).

➤ Accounts can be less detailed for small/medium sized companies (*CA(ASMCMAA)R 1997*).

- An Auditor's report may not be necessary for certain companies (see p.257).

b) **Director's report** (*s.234*)

➤ Duty to submit this for each financial year.

c) **Annual return**

➤ Duty to submit this to the Registrar within 28 days of the 'return date' (*s.363*). (The 'return date' is fixed 1 year after incorporation, and thereafter 1 year after the last return.)

➤ This shows amongst other things, the address of the registered office, main business activities, details of directors and the company secretary (*s.364* and *C(CAR)R 1999*) .

d) **Register of Directors**

➤ Contains name, address, business occupation, date of birth, nationality, other directorships.

e) **Register of Directors' Interests in the company**

➤ Number of shares and debentures held by directors, their spouses and children under 18.

➤ Information must be given within 5 days of joining the board or gaining the interest.

➤ Company secretary updates it.

4 **Duty to consider the interests of employees** (*s.309*)

➤ Directors must consider employees' interests and balance these against members' interests.

➤ Employees do not have the right to enforce this.

5 **Duty to comply with rules on stationery** (*s.305*)

➤ All directors' names must appear, or none of them.

6 **Statutory restrictions**

The following topics have statutory restrictions where directors are concerned:

a) **Gratuitous compensation** (*s.312*)

➤ A 'golden handshake' must have prior approval of members by ordinary resolution (*s.312*).

➤ Redundancy rights, compensation for unfair dismissal and breach of contract are unaffected.

b) **Service contracts** (*s.319*)

➤ These may not exceed 5 years, unless approved by members' ordinary resolution (see p.251).

c) **Substantial property transactions** (*s.320*)

➤ Directors' transactions with the company are forbidden if an asset is of 'requisite value':

a) over £100,000, *or*

b) between £2,000 and £100,000 *and* representing more than 10% of the company's net assets as shown in the latest accounts (or if no accounts, 10% of paid up share capital).

➤ BUT the transaction is permitted if members authorise it, by passing an ordinary resolution.

◆ If members' approval is not gained, the contract is voidable. Any director who authorised it must indemnify the company for any loss, and account to it for any profit.

d) **Contract with a sole member who is a director** (*s.322B*)

➤ The contract must be written, or the terms should be set out in a memorandum, or in the minutes of the first board meeting after the contract is made.

➤ The company and defaulting officers are liable to be fined if this is not done.

e) **Restriction on loans to directors** (*s.330*)

➤ These are forbidden, unless the amount concerned is very small.

➤ *s.330* does not make it a criminal offence to make such loans. It is often ignored in practice.

➤ *s.330* gives the company redress (for profit or losses accruing to the company due to the transaction) against a director who receives the loan and against directors who authorised it.

D. Board meetings

Board meetings

- A board meeting may be called by *any* director at *any* time (*Art.88*).
- Notice must be 'reasonable' and given to every director who is in the country. (Oral notice is sufficient.)
    - What is 'reasonable' depends on the issue to be discussed and the make-up of the board.
        - In practice 'reasonable' is very often taken to be 7 days.

1 Votes

- One per director.
- Resolutions are passed by a simple majority.
- *Art.88* gives the chairman a casting vote, but a special resolution may remove this, in which case the negative view takes precedence and a resolution is defeated.
- Personal interests may stop a director voting (*Art. 94*). A *s.317* declaration must be made to avoid criminal liability.
    - Even a single director at a board meeting of one must make this declaration and note it in the minutes - *Neptune (Vehicle Washing Equipment) Ltd. v. Fitzgerald [1995] 3 All ER 811, Ch.D.*
- *Art.94* permits voting if the director is buying shares in the company or lending it money, otherwise it forbids him to vote if he has an interest, *unless* it comes within the 4 exceptions listed in *Art.94.*
- The board has powers of management (*Art.70*).
    - In a deadlock, the Board should summon a general meeting.

2 Quorum

- 2 constitute a quorum, unless directors themselves or a special article dictate otherwise (*Art.89*).
- A director with a personal interest does not qualify as part of a quorum (*Art.95*).

3 Minutes

- Minutes must be kept of every board meeting (*Art.100, s.382(1)*).

4 Written resolutions

- Written resolutions avoid the need for a meeting, but consent must be unanimous (*Art.93*).
    - Under *Art. 94,* a written resolution cannot be used if there is a director who cannot vote. However, this restriction is often ignored in practice.

E. Company officers

1 **Chairman**

- The board elects a chairman and may remove the chairman at any time (*Art.91*).
- The chairman has a casting vote, but this is revocable by special article (*Art.88*).
- The casting vote can be used if directors' votes are tied, but it may *not* be used to create a tie.
- The chairman resolves disputes over whether a board meeting is quorate, and over voting rights.

2 **Managing director**

- The managing director is entrusted with the company's daily administration, but the board may alter or withdraw a managing director's powers at any time (*Art.72*).
- The managing director is a member of the board, but he does not need to retire by rotation at every third AGM as the other directors do (*Art.84*).

3 **Company secretary**

- It is compulsory to have a company secretary (*s.283*).
- The first secretary is named on *Form 10*.
- Subsequent secretaries are appointed by the board (*Art.99*).
- The board sets the terms of the appointment (*Art.99*).
- The secretary has ostensible authority (and probably actual authority) to act in administrative matters (*Panorama v. Fidelis* [1971] 2 QB 711). This includes keeping the statutory books.
- The board can remove the secretary at any time. Compensation depends on the terms of employment (*Art.* 99).

4 **Auditor**

The need for an auditor in a small company (*s.246 and s.249A*)				
Balance sheet	Over £1.4 million	£1.4 million or less		Shareholders holding at least 10% of shares can insist on an audit
Turnover	Any	Greater than £1 million	£1 million or less	
Need for an auditor?	✓	✓	✗	

- Directors appoint an auditor before the first AGM.
  - The auditor must be a certified or chartered accountant who is independent of the company.
- At the end of the first AGM, the auditor's office ends. The members decide who will act as auditor until the next AGM (*s.384*).
- Under the elective regime, the auditor is appointed within 28 days of the annual accounts being sent to members - he is deemed to be returned to office (*s.385A*).
- Members can remove the auditor at any time by an ordinary resolution at a general meeting (*s.391*). The procedure is the same as for the removal of a director (see p.252).
- The auditor may resign by sending a written notice to the company's registered office (*s.392*). This notice must state whether there are suspicious circumstances. This prevents an auditor abandoning members to a fraud (*s.394*).

F. Liability

> *s.727* - a court may excuse a director either wholly or partly from liability if it is fair to do so

1 **Generally**

A director is ***not*** personally liable, *except* if he ...

- ➤ **... gives a personal guarantee.**
  - This will occur in a small company where the banks insist on a personal guarantee to back loans.
- ➤ **... acts while disqualified by court order.**
  - He will be liable for all debts the company incurs during this period.
- ➤ **... trades 'fraudulently' (*IA s.213*)** (see p.285).
  - This means the director is knowingly party to fraudulent trading.
  - An action under this section is only possible during liquidation when the liquidator may petition the court for the director to contribute to the company's assets.
- ➤ **... trades 'wrongfully' (*IA s.214*)** (see p.285).
  - The director knows or ought to know that the company's insolvency is likely, *and*
  - The director fails to act to minimise the loss of creditors, *and*
  - The director may be required to contribute to the company's assets during liquidation.
- ➤ **... breaches a warranty of authority.**
  - The director purports to act for the company, but acts *ultra vires*.
  - If the director has ostensible authority, the company is bound.
- ➤ **... delegates wrongfully.**
  - A director delegates a function(s) to employees whom he should have known to be incompetent.
- ➤ **... breaches a fiduciary/statutory duty** (see pp.254 - 255).

2 ***Ultra vires* acts (ie: acts outside the objects clause of the company's memorandum)**

a) **Company acts *ultra vires*** (*s.35*)

- ➤ The company is bound provided its agent had actual or ostensible authority to act (see p.300).
- ➤ The directors are liable for a breach of duty.
- ➤ Members can ratify a breach and indemnify directors by passing special resolutions.

b) **Agent acts *ultra vires*, but within the *company's* power** (*s.35A*)

- ➤ **Board of directors:** power to bind the company (and to authorise others to do so) is unfettered.
  - Provided a third party acts in good faith the company will be bound.
  - Members can ratify the directors' acts with an ordinary resolution.

c) **Agent (eg: unauthorised director or company secretary)**

- ➤ If the agent has 'ostensible' authority the company is bound.
- ➤ Members can ratify the act with an ordinary resolution.

Note:

- ➤ Although Companies House is a public register, third parties are not fixed with constructive notice of a company's constitution (*s.35B*).
- ➤ Members can seek an injunction to prevent an *ultra vires* act being committed (*s.35(2)*).
- ➤ Notwithstanding personal liability, an agent or director will not be subject to a penalty unless the company actually incurs a loss due to their actions.

Party	Act	Actual authority?	Apparent authority?	Company bound?	Can board ratify?	Director liable?
Board	*intra vires*	✓ (always for IV)	✓ (Board always has this)	✓ (*s. 35, 35A and 35B*)	Ratification by the Board if within the Board's power else ratification by an appropriate resolution at a GM (unless a fraud on the minority)	✗
Board	*ultra vires*	✗ (always for UV)	✓ (Board always has this)	✓ (*s. 35, 35A and 35B*)	A special resolution is needed to ratify a UV act (effectively changing the objects clause)	✓
Single Director	*intra vires*	✓	✓ (must be if Board has actual authority)	✓	Ratification by the Board if within the Board's power else ratification by an appropriate resolution at a GM (unless a fraud on the minority)	✗
Single Director	*intra vires*	✗	✓	✓	Ratification by the Board if within the Board's power else ratification by an appropriate resolution at a GM (unless a fraud on the minority)	✓
Single Director	*intra vires*	✗	✗	✗ No because it is not an act done with the authority of the Board s.35, s35A, 35B do not apply	Ratification by the Board if within the Board's power else ratification by an appropriate resolution at a GM (unless a fraud on the minority)	✓
Single Director	*ultra vires*	✗ (always for UV)	✓	✓	A special resolution is needed to ratify a UV act (effectively changing the objects clause)	✓
Single Director	*ultra vires*	✗ (always for UV)	✗	✗ No because it is not an act done with the authority of the Board s.35, s35A, 35B do not apply	A special resolution is needed to ratify a UV act (effectively changing the objects clause)	✓
Unauthorised agent	*intra vires* or *ultra vires*	✗	✗	✗	✗	Not applicable

Instructions for use of this box:

Read it from left to right
- grey areas indicate a choice that has to be made depending on circumstances
- non-grey areas indicate consequences that automatically flow from whatever is on the left

IV = *intra vires*
UV = *ultra vires*

IV Finance

➤ This section examines 2 methods by which companies raise money: by loans and by shares.

A. Debentures

➤ Directors and a lender take the following steps to grant a debenture:

Steps	
1	Check whether the company has authority to borrow (this applies to the directors).
2	Make searches (this applies to the lender).
3	Agree the type of the security.
4	Agree the terms of the debenture.
5	Follow the procedure for granting the debenture.
6	Register the debenture.
7	Comprehend the lender's remedies.
8	Redeem the debenture.

These steps are expanded below

1 **Check whether the company has authority to borrow (this applies to the directors)**

➤ A company may not borrow money unless it has the power under its memorandum or articles to do so.

- ◆ A 'general trading company' has implied authority, but the large City institutions prefer there to be actual authority in the articles.

➤ The directors should check they have power in the memorandum/articles to borrow.

- ◆ *Art. 70* gives directors the power to borrow.

2 **Make searches (this applies to the lender)**

➤ The lender should make a search of the Charges Register at Companies House which lists the date on which any charge was created, the amount of the security, the property subject to the charge and the holder of the charge.

- ◆ If these particulars are given incorrectly on the Register, then registration is void against an administrator, liquidator or purchaser for value.

➤ The lender should also check at Companies House to ensure that:

- ◆ the directors have power to borrow - he should inspect the memorandum and articles.
  - Although this is sensible, it is not *necessary* as *s.35* says that the company has power ostensibly and a third party does not need to check whether it *actually* has such power.
- ◆ the directors have been properly appointed - he should inspect *Form 10* and *Form 288a* which will confirm the authorisation of particular individuals to act on the company's behalf.
- ◆ the property is not already subject to a prior charge on the Charges Register.

  Note: the lender should ask the holder of a floating charge for a 'letter of non-crystallisation', stating that the charge has not crystallised.

➤ The lender should search HM Land Registry and the Land Charges Department. Both keep records of charges over land. A 'purchaser' for value is only fixed with notice of charges which appear on *these* registers, irrespective of whether the charge is also registered at Companies House.

3 **Agree the type of security**

a) **A fixed charge** is a charge over specified property. It prevents the company disposing of that asset without the debenture holder's agreement.

b) **A floating charge** hangs over a class of property. The company may dispose of the property in the class without the debenture holder's agreement. If an event specified in the debenture occurs, the charge 'crystallises' and the property in the class becomes 'fixed'. At this point the rules for a fixed charge apply. Examples of when a charge may crystallise include when:

- a winding up petition is presented to a court (*s.463*), *or*
- there is a members' resolution to voluntarily wind up the company (*s.463*), *or*
- a receiver is appointed by the court, or by a debenture holder under a power in the debenture, *or*
- any other event specified in the debenture occurs.

c) **A personal guarantee** may be required from the directors, in which case they will be personally liable if the company defaults.

- The director concerned must make a *s.317* declaration at the board meeting when the loan is discussed (see p.254).

4 **Agree the terms of the debenture**

- **Repayment date:** on a fixed date *or* on the occurrence of a specified event.
- **Interest:** when payable and how the rate will be calculated.
- **Conditions:** if the charge is a floating one, the lender will impose a condition preventing the subsequent creation of a fixed charge over the property as this would take priority over the floating charge on liquidation.
  - The company is responsible for registering this prohibition.
- **Power to appoint a receiver and an administrative receiver:** to be exercised if the company defaults on interest or capital repayments.
  - **A receiver** has power to sell assets (and it is usual to have power to appoint one for a fixed charge).
    - A receiver should be expressly empowered to:
      - sell assets, *and*
      - manage the company, *and*
      - take legal proceedings in its name.
  - **An administrative receiver** has management powers (and it is usual to have power to appoint one for a floating charge).
- **Any other powers:** eg: power to sell the security, power to run the business, etc.

5 **Follow the procedure for granting the debenture**

- The board resolves to grant the debenture.
- 2 directors sign the debenture.

6 Register the debenture as a charge (*ss. 395-397*)

(NB: The Companies Act 1989 imposes a new regime for registration, but this is not yet in force. Below are the present rules that are still in force.)

- Register the charge at Companies House and pay the fee.
  - If appropriate, register it also with HM Land Registry or the Land Charges Department.
- It is the company's duty to register the charge, but anyone interested in it may do so.
  - The security of an *un*registered charge is void against:
    - an administrator,
    - a liquidator,
    - a creditor of the company - the creditor ranks as an unsecured creditor,
    - a person who has registered a proprietary right or interest in the property subject to the charge.
  - A second charge which is registered, takes precedence over a first unregistered charge.
- The debenture should be registered at Companies House within 21 days (*s.395*).
  - The *Companies Act 1985* requires the registration of 'prescribed particulars' of the charge and the instrument of the charge at Companies House.
- Late registration
  - Either seek leave of the court for late registration (*s.404*) or take out a fresh charge.
- Incorrect registration
  - Corrupted register entries do not offer protection so the lender should check a copy of the entry.
  - Errors can be corrected (*s.404*). Although alterations are not retrospective, the court can order that the alteration should be valid if it does not prejudice a third party.

7 Comprehend the lender's remedies

- If remedies are required, then appoint an administrative receiver.
  - An administrative receiver should notify the following of his appointment: the company, creditors and the Registrar (*IA s.46*).

8 Redeem the debenture

- The company sends a memorandum of discharge, usually *Form 403*, to the Registrar (*s.403*).
- The lender endorses a receipt for repayment on the debenture.

B. Shares

1 Share capital

Money from sale of shares
➤ The company can use the money raised from the sale of shares as it sees fit.
➤ If the company receives money for the shares above the nominal value, the extra consideration is paid into a share premium account (*s.130*).
➤ If the company receives money for the shares below the nominal value, the shareholder must pay the company a sum equal to the discount in the shares plus interest (*s.100*).

a) Types of shares

- **Fully paid:** the shareholder has paid the company the share's nominal value.
- **Partly paid:** the shareholder has paid the company only part of the share's nominal value.
  - If the company goes into liquidation, the shareholder will have to pay creditors whatever sum remains unpaid.
  - Redeemable shares cannot be partly paid (*Art.3*).

b) Issue of new shares (allotment)

Steps

1 A board meeting resolves to issue shares.

2 A general meeting is called to obtain shareholders' approval if:

a) the authorised share capital needs to be increased. This can be done provided:
- the articles permit it (*Art.32* does), *and*
- the members pass an ordinary resolution.

b) the directors lack valid authority to allot shares under *s.80*. This authority can be either granted:
- by an ordinary resolution (this must be filed with the Registrar). This lasts for a maximum of 5 years unless an elective resolution is in force - see p.243.
- by the articles (although an ordinary - ***not** a special* - resolution can revoke this).

c) the directors wish to suspend pre-emption rights under *CA s.89*.

CA s.89

➤ The company must offer existing shareholders the shares on a pro rata basis for 21 days. After 21 days, any shares not allotted can be taken by third parties (but not on terms more favourable than those offered to shareholders).

- The directors will want to disapply *s.89* rights where:
  - the consideration is wholly in cash, *or*
  - the directors do not intend to offer existing members the chance to take up their pro rata entitlement (*either* because members are unlikely to do so, *or* because the directors wish to broaden the company's membership), *or*
  - the directors do not wish to keep the share offer open for 21 days.

  Note: *s.89* authority is only valid provided that the *s.80* authority in force when the *s.89* authority was granted is still valid.

Suspending pre-emption rights - 3 methods

1 Insert a special article.

2 Pass a special resolution. A written circular (which is usually sent out with a notice of a GM) to shareholders before the meeting must explain:
   a) the reason for suspending *s.89* pre-emption rights,
   b) the consideration for the shares,
   c) a justification for the value of the consideration being asked for the shares.

3 Use a written resolution: the circular is the same as that for passing a special resolution.

3 File with the Registrar the memorandum if this has been amended, *Form 123* (increase of share capital), any special resolutions and any ordinary resolutions that increase the authorised share capital, or that give or revoke *s.80* authority to allot shares.

4 The board resolves to issue shares. Any offer for those shares must come from a prospective shareholder, and must *not* be offered by the company to the public.

5 Payment need not be in cash, but if the consideration takes any other form, the written contract and *Form 88(2)* are filed with the Registrar.
- Where the contract is oral, *Form 88(3)* is used.

6 The board resolves to seal share certificates.

2 Acquisition and transmission of shares

a) Transfer of shares

Steps

1 **The donor or vendor completes and signs a stock transfer form.**

- ➤ If the shares are partly paid, the transferee also signs the form.
- ➤ Unless the shares are a gift, stamp duty (0.5%) is due (*Finance Act 1986 s.64*).

2 **The transferee sends the stock transfer form to the company.**

3 **The company amends the Register of Members and issues a certificate in the transferee's name within 2 months (*s.183*).**

- ➤ Directors can refuse to transfer the shares if they are empowered to do so by a special article.
  - ◆ Table A (*Art.24*) does *not* permit this if the shares are fully paid.
  - ◆ The directors may refuse under *Art. 24* if *either*:
    a) the shares are partly paid and the directors do not approve of the transferee, *or*
    b) the company has a lien over them, *or*
    c) there is a procedural irregularity such as:
      - the transfer is not lodged at the registered office with the share certificate, *or*
      - the transfer relates to more than one class of share, *or*
      - the transfer is in favour of more than 4 transferees.
  - ◆ The directors must act in good faith and decide within a reasonable time (under 2 months) (*s.183*).
  - ◆ If the directors refuse, and they are acting *ultra vires, or* the transferee shows they are acting in bad faith, the court will order the register to be rectified.
  - ◆ If the directors validly refuse to transfer shares, this does not entitle the transferee to seek damages or recission of the contract to purchase the shares. In such a case:
    - the transferor remains the legal owner of the shares and holds them on trust for the transferee.
    - the transferor receives notice of general meetings, and he may both vote and receive dividends, but he must act as the transferee instructs.

4 **If the transferee is a director:**

- ➤ he must inform the company in writing within 5 days (*s.324*), and the Register of Directors' Interests is amended (*s.325*).

5 **The company records the transfer on the annual return.**

b) Transmission of shares

- ➤ Transmission of shares occurs when a member dies.
- ➤ Shares vest automatically in PRs or trustees in bankruptcy by operation of law. However, although the PRs or trustees control the beneficial interest, they are not members of the company and so cannot vote or receive dividends. They can *either*:
  i) elect for registration as members in their own right, *or*
  ii) nominate a transferee (ie: transfer the shares to a beneficiary or creditor who can then apply for registration as a member).

3 Reducing share capital - 3 methods

a) Reduce share capital (*ss.135-137*)

- This requires a special resolution and the court's consent.
- The company can:
  - cancel further liability on partly paid shares, *or*
  - repay to members surplus capital without reducing the capital available to repay creditors, *or*
  - reduce the value of the shares in line with capital losses. (This does not prejudice creditors as it merely represents an admission of losses that have been incurred.)

b) Buy back its own ordinary shares which have been issued (*s.162*)

- Repurchased shares are effectively cancelled.
- It is only possible to buy back ordinary shares if:

Conditions for buy-back of shares

  - the articles permit it (*Art.35* does), *and*
  - the members pass a special resolution to do so (the shares affected carry no voting rights), *and*
  - the company has money available which will be from one of the following sources:
    - i) distributable profits ('in reserves') (*s.168*), *or*
    - ii) an issue of shares (*s.171*), *or*
    - iii) capital (*s.173*), but only if:
      - there is no other possible source of finance, *and*
      - shareholders pass a second special resolution approving the use of capital (the shares affected carry no voting rights), *and*
      - creditors are notified, *and*
      - the directors make a statutory declaration of the company's solvency for the next year.

    NB: *Art. 35* in *Table A* specifically permits it (subject of course to the above), *and*
  - the contract is available at the registered office for 15 days before a general meeting and 10 years after it (*s.169(4)*), and is at the general meeting itself (*s.164*).
- *Form 169* is sent to the Registrar. It states the number of shares bought and the nominal value of the shares.
- Note: a) if the directors make the statutory declaration erroneously, they may be personally liable together with the purchaser of the shares to compensate the company's creditors.

  b) a vendor shareholder cannot vote at the meeting.

c) Issue redeemable shares (*s.159*)

- The company can buy back this type of share if:
  i) the shares are fully paid up, *and*
  ii) it has already issued non-redeemable shares.
- *Art. 3* permits the issue of redeemable shares, but a special article must set out terms on which the shares are redeemable, eg: whether at the company's or a shareholder's behest.
- The members pass a special resolution to amend the articles, to state the terms and manner of the issue. *(NB: s.159A is not yet in force, but will require all companies to state the terms and manner of such an issue in the articles.)*
- The members can approve an issue of redeemable shares by ordinary resolution.

Note on taxation (*TA 1988 ss.219-224*)

➤ Money received by an individual from the company is usually classified as a 'distribution' subject to income tax under Schedule F (see p.76).

➤ However, on a redemption, repayment or purchase of shares by a company, the individual is treated as having made a disposal for capital gains tax purposes rather than having received income under Schedule F if:

a) the owner of the shares is domiciled, resident and ordinarily resident in the UK during the year of assessment in which the transaction occurs (*TA 1988 s.220(1)*), *and*
b) has possessed the shares for 5 years (*TA 1988 s.220(5)*), *and*
c) the sale 'substantially' reduces his holding or that of his associates (partners, close relatives, etc) (*TA 1988 s.222(1), s.224*),

and the transaction was either:

'wholly or mainly for the purposes of benefiting a trade carried on by the company' and not ' to enable the owner of the share to participate in a company's profits without receiving a dividend or for the avoidance of tax' (*TA 1988 s.219(1)(a)*)

or

i) the money received is applied to pay IHT within 2 years of death, *and*
ii) the IHT arises on death, *and*
iii) undue hardship would arise if the company did not repurchase the shares.

4 Prohibition on financial assistance for purchasing shares *(s.151)*

➤ A company is prohibited from helping a third party to buy its shares.
  - It is a criminal offence incurring imprisonment of up to 2 years and/or a fine.
  - Such transactions are void and unenforceable.

➤ Such 'financial assistance' is defined by a list given in *s.152(1).*

➤ A whole set of exceptions is listed in *s.153*, but many exceptions have been cut back due to recent case law. However, although a company is restricted by *s.151,* it *can* give financial assistance if it goes through the 'whitewash procedure' (*ss.155-158*). It can do this if:

a) the articles permit it, *and*
b) the directors make a statutory declaration that the company is solvent and will remain so over the next year, *and*
c) the members consent by special resolution (within 1 week of the statutory declaration), *and*
d) the auditor confirms the directors' statutory declaration.

Note: if the borrower is a director then a loan is forbidden by *s.330*. The *CA 1985* does not impose a criminal penalty, but it imposes an obligation on the directors who authorise the loan to indemnify the company for any resulting loss (see p.255).

➤ The House of Lords considered *s.151* in considerable detail in *Brady v. Brady* [1989] AC 755, but a pragmatic approach is to be found in a judgment of Hoffmann J in *Charterhouse Investment Trust Ltd v. Tempest Diesels Ltd* [1986] BCLC 1, where he emphasises that the 'commercial realities of each transaction' should be examined to determine if financial assistance is being given.

5 **Dividends**

➤ The directors consider the payment of a 'final' dividend after the accounts have been completed, and recommend it to a general meeting. The accounts for the calculation of a final 'dividend' must be the last set for the financial year, prepared in accordance with *s.226* (ie: audited, put before the members, filed with the Registrar, etc).

➤ At any time during an accounting period, the directors can decide to declare an 'interim' dividend if this appears 'justifiable by the profits of the company available for distribution' (*Art.103*). For the payment of an 'interim' dividend, the company can prepare 'interim' accounts.

➤ Dividends can only be paid if there are 'profits available' (*s.263*).

- There are 'profits available' if the undistributed trading profit which has accumulated during the past year and previous years exceeds the total amount of debts which have fallen due over the past year and previous years.
- In addition to the normal accountancy rules which are applied in working out the extent of profits and losses, there are some statutory rules (*s.263*):
  - capitalised profit (ie: profit used to repay bonus shares or buy back shares) *is not* treated as profit.
  - loss written off against a reduction of share capital *is not* treated as a loss.
  - a provision against anticipated losses (ie: the reduction in the value of wasting assets) *is* treated as a loss (*s.275*).

➤ A general meeting votes upon whether to accept the directors' recommendation; it may not vote for a higher dividend than the directors propose (*Art.102*).

➤ Members can sue the company for unpaid 'final' dividends as a debt which is owed to them from the date when the dividend was declared. There is no debt action for unpaid 'interim' dividends as members may not expect these as of right until the money is actually paid to them.

➤ Members knowingly in receipt of dividends paid when there are insufficient 'profits available' must refund the money to the company (*s.277*).

- Directors are personally liable for breach of duty if any such sums are unrecovered after the company has paid a dividend without sufficient 'available profits'.

C. Comparison of shareholding and debenture holding

	Shareholder	Debenture holder
Management control	✓ The investor may attend GMs and vote to influence how the company is run	✗ The lender usually has no right to vote at meetings
Income	✗ Dividends cannot be paid unless the company makes a profit	✓ The amount of interest and its payment dates are guaranteed. If insufficient profits are available, interest will have to be paid out of capital
Security	✗ The capital will not be repaid unless the company buys back its own shares or issue redeemable shares ✗ The value of the capital may fluctuate ✓ The capital may go up (or down!)	✓ The capital will be repaid on a predetermined date *or* when the debenture holder demands it ✓ The capital sum will normally remain set at the amount of the loan ✗ The capital sum will not appreciate
	✗ Capital is not returned if the company is insolvent on winding up	✓ Capital will be recovered on insolvency if the debenture is secured
Investment's marketability	✗ The articles may restrict the transfer of shares	✓ The debenture can be sold to anyone
Tax	✗ Dividends are not tax deductible	✓ Interest on the loan may be deductible as a debit on a 'loan relationship' (see p.95)

Summary of company procedure

Transaction	Authority	Resolution	Internal procedures	External procedures
Appoint directors for at least 5 years	*s.319*	Ordinary	The contract is kept at the registered office for 15 days before the meeting and at the meeting itself	
Allot shares (if this power is not in the articles)	*s. 80*	Ordinary		File resolution. Within 1 month of allotment, file *Form 88(2)* and the contract if consideration is in kind, or *Form 88(3)* if the contract is oral
Remove statutory pre-emption rights	*s. 95*	Special		File resolution
Introduce elective regime	*ss.379A-380*	Elective		File resolution
Cancel elective regime	*s.379A*	Ordinary		File resolution
Change company name	*s.28*	Special	Alter memorandum	File amended memorandum and resolution
Select business name		Board resolution	Alter stationery as appropriate	
Increase nominal share capital	*s.121*	Ordinary		File resolution, *Form 123* and amended memorandum
Change objects	*s.4*	Special		File amended memorandum and resolution
Change articles	*s.5*	Special		File amended articles and resolution
Remove a director	*s.303*	Ordinary	Complainant gives the board special notice 28 days before an EGM. The board gives a copy of this notice to the director The board should resolve to call an EGM with 21 days' notice (arguably 14 is sufficient). A director can make a written representation which the board circulates to members Alter the Register of Directors and the Register of Directors' Interests	File *Form 288b*
Remove an auditor	*s.391*	Ordinary	Special notice procedure as for the removal of a director	Give the Registrar notice within 14 days of the resolution
Alter minimum directors from 2	*Art.64*	Special		File resolution
Fix salary of non-executive director	*Art.82*	Ordinary		File resolution
Relax quorum requirement for a director voting on own service contract	*Art.97*	Alter articles by special resolution. Or temporarily relax rules under the *Art.96* ordinary resolution procedure		File resolution if it is a special resolution
Reduce share capital	*ss.135-137*	Special		File resolution. Obtain the court's consent
Sanction a 'substantial property transaction'	*s.320*	Ordinary	After the transaction it may be necessary to alter the Register of Directors' Interests	

Transaction	Authority	Resolution	Internal procedures	External procedures
Gratuitous payment to a director	*s.312*	Ordinary		
Retirement by rotation		No resolution This is automatic (*Art.76*)		
Repurchase ordinary shares	*s.162*	Special	Update Register of Members, Register of Directors' Interests	*Form 169* (stating number of shares and nominal value)
Financial assistance to buy shares	*s.155*	Special	Statutory declaration of solvency by the directors, confirmed by the auditor	File resolution and statutory declaration
Approve dividend	*Art.102*	Ordinary		
Absolve liability for *ultra vires* act		Special		File resolution
Grant indemnity for *ultra vires* act		Special		File resolution
Absolve liability for exceeding actual authority		Ordinary		
Issue of a debenture		Board resolution	The board resolves to take out the loan and to affix the company seal. 2 directors, *or* 1 director and the company secretary sign the agreement. Update Register of Charges	Register with *Form 395* at Companies House within 21 days. Charges over land should be registered with the Land Charges Department or HM Land Registry
Redemption of a debenture		Board resolution	Lender endorses receipt on the debenture Update Register of Charges	File statutory declaration and memorandum of satisfaction (*Form 403*) that the debt has been repaid
Voluntary winding up - company is insolvent	*IA s.84* *IA s.378*	Extraordinary	see p.283	File the extraordinary resolution
Winding up - company is solvent	*IA s.84*	Special	see p.283	File the special resolution
Approve voluntary arrangement	*Insolvency Rules*	Ordinary (members) 75% by value (unsecured creditors)	see p.281	
Move registered office		Board resolution		File *Form 287*

Note:

a) the table on the previous page and the table on this page assume that Table A is in force and has not been amended

b) every members' resolution which is passed concerning the company's management will need a separate board resolution if it is to be executed

c) written resolutions are an acceptable alternative to members' resolutions passed at meetings in all cases *except* those listed on p.249

d) a complete list of which resolutions are to be filed can be found in *s.380*

D Public companies

Advantages and extra stringencies associated with plcs

Pros

- ✓ Shares and debentures may be offered to the public.
  (There is a criminal penalty for a private company which does this (*s.81*).)
- ✓ Prestige.
- ✓ The company may apply for listing of its securities if it has:
  - traded for at least 3 years and at least 25% of its shares are held by the public.

  (*Chapter 3 of the Listing Rules of the Financial Services Authority will apply.*)

Cons

- ✗ Costs of changing name on memorandum *and* stationery.
- ✗ The rules of the City Code on Takeovers and Mergers will apply. Rule 9 of the Code obliges anyone who alone, or in concert with others, acquires 30% of the shares to make a bid for all the share capital.
- ✗ Non-cash consideration for shares must be independently valued within 6 months (*s.44* and *s.103*).
- ✗ There is no elective regime.
- ✗ The prohibition on loans to directors (and associates) extends to quasi-loans & credit transactions (*ss.330-331*).
- ✗ Criminal penalties: loans to directors (*s.342*), giving unlawful financial assistance (*s.151*).
- ✗ There is an absolute bar on financial assistance to buy shares (*s.151*).
- ✗ The company must call an EGM if 'net assets' fall to 50% or less of the share capital (*s.142*).
- ✗ The company needs a special resolution, or article to disable statutory pre-emption rights (*s.95*).
  (A private company may do this in its memorandum or articles (*s.91*).)
- ✗ Dividend rules are stricter. A plc may only make a distribution when distributable profits equal accumulated realised profits less accumulated realised losses, plus the excess of unrealised losses over unrealised profits.
- ✗ A plc may not redeem or purchase shares from capital (*s.171*).
- ✗ 7 months to lay AGM accounts after accounting period ends (rather than 10 as for private companies) (*s.244*).
- ✗ Written resolutions are not available.
- ✗ Minimum of 2 directors (*s.282*).
- ✗ Directors may not be appointed over 70. They must leave office at the AGM after their 70th birthday, unless members agree otherwise (*s.293*).
- ✗ The directors' report must contain a statement of the company's policy and practice on the payment of its suppliers (*CA(DR)(SPP)R 1997*).
- ✗ For listed companies: there is a new Combined Code of conduct for directors (made up of the Cadbury and Greenbury codes and reflecting the Hampel and Turnbull reports - see p.274).

➤ From 1st May 2000, admission to listing is the responsibility of the FSA and admission to trading will be the responsibility of the London Stock Exchange. However, a condition of admission to each is a listing with the other.

Conversion to a plc

Requirements

1. Issued share capital is a minimum of £50,000.
2. At least 25% (£12,500) of the share capital is fully paid to the nominal value and the whole of any premium (*s.45*).
3. The memorandum must state that the company is a public limited company and the name must include 'plc'.

Procedure

Steps

1. Special resolutions to (a) re-register as a plc, *and* (b) alter the memorandum, adding 'plc' to the company's name.
2. Apply for registration as a plc.
3. Adopt a new memorandum and articles suitable for a public company.
4. Send to the Registrar (*s.43*):
   - a printed copy of the new memorandum and articles,
   - a copy of the latest balance sheet,
   - an auditor's report that the company's net assets are not less than its capital balance sheet,
   - a statutory declaration made by a company secretary or director that the net asset value in the auditor's report is accurate and that the requirements of the *Companies Acts* have been complied with.
5. The Registrar issues a certificate of incorporation as a plc.

E Converting businesses

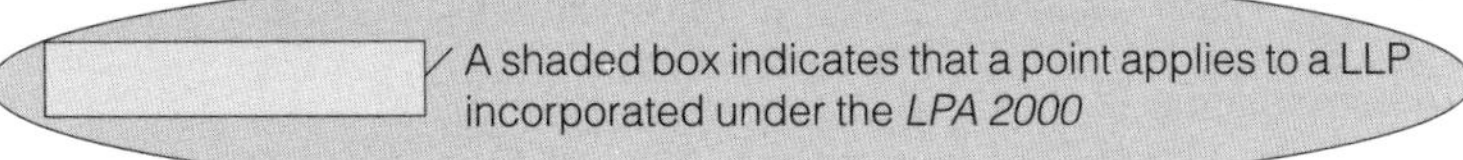
A shaded box indicates that a point applies to a LLP incorporated under the *LPA 2000*

Converting sole trader to partnership	Converting a partnership to a company/LLP
Formalities	
➤ Draw up a partnership agreement ➤ Decide on the ownership of capital assets, which can be: ◆ leased or licensed to the firm ◆ owned by the partners jointly - this requires a transfer or conveyance ◆ held on trust by a partner for all the partners ➤ Comply with *BNA 1985*	➤ Purchase or create a company/LLP ➤ Observe the formalities for board and shareholder meetings ➤ Draw up a contract for sale of the business: ◆ listing the assets being sold, consideration and method of payment ◆ stating the company's acceptance of the seller's title to assets ◆ recording the company's acceptance of stock in its current condition ◆ apportioning the value of assets ◆ providing an indemnity from the company in respect of business liabilities. ➤ Comply with *BNA 1985*, and *CA ss.25-30* (see p.228 and p.240)
Income tax	
	➤ The seller may incur a 'balancing charge' on the sale of capital assets under Schedule D Case VI. If the ex-partners are controlling shareholders, then they and the company and partners may elect for the company to inherit the business's writing down allowance (there are 2 years in which to make this election) (*CAA 2001 s.266*) If this election is made, no 'balancing charge' is deemed to arise on the discontinuance of trade by the partnership (*CAA 2001 s.267(2)*) ➤ Unrelieved trading losses can be carried forward and offset against any salary or dividends paid by the company to the vendor, as long as shares in the company provided most of the consideration for the sale (*TA 1988 s.386*)
Capital taxation	
➤ A sole trader going into partnership may be disposing of chargeable assets. Consider: ◆ annual exemption ◆ hold-over relief on a *gift* ◆ retirement relief ◆ taper relief	➤ Insofar as shares are consideration for the transfer of assets, gains can be 'rolled-over' into shares on condition that all the business's assets (except cash) are sold to the company and that the shares issued by the company qualify for the Enterprise Investment Scheme (*TCGA 1992 ss.150-150C, Sch.5B*). This has disadvantages: ◆ any subsequent gain may be liable to double taxation ◆ assets transferred to the company are available to creditors if it becomes insolvent, and so might not be recoverable
Stamp duty	
➤ Stamp duty is less likely to be applicable as title to assets may not be transferred unless goodwill is assigned, etc	➤ Stamp duty may be due on an instrument transfering or agreeing to transfer an interest in certain property, see pp.119-120 ◆ There is an exemption for a transfer to a LLP within 1 year of incorporation (*LPA 2000 s.12*)
VAT	
➤ If the company is not registered *before the sale*, the seller must charge VAT unless the business is transferred as a going concern (*VATA s.49*)	
Employees	
Transfer of Undertakings (Protection of Employment) Regulations 1981 ➤ When the business is taken over, the employees retain all the rights they enjoyed previously	

F Choice of business medium

➤ The choice of business medium determines how a business is financed and run.

➤ Issues that concern clients include:
- the different liabilities assumed by sole traders or partners (as opposed to shareholders).
- the amount of statutory control over the business.
- how easily profits may be extracted from the business.
- working out what tax is payable by the business and what tax is payable by the individuals involved (although this depends on whether they are sole traders, directors or shareholders.)

➤ As a general rule:
- Partnerships are better initially when profits are low (because of lower running costs and start-up relief).
- Companies are usually better initially when profits are expected to be higher.

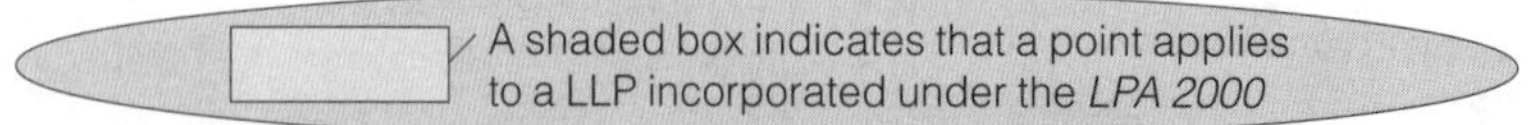
A shaded box indicates that a point applies to a LLP incorporated under the *LPA 2000*

	Sole trader or partnership	Company
	General matters	
Personal liability for debts	✗ Unlimited liability ✗ A partner and a sole trader are personally liable for debts the business incurs Note: A novation agreement or an indemnity only protects if the guarantor is solvent NB:Under the self assessment regime, partners are in most cases no longer jointly and severally liable for income tax	✓ Limited liability ✓ Members are only liable to the extent of the fully paid up value of the shares ➤ Directors are not personally liable *unless* they: ◆ give a personal guarantee ◆ breach their fiduciary duty to the company ◆ trade wrongfully or fraudulently (*IA 1986 ss.213-214*) ◆ breach certain statutory administrative requirements ◆ sign a document giving an incorrect company name
Finance	✗ Can only create fixed charges ✗ A new partner is liable for future debts	✓ Can create a floating charge ✓ A new investor in shares only incurs limited liability
Management	✓ Flexibility: the business can be organised as the participants wish ✗ All partners have apparent authority to bind the firm	✓ Management is largely divorced from capital investment ✓ Shareholders have no authority to act for the company
Status		✓ Often seen by clients as more substantial and 'solid'
Setting-up and initial cost	✓ Theoretically free as acting in a certain way is enough to start a partnership ✗ For a partnership, an agreement ought to be drawn up, so in practice this is not a viable 'short-cut'	✗ Many statutory requirements must be fulfilled: ◆ the formalities at start-up, *and* ◆ the ongoing formalities
Statutory control	✓ This is minimal	✗ The inconvenience of maintaining the required registers, minutes, annual returns, etc ✗ The expense of professional advice to ensure compliance with statutory requirements ✗ Restrictions on certain activities: ◆ purchase and redemption of its own shares ◆ paying dividends solely out of 'available' profit as defined by *CA1985 s.263*
Publicity	✓ Need reveal only the partners' names and their addresses for the service of documents	✗ Information filed at Companies House is open to public inspection. This includes annual accounts, but for a 'small company' a profit and loss account does not have to be filed, and smaller companies do not need audits (see p.257)

A shaded box indicates that a point applies to a partner in a LLP incorporated under the *LPA 2000*

Sole trader or partnership	Company	Director
Income tax / National insurance contributions		
✓ Expenses are more generous: anything 'wholly and exclusively for the purposes of the trade'		✓ Expenses: 'wholly, exclusively *and necessarily* in the performance of an employee's duties'
£0-£1,880 at 10% £1,881 - £28,400 at 22% £28,400+ at 40% ✗ Profit £28,400+ at 40% not 22.5-32.5%	£0-£10,000 at 10% £10,000 to £50,000 at 22.5% £50,001 to £300,000 at 20% £300,001- £1,500,000 at 32.5% £1,500,000+ at 30% ✓ Reinvestment is easier if profits are taxed in the 10% or 20% bands	£0-£1,880 at 10% £1,881 - £28,400 at 22% £28,400+ at 40%
✓ Start-up relief over first 4 years ✓ Losses can be set against an individual's income or gains from other sources	Check whether *FA 2000 Sch 12* applies (see p.98).	
A sole trader/partner pays Class 4 contributions related to profit and Class 2 contributions at a flat rate ✓ Neither Class 4 or 2 qualify for tax relief, but the overall burden is less ✗ Benefits are poorer than for employees	✓ A company may claim tax relief on secondary national insurance contributions	✗ No tax relief on national insurance contributions ✓ Benefits are more generous than for a self-employed person
✓ Interest on a loan to buy into a partnership/LLP may be set against income tax as a 'charge on income' (*TA 1988 s.362*)	✓ Interest on a loan to buy shares may be a 'charge on income' (see p.76)	

Sole trader or partner	Director/Shareholder	Company
Capital gains tax		Corporation tax
✓ Annual exemption and taper relief		✗
✓ Roll-over relief on the replacement of 'qualifying assets'	✓ Roll-over relief on replacement of 'qualifying assets' *if* the company is a personal trading company	✓
✓ Retirement relief	✓ Retirement relief *if* the company is a personal trading company *and* a shareholder has worked full-time *and* the company owns the asset (being phased out by 2003)	✗
✓ Hold-over relief on a gift of business assets	✓ Hold-over relief on a disposal of assets used by the company (other than shares) not at arm's length provided the company is a personal trading company	✗
Double taxation		
✓ A trader or partner only pays CGT once	✗ The company pays corporation tax on gains and a shareholder pays capital gains tax on corresponding rises in share value ✓ This can be alleviated or prevented if a company distributes capital profit ✗ If a shareholder owns assets and licenses/leases them to the company he is only taxed once, but retirement relief may not be available	
Inheritance tax		
✓ Business property relief ✓ The instalment option is always available on business assets	✗ Business property relief is not always available, see p.xx ✗ The instalment option is only available if *either* the transfer concerns a controlling holding *or* other conditions are satisfied	Generally not applicable (unless a close company, etc)

Reform of corporate governance

Company law generally

- ➤ The Hampel Committee Report on Corporate Governance was published on 28 January 1998.
- ➤ After the publication, the government announced that it would launch a consultation exercise for a major review of company law which will probably take the form of a new *Companies Act*.

The Hampel Committee Report on Corporate Governance

- ➤ The Hampel Committee Report on Corporate Governance was a continuation of the review process started by the Cadbury and Greenbury committees.
  - ◆ Cadbury reported in December 1992 on financial aspects of corporate governance.
    - Cadbury produced a code of best practice aimed so that companies achieve high standards of corporate behaviour.
    - The code provides that:
      - the Board retains control over the company and monitors executive management
      - the responsibilities on the Board should be clearly divided
      - non-executive directors should carry significant weight in the Board's decisions.
    - Cadbury recommended that the Boards of UK listed companies should comply with the code.
  - ◆ Greenbury was established by the Confederation of British Industry to consider directors' remuneration and emoluments.
    - Greenbury produced another code of best practice.
    - The code provides that:
      - the Board of a listed company should establish a remuneration committee made up of non-executive directors to determine remuneration policy.
- ➤ The aims of the Hampel Committee were:
  - ◆ to review the implementation and effect of the Cadbury code, *and*
  - ◆ to review the role of executive and non-executive directors, *and*
  - ◆ to push further the Greenbury recommendations, *and*
  - ◆ to comment on shareholders' roles in corporate governance, *and*
  - ◆ to comment on auditors' roles in corporate governance, *and*
  - ◆ to cut back on the regulatory burden on companies.
- ➤ The main recommendations of the Hampel Committee were:
  - ◆ the annual report of a company should indicate how the broad principles of corporate governance are applied by the company, *and*
  - ◆ companies should have transparent governance policies, *and*
  - ◆ the principles of governance should be applied flexibly and with common sense, *and*
  - ◆ a comprehensive 'Combined Code' combining the best of the previous codes and the new Hampel recommendations should be attached to the *Listing Rules*, *and*
    - The full 'Combined Code' as adopted by the UK Listing Authority (from 1 May 2000 this is the Financial Services Authority) (and which includes measures recommended by the Turnbull report) specifies quite detailed rules for directors, directors' remuneration, shareholders and the AGM and company accountability and audit.
  - ◆ the UK Listing Authority should take charge of amending and updating this code.

G Insolvency

All references in this section are to the Insolvency Act 1986, unless stated otherwise.

I	Personal insolvency	III	LLP insolvency
II	Partnership insolvency	IV	Corporate insolvency

I Personal insolvency

A. Voluntary arrangement

- ✓ Avoids stigma and disability of bankruptcy.
- ✓ Cheaper and quicker.
- ✓ Creditors retain the option of petitioning the court if a debtor defaults.
- ✗ The supervisor of the voluntary arrangement does *not* have power to set aside transactions.
- ✗ Creditors may not get paid in full.

➤ This is commonly referred to as an 'IVA'.

➤ The debtor may apply for a moratorium (called an 'interim order'). This prevents unsecured creditors starting bankruptcy proceedings or seizing assets. In return, the debtor agrees to a voluntary repayment plan.

➤ A resolution for a voluntary arrangement must be passed by a majority of at least 75% (by value) of the creditors present in person or by proxy. The resolution binds every unsecured creditor who had notice of, and was entitled to vote at the meeting, or who is a party to the arrangement. *The last sentence will be replaced with: The resolution binds every unsecured creditor (but if an unsecured creditor did not have notice of the meeting, he may apply to the court for relief) (s.262) [not yet in force].*

➤ A debtor may enter a voluntary arrangement at any time before a bankruptcy petition by the debtor is pending (*s.253(5)*).

➤ A voluntary arrangement may take the form of a 'composition', ie: the creditor and debtor agree the payment of a lesser sum in full satisfaction of the claim. Alternatively, it can take the form of a 'scheme of arrangement' which can be on any terms acceptable to the parties (eg: sale of assets, etc).

Steps

1. The debtor appoints an insolvency practitioner known as a 'nominee' to investigate his finances.
2. The debtor prepares a proposal for the intended nominee setting out, inter alia:
   i) the terms of the IVA, *and*
   ii) a statement of affairs containing particulars of his creditors, debts, other liabilities, assets and other information as may be prescribed.
3. The proposal is sent to the intended nominee, who then decides whether to act as nominee.
4. The debtor may apply for an interim order (the moratorium described above). This usually lasts for 14 days but can be extended (*ss.255(6), 256(4)*).
5. The nominee prepares a report on the proposal to the court including whether a creditor's meeting should be held *(and giving the nominee's opinion on whether the proposal has a reasonable prospect of being approved and implemented (s.256(1) [not yet in force]).*

Steps

6 The court considers whether, based on the nominee's recommendation, a creditors' meeting is necessary to obtain their approval (*s.258*).

- **If an interim order has been made:** If a meeting is necessary, then during the period of the interim order, creditors can examine the proposed voluntary arrangement.
- ***An interim order has not been made or applied for:*** *If a meeting is necessary, then creditors can examine the proposed voluntary arrangement (IA s.256A-258) [not yet in force].*
- 75% (by value) of creditors at the meeting must agree to the IVA (*Insolvency Rules*).

7 Provided that consent is obtained, a bankruptcy order is avoided, and the nominee is appointed as the debtor's 'supervisor' to ensure the IVA is carried out in accordance with its terms (*s.263*).

B. Bankruptcy

Steps

1 A petition is made to a court with insolvency jurisdiction, by any of the following:

a) **Creditor (1) (*s.267*) ...**

i) ... who is owed £750 or more, *and*

ii) the debt is for a liquidated sum payable now, or at a certain future time, and is unsecured, *and*

iii) the debtor is unable to pay or has no reasonable prospect of doing so.

- The evidence for this is:
  - 1) there is evidence of the debtor's failure to comply with a statutory demand within 3 weeks, *and*

    2) there is no outstanding application to set aside a statutory demand.

or • the debtor has failed to satisfy execution of a judgment debt.

b) **Creditor (2) ...**

... who is bound by a voluntary arrangement where the debtor has not complied with the arrangement, or the debtor has entered the scheme giving misleading information.

c) **Debtor ...** with a statement of affairs showing that he is unable to pay his debts (*s.272*).

2 A bankruptcy order is made at a court hearing (at least 14 days must elapse between service of the petition and the hearing), or the court may appoint an insolvency practitioner to investigate the possibility of an IVA. A bankruptcy order will be entered into the public register of bankruptcy orders.

3 The courts appoints an official receiver (*s.287*) until the bankrupt's estate vests in the trustee in bankruptcy.

- If a creditor began the action, the debtor has 21 days to submit a statement of affairs (*s.288*).

4 A creditors' meeting is held at the official receiver's discretion *or* if 25% of creditors (by value) request it (*s.294*).

5 A trustee in bankruptcy is appointed by the creditors at the meeting, *or* if no meeting is called or no appointment is made by creditors, the official receiver will act as the trustee in bankruptcy (*s.293*).

6 The bankrupt's property vests in the trustee (see chart on next page '*Property vesting in the trustee*') (*s.306*).

7 The function of the trustee is to get in, realise, and distribute the bankrupt's estate to satisfy the creditors (see chart overleaf for '*Trustee's powers to gather assets*').

8 The bankruptcy order is discharged, usually after 3 years, although this may be delayed if the bankrupt has not co-operated, or where the bankrupt has been an undischarged bankrupt at any time within the preceding 15 years (*s.279*). 2 years (and in some circumstances 3 years) after the bankruptcy order is discharged the entry in the register of bankruptcy orders is deleted.

Property vesting in the trustee in bankruptcy	
Property retained by the bankrupt	Property vesting in the trustee
➤ Any right which is purely personal, rather than proprietary ➤ Tools of a trade, vehicle (*s.283(2)*) ➤ Bankrupt's and family's furniture, bedding and clothing (*s.283(2)*) **Note:** the above might be replaced by functional cheaper versions ➤ Trust property eg: trust property held for a minor	➤ All other property **Note:** If the debtor only partly owns his house, the trustee in bankruptcy will need an order for sale from the court (*LPA 1925 s.30*)

- ➤ Initially the bankrupt can usually continue to occupy the family home *if either:* (*ss.336-338*)
  - a) a spouse has a right of occupation under the *MHA/FLA, or*
  - b) the bankrupt is living with minors and therefore has a right of occupation under the *MHA/FLA*
- ➤ During the first year a possession order is unlikely to be granted as the needs of the children are paramount
- ➤ **After 1 year, an order for possession will probably be granted as the creditors' interests now become paramount**

Trustee's powers to gather assets			
Transaction	Time of transaction	Defence	Effect
At an undervalue (*ss.339, 341*)	With an unconnected person ➤ Within 5 years prior to bankruptcy, *and* the debtor is insolvent at the time or became so as a result of the transaction		All such property is 're-claimed' under a court order by the trustee, and distrib-uted to the creditors
	With an associate ➤ Within 2 years prior to bankruptcy	a) The debtor was not insolvent at the time, *or* b) the debtor did not become insolvent as a result of the transaction	
To create a preference (*ss.340, 341*)	With an unconnected person ➤ Within 6 months prior to bankruptcy, *and* the debtor was insolvent at the time or became so as a result of the transaction, *and* the debtor intended to prefer, *and* the creditor was thus put in a better position	The debtor did not intend to prefer, or pressure was exerted to prefer	
	With an 'associate': ➤ Within 2 years prior to bankruptcy, *and* the debtor was insolvent at the time or became so due to this transaction (pre-sumed), *and* the creditor was put in a better position as a result (presumed)	a) The debtor was not insolvent at the time, *or* b) the debtor did not become insolvent as a result of the transaction The debtor did not intend to prefer, or pressure was exerted to prefer	
At an undervalue to defraud creditors (*s.423*)	No time limit		

- ➤ 'Onerous' contracts or property - if an interested third party serves notice, a trustee must disclaim the contract or property within 28 days, otherwise he loses this right to disclaim and will be deemed to have adopted any contract (*s.316*)
  - ◆ Third parties who lose from a disclaimed contract claim loss from the bankrupt's estate
- ➤ Any disposition made between the day of presentation of the petition and the vesting of the bankrupt's estate in the trustee is void unless the court consents (*s.284*)

A trustee is *not* entitled to pursue:

- ➤ sale proceeds from a fully enforced judgment order obtained before the bankruptcy order was made (*s.346*)
- ➤ goods which, before a bankruptcy order was made, a landlord has distrained for up to 6 months arrears of rent (*s.347*)

Disabilities (ie: things the bankrupt may not do)

- Take credit above £250 without disclosing his bankruptcy - this is a criminal offence (*s.360*).
- Trade under a non-bankrupt name without disclosing the bankrupt name - this is a criminal offence (*s.360*).
- Retain membership of a partnership - consequences depend on the partnership agreement.
- Retain directorships - *Art. 81* of Table A provides for this, and *CDDA 1986 s.11* requires it.
- Perform any of the the following occupations:

i) barrister	iv) Member of Parliament
ii) solicitor	v) local authority member
iii) Justice of the Peace	vi) insolvency practitioner

Order of distribution

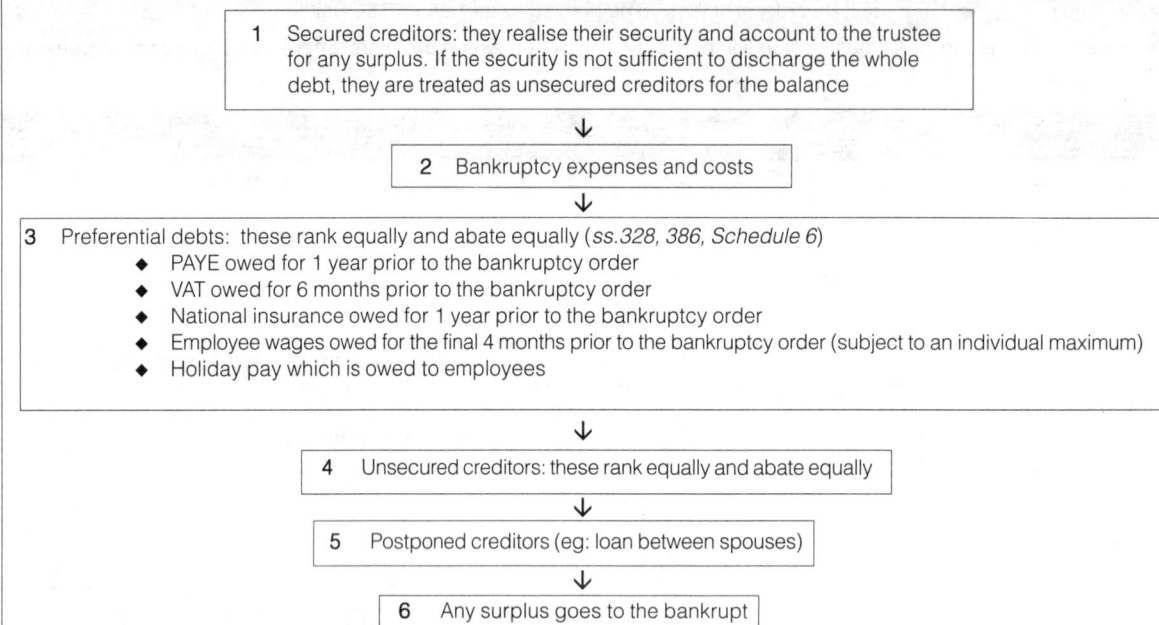

1 Secured creditors: they realise their security and account to the trustee for any surplus. If the security is not sufficient to discharge the whole debt, they are treated as unsecured creditors for the balance

↓

2 Bankruptcy expenses and costs

↓

3 Preferential debts: these rank equally and abate equally (*ss.328, 386, Schedule 6*)
- PAYE owed for 1 year prior to the bankruptcy order
- VAT owed for 6 months prior to the bankruptcy order
- National insurance owed for 1 year prior to the bankruptcy order
- Employee wages owed for the final 4 months prior to the bankruptcy order (subject to an individual maximum)
- Holiday pay which is owed to employees

↓

4 Unsecured creditors: these rank equally and abate equally

↓

5 Postponed creditors (eg: loan between spouses)

↓

6 Any surplus goes to the bankrupt

II Partnership insolvency

Insolvent Partnerships Order 1994, Insolvency Act 1986

- The provisions of the *IA* regarding company voluntary arrangements apply to partnerships.
- The provisions of the *IA* regarding administration orders apply to partnerships.
- The partnership is treated as an unregistered company even though a partnership is not a legal person in its own right. There are different treatments for creditors' and members' winding up petitions.
- The law of bankruptcy does not apply to the firm, but individual partners may be subject to bankruptcy orders, whereupon the official receiver becomes trustee.

III LLP insolvency

- The *IA 1986* applies to a LLP broadly as it does to a company incorporated under the *Companies Acts*.
  - *LLPR 2001 r.5* and *Sch. 3* apply the *IA 1986* (with appropriate modifications) to LLPs.

IV Corporate insolvency

A. Alternatives to liquidation

There are 4 alternatives:

1 The company is declared defunct.

2 An administrative receiver, or receiver, is appointed by a debenture holder.

3 An administration order is made.

4 A voluntary arrangement is made.

1 The company is declared defunct (*CA ss.652-653*)

- The company has ceased trading.
- The Registrar of Companies can act on his own initiative to strike off the company.
- The Registrar must advertise his intention to strike off the company.
- For up to 20 years, a member or creditor who is prejudiced may apply for the company's restoration to the register.
- The liability of every director, managing officer and member of the company continues, and may be enforced as if the company had not been dissolved (*s.652(6)(a)*).

2 An administrative receiver, or receiver, is appointed by a debenture holder

Most debentures allow a debenture holder to appoint an **administrative** receiver in the event that he is not paid sums he is owed under the debenture, provided that the holder has security (floating charge or a fixed and floating charge) over all, or substantially the whole of the assets of the company. (If he does not have such security, he might still appoint a receiver - different from an administrative receiver.)

The *aim* of a receiver is **to recover the debenture holder's debt, interest and his own costs though he is the agent of *the company.***

- Only an insolvency practitioner can be appointed as an administrative receiver. His powers are laid down under statute but are generally augmented in the debenture.

Steps

1 The debenture holder appoints the administrative receiver, who must formally accept.

2 The administrative receiver must notify the company, the Registrar of Companies and known creditors of his appointment (*s.46*).

3 Floating charges crystallise, preventing the company from dealing with the assets concerned.

- The receiver must cede priority to fixed chargees and preferential creditors (if security is by way of a floating charge).

4 The directors give the administrative receiver a statement about the company's affairs.

5 The administrative receiver can *only* set aside transactions that were used to defraud creditors.

6 The administrative receiver produces final reports and accounts.

7 The court can remove an administrative receiver, or he can resign (*s.45*), but the debenture holder cannot dismiss him.

3 An administration order is made

The *aim* of an administration order is **to avoid or postpone the liquidation or receivership of a company.**

Steps

1 Petition: the directors, members, creditors or the supervisor of a voluntary arrangement, may petition the court for an administration order (*s.9*).

2 Notice is given to any person entitled to appoint an administrative receiver. If an administrative receiver is validly appointed at this stage, the petition will be dismissed.

3 If the court is satisfied that grounds exist and that no administrative receiver has been appointed, an administration order is made appointing an insolvency practitioner as administrator.

4 The directors give the administrator a statement of the company's affairs.

5 The administrator (within 3 months of the order) draws up proposals based on the statement.

6 A meeting of the company's unsecured creditors must approve the proposals by more than 50%.

7 The administrator manages the company accordingly, and may set aside transactions to defraud creditors, transactions at an undervalue, and preferences.

8 If the administrator achieves the aims of the order, or if he realises that it is impossible, he can ask the court to discharge the order (*s.18*).

a) From the time of the petition there is a moratorium preventing (*s.10*):

i) the company being put into liquidation (by the court or voluntarily).

ii) the enforcement, without the court's consent, of any security against the company's property, (ie: no repossession of hire purchase goods or supplied under retention of title clauses).

iii) a landlord or other person to whom rent is payable exercising any right of forfeiture by peaceable re-entry for premises let to the company if the company has failed to comply with any term or condition of its tenancy of such premises (except with the leave of the court and subject to such terms as the court may impose).

iv) any legal proceedings being commenced or continued without the court's consent.

NB: However, a debenture holder entitled to appoint an administrative receiver (see p.279) has the right to appoint an administrative receiver after the petition for the order, but before the order is granted - this generally requires the petition to be dismissed and so means that the debenture holder can veto the granting of an administration order.

b) Grounds for an order (*s.8)*

➤ If the court is satisfied that the company is insolvent, or on the verge of insolvency, and the making of the order is likely to achieve one or more of the following:

i) the survival of the company, and the whole or any part of its undertaking, as a going concern, *or*

ii) the approval of a company voluntary arrangement, or

iii) the sanctioning under *CA s.425* of a compromise or arrangement, or

iv) a better realisation of the company's assets than would be achieved on liquidation.

c) Consequences of the order (*s.11*)

➤ On making the order:

i) any outstanding petitions for winding up the company are dismissed, *and*

ii) any administrative receiver of the company immediately vacates his office, *and*

iii) a receiver who is not an administrative receiver stays in office unless the administrator requires him to vacate.

➤ While the order is in force:

i) no resolution can be passed, or order made, to wind up the company, *and*

ii) no administrative receiver may be appointed, *and*

iii) no steps may be taken to enforce any security over the company's property or to repossess goods held under a hire purchase agreement, or supplied on retention of title terms, without the consent of the administrator or leave of the court, *and*

iv) no other proceedings and no distress, execution or other legal process may be commenced or continued against the company without the administrator's consent or leave of court (ie: a moratorium is imposed on creditors seeking to enforce their claims against the company).

d) Role of the administrator who is appointed

➤ The administrator acts in the company's name as the company's agent. He is there to manage the company, investigate its affairs and draw up proposals. He has a liquidator's powers (see 'Liquidator's powers to recover assets', p.285) to set aside:

- preferences,
- transactions at an undervalue,
- floating charges, and
- unregistered charges.

➤ The directors remain in office, unless the administrator removes them, but cannot use their powers in a manner which would interfere with the administrator.

4 A voluntary arrangement is made (*ss.1-7*)

The *aim* of a company voluntary arrangement ('CVA') is **for the company to agree on a binding plan to repay debts whereby the company can survive and continue trading.**

Steps

1 *A 'small company' may apply for a moratorium on actions against it (Sch. A1) [not yet in force].*

2 The directors draft a proposal for a composition or scheme of arrangement.

3 An insolvency practitioner, called a 'nominee', submits a report to the court, stating whether *(in his opinion the proposal has a reasonable prospect of being approved and implemented (Sch. A1 [not yet in force] and whether)* meetings of shareholders and creditors should be held to consider his proposals. Unless the court directs otherwise, meetings of shareholders and creditors are held.

- Consent must be obtained from 50% or more of the members who are present and voting, and 75% (by value) of the unsecured creditors who are present and voting.
- *However, a decision by the creditor's meeting to approve the CVA will prevail over a member's meeting to reject the CVA, subject to a right by a member to challenge this in court (s.4A) [not yet in force].*

3 If approved, this approval is reported to the court.

4 The 'nominee' now becomes the 'supervisor' and carries out the CVA.

➤ Consequences:

- A voluntary arrangement is binding on every creditor who had notice of, and was entitled to attend and vote at the meeting.
- It is *not* binding on secured creditors *unless* they agree to be bound by the arrangement.
- If the company defaults, creditors or members can petition to have the company wound up.

CVA 'small' company moratorium (IA 1986 Schedule A1) [not yet in force]

➤ *A 'small company' may apply for a moratorium by filing certain documents with the court.*

- *A small company has at least 2 of 3 conditions applicable to it in the year ending with the date of filing, or in the financial year of the company which ended last before that date (CA s.247):*
  a) turnover is not more than £2.8 million,
  b) the balance sheet total is not more than £1.4 million,
  c) there are not more than 50 employees.
- *A small company cannot apply for a moratorium if:*
  - *an administration order is in force in relation to the company, or*
  - *the company is being wound up, or*
  - *there is an administrative receiver of the company, or*
  - *a voluntary arrangement has effect in relation to the company, or*
  - *there is a provisional liquidator of the company, or*
  - *a moratorium has been in force for the company at any time during the period of 12 months ending with the date of filing, and*
    i) no voluntary arrangement had effect at the time at which the moratorium came to an end, or
    ii) a voluntary arrangement in force at any time in that period has come to an end prematurely.

➤ ***The moratorium starts*** *when certain documents are filed with the court.*

➤ ***The moratorium ends*** *at the earlier of 28 days after it begins or at the end of the day on when the CVA meetings are first held (or, if the meetings are held on different days, the later of those days). A meeting to establish a CVA may extend the moratorium for a further 2 months from the CVA meeting.*

➤ *While the moratorium is in force:*

- *no petition may be presented for the winding up of the company, and*
- *no meeting of the company may be held except with the nominee's consent or leave of the court and subject (where the court gives leave) to such terms as the court may impose, and*
- *no resolution may be passed or order made for the winding up of the company, and*
- *no petition for an administration order in relation to the company may be presented, and*
- *no administrative receiver of the company may be appointed, and*
- *no landlord may exercise any right of forfeiture by peaceable re-entry for premises let to the company (if the company has failed to comply with any term or condition of its tenancy of such premises), except with the leave of the court, and*
- *nothing else may be done to enforce security over the company's property, or to repossess goods in its possession under any hire purchase agreement, except with the leave of the court, and*
- *no other proceedings or execution or other legal process may be started or continued, and no distress may be levied, against the company or its property except with the leave of the court, and*
- *there are special rules relating to an uncrystallised floating charge (not dealt with here), and*
- *security granted by the company may only be enforced if, at the time it was granted, there were reasonable grounds for believing that it would benefit the company.*
- *business correspondence must carry a statement of the nominee's name and that the moratorium is in force (but if not done transactions are still enforceable by third parties), and*
- *the company may not obtain credit of £250 or more from a person who has not been informed that a moratorium is in force, and*
- *there are several other restrictions on what the company may do during this time.*

B. Liquidation

1 **Voluntary liquidation**

Sometimes a company may be wound up following criteria laid down in the articles (eg: to enable the shareholders to extract their capital, or to facilitate restructuring of a group of companies). Otherwise it may be wound up after a special resolution has been passed to wind up the company, or after an extraordinary resolution has been passed due to its perceived liabilities.

Steps

1 The directors prepare a statement of affairs.

2 *Either*:

a) the company is ***solvent.*** This is known as a members' voluntary liquidation since the members will control the winding up of the company.

The directors make a statutory declaration that the company will be able to pay its debts, including interest, within a period not exceeding 1 year (and this must be done within 5 weeks prior to passing a resolution to wind up the company) (*s.89*). They summon a general meeting (*s.89*) at which the members may:

i) pass a special resolution to wind up the company (*s.84*), and advertise the fact in the *London Gazette* within 14 days of the resolution being passed (*s.85*), *and*

ii) pass an ordinary resolution to appoint a liquidator (*s.91*).

or:

b) the company is ***insolvent***. This is known as a creditors' voluntary liquidation. It is not a remedy available to creditors, but rather it is a procedure supervised by creditors.

The members pass an extraordinary resolution to wind up the company (*s.84, CA s.378*), and the resolution is advertised in the *London Gazette* (*s.85*). Separate meetings are held for creditors and members to appoint a liquidator - generally all meetings are held on the same day.

- The creditors should meet within 14 days of the members' general meeting (*s.98*), where they are shown a statement of affairs by the directors (*s.99*).
- The creditors may appoint a liquidator.
- The creditors' choice of liquidator takes priority over that of the members (*s.100*).

3 The liquidator advertises his appointment and notifies the Registrar of Companies (*s.109*).

4 The liquidator has the same powers and duties as in the case of a compulsory insolvency (see p.285).

5 After the company's assets have been distributed, the liquidator makes final reports prior to dissolution to a meeting of members (members' voluntary winding up)(*s.94*), *or* to meetings of members and creditors (creditors' voluntary liquidation)(*s.106*).

6 The liquidator sends the final return to the Registrar of Companies (*ss.94(3), 106(3)*).

7 The Registrar dissolves the company 3 months after receiving the liquidator's final return (*s.201*).

2 **Compulsory liquidation** (for unsecured creditors. Secured creditors usually have more specific remedies, eg: appointing an administrative receiver or receiver)

Steps

1 A creditor *or* the company petitions the Chancery Division of the High Court on one of 7 statutory grounds (*ss.122 (a)-(g)*) (eg: the company is unable to pay its debts).

- The company is *presumed* to be unable to pay its debts if:
  - a statutory demand has been served by a creditor (minimum debt of £750) and is outstanding for 3 weeks, *or*
  - execution has been issued for an unsatisfied judgment debt.
- If this presumption does not arise, insolvency must be shown to the court by taking into account actual, prospective and contingent liabilities.

2 The court has discretion to grant a winding up order (*s.125*).

3 The court appoints an official receiver. He is the liquidator until another is appointed (*s.136*). He:

- takes the board's powers and is obliged to alter the company's notepaper so that the insolvency is apparent to third parties (*s.188*).
- advertises his appointment in the *London Gazette* and the local paper.
- notifies the Registrar of Companies and the company itself of his appointment.

4 The directors present a statement of affairs to the official receiver (or liquidator) within 14 days of the order. He reports to the court on the reasons and causes for the failure, and generally the position, dealings, etc, of the company, and any suspicious circumstances (*ss.131-132*).

5 The receiver calls separate members' and creditors' meetings, and may nominate an alternative liquidator to the official receiver (*s.136(5)*).

- The official receiver *must* call a creditors' meeting if 25% (by value) request it (*s.136(5)*).
- The creditors' nomination as liquidator takes priority.

6 The liquidator takes the board's powers and collects in all property of the company (see '*Liquidator's powers to recover assets' on the next page*) (Powers are listed in *Schedule 4* of the *IA).*

7 The liquidator distributes assets (see p.286 for the '*Order of distribution*').

8 After distribution, the liquidator notifies the Registrar of Companies, who dissolves the company 3 months later (*s.202*).

9 The liquidator makes a final report to the creditors' and the members' meetings (*s.146*).

Distribution

➤ Property does NOT vest in the liquidator (as he is the company's agent), but he is under a duty to take it all into his possession.

➤ Legal proceedings against the company cannot proceed without leave of court. Leave will be refused, for example, if it give a creditor a chance to 'promote' himself from an unsecured position.

Order of distribution

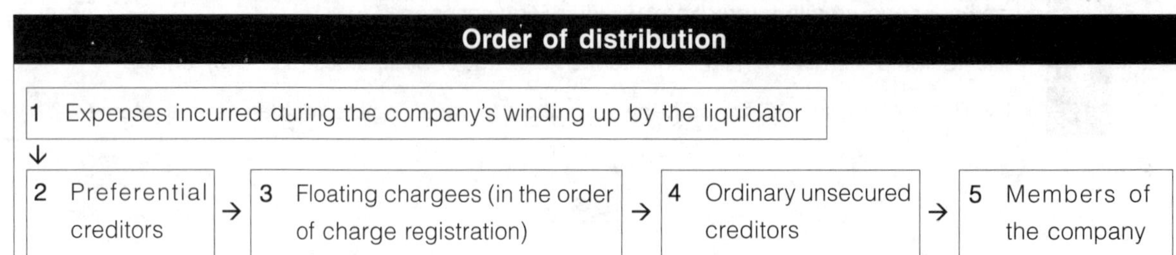
1 Expenses incurred during the company's winding up by the liquidator
2 Preferential creditors
3 Floating chargees (in the order of charge registration)
4 Ordinary unsecured creditors
5 Members of the company

Liquidator's (and administrator's for *ss. 238, 239, 423*) powers to recover assets

Transaction	Requirements	Defence	Effect
At an undervalue (*s.238*)	Within 2 years prior to the insolvency + the company was insolvent at the time or became so as a result of this transaction (presumed if with a connected person)	A bad bargain was: ➤ in good faith ➤ on reasonable grounds ➤ for genuine commercial reasons	He can set aside the transaction. (It is actually more complicated than this, but it holds true in general terms)
To create a preference (*s.239*)	Within 6 months prior to the onset of insolvency + the company was insolvent at the time or became so as a result of this transaction + voluntary act + desire to prefer + creditor put in a better position as a result		
	Within 2 years prior to the onset of insolvency for a transaction with a 'connected person' + insolvent at the time or became so as a result of this transaction + voluntary act + creditor put in a better position as a result	Pressure was exerted on the company (no desire to prefer)	
At an undervalue to defraud creditors (*s.423*)	An attempt to put assets beyond the reach of the person making, or who at some time, may make a claim, or otherwise prejudicing the interests of such a person	None	
Fraudulent trading (*s.213*)* Criminal offence *CA s.458*	➤ A positive act ➤ The business has been carried on with intent to defraud creditors or for a fraudulent purpose	No such intention	The court will require an offender to contribute to the company's assets insofar as it thinks it proper in the circumstances
Wrongful trading (*s.214*)*	➤ A director knew, or ought to have concluded that there was no reasonable prospect of the company avoiding insolvency; *and* ➤ did not take every step he ought to have taken to minimise loss to creditors	On becoming aware, he took every step that a reasonably diligent person would have, to minimise loss to creditors	

* The liquidator alone can seek an order under these sections

Charges

Fixed charge: is void against the liquidator if unregistered (or registered after 21 days of creation of charge) (*CA s.395*)

Floating charge: is void against the liquidator if:

- unregistered (or registered after 21 days of creation of the charge) *(CA s.395), or*
- (except to the extent of the value of consideration provided to the company in money or money's worth at the same time, or after the creation of the charge):
  - (if in favour of a connected person) the charge was created within 2 years of liquidation,
  - *or* (if in favour of an unconnected person):
    - i) the charge was created within 1 year of liquidation, *and*
    - ii) the charge was created at a time when the company was insolvent or became insolvent as a result (*IA s.245*).

Note: there are proposed changes to the registration requirements by the *CA 1989*, see p.262

A liquidator may not pursue sale proceeds of a fully enforced judgment order obtained before the bankruptcy order. If the order is not fully enforced, the sheriff will transfer any seized goods to the liquidator (*s.183*)

A liquidator may set aside 'onerous contracts', or disclaim 'onerous property', provided he replies to any inquiry by an interested third party within 28 days (*s.178*). 'Onerous' means that it is a drain on the company's assets or cash flow

H Trading and competition

All references to Articles in the EU Treaties' are to the consolidated version, following the Amsterdam Treaty renumbering.

Any business will enter into contracts. Therefore drafting and negotiating are important skills to acquire. Whether contracts are enforceable is also a vital issue and this will in part depend on the following legislative regimes:

I EU competition law

II UK competition law

III Free movement of goods (*Articles 28-30* of the Treaty of Rome)

IV Contracts for the sale of goods and supply of services

I EU competition law

A. *Article 82* - abuse of a dominant position

Article 82

- ➤ This article prohibits abuse by one or more undertakings of a dominant position ...
  - ◆ ... within the EU or a substantial part of it ...
  - ◆ ... which may affect trade between member states.
- ➤ A market share of 40% and more is a good indication that an undertaking is dominant in that market.
  - ◆ Markets can be defined widely or narrowly (eg: passenger aircraft or commuter aircraft).
  - ◆ A market is evaluated:
    - geographically, *and*
    - by product market
      - ■ The test is 'what other product, if any, can be substituted for the product in question, given the nature of it, its price and its intended use?' (*United Brands v. Commission* [1978] ECR 207).

Avoiding infringement of _Article 82_

- ➤ If dominant in the market, an undertaking should not abuse its position.
- ➤ The European Commission ('Commission') can grant negative clearance. This is a declaration that an agreement does not contravene *Article 82.*
  - ◆ This is the only option open to an undertaking to avoid infringement.

B. *Article 81* - restriction or distortion of competition

Article 81

- This article prohibits agreements, decisions and concerted practices ...
  - ... between undertakings or associations of undertakings ...
  - ... which have as their object *or* effect ...
  - ... prevention, restriction or distortion of competition within the EU.
- Such agreements are void (but *Article 81(2)* permits severance of an offending term if national law permits this. UK law does permit this).

Avoiding infringement of *Article 81*

- **Agencies** (Commission Announcement 24 December 1962) - there is no infringement if:
  - the principal and agent are pursuing the same economic interest, *and*
  - the agent does not take the financial risk, and does not act independently of the principal.
- **Agreements between parents and subsidiaries**
  - These are *usually* treated as one 'undertaking', and therefore are not caught by *Article 81*.
- **Agreements of 'minor importance' (which are not 'black-listed' agreements)**
  - Agreements under this Commission Notice (*OJ C 372 on 9/12/1997*) do not infringe *Article 81*.

    Ie: where the parties' combined share of the relevant market is do not exceed 5% (for horizontal agreements) or 10% (for vertical agreements) of the total market in the agreement area.
  - The Commission is not bound by the Notice, but compliance with it will avoid heavy fines.
- **Block exemptions**
  - These allow parties to certain types of agreement to include anti-competitive/*Article 81* infringing provisions in their agreements. However, they will be permitted, if the agreement is drafted strictly in accordance with a block exemption. Block exemptions list forbidden 'black' clauses (eg: export bans) which must be avoided and permitted 'white' clauses (eg: certain territorial restrictions).
  - Examples of block exemptions are:
    - *Regulation 2790/1999* - vertical agreements (see also p.301)
    - *Regulation 2658/2000* - specialisation agreements (horizontal agreements)
    - *Regulation 2659/2000* - research and development agreements (horizontal agreements)
    - *Regulation 240/1996* - new technology transfer
- **Notification to the Commission:** this protects against fines in respect of the period from the date of notification until the Commission's 'first adverse reaction' (ie: possibly before its final ruling).
  - The Commission then has 3 options:

    a) **Negative clearance:** a declaration that *Article 81* is not infringed.

    b) **Individual exemption:** granted under *Article 81(3)* if the agreement can be justified because it will 'contribute to the improvement of production or distribution of goods, or to promoting technical or economic progress, while allowing consumers a fair share of the resulting benefit'. An exemption binds the Commission, but few are granted and the process is lengthy.

    c) **Comfort letter:** a non-binding reassurance that *either Article 81* is not infringed, *or* a block exemption covers the agreement, *or* the Commission is closing its files for the moment.

C. Enforcement of EU competition law

Enforcement *of EU competition law (Regulation 17/62)*

- The Commission may *request* information informally or formally.
  - Non co-operation is punishable by a fine.
- The Commission can *investigate* informally or formally ('dawn raids' on premises).
  - Obstruction of an investigation is punishable by fine. BUT the Commission has to hold a hearing to consider the merits of a case before imposing a fine.
- Fines for infringements of EU competition law may be up to 1 million Euros, or a greater sum up to 10% of an undertaking's worldwide turnover during the preceding year (*Regulation 17/62, Art.15(2)*).
  - The amount depends on the seriousness of the abuse, the party's position in the market, the size of the offender, and any mitigating factors such as co-operation with the Commission.
  - An undertaking may appeal against the Commission's ruling. The appeal is to the Court of First Instance for a 'preliminary' ruling, but the European Court of Justice (ECJ) is the final authority.
- The remedies obtainable in UK courts are uncertain. Cases have stated that injunctions or damages for breach of statutory duty may be available.
- Commission enforcement powers have been much strengthened by *CA 1998*.

D. European merger control

- European merger control legislation provides for a system of merger control for mergers with a 'Community dimension' and is based on pre-notification to the Commission for evaluation and sanction.
  - The Merger Control Regulation 4064/89 came into force on 21 September 1990.
  - Since its adoption, there has been a specific community law regime against significant mergers.
  - Regulation 4064/89 is read in light of implementing Regulation (2367/90) and various Notices.
  - 'Community dimension' is assessed in terms of worldwide turnover, EC turnover, and in some cases, national turnover).
    - Purely national mergers are excluded from the European legislation but may be subject to national legislation.
- The Commission can assess, on competition grounds, any concentration with a Community dimension.
- A concentration is incompatible with the common market only if:
  a) it is within the defined limits, *and*
  b) it creates or strengthens a dominant position, *and*
  c) as a result competition is effectively impeded.
  - There is no *presumption* that a concentration with a community dimension is incompatible with the common market.
    - This is the case whatever the levels of market share and whatever the size of undertakings.
- The Commission's enforcement powers are detailed in the box in 'C' above.
- Before a decision is reached, the parties must be told the case against them and have a chance to respond.
- If the Commission prohibits a merger, the decision can be appealed to the European Court of Justice within 2 months.
- The *scope* of the Merger Control Regulation was extended on 1 March 1998 by Regulation 1310/97.

II UK competition law

A. *Competition Act 1998* - General

- The Director General of Fair Trading (DGFT) is the enforcing body under the *CA 1998.*
  - Appeals from the DGFT are to the Competition Commission.
- *CA 1998 s.60* puts an obligation on UK competition authorities to ensure there is no inconsistency with European competition law and to have regard to any statement/decision of the EC Commission.
- Exclusions: certain agreements are excluded from the Chapter I and II prohibitions.
  - Eg: if they are subject to EC Merger Regulation or are one of a defined list (eg: where there is competition scrutiny under other enactments).

Enforcement of UK competition law

- The DGFT has sweeping powers of investigation and enforcement similar to those of the European Commission (see p.288) but also backed by criminal sanction.
- The DGFT has power to give such directions as it sees fit to end any infringment (enforced by courts).
  - The DGFT can also give interim measures directions, pending the completion of an investigation.
- Fines for infringements of UK competition law may be up to 10% of an undertaking's turnover in the UK during the preceding year.
  - There is immunity for 'small' agreements and for 'conduct of minor significance', but not if the agreement or conduct is in respect of price fixing.
  - The amount of the fine depends on the seriousness of the abuse, the party's position in the market, the size of the offender, and any mitigating factors such as co-operation with the DGFT.
  - An undertaking may appeal against the DGFT's ruling to the Competition Commission.
- If there is any overlap between European penalties and those which the DGFT seeks to impose, the DGFT must take the European penalties into account so there is no 'double jeopardy'.

B. *CA 1998* -The Chapter II prohibition

The Chapter II prohibition

- This is modelled on the *Article 82* regime but certain EU principles are not relevant eg: EU market principles and objectives.
- The Chapter II prohibition provides that any conduct on the part of one or more undertakings which amounts to the abuse of a dominant position in a market is prohibited if it may affect trade within the UK.
  - A market share of 40% or more is a good indication that an undertaking is dominant in that market.
    - Markets can be defined widely or narrowly (eg: passenger aircraft or commuter aircraft).
    - A market is evaluated:
      - geographically *and*
      - by product market.

Avoiding infringement of the Chapter II prohibition

- If dominant in the market, an undertaking should not abuse its position.
- **Minor conduct:** There is limited immunity from penalty for conduct of minor significance (ie: conduct by an undertaking whose applicable turnover does not exceed £50 million) (*CA(SACMS)R*).
- DGFT can decide that an arrangement does not infringe but there is no power to grant exemptions.
  - This is the only option open to an undertaking to avoid infringement.

C. *CA 1998* -The Chapter I prohibition

CA 1998 - The Chapter I prohibition

➤ This is modelled on the European *Article 81* regime but certain EU principles are not relevant eg: EU market principles and objectives.
- ◆ **Note:** for agreements made before 1 March 2000, Chapter I does not apply before 1 March 2001.

➤ The Chapter I prohibition prohibits agreements, decisions and concerted practices ...
- ◆ ... between undertakings or associations of undertakings ...
- ◆ ... which have as their object *or* effect ...
- ◆ ... prevention, restriction or distortion of competition within the UK.

➤ Such agreements are void (but offending terms may be severed).

➤ Some agreements are not caught, eg: mergers, vertical agreements, land agreements etc.

Avoiding infringement of the Chapter I prohibition

➤ Outside scope
- ◆ Generally, the DGFT says there is no 'appreciable effect' if the parties' combined share of the relevant market is not greater then 25%.
  - A market share of less than 25% will have 'appreciable effect' if the agreement fixes prices, sets minimum resale prices or is part of a network of agreements that have a cumulative effect.

➤ "Small agreements"
- ◆ There is limited immunity from penalty for "small agreements" (ie: all agreements between undertakings where their combined applicable turnover does not exceed £20 million) (*CA(SACMS)R*).

➤ Exemptions - 3 types (*ss. 4-11*):
- Individual exemptions (application must be made for one by notifying the DGFT - see below).
- Block exemptions which have been made by the DGFT.
- Parallel exemptions (which are EU individual or block exemptions - see p.287).

➤ **Notification to the EC Commission** (see p.287): this gives immunity from fines in *CA 1998* but infringments may still be investigated by DGFT.

➤ **Notification to the DGFT:** this protects against fines in respect of the period from the date of notification until at least the date when the application is determined.
- ◆ The DGFT has 3 options:
  a) **Decision:** a declaration that the Chapter 1 prohibition is not infringed (a similar procedure to 'negative clearance' from the EC Commission (see p.287)). These appear on a public register.
  b) **Individual exemption:** if the agreement can be justified because it 'contributes to the improvement of production or distribution of goods, or to promoting technical or economic progress, while allowing consumers a fair share of the resulting benefit'. This is similar to the European individual exemption (see p.287). An appropriate sectorial regulator can also grant one.
  c) **Guidance :** a non-binding reassurance that the Chapter I prohibition is not infringed, *or* a block exemption covers the agreement, *or* the DGFT is closing its files for the moment. This is similar to a comfort letter (see p.287).

D. Common law restraint of trade doctrine

➤ The restraint of trade doctrine prevents restrictive covenants being enforceable *unless*:
- ◆ they are reasonably limited as to time, space and scope, *and*
- ◆ they are reasonably necessary in the context of the whole agreement.

III Free movement of goods

Treaty of Rome - *Articles 28 and 29*

➤ *Articles 28* and *29* prohibit quantitative restrictions on imports and exports and all measures having equivalent effect.

- 'Equivalent effect' means 'all trading rules enacted by member states that are capable of hindering, directly, or indirectly, actually or potentially, intra-community trade' (*Procureur du Roi v. Dassonville* [1974] ECR 837).
- The measure must have some discriminatory effect (ie: putting imports at a disadvantage (*Re Keck and Mithouard* (Joined Cases C-267/91 and C-268/91) [1993] ECR I-6097; [1995] 1 CEC 298).
  - Before *Keck* it had been held that some marketing provisions had infringed *Article 28. Keck* seems to say that rules about selling arrangements/marketing probably do not come within *Article 28* and so it is not clear how the courts will treat such rules now.
- *Article 28* applies not only to the official laws of the state, but also when the state acts through another undertaking or 'bodies established or approved by an official authority' (*Re Peter Vriend* [1980] ECR 327, *Commission v. Ireland* [1982] ECR 4005).
- The effect can be indirect and need not be the main purpose of the legislation (*Torfaen Borough Council v. B & Q plc* [1989] ECR 765) (one of the Sunday trading cases), and it includes bureaucratic procedures (*Rewe-Zentralfinanz GmbH v. Landwirtschafiskammer* [1975] ECR 843).
- Discrimination against national goods is allowed since *Article 28* is not meant to give a level playing-field, but rather to avoid discrimination against imports (*Nederlandse Bakkerij Stichting v. Edah BV* [1986] ECR 3359).

Two classes of exception to *Article 28*

1 Rule of reason (if both domestic and imported products are affected)

➤ National legislation for 'fiscal supervision, the protection of public health, the fairness of commercial transactions and the defence of the consumer' (*Rewe-Zentral AG v. Bundesmonopolverwaltung fur Branntwein (Re Cassis de Dijon*) [1979] ECR 649), and the protection of the environment (*Commission v. Denmark* [1989] CMLR 619) will not infringe *Article 28.*

➤ The 'rule of reason' test. Is the restriction ...

a) ... justifiable under EU law, *and* ...

b) ... in proportion to its declared aim? (ie: is the effect 'direct, indirect or merely speculative' and does it 'impede the marketing of imported products more than the marketing of national products' (*Stoke-on-Trent City Council v. B & Q plc* [1993] 1 All ER 481))?

2 *Article 30* (ex *Article 36*)

➤ Certain laws will escape the prohibition of *Articles 28* and *29*. Such laws must be:

- to uphold public morality in a state (*R. v. Henn & Darby* [1979] ECR 3795 (pornography import)), *or*
- on grounds of public policy, *or*
- to maintain public security (internal and external), *or*
- to protect public health, *or*
- to protect national treasures, *or*
- to protect intellectual property rights →

BUT such laws must not *either:*

a) constitute a means of arbitrary discrimination, *or*

b) be a disguised restriction on trade between member states.

IV Contracts for the sale of goods and supply of services

A. Terms implied by statute and regulation (generally)

- Terms may be implied by the 3 statutes listed in the following table where a contract for sale or supply of goods and/or services (*SGA s.55*) is silent as to certain matters.
- Other statutes/regulations also mandate certain rules in contracts (eg: *LPCD(I)A 1998* and *CP(DS)R 2000*.

Term	*SGA 1979* amended by *SSGA 1994/5*	*SGSA 1982* amended by *SSGA1994*			*SG(IT)A 1973*	When a term is implied into a contract *and* a few details as to the nature of the term
	Contract for sale of goods	Contract for hire	Contract for transfer of goods Contract for work + materials	Contract for services	Contract for hire purchase	
Description	*s.13*	*s.8*	*s.3*		*s.9*	Goods/services must correspond with description (if sold by description)
Satisfactory quality	*s.14(2)* *s.14(2A)*	*s.9(2)* *s.9(3)*	*s.4(2)* *s.4(3)*		*s. 10(2)*	Implied when dealing in the course of seller's business. Not applicable to: a) defects shown to the customer, *or* b) defects which the customer's examination ought to have revealed
Fitness for purpose	*s.14(3)*	*s.9(4)* *s.9(5)*	*s.4(4)* *s.4(5)* *s.4(6)*		*s.10(3)*	Implied when dealing in the course of seller's business, except where defects are specifically drawn to the attention of the customer, or the customer examines the goods
Title	*s.12*	*s.7* (Possession)	*s.2*		*s.8*	Always implied
Price	*s.8*					See p.293
Payment	*s.10*					See p.293
Ownership	*ss.16-18*					See p.293
Risk	*s.20*					See p.294
Delivery	*s.29*					See p.294
Sample	*s.15*	*s.10*	*s.5*		*s.11*	Always implied on a sale by sample
Reasonable care and skill				*s.13*		Implied when dealing in the course of the seller's business
Within reasonable time				*s.14*		Implied when dealing in the course of the seller's business. Not applicable if the time is fixed by contract, or is left to be agreed in the manner set out in the contract, *or* is determined by a course of dealing between the parties
Reasonable charge				*s.15*		Always implied. Not applicable if charge is fixed by contract, or is left to be agreed in the manner set out in the contract, *or* is determined by a course of dealing between the parties

B. *Sale of Goods Act 1979*

➤ When a sale of goods contract is formed, sometimes not all terms that are supposed to be included, are in fact included. *The following defaults only apply where the contract does **not** make provision.*

<table>
<tr><th colspan="3">Sale of Goods Act 1979</th></tr>
<tr><th>s.</th><th>Area</th><th>Content</th></tr>
<tr><td colspan="3">Formation of the contract</td></tr>
<tr><td>2</td><td>Definition</td><td>A contract for sale of goods is a contract by which the seller (S) transfers or agrees to transfer the property in goods to the buyer (B) for a money consideration, called the price</td></tr>
<tr><td>8</td><td>Price</td><td>Where price is not agreed, or determined by fact, B must pay a reasonable price</td></tr>
<tr><td>10</td><td>Time of payment</td><td>Not of the essence
Note: other stipulations as to time depend on the terms of the contract</td></tr>
<tr><td>15</td><td>Sale by sample</td><td>2 implied terms:
◆ the bulk corresponds with the sample in quality
◆ the goods are free from any defect not apparent on a reasonable examination of the sample</td></tr>
<tr><td colspan="3">Effect of the contract</td></tr>
<tr><td>16
17
18</td><td>Ownership</td><td>Ownership passes when the parties intend it to pass
◆ If the parties do not express an intention as to when ownership passes, the time it does pass depends on the type of contract:
<table>
<tr><th>Rule</th><th>Type of contract</th><th>Ownership passes</th></tr>
<tr><td>1</td><td>Unconditional contract for specific goods in a deliverable state</td><td>When the contract is made</td></tr>
<tr><td>2</td><td>Contract for specific goods to be put into a deliverable state</td><td>When they are in a deliverable state and B is told of this</td></tr>
<tr><td>3</td><td>Contract for specific goods where something must be done to ascertain the price</td><td>When the price is set and B is told what it is</td></tr>
<tr><td>4</td><td>Goods on approval for sale and return</td><td>When either:
◆ B indicates his acceptance of the goods to S, or
◆ B's conduct implies that he accepts the sale transaction or
◆ B retains the goods beyond a reasonable period (or agreed time) without rejecting them</td></tr>
<tr><td>5</td><td>Unascertained goods</td><td>When goods are available and unconditionally appropriated to the contract (ie: ascertained)</td></tr>
<tr><td colspan="3">Specific goods: 'goods identified and agreed on at the time the contract of sale is made' (SGA s.61(1))</td></tr>
</table></td></tr>
<tr><td>19

Note: the importance of retention of title clauses is manifest on insolvency; their purpose is either to recover goods when a business becomes insolvent, or failing that, to put the debtor in a strong position in negotiations with the receiver</td><td>Reservation of title</td><td>◆ S may reserve title to 'specific goods' or those 'appropriated to the contract' by a 'retention of title clause'
◆ There are 3 types of these clauses, known collectively (and confusingly!) as 'Romalpa' clauses.
a) Retention of title clause: title is reserved until payment is received
b) 'All moneys clause': title does not pass until all moneys owing to S, whether under this contract or any other contract, are paid
c) A true 'Romalpa' clause: title is retained in the goods, and S is permitted to trace the purchase price into the hands of a third party to whom the goods are sold
● a) and b) are generally upheld by the courts
● c) succeeded on particular facts once when a fiduciary relationship was found between S and B (Aluminium Industrie v. Romalpa Aluminium Ltd [1976] 2 All ER 552). Attempts to copy it have failed and the Courts construe c) as an unregistered (ie: void) charge
◆ To stand a chance of being effective (ie: to stand a chance of being construed as more than just a charge that is void and being construed instead as a right to repossession) a clause should:
● reserve full legal title to the goods (equitable and/or beneficial title are insufficient), and
● entitle the seller to enter the buyer's property to inspect and repossess the goods, and
● oblige the buyer to store the goods separately, or label them, so they can be identified as being appropriated to the contract</td></tr>
</table>

Sale of Goods Act 1979 (cont.)		
s.	Area	Content
		Effect of the contract (cont.)
20	Risk	◆ Goods are at the risk of S unless property is transferred to B ◆ If property has been transferred to B, goods are at B's risk whether delivery has been made or not ◆ If goods are delayed due the fault of one party, the goods are at the risk of the party at fault
20A	Undivided shares in bulk	When goods within a bulk become identified *and* the price has been paid for the goods in the bulk, *then* ◆ property in undivided share is transferred to B, *and* ◆ B becomes an owner in common of the bulk
21	Capacity to pass property	One cannot give what one does not have - *nemo dat quod non habet.* (Exceptions include factors, S in possession after sale, and motor vehicles (*HPA 1964 s.27(5)(a)*))
		Performance of the contract
27 *28*	Duties	S must deliver the goods and B must accept and pay for the goods Delivery and payment are concurrent (ie: cash on delivery)
29 *31*	Delivery	**Place of delivery:** S's place of business (or if not, his residence) **Note:** if the goods are specific goods and they are known to be at another place, delivery is at that other place **Note:** delivery to an independent carrier is counted as delivery to B **Delivery time:** S must send the goods within a reasonable time and at a reasonable hour
30	Wrong quantity delivered	**Smaller quantity than expected:** B may reject all the goods (unless he is not a consumer and the shortfall is only slight) B may accept all the goods. If so, he must pay for them at the contract rate **Larger quantity than expected:** B may accept the right quantity and reject the excess B may reject the whole (unless he is not a consumer and the excess is only slight) B may accept all the goods. If so, he must pay for them at the contract rate
31 *34* *35* *35A* *36*	Acceptance ?	**B accepts the goods by:** ◆ intimating to S that he accepts, *or* ◆ after the goods have been delivered, acting in a manner inconsistent with the ownership of S **B rejects the goods:** ◆ B has a right to reject the goods if he has not had a reasonable opportunity to examine the goods (this cannot be waived if B is a consumer) ◆ B has a right to reject part of the goods ◆ B is not bound to return rejected goods ◆ B does not have to accept the goods if they unexpectedly arrive in instalments
41 *42* *44* *45*	Unpaid seller	**An unpaid seller, if he has received no payment, or tender of payment may:** ◆ have a lien on the goods or part of them for the price, *or* ◆ (if B is insolvent) stop the goods in transport, *or* ◆ (if the goods are perishable and S informs B he has not been paid) re-sell the goods
		Remedies
49 *50* *15A*	Things go wrong	**Remedies for S** ◆ **Property has passed and S has received no payment** - S sues for the price ◆ **Property has passed and payment time has passed without payment** - S sues for the price ◆ **B wrongfully refuses to accept the goods** - S sues for damages and losses 'directly and naturally' flowing from B's breach of contract **Remedies for B** ◆ **S does not deliver** - B sues for damages and losses 'directly and naturally' flowing from S's breach of contract ◆ **S breaches a warranty** - S sues for damages **Note:** if S breaches *ss. 13-15* (see p.292) and B is a non-consumer, and the breach is slight, this may be treated as a breach of warranty.

C. *Late Payment of Commercial Debts (Interest) Act 1998*

➤ *LPCD(I)A 1998* gives a creditor a statutory right to claim interest on debts paid late (*s. 1*) under contracts for the sale or hire of goods or services where purchaser and supplier both act in the course of business.

- 'Business' includes professions and government departments or local/public authorities.
- Exempt contracts include consumer credit agreements, mortgages, charges or security (*s. 2*).

➤ Interest starts to accrue on (*s. 4*):

either the day after the contractual date for payment,

or if none, 30 days from the later of:

- delivery of the invoice for payment, *or*
- delivery/performance of the relevant goods/services .

- The rate of interest is 8% *above the official dealing rate.*
- There are slightly different rules for advance payments (not dealt with here).

➤ Contracting-out of *LPCD(I)A 1998* before the debt is created is not permitted unless there is a substantial contractual remedy for late payment in the contract *(s. 8).* It will not be substantial if it is insufficient either:

a) to compensate the supplier for late paymen or to deter late payment, *and*

b) it would be unfair or unreasonable to allow the remedy to be relied upon.

➤ *LPCD(I)A 1998* is being phased in, in stages:

- At present, in relation to a commercial contract for goods or services, a small business supplier has the right to claim interest against business purchasers and the public sector
- *From 1 November 2002, it is intended that all businesses will have the right to claim interest against all businesses (large and small) and the public sector [not yet in force].*

Note: A small business has 50 or less employees on the date on which payment becomes late.

D. *Consumer Protection (Distance Selling) Regulations 2000*

➤ There are many types of distance sales, including those made over the Internet. *CP(DS)R 2000* implements (most of) Euro Directive 97/7/EC on the protection of consumers in relation to distance contracts.

➤ *CP(DS)R 2000* applies to contracts for goods or services to be supplied to a consumer where the contract is made exclusively by means of distance communication (ie: any means used without the simultaneous physical presence of the consumer and the supplier (*reg. 4*).

- *CP(DS)R 2000* do not apply to 'excepted contracts' ie: contracts (*reg. 5*):
  - for the sale an interest in land except for a rental agreement, *or*
  - relating to financial services, *or*
  - concluded by means of an automated vending machine or automated commercial premises, *or*
  - concluded with a telecommunications operator through a public pay-phone, *or*
  - concluded at an auction.
- Most of *CP(DS)R 2000* do not apply to contracts for the supply of groceries by regular delivery or contracts for the provision of accommodation, transport, catering or leisure services (*reg. 6*).

➤ The contract must be performed within 30 days, subject to agreement between the parties. If the supplier cannot supply the goods/services ordered, he may offer substitutes if set conditions are met (*reg. 19*).

➤ The Director General of Fair Trading and Trading Standards Departments must consider complaints about a breach of *CP(DS)R 2000* (*regs. 26-27*).

- In good time **prior to the conclusion of the contract** the supplier must (*reg. 7*):
  - provide to the consumer the following information in a clear and comprehensible manner:
    - the supplier's identity and, if the contract requires advance payment, the supplier's address, *and*
    - a description of the main characteristics of the goods or services, *and*
    - the price of the goods or services including all taxes and delivery costs where appropriate, *and*
    - the arrangements for payment, delivery or performance, *and*
    - the existence of a right of cancellation (except in the excpetional cases - see below), *and*
    - the cost of using the means of distance communication, if not at the basic rate, *and*
    - the period for which the offer or the price remains valid, *and*
    - where appropriate, the minimum duration of the contract, in the case of contracts for the supply of goods or services to be performed permanently or recurrently, *and*
  - inform the consumer if he proposes that, if the goods/services ordered by the consumer are unavailable, he will provide substitutes of equivalent quality and price, *and*
  - inform the consumer that the cost of returning any such substitute goods to the supplier in the event of cancellation by the consumer will be met by the supplier.
- The supplier must confirm in writing, or on other durable medium available and accessible to the consumer, most of the information already given **and** some additional information (eg: conditions and procedures relating to the cancellation rights and information on after-sales services/guarantees) (*reg. 8*).
  - The supplier must inform the consumer prior to conclusion of a contract for services that he will not be able to cancel once performance of the service has begun with his agreement (*reg. 8(3)*).
- There must be a "cooling off period" so the consumer can cancel the contract by giving notice of cancellation. The effect of this notice is that the contract is treated as if it had not been made (*regs .10-12*).
  - If the supplier gives the specified information on time, the cooling-off period is: (for services) 7 working days from the day after the date of the contract, or (for goods) from the day after the date of delivery.
  - If the supplier fails to supply the required information, the cooling-off period is extended by 3 months.
  - If the supplier complies with the information requirement later than he should have done but within 3 months, the cooling-off begins from the date he provided the information.
- There is no cancellation right (unless the parties agree) if the contract is for the supply of (*reg. 13*):
  - services, if the supplier has complied with *reg. 8(3)* and performance of the contract has begun with the consumer's agreement before the end of the applicable cancellation period, *or*
  - goods/services where price depends on financial market fluctuations outside the supplier's control, *or*
  - goods made to the consumer's specifications or clearly personalised or which by reason of their nature cannot be returned or are liable to deteriorate or expire rapidly, *or*
  - audio or video recordings or computer software if they are unsealed by the consumer, *or*
  - newspapers, periodicals or magazines, *or*
  - gaming, betting or lottery services.
- If the consumer cancels, the consumer must be reimbursed within a maximum of 30 days (*reg. 14*).
  - If the consumer cancels the contract, a related credit agreement is automatically cancelled (*reg. 15*).
  - On cancellation, the consumer must restore goods to the supplier if he collects them, but meanwhile the consumer must take reasonable care of them. The consumer does not have to return goods but if he breaches a requirement under the contract, he must pay the supplier's recovery costs (*reg. 17*).
- If the consumer's payment card is used fraudulently, he may cancel the payment. If the payment has already been made, he is entitled to a re-credit or to have all sums returned by the card issuer (*reg. 21*).

E. Exclusion clauses

➤ A clause which successfully excludes or limits liability must have overcome certain hurdles:

1 **Common law rules**

- **Incorporation:** the clause must be properly incorporated into the contract (ie: reasonable steps must be taken to draw the term to the promisee's attention).
- **Construction:** the clause must cover the breach which occurs.
- **Particular common law rules:** the *'contra proferentem'* rule - any ambiguity in a term of the contract is interpreted against the party attempting to rely on the exclusion.

2 **Some statutory/regulatory rules - background**

- Certain rules cannot be contracted out of. For example, the *CP(DS)R 2000, the Unfair Contract Terms Act ('UCTA')* and *the Unfair Terms in Consumer Contracts Regulations 1999 ('UTCC')*.
- *CP(DS)R 2000* has been dealt with on the previous 2 pages.
- *UCTA* has been in English law since 1977. *UTCC* on the other hand, is a relatively recent development and is based on a European directive.
  - ◆ There are 3 problems with having these 2 sources of legislation:

    a) There is a degree of overlap because:
       - *UCTA* covers exclusion and limitation of liability clauses in business and consumer contracts.
       - *UTCC* covers unfair terms in consumer contracts which have not been individually negotiated.
         - ▪ An 'unfair term' is a term which is contrary to the requirement of good faith and causes a significant imbalance in the parties' rights/obligations to the detriment of the consumer.

    b) Key concepts such as 'consumer' are defined differently in both pieces of legislation.

    c) The list of contracts exempted from each legislative regime is different and must be checked.

UCTA and *UTCC*

➤ Where there is a **consumer contract** containing an **unfair exemption clause,** there is an overlap between the *UCTA* and *UTCC* and both must be checked against the contract.

- ◆ The procedure is as follows:

Steps	
1	Check definitions in *UCTA*
2	Check *UCTA* (see box overleaf)
3	Tighten the contract to comply with *UCTA*
4	Check definitions in *UTCC*
5	Check *UTCC* (if a consumer contract) (see box overleaf)
6	Tighten the contract to comply with *UTCC*

➤ *UCTA* does not apply to International Supply Agreements (*s.26 UCTA 1977*).

(Step 2) - *Unfair Contract Terms Act 1977* - contents		
	Attempted exclusion	Effect
s.2	a) The common law duty of care, *or* b) liability under the *Occupiers Liability Act 1957*	Void for death *or* personal injury Valid for other loss if the clause satisfies the requirement of reasonableness'
s.3	General exclusion of liability NB: This section is only applicable if one party 'deals as a consumer' and/or uses the other's standard written terms ➤ Covers 2 parties dealing in business ➤ Not applicable to implied terms	Entitles the promisor to offer performance of the contract 'substantially different from that which was reasonably expected of him', subject to the 'requirement of reasonableness'
s.6	*SGA* or *SG(IT)A* implied terms: ◆ Description, satisfactory quality, fitness for purpose, sample	Exclusion is void against purchaser 'dealing as a consumer', but otherwise it is valid if it satisfies the 'requirement of reasonableness'
	SGA or *SG(IT)A* implied terms: ◆ Title	Always void
s.7	Where possession or ownership of goods passes under a contract which is not a sale of goods or hire purchase contract, ◆ any term is implied by law, *or* ◆ *s.2* of the *SGSA* (Title), *or* ◆ right to transfer goods	◆ Exclusion is void if a party is dealing as a consumer, otherwise a clause is valid subject to satisfying the 'requirement of reasonableness' ◆ *s.2 SGSA* (Title) is not excludable ◆ Subject to 'reasonableness'

Requirement of reasonableness (*s.11*) is ...

'... a fair and reasonable [term] ... having regard to the circumstances which were, or ought reasonably to have been, known to or in the contemplation of the parties when the contract was made'

➤ Although the guidelines exist in *Schedule 2* to define reasonableness, they are only obligatory for *ss.6-7*. Nevertheless, the courts frequently use them in other cases too. They include:
- ◆ the customer's knowledge
- ◆ the bargaining position of the parties
- ◆ whether the contract involved the customer making a special order

(Step 5) - *Unfair Terms in Consumer Contracts Regulations 1999* - contents	
Section	Breakdown of the section
r.3	Interpretation clause. Includes the definition of: ◆ seller/supplier (any natural/legal person acting for purposes relating to his trade, business or profession), ◆ consumer (any natural person acting for purposes outside his trade, business or profession - different to *UCTA*)
r.4	Regulations apply to unfair terms in contracts between a seller/supplier and a consumer ***but*** subject matter of the contract and price are not tested for fairness (*r.6(2)*)
r.5	Key concept of an 'unfair term' which is a term 'contrary to . . . good faith [which] causes a significant imbalance in . . . rights . . . to the detriment of the consumer'
r.6	To see if a term is unfair, it must be looked at in context at the time it was made
r.7	Terms must be in plain, intelligible language; if not, the term will be construed in the consumer's favour
r.8	Unfair terms do not bind a consumer.
r.10-15	The Director General of Fair Trading considers any complaints made and has various powers
Schedule 2	Examples of unfair terms

➤ The Office of Fair Trading (OFT) has published a bulletin covering the following topics:
- ◆ the most common unfair terms in consumer contracts
  - eg: • entire agreement clauses
  - • penalty clauses
  - • variation of price clauses
- ◆ terms that have been successfully excluded after OFT intervention
  - • eg: 'The Council accepts no liabiility for loss or damage to cars parked in this car park ... howsoever caused.'

I Commercial agreements

I Third party rights in contracts

➤ Under *C(ROTP)A 1999,* if a contract is made with the purpose of conferring a benefit on a third party, under certain circumstances that person has a right to sue for breach of contract.

II Agency agreements

A. 3 types of agency

3 types of agency			
Classical sales agency	P authorises A to enter into contracts with C on behalf of P	P → A ↖↘ ↓ C	Note: in this chapter P=Principal A=Agent C=Customer
Marketing agency	P authorises A to introduce customers (C) to P	P → A ↖ ↓ C	
Note: a del credere agent guarantees C's performance for an additional commission			

B. Legislative rules

Commercial Agents (Council Directive) Regulations 1993	
Effect - on all commercial agents operating in the UK after 1 January 1994	*Regulation*
◆ oblige the principal and the agent to exchange certain information	*3-4*
◆ govern the amount of commission paid to an agent and the method of payment	*6-12*
◆ provide for compensation to be paid to the agent on termination especially where: a) the agent has been deprived of commission which proper performance of his duties would have procured for him, while the principal retains substantial benefits linked to the agent's activities, *or* b) the agent has been unable to amortise the costs and expenses that he had incurred in the perfomance of the contract on the principal's advice ◆ give the parties a choice between an indemnity or compensatory arrangement on termination ● Where no preference is expressed, the agent will be entitled to compensation (*rr. 17-18*) ● The right to damages, as well as an indemnity (linked to the fruits of the agent's efforts), is preserved	*13-19*
◆ renders any attempt to restrain an agent's trade after termination void, unless it: a) is contained in a written agreement b) defines a geographical area where the agency operates *or* the area in which customers are situated c) ceases no more than 2 years after termination	*20*
Note a) agencies in other EU member states may be governed by a version of the *Regulations* enacted in accordance with that state's laws. Complicated questions of jurisdiction and applicable law determine which courts (UK or foreign) will enforce which set of legislation (UK, local state or EU directive) b) certain classes of agent, such as unpaid agents, insolvency practitioners and those whose 'activities as agents are considered to be secondary' are excluded from the *Regulations*	

C. The law of agency - basic principles

➤ An agency agreement can be oral or written, express or implied.

1 Authority

➤ **Actual authority:** this can be given expressly *or* impliedly.

➤ **Ostensible authority.** Four conditions must be satisfied (*PA ss.5-8*):

subjective test:
a) C knows or believes he is dealing with A, *and*
b) C is unaware that 'A' is not actually authorised, *and*

objective test:
c) 'A' would usually be expected to be authorised to enter into such a transaction, *and*
d) P's type of business is consistent with the nature of the transaction.

2 Liability

➤ **When A is authorised to act**

- P is liable for A's acts.
- A is not liable unless the contrary is agreed, expressly or implicitly, by A and P *or* A and C.

➤ **When A is *un*authorised to act**

- Generally, P is not liable to C for A's acts.
- If A has ostensible authority, but has exceeded his actual authority, P will be liable and A may be liable to P and C for breach of warranty of authority.

3 Ratification of A's acts

➤ **P can 'ratify'** (ie: agree to be bound by) **a contract by an unauthorised A if:**

a) C could identify P when the contract was agreed, *and*
b) P has contractual capacity at the date of the contract and the date of ratification, *and*
c) the act is capable of ratification (ie: not illegal), *and*
d) ratification occurs within a reasonable time.

4 Non-disclosure of agency

➤ **If A does not disclose his agency, P can always intervene *unless*:**

a) the contract between A and C, expressly or impliedly excludes an agency, *or*
b) C wished to contract with A, *or*
c) the 'personality' of the parties is central to the contract.

5 Termination

➤ The agency agreement can be terminated by *either* A *or* P at any time subject to the contract.

➤ If P who is a debtor gives a creditor authority to act as an agent, then while the debt remains outstanding, the agency is irrevocable (*Greer v. Downs Supply Co* [1927] 2 KB 28).

➤ The contract is terminated by the death or mental incapacity of A or P, but A is protected if he acts in ignorance of P's incapacity (*PAA 1971 s.5(1)*).

6 Payment

➤ Payment to A by C does not discharge a debt owed to P by C unless *either* A has authority (actual or apparent) to receive the payment, *or* P is undisclosed.

➤ Payment by P to A does not discharge a debt owing to C unless C misleads P into thinking that the money is to reimburse A for money already paid to C.

III Distribution agreements

A. Types of distribution agreement

➤ Distribution agreements with anti-competitive provisions may infringe European/UK competition law. Eg:

1 **Exclusive distribution** - distributor alone may distribute supplier's goods in a particular territory, but supplier may still make passive sales in the territory.

2 **Sole distribution** - as in 1, but supplier can actively sell within the 'exclusive territory'.

3 **Selective distribution** - supplier attempts to retain control over the sales that his distributor makes.

4 **Exclusive purchasing** - distributor promises to buy goods from a sole supplier for an 'exclusive territory'.

B. Relevant law

black clauses

white clauses

➤ See pp. 286-290 for relevant law and possible ways to avoid infringement.

Block exemption covering vertical agreements (*Regulation 2790/1999*)

➤ Vertical agreements are agreements or concerted practices entered into by 2 or more undertakings each of which operates at a different level of the supply or production chain, which relate to the conditions under which a party may purchase, see or resell certain goods or services, and which contain restrictions within the scope of *Article 81(1)*.

➤ The exemption only applies if the market share held by the supplier does not exceed 30 % of the relevant market on which it sells the contract goods or services.

➤ If a vertical agreement contains exclusive supply obligations, the exemption only applies if the market share held by the buyer does not exceed 30 % of the relevant market on which it purchases the contract goods or services.

➤ The exemption does not apply to vertical agreements which, directly or indirectly, in isolation or in combination with other factors under the control of the parties, have as their object a restriction on:

- ◆ the buyer's ability to determine its sale price (even though the supplier may impose a maximum sale price or recommend a sale price, provided that it does not amount to a fixed or minimum sale price due to pressure), *or*
- ◆ active or passive sales to end users by members of a selective distribution system operating at the retail level of trade, without prejudice to the possibility of prohibiting a member of the system from operating out of an unauthorised place of establishment, *or*
- ◆ cross-supplies between distributors within a selective distribution system, including between distributors operating at different level of trade, *or*
- ◆ limitation, agreed between a supplier of components and a buyer who incorporates those components, which limits the supplier to selling the components as spare parts to end-users or to repairers or other service providers not entrusted by the buyer with the repair or servicing of its goods, *or*
- ◆ the territory into which the buyer may sell the contract goods or services.

NB: the following restrictions *are* allowed - restrictions on:

- active sales into the exclusive territory or to an exclusive customer group reserved to the supplier or allocated by the supplier to another buyer, where such a restriction does not limit sales by the customers of the buyer.
- sales to end users by a buyer operating at the wholesale level of trade.
- sales to unauthorised distributors by the members of a selective distribution system.
- the buyer's ability to sell components, supplied for the purposes of incorporation, to customers who would use them to manufacture the same type of goods as those produced by the supplier.

➤ The exemption does not apply to the following direct or indirect obligations contained in vertical agreements:

- ◆ an obligation which is indefinite or exceeds 5 years. A non-compete obligation which is tacitly renewable beyond 5 years is deemed to have been concluded for an indefinite duration. However, there are slightly different rules for where contract goods or services are sold by the buyer from premises and land owned by the supplier or leased by the supplier from third parties, *or*
- ◆ an obligation forbidding members of a selective distribution system from selling brands of competing suppliers, *or*
- ◆ an obligation forbidding the buyer, after termination of the agreement, from manufacturing, purchasing, selling or reselling goods or services, unless such an obligation:
  - relates to goods or services which compete with the contract goods or services, *and*
  - is limited to the premises and land from which the buyer has operated during the contract period, *and*
  - is indispensable to protect know-how transferred by the supplier to the buyer, and provided that the duration of such non-compete obligation is limited to a period of 1 year after termination of the agreement (this obligation is without prejudice to the possibility of imposing a restriction which is unlimited in time on the use and disclosure of know-how which has not entered the public domain).

IV Choosing the right type of agreement

	Agency agreement	Distribution agreement
Supervision	This depends on the type of agency: **classical sales agency:** requires more supervision over the agreement **marketing agency:** requires less supervision over the agreement ✗	There is no need for day to day supervision, and the principal specifies any detailed requirements in the agreement. These are preferable if the principal wishes to deal in a new geographical market with minimum expense and inconvenience ✓
Goods	Suitable for goods which are ordered on a 'one-off' basis to a customer's individual specification	Suitable for standard ranges of goods which do not require specialist after-sales support
Prices	➤ The supplier sells directly to the retailer ➤ The supplier controls the price ➤ The agent takes commission ✓	➤ The supplier sells to the distributor who marks up the resale price ➤ The supplier can 'recommend', but cannot control the price as *Article 81* and *CA 1998* prohibit price-fixing ✗
Risk	P takes the risk, A gets the commission ✗	The distributor takes the risk ✓
Marketing	The supplier retains tight control over marketing ✓	The supplier has less say; the distributor has more freedom of action ✗
Enforcing contracts	This is difficult as the supplier sells to many customers ✗	This is straightforward as there is only one buyer - the distributor ✓
Liability	This depends on the type of agency: **classical sales agency:** the principal is directly liable in contract to customers **marketing agency:** the agent has no actual authority to act on the principal's behalf ✗	The principal is only liable in contract to the distributor The principal may be liable to consumers under the *CPA 1987* or *GPSR 1994* ✓
Protection of a territory	As a principal and agent are separate undertakings, the agent can be given an 'exclusive territory' ✓	**Passive sales** cannot be banned (*either* those by a distributor outside his territory, *or* by a supplier within the territory) **Active sales** by either party in contravention of an 'exclusive territory' can usually be banned ✗
Article 81 problems	Usually non-applicable as principal and agent are counted as one undertaking ✓	This can be a problem, unless use is made of a block exemption ✗
Taxation	An overseas business trading through an agency in the UK may be subject to corporation tax	This depends on the agreement's wording, and the extent of the principal's presence in the UK
Compensation	The agent may seek compensation for termination under *CA(CD)R 1993* ✗	The only remedies are those usually available in contract and tort ✓

✓ advantage ✗ disadvantage

Franchise

➤ These are suitable vehicles for exploiting a 'business format' (eg: Pizza Hut).

- The franchisor can control closely many aspects of the product, and thus protect and foster his goodwill without incurring the capital costs of expanding in new markets
- The franchisee also benefits from the accumulated goodwill. He contributes his own capital. His freedom to innovate is rather limited by the franchise

Licence

➤ These enable the exploitation of intellectual property rights by permitting a third party to use a process, or manufacture a product

- The licensor is spared the difficulties and capital investment involved in manufacture
- A licence (possibly combined with a distribution agreement) may be vital where national laws insist that products are manufactured within a given area

J Employment

Employers, employees, or self-employed businessmen will need to be aware of 'free movement of workers' and of 'residence rights' in EU member states. Both employers and employees may seek advice on the 'rights to equal treatment of workers' and on 'UK employment legislation'. Finally, with the state reducing its retirement provisions, clients should receive advice on 'pensions in the UK'.

I Free movement of workers (EU law)

Treaty of Rome - *Article 39*

- This article prohibits discrimination based on nationality between workers of member states, for employment, or remuneration and other conditions of work and employment.

Derogation and exclusions (*Article 39(3)-(4)*)

- *Article 39(3)* allows a member state to refuse to comply with the rights set out in *Article 39* on the grounds of public policy, public security or public health. The state must show that the individual's personal conduct presents a current threat in one of these respects. *Directive 64/221* says that derogation on these grounds must be based 'exclusively on the personal conduct of the individual concerned' and 'shall not be invoked to serve economic ends.'
- *Article 39(4)* excludes jobs in the public service 'involving the exercise of official authority and functions relating to safeguarding the general interests of the state' (*Commission v. Belgium* [1980] ECR 3881). The term 'public service' cannot be interpreted widely so as to erode the principle of freedom of movement for workers (*Commission v. France* [1984] ECR 307).

II Residence rights (EU law)

1 If employed

- A citizen of a member state has an absolute right of residence in any other member state where he is employed on a full or part-time basis (*Levin v. Staatssecrestaris van Justitie* [1982] ECR 1035).
- Notwithstanding an involuntary loss of work, an EU citizen is entitled to a 5 year residence permit (*Directive 68/360*), and his right of residence is unimpaired by incapacity due to disability or reaching the retirement age, subject to certain criteria (*Regulation 1251/70*).

2 If 'voluntarily' unemployed

- A citizen of a member state has a right of residence for as long as the individual and the members of his family are not a burden on the social assistance system of the host state (*Directive 90/364*).

III Rights of workers to equal treatment (EU law)

1 **To enter to look for work**

- *Article 39* extends to the right to move freely in search of employment.
- Deportation is allowed if someone is jobless after 6 months and cannot support himself, unless he can show he had genuine chances of being engaged (*R. v. IAT, ex parte Antonissen* [1991] 2 CMLR 373).

2 **Conditions of work:** there must be no discrimination against citizens of other member states for:

- **employment, dismissal, social and taxation status, training, and union membership** (*Regulation 1612/68*): the right to these must be the same as for any citizen of the host state.
- **social security benefits:** entitlement is the same as for a national of the host state subject to the individual having made contributions to similar schemes in other member states (*Regulation 1408/71*).

3 **Right to bring a family**

- A spouse, children under 21 and dependant relatives may enter *with a worker* (*Regulation 1612/68*).
- A spouse, children up to 21 and dependants can enter *with a self-employed person* who provides 'services' (*Directive 73/148*).
- The right to bring a family is only lost if *Article 39(3)* permits a member state to exclude the worker himself, or if the couple divorce (*Diatta v. Land Berlin* [1985] ECR 567).
- A returning national may bring a spouse that he/she married in another member state notwithstanding any obstacles to this in national law (*R. v. IT & Surinder Singh, ex parte Home Sec.*[1982] 3 All ER 798).

4 **Mutual recognition of qualifications**

- A diploma after 3 years' higher professional education or training is accepted in all member states. If national criteria differ substantially, the individual can submit to an aptitude test *or* an 'adaptation' period of up to 3 years (*Directive 89/48*).

5 **Recipients of services**

- Recipients of services have a right to seek services from another member state (*Article 49* and *Luisi v. Ministero del Tesoro* [1984] ECR 377). This embraces the right to vocational training at no extra fee due to nationality (*Gravier v. City of Liege* [1985] ECR 593).

6 **Fundamental Bill of Rights**

- The Charter of Fundamental Rights was proclaimed on 7 December 2000 and in 7 Chapters sets out the fundamental rights of European citizens. It is designed to make existing EU rights more visible.

IV UK employment legislation - statutory rights

a) **Employment Relations Act 1999**

- Contains greater employee rights (eg: unfair dismissal compensation capped at £51,700; inability to contract out of unfair dismissal on expiry of a fixed term contract); greater family-friendly provisions (eg: extended maternity leave; a proposal to extend the SMP period from 18 to 26 weeks); right to 13 weeks parental unpaid leave after 1 years' continuous service; a proposal of 2 weeks' paid paternity leave (at £100 per week) for those with 26 weeks' service; a proposal to allow paid adoption leave; reasonable time off for domestic incidents) and greater collective rights (eg: trade union recognition for collective bargaining; prohibition on blacklisting of trade unionists for recruitment).
- In principle, part time workers cannot be treated less favourably than full-time workers of the same employer under the same employment contract (*PTWDR*).

b) **Employment Rights Act 1996 s.1**

➤ The employer must provide the employee with a written statement within 2 months of employment commencing. The statement must contain certain particulars as follows:

Statement of employment	
◆ the name of the employer ◆ the name of the employee ◆ the date that employment began ◆ the period of 'continuous employment' for statutory purposes ◆ pay and how the pay is timed ◆ the hours of work ◆ holiday time (and any holiday pay) ◆ sickness time (and any sickness pay) ◆ pensions	◆ notice periods ◆ job title ◆ place of work ◆ expected length of employment ◆ any collective agreements ◆ certain details if the employee must work outside the UK for more than 1 month ◆ disciplinary procedures ◆ complaints procedures

c) **Human Rights Act 1998** (and see p.26)

➤ HRA's impact is likely to be felt most in relation to Art.8 (right to family and private life) and Art.14 (right not to be discriminated against). Workers in the public sector may rely on the HRA directly. Workers in the private sector may rely on the HRA indirectly, in support of other employment law claims.

d) **Equal Pay Act 1970**

➤ An employer must provide equal pay for men and women employed to do the same/comparable work.

e) **Sex Discrimination Act 1975, Sex Discrimination Act 1986, Race Relations Act 1976**

➤ An employer must not to discriminate directly or indirectly on grounds of sex, race, or marital status.

f) **Disability Discrimination Act 1995**

➤ It is unlawful (unless justified) to discriminate against disabled employees or potential employees, whether in recruitment, working conditions or promotion prospects. There is also a duty to take reasonable steps to prevent a disabled person being disadvantaged by the employer's working arrangements or physical features of the work premises. (NB: this latter duty is limited to certain sizes of business. However the 'small employer' exemption is likely to be lowered significantly from October 2004).

g) **Health and Safety at Work Act 1974 (and the common law duty to take reasonable care for the health and safety of the employee at work)**

➤ The employer has a duty to provide the employee with a safe place of work, safe equipment and to provide a Health and Safety policy. Breach leads to criminal prosecution.

➤ The employee can sue for damages for breach of common law duty *and* breach of statutory duty.

h) **Transfer of Undertakings (Protection of Employment) Regulations 1981**

➤ These regulations apply when a business is transferred as a 'going concern'.

- ◆ The contract of employment of any employee employed by the seller of a business immediately before the transfer is not ended by the transfer.
- ◆ The employer's liability and obligations under the contract are transferred to the seller.

i) **Collective Redundancies and Transfer of Undertakings (Protection of Employment) Amendment) Regulations 1995 and 1999**

➤ All business transfers and certain redundancies oblige an employer to consult with employees either through a trade union or elected employee representatives.

j) **Trade Union and Labour Relations (Consolidation) Act 1992**

k) **Asylum and Immigration Act 1996 (s.8)**

➤ It is a criminal offence for an employer to employ a person who either has not been granted leave to remain in the UK or whose leave is not 'valid and subsisting'.

l) **Working Time Regulations 1998**

- These set limits on average weekly working hours and set minimum rest periods and holidays.

m) **Transitional Information and Consultation of Employees Regulations 1999**

- These regulations establish European Works Councils and a procedure to inform and consult with employees in EU-scale enterprises.

n) **Data Protection Act 1998**

- This replaces the *Data Protection Act 1984*. It extends protection to certain manual records, introduces stricter conditions for processing sensitive data and restricts transfer of data outside the EEA.

Some rights before and on being made redundnant

a) **Wrongful dismissal - Notice rights (*ERA 1996 ss.86-93*)**

- This means **the employer has failed to give the employee the necessary period of notice.**
- The employee can claim damages.
- The contract will normally stipulate the correct notice period that should have been given.
  - There is a statutory minimum period of notice.

b) **Unfair dismissal (*ERA 1996 ss.94-134*)**

- This means **the employer has dismissed the employee for an unfair reason (after a minimum of 1 year's continuous service).**
- To determine if the reason for dismissal is fair the employer must show: **a)** the reason *and* **b)** that the reason falls within a defined list in *s.98(2)* or is substantial enough so as to justify dismissal *and* **c)** that he acted reasonably (*s.98*). *Ss 99-104* contains reasons that do not justify dismissal eg: pregnancy.
- The employee can claim:
  - reinstatement, *or*
  - re-engagement in the service of the employer, *or*
  - compensation according to a statutory formula.

c) **Redundancy (*ERA 1996 ss.135-181*)**

- This means that the employee is made redundant after 2 years of qualifying service.
- The employee can claim a redundancy payment calculated by a statutory formula.

Factors

- The following are some employment-related factors to consider when starting a business:
  - the number of employees and the responsibility for them
  - the terms of any contracts of employment
  - employment legislation (see the previous and this page)
  - health and safety legislation
  - insurance legislation
    - This will include the statutory duties to obtain and display a certificate of insurance in respect of employees and accidents
    - This may include motor insurance
  - allowing employees time off to perform statutory duties including:
    - public duties (eg: jury service or acting as a magistrate)
    - trade union duties
  - the need to provide personnel services (sometimes called human resources) for employees
  - the need to deal with payroll and the implementation of PAYE machinery

V Pensions in the UK

Pensions - general points

- Pensions can be provided via an Inland Revenue approved or unapproved arrangement.
- Pension schemes (both employer-operated and personal schemes) can elect to contract out of the State Earnings Related Pension Scheme (SERPS).

A. Rules for directors and employees

- Of the various options available, an 'exempt approved retirement benefits scheme' is one of the most popular. These are approved by the Inland Revenue Superannuation Funds Office.
- A qualifying scheme benefits as follows (*TA ss.590-612*):

  a) an employee can deduct annual contributions from *Schedule E, and*

  b) an employer's contributions may be deducted from profits under *Schedule D Cases I and II, and*

  c) income on the scheme's investments and deposits is not subject to income tax, *and*

  d) pensions/annuities under the scheme are charged under *Schedule E* and deducted through PAYE.
- If an employer does not operate an occupational scheme, or an individual desires to have another pension in respect of earnings not earned from an employer, he can make provision as an individual.
- Individuals who have made national insurance contributions for 90% of their working life with an employer who has not contracted out of the government scheme, are eligible for a state pension.

B. Rules for sole traders and partners

1 **Annuity contracts** (created on, or before, 29 June 1988 and which are still effective (*TA s.618(1)*))

- Contributors under the age of 51 are entitled to tax relief at 17.5% of their net relevant earnings (*TA s.619*); the rate of relief for older contributors rises to a maximum of 27.5% (*TA s.626*).
- The annuity is liable to income tax. Capital gains tax is not payable on a lump sum on retirement, but this must not exceed triple the value of the annuity payable after the lump sum has been deducted, and, is subject to a ceiling of £150,000 (*TA s.618(2)*).

2 **Partnership annuities** (*TA s.628*)

- A partnership may agree to pay an annuity to a partner, his spouse or dependants. This is paid net of basic rate tax (22%).
  - A partner can set the payment off against his 'total income' as a 'charge on income'.
- As an alternative to paying an annuity, the partnership may appoint a retiring partner as a consultant.
  - This retains the value of goodwill the partner has acquired, so his fees would be a deductible expense.

3 **State pensions**

- Unless an individual or an employer's scheme contracts out of SERPS, the individual will receive a state pension in respect of his past national insurance contributions.

4 **Personal pensions** (begun after 1 July 1988)

➤ A contributor under the age of 36 is given tax relief up to 17.5% of his 'net' earnings.

- If aged 36 or over, the relief increases proportionately with the passing years up to 40% for those aged 61 or more *(TA s.640).*
- Contributions are subject to an earnings cap of £95,400 in 2001/2002.

➤ For pension schemes begun before 27 July 1989, a lump sum payment to a pensioner may not exceed £150,000. For subsequent schemes, the limit is set at 25% of the total benefit provided and the value of rights protected by the *Pensions Schemes Act 1993* (*TA s.635*).

➤ Lump sum death benefits must be payable before the member reaches the age of 75 (*TA s.637*).

➤ Contributions can be carried back *(s.641)* or forward *(s.642)* utilising relief from one year to another.

'Stakeholder' pensions (from 6 April 2001)

➤ An employer with 'relevant employees' (eg: more than 5 employees) will be obliged to offer those employees access to a stakeholder pension.

- An employer will not have to offer access to a stakeholder pension if all its employees have access to a personal pension and certain conditions are fulfilled (eg: the employer contributes at least 3% of the employee's basic pay to the scheme and there are no penalties/charges if the employee leaves the scheme).

➤ The main features of a stakeholder pension are that:

- a person can contribute up to £3,600 a year even if he or she is not earning (ie: a child, non-earning spouse, carer, can have a stakeholder pension) (*TA s.632A(4)-(9)*).
- contributions may be made by a person who is a member of an occupational pension scheme if that person (*TA s.632A(4)-(9)*):
  a) is not a controlling director of a company in the tax year in which payments begin (or in any of the 5 immediately preceding tax years), and
  b) does not have earnings from pensionable employment exceeding a 'remuneration limit' for at least one of the 5 years preceding the year in which an election for partial concurrency is made. The 'remuneration limit' is currently £30,000.
- contributions over £3,600 can be made based on earnings (these higher level contributions can be continued for up to 5 years after the person has ceased earning (*TA s.646B-D*)).
- it will be possible to carry back (but not carry forward) contributions (*TA s.641A*).
- up to 10% of the amount contributed can be used to purchase life assurance.
- the annual charge for the management of the fund may not exceed 1%.
- contributions will be paid net of basic rate tax (currently 22%); the scheme manager will reclaim the tax from the Inland Revenue (*TA s.639(4A)*).
  - Higher rate (40%) relief will be given by means of extending the basic rate band, rather than by deduction or set off (*TA s.639(5A)*).

➤ Trustees of existing retirement benefit schemes may, on or after 1 October 2000, apply to the Board of the Inland Revenue to convert a scheme so that it operates under the new personal pension (ie: stakeholder) rules (*TA Sch. 23ZA*).

Civil Litigation

This chapter examines:

Note: use this chart as a 'map' to sections 'B' to 'I'

The tracks

Rules of the court

➤ Rules of court procedure are governed by the **Civil Procedure Rules (*CPR*)** (exceptions are in *r.2.1*).

- The *CPR* are divided into over 55 Parts.
- Definitions of terms in the *CPR* are listed in *r.2.3* and also in a glossary at the back.
- Each *Part* contains rules - we use notation as follows: eg: *r.7.2(2)* refers to rule 7.2(2) in *Part 7*.
- Each *Part* is supplemented by a practice direction - we use notation as follows: *eg: PD7: 8.2* refers to paragraph 8.2 in the Practice Direction that supplements *Part 7*.

➤ For some purposes, some of the old rules that existed prior to the CPR are retained.

- For the High Court, these are the Rules of the Supreme Court (*RSC*) now in *Schedule 1* to the *CPR*.
- For the county courts, these are the County Court Rules (*CCR*) now in *Schedule 2* to the *CPR*.

A First steps

I Is the claim viable?

II Are there any alternatives to starting proceedings in the UK courts?

III How will the client finance the action?

IV Has the relevant pre-action protocol (if any) been considered?

<table>
<tr><td colspan="4">I Is the claim viable?</td></tr>
<tr><th rowspan="2">Contract</th><th colspan="3">Tort</th></tr>
<tr><th>Negligence</th><th>Personal injury</th><th>Latent damage</th></tr>
<tr><td colspan="4">1 Is the defendant worthy of attention?</td></tr>
<tr><td colspan="4">Is the defendant i) traceable and ii) solvent?</td></tr>
<tr><td colspan="4">2 How strong is the claimant's case?</td></tr>
<tr><td colspan="4">Does the evidence i) show all the elements required in law, and ii) prove these elements on the balance of probabilities?</td></tr>
<tr><td colspan="4">3 Has the limitation period expired? (LA 1980)</td></tr>
<tr><td>6 years from the breach of contract (s.5)</td><td>6 years from when the damage occurs (s.2)</td><td>3 years from (s. 11):
a) the date of the accident, or
b) the date of knowledge that (s. 14):
i) the injury is significant enough for proceedings +
ii) an injury is due to the defendant's fault +
iii) the defendant's identity becomes known</td><td rowspan="4">Either:
a) 6 years from the date on which the cause of action accrues (s. 14A), or
b) (if later than a)), 3 years from the date that a claimant could start proceedings because a claimant now has:
i) the knowledge* required for bringing an action, and
ii) a right to bring such an action (ie: recovery from a defendant seems realistic)
(NB: it must not be more than 15 years from the date of the breach)
*Knowledge means knowledge of the facts such that an action may be brought eg: the identity of the defendant and that the damage was due to the defendant's fault, etc</td></tr>
<tr><td colspan="3">For death and personal injury, the court has discretion to override the limitation period (s.33)</td></tr>
<tr><td colspan="3">4 What damages are available?</td></tr>
<tr><td>Generally
Loss which flows naturally from the breach

Loss which was within the reasonable contemplation of the parties at the time the contract was made

There is a duty on the claimant to mitigate loss

Debt claims
If the action is a claim for debt, the one claiming the sum outstanding does not have the duty to mitigate his loss, which applies to all other types of damages</td><td>Direct loss and consequential loss which is a reasonably foreseeable consequence of the negligence
Note: It is doubtful whether pure economic loss can be recovered</td><td>a) Special damages: liquidated claims for actual financial loss up to the date of the trial
b) General damages: unliquidated, compensating for:
i) past and future non-financial loss, and
ii) future financial loss
c) (SS(RB)A 1997): if the claimant receives state benefits:
i) then the defendant obtains a certificate of recoverable benefits from the Department of Social Security (DSS) Compensation Recovery Unit (CRU)
ii) the defendant is obliged to pay to the CRU the full amount of certain benefits listed which have been paid to the injured person
iii) where part of the compensation payment itself from the defendant to the claimant is in respect of a particular kind of loss, (loss of earnings, cost of care, loss of mobility) and benefits have been paid to the claimant for this kind of loss, the defendant may deduct the relevant benefits from the compensation payment (ie: the claimant is paid damages net, less the sum due to the DSS which the defendant forwards to the CRU within 14 days of the claimant receiving compensation
NB: No deductions are possible for pain and suffering ie: the victim keeps all the damages for pain and suffering</td></tr>
<tr><td colspan="4">5 Does the claim carry interest?</td></tr>
<tr><td>Interest is given from:
a) the date when the action arose to judgment or
b) date of payment (if sooner) either
i) at the contract rate, or
ii) at a court's discretion (unlikely to exceed the judgment debt rate)
<u>Debt claims</u>
High Court: 8% from final judgment date
County Court: see rules on p.398</td><td>At the Court's discretion</td><td>Judgment for a sum ...
a) ...over £200: a court must award interest (but will not do if it has a special reason (SCA 1981s.35A)
b) ...£200 or less: at the court's discretion
The rate is usually:
i) 0% for future loss of earnings
ii) 2% from the service of the claim form to the trial, for pain, suffering and loss of amenity
iii) half the court's average Special Account average rate from the accident to the start of trial for 'special damages'</td><td>At the Court's discretion</td></tr>
<tr><td colspan="4">6 What other remedies are possible?</td></tr>
<tr><td colspan="4">Eg: possession orders, injunctions, etc.</td></tr>
</table>

II Are there any alternatives to starting proceedings in the UK courts?

1 **Negotiation**
2 **Alternative dispute resolution (ADR)**
3 **Motor Insurers' Bureau**
4 **Statutory demand**
5 **Insurance (motor accidents)**
6 **Criminal Injuries Compensation Authority**
7 **Criminal compensation order**
8 **Arbitration under *Arbitration Act 1996***
9 **Application in a foreign jurisdiction**
10 **Trade schemes**

1 Negotiation

➤ This is always better than litigation and should normally be conducted 'without prejudice'.

2 Alternative dispute resolution (ADR)

➤ It is the duty of a solicitor to put the possibility of ADR to the client (see p.313).

- ◆ There are many types of ADR, eg: mediation, neutral evaluation, expert determination, etc.

➤ In mediation, a third party mediates and the mediation may or may not be binding.

- ◆ If no binding agreement is reached, then arbitration or litigation is possible later.

➤ ADR is usually quicker, cheaper and less destructive of the parties' relationship than litigation.

3 Motor Insurers' Bureau ('MIB')

➤ There are 2 schemes:

Victims of *uninsured* drivers	Victims of *untraced* drivers
Commence proceedings ↓ Notify the MIB within 7 days of commencing proceedings ↓ If 7 days after final judgment against the defendant driver the claim is not satisfied, the MIB will meet the claim together with costs ↓ Judgment must be assigned to the MIB so they may try and recover from the insured driver	The death or injury must not have been caused deliberately by the untraced driver ↓ Notify the police within 14 days of the accident or as soon as reasonably possible ↓ Notify the MIB by letter within ***3 years*** of the accident ↓ The MIB itself investigates the merit of the claim ↓ Negligence *must* be proved ↓ The MIB will cover death, bodily injury or emergency hospital treatment and there is no need to prove these costs. (Note: loss of earnings *is* recoverable)
The first £175 of property damage is not covered	Property damage is *not* recoverable Queen's Counsel hears appeals against the amount of damages by way of arbitration For claims up to £50,000, an accelerated process allows the claimant and the MIB to reach a compromise, but there is no full investigation and no right of appeal
◆ The MIB pays to the CRU money owed to NHS trusts and hospitals (*RT(NC)A 1999*).	

4 Statutory demand (see p.276)

5 Insurance (motor accidents)

➤ The decision how to claim depends on the type of insurance policy concerned:

a) **Compulsory risks** (required by *RTA 1988*). Such insurance covers ...

- ... death or injury to any other person, *and*
- ... property damage up to £250,000, excluding damage to the insured vehicle and its contents, *and*
- ... the cost of emergency hospital treatment.

b) **Third party, fire and theft.** Such insurance additionally covers...

- ... the insured against these risks.

c) **Comprehensive.** Such insurance additionally covers...

- ... damage to the insured's vehicle and limited compensation for a driver's injuries.

➤ Claims against the insured's own insurance (*only* if the policy is 'comprehensive').

- A 'no-claims' bonus may be lost, increasing the premium payable on the policy in the future.
- The insured may have to pay an 'excess' as a contribution to damages.
- The insurance company may insist that the insured lends their name to any legal proceedings.
- If the other party has 'comprehensive' insurance, the companies may agree between themselves to cover the costs of their own insured - the claimant has no control over the settlement they reach. This is called 'knock for knock'.
- The claimant may also choose to proceed against the other party or their insurer's for any *un*insured losses, eg: the amount of the excess *or* loss of any discount given by a no claims bonus.

➤ Claims against the other party's insurance.

- Provided the claimant serves a notice on the defendant's insurers within 7 days of commencing proceedings, he can recover damages from them, even if they are entitled to avoid *or* cancel the policy (*ss.151-152 RTA 1988*).

➤ Insurance is not necessarily an alternative to proceedings in the courts because of subrogation of rights - the insurer may still bring the action, leading to litigation.

6 Criminal Injuries Compensation Authority

➤ The Criminal Injuries Compensation Authority is a body that was set up in 1964 to award, *ex gratia*, compensation to the victims of crime. Awards are normally small but in some severe cases may be substantial.

➤ There is a fixed scale of awards (see *CICA 1995*). The absolute maximum it may award is £500,000.

7 Criminal compensation order (*PCC(S)A 2000 ss.130-134*)

➤ This is available for personal injury losses or damage following a criminal offence (other than loss due to accident arising out of there being a personal motor vehicle on a road). Compensation may be payable for damage which is not covered by the MIB.

- Magistrates' Court: fine up to £5,000 for each offence.
- Crown Court: fine unlimited, taking account of the defendant's means.

8 Arbitration under *Arbitration Act 1996*

➤ This may or may not be a cheaper and faster option than litigation. It depends on the case and the circumstances. The procedures are governed by *Arbritration Act 1996* (not dealt with here).

➤ It is binding and appeal lies to the courts.

9 **Application in a foreign jurisdiction** - (*CJJA 1982* & *PIL(MP)A 1995*)

➤ A person domiciled in the UK, or a company based in the UK, may sue in the UK.

➤ But a UK claimant may sue abroad if:

- for contractual claims: *either* the defendant is domiciled abroad, *or* the cause of action arose abroad, *or* a foreign law or jurisdiction is stipulated in the contract.
- for tortious claims: *either* the tort occurred abroad, *or* the damage was suffered abroad.

NB: Consider the costs and remedies, and the likelihood of enforcement in foreign jurisdictions.

10 **Trade schemes**

➤ These are operated by various trade and professional bodies and include:

- Royal Institute of Chartered Surveyors (RICS).
- Association of British Travel Agents (ABTA).
- British Association of Removers.

III How will the client finance the action?

➤ The client may be eligible for LSC funded help. If not, the solicitor should:

a) explain that the client is responsible for all the solicitor's costs and that if the case is lost he may have to pay the other side's costs. Even if the client is successful, costs are at the court's discretion and will not be awarded to the client automatically - the client will have to meet any shortfall, *and*

b) ask the client for a 'payment on account' to finance preparatory work, expert's reports, etc.

IV Has the relevant pre-action protocol (if any) been considered?

➤ Pre-action protocols are intended to improve pre-action contact between the parties, to ease exchange of information between the parties and to allow both sides to more fully investigate a claim at an earlier stage. All this is to encourage early settlement.

➤ The extent to which a party has (or has not) complied with any relevant pre-action protocol, is one of the factors a Court will consider when making orders as to costs (see p.390) and sanctions (see p.319) and giving directions to manage proceedings (see pp. 371 and 373).

➤ There are currently 5 pre-action protocols for:

- personal injury cases which are likely to be allocated to the fast track
- clinical negligence cases
- construction and engineering disputes
- defamation
- professional neligence

➤ There is also a pre-action protocol PD *which contains some rules of general application in all cases.*

- Eg:'In cases not covered by any approved protocol, the Court will expect the parties, in accordance with the overriding objective and ... [other] matters ... to act reasonably in exchanging information and documents relevant to the claim and ... in trying to avoid the necessity for the start of proceedings.'
- Eg:'Where a person enters into a funding arrangement ... he should inform other potential parties to the claim that he has done so' (and failure to do so means he cannot recover any additional liability).

After the first client meeting

1 Write to the client confirming instructions (giving information required by *SPR r.15* - see p.6).

2 Consider possibiltites for settlement. Discuss possible approaches with the client to avoid litigation.

3 Take some general statements from the client and witnesses to get a 'feel' for the case.

4 Make a site visit, if relevant, as soon as possible and take appropriate photographs, etc.

5 Consider whether experts may be needed and prepare possible names (see p.387).

6 Research any relevant law.

7 **Road traffic accident cases only**

- Write to the Chief Superintendent requesting a copy of the police accident report.
- Obtain a certificate of conviction from the court (if appropriate).
- Serve a *s.151/s.152* notice on the defendant's insurers before issuing proceedings or within 7 days after issuing proceedings.

8 **Personal injury cases only:**

- Comply with the relevant pre-action protocol. Prepare the calendar with appropriate reminders.
- Write to the client's employer for details of gross and net salary over the 26 weeks prior to the accident, the employee's prospects and details of the employment contract.
- Write to the Inland Revenue to claim a tax rebate (if appropriate).
- Notify the Compensation Recovery Unit within 14 days of receiving a letter before action.

9 Send a letter before action to the defendant stating:

a) for whom the solicitors are acting, *and*

b) the factual circumstances by which the claim has arisen, *and*

c) the action the solicitors are preparing to take, *and*

d) brief details of any loss, injury or damage.

- The letter should demand either settlement *or* a response within 7 to 14 days, failing which proceedings will be issued. The letter should warn that any claim will include interest and costs.

10 Negotiate or propose some other means of reaching a settlement (eg: ADR or *Part 36* - see p.358)

- Before proceedings are issued the solicitor has no implied authority to settle.
- After proceedings have been issued the solicitor has implied authority to settle; however, the client's express authority should always be sought (ideally in writing).
- Negotiations should normally be conducted 'without prejudice' so that nothing in the negotiations will be admissible in court.

11 Consider drawing up formal 'Instructions to Counsel' and arranging a conference (see p.385).

12 Consider forcing the potential defendant or a third party to give information by applying for an order for pre-action disclosure (see p.375)

- ask the defendant to co-operate by letter. This should save the claimant costs.
- An order can be made against *anyone* who holds property central to the case.
- An order might permit: photography, detention and custody, inspection, testing, and sampling.

Overview of proceedings (early stages)

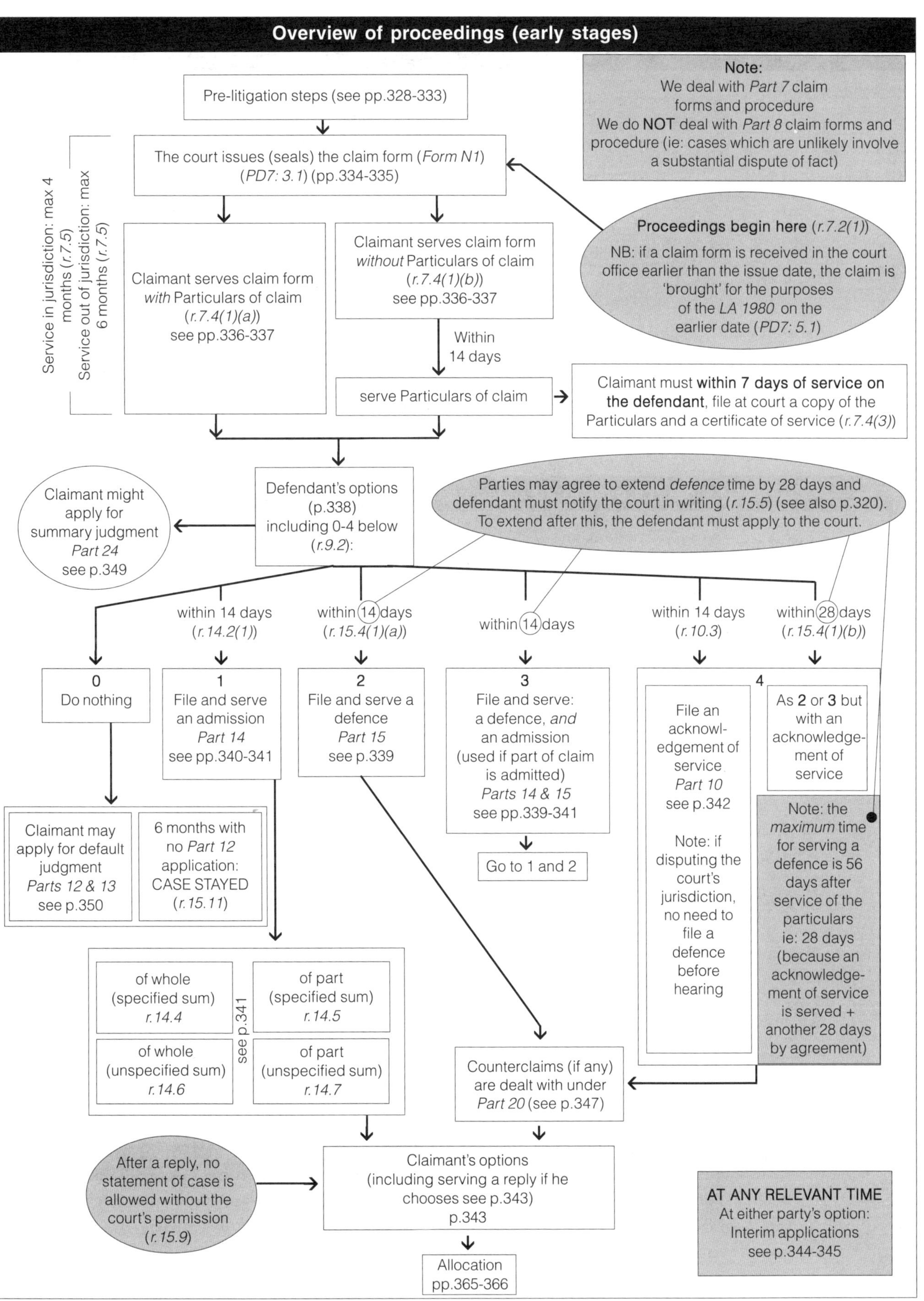
Note:
We deal with Part 7 claim forms and procedure
We do NOT deal with Part 8 claim forms and procedure (ie: cases which are unlikely involve a substantial dispute of fact)
Pre-litigation steps (see pp.328-333)
The court issues (seals) the claim form (Form N1) (PD7: 3.1) (pp.334-335)
Service in jurisdiction: max 4 months (r.7.5)
Service out of jurisdiction: max 6 months (r.7.5)
Proceedings begin here (r.7.2(1))
NB: if a claim form is received in the court office earlier than the issue date, the claim is 'brought' for the purposes of the LA 1980 on the earlier date (PD7: 5.1)
Claimant serves claim form with Particulars of claim (r.7.4(1)(a)) see pp.336-337
Claimant serves claim form without Particulars of claim (r.7.4(1)(b)) see pp.336-337
Within 14 days
serve Particulars of claim
Claimant must within 7 days of service on the defendant, file at court a copy of the Particulars and a certificate of service (r.7.4(3))
Defendant's options (p.338) including 0-4 below (r.9.2):
Claimant might apply for summary judgment Part 24 see p.349
Parties may agree to extend defence time by 28 days and defendant must notify the court in writing (r.15.5) (see also p.320). To extend after this, the defendant must apply to the court.
within 14 days (r.14.2(1))
within 14 days (r.15.4(1)(a))
within 14 days
within 14 days (r.10.3)
within 28 days (r.15.4(1)(b))
0 Do nothing
1 File and serve an admission Part 14 see pp.340-341
2 File and serve a defence Part 15 see p.339
3 File and serve: a defence, and an admission (used if part of claim is admitted) Parts 14 & 15 see pp.339-341
Go to 1 and 2
4
File an acknowledgement of service Part 10 see p.342
Note: if disputing the court's jurisdiction, no need to file a defence before hearing
As 2 or 3 but with an acknowledgement of service
Note: the maximum time for serving a defence is 56 days after service of the particulars ie: 28 days (because an acknowledgement of service is served + another 28 days by agreement)
Claimant may apply for default judgment Parts 12 & 13 see p.350
6 months with no Part 12 application: CASE STAYED (r.15.11)
of whole (specified sum) r.14.4
of part (specified sum) r.14.5
of whole (unspecified sum) r.14.6
of part (unspecified sum) r.14.7
see p.341
Counterclaims (if any) are dealt with under Part 20 (see p.347)
After a reply, no statement of case is allowed without the court's permission (r.15.9)
Claimant's options (including serving a reply if he chooses see p.343) p.343
Allocation pp.365-366
AT ANY RELEVANT TIME
At either party's option: Interim applications see p.344-345

B Court matters applicable throughout litigation

I General powers of the court

A. The court's overriding objective

The court's overriding objective in applying the *CPR* (*r.1*)

- The *CPR* are a new procedural code with the overriding objective of enabling the court to deal with cases justly.
  - 'justly' means:
    - a) ensuring that the parties are on an equal footing, *and*
    - b) saving expense, *and*
    - c) dealing with the case in ways which are proportionate:
      - i) to the amount of money involved, *and*
      - ii) to the importance of the case, *and*
      - iii) to the complexity of the issues, *and*
      - iv) to the financial position of each party, *and*
    - d) ensuring that a case is dealt with expeditiously and fairly, *and*
    - e) allotting to a case an appropriate share of the court's resources, while taking into account the need to allot resources to other cases.
- The court must seek to give effect to the overriding objective when it:
  - exercises any power given to it by the *CPR, or*
  - interprets any rule.
- The parties are required to help the court to further the overriding objective.
- The court must further the overriding objective by actively managing cases.

Decisions under pre-*CPR* cases

- Any decisions under the old *RSC* or *CCR* rules will not necessarily be followed, even on identical wording (*Lombard Natwest Factors v Sebastian Arbis* [2000] BPIR 79, *BCCI (in liquidation) v (1) Munwar Ali (2) Sultana Khan, Sub nom the Stigma Claims* (1999) 149 NLJ 1734).

B. Case management powers

The court's general powers of case management (*r.3.1*)

➤ The court has these additional general powers of management (unless a rule provides otherwise):

- to extend or shorten the time for compliance with any rule, practice direction or court order (even if an application for extension is made after the time for compliance has expired),
- to adjourn or bring forward a hearing,
- to require a party or a party's legal representative to attend the court,
- to hold a hearing and receive evidence by telephone or by using any other method of direct oral communication,
- to direct that part of any proceedings (eg: a counterclaim) be dealt with as separate proceedings,
- to stay the whole or part of any proceedings or judgment either generally or until a specified date or event,
- to consolidate proceedings,
- to try 2 or more claims on the same occasion,
- to direct a separate trial of any issue,
- to decide the order in which issues are to be tried,
- to exclude an issue from consideration,
- to dismiss or give judgment on a claim after a decision on a preliminary issue,
- to take any other step or make any other order for the purpose of managing the case and furthering the overriding objective.

➤ When the court makes an order, it may:

a) make it subject to conditions, including a condition to pay a sum of money into court, *and/or*

b) specify the consequence of failure to comply with the order or a condition.

➤ A power of the court under the *CPR* to make an order includes a power to vary or revoke the order.

The court's powers to make an order of its own initiative (*r.3.3*)

➤ Except where a rule or some other enactment provides otherwise, the court may exercise its powers on an application or of its own initiative (*Part 23*).

- Where the court proposes to make an order of its own initiative it *may* (but does not have to) give any person likely to be affected an opportunity to make representations.
  - If it does so it must set the time by and the manner in which the representations must be made.
  - The court must give each party likely to be affected by the order at least 3 days' notice of the hearing.

➤ A party affected by the order may apply to have it set aside, varied or stayed.

- This application must be made:

  a) within such period as may be specified by the court, *or*

  b) if the court does not specify a period, not more than 7 days after the date on which the order was served on the party making the application.

C. Power to strike out a statement of case (*r. 3.4*)

<table>
<tr><th colspan="3">Striking out a statement of case</th></tr>
<tr><td>Grounds
(r.3.4(2))</td><td colspan="2">1 A statement of case (or part of a statement of case) discloses no reasonable grounds for bringing or defending a claim (r.3.4(2)(a)), or
Eg: the particulars of claim set out no facts indicating what the claim is about, or are incoherent and make no sense, or do not disclose no legally recognisable claim against the defendant (PD3.4: 1.4)
Eg: a defence consists of a bare denial, sets out no coherent statement of facts, or those facts (being coherent) would not even if true amount in law to a defence (PD3.4: 1.6)
or 2 A statement of case (or part of a statement of case) is an abuse of the court's process or is otherwise likely to obstruct the just disposal of proceedings (r.3.4(2)(b)), or
Eg: a claim is vexatious, scurrilous, or obviously ill-founded (PD3.4: 1.5).
or 3 There has been a failure to comply with a a rule, practice direction or court order (r.3.4(2)(c))</td></tr>
<tr><td rowspan="3">Procedure

(if court acts of its own volition on grounds set out in r.3.4(2(a)(-(b)))</td><td>Striking out a claim (PD3.4: 2)</td><td>Striking out a defence (PD3.4: 3)</td></tr>
<tr><td>➤ A court officer must issue a claim form, but before returning the form to the claimant or taking any step to serve it on the defendant, the officer may consult a judge if the officer believes that there may be grounds for the claim to be struck out.
➤ The judge may make an order of his own initiative to ensure that the claim is disposed of or proceeds in a way which accords with the rules: this includes an order that:
◆ the claim be stayed until further order, or
◆ the claim form be retained by the court and not served until the stay is lifted, or
◆ no application by the claimant to lift the stay be heard unless the claimant files other documents (eg: a witness statement).</td><td>➤ A court officer may consult a judge if the officer believes that there may be grounds for the defence to be struck out.
➤ The judge may either:
◆ make an order of his own initiative (eg: striking out the defence or extending the time for the defendant to file a defence), or
◆ make an order under for further information r.18.1 (see p.351)</td></tr>
<tr><td colspan="2">➤ A court may exercise its powers under r.3.4(2) at any time of its own volition
➤ If a judge acts of his own volition, he may decide to hold a hearing before making an order</td></tr>
<tr><td>Order to strike out</td><td colspan="2">➤ The court may make any consequential order it considers appropriate (r.3.4(3))
➤ If a claimant's statement of case (or part of a statement of case) is struck out, and
... the claimant has been ordered to pay costs to the defendant, and
... before the claimant pays those costs, the claimant starts another claim against that defendant arising out of facts which are substantially the same as those relating to the struck out claim, ...
... the court may on the defendant's application stay the second claim until the costs of the struck out claim have been met (r.3.4(4)).</td></tr>
<tr><td>Judgement without trial after striking out
(r.3.5)</td><td colspan="2">➤ If a party's statement of case (or part of its statement of case) is struck out as a term of a court order and that party does not comply with that order, then ...
Either...
... if the order relates to the whole statement of case, a party may obtain costs by filing a request for judgment provided that if the party wishing to obtain judgment is the claimant, the claim is for:
● a specified amount of money, and/or
● an amount of money to be decided by the court, and/or
● delivery up of certain goods where the claim form gives the defendant the alternative of paying their value
OR
... a party must make an application under Part 23 (see p.344) if he wishes to obtain judgment.
➤ A party may apply within 14 days after receiving a judgment under r.3.5 to have that judgment set aside (r.3.6(1)-(2)).
➤ The court must set aside judgment if the right to enter judgment had not arisen at the time when judgment was entered (r.3.6(3).
➤ If an application to set aside is made for any other reason, r.3.9 applies (r.3.6(4))</td></tr>
</table>

D. Sanctions - powers and procedure

- Where a party has failed to comply with a rule, *PD* or court order, any sanction for failure to comply has effect unless the party in default applies for and obtains relief from the sanction (*r.3.8(1)*).
- Where the sanction is the payment of costs, the party in default may only obtain relief by appealing against the order for costs (*r.3.8(2)*).

Sanctions for non-payment of certain fees (*r.3.7, PD3B*)

- A fee is usually payable by the claimant to the court:
  a) ◆ on the filing of the allocation questionnaire, *or*
  ◆ where the claimant is not required to file an allocation questionnaire,
  and b) ◆ on the filing of the listing questionnaire, *or*
  ◆ where the claimant is not required to file a listing questionnaire.
- If the fee is not paid (or no exemption has been applied for), the court will serve a notice on the claimant specifying the date by which the claimant must pay the fee.
- After the notice, if the claimant does not pay the fee (or make an application for an exemption from or remission of the fee) by the date specified in the notice:
  - the claim is struck out (and the court sends the defendant a notice of this), *and*
  - the claimant is liable for the defendant's costs (unless the court orders otherwise), *and*
  - any interim injunction which the court granted may cease to have effect 14 days after the date on which the claim is struck out (see *r.25.11*).

Obtaining relief from sanctions (*r.3.9*)

- On an application for relief from sanctions (which must be supported by evidence) the court will consider all the circumstances including:
  - the interests of the administration of justice,
  - whether the application for relief has been made promptly,
  - whether the failure to comply was intentional,
  - whether there is a good explanation for the failure,
  - how much a party in default has complied with other rules, *PD*s, court orders, pre-action protocols,
  - whether the failure to comply was caused by the party or his legal representative,
  - whether the trial date or the likely trial date can still be met if relief is granted,
  - the effect which the failure to comply had on each party,
  - the effect which the granting of relief would have on each party.

Sanctions for non-compliance with case management directions (*PD28: 5, PD29: 7*)

- Where a party has failed to comply with a case management direction given by the court, any other party may apply for an order to enforce compliance or for a sanction to be imposed or both of these.
- A party applying for such an order must not delay and must first warn the other party of his intention.
- The court may take any such delay into account when it decides whether to make an order imposing a sanction or whether to grant relief from a sanction imposed by the rules or any *PD*.
  - Postponement of a trial is a last resort and will be for the shortest time possible. The court may require a party *and* his legal representative to attend where such an order is sought. Other than in exceptional circumstances, the court will not allow failure to comply with directions to lead to postponement. The court will assess steps each party should take to prepare for trial, directs those steps be taken in the shortest possible time and impose a sanction for non-compliance.
  - The court will not postpone any other hearing without a very good reason, and the failure of a party to comply on time with directions previously given will not be treated as a good reason.

II Provisions as to time

Provisions as to time (*r.2.8 - 2.11*)

- **days:** time expressed in the *CPR* as a number of days means clear days.
  - **'clear days'** do not include:
    a) the day on which the period begins, *and*
    b) (if the end of the period is set by reference to an event), the day on which that event occurs.
  - Where the specified period is 5 days or less *and includes* a Saturday or Sunday; *or* a Bank Holiday, Xmas Day or Good Friday; then that day does not count.
- **month:** 'month' in any judgment, order, direction or other document, means a calendar month.
- **time limits (1):** Where the court gives a judgment, order or direction with a time limit, the last date for compliance must, wherever practicable:
  - be expressed as a calendar date, *and*
  - include the time of day by which the act must be done.
- **time limits (2):** Where the date by which an act must be done is inserted in any document, the date must, wherever practicable, be expressed as a calendar date.

Time limits may be varied by the parties (*r.2.11*)

- Unless the court orders otherwise, any time limits specified by the *CPR* or by the court for a person to do any act may be varied by the written agreement of the parties.
  - Exceptions are:
    - any sanctions imposed (see p.319) have effect unless defaulting party obtains relief, *or*
    - when the *CPR* specifies the sanctions for failure to comply with a fixed time (*r.3.8(3)*), *or*
    - variation of the times in a case management timetable for fast track and multi-track, *or*
    - time limits for an appeal to the Court of Appeal (see p.403).

III Documents for court

Documents for court (*r.5.2, 5.3*)

- A document should be legible, duly authorised and must not be unsatisfactory for a similar reason.
- If a document must be signed, it may be manual, printed by computer or another mechanical means.
- Every document prepared by a party for filing or use at the court:

must be (*PD5: 2.2*):
- (unless impracticable), on A4 paper of durable quality having a margin not less than 3.5 cm wide, *and*
- fully legible and should normally be typed, *and*
- where possible, bound securely so as not to hamper filing or otherwise each page should be endorsed with the case number, *and*
- so that pages have consecutive numbering, *and*
- divided into numbered paragraphs, *and*
- such that all numbers, including dates, are expressed as figures, *and*
- give in the margin the reference of each document mentioned that has already been filed.

may be filed at court by fax (and there is no need also to send a copy by post or in the DX) (*PD5: 5.3*) ***BUT***:
- Faxes should not be used to send letters or documents of a routine or non-urgent nature.
- If a fax is sent after 4pm, it is treated as filed the next day that the court office is open.
- The following documents may *not* be faxed unless there is an unavoidable emergency:
  - documents that attract a fee (and the nature of the emergency must be explained in the fax together with an undertaking to make payment), *or*
  - a *Part 36* payment notice (and the nature of the emergency must be explained in the fax together with an undertaking to make payment), *or*
  - a document relating to a hearing less than 2 hours ahead, *or*
  - trial bundles or skeleton arguments.

IV Statements of case

A. Statements of case generally

Statements of case

- ➤ Statements of case are documents that all the parties produce, which contain formal statements of a party's case.
  - ◆ Statements of case focus the parties and the court on the pertinent issues.
- ➤ A subsequent statement of case must not contradict or be inconsistent with an earlier one
  - ◆ eg: a reply to a defence must not bring in a new claim. Where new matters arise, the appropriate course may be to seek the court's permission to amend the statement of case (*PD16: 10.2*).
- ➤ Time limits for service of statements of case are often (and usually) extended by agreement between the parties (see p.320).

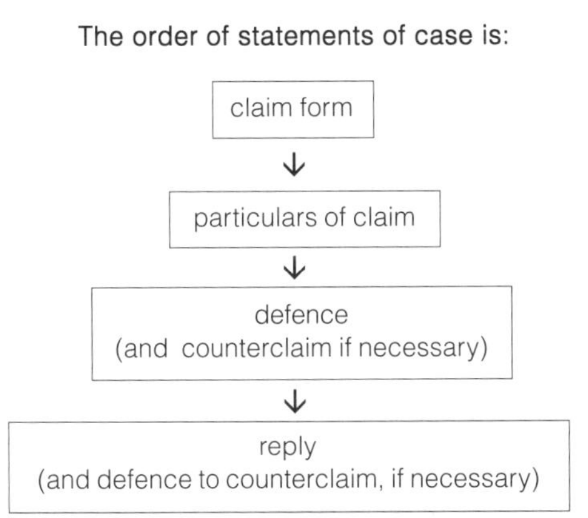
The order of statements of case is:
claim form
particulars of claim
defence
(and counterclaim if necessary)
reply
(and defence to counterclaim, if necessary)

Every statement of case must be headed with the title of the proceedings stating (*PD7: 4.1*):

- ◆ the claim number of the proceedings
- ◆ the court or Division in which they are proceeding
- ◆ the full name of each party
- ◆ his status in the proceedings (ie: claimant/defendant)

Where there is more than 1 claimant and/or more than 1 defendant, the parties should be described in the title as follows (*PD7: 4.2*):

(1) AB
(2) CD
(3) EF
Claimants

(1) GH
(2) IJ
(3) KL
Defendants

Clinical negligence practice tip

- ➤ In clinical negligence claims, the words 'clinical negligence' should be inserted at the top of every statement of case (*PD16: 10.3*).

6 practice rules for statements of case

1. State all material facts
2. State facts relevant to the action
3. State facts, not evidence (*Practice Direction (Civil Litigation: Case Management) 1995*)
   - ◆ One exception to this rule is criminal convictions (see p.336)
4. Refer to any point of law on which the claim/defence is based (*PD16: 14.3*)
5. Give the name of any witness a party proposes to call (*PD16: 14.3*)
6. Attach to or serve with the statement of case a copy of any document which is necessary to the claim/defence (including any expert's report) (*PD14: 16.3*)

B. Amendments to statements of case

➤ Amendments generally take effect retrospectively from the date of the original document.

➤ Limited amendments only are allowed (see box below) if:

- the limitation period has expired, *or*
- parties are to be amended.

➤ In practice, amendments are often agreed (subject to costs). However, a party applying for an amendment will usually be responsible for the costs of and arising from the amendment.

If a party has amended his statement of case where permission of the court was not required, the court may disallow the amendment (*r. 17.2*)

What to do when amending

➤ Any amended statement of case (and its court copy) must be endorsed as follows (*PD17: 2.1*):

- *where the court's permission is required:*
  'Amended [Particulars of Claim *or other*] by Order of [Master .....][District Judge .... *or other*] dated......'
- *where the court's permission is **not** required:*
  'Amended [Particulars of Claim *or as may be*] under *CPR* [rule 17.1(1) or (2)(a)] dated..........' (see box below).

➤ The statement of case in its amended form need not show the original text, but the court may direct that the amendments should be shown *either* (*PD17: 2.2*):

- by coloured amendments, either manuscript or computer generated, *or*
- by use of a numerical code in a monochrome computer generated document.

➤ Where colour is used, the text to be deleted should be struck through in colour and any text replacing it should be inserted or underlined in the same colour (*PD17: 2.3*).

- The order of colours for successive amendments is: red, green, violet and yellow (*PD17: 2.4*).

➤ All amendments must carry a statement of truth (see p.324).

Amending before service

- A statement of case may be amended any time before service of it on any other party (*r. 17(1)*).

Amending after service

- After service, a party may amend a statement of case only:
  - (*r. 17.1(2)(a)*): with written consent of all other parties, *or*
  - (*r. 17.1(2)(b)*): with the permission of the court (but subject to substitution of parties and limitation rules below).
- The court may give consequential directions (*r. 17.3*)).

- Procedure (*PD17: 1*):

Steps

1. Usually the court will hold a hearing unless the parties agree otherwise between themselves.
2. When making an application to amend a statement of case, the applicant should file with the Court: a) the application notice *and* b) a copy of the statement of case with proposed amendments.
3. Where permission to amend is given, the applicant, within 14 days of the date of the order (or other period directed by the court), must file with the court the amended statement of case.
4. If the substance of the statement of case is changed by reason of the amendment, the statement of case should be re-verified by a statement of truth.
5. The amender should serve a copy of the order and the amended statement of case on every party to the proceedings, unless the court orders otherwise.

NB: if changing the parties use the procedure steps on the facing page instead

Amending after limitation expiry

➤ After a limitation period has expired, the only amendment a court may allow is one (*r. 17.4*):

- whose effect is to add/substitute a new claim, *but only if* the new claim arises out of the same (or substantially the same) facts as a claim in respect of which the party applying for permission has already claimed a remedy, *or*
- to correct a mistake as to the name of a party, *but only if* the mistake was genuine and not one which would cause reasonable doubt as to the identity of the party in question, *or*
- to alter the capacity in which a party claims if the new capacity is one which that party had when the action started or has since acquired.

➤ The court may add/substitute a party only if (*r. 19.5(2)*):

- the relevant limitation period was current when the proceedings were started, *and*
- a) the new party is to be substituted for a party who was named in the claim form in mistake for the new party, *or*
  b) the claim cannot properly be carried on by or against the original party unless the new party is added or substituted as claimant or defendant, *or*
  c) the original party has died or is under a bankruptcy order and his interest/liability has passed to the new party

Note: For personal injuries, the court may add/substitute a party where it directs that (*r. 19.4*) *LA 1980 s. 11/s. 12* does not apply to the claim by/against the new party or the issue of whether those sections apply shall be determined at trial.

Adding or substituting a party (after service)

The court may (*r. 19.2*):

- **Add** a party if:
  a) it is desirable to add the new party so that the court can resolve all the matters in dispute in the proceedings, *or*
  b) there is an issue involving the new party and an existing party which is connected to the matters in dispute in the proceedings, and it is desirable to add the new party so that the court can resolve that issue

- **Substitute** a party if:
  a) the existing party's interest or liability has passed to the new party, *and*
  b) it is desirable to substitute the new party so that the court can resolve the matters in dispute

Note: To substitute a party, an application may be made without notice (*r. 19.4*)

Procedure for adding/substituting parties (*r. 19.4*):

Steps	
1*	An application for permission to amend may be made by: a) an existing party, *or* b) a person who wishes to become a party.
2	If adding/substituting *the claimant*, the applicant files: a) the application notice, *and* b) the proposed amended claim form and particulars of claim, *and* c) the signed, written consent of the new claimant to be added/substituted, *and* **Note:** if this consent is not filed, the order and the addition/substitution of the new party as claimant, will not take effect until the signed, written consent of the new claimant is filed. d) evidence setting out the proposed new party's interest in or connection with the claim (*PD19:1.3*). ◆ **Substitution only:** evidence must also show the stage the proceedings have reached and what change has occurred to cause the transfer of interest or liability (*PD19: 5.2*).
3a	**Addition only:** the application notice is filed under *r.23.3* and served under *r.23.4* (*PD19: 1.4*) (see pp.344-345).
3b	**Substitution only:** the application notice is filed under *r.23.3* (*PD19: 1.4*) (see p.344).
4*	The hearing is held (if appropriate).
5*	An order giving permission to amend will, unless the court orders otherwise, be drawn up (*PD19: 1.5*).
6*	The order must be served on: a) all parties to the proceedings, *and* b) any other person affected by the order. It will be served by the court unless the parties wish to serve it or the court orders them to do so (*PD19: 1.5*)
7*	The court may give consequential directions about: a) filing and serving the claim form on any new defendant, *and/or* b) serving relevant documents on the new party, *and/or* c) the management of the proceedings.
8a	If adding/substituting *a claimant*, the court may direct (*PD19: 3*): a) a copy of the order to be served on every party and any other person affected by the order, *and/or* b) copies of the statements of case + any documents referred to in those to be served on the new party, *and/or* c) the applicant must file, within 14 days an amended claim form and particulars of claim.
8b	If adding/substituting *a defendant*, the court may direct (*PD19: 3*): a) the claimant to file with the court, within 14 days (or as ordered), an amended claim form and particulars of claim for the court file, *and/or* b) a copy of the order to be served on all parties to the proceedings and any other person affected by it, *and/or* c) the amended claim form + particulars of claim, forms for admitting, defending, acknowledging the claim + statements of case + any other documents referred to in those, must be served on the new defendant, *and/or* d) unless the court orders otherwise, the amended claim form + particulars of claim must be served on defendants. **Note:** A new defendant does not become a party until the amended claim form has been served on him.

laimant

laimant

efendant

Removing a party (after service)

The Court may (*r. 19.2*):

- **Delete** a party if: it is not desirable for that person to be a party

Procedure: the steps in the table above with a '*' apply here, with the following amendments (*PD19: 4*):

Steps	
2	Replace steps 2 and 3 above with: the claimant must file with the court an amended claim form and particulars of claim.
8	Replace step 8 above with: a copy of the order must be served on every party and on any other person affected by the order.

V Statements of truth (*Part 22*)

➤ **In the following documents:** The following documents must be verified by a statement of truth:

- all statements of case (claim form, particluars of claim, defence, counterclaim reply etc.), *and*
  - if a statement of case is amended, the amendments must be verified by a statement of truth.
- a response providing further information, *and*
- witness statements (including expert's reports), *and*
- application notices if an applicant wishes to rely on matters set out in it as evidence.

Note: A statement of truth not contained in the document it verifies, must clearly identify that document.

➤ **What it is:** A statement of truth is a statement that the party putting forward the document (or in a witness statement, the maker of the witness statement) believes that the facts stated in the document are true.

- **Litigation friends:** If a party is conducting proceedings with a litigation friend, the statement of truth is a statement that the litigation friend believes the facts stated in the document being verified are true.

➤ **Who signs it:** The statement of truth must be signed by:

- in the case of a statement of case, a response or an application, the party or litigation friend, *or* the solicitor on behalf of the party or litigation friend, *or*
- in the case of a witness statement, the maker of the statement.

Note 1: Signature by a registered company - signature must be by a person holding a senior position in the company/corporation who must state the office/position he holds. A senior position means a director, the treasurer, secretary, chief executive, manager or other officer of the company/corporation.

Note 2: Signature by partnership - signature must be by any of the partners, or a person having the control or management of the partnership business.

Note 3: Signature by solicitor - if a party has a solicitor, the solicitor may sign but the statement refers to the *client's belief*, not his own. The solicitor must sign his own name, *not* that of his firm. He must state the capacity in which he signs and the name of his firm where appropriate. The court takes it to mean:

- that the client on whose behalf he has signed had authorised him to do so, *and*
- that before signing he explained to the client that in signing the statement of truth he would be confirming the client's belief that the facts stated in the document were true, *and*
- that before signing he informed the client of the possible consequences if it should subsequently appear that the client did not have an honest belief in the truth of those facts (see below).

NB: Examples of who should sign are given in *PD22: 3.11*.

➤ **Failure to put in a statement of truth:**

- **statement of case:** the statement of case shall remain effective unless struck out, *but* the party may not rely on the statement of case as evidence of any of the matters set out in it.
- **witness statement:** the court may direct that it shall not be admissible as evidence.

➤ **Penalty for false statement:** contempt of court proceedings may be brought against the signer (*r.32.14*).

Form of the Statement of Truth (*PD22*)

➤ **For a statement of case**, a response, an application notice or a notice of objections:
'[I believe][the (claimant etc.) believes] that the facts stated in this [name document being verified] are true.'

➤ **For a witness statement:** 'I believe that the facts stated in this witness statement are true.'

➤ If the statement of truth is contained in a separate document, that document must be headed with the title of the proceedings and claim number. The document being verified should be identified as follows:

- **claim form:** 'the claim form issued on [date]'
- **particulars of claim:** 'the particulars of claim issued on [date]'
- **statement of case:** 'the [defence or as may be] served on the [name of party] on [date]'
- **application notice:** 'the application notice issued on [date] for [set out the remedy sought]'
- **witness statement:** 'the witness statement filed on [date] or served on [party] on [date]'

VI Service of documents

A. Address for service (subject to 'alternative' service below)

➤ If an address for service is given:

- A party must give an address for service which is (*r. 6.5(4)*):

a) the business address of his solicitor, *or*

b) the address of his residence or place of business.

➤ If an address for service is *not* given:

- If party has a solicitor:
  - if it is the claim form: the address is the business address of the solicitor if the solicitor is authorised to accept service (*PD6: 6.16*).
  - if it is not the claim form: the address is the business address of the solicitor (*r.6.5(5)*).
- If party has no solicitor: the document should be served as follows (*r. 6.5(6)*):

Address for service if address not given and no solicitor	
Nature of party to be served	Place of service
Individual	◆ usual or last known residence
Proprietor of a business	◆ usual or last known residence, *or* ◆ place of business or last known place of business
Individual suing/being sued in the firm name	◆ usual or last known residence, *or* ◆ principal or last known place of business of the firm
Company registered in England and Wales	◆ principal office of the company, *or* ◆ any place of business of the company within the jurisdiction which has a real connection with the claim

'Alternative' service

➤ The court may make an order permitting service by an alternative method is a normal service method cannot be used (*r. 6.8*).

- An application for this:

  a) may be made without notice, *and*

  b) must be supported by evidence.

  - The evidence required is (*PD6: 9.1*):
    - the reason for seeking an order for an alternative method of service, *and*
    - what steps have been taken to serve by other permitted means.

➤ Such an order must specify the method of service *and* the date when the document will be deemed to be served.

B. Service of documents on children and patients

➤ There are special rules for service on children/patients (we list no detail here) (*r.6.6*). Very generally:

- Service on a child is through a parent, guardian or person with whom the child lives, *and*
- Service on a patient is on the *MHA 1983* authorised person or if none, the person with whom the defendant resides or in whose care he is, ...

... BUT once a litigation friend is appointed, service is on the litigation friend.

C. Who will serve the document and how?

➤ The court will serve a document which it has issued or prepared *unless* (*r. 6.3*):

Party service

a) a rule provides that a party must serve the document in question, *or*
b) the party on whose behalf the document is to be served notifies the court that he will serve it himself,
c) a *PD* provides otherwise, *or*
d) the court orders otherwise, *or*
e) the court has failed to serve and has sent a notice of non-service to the party on whose behalf the document is to be served.

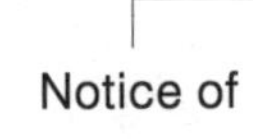

Notice of non-service

- ◆ Where a document is to be served by the court and it cannot serve it, the court must send **a notice of non-service** to the party who requested service stating the method it attempted (*r. 6.11*).
  - Where a party receives notice of non-service of a document by the court, he must endeavour to serve the document himself as the court is under no further duty to effect service (*PD6: 8.2*).

➤ Where the court serves a document, it may decide which of the methods of service it will use.

- ◆ The method will normally be by first class post (*PD6: 8.1*).
- ◆ Where the court serves a claim form, delivers a defence or notifies a claimant that the defendant has filed an acknowledgment of service, the court also serves/delivers a copy of any filed notice of funding provided it was filed at the same time as the other document being delivered/served and copies were provided for service (*PD6: 8.3*).

➤ **Filing:** Where a party prepares a document which is to be served by the court, that party must file a copy for the court, and for each party to be served.

Extra rules for service of a claim form (*r.6.13 - 6.14*)

➤ **Claim form served by the court:**

- ◆ Where a claim form is to be served by the court, the claim form must include the defendant's address for service (and if the defendant's solicitor is authorised to accept service, the defendant's address for service may be the business address of the defendant's solicitor), *and*
- ◆ the court must send the claimant a notice which includes the deemed date of service.

➤ **Claim form served by the claimant:**

- ◆ claimant must file a certificate of service within 7 days of service of the claim form, *and*
- ◆ he may not obtain judgment in default unless he has filed the certificate of service.

Service on companies and partnerships

Service on a company (*r. 6.4(4), PD6: 6.1 - 6.2*)	Service on a partnership (*r. 6.4(5), PD6: 4.1, 4.2*)
➤ A document is served by: ◆ **leaving a document at or posting it to an authorised place (*s. 725 CA 1985*) (*r. 6.2(2)*)**, *or* ◆ leaving it with a person holding a senior position within the company or corporation • a senior position is: 1) for a registered company: a director, the treasurer, secretary, chief executive, manager or other officer of the company or corporation. 2) for a non-registered company: a director, the treasurer, secretary, chief executive, manager or other officer of the company or corporation, the mayor, chairman, president, town clerk or similar officer of the corporation.	➤ A document is served personally on a partnership where partners are being sued in the name of their firm by leaving it with: ◆ **a partner, *or*** ◆ a person who, at the time of service, has the control or management of the partnership business at its principal place of business. ➤ A claim form or particulars of claim which are served by leaving them with a person at the principal or last known place of business of the partnership, must *at the same time,* serve a notice specifying whether that person is being served: 1) as a partner, *or* 2) as a person having control or management of the partnership business, *or* 3) as both.

Types of service and when service takes effect

NB: The rules below apply unless the text later specifies otherwise (*r. 6.1*)

Method of service (*r. 6.4*)	When service takes effect (*r. 6.7*)	Rules about the method of service
Personal	When delivered but if served after 5pm on a business day or at the weekend or a bank holiday, then the next business day	➤ A document may be served personally (*r. 6.4*), *but* ◆ ***must*** be served on a solicitor if: a) he is authorised to accept service, *and* b) has notified the party serving the document in writing that he is authorised **Note for whole box:** See the provisions about time on p.320
Delivery to a permitted address	Day after it was delivered to or left at the permitted address	
First class post	Second day after posting	
Leaving at a DX	Second day following day it is left	➤ A document can only be sent by DX if (*PD6: 2.1, 2.2*): a) the other party's address for service includes a DX number, *and* b) the other party's writing paper (or that of his legal representative) has a DX number, *and* c) the other party (or his legal representative) has not indicated in writing that they are unwilling to accept service by DX
Fax sent before 4 pm on a business day	Same day	➤ A fax can only be sent if (*PD6: 3.1, 3.2*): ◆ the other party (or his legal representative) has previously indicated in writing: i) that he is willing to accept service by fax, *and* ii) the fax number to which the fax should be sent. Note: If the other party is acting by a legal representative, the fax must be sent to the legal representative's business address. ◆ Where a legal representative's fax number is given with the business address, it is deemed to be the business fax number (*PD6: 3.2*). ◆ The party serving need not send a copy by post or DX as well, but if he does not and the document is proved not to have been received then the court may, on any application arising out of that non-receipt, take account of the fact that a hard copy was not sent (*PD6: 3.4*).
Fax sent after 4 pm on a business day, *or* Fax sent on a non-business day	Next business day	
Other means of electronic communication	Second day after the day on which it is transmitted	➤ Other electronic communication can used if (*PD 6: 3.2 - 3.4*): a) the party serving the document and the other party are both acting by legal representative, *and* b) the document is served at the legal representative's business address, *and* c) the legal representative who is to be served has previously expressly indicated in writing to the party serving his willingness to accept service by this means and has provided his e-mail address *or* other electronic identification. ◆ Where a legal representative's electronic address or identification is given in conjuction with the business address, the electronic address will be deemed to be at the business address (*PD 6: 3.2*). ◆ The party serving need not send a copy by post or DX as well, but if he does not and the document is proved not to have been received then the court may, on an application arising out of that non-receipt, take account of the fact that a hard copy was not sent (*PD 6: 3.4*).

Certificate of service (*r. 6.10*)

➤ Where a rule, PD or order requires a certificate of service, the certificate must state:

a) that the document has not been returned undelivered, *and*

b) details which depend on the service method (eg: for fax service, the date & time of transmission).

C Starting proceedings

I Identifying the parties (and some extra procedural points that result)

1 Joint claimants (*r.19.3*)

➤ Where a claimant claims a remedy to which someone else is jointly entitled , all persons jointly entitled must be parties unless the court orders otherwise.

- If any person does not agree to be a claimant, he must be made a defendant, unless the court orders otherwise.

2 Joining possible claims

➤ A claimant may use a single claim form to start all claims which can be conveniently disposed of in the same proceedings (*r.7.3*). A claimant does not need leave of the court for this.

3 If claimant/defendant is trading under another name

4 If claimant/defendant is suing/being sued in a representative capacity

5 If claimant/defendant is a firm

see p.334

6 If claimant/defendant is a company registered in England & Wales - see pp.326 and 334

7 If claimant/defendant is a partnership - see p.326

➤ Suing partners in the firm name:

✓ makes service easier, *but*

✗ leave is needed for enforcing judgment against the individual partners' own assets.

8 Claimant or defendant is a patient within *MHA 1983* (*Part 21* and *PD21*)

➤ A patient must bring or defend proceedings by a litigation friend (*r.21.2(1), PD21: 1.2*) (see p.329).

➤ The patient is referred to in the title as 'X (by Y his litigation friend)' (*PD21: 1.3*).

➤ If the patient has no litigation friend (*r.21.3(2)*):

- prior to service of claim form, no applications are allowed without the court's permission, *and*
- during proceedings, no steps are allowed without the court's permission *except*: issuing and serving the claim form and applying for appoinment of a litigation friend.

➤ If a party becomes a patient during proceedings, no party may take any step in the proceedings without the permission of the court until the patient has a litigation friend (*r.21.3(3)*).

➤ When a party ceases to be a patient, the litigation friend's appointment continues until it is ended by a court order (*r.21.9*).

9 Insurers

➤ In a road traffic accident case, if insurers are involved, the claimant must send a *s.151/152 RTA 1988* notice to the defendant's insurers within 7 days of issuing proceedings. This enables the defendant's insurers to defend the claim, and for the claimant to claim against them if he wins.

10 Claimant or defendant is a child (ie: under 18 - a minor) (*Part 21* and *PD21*)

➤ A child must bring or defend proceedings by a litigation friend *unless* the court has made an order permitting the child to do so on his own behalf (*r. 21.2(2), PD21: 1.4*).

➤ Where the child (*PD21: 1.5*):

- has a litigation friend, the child is referred to in the title as 'X (a child by Y his litigation friend)', *or*
- conducts proceedings on his own behalf, the child is referred to in the title as 'X (a child)'.

➤ If the child has no litigation friend, and the court has not ordered an exemption (*r. 21.3(2)*):

- prior to service of the claim form, no applications are allowed without the court's permission, *and*
- during proceedings, no steps are allowed without the court's permission except: issuing and serving the claim form and applying for appoinment of a litigation friend.

➤ The litigation friend is personally liable for costs, but is usually indemnified for these by the child.

➤ When a child (who is not a patient) reaches 18, a litigation friend's appointment ceases (*r. 21.9*). The child may adopt or repudiate proceedings on coming of age during the proceedings.

➤ No settlement, compromise or payment and no acceptance of money paid into court is valid, without the approval of the court. Any money won by the child will be dealt with by direction of the court but will usually be paid into court and invested until the child is 18 (although sums may be drawn and paid earlier to the child for his immediate needs) (*r. 21.10-21.11*).

A litigation friend (*Part 21, PD: 21*)

➤ **Duties:** a litigation friend must:
- fairly and competently conduct proceedings on behalf of the child or patient, *and*
- have no interest adverse to that of the child or patient, *and*
- where the child or patient is a claimant, undertake to pay any costs which the child or patient may be ordered to pay in relation to the proceedings (subject to any right he may have to be repaid from the assets of the child or patient).

➤ **What to file (1):** to become a litigation friend *without a court order* the potential litigation friend must (*PD21: 2.3*):
- (for a patient with *MHA* authorisation) file an official copy of the order/other document which constitutes the authorisation under *MHA 1983*, *or*
- (for a child or a patient without *MHA* authorisation) file a certificate of suitability stating:
  a) that he consents to act, *and*
  b) that he knows or believes that the [claimant] [defendant] is a [child][patient], *and*
  c) (for a patient only) the grounds of his belief and if his belief is based upon medical opinion attaching any relevant document to the certificate, *and*
  d) that he can fairly and competently conduct proceedings on behalf of the child or patient and has no interest adverse to that of the child or patient, *and*
  e) where a claimant, an undertaking to pay any costs which the child or patient may be ordered to pay in relation to the proceedings, subject to any right he may have to be repaid from the assets of the child or patient, *and*
  f) which he has signed in verification of its contents.

➤ **What to file (2):** the litigation friend must serve a certificate of suitability (*PD21: 2.4, 2.4A*):
- for a child (who is not a patient), on one of the child's parents/guardians or none, on the person with whom the child resides or in whose care the child is, *and*
- for a patient, on the person authorised under *MHA 1983* to conduct proceedings on behalf of the patient or if none, on the person with whom the patient resides/in whose care the patient is (NB: 'c' in the above list can be ignored).

➤ **When to serve/file** (*r. 21.5*):
- for claimant: serve authorisation or certificate of suitability with a certificate of service (see p.327) when the claim form is issued.
- for defendant: file authorisation or certificate of suitability with a certificate of service (see p.327) at the time when first taking a step in the proceedings on behalf of the defendant.

➤ **Who to serve:** the litigation friend must serve on every person on whom the claim form should be served (*r. 21.5*).

II Selecting the court

A. Courts generally

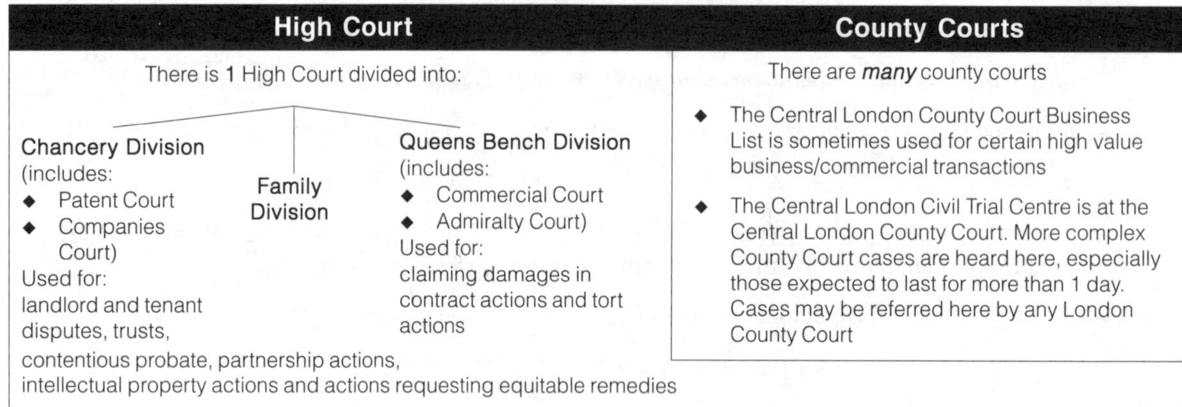

High Court
County Courts
There is 1 High Court divided into:
Chancery Division
(includes:
◆ Patent Court
◆ Companies Court)
Used for:
landlord and tenant disputes, trusts,
Family Division
Queens Bench Division
(includes:
◆ Commercial Court
◆ Admiralty Court)
Used for:
claiming damages in contract actions and tort actions
contentious probate, partnership actions,
intellectual property actions and actions requesting equitable remedies
There are many county courts
◆ The Central London County Court Business List is sometimes used for certain high value business/commercial transactions
◆ The Central London Civil Trial Centre is at the Central London County Court. More complex County Court cases are heard here, especially those expected to last for more than 1 day. Cases may be referred here by any London County Court

B. Where to *start* a claim (*PD7: 2)*

➤ In general (*and subject to the rest of the rules in this section*), any action which both the High Court and the county courts have jurisdiction to deal with may be started in either the High Court or a county court.

- Note: in calculating the *value* of a claim in this section see the large grey box on p.335.
- The jurisdiction of the High Court and the county courts is as follows:

The jurisdiction of the courts (*CCA 1984, SI 1991/724*) - commencement of a claim

Jurisdiction of the High Court	Jurisdiction of the county courts
Tort claims over £15,000 (Note overlap with county courts)	Tort claims up to £50,000 (*CCA 1984 s.15*)
Contract claims over £15,000 (Note overlap with county courts)	Contract claims up to £50,000 (*CCA 1984 s.15*)
Personal injury claims worth £50,000 or more	Personal injury claims worth under £50,000 (*SI 1991/724*)
Libel (unless the parties agree otherwise)	Equitable interests and land charges disputes where the property has a value of £30,000 or less (*CCA 1984 s.23*)
Slander (unless the parties agree otherwise)	
Search orders (authorises a party to search for documents or property at their opponent's premises)	
Freezing injunctions (to freeze assets)	
Judicial review	

➤ **Claims of damages or a specified sum: the £15,000 rule**

- worth more than £15,000 *may* be commenced in the High Court or the county courts (up to £50,000).
- worth £15,000 or less *must* be commenced in the county courts.

➤ **Personal injury action: the £50,000 rule**

- worth £50,000 or more - *must* be commenced in the High Court
- worth less than £50,000 - *must* be commenced in the county courts.

➤ **Claimant's belief:** the High Court (and not a county court) should hear a case if (subject to the above) a claimant believes the following factors are of a sufficiently high level:

Claimant's factors

1. Financial value of the claim and the amount in dispute
2. Complexity: of facts, legal issues, remedies or procedures involved
3. Importance of the outcome: to the public in general

C. Transfer of a claim after the claim has been started (*Part 30*)

➤ A claim will usually proceed in the court in which it was commenced.

➤ However, in certain cases the claim can be transferred to a different court. This happens if a court does not have jurisdiction (see the table on the previous page) or if the following rules apply:

1 County Court transfer to another County Court (*r.30.2(1)-(3)*)

➤ A county court may order proceedings before that court, or any part of them (eg: a counterclaim) to be transferred to another county court if it is satisfied that:

a) an order should be made having regard to the 'transfer criteria' (see box on p.332), *or*

b) the following proceedings could be more conveniently or fairly taken in that other county court:

- the detailed assessment of costs, *or*
- the enforcement of a judgment or order, *or*

application is made to the court where the claim is proceeding

c) proceedings have been started in the wrong county court in which case the Court may order they:

- be transferred to the county court in which they ought to have been started, *or*
- continue in the county court in which they have been started, *or*
- be struck out.

d) the rules for 'Automatic Transfers' apply (claim is for a specified amount, was commenced in a court which is not the defendant's home court, has not otherwise been transferred to another defendant's home court under an application to set aside or vary default judgment and the defendant is an individual) - see p.365 for detail.

2 Hign Court transfer within itself (*r.30.2(4)-(6)*)

➤ The High Court may, having regard to the 'transfer criteria' (see box overleaf), order proceedings in the Royal Courts of Justice (RCJ) or a district registry (DR) , or any part of such proceedings (eg: a counterclaim) to be transferred:

- from the RCJ to a DR, *or*
- from a DR to the RCJ, *or*
- from a DR to another DR.

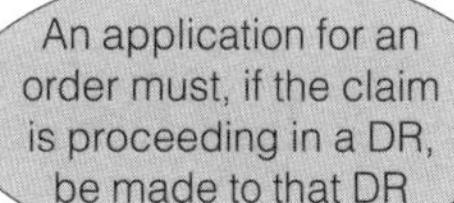

An application for an order must, if the claim is proceeding in a DR, be made to that DR

➤ A DR may order proceedings before it for detailed assessment of costs to be transferred to another DR if it is satisfied that the proceedings could be more conveniently or fairly taken in that other DR.

3 High Court transfer to a County Court

➤ Discretionary transfer: the High Court can transfer whatever it wants to a County Court (*CCA 1984 s.40*).

- This might occur in the following types of cases:

  a) cases that *could* only be started in the High Court, eg: slander, libel.

  b) cases that *should* never have started in the High Court *must* be moved to a county court (*CCA 1984 s.40*), eg: a personal injury action worth less than £50,000.

  c) cases that can be heard in either court.

➤ Automatic transfer: there will be automatic transfer to a County Court unless a 'statement of value' showing the action is worth at least £15,000 (or a statement saying why the action ought to be heard in the High Court) is delivered at the appropriate time.

4 General power of High Court to transfer to a county court and a county court to High Court

➤ Generally, the High Court has power to transfer cases to a county court and a county court has power to transfer cases to the High Court (*CCA 1984 ss.40-42*). It must take account of the 'transfer criteria' (*r.30.3*).

Transfer criteria (*r.30.3*)

➤ The following are matters which the court must have regard to when considering whether to make a transfer order:

- the financial value of the claim and the amount in dispute, if different, *and*
- whether it would be more convenient or fair for hearings (including the trial) to be held in some other court, *and*
- the availability of a judge specialising in the type of claim in question, *and*
- whether the facts, legal issues, remedies or procedures involved are simple or complex, *and*
- the importance of the outcome of the claim to the public in general, *and*
- the facilities available at the court where the claim is being dealt with and whether they may be inadequate because of any disabilities of a party or potential witness, *and*
- whether the making of a declaration of incompatibility under *HRA 1998 s.4* has arisen or may arise, *and*
- High Court Factors - ie: factors that might include a court more to having a case heard in the High Court (*PD29:2.6*):
  - professional negligence claims.
  - Fatal Accident Act claims.
  - fraud or undue influence claims.
  - defamation claims.
  - claims for malicious prosecution or false imprisonment.
  - claims against the police.
  - contentious probate claims.

Transfer procedure (*r.30.4*)

➤ Where the Court orders proceedings to be transferred, the court from which they are to be transferred must give notice of the transfer to all the parties.

Application to set aside a transfer order (*PD30: 6*)

➤ Where a party may apply to set aside an order for transfer the application should be made to the Court which made the order.

➤ Such application should be made in accordance with *Part 23* - see p.344.

III Hearings

Hearings - miscellaneous provisions (*Part 39*)	
In public (*r.39.1*) Note: see also telephone hearings p.346	➤ A hearing is in public, *unless* ◆ publicity would defeat the object of the hearing, *or* ◆ the hearing involves matters relating to national security, *or* ◆ confidential information is involved and publicity would damage that confidentiality, *or* ◆ privacy is necessary to protect the interests of a child or patient, *or* ◆ it is the hearing of an application made without notice and a public hearing would be unjust to the respondent, *or* ◆ the hearing involves uncontentious matters arising in the administration of trusts or a deceased person's estate, *or* ◆ the court considers a private hearing necessary in the interests of justice. ➤ The court may order the identity of a party or witness not be disclosed if this is necessary to protect the interests of that party or witness.
Failure to attend trial (*r.39.3*)	➤ The court may proceed in a party's absence, *but* ◆ if no party attends, the court may strike out the whole of the proceedings. ◆ if the claimant does not attend, the court may strike out the claim and any defence to a counterclaim. ◆ if the defendant does not attend, it may strike out the defence and/or counterclaim (*r.39.3(1)*). ➤ If a court strikes out proceedings (or any part of proceedings) under *r.39.3* it may subsequently restore them (*r.39.3(2)*). ➤ A party who does not attend and has a order or judgment made against it under *r.39.3* may apply for that order or judgement to be set aside (*r.39.3(3)*). ◆ An application for proceedings to be restored or an order/judgment to be set aside must be supported by evidence (*r.39.3(4)*) ◆ The court may only grant an application to restore proceedings or set aside an order/ judgment if the applicant: a) acted promptly when he found out that the claim had been struck out or the order/ judgment set aside, *and* b) had a good reason for not attending the trial, *and* c) has a reasonable prospect of success at trial (*r.39.3(5)*)
Timetable for trial (*r.39.4*)	➤ When the court sets a timetable for a trial under: ◆ *r.28.6* (Fast track) (see p.370), *or* ◆ *r.29* (Multi track) (see p.372) ... ... it will do so in consultation with the parties.
Trial bundles (*r.39.5*)	➤ A claimant must file a trial bundle containing documents required by any relevant practice direction and any court order, unless the court orders otherwise. ➤ The trial bundle must be filed not more than 7 days and not less than 3 days before the start of the trial (see p.384).
Representation at trial of companies/ corporations (*r.39.6*)	➤ An employee may represent a company or corporation at trial if that employee has been authorised by the company or corporation to appear at trial on its behalf and the court gives permission.

IV Initial documents needed to file with the claim form

➤ Documents to file with the claim form include:
- the particulars of claim (if not on the claim form or if not being served after the claim form), *and*
- for a legally assisted claimant, a notice of funding + any amendments (*PD:Costs 19*), *and*
- the relevant defence / admission / acknowledgment of service forms, *and*
- the fee, *and*
- any relevant litigation friend documents (see p.329).

V The claim form (*Part 7*)

A. General

➤ Proceedings are started when the court issues a claim form at the request of the claimant (*r.7.2(1)*).

- A claim form is issued on the date entered on the form by the court (*r.7.2(2)*).

➤ Drafting the claim form must be done on *Form N1* (*PD7: 3.1*).

➤ There are 2 other ways of starting claims. These are where there is:

- no substantial dispute of fact. *Part 8* procedures apply and *Form N208* (*PD7: 3.1*) is used as the claims form. *Part 8* proceedings are not dealt with in this book.
- a specialist jurisdiction (known as a 'list') (eg: the Commercial Court) (not dealt with in this book).

B. Procedure for the claimant's solicitors to issue the claim form

Steps

1. prepare at least 3 copies of the claim form and all documents accompanying it (see steps 4 and 5 below); one for the claimant, one for each defendant and one for the court.
2. sign the copies.
3. prepare the 'Response Pack' consisting of: 1) the correct admissions form; 2) the correct defence form *and* ; 3) the acknowledgement of service form.
4. if the claimant is legally funded, prepare the notification of legal funding and copies (*PD:Costs 19*).
5. if the claimant is a child or a patient, prepare the litigation friend documents (see p.329).
6. prepare the court fee - cheques are payable to 'HM Paymaster General'.
7. take, or send (include the SAE if so), the claim form and response pack and any of the above documents to the court, together with the court fee.
8. The court will issue a claim number, seal the documents and issue the claim form.
9. Once issued the claim form can be served within 4 months (within the jurisdiction) (see p.315).

Filling in the parties on the claims form

Party	Wording on claim form
Individual	➤ Insert all known forenames and surname, whether Mr, Mrs, Miss, Ms or Other (eg: Dr) and residential address (**including** postcode and telephone number) ➤ Where the defendant is a proprietor of a business, a partner in a firm or an individual sued in the name of a club or other unincorporated association, the address for service should be the usual or last known place of residence **or** principal place of business of the company, firm or club or other unincorporated association
Child (ie: under 18) *or* patient under *MHA 1983*	➤ See pp.328-329 for correct form in title and procedure
Trading under another name	➤ Insert the words: 'trading as' and the trading name, eg: 'Mr X trading as X's dairies'
Suing or being sued in a representative capacity	➤ State the capacity, eg: 'Mr X as the representative of Ms Y (deceased)'
A firm	➤ Insert the firm name followed by 'a firm', eg: 'X - a firm' ➤ Insert an address for service which is either a partner's residential address or the principal or last known place of business
A company registered in England and Wales	➤ Insert the company name and an address which is either the company's registered office **or** any place of business that has a real, or the most, connection with the claim eg: the shop where goods were brought ➤ Verify the company's details with a company search

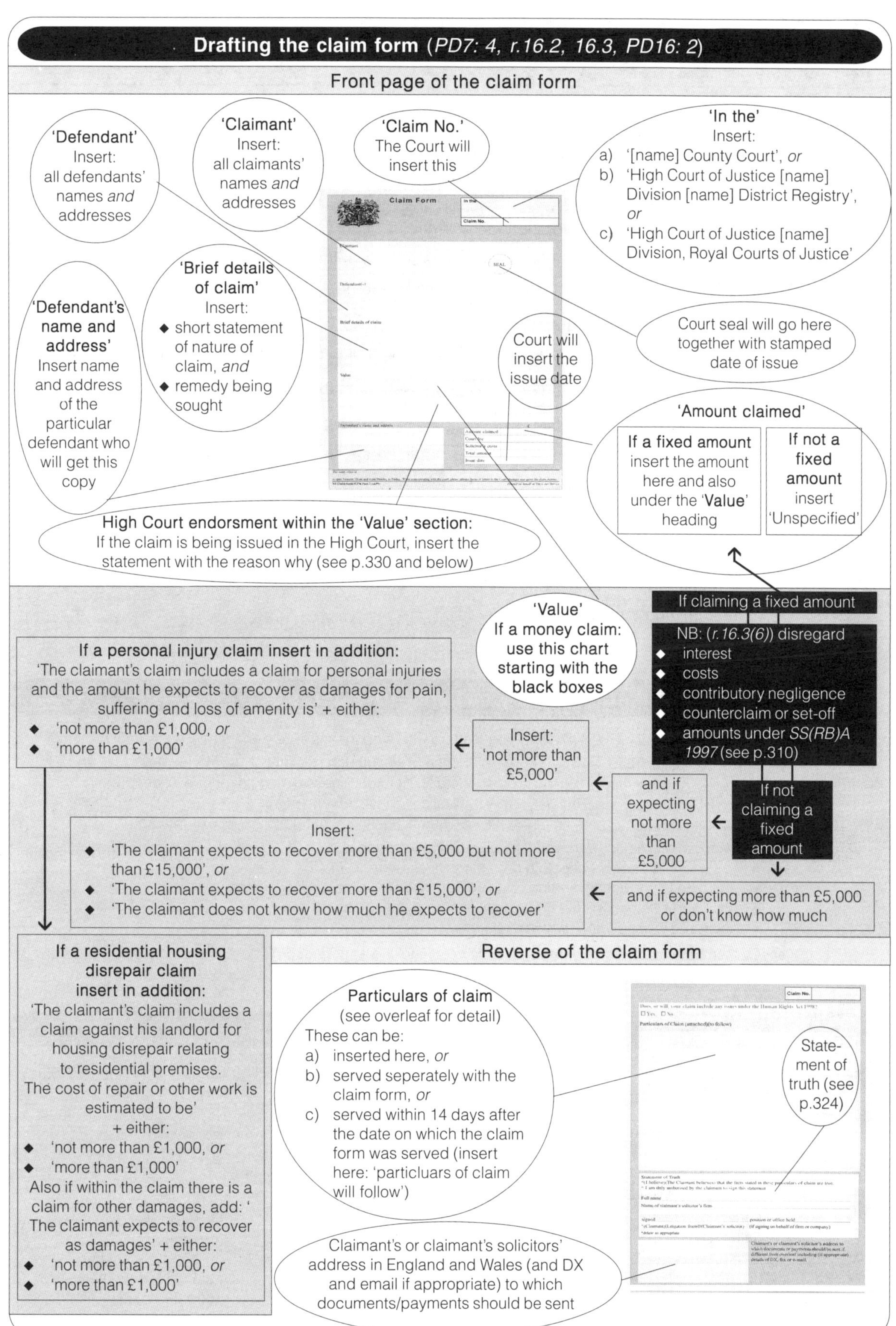
Drafting the claim form (PD7: 4, r.16.2, 16.3, PD16: 2)
Front page of the claim form
'Defendant' Insert: all defendants' names and addresses
'Claimant' Insert: all claimants' names and addresses
'Claim No.' The Court will insert this
'In the' Insert:
a) '[name] County Court', or
b) 'High Court of Justice [name] Division [name] District Registry', or
c) 'High Court of Justice [name] Division, Royal Courts of Justice'
'Defendant's name and address' Insert name and address of the particular defendant who will get this copy
'Brief details of claim' Insert:
◆ short statement of nature of claim, and
◆ remedy being sought
Court will insert the issue date
Court seal will go here together with stamped date of issue
'Amount claimed'
If a fixed amount insert the amount here and also under the 'Value' heading
If not a fixed amount insert 'Unspecified'
High Court endorsment within the 'Value' section: If the claim is being issued in the High Court, insert the statement with the reason why (see p.330 and below)
'Value' If a money claim: use this chart starting with the black boxes
If claiming a fixed amount
NB: (r.16.3(6)) disregard
◆ interest
◆ costs
◆ contributory negligence
◆ counterclaim or set-off
◆ amounts under SS(RB)A 1997 (see p.310)
If a personal injury claim insert in addition: 'The claimant's claim includes a claim for personal injuries and the amount he expects to recover as damages for pain, suffering and loss of amenity is' + either:
◆ 'not more than £1,000, or
◆ 'more than £1,000'
Insert: 'not more than £5,000'
and if expecting not more than £5,000
If not claiming a fixed amount
Insert:
◆ 'The claimant expects to recover more than £5,000 but not more than £15,000', or
◆ 'The claimant expects to recover more than £15,000', or
◆ 'The claimant does not know how much he expects to recover'
and if expecting more than £5,000 or don't know how much
If a residential housing disrepair claim insert in addition: 'The claimant's claim includes a claim against his landlord for housing disrepair relating to residential premises. The cost of repair or other work is estimated to be' + either:
◆ 'not more than £1,000, or
◆ 'more than £1,000'
Also if within the claim there is a claim for other damages, add: ' The claimant expects to recover as damages' + either:
◆ 'not more than £1,000, or
◆ 'more than £1,000'
Reverse of the claim form
Particulars of claim (see overleaf for detail)
These can be:
a) inserted here, or
b) served seperately with the claim form, or
c) served within 14 days after the date on which the claim form was served (insert here: 'particluars of claim will follow')
Statement of truth (see p.324)
Claimant's or claimant's solicitors' address in England and Wales (and DX and email if appropriate) to which documents/payments should be sent
Claim Form
Claim No.

VI Particulars of claim

➤ Particulars of claim form the main statement of case that sets out the claimant's case.

➤ Particulars of claim must (*r.7.4*):

a) be contained in the claim form, *or*

b) be served with, but seperate to, the claim form, *or*

c) be served on the defendant within 14 days after service of the claim form (provided it is still within the time that the claim form could be served - ie: within 4 months after its date of issue - see p.315).

- If the particulars of claim are not included in or have not been served with the claim form, the claim form must also contain a statement that particulars of claim will follow (*PD7: 6.1, PD16: 3.3*).

◆ If practicable, the particulars of claim should be set out in the claim form (*PD16: 3.1*).

➤ Where the claimant serves particulars of claim at a different time to the claim form, he must, within 7 days of service on the defendant, file a copy of the particulars with the court, together with a certificate of service (see p.315) (*r.7.4(3)*).

➤ When particulars of claim are served on a defendant, whether they are contained in the claim form, served with it or served subsequently, they must be accompanied by (*r.7.8(1)*):

a) a form for defending the claim, *and*

b) a form for admitting the claim, *and*

c) a form for acknowledging service.

Compulsory matters (*PD16: 9.1, 9.2*)

➤ The claimant must set out specifically the following matters where he wishes to rely on them in support of his claim

- any allegation of fraud
- the fact of any illegality
- details of any misrepresentation
- details of all breaches of trust
- notice or knowledge of a fact
- details of unsoundness of mind or undue influence
- details of wilful default
- any facts relating to mitigation of loss or damage
- **Conviction:** a claimant who wants to rely on evidence under *s.11 CEA 1968* of a conviction must include:
  - a statement that he wants to rely on a convition under *s.11 CEA 1968* , *and*
  - the type of conviction, finding or adjudication and its date, *and*
  - the court which made the conviction, finding or adjudication, *and*
  - the issue in the claim to which it relates.
- **Certain special types of damages:** a claimant seeking aggravated damages, exemplary damages or provisional damages must include a statement to that effect and the grounds for claiming them

Interest (*r.16.4*)

➤ A claimant seeking interest must state the following:

a) a statement to that he is seeking interest, *and*

b) a statement that:

i) that he is seeking interest under the terms of a contract, *or*

ii) that he is seeking interest under an enactment (state which), ★ *or*

iii) that he is seeking interest on some other basis (state which) (eg: see p.310), *and*

c) (if the claim is for a specified amount of money), he must state:

i) the percentage rate at which interest is claimed, ★ *and*

ii) the date from which it is claimed, *and*

iii) the date to which it is calculated (must not be later than the date the claim form is issued), *and*

iv) the total amount of interest claimed to the date of calculation, *and*

v) the daily rate at which interest accrues after that date

High Court interest is sought under *SCA 1981 s.35A*

County Court interest is sought under *CCA 1984 s.69*

For debt actions, interest may have been set by an agreement - if not then the rate is set by statutory instrument (now 8%) (see p.398)

Drafting the particulars of claim (*r.7.4, PD7A: 6, r.16.4, PD16: 3-10*)

Particulars of claim which are served separately from the claim form must contain (*PD16: 3.8*):

- the name of the court in which the claim is proceeding, *and*
- the claim number, *and*
- the title of the proceedings, *and*
- the claimant's address for service.

Give a concise statement of the facts on which the claimant relies (*r.16.4*)

- It is good practice to set this out as numbered paragraphs
- Examples of typical facts (in addition to the compulsory matters) to include are set out below:

Breach of contract	Problem with goods	Personal injury
◆ whether contract is oral or written ◆ date of + parties to the contract ◆ purpose of the agreement ◆ consideration (unless under seal) ◆ the term breached	◆ price of the goods ◆ date the goods were sold ◆ particulars of goods ◆ date delivery was due	◆ date and place of the accident ◆ names of those involved ◆ allegation of negligence (with 'particulars of negligence')

Compulsory matters which must specifically be stated if relied on (*PD16: 9.1*):

Breach of contract claims (*PD16: 8*)	Personal injury claims (*PD16: 4*)
Written agreement: ◆ attach or serve a copy of the contract/ documents constituting the agreement (**Note:** the original(s) should be available at the hearing) ◆ attach any general conditions of sale incorporated in the contract (but where any of the above are bulky, attach or serve only the relevant parts of the contract/ documents). **Oral agreement:** ◆ set out the contractual words used and state by whom, to whom, when and where they were spoken **Agreement by conduct:** ◆ specify the conduct relied on and state by whom, when and where the acts constituting the conduct were done	◆ state the claimant's date of birth ◆ state brief details of the claimant's personal injuries ◆ attach a schedule of details of any past and future expenses and losses which he claims ◆ (if relying on evidence of a medical practitioner) attach or serve a report from a medical practitioner about the personal injuries which he alleges in his claim ◆ (if a provisional damages claim), add a statement: 1) that he is seeking an award of provisional damages under either *SCA 1981 s.32A* or *CCA 1984 s.51*, *and* 2) that there is a chance that at some future time the claimant will develop some serious disease or suffer some serious deterioration in his physical or mental condition, *and* 3) specifying the disease or type of deterioration in respect of which an application may be made at a future date. (see p.357 (*Part 41*) for more details)

Fatal accident claims (*PD16: 5*)	Others claims(*PD16: 6-7, r.19.5A*)
◆ state that the claim is brought under the *FAA 1976* ◆ state the dependents on whose behalf the claim is made ◆ state the date of birth of each dependent ◆ state details of the nature of the dependency claim **Note:** A fatal accident claim may include a claim for damages for bereavement. The claimant may also bring a claim under the *LR(MP)A 1934* on behalf of the estate of the deceased	For: ◆ Recovery of land ◆ Hire purchase claims ◆ Wrongful interference with goods certain details must be included (not listed here)

A claimant who wishes to rely on certain matters must specifically state them (see 'Compulsory matters' box on the facing face)

A claimant who seeks interest must state he is seeking interest and add certain details (*r.16.4*) (see 'Interest' box on the facing page)

Add the prayer for relief headed 'AND THE CLAIMANT CLAIMS:' Specify exactly what the claimant wants the court to order

Add a statement of truth (see p.324) (*PD16: 3.4*)
'[I believe][the claimant believes] that the facts stated in these particulars of claim are true.'

D Defendant's options

Including:

- an interim injunction
- an interim declaration
- an order for the detention, custody or preservation of property or inspection or taking of a sample or carrying out of an experiment on or with property, *and* authorising a person to enter land in the possession of a party to carry out that order.
- a 'freezing injunction
- a 'search order'.
- an order for disclosure of documents or inspection of property
- an order for an interim payment made under *r.25.6* (see p.356).

Claiming additional liability if legally funded (*PD:Costs 19*)

Note: A party who will claim an additional liability under a funding arrangement must give other parties information about this (eg: in the defence, acknowledgement etc.), but there is no need to specify the amount of additional liability separately nor to state how it is calculated until it is assessed.

I Defence and counterclaim

A. The defence

Times for filing/serving are set out on p.315

➤ A defence is the statement of case setting out the defence to the claimant's particulars of claim.

➤ **Dealing with the claimant's allegations:** In his defence, the defendant must state (*r. 16.5*):
- which allegations he admits, *and*
- which allegations he is unable to admit or deny, but which he requires the claimant to prove, *and*
- which of the allegations in the particulars of claim he denies.
  - He must state his reasons for denying any allegation, *and*
  - if he is putting forward a different version of events, he must state his own version.

➤ **Failing to deal with an allegation:** If the defendant is silent as to an allegation (*r. 16.5*):

a) if the claim includes a money claim, it is deemed that he requires any allegation relating to the amount of money claimed be proved by the claimant *unless* the defendant expressly admits the allegation.

b) if he has set out in his defence *the nature of his case in relation to the issue to which that allegation is relevant*, it is counted as if he requires that allegation to be proved.

c) if a and b above do not apply, it is counted *as if admits that allegation.*

See p.318 Ground 1 for consequences of a bare denial

➤ **Disputing the statement of value in the statement of claim:** the defendant must state why he disputes it *and* (if he can), give his own statement of the value of the claim (*r. 16.5*).

➤ **Representative capacity** (*r. 16.5*): if a defendant acts in a representative capacity, he must state what it is.

➤ **Address for service** (*r. 16.5*): the defendant must give an address for service *unless* he has filed an acknowledgment of service under *Part 10* (see p.342).

➤ **Statement of truth:** the defence must be verified by a statement of truth (see p.324) (*PD16: 12*, *Part 22*).
- The wording is: '[I believe][the defendant believes] that the facts stated in the defence are true.'

➤ **A defence of set-off** (*r. 16.6*): where a defendant contends he is entitled to money from the claimant *and* relies on this as a defence to the whole or part of the claim, the contention may be included in the defence and set off against the claim, whether or not it is also a *Part 20* claim (see pp.347-348).

Compulsory matters to insert in the defence (*PD16: 13, 14.1*)

The defendant must set out specifically the following matters where he wishes to rely on them in support of his claim:

- **Limitation defence:** the defendant must give details of the expiry of any relevant limitation period he has relied on
- **Personal injuries claim:**
  - where claimant attached a medical report about his alleged injuries, defendant should:
    a) state in the defence whether, concerning the matters in the medical report, he:
      - agrees with those matters, *or*
      - disputes those matters (giving his reasons), *or*
      - neither agrees nor disputes but has no knowledge of those matters, *and*

    b) if he has obtained his own medical report on which he intends to rely, attach his own medical report to his defence.
  - where claimant included a schedule of past and future expenses and losses, defendant should include in, or attach to, his defence a counter-schedule stating which items he:
    - agrees, *or*
    - disputes (supplying alternative figures where appropriate), *or*
    - neither agrees nor disputes but has no knowledge of

B. The counterclaim

➤ Where a defendant serves a counterclaim (i.e. a *Part 20* claim - see pp.347-348) the defence and counterclaim should normally form one document with counterclaim following on from the defence.

II Admissions

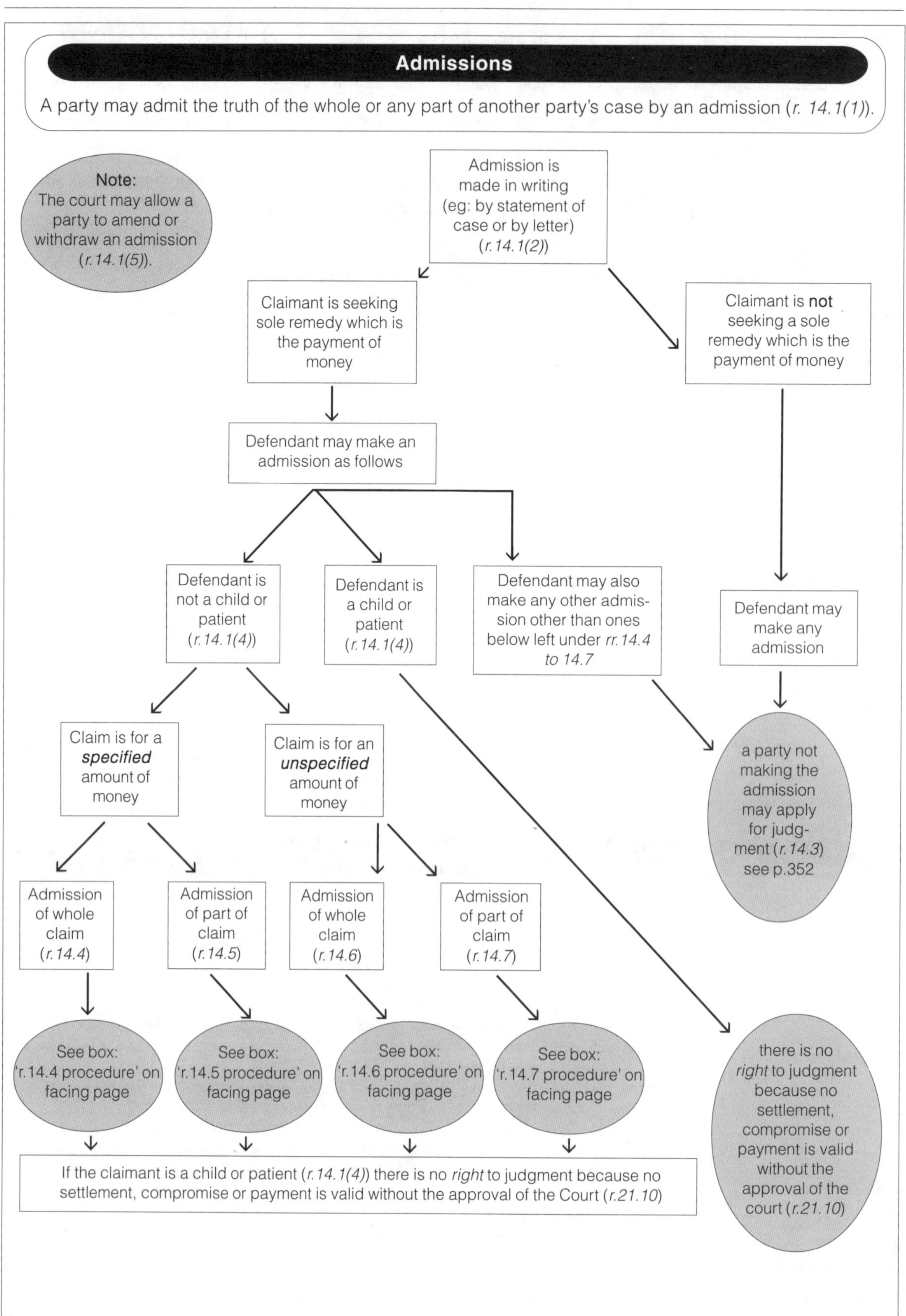
Admissions
A party may admit the truth of the whole or any part of another party's case by an admission (r. 14.1(1)).
Note:
The court may allow a party to amend or withdraw an admission (r. 14.1(5)).
Admission is made in writing (eg: by statement of case or by letter) (r. 14.1(2))
Claimant is seeking sole remedy which is the payment of money
Claimant is not seeking a sole remedy which is the payment of money
Defendant may make an admission as follows
Defendant is not a child or patient (r. 14.1(4))
Defendant is a child or patient (r. 14.1(4))
Defendant may also make any other admission other than ones below left under rr. 14.4 to 14.7
Defendant may make any admission
a party not making the admission may apply for judgment (r. 14.3) see p.352
Claim is for a specified amount of money
Claim is for an unspecified amount of money
Admission of whole claim (r. 14.4)
Admission of part of claim (r. 14.5)
Admission of whole claim (r. 14.6)
Admission of part of claim (r. 14.7)
See box: 'r. 14.4 procedure' on facing page
See box: 'r. 14.5 procedure' on facing page
See box: 'r. 14.6 procedure' on facing page
See box: 'r. 14.7 procedure' on facing page
there is no right to judgment because no settlement, compromise or payment is valid without the approval of the court (r. 21.10)
If the claimant is a child or patient (r. 14.1(4)) there is no right to judgment because no settlement, compromise or payment is valid without the approval of the Court (r. 21.10)

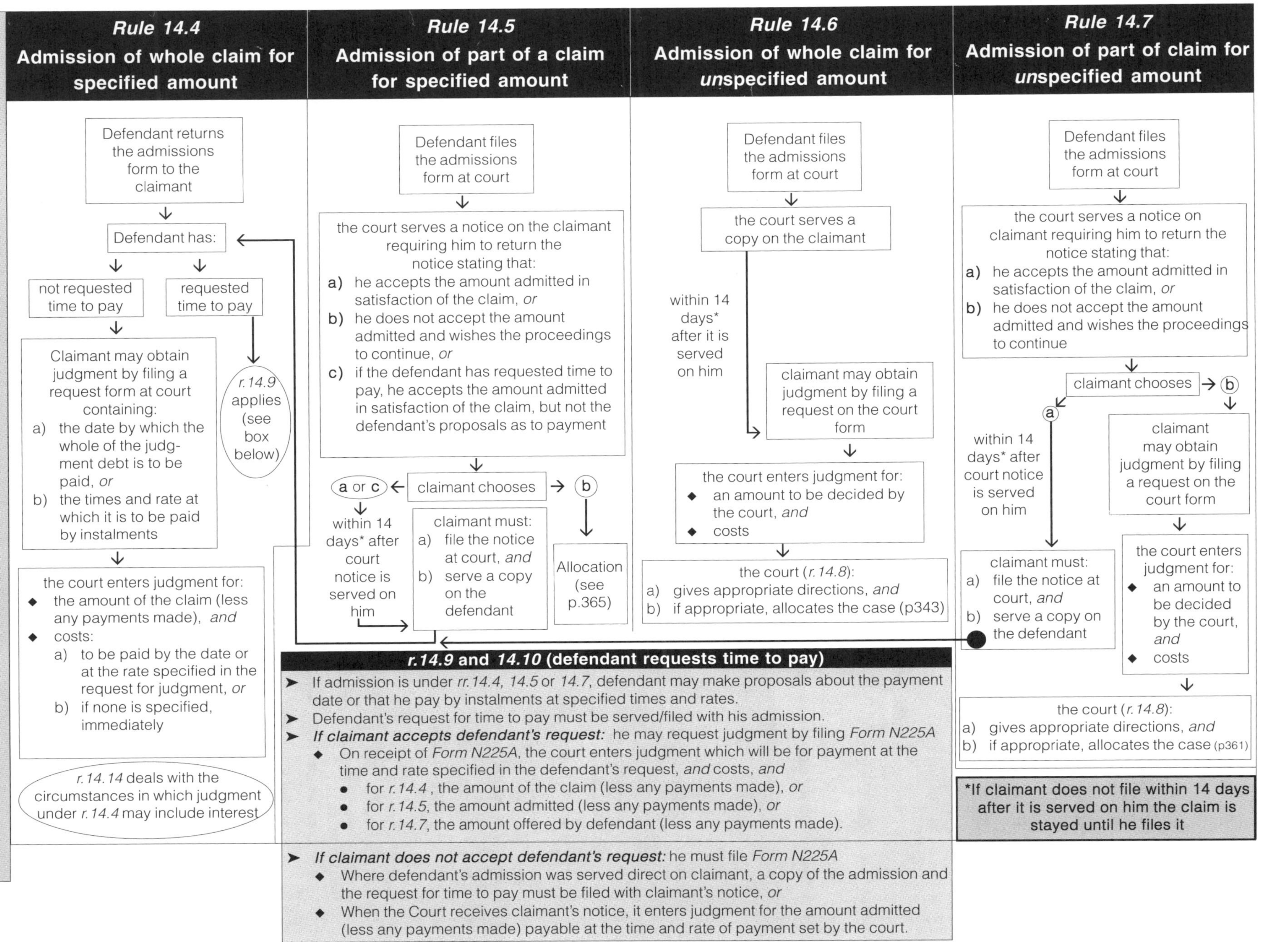

Rule 14.4
Admission of whole claim for specified amount
Defendant returns the admissions form to the claimant
Defendant has:
not requested time to pay
requested time to pay
r.14.9 applies (see box below)
Claimant may obtain judgment by filing a request form at court containing:
a) the date by which the whole of the judgment debt is to be paid, or
b) the times and rate at which it is to be paid by instalments
the court enters judgment for:
◆ the amount of the claim (less any payments made), and
◆ costs:
a) to be paid by the date or at the rate specified in the request for judgment, or
b) if none is specified, immediately
r.14.14 deals with the circumstances in which judgment under r.14.4 may include interest
Rule 14.5
Admission of part of a claim for specified amount
Defendant files the admissions form at court
the court serves a notice on the claimant requiring him to return the notice stating that:
a) he accepts the amount admitted in satisfaction of the claim, or
b) he does not accept the amount admitted and wishes the proceedings to continue, or
c) if the defendant has requested time to pay, he accepts the amount admitted in satisfaction of the claim, but not the defendant's proposals as to payment
a or c
claimant chooses
b
within 14 days* after court notice is served on him
claimant must:
a) file the notice at court, and
b) serve a copy on the defendant
Allocation (see p.365)
Rule 14.6
Admission of whole claim for unspecified amount
Defendant files the admissions form at court
the court serves a copy on the claimant
within 14 days* after it is served on him
claimant may obtain judgment by filing a request on the court form
the court enters judgment for:
◆ an amount to be decided by the court, and
◆ costs
the court (r.14.8):
a) gives appropriate directions, and
b) if appropriate, allocates the case (p343)
Rule 14.7
Admission of part of claim for unspecified amount
Defendant files the admissions form at court
the court serves a notice on claimant requiring him to return the notice stating that:
a) he accepts the amount admitted in satisfaction of the claim, or
b) he does not accept the amount admitted and wishes the proceedings to continue
claimant chooses
a
b
within 14 days* after court notice is served on him
claimant must:
a) file the notice at court, and
b) serve a copy on the defendant
claimant may obtain judgment by filing a request on the court form
the court enters judgment for:
◆ an amount to be decided by the court, and
◆ costs
the court (r.14.8):
a) gives appropriate directions, and
b) if appropriate, allocates the case (p361)
*If claimant does not file within 14 days after it is served on him the claim is stayed until he files it
r.14.9 and 14.10 (defendant requests time to pay)
➤ If admission is under rr.14.4, 14.5 or 14.7, defendant may make proposals about the payment date or that he pay by instalments at specified times and rates.
➤ Defendant's request for time to pay must be served/filed with his admission.
➤ If claimant accepts defendant's request: he may request judgment by filing Form N225A
◆ On receipt of Form N225A, the court enters judgment which will be for payment at the time and rate specified in the defendant's request, and costs, and
● for r.14.4, the amount of the claim (less any payments made), or
● for r.14.5, the amount admitted (less any payments made), or
● for r.14.7, the amount offered by defendant (less any payments made).
➤ If claimant does not accept defendant's request: he must file Form N225A
◆ Where defendant's admission was served direct on claimant, a copy of the admission and the request for time to pay must be filed with claimant's notice, or
◆ When the Court receives claimant's notice, it enters judgment for the amount admitted (less any payments made) payable at the time and rate of payment set by the court.

See p.352 for how to obtain judgement on admissions

III Acknowledgement of service (*Part 10*)

➤ A defendant must file an acknowledgment of service (*Form N9*) if:

- he is unable to file a defence within the period specified (see p.315 and below), *or*
- he wishes to dispute the court's jurisdiction (see below).

Note: A defendant who files an acknowledgment of service does not, by doing so, lose any right that he may have to dispute the court's jurisdiction (see below) (*r. 11(3)*).

➤ **Period:** The general rule is that the period for filing an acknowledgment of service is:

- where the defendant is served with a claim form which states that particulars of claim are to follow, 14 days after service of the particulars of claim, *and*
- in any other case, 14 days after service of the claim form.

➤ The claimant may obtain default judgment (see p.350) if:

- a defendant fails to file an acknowledgment of service within the period specified above, *and*
- does not within that period file a defence (see p.339) or serve or file an admission (see pp.340-341).

➤ On receipt of an acknowledgment of service, the court must notify the claimant in writing.

➤ An acknowledgment of service must be signed by the defendant or his solicitor and include the defendant's address for service, or if represented by a solicitor, his solicitor's address.

IV Disputing the court's jurisdiction (*Part 11*)

➤ A defendant may apply to the court for an order declaring that the court has no such jurisdiction or should not exercise any jurisdiction which it may have, if he:

- disputes the court's jurisdiction to try the claim, *or*
- argues that the court should not exercise its jurisdiction.

➤ A defendant making such an application *must* first file an acknowledgment of service (see above).

➤ **Period:** An application must be made within the defence-filing period (must be supported by evidence).

- The defendant accepts that the court has jurisdiction to try the claim if he:
    - files an acknowledgment of service, *and*
    - does not make such an application within the period for filing a defence.

➤ **Court makes a declaration:** that it has no jurisdiction/will not exercise its jurisdiction and may also:

- set aside the claim form, *and/or*
- set aside service of the claim form, *and/or*
- discharge any order made before the claim was commenced or served, *and/or*
- stay the proceedings.

➤ **Court does not make a declaration, then:**

- the acknowledgment of service ceases to have effect, *and*
- the defendant may file a further acknowledgment of service within 14 days or such other period as the court may direct.
    - If the defendant does file a further acknowledgment of service, he is treated as having accepted that the court has jurisdiction to try the claim.

Note: Where a defendant disputes the court's jurisdiction, he need not file a defence before the application hearing.

E Claimant's options

Including:

- an interim injunction
- an interim declaration
- an order for the detention, custody or preservation of property or inspection or taking of a sample or carrying out of an experiment on or with property, *and* authorising a person to enter land in a party's possession to carry out the order.
- a 'freezing injunction'
- a 'search order'
- an order for disclosure of documents or inspection of property
- an order for an interim payment made under *r.25.6* (see p.356).

Claiming additional liability if legally funded (*PD:Costs 19*)

Note: A party who will claim an additional liability under a funding arrangement must give other parties information about this (eg: in the claim form etc.), but there is no need to specify the amount of additional liability separately nor to state how it is calculated until it is assessed.

Reply and defence to counterclaim (*r.15.8, r.16.7*, ***PD15: 3.2A***)

- If a claimant files a reply to the defence, he must (*r.15.8*):
  - file his reply when he files his allocation questionnaire, *and*
  - serve his reply on the other parties at the same time as he files it.
- A statement of truth is required (see p.324).
- A claimant filing a reply to a defence who fails to deal with a matter raised in the defence, is taken to require that matter to be proved (*r.16.7*).

If the allocation questionnaire filing date is later than the defence to counterclaim filing date, the court normally orders the defence to counterclaim to be filed by the same date as the reply. If the court does not order this, the reply and defence to counterclaim may form separate documents

- A claimant who does not file a reply to the defence is not taken to admit matters raised in it (*r.16.7*).

F Applications for court orders (*Part 23*)

I Generally

- An 'application notice' is a document in which an applicant states his intention to seek a court order (*r.23.1*).
- An applicant must file an application notice *unless*:
  a) a rule or *PD* permit otherwise, *or*
  b) the court dispenses with the requirement for an application notice (*r.23.3*).

- An application should be made as soon as it is apparent that it is necessary or desirable (*PD23: 2.7*).
- Whenever possible, an application should be made so that it can be considered at any other hearing (eg: case management conference, allocation or listing hearing) for which a date has already been fixed or is about to be fixed (*PD23: 2.8*).
  - If a date for a hearing has been fixed and a party does not have sufficient time to serve an application notice, he must inform the other parties and the court (in writing) as soon as possible of the nature of the application and the reason for it (*PD23: 2.10*) (unless circumstances require secrecy (*PD 23: 4.2*).
    - The party wishing to make the application should make the application orally at the hearing.
  - At the hearing, the court may wish to review the conduct of the case and give any necessary case management directions (*PD23: 2.9*).
    - The parties must be ready to assist the court and answer questions the court asks for this purpose.

II Making an application

A. Which court?

Which court?

- An application must be made to the court in which the claim was started (*r.23.2) unless*:

a claim has not been started →	... the court in which the claim is most likely to be started (except when there is good reason otherwise)
the claim has been transferred to another court →	... the court to which the claim has been transferred
the parties have been notified of a fixed date for a trial →	... the court where the trial is to take place
proceedings to enforce judgement have begun →	... any court which is dealing with the enforcement of the judgement (unless a practice direction provides otherwise)

B. The application notice - contents, form and procedure

<table>
<tr><th colspan="2">Application notice - contents, form and procedure</th></tr>
<tr><td>Contents and Form</td><td>

➤ An application notice must state the order an applicant seeks and (briefly) why the applicant seeks the order (*r.23.6*).
➤ An application notice must be signed and include (*PD 23: 2.1*):
◆ the title of the claim, *and*
◆ the reference number of the claim, *and*
◆ the full name of the applicant, *and*
◆ where the applicant is not already a party, the address for service, *and*
◆ a request for a hearing or a request that the application be dealt with without a hearing.
➤ An application notice must be verifed by a statement of truth (*Part 22*) if the applicant wishes to rely on matters set out in the application as evidence.
</td></tr>
<tr><td>Procedure</td><td>

Steps
1 The applicant files the application notice at court.
2 A copy of the application notice must be served on each respondent (unless a rule, *PD* or court order provide otherwise) (*r.23.4*).
A copy an application notice must be served as soon as practicable after the notice is filed and (unless a rule or *PD* specify otherwise) must be served at least 3 days before the court is to deal with the application (*r.23.7(1)*).
◆ If an application notice is served and the period of notice is shorter, the court may direct that sufficient notice has been given (*r.23.7(4)*).
3a **Hearing requested**: on receipt of the application notice the court notifies the applicant of the time and the date for the hearing (*PD 23: 2.1*).
3b **Request for no-hearing**: as the Master or District Judge determines, the court *either:*
◆ if the application **is suitable** for consideration without a hearing, informs the applicant and the respondent and gives directions for the filing of evidence, *or*
◆ if the application **is not suitable** for consideration without a hearing, notifies the applicant and the respondent of the time and date for the hearing and may give directions as to the filing of evidence (*PD 23: 2.3-2.5*).
• The court may deal with the application without a hearing if *either* (*r.23.8*):
■ the parties agree to the terms of the order sought, *or*
■ the parties agree that the court dispose of the application without a hearing, *or*
NB: the parties should inform the court in writing and each party should confirm that all evidence and other material on which that party relies has been disclosed to the other parties to the application (*PD23: 11.1*).
■ the court does not consider that a hearing would be appropriate.
➤ If the court is to serve a copy of the application notice, the applicant must file a copy of any written evidence in support when he files the notice itself (*r.23.2(7)*).
➤ An application notice must be served with:
◆ a copy of any written evidence in support (unless that evidence has already been filed or served on the respondent) (*r.23.7(5)*), *and*
◆ a copy of any draft order which the applicant has attached to the application, *and*
◆ a statement of costs at least 24 hours before any interim hearing (*PD:Costs 13.5*).
➤ **Costs of interim hearings are routinely assessed at the conclusion of the hearing by summary assessment - see p.393.**
</td></tr>
</table>

C. Applications made without service of an application notice

➤ A court may dispose of an application without notice only (*PD 23: 3*):

- where there is exceptional urgency, *or*
- where the overriding objective is best furthered by doing so, *or*
- by consent of all the parties, *or*
- with the court's permission, *or*
- where the date for a hearing has been fixed and there is not sufficient time to serve a notice (*PD23: 2.10*), *or*
- where a court order, rule, or *PD* permits.

➤ If the court makes an order (granting or dismissing the application) a copy of the application notice and any evidence in support must be served ...

... on any party or person against whom the order was made and against whom the order was sought ...

... *unless* the court orders otherwise (*r.23.9(2)*).

➤ An order granted with respect to an application made without notice must contain a statement of the right to have the order set aside or varied (*r.23.9(3)*).

➤ A person who was not served with a copy of an application notice may apply to have the order set aside or varied *(23.10(1)*).

- This must application to set aside or vary must be made within 7 days after the date on which the order was served on the person who wishes to make that application for set aside/variation (*r.23.10(2)*).

Telephone hearings (*PD23: 6.1, 6.1A, 6.2-6.5*)

➤ The court may order an application (or part of an application) to be dealt with by telephone hearing only if all the parties have consented and no party is acting in person; if a court so orders it will allocate a time and give any directions necessary for the telephone hearing.

➤ No representative of a party may attend the judge in person without the other party's agreement.

➤ If a telephone application is sought, the application notice should indicate this. If it does not indicate this, a request for a telephone hearing should be made as early as possible.

➤ The following directions may apply to telephone hearings:

- The applicant's legal representative must arrange the conference by BT's conference call 'call out' system (or a comparable system) for the precise time fixed by the court (giving the operator the telephone numbers of all those participating and the sequence in which they are to be called).
- The sequence in which the participant's are to be called is:
  a) the applicant's legal representative and (if on a different number) his counsel, *then*
  b) the legal representative (and counsel) of all the other parties, *then*
  c) the judge.
- The applicant's legal representative must arrange for the call to be recorded on tape by the telecommunications provider and must send the tape to the court.
- Each speaker must remain on the line after being called by the operator (the call may be 2 or 3 minutes before the time fixed for the application).
- When the judge has been connected the applicant's legal representative introduces the parties in the usual way.
- The judge may require a party to use a handphone if the use of a speakerphone causes the judge or any party difficulty in hearing what is said.
- The telephone charges debited to the account of the party initiating the call are treated as part of the costs of the application.

III The applications

A. Making a *Part 20* claim (*Part 20*)

Purpose: A *Part 20* claim is a claim other than a claim by a claimant against a defendant (*r.20.2*).

- *Part 20* claims include:
  - a) a **counterclaim** by a defendant, *and/or*
  - b) a claim by a defendant for a **contribution** or **indemnity** or some other remedy, *and/or*
  - c) any claim made by a person who is the subject of a *Part 20* claim and is not already a party.

Procedure for making a *Part 20* claim

Counterclaims: Against claimant (*r.20.4*)	Counterclaims: Other (*r.20.5*)	Contribution/Indemnity (*r.20.6*)	Other (*r.20.7*)
Defendant files particulars of the counterclaim. If the *Part 20* claim is filed with the defence, court's permission is not needed. If the *Part 20* claim is **not** filed with defence, the court's permission is needed	Defendant applies to court for an order that the person be added as a defendant to the counterclaim. The application is without notice (unless the court orders otherwise). When making the order, the court will give case management directions	A defendant who has filed a defence or acknowledgement of service files a notice containing a statement of the nature and grounds of his claim	A defendant does not need the court's permission to make a *Part 20* claim if a that claim is issued before or at the same time as he files his defence (otherwise the court's permission is needed). A *Part 20* claim is made when the court issues a *Part 20* claim form. Particulars of a *Part 20* claim must be contained in or served with the claim form

Application for the court's permission to issue a *Part 20* claim

➤ An application must be supported by evidence stating (*PD20: 2*):
- the stage which the action has reached (including, where possible, a timetable of the action to date; if delay is a factor in the application, an explanation should be given), *and*
- the nature of the *Part 20* claim or details of the question/issue which needs to be decided, *and*
- a summary of the facts on which the *Part 20* claim is based, *and*
- the name and address of the proposed *Part 20* defendant.

Service of *Part 20* claim (*r.20.8*)

Counterclaims (*r.20.8(1)(a)*)	Contribution/Indemnity (*r.20.8(2)*)	Other (*r.20.8(1)(b)*)
On every other party when a copy of the defence is served	Not applicable	On the person against whom it is made within 14 days after the date on which the party making the *Part 20* claim files his defence

➤ If the claim form is served on a non-party it must be accompanied by (*r.20.12(1)*):
- a form for defending the claim, *and*
- a form for admitting the claim, *and*
- a form for acknowledging service, *and*
- a copy of every statement of case which has been served in the proceedings and such other documents as the court may direct.

➤ A person who is not already a party to the proceedings becomes a party on service of the *Part 20* claim (*r.20.10(1)*).

➤ A copy of the *Part 20* claim form must be served on every existing party (*r.20.12(2)*).

(A. continued...) Conduct of a *Part 20* claim (*Part 20*)

Should a *Part 20* claim be a separate claim?

➤ When considering whether to permit a *Part 20 claim* to be made, to dismiss a *Part 20 claim* or to require a *Part 20* claim to be dealt with separately, the court may have regard to (*r.20.9(1)-(2)*):

- the connections between the *Part 20* claim and the claim made by the claimant against the defendant, *and*
- whether the *Part 20* claimant seeks substantially the same remedy as the claimant seeks from him, *and*
- whether the *Part 20* claimant wants the court to decide any question connected with the subject matter of proceedings: i) between existing parties, but also between existing parties and a person not already a party, *or* ii) against an existing party in a different capacity to that in which that existing party is already a party to the proceedings.

General application of *CPRs*

➤ The *CPRs* generally apply to the *Part 20* claim as to any other claim, *except* that (*r.20.3*):

All claims

- the general rules applicable to time limits for serving a claim form (see p.315) do not apply (see previous page for the rules which do apply).
- the claim need not include a statement of value (which would otherwise be needed under *r.16.3(5)*) to commence a claim in the High Court, see p.335).
- The preliminary stage of case management, at allocation (see p.365), does not apply.

For counterclaims

- *Part 14* (Admissions) applies (see pp.318-319).
- *Part 12* (Default judgment) applies (see p.328).

Claims other than counterclaims

- *r.14.3-14.14* (Admissions - see pp.318-319) do not apply.
- *Part 12* (Default judgment - see p.328) does not apply, *but ...* (*r.11(3)*):

... if the claim is not being made by a defendant for a contribution or indemnity and the party against who the *Part 20* claim is made fails to file an acknowledgment of service or defence in respect of the *Part 20* claim *then ...*

a) the party against whom the *Part 20* claim is made is deemed to admit the *Part 20* claim and is bound by any judgment in the main proceedings so far as that judgment is relevant to any matter arising out of the *Part 20* claim, *and*

b) if default judgment is given against the *Part 20* claimant, the *Part 20* claimant may obtain judgment in respect of the *Part 20* claim by filing a request in the relevant practice form.

NB: The court's permission is needed to enter judgment under 'b' if the *Part 20* claimant has not satisfied the default judgment against him *or* wishes to obtain judgment for any remedy other than a contribution or indemnity (*r.20.11(3)*).

An application for the court's permission may be made without notice, unless the court directs otherwise (*r.20.11(4)*).

A court may at any time set aside or vary a judgment under 'b'.

Case managment (*r.20.13, PD20: 5*)

➤ Where a defence to a *Part 20* claim is filed the court considers the conduct of the case and gives appropriate directions (*r.20.13(1)*).

- When the defence is filed the court arranges a hearing and gives notice of the hearing to each party likely to be affected by any order made at the hearing (*PD20: 5.1-5.2*).

➤ At the hearing, the court may (*PD20: 5.3*):

- treat the hearing as a summary judgment hearing.
- order the dismissal of the *Part 20* proceedings.
- give directions as to how a claim or issue set out in or arising from the *Part 20* claim should be dealt with.
- give directions as to the extent to which the *Part 20* defendant is to be bound by any judgment or decision in the action.
  - When giving directions, the court must ensure as far as practicable the claims are managed together (*r.20.13(2)*)

B. Summary judgment (*Part 24*)

Purpose: the claimant or defendant seeks judgment quickly and cheaply without the expense and delay of a trial

Grounds (*r.24.2*)

A **claimant** has no real prospect of succeeding on the claim or an issue

A **defendant** has no real prospect of successfully defending the claim or issue

\+ There is no other compelling reason why the cause or issue should be disposed of at trial

Procedure (*r.24.4*)

- ➤ A claimant may not apply until the defendant has filed an acknowledgement of service or a defence *unless* the court gives permission or a *PD* provides otherwise (eg: the claimant seeks an order for specific performance (*PD24: 7.1(b)*)).
- ➤ An application must (*PD24:2(3)*):
  - a) identify concisely any point of law or provision in a document on which the applicant relies, *and/or*
  - b) state that it is made because the applicant believes that on the evidence the respondent has no real prospect of succeeding on the claim or issues, or of successfully defending the claim or issue

  \+ The applicant knows of no other reason why the disposal of the claim or issue should await trial

  - If the application relies on written evidence but does not contain that written evidence, the application should identify that evidence (*PD24: 2(4)*).
  - The application should draw the respondent's attention to *r.24.5(1)* governing evidence (*PD24: 2(4)*).
- ➤ If a claimant applies before a defence has been filed, the defendant need not file a defence before the hearing.
- ➤ The parties will have at least 14 days notice of the date fixed for the hearing and the issues which it is proposed that the court will decide.

Evidence (*r.24.5*)

Hearing fixed as a result of an application by a party		Hearing fixed by the court of its own volition	
Respondent (*r.24.5(1)*)	Applicant (*r.24.5(2)*)	Any party (*r.24.5(3)(a)*)	Any party in reply (*r.24.5(3)(b)*)
At least 7* days before the hearing file written evidence and serve copies on the other parties to the application ...	At least 3 days before the hearing file written evidence and serve copies on the respondent ...	At least 7* days (unless the court orders otherwise) before the hearing file written evidence and serve copies on the other parties to the application ...	At least 3 days (unless the court orders otherwise) before the hearing file written evidence and serve copies on the respondent ...

... unless evidence has already been filed or served on the appropriate party (*r.24.5(4)*)

* 4 days before the hearing if an order for specific performance is sought (*PD24: 7.3*).

Possible orders (*r.24.6*)

- ➤ The orders which the court (usually a Master or a District Judge) may make include (*PD24: 3(1), 5.1*):
  - a) judgment on the claim.
  - b) striking out or dismissal of the claim.
  - c) dismissal of the application.
  - d) a conditional order.
    - Eg: an order requiring a party to pay money into court or take a specified step *and* providing for that party's claim to be dismissed or statement of claim struck out if he does not comply (*PD 24: 5.2*).
    - Made if it appears possible but improbable that a claim/defence will succeed (*PD 24: 4*).
- ➤ If the application is not dismissed or an order is not made disposing of the claim, the court will give case management directions (*PD24: 10*).

Summary judgment is **not** available against a defendant in proceedings (*r.24.3*):

- ◆ for possession of residential premises against a tenant, or mortgagor or a person holding over after the tenancy ends, *or*
- ◆ for an admiralty claim *in rem*.

C. Default judgment (*Parts 12 and 13*)

Purpose: The claimant wants to obtain judgment when the defendant (*r. 12.1-12.2*):

a) has failed to file an acknowledgement of service, *or*

b) has failed to file a defence ...

but not for a claim under the *CCA 1974*, under the *Part 8* procedure, *or* where a *PD* provides that a claimant may not obtain default judgment (eg: *PD12: 1.2-1.3*) *or* for non-counterclaim *Part 20* claims (*r.20.3(3)*).

Grounds

➤ The claim has been properly served and (*r. 12.3(1)-(2)*):

a) the defendant has not filed an acknowledgment of service or a defence and the time limit has expired, *or*

- A certificate of service on the court file is sufficient evidence that particulars of claim have been served on the defendant (*PD12: 4.1*)

b) an acknowledgment of service has been filed but a defence has not been filed and the time limit has expired, *or*

c) in a counterclaim made under *r.20.4* (see p.347) a defence has not been filed and the time limit has expired...

... *provided that* it is not the case that (*r. 12.3(3)*):

- the defendant has applied for summary judgment and that application has not been disposed of, *or*
- the defendant has applied to have the claimant's statement of claim struck out under *r.3.4* (see p.318), and that application has not been disposed of, *or*
- the defendant has satisfied the whole claim (including costs), *or*
- it is a money claim and the defendant has filed or served on the claimant an admission of liability to pay all the money claimed with a request for time to pay.

Procedure

➤ The claimant **files a request** on the relevant practice form if the claim is for (*r. 12.4(1)*):

a) a specified amount of money, *and/or*

b) an amount of money to be decided by the court, *and/or*

c) delivery of goods (if the claim form gives the defendant the alternative of paying their value.

> The **request** may specify the date by which the debt is to be paid, or the time/rate for instalments (*r. 12.5(1)*) and interest (*r. 12.6(1)*)

➤ The claimant **makes an application** under *Part 23* (see p.344) if the claim (*r. 12.4(2)*):

- includes a claim for any remedy other than those set out in a) to c) above, *or*
- the claimant seeks a judgment for costs (which are not fixed costs - see p.392) only (*r. 12.9*), *or*
- is against a child, a patient, the Crown, a claim in tort by one spouse against the other (*r. 12.10(a)*), *or*
- is against a defendant who has not filed an acknowledgment of service *and* is a State, diplomat, immune under the *IOA 1968* or *IOA 1981*, *or* has been served out of the jurisdiction (in certain circumstances), *or* is domiciled in Scotland, Northern Ireland or a territory to which the Brussels or Lugnano Conventions apply (*r. 12.10(b)*).

Judgment (on a request)

➤ If a claim is for a specified sum of money, the judgment is for the amount of the claim (less any payments made) and costs (*r. 12.5(2)*):

a) to be paid by the date or at the rate specified in the request, *or*

b) if no date/rate are specified, immediately.

➤ If a claim is for an unspecified amount of money, judgment is for an amount to be decided by the court and costs (*r. 12.5(3)*).

➤ If a claim is for the delivery of goods the judgment requires the defendant to deliver the goods (or if he does not) to pay the amount decided by the court and costs (*r. 12.5(4)*).

- If judgment is for an amount decided by the court, it gives directions and may allocate the case (*r. 12.7*).

Setting aside a judgment in default

Procedure

If a claimant has good reason to believe that the particulars of claim did not reach the defendant before the claimant entered judgment, the claimant must file a request for the judgment to be set aside *or* apply to the court for directions (*r. 13.5(2)*)

Grounds

➤ The court **must** set aside judgment if (*r. 13.2*):

a) any of the conditions for obtaining that judgment were not satisfied, *or*

b) the whole of the claim was satisfied before judgment was entered.

➤ The court **may** set aside judgment if (*r. 13.3*):

a) the defendant has a real prospect of successfully defending the claim, *or*

b) there is some other good reason why the judgment should be set aside or varied or the defendant should be allowed to defend the claim

D. **Further information** (*Part 18*)	
Purpose: to clarify any matter which is in dispute in proceedings or provide additional information with regard to such a matter - even if the matter is not contained in or referred to in the statement of case	
Format of request	➤ A written request specifying the clarification or information sought, stating the time by which a response must be served (the time for response must be 'reasonable' (*PD18: 1.1*)). ➤ The request: ◆ must be concise and strictly confined to matters 'reasonably necessary and proportionate' (*PD18: 1.2*), *and* ◆ should take the form of a single comprehensive document, not be piecemeal (*PD18: 1.3*), *and* ◆ should be a separate document *unless* it is brief *and* the reply is likely to be brief, in which case it may in the form of a letter (*PD 18:1.4*), *and* ◆ should (*PD 18:1.6(a)*): • be headed with name of the court, the title and number of the claim, *and* • in the heading state it is a request under *Part 18*, identify both parties, use separate numbered paragraphs for each request, *and* • identify each document and the paragraph/words to which a request relates. ➤ If convenient, numbered paragraphs should appear on the left of the page so that a response may appear on the right (if the request is in this form any extra copy should be served for use by the respondent) (*PD18: 1.6(2)*).
Format of reply	➤ In writing, dated, signed by the respondent or his legal representative (*PD18: 2.1*). ➤ A point by point reply to the request. ➤ For each point, repeat the request verbatim and provide a reply (unless the format suggested in *PD18: 1.6(2)* is used (see above)). ➤ A response must be verified by a statement of truth (*PD18: 3*) (see p.324). ➤ The person making a reply must file it at court and serve it on the other parties. ➤ If a party objects to complying with a request or is unable to do so within the time stated in that request, that party must (*PD18: 4*): ◆ promptly inform the party making the request, *and* ◆ give reasons (eg: disproportionate expense), *and* ◆ give a date by which he expects to be able to comply.
Court application	➤ An application under *Part 23* (see p.344), with (*PD18: 5*): ◆ the text of the order sought, *and* ◆ a description of the response, if any ... *plus* ... ◆ costs if sought (*PD18: 5.8*). ➤ If a party has not responded to a request served on him and at least 14 days have passed since the request was served and the time stated in it for a response has expired (*PD18: 5.5*): ◆ the applicant need not serve a copy of the application notice on the party to whom the request was made, *and* ◆ the court may deal with the application without a hearing ... *otherwise* ... ... the application notice and any order made must be served on all other parties to the claim (*PD18: 5.6-5.7*)

E. Judgment on admissions

Purpose: to reduce/avoid the expense of a trial by resolving agreed issues beforehand

Time	➤ If a claim form states that particulars of claim will follow, 14 days after the service of those particulars *otherwise* 14 days after service of the claim form (*r. 14.2*) (see p.315).
Procedure	➤ A party gives written notice that it admits the whole or part of another party's case (*r. 14.1(1)-(2)*). ➤ The claimant may enter judgment (*r. 14.1(4)*) (see p.336-337). If the claim relates to a specified amount of money, or an unspecified amount of money (*r. 14.4-14.7*): Steps 1 The defendant files the relevant *Practice Form* with the court. 2 The court serves a notice on the claimant, requiring him to return the notice. 3 Within 14 days the claimant must file the notice and serve a copy on the defendant (otherwise proceedings are stayed until the notice is filed). ➤ A defendant may request time to pay (*r. 14.9-14.13, PD 14: 5-6*). ◆ A claimant will not accept a defendant's proposals for payment must file a notice in set form. ◆ The court determines the time and rate of payment. ● If the amount outstanding is less than £50,000 a court officer may make this determination (there is no hearing). ● A judge may make this determination at a hearing. If a judge holds a hearing: ■ the court gives each party at least 7 days' notice of the hearing, *and* ■ where the claim was not started at the defendant's home court or subsequently transferred there, it will transferred there if: a) the claim is for a specified amount of money, *and* b) the defendant is an individual, *and* c) the claim was not started in a specialist list. ● If a court officer makes the determination, or a judge does so without a hearing, either party may apply for a redetermination within 14 days of service of the determination on the applicant.

F. Discontinuance (*Part 38*)

Purpose: Discontinuance halts the action.

The defendant is entitled to costs (other than in respect of claims allocated to the small claims track) to the date notice of discontinuance is served on him for the part of the proceedings that are discontinued (*r.38.6*) ←

Claimant's right to discontinue	➤ The claimant may discontinue without seeking leave. *But* if the court has granted an interim injunction or any party has given an undertaking to the court the claimant must obtain the court's permission (*r.38.2(2)(a)*). ➤ If the claimant has received an interim payment *either* the defendant must consent in writing *or* the court gives permission (*r.38.2(2)(b)*). ➤ If there is more than one claimant, *either* every other claimant must consent in writing *or* the court gives permission (*r.38.2(2)(c)*).
Claimant	a) File a notice of discontinuance (*r.38.3(1)(a)*): ◆ stating that a copy has been served on every other party (*r.38.3(2)*). ◆ (if the consent of another party is needed), attaching a copy of that consent (*r.38.3(3)*). ◆ (if there is more than 1 defendant), stating against which defendant the claim is discontinued (*r.38.3(4)*). b) Serve a copy of the notice on every party to the proceedings (*r.38.3(1)(b)*).
Defendant	➤ May apply to have a notice of discontinuance set aside (*r.38.4(1)*). ➤ An application may not be made more than 28 days after the date on which the notice was served on that defendant (*r.38.4(2)*).
Consequences	1) The permission of the court is need for the claimant to subsequently make a claim against the same defendant if (*r.38.7*): a) the claimant discontinued the claim after the defendant filed a defence, *and* b) the new claim arises out of facts which are the same, or substantially the same, as those out of which the original claim arose. 2) If proceedings are only partly discontinued *and* the claimant fails to pay costs under *r.38.6* within 21 days of the date on which the parties agreed costs *or* the court ordered the costs to be paid, the court may stay the rest of the proceedings until the costs are paid (*r.38.8*).

IV Consent orders

Consent orders (and judgments) (*r.40.6*)

Purpose: To obtain a court order without a hearing, thus saving time and costs.

- A consent order (or judgment) is drawn up in the terms agreed, expressed as being 'By Consent', and signed by the legal representative acting for each of the parties to whom the order relates, or by a litigant in person (*r.40.6(7)*).
- A consent order (or judgment) may be drawn up and sealed by a court officer if (*r.40.6(2)*):
  a) none of the parties is a litigant in person, *and*
  b) the court's approval is not required by the *CPR*, a *PD* or any enactment, *and*
  c) *either* (*r.40.6(3)*):
    i) the order (or judgment) is for:
      - payment of an amount of money (including damages or the value of goods to be decided by the court).
      - delivery up of goods with or without the option of paying the value of the goods or the agreed value.

    ii) the order is for:
      - dismissal of any proceedings (wholly or in part).
      - stay of proceedings (the terms agreed may be recorded in a schedule to the order, or elsewhere).
      - stay of enforcement (unconditionally, or on condition that money due is paid by instalments specified in the consent order).
      - setting aside of a default judgment (*Part 13*) which has not been satisfied.
      - payment out of money which has been paid into court.
      - discharge from liability of any party.
      - payment, assessment or waiver of costs, or such other provision for costs as may be agreed.

      NB: see p.396 for the drawing up and filing of judgments and orders - those rules apply to judgments and orders entered and sealed by a court officer (*r.40.6(4)*).
- If a court officer may not draw up and seal a consent order (or judgment), any party may apply for an order (or judgment) in the terms agreed (*r.40.6(5)*).
  - The court may deal with the application without a hearing (*r.40.6(6)*).

Form of consent order (*PD40B: 3.4*)

- A consent judgment or order must:
  - be drawn up in the terms agreed, *and*
  - bear on it the words **'By Consent'**, *and*
  - be signed by:
    - solicitors or counsel acting for each of the parties to the order, *or*
    - where a party is a litigant in person, the litigant.

A special type of consent order (previously known as a Tomlin order)

- **Purpose:** To stay the action by consent of both parties on terms set out in a schedule to a court order.
- **Procedure:** Both parties submit a consent order. The agreement terms are set out in a schedule to the order.
  - If enforcement is necessary, an application can be made to court for specific performance or an injunction.
- Any payment to be made under an order is *not* treated as being paid under a judgment, so statutory interest is not available as it is on judgments under *JA 1838 s.17*.

V Declaratory judgments

- The court may make binding declarations whether or not any other remedy is claimed (*r.40.20*).

G Interim remedies (*Part 25*)

I Generally
II Making an application

I Generally

- An order may be made at any time (including before proceedings are started and after judgment) (*r.25.2(1)*).
  - Before a claim is made, a court will only grant an interim remedy if the matter is urgent *or* it is desirable to do so in the interests of justice (*r.25.2(2)(b)*).
- If a court grants an interim remedy it may give directions that a claim be commenced (*r.25.2(3)-(4)*).
- A defendant may not apply for an interim order before he has filed an acknowledgment of service or a defence (*r.25.2(2)(c)*), unless he has the court's permission.

Types of order

- A court may grant interim remedies which include (*r.25.1*):
  a) an interim injunction (prohibiting a person from doing, or requiring a person to do, something).
  b) an interim declaration.
  c) an order for the:
     i) detention, custody or preservation of property, *and/or*
     ii) inspection of property, *and/or*
     iii) taking of a sample of property, *and/or*
     iv) carrying out of an experiment on or with property, *and/or*
     v) sale of property which is perishable or which it is desirable to sell quickly, *and/or*
     vi) payment of income from property until the claim is decided, *and*
     ... authorising a person to enter land in the possession of a party to carry out an order under i) to vi) above.
  d) an order to deliver up goods (under *Torts (Interference with Goods) Act 1977*).
  e) an order (known as a 'freezing injunction'), restraining a party from:
     i) removing from the jurisdiction assets located here, *or*
     ii) dealing with any assets (irrespective of whether the assets are located in the jurisdiction ...
     ... directing a party to provide information about assets which are, or may be, the subject of an injunction under i) or ii) above.
  f) an order requiring a party to admit another party to premises to preserve evidence etc. made under *CPA 1997 s.7* (known as a 'search order').
  g) an order for disclosure of documents or inspection of property before a claim has been made under *SCA 1981 s.33* or *CCA 1984 s.52*.
  h) an order for disclosure of documents or inspection of property against a non-party made under *SCA 1981 s.34* or *CCA 1984 s.53*.
  i) an order for an interim payment made under *r.25.6* (see p.356).
  j) an order for a specified fund to be paid into court or secured, where there dispute over a party's right to the fund.
  k) an order permitting a party seeking to recover personal property, to pay money into court pending the outcome of proceedings and directing that, if he does, the property shall be given to him.
  l) an order directing a party to prepare and file accounts relating to a dispute.

II Making an application

- A court may grant an interim remedy on an application made without notice, if it appears that there are good reasons for not giving notice (*r.25.3(1)*).
- An application must be supported by evidence, unless the court orders otherwise (*r.25.3(2)*).
  - If notice has not been given, evidence in support of the application must state reasons why notice has not been given.
- The general rules relating to applications in *Part 23* apply (see pp.344-346).

A. Injunctions

1 Jurisdiction

- The judge with jurisdiction to conduct the trial has the power to grant an injunction (*PD25 II: 1.3*).
  - However, in the High Court, Masters and District Judges may grant injunctions (*PD25 II: 1.2*):
    a) by consent (a Master or District Judge may, with consent, vary or discharge an order granted by any judge (*PD25 II: 1.4*)), *and*
    b) in connection with a charging order and the appointment of a receiver, *and*
    c) in aid of execution of judgments.
- A High Court judge, or any other judge duly authorised, may grant 'search orders' and 'freezing injunctions' (*PD25 II: 1.1*).

2 Making an application

- The application notice must state the order sought *and* the date, time and place of hearing (*PD25 II: 2.1*).
  - For court service, the applicant must file sufficient copies for the court and each respondent (*PD25 II: 2.3*).
  - A draft order should be filed, plus a disk containing the draft in a format specified in the *PD* (*PD25 II: 2.4*).
- The application notice and evidence must be served as soon as practicable after issue (*PD25 II: 2.2*) and in any event not later than 3 days before the hearing.

3 Evidence

- Evidence must generally be set out (*PD 25 II: 3.2*):
  a) in a witness statement, *or*
  b) a statement of case (if it is verified by a statement of truth), *or*
  c) the application itself (if it is verified by a statement of truth).
- However, an application for a 'freezing injunction'/'search order' must be supported by affidavit.
- In either case, all material facts of which the court should be aware should be set out (including, if appropriate, why notice is not given) (*PD25 II: 3.3-3.4*).

4 Urgent applications without notice

- These are usually dealt with at a hearing, but in cases of 'extreme urgency' may (where the applicant is acting by counsel or solicitors) be by telephone (*PD25 II: 4*).

B. Interim payments	
Purpose:	The claimant wants an advance from the defendant against a debt or damages
Note:	a) before applying to court, it is wise to negotiate with an insurance company for a voluntary payment b) if resolving the case takes longer than expected, the claimant can make additional applications
Conditions	➤ The court is satisfied that *either* (*r.25.7(1)*): a) the defendant has admitted liability to pay damages or a sum of money to the claimant, *or* b) the claimant has obtained judgment for damages or a sum of money (not costs) to be assessed, *or* c) the claimant would obtain judgment for a substantial amount of money, *or* d) the claimant is seeking an order for possession of land *and* the defendant would be liable to pay the claimant a sum for the use and occupation of the land while the claim is pending. ➤ For personal injuries claims, the defendant is (*r.25.7(2)*): a) insured in respect of the claim *or* its liability will be met by an insurer (under *RTA 1988 s.151* or by an insurer acting under the Motor Insurers' Bureau Agreement or the MIB acting for itself - see p.311), *or* b) a public authority
Amount	➤ A 'reasonable proportion of the damages' which 'the court considers just' taking account of (*r.25.7(4)-(5)*): a) the sum likely to be recovered by the claimant, *and* b) any contributory negligence, *and* c) any counterclaim or set-off on which the defendant is likely to rely.
Legal help	➤ Interim payments are paid directly to the claimant ie: are *not* subject to a statutory charge (see pp.8-14)
Time	➤ The time for acknowledging service has expired (ie: 14 days after service of claim) (*r.25.6(1)*)
Applicant	➤ A copy of the application notice must be served at least 14 days before a hearing and be supported by evidence (*r.25.6(3)*) which deals with (*PD25 IP: 2.1*): a) the sum of money sought by way of interim payment, *and* b) the items or matters in respect of which interim payment is sought, *and* c) the sum of money for which final judgment is likely to be given, *and* d) the reasons for believing the conditions set out in *r.25.7* (see above) are satisfied, *and if appropriate* e) any other relevant matters (eg: why the plaintiff needs the money), *and* f) states, in a personal injury action, details of special damages and past and future loss, *and* g) in a claim under the *FAA 1976*, details of the persons on whose behalf the claim is made. ➤ A medical report or statement of special damages should be exhibited (*PD25 IP: 2.2*).
Respondent/ Applicant	➤ The respondent may serve written evidence in reply. ◆ The respondent must file the evidence and serve copies on every other party to the application at least 7 days before the hearing (*r.25.6(4)*). ◆ If the order is not by consent and the defendant is liable to pay recoverable benefits to the Secretary of State under the *SS(RB)A 1997*, the defendant should obtain a certificate of recoverable benefits (and this certificate should be filed at the hearing of the application) *(PD25 IP: 4*). ➤ An applicant wishing to rely on written evidence in reply must file written evidence and serve a copy on the respondent at least 3 days before the hearing (*r.25.6(5)*).
Conse-quences	1) The secrecy rule applies after this order - ie: the trial judge is not told about it until liability and quantum are resolved, unless the defendant agrees (*r.25.9*). 2) A preamble to a final judgment should set out the amounts and dates of any interim payment(s). Any final judgment is reduced by the amount of any interim payment(s) (*PD25 IP: 5*). 3) The court may order the claimant to repay the defendant (with interest) any surplus if the final award exceeds the interim payment (*r.25.8*).

C. Security for costs (*r.25.12 - 25.15*)

Purpose: to order the claimant (or another person) to give security (in any form the court may direct) for the costs incurred by the defendant in the action or in other proceedings

Procedure	Application supported by written evidence.
Grounds	◆ The court is satisfied that, having regard to all the circumstances of the case, it is just to make an order, *and* ◆ a) The claimant is an individual: • who is ordinarily resident outside the jurisdiction, *and* • is not a person against whom a claim can be enforced under the Brussels Conventions or the Lugano Convention, *or* b) the claimant is a company, or other incorporated body: • which is ordinarily resident out of the jurisdiction, *and* • is not a body against whom a claim can be enforced under the Brussels Conventions or the Lugano Convention, *or* c) the claimant is a company or other body and there is reason to believe that it will be unable to pay the defendant's costs if ordered to do so, *or* d) the claimant has changed his address since the claim was commenced with a view to evading the consequences of litigation, *or* e) the claimant failed to give his address in the claim form, or gave an incorrect address in that form, *or* f) the claimant is acting as a nominal claimant and there is reason to believe that he will be unable to pay the defendant's costs if ordered to do so, *or* g) the claimant has taken steps in relation to his assets that would make it difficult to enforce an order for costs against him.

An LSC funded claimant

Where a legally funded client who has Cost Protection (see p.394) is required to give security for costs, the amount of that security shall not exceed the amount (if any) which is a reasonable one having regard for all the circumstance's (including the client's financial resources and his conduct).
(*CLS(C)R 2000 r.6*)

D. Provisional damages in personal injury claims (*Part 41*)

Purpose: In a personal injury action, a claimant may want to claim provisional damages to pay expenses until trial.

Grounds	a) The particulars of claim include a claim for provisional damages, *and* b) the court is satisfied that the injured person will not develop disease or suffer deterioration *and* the injured person is entitled to apply for further damages at a future date if he develops the disease or suffers the deterioration.
Order (*r.41.2*)	◆ Must specify (each) disease or (each) type of deterioration in respect of which an application may be made at a future date and the period within which each application may be made (a claimant may subsequently make more than one application to extend this time).
Claimant (*r.41.3*)	◆ The general rules for making an application for an interim payment under *Part 25* (see p.356) apply to an application under *Part 41*. ◆ Only 1 further application may be made in respect of each disease or type of deterioration specified in the award of special damages. ◆ The claimant must give at least 28 days notice to the defendant of his intention to apply for further damages. • If the claimant knows that the defendant is insured and the identity of the insurers, the claimant must also give 28 days written notice to the insurers. ◆ Within 21 days after the end of the 28 day period, the claimant must apply for directions.

H Offers to settle/payments into court (*Parts 36-37*)

I General caveat as to *Part 36* consequences
II Form and content of a *Part 36* offer/payment notice
III Making a *Part 36* offer/payment
IV Accepting a *Part 36* offer/payment
V Consequences

Calderbank offer - costs control

➤ This is used where a payment into court is not suitable to resolve a claim (*Calderbank v. Calderbank* [1975] All ER 333).

➤ The defendant makes a written offer 'without prejudice save as to costs'.
- If the offer is not accepted, the offer letter remains secret from the trial judge until liability and quantum are resolved.
- If the damages offered in the letter are not exceeded by the judgment, then the judge may ask the claimant to pay both sides' costs from the date of the offer.

I General caveat as to *Part 36* consequences

➤ Nothing in *Part 36* prevents a party making an offer to settle in any way he chooses (*r.36.1(2)*).
- An offer not made in accordance with *Part 36,* (eg: a Calderank offer) only has the consequences set out in Section V below if the court so orders.

➤ Offers to settle and payments made into court in accordance with *Part 36* have the consequences set out in Section V below.

➤ While a claim is on the small claims track, an offer to settle or a payment into court in accordance with *Part 36* do not have the consequences set out in Section V below unless the court so orders (*r.36.2(5)*).

II Form and content of a *Part 36* offer/payment notice

➤ A defendant's offer to settle a money claim will only have the consequences set out in *Part 36* if it made by way of a *Part 36* payment (*r.36.3(1)*).
- If a payment-out of court to a claimant following a *Part 36* offer or a *Part 36* payment would be a compensation payment within *SS(RB)A 1997*, a defendant to a money claim may make an offer which shall have the consequences set out in Section V below **even if that defendant does not make a *Part 36* payment** if:

  a) at the time the offer is made the offeror has applied for, but not received, a certificate of recoverable benefits, *and*

  b) the offeror makes a *Part 36* payment not more than 7 days after the offeror receives the certificate (*r.36.23(2)*).

➤ If a claim includes a money claim and a non-money claim, and a defendant wishes to make an offer to settle the whole claim which will have the consequences set out in *Part 36*, that defendant must (*r.36.4*):

a) make a *Part 36* payment in respect of the money claim, *and*

b) make a *Part 36* offer in relation to the non-money claim.

A *Part 36* Offer (*r.36.5*)

➤ May:

- relate to the whole claim, or any part of the claim, or any issue which arises out of the claim (*r.36.5(2)*).
- be made by reference to an interim payment (*r.36.5(5)*).
- if made by a defendant, be limited to liability up to a specified proportion (*r.36.5(4)*).

➤ Must:

- be in writing (*r.36.5(1)*) and give the additional information set out below, *and*
  - **if made not less than 21 days before trial**, be expressed to remain open for 21 days from the date on which it is made and provide that it may only be accepted after 21 days if the parties agree liability for costs or the court gives permission (*r.36.5(6)*)
  - **if made less than 21 days before trial**, state that acceptance requires agreement by the parties as to costs or the court's permission (*r.36.5(7)*

A *Part 36* Payment notice (*r.36.6*)

➤ Must:

- give the additional information set out below, *and*
  - state the amount of the payment (*r.36.6(2)(a)*).
  - if the claim includes a claim for provisional damages, the notice must state whether the defendant is offering to agree to the making of an award for provisional damages. If the defendant offers to accept such an award, the notice must state (*r.36.7(3)(a)-(c)*):
    a) that the defendant pays the sum on the assumption that the injured person will not develop disease or suffer disease or suffer deterioration specified in the notice, *and*
    b) the offer is subject to the condition that the claimant must make any claim for further damages within a limited period (the period must be states).
  - if the defendant wishes to settle a claim which includes both a claim for money and a non-money claim (*r.36.4(3)*):
    a) identify the document containing the terms of the *Part 36* offer, *and*
    b) state that notice of acceptance of the payment will be treated as acceptance also of the *Part 36* offer.
  - if money is recoverable under *SS(RB)A 1997* as a compensation payment state (*r.36.23*):
    a) the amount of gross compensation, *and*
    b) the name and amount of any benefit by which the gross amount is reduced in accordance with *SS(RB)A 1997 s.8, Sch. 2, and*
    c) that the sum paid in is the net amount after deduction of the benefit.

A Part 36 Payment must be accompanied by a Part 36 Payment notice

Additional information for inclusion in an offer or payment notice

➤ An offer and a payment notice must both:

- state whether the offer/payment relates to the whole of the claim, or to part of it, or to an issue which arises in the claim (and which part or issue) (*r.36.5(3)(a)*), *36.6(2)(b)*).
- state whether the offer/payment takes into account any counterclaim (*r.36.5(3)(b)*), *36.6(2)(c)*).
- if the offer/payment is expressed not to include interest, state whether interest is offered/included and if so, the amount offered/included, the rate(s) offered/included and the period(s) for which it is offered/included (*r.36.5(3)(c), 36.6(2)(e)22(2)*).
  - Unless an offer/payment notice indicates otherwise the offer/payment is treated as including interest until the last date on which it could be accepted without needing the court's permission (*r.36.22(1)-(2)*).

III Making a *Part 36* offer/payment

1 Generally

- A *Part 36* offer or a *Part 36* payment may be made at any time after proceedings have started (*r.36.2(4)*); a *Part 36* payment may not be until proceedings have started (*r.36.3(2)*).
  - File with a *Part 36* payment notice: a cheque payable to Her Majesty's Paymaster General (County Court or a District Registry) or the Accountant General of the Supreme Court (Royal Courts of Justice) *plus* , in the Royal Courts of Justice, a sealed copy of the claim form and Courts Funds Office *form 100 (PD 36:4.1)*.
- An offeror making a *Part 36* payment must file a certificate of service (*r.36.6(4)*) (see p.337).
  - A defendant may choose to treat the whole or part of the sum paid into court as a *Part 36* payment if *either* (*r.37.2(1)-(2)*):

    a) the court makes an order subject to conditions (including that a sum of money be paid into court) and specifies the consequence of failure to comply with the order or condition (*r.3.1(3)* see p.360), *or*

    b) the court orders a party to pay a sum into court as that party has failed without good reason to comply with a rule, *PD* or pre-action protocol (*r.3.1(5),* see pp.313, 360), *then ...*

    - If a defendant so chooses, he must file a *Part 36* payment notice (*r.37.2(3)*).
- The court will serve the *Part 36* payment notice on the offeree unless the offeree informs the court that, when the money is paid into court, the offeror will serve the notice (*r.36.6(3)*).
- If a party makes a payment into court under a court order, the court will notify every other party of that payment (*r.37.1(1)*).

2 Timing an offer/payment

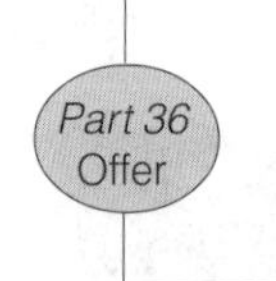

- A *Part 36* offer is made when received by the offeree (*r.36.8(1)*).
  - An improvement of a *Part 36* offer is effective when received by the offeree (*r.36.8(3)*).
  - If a *Part 36* offer is withdrawn it will not have the consequences which a *Part 36* offer otherwise has (*r.36.5(8)*).

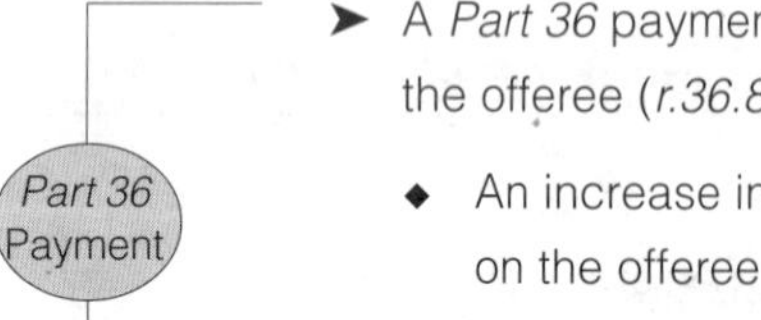

- A *Part 36* payment is made when written notice of the payment into court is served on the offeree (*r.36.8(2)*).
  - An increase in a *Part 36* payment is effective when notice of the increase is served on the offeree (*r.36.8(4)*).
  - A Part 36 payment may only be withdrawn or reduced with the court's permission (*r.36.6(5)*).

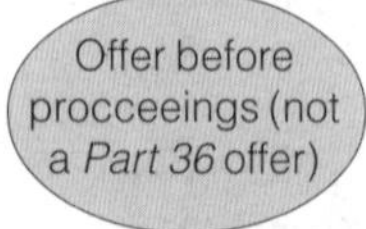

- An offer to settle made before the commencement of proceedings (and which is therefore **not** a *Part 36* offer) is made when received by the offeree (*r.36.10(5)*) (see further Section V below).

3 Clarifying an offer/payment

- Within 7 days of a *Part 36* offer or a *Part 36* payment being made, the offeree may ask for clarification (*r.36.9(1)*).
  - An offeror has 7 days from receipt of a request for clarification to provide that clarification (*r.36.9(2)*).
    - If clarification is not provided within this time then (assuming the trial has not started) the offeree may apply for an order that the offeror provide the requested clarification (*r.36.9(2)*).

IV Accepting a Part 36 offer/Part 36 payment

A. Generally

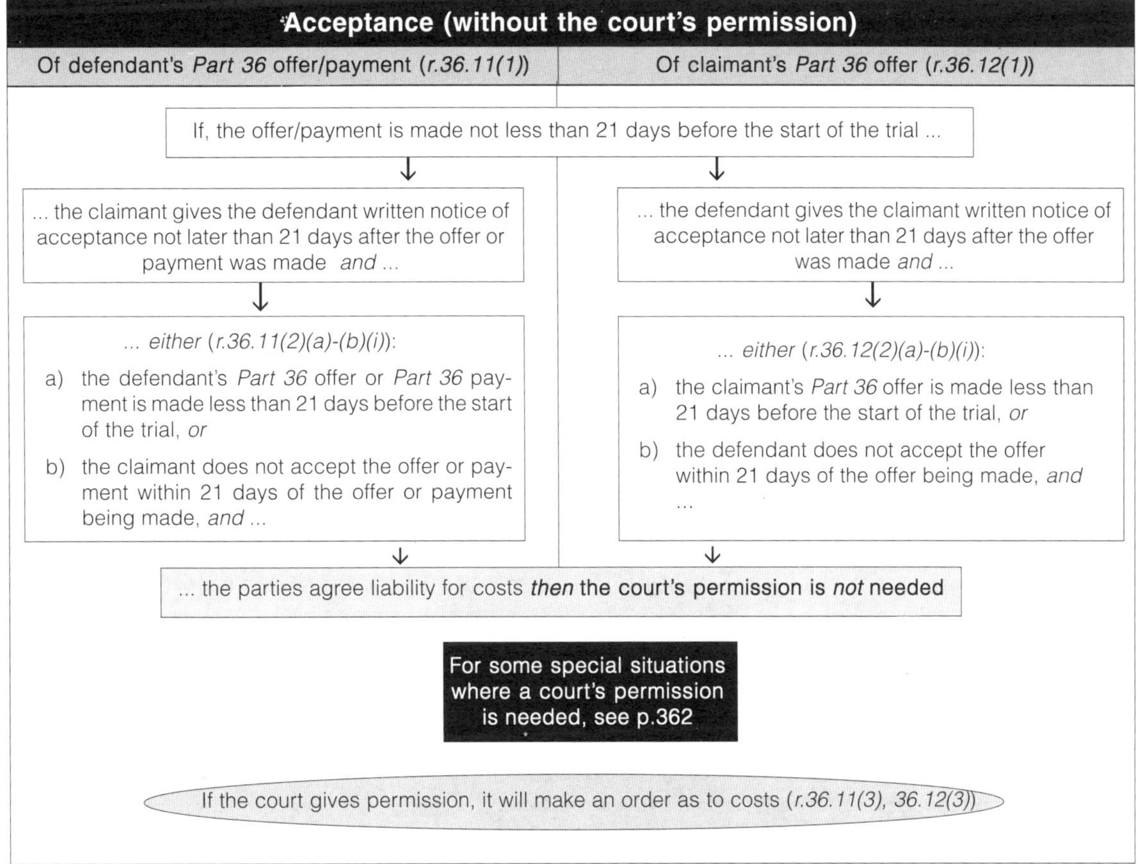

Acceptance (without the court's permission)
Of defendant's *Part 36* offer/payment (*r.36.11(1)*)
Of claimant's *Part 36* offer (*r.36.12(1)*)
If, the offer/payment is made not less than 21 days before the start of the trial ...
... the claimant gives the defendant written notice of acceptance not later than 21 days after the offer or payment was made *and* ...
... the defendant gives the claimant written notice of acceptance not later than 21 days after the offer was made *and* ...
... *either* (*r.36.11(2)(a)-(b)(i)*):
a) the defendant's *Part 36* offer or *Part 36* payment is made less than 21 days before the start of the trial, *or*
b) the claimant does not accept the offer or payment within 21 days of the offer or payment being made, *and* ...
... *either* (*r.36.12(2)(a)-(b)(i)*):
a) the claimant's *Part 36* offer is made less than 21 days before the start of the trial, *or*
b) the defendant does not accept the offer within 21 days of the offer being made, *and* ...
... the parties agree liability for costs *then* the court's permission is *not* needed
For some special situations where a court's permission is needed, see p.362
If the court gives permission, it will make an order as to costs (*r.36.11(3), 36.12(3)*)

➤ **Time of accepting an offer/payment:** a *Part 36* offer or a *Part 36* payment is accepted when notice of acceptance is received by the offeror (*r.36.8(5)*).

- Where an offer is made to settle the whole of a claim which comprises a money claim and a non-money claim, acceptance of the *Part 36* payment is treated as acceptance of the *Part 36* offer relating to the non-money claim (*r.36.4(4)*).
- If the claim includes a claim for provisional damages a claimant must, within 7 days of accepting a *Part 36* payment, apply to the court for an order for an award of provisional damages under *Part 41 r.41.2* (*r.36.7(5)*).
  - Money paid into court may not be paid out until this *Part 41* application is disposed of (*r.36.7(6)*).

B. Special situations

1 **Claim made by or on behalf of/against a child or patient (*r.36.18*)**

➤ Permission of the court is required to accept a *Part 36* offer or a *Part 36* payment.

➤ A court order is required for the payment out of a sum in court.

- If the court gives a claimant permission after a trial has started, the order deals with the whole costs of proceedings.

2 ***Part 36* offer or *Part 36* payment made by some, but not all, defendants (*r.36.17*)**

➤ A claimant **must** apply to court for:

- an order permitting a payment out in respect of any sum held in court, *and*
- such order as to costs as the court considers appropriate, *unless either:*

a) **defendants are sued jointly or in the alternative**, in which case the claimant need not seek the permission of the court (ie: *r.36.11(1)*, see top left of the box on p.361), where:

- the claimant discontinues against those defendants who have not made the offer/payment, *and*
- those defendants give written consent to the acceptance of the offer/payment, *or*

b) **a claimant alleges that the defendants have a several liability**, in which case the claimant may accept the offer/payment in accordance with (*r.36.11(1)*) (see top left of the box on p.361) and continue his claim against the other defendants if he is entitled to do so.

3 **Offer to settle made before proceedings commence (*r.36.10(4)*)**

➤ An offeree needs permission of the court to accept such an offer (or an associated payment) once proceedings have begun (*r.36.17*).

V Consequences

A. Offer to settle made before proceedings commence

➤ When making any order as to costs the court will consider any offer made before proceedings, if that offer (*r.36.10(2)-(3)*):

a) is expressed to be open for at least 21 days after the date on which it is made, *and*

b) if made by the defendant in the proceedings, includes an offer to pay the costs of the offeree up to the date 21 days after the date it was made, *and*

c) if the offeror is a defendant to a money claim:

i) the offeror makes a *Part 36* payment within 14 days of service of the claim form, *and*

ii) the amount of that *Part 36* payment is not less than the amount offered before proceedings began.

B. Prior to judgment

1 **Permission of the court not needed to accept *Part 36* offer or *Part 36* payment - costs**

➤ **Defendant accepts claimant's offer:** claimant entitled to costs up to the date on which the defendant serves notice of acceptance (*r.36.14*).

➤ **Claimant accepts defendant's offer or payment:** claimant entitled to costs up to the date of serving notice of acceptance (unless the court orders otherwise) (*r.36.13(1)*).

- If a *Part 36* offer or *Part 36* payment relates to only part of a claim and when the claimant serves notice of acceptance the claimant abandons the remainder of the claim, the claimant is entitled to costs up to the date of serving the notice of acceptance (unless the court orders otherwise) (*r.36.13(2)*).
- If the *Part 36* offer or *Part 36* payment states that a defendant's counterclaim has been taken into account in the offer/payment, the claimant's costs include any costs attributable to the counterclaim (*r.36.13(3)*).
- Costs under *r.36.13* are payable on a standard basis, if not agreed (*r.36.13(4)*) (see p.390).

2 **Permission of the court needed to accept *Part 36* offer or *Part 36* payment - costs**

➤ Costs are as the court orders.

3 **Effect of acceptance**

➤ The claim is stayed (*r.36.15(1)*).

- If the court's approval is needed the stay does not take effect until approval is given (*r.36.15(4)*). If approval is not needed the stay takes effect on acceptance.

➤ If the acceptance of a ***Part 36* offer** relates to **the whole claim** the stay is upon the terms of the offer and either party may apply to enforce those terms (*r.36.15(2)*).

➤ If a ***Part 36* offer** or a ***Part 36* payment** relate to **part of the claim,** the claim is stayed as to that part and the court decides costs (unless the parties have done so) (*r.36.15(3)*).

➤ Where a ***Part 36* offer** has been made and a party alleges that another party has not offered the terms and the party making the allegation may claim a remedy for breach of contract by apply to court without the need to start new proceedings (unless the court orders otherwise) (*r.36.15(6)*).

➤ Where a *Part 36* payment is accepted, the claimant obtains payment by making a request for payment in the practice form (*r.36.16*).

- If a payment to a claimant is a compensation payment (as defined in *SS(RB)A 1997 s.1*), the court may treat the money paid into court as being reduced by any sum equivalent to any recoverable benefits paid to the claimant since the date of the payment into court and may direct payment out accordingly (*r.36.23(5)*).

C. At trial

1 **The judge**

➤ The judge is generally not told that a *Part 36* payment has been made until all questions of liability and the amount of money to be awarded have been decided (*r.36.19(2)*).

- Circumstances where the judge may be told include where (*r.36.19(3)*):
  - the proceedings have been stayed following the acceptance of a *Part 36* offer/payment.
  - liability has been determined (before any assessment of the money claimed) and the fact that a *Part 36* payment has (or has not) been made may be relevant to costs in respect of the liability issue.

2 **Claimant does not do better than a *Part 36* offer (ie: judgment is not more advantageous than the terms of the offer) or a *Part 36* payment**

➤ Claimant pays the defendant's costs incurred after the latest date when the offer/payment could have been accepted without needing the court's permission (unless the court considers this unjust) (*r.36.20(2)*).

- Where a payment to a claimant is a compensation payment (as defined in *SS(RB)A 1997 s.1*), that claimant fails to better a *Part 36* payment if he fails to obtain judgment for more than the gross sum specified in the payment notice (*r.36.23(4)*).

3 **Claimant does better than a *Part 36* offer (ie: judgment is more advantageous than the terms of the offer)**

➤ The court may (unless it considers it unjust to do so (*r.36.21(4)*)) award the claimant:

a) **interest** for some or all of the period starting with the latest date on which the defendant could have accepted the offer without needing the court's permission (*r.36.21(2)*).

- Interest may not exceed a rate 10% above the base rate set by the Bank of England which is used as the basis for other banks' lending rates.
- The court may not award interest on interest.

b) **costs on an indemnity basis** (see p.390) from the latest date when the defendant could have accepted the offer without needing the court's permission and interest on those costs not exceeding 10% above the base rate set by the Bank of England as the basis for other banks' lending rates (*r.36.21(3)*).

➤ In considering whether it would be unjust to make the orders referred to in a) and b) above, the court takes into account all the circumstances including the (*r.36.21(5)*):

- terms of any *Part 36* offer.
- stage in proceedings when any *Part 36* offer/payment was made.
- information available to the parties at the time any *Part 36* offer/payment was made.
- parties' conduct with regard to giving or refusing to give information to enable a *Part 36* offer/payment to be evaluated.

Where a claim includes a claim under the *Fatal Accidents Act 1976* and the *Law Reform (Miscellaneous Provisions) Act 1934* the court has power to apportion money paid into court between the different claims (*r.37.4*)

I Allocation (and automatic transfer) (*Part 26*)

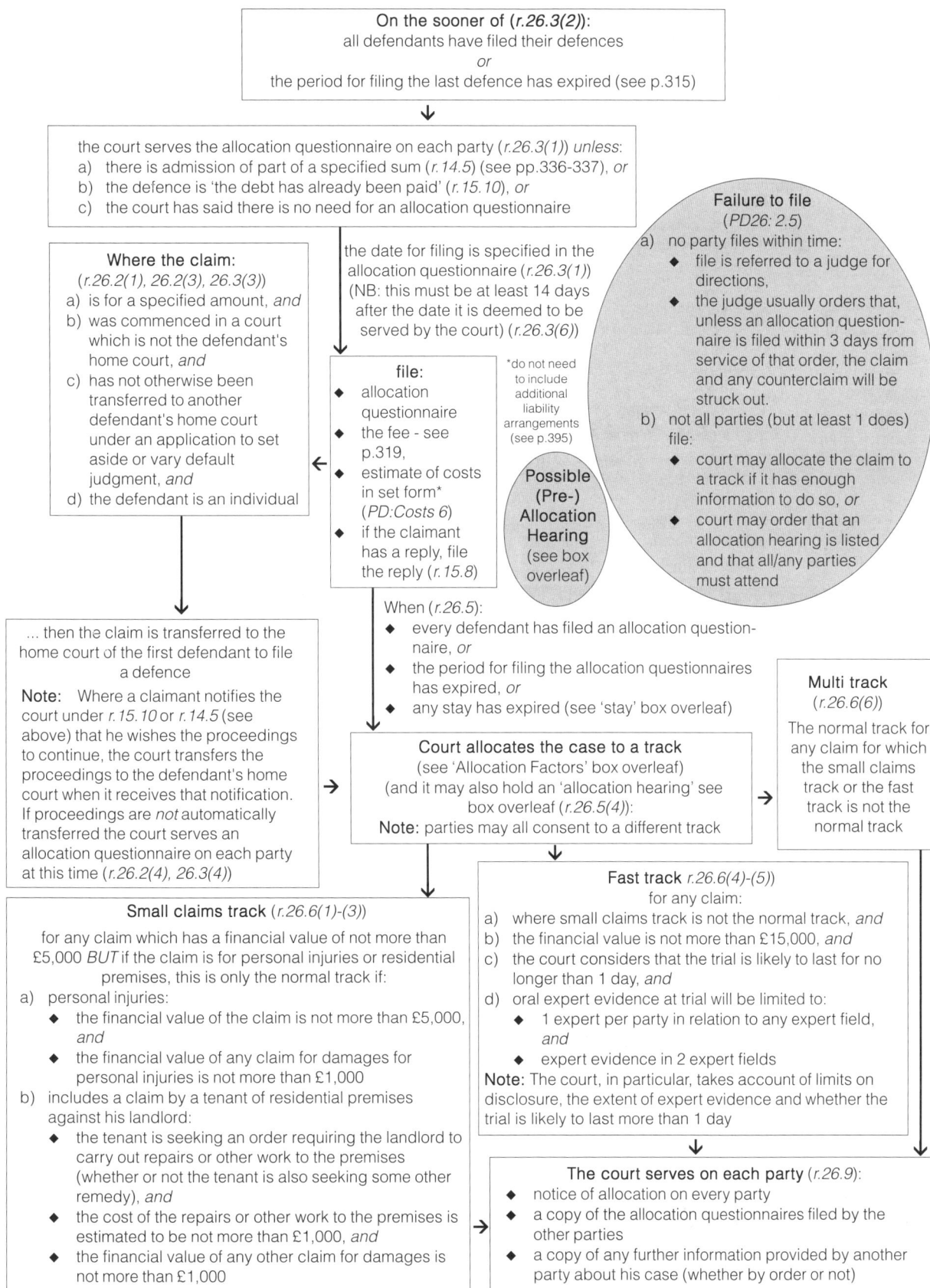

On the sooner of (*r.26.3(2)*):
all defendants have filed their defences
or
the period for filing the last defence has expired (see p.315)

the court serves the allocation questionnaire on each party (*r.26.3(1)*) *unless*:
a) there is admission of part of a specified sum (*r. 14.5*) (see pp.336-337), *or*
b) the defence is 'the debt has already been paid' (*r. 15.10*), *or*
c) the court has said there is no need for an allocation questionnaire

the date for filing is specified in the allocation questionnaire (*r.26.3(1)*) (NB: this must be at least 14 days after the date it is deemed to be served by the court) (*r.26.3(6)*)

Failure to file
(*PD26: 2.5*)
a) no party files within time:
- file is referred to a judge for directions,
- the judge usually orders that, unless an allocation questionnaire is filed within 3 days from service of that order, the claim and any counterclaim will be struck out.

b) not all parties (but at least 1 does) file:
- court may allocate the claim to a track if it has enough information to do so, *or*
- court may order that an allocation hearing is listed and that all/any parties must attend

file:
- allocation questionnaire
- the fee - see p.319,
- estimate of costs in set form* (*PD:Costs 6*)
- if the claimant has a reply, file the reply (*r. 15.8*)

*do not need to include additional liability arrangements (see p.395)

Possible (Pre-) Allocation Hearing (see box overleaf)

Where the claim:
(*r.26.2(1), 26.2(3), 26.3(3)*)
a) is for a specified amount, *and*
b) was commenced in a court which is not the defendant's home court, *and*
c) has not otherwise been transferred to another defendant's home court under an application to set aside or vary default judgment, *and*
d) the defendant is an individual

... then the claim is transferred to the home court of the first defendant to file a defence

Note: Where a claimant notifies the court under *r. 15.10* or *r. 14.5* (see above) that he wishes the proceedings to continue, the court transfers the proceedings to the defendant's home court when it receives that notification. If proceedings are *not* automatically transferred the court serves an allocation questionnaire on each party at this time (*r.26.2(4), 26.3(4)*)

When (*r.26.5*):
- every defendant has filed an allocation questionnaire, *or*
- the period for filing the allocation questionnaires has expired, *or*
- any stay has expired (see 'stay' box overleaf)

Court allocates the case to a track
(see 'Allocation Factors' box overleaf)
(and it may also hold an 'allocation hearing' see box overleaf (*r.26.5(4)*):
Note: parties may all consent to a different track

Multi track
(*r.26.6(6)*)
The normal track for any claim for which the small claims track or the fast track is not the normal track

Small claims track (*r.26.6(1)-(3)*)

for any claim which has a financial value of not more than £5,000 *BUT* if the claim is for personal injuries or residential premises, this is only the normal track if:

a) personal injuries:
- the financial value of the claim is not more than £5,000, *and*
- the financial value of any claim for damages for personal injuries is not more than £1,000

b) includes a claim by a tenant of residential premises against his landlord:
- the tenant is seeking an order requiring the landlord to carry out repairs or other work to the premises (whether or not the tenant is also seeking some other remedy), *and*
- the cost of the repairs or other work to the premises is estimated to be not more than £1,000, *and*
- the financial value of any other claim for damages is not more than £1,000

Fast track *r.26.6(4)-(5)*
for any claim:
a) where small claims track is not the normal track, *and*
b) the financial value is not more than £15,000, *and*
c) the court considers that the trial is likely to last for no longer than 1 day, *and*
d) oral expert evidence at trial will be limited to:
- 1 expert per party in relation to any expert field, *and*
- expert evidence in 2 expert fields

Note: The court, in particular, takes account of limits on disclosure, the extent of expert evidence and whether the trial is likely to last more than 1 day

The court serves on each party (*r.26.9*):
- notice of allocation on every party
- a copy of the allocation questionnaires filed by the other parties
- a copy of any further information provided by another party about his case (whether by order or not)

Allocation Factors (*r.26.7-26.8*)

- When deciding the track for a claim, the court shall have regard to:
  - the financial value, if any, of the claim.
    - The court may direct the claimant to justify the amount.
    - The amount should disregard:
      - any amount not in dispute, *and*
        1. Note: an amount for which the defendant does not admit liability is in dispute.
        2. Note: a part amount for which judgment has been entered (eg: summary judgment) is not in dispute.
        3. Note: a part amount claimed as a distinct item which the defendant admits he is liable for is not in dispute.
        4. Note: a sum offered and accepted in satisfaction of any item which is part of the claim is not in dispute.

        Note: Therefore, if there is a claim above £5,000 and the defendant makes, before allocation, an admission that reduces the amount in dispute to a figure below £5,000, the small claims track is the normal track. As to recovery of pre-allocation costs, the claimant can, before allocation, apply for judgment with costs on the amount of the claim that has been admitted.
      - any claim for interest, *and*
      - costs, *and*
      - any contributory negligence.
    - Where 2 or more claimants have started a claim (using 1 claim form) against the same defendant and each claimant's claim is separate from the other claimants, the court considers the financial value of each separately.
  - the nature of the remedy sought.
  - the likely complexity of the facts, law or evidence.
  - the number of parties or likely parties.
  - the value of any counterclaim or other *Part 20* claim (see p.347) and the complexity of any matters relating to it.
    - If there is more than 1 money claim (eg: where there is a *Part 20* claim) the court will not generally aggregate the claims but generally regards the largest of them as determining the financial value of the claims.
  - the amount of oral evidence which may be required.
  - the importance of the claim to persons who are not parties to the proceedings.
  - the views expressed by the parties (including any other information the parties may provide).
  - the circumstances of the parties.

Stay (*r.26.4, PD26: 3*)

- When filling in the allocation questionnaire, a party may request the proceedings be stayed while all try to settle.
- The court will stay proceedings for 1 month (unless it extends it further) if:
  - all parties request a stay, *or*
  - the court, on its own, considers that such a stay would be appropriate.
- The parties may apply to extend any stay. (This may be by letter to the court.)
  - The extension is generally for no more than 4 weeks unless clear reasons are given to justify a longer time.
- After a stay, the claimant must tell the court if a settlement has been reached.
- **No settlement:** If the claimant does not tell the court by the end of the period of the stay that a settlement has been reached, the court gives such directions as it considers appropriate.
- **Settlement:** Where the whole proceedings are settled during a stay, any of the following are treated as an application for the stay to be lifted:
  a) an application for a consent order (in any form) to give effect to the settlement, *or*
  b) an application for the approval of a settlement where a party is a person under a disability, *or*
  c) giving notice of acceptance of money paid into court in satisfaction of the claim or applying for money in court to be paid out.

Allocation Hearings or Pre-Allocation Hearings (*PD26: 2.4, 5, 6*)

- When there is *any* type of hearing or a special allocation hearing, the court may at any time before allocation:
  - dispense with the need for allocation questionnaires, hold an allocation hearing, make an order for allocation and give directions for case management, *or*
  - fix a date for allocation questionnaires to be filed and give other directions.
- Where the court orders a *special* allocation hearing, it gives the parties at least 7 days notice and brief reasons.
- A legal representative at an allocation hearing should be the person responsible for the case and *must* be familiar with the case and able to provide the court with information it is likely to need to take decisions about allocation and case management. He must also have sufficient authority to deal with any issues that arise.
- The court may also deal with summary disposal of issues at any pre-allocation hearing (eg: summary judgment).

The duty of consultation (*PD26: 2.3*)

- The parties should consult each other and co-operate in completing the allocation questionnaires.
- They should try to agree the case management directions which they will invite the court to make.
  - The process of consultation must not delay the filing of the allocation questionnaires.

J Small claims track (*Part 27*)

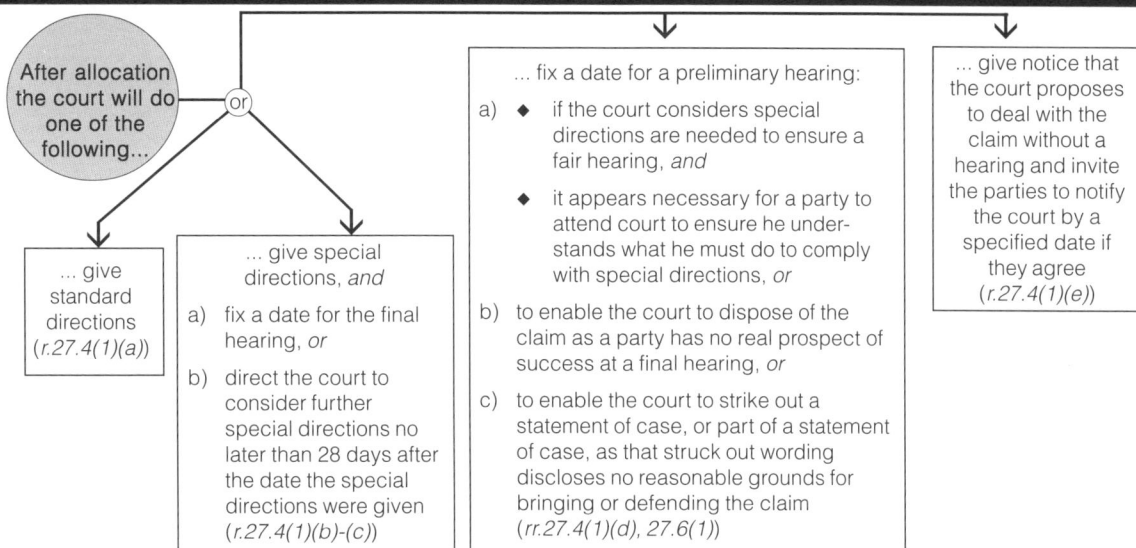

After allocation the court will do one of the following... or

... give standard directions (*r.27.4(1)(a)*)

... give special directions, *and*

a) fix a date for the final hearing, *or*

b) direct the court to consider further special directions no later than 28 days after the date the special directions were given (*r.27.4(1)(b)-(c)*)

... fix a date for a preliminary hearing:

a) ◆ if the court considers special directions are needed to ensure a fair hearing, *and*

◆ it appears necessary for a party to attend court to ensure he understands what he must do to comply with special directions, *or*

b) to enable the court to dispose of the claim as a party has no real prospect of success at a final hearing, *or*

c) to enable the court to strike out a statement of case, or part of a statement of case, as that struck out wording discloses no reasonable grounds for bringing or defending the claim (*rr.27.4(1)(d), 27.6(1)*)

... give notice that the court proposes to deal with the claim without a hearing and invite the parties to notify the court by a specified date if they agree (*r.27.4(1)(e)*)

The court gives the parties at least 21 days' notice of the date fixed for the final hearing (unless the parties agree to accept less notice), and informs them of the time allowed for the final hearing (*r.27.4(2)*)

Standard Directions

These are directions that include:

a) each party, at least 14 days before the date fixed for the final hearing, must file (at the court office) and serve on every other party copies of all documents (including expert's reports) on which he intends to rely at the final hearing (*r.27.4(3)*) (this includes signed witness statements (*PD27: App. A Forms B-E*)),

b) the original documents shall be brought to the hearing (*PD27: App. A Form A*)

c) the court must be informed immediately if the case is settled by agreement (*PD27: App. A Form A*)

Special Directions

Claims arising out of road accidents

The court directs that before the date of the hearing the parties shall try to agree the cost of the repairs and any other losses claimed, subject to the court's decision about whose fault the accident was (*PD27: App. A Form B*).

Claims arising out of building disputes, vehicle repairs and similar contractual claims

The court directs that:

a) the [claimant/defendant] shall deliver to the court [no later than] [with his copy of the documents] [a list of all items of work which he complains about and why, and the amount claimed for putting each item right]/[a breakdown of the amount claimed, showing work done and materials supplied], *and*

b) before the date of the hearing the parties shall try to agree the nature and cost of remedial work, subject to the court's decision about any other issue (*PD27: App. A Form C*).

Tenant's claim for return of deposits/ landlord's claim for damage caused

a) the [claimant/defendant] shall delivery copy documents showing each item of loss or damage for which he claims, and the amount he claims for the replacement or repair, *and*

b) before the date of the hearing the parties shall try to agree the nature and cost of any repairs and replacements, subject to the court's decision about any other issue (*PD27: App. A Form D*).

Other special directions are set out in *PD27: App. A Form F*

Holiday and wedding claims

If either party intends to show a video he must contact the court at once to make arrangements for him to do so and provide the other party with a copy of the video or an opportunity to see it (if he asks) at least 2 weeks before the hearing (*PD27: App. A Form E*)

1 Conduct of a hearing

- The court may, if all the parties agree, deal with the claim without a hearing (*r.27.10*).
- The court may adopt any method of proceeding at a hearing that it considers fair (*r.27.8(1)*).
  - Hearings are informal (*r.27.8(2)*).
- Strict rules of evidence do not apply (*r.27.8(3)*).
  - The court need not take evidence on oath (*r.27.8(4)*).
  - The court may limit cross-examination (*r.27.8(5)*).
    - Eg: a judge may (*PD27: 4.3*):
      - ask questions of any witness before allowing another person to do so, *or*
      - refuse to allow cross-examination of any witness until all the witnesses have given evidence-in-chief, *or*
      - limit cross-examination of a witness to a fixed time/subject/issue.
- The court must give reasons for its decision (*r.27.8(6),* see also *PD27: 5.1-5.8*).
- The hearing will generally be conducted in public (*PD27: 4.1(1)*).

2 Representation

- A case may be presented by a party, a lawyer or a lay representative (*PD27: 3.2(1)*).
  - A 'lay representative' is a person other than a barrister, a solicitor or a legal executive employed by a solicitor (*PD27: 3.1(2)*)
- A lay representative may not exercise his right of audience (*LR(RA)O 1999*, *PD27: 3.2(2)*):

  a) if his client does not attend the hearing, *or*

  b) at any stage after judgment, *or*

  c) on an appeal brought against any decision made by the district judge in the proceedings.

    - The court has a general discretion to hear anybody, even in circumstances excluded by the *LR(RA)O 1999* (*PD 27:3.3(3)*).
- A corporate party may be represented by any of its officers or employees (*PD27: 3.2(4)*).

3 Experts

- An expert may not give evidence at a hearing without the court's permission (*r.27.5*).

4 Non-attendance

Party does not attend and gives the court written notice (an '**Excuse Notice**'), at least 7 days before the hearing that he will not attend and in that notice requests the court to decide the claim in his absence	**Claimant** does not attend the hearing *and* no Excuse Notice is given	**Defendant** does not attend the hearing *or* give an Excuse Notice *and* the claimant attends or gives an Excuse Notice
↓	↓	↓
The court will take into account that party's statement of case and any other documents that party has filed with the court (*r.27.9(1)*)	The court may strike out the claim (*r.27.9(2)*)	The court may decide the claim on the basis of the claimant's evidence alone (*r.27.9(3)*)

If neither party attends, or gives notice, the court may strike out the claim and any defence or counterclaim (*r.27.9(4)*)

The court has a general power to adjourn a hearing, eg: a party wishes to attend but cannot do so for a good reason (*PD27: 6.2*)

Setting aside judgment and rehearing under *Part 27*

➤ A party may apply for an order setting aside judgment and for the claim to be reheard if (*r.27.11(1)*):

a) he was not present or represented at the hearing of the claim, *and*

b) did not give an Excuse Notice.

Procedure	➤ Party applies not more than 14 days after the day on which notice of the judgement was served on him (*r.27.11(2)*).
Grounds	➤ The court may grant the application only if the applicant (*r.27.11(3)*): a) had a good reason for not: i) attending, *or* ii) being represented, *or* iii) giving an Excuse Notice, *and* b) has reasonable prospect of success at the hearing.
Order	➤ The court fixes a new hearing for the claim. ➤ The new hearing may take place immediately after the hearing of the application and may be dealt with by the same judge.

Appeals under the small claims track

➤ An appeal from a decision of a small claims track court is made under *Part 52* as for other appeals (see p.403).

➤ However, for a small claims track appeal, unlike for other appeals:

- the appellant only needs to file the following documents (and no other documents are required) (*PD52: 5.8A*):
  - a sealed copy of the order being appealed, *and*
  - the order giving or refusing permission to appeal (and the reasons), *and*
  - a record of the reasons of the judgement of the lower court.
- the respondent may provide a skeleton argument, but is not required to do so (*PD52: 7.7A*).

K Fast Track

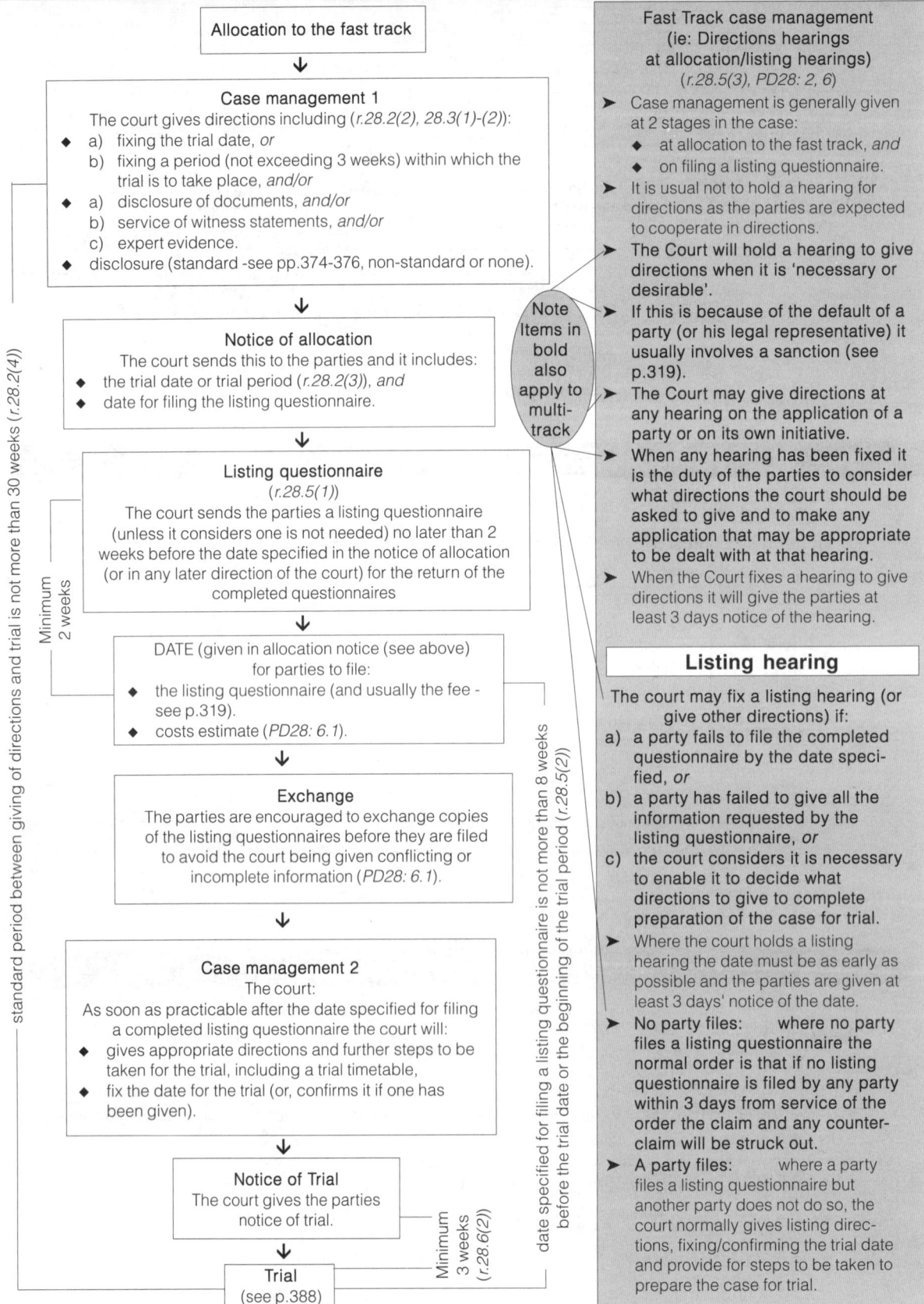

Allocation to the fast track

Case management 1

The court gives directions including (*r.28.2(2), 28.3(1)-(2)*):

- a) fixing the trial date, *or*
  b) fixing a period (not exceeding 3 weeks) within which the trial is to take place, *and/or*
- a) disclosure of documents, *and/or*
  b) service of witness statements, *and/or*
  c) expert evidence.
- disclosure (standard -see pp.374-376, non-standard or none).

Notice of allocation

The court sends this to the parties and it includes:

- the trial date or trial period (*r.28.2(3)*), *and*
- date for filing the listing questionnaire.

Listing questionnaire

(*r.28.5(1)*)

The court sends the parties a listing questionnaire (unless it considers one is not needed) no later than 2 weeks before the date specified in the notice of allocation (or in any later direction of the court) for the return of the completed questionnaires

DATE (given in allocation notice (see above) for parties to file:

- the listing questionnaire (and usually the fee - see p.319).
- costs estimate (*PD28: 6.1*).

Exchange

The parties are encouraged to exchange copies of the listing questionnaires before they are filed to avoid the court being given conflicting or incomplete information (*PD28: 6.1*).

Case management 2

The court:

As soon as practicable after the date specified for filing a completed listing questionnaire the court will:

- gives appropriate directions and further steps to be taken for the trial, including a trial timetable,
- fix the date for the trial (or, confirms it if one has been given).

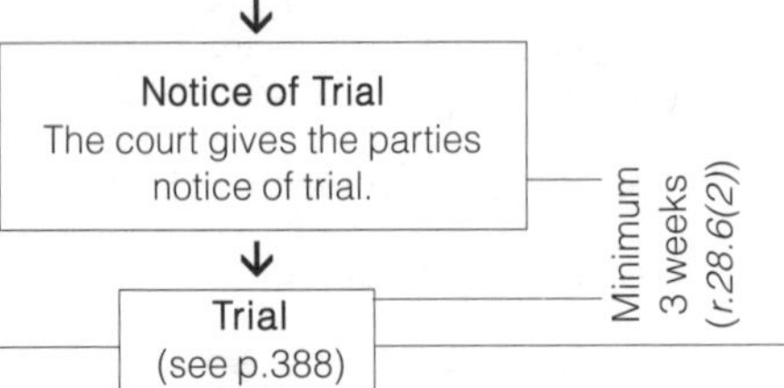

standard period between giving of directions and trial is not more than 30 weeks (*r.28.2(4)*)

Minimum 2 weeks

date specified for filing a listing questionnaire is not more than 8 weeks before the trial date or the beginning of the trial period (*r.28.5(2)*)

Note Items in bold also apply to multi-track

Fast Track case management (ie: Directions hearings at allocation/listing hearings)

(*r.28.5(3), PD28: 2, 6*)

- ➤ Case management is generally given at 2 stages in the case:
  - at allocation to the fast track, *and*
  - on filing a listing questionnaire.
- ➤ It is usual not to hold a hearing for directions as the parties are expected to cooperate in directions.
- ➤ **The Court will hold a hearing to give directions when it is 'necessary or desirable'.**
- ➤ **If this is because of the default of a party (or his legal representative) it usually involves a sanction (see p.319).**
- ➤ **The Court may give directions at any hearing on the application of a party or on its own initiative.**
- ➤ **When any hearing has been fixed it is the duty of the parties to consider what directions the court should be asked to give and to make any application that may be appropriate to be dealt with at that hearing.**
- ➤ When the Court fixes a hearing to give directions it will give the parties at least 3 days notice of the hearing.

Listing hearing

The court may fix a listing hearing (or give other directions) if:

a) a party fails to file the completed questionnaire by the date specified, *or*

b) a party has failed to give all the information requested by the listing questionnaire, *or*

c) the court considers it is necessary to enable it to decide what directions to give to complete preparation of the case for trial.

- ➤ Where the court holds a listing hearing the date must be as early as possible and the parties are given at least 3 days' notice of the date.
- ➤ **No party files: where no party files a listing questionnaire the normal order is that if no listing questionnaire is filed by any party within 3 days from service of the order the claim and any counter-claim will be struck out.**
- ➤ A party files: where a party files a listing questionnaire but another party does not do so, the court normally gives listing directions, fixing/confirming the trial date and provide for steps to be taken to prepare the case for trial.

Directions on allocation (*PD28: 3-4*)

- The court's first concern is to ensure that issues between parties are identified and necessary evidence is prepared + disclosed. If in doubt about directions, the court holds a hearing (listed as promptly as possible).
- The court may have regard to any document filed with an allocation questionnaire containing further information *provided* that the document states either that its contents have been agreed with every other party or that it has been served on every other party and when it was served.

Agreed directions	No agreed directions
The court may approve these if: ◆ the parties have filed these, *and* ◆ the court considers that they are suitable, *and* ◆ they set out a timetable (referring to calendar dates) for steps to prepare the case, *and* ◆ they include a date or a trial period (which must not be longer than 3 weeks) when it is proposed that the trial will take place (where the latest proposed date for the trial or the end of the trial period is not later than 30 weeks from the date of the directions order, *and* ◆ they include provisions about disclosure of documents, *and* • these may limit disclosure to standard disclosure between all parties or to less than that, *and/or* • these may direct that disclosure take place by supply of copy documents without a list (but it must in that case either direct that the parties must serve a disclosure statement with the copies or record that they have agreed to disclose in that way without such a statement) ◆ they include provision about both factual and expert evidence (eg: none is required), *and* ◆ they contain other appropriate provisions.	The court's general approach is: ◆ to give directions for the filing and service of any further information required to clarify either party's case, ◆ to direct standard disclosure (see pp.374-376) between the parties, ◆ to direct the simultaneous exchange of witness statements, ◆ to give directions for a single joint expert unless there is good reason not to do so, ◆ if no directions for a single expert are given: • to direct simultaneous exchange of experts' reports • (if experts' reports are not agreed) to direct a discussion between experts and preparation of a report. **Note:** If the court does not approve agreed directions but gives directions itself without a hearing, it takes the parties' proposed directions into account in deciding on directions

- **Typical timetable:** (periods from notice of allocation)
  - Disclosure — 4 weeks
  - Exchange of witness statements — 10 weeks
  - Exchange of experts' reports — 14 weeks
  - Sending of listing questionnaires by the Court — 20 weeks
  - Filing of completed listing questionnaires — 22 weeks
  - Hearing — 30 weeks

If the court thinks that some/all steps in the timetable are unnecessary it may omit them - eg: if pre-action protocols have been complied with or other steps have already been taken

- **Varying the Court's directions** - the procedure is outside this book but is set out in *r.28.4* and *PD28: 4*.

Directions on listing (*PD28: 7*)

- The court must confirm or fix the trial date, specify the place of trial and give a time estimate.
  - The trial date must be fixed and the case listed on the footing that the hearing will end on the same calendar day as that on which it commenced.
- The parties should seek to agree directions (see practice box above) and may file the proposed order. (The court may make an order in those terms or it may make a different order.)
  - Agreed directions should include provisions about evidence (including expert evidence - see p.387), a trial timetable and time estimate, preparation of a trial bundle, other matters needed to prepare the case for trial.
- **Varying the Court's directions** - the procedure is outside this book but is set out in *r.28.4* and *PD28: 4*.

Fast track standard directions (*PD28: Appendix*)

- Standard Directions are listed in the Appendix to *PD28* but include provisions on:
  - FURTHER STATEMENTS OF CASE
  - REQUESTS FOR FURTHER INFORMATION
  - DISCLOSURE OF DOCUMENTS
  - WITNESSES OF FACT
  - QUESTIONS TO EXPERTS
  - REQUESTS FOR INFORMATION ETC.
  - DOCUMENTS TO BE FILED WITH LISTING QUESTIONNAIRES
  - DATES FOR FILING LISTING QUESTIONNAIRES AND THE TRIAL
  - DIRECTIONS FOLLOWING FILING OF LISTING QUESTIONNAIRE

L Multi-Track

Allocation to the multi-track

Case management 1
The court (*r.29.2(1)-(2)*):
- a) gives directions for the management of the case and sets a timetable for the steps to be taken between the giving of directions and the trial, *or*
  b) fixes:
  i) a case management conference, *and/or*
  ii) a pre-trial review.
- gives any other directions relating to case management.
- fixes the trial date or period in which the trial is to take place.

Notice of allocation
The court sends this to the parties and it includes (*r.29.2(23)*):
- the trial date or trial period, *and*
- date for filing the listing questionnaire.

Listing questionnaire
(*r.29.6(1)* and *(4)*)
The court sends the parties a listing questionnaire (unless it considers one is not needed) no later than 14 days before the date specified in the notice of allocation (or in any later direction of the court) for the return of the completed questionnaires

Minimum 14 days

DATE (given in allocation notice (see above) for parties to file:
- the listing questionnaire(and usually the fee - see p.319).
- costs estimate (*PD29: 8.1*).

date specified for filing a listing questionnaire is not more than 8 weeks before the trial date or the beginning of the trial period (*PD29: 8.1(3)*)

Exchange
The parties are encouraged to exchange copies of the listing questionnaires before they are filed to avoid the court being given conflicting or incomplete information (*PD29: 8.1(5)*)

→

Pre-trial review
The Court *may* (but does not have to) decide to:
- hold a pre-trial review, *or*
- cancel a previously fixed pre-trial review.

If so, it serves a notice of its decision at least 7 days before the date fixed for the hearing/ cancelled hearing

←

Case management 2
The court (*r.29.8, PD29: 8.1(6)*):
As soon as practicable after:
a) each party has filed a completed listing questionnaire, *or*
b) the court has held a listing hearing, *or*
c) the court has held a pre-trial review,
the court will:
- set a trial timetable (*unless* one has already been fixed, or the court considers that it would be inappropriate to do so),
- fix or confirm the date for the trial or the week within which the trial is to begin.

→

Notice of Trial
The Court gives the parties notice of the trial timetable and the date or trial period

←

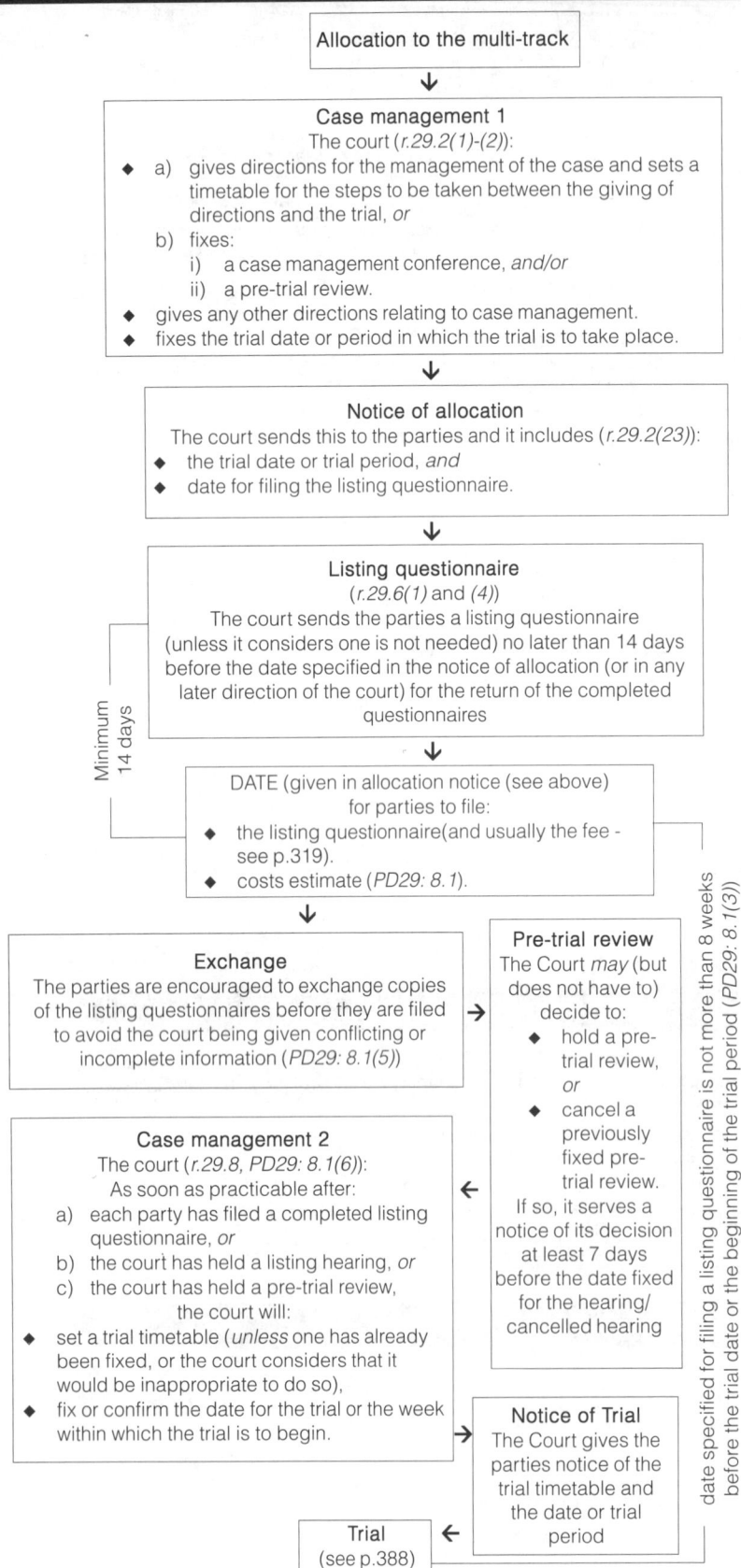

Trial
(see p.388)

Multi-Track case management (ie: Directions hearings)
(*r.29.3, PD29: 3, 5, 8*)

➤ Any time after the claim has been allocated the court may fix:
- a case management conference, *or*
- a pre-trial review.

Note: at such hearings, if a party is legally represented, that representative must be familiar with the case and have authority to deal with any issues that are likely to arise.

➤ A party must apply to court if he wishes to vary any dates fixed for:
- a case management conference
- a pre-trial review
- return of a listing questionnaire
- the trial
- the trial period.

Note: Any date set by the court or the *CPR* for doing any act may not be varied by the parties if it makes it necessary to vary any of these dates.

➤ The court may give directions without a hearing.

➤ Whether or not the court has fixed a trial date or period, it may either:
- give directions for certain steps to be taken and fix a date for a case management conference or a pre-trial review to take place after they have been taken, *or*
- fix a date for a case management conference.

➤ **Items in bold in the case management box for 'Fast Track' apply here.**

➤ If the court fixes a hearing to give directions it gives the parties at least 3 days' notice of the hearing unless a pre-trial review (see chart left).

➤ Where a party applys for a direction not included in a set case management timetable he must do so as soon as possible so as to minimise the need to change the timetable.

Listing hearing

➤ **Items in bold in this section under 'Fast Track' apply here too.**

➤ Where the court holds a listing hearing the date must be as early as possible and the parties are given at least 3 days' notice of the date (unless a pre-trial review - see left).

➤ **A party files:** where a party files a listing questionnaire but another party does not do so, the court will fix a listing hearing. Whether or not the defaulting party attends the hearing, the court will normally fix or confirm the trial date and make other orders about the steps to be taken to prepare the case for trial.

Directions on allocation (*PD29: 4*)

- The court tailors directions to the needs of the case and the steps which the parties have already taken to prepare the case of which it is aware. In particular it will have regard to the extent to which any pre-action protocol has or (as the case may be) has not been complied with.
- The court's first concern is to ensure that issues between parties are identified and necessary evidence is prepared + disclosed. If in doubt about directions, the court holds a hearing (listed as promptly as possible).
- The court may have regard to any document filed with an allocation questionnaire containing further information *provided* that the document states either that its contents have been agreed with every other party or that it has been served on every other party and when it was served.

Agreed directions	No agreed directions
The court may approve these if: ◆ the parties have filed these, *and* ◆ the court considers they are suitable, *and* ◆ they set out a timetable (referring to calendar dates) for steps to prepare the case, *and* ◆ they include a date/trial period (which must not be later than reasonably necessary), *and* ◆ they include provisions about disclosure of documents, *and* • these may limit disclosure to standard disclosure between all parties or to less than that, *and/or* • these may direct that disclosure take place by supply of copy documents without a list (but it must in that case either direct that the parties must serve a disclosure statement with the copies or record that they have agreed to disclose in that way without such a statement) ◆ they include provision about both factual and expert evidence (eg: none is required), *and* ◆ they contain other appropriate provisions.	The court's general approach is: ◆ to give directions for the filing and service of any further information required to clarify either party's case, ◆ to direct standard disclosure (see pp.374-376), ◆ to direct the simultaneous exchange of witness statements, ◆ to give directions for a single joint expert unless there is good reason not to do so, ◆ if no directions for a single expert are given: • to direct simultaneous exchange of experts' reports • (if experts' reports are not agreed) to direct a discussion between experts and preparation of a report NB: if expert evidence is required on issues of liability and amount of damages, the court may direct that the exchange of reports that relate to liability are exchanged simultaneously and those relating to amount of damages are exchanged sequentially. ◆ to list a case management conference after the date for compliance with directions, ◆ to specify a trial period. **Note:** If the court does not approve agreed directions but gives directions itself without a case management conference, it takes any proposed directions into account in deciding on directions.

- **Varying the Court's directions** - the procedure is outside this book but is set out in *PD29: 6*.

Directions on listing (*PD29: 9*)

- The court must fix the trial date or week, give a time estimate and fix the place of trial.
- The parties should seek to agree directions and may file the proposed order. (The court may make an order in those terms or it may make a different order.)
  - Agreed directions should include provisions about evidence (especially expert evidence - see p.387), a trial timetable and time estimate, preparation of a trial bundle, other matters for preparation for trial.
- **Varying the Court's directions** - the procedure is outside this book but is set out in *PD29: 6*.

What happens at a Case Management conference? (*PD29: 5*)

- A review of the steps taken in the preparation of the case (especially compliance with any directions).
- The court gives directions about steps to progress of the claim in accordance with the overriding objective.
- The court records agreements reached between parties about issues + conduct of the claim.
- Topics usually considered include:
  - whether the claimant has made his claim clearly (especially any amount he is claiming),
  - whether any amendments are required to the claim, a statement of case or any other document,
  - what disclosure of documents (if any) and factual evidence is necessary,
  - what expert evidence is reasonably required and how and when it should be obtained and disclosed,
  - what arrangements should be made to clarify, obtain further information or put questions to experts,
  - whether it is just and saves costs to order a split trial or the trial of one or more preliminary issues.
- The court will not at this stage give permission to use expert evidence unless it can identify each expert by name or field in its order and say whether his evidence is to be given orally or by the use of his report.
  - A party who obtains expert evidence before obtaining a direction about it does so at his own risk as to costs, *except* where he obtained the evidence in compliance with a pre-action protocol.
- The parties and their legal advisers should:
  - ensure that all documents that the court is likely to ask to see are brought to the hearing,
  - consider whether the parties should attend,
  - consider whether a case summary will be useful (containing a brief chronology of the claim, the issues of fact which are agreed or in dispute and the evidence needed to decide them, maximum 500 words and prepared by the claimant and agreed with the other parties if possible) , *and*
  - consider what orders each wishes to be made and give notice of them to the other parties.

M Disclosure and Inspection (*Part 31*)

I Generally

➤ 'Disclosure' is a statement by a party that a document exists or has existed (*r.31.2*).

➤ The duty to disclose is limited to a document which is or has been in a party's control (*r.31.8*), ie:

a) it is or was in his physical possession, *or*

b) he has or has had a right to possession of it, *or*

c) he has or has had a right to inspect or take copies of it.

Documents and copies

➤ A 'document' is anything in which information of any description is recorded (*r.31.4*).

- ◆ A 'copy' is anything onto which information recorded in a document has been copied (by whatever means, whether directly or indirectly) (*r.31.4*).
  - A copy which contains a modification, obliteration or other marking or feature on which a party intends to rely or which adversely affects his case or another party's case or supports another party's case is a separate document (*r.31.9*).
  - A party need not disclose more than one copy of a document (*r.31.9*).

➤ Any duty of disclosure continues until the proceedings are concluded (*r.31.11(1)*).

- ◆ If a document comes to a party's notice during proceedings, he must immediately notify every other party (*r.31.11(2)*).
- ◆ Disclosure and/or inspection may take place in stages if the parties agree or the court so directs (*r.31.13*).

➤ A party may not rely on any document which he fails to disclose or to which he does not permit inspection, unless the court gives permission for him to rely on it (*r.31.21*).

Claim to withhold disclosure or inspection (*r.31.19*)

➤ A person may apply, without notice (and supported by evidence), for an order pemitting him to withhold disclosure of a document on the ground that disclosure would damage the public interest.

Order for specific disclosure or inspection (*r.31.12*)

➤ A court may make an order for specific disclosure or inspection (*r.31.12(1)*).

Discovery	Inspection
➤ An order that a party must (*r.31.12(2)*): ◆ disclose documents or classes of documents specified in the order, *and/or* ◆ carry out a search to the extent specified in the order, *and/or* ◆ disclose any documents located as a result of that search.	➤ An order that a party must permit inspection of a document (or class of documents) which that party disclosed, being a document which: ◆ adversely affects his own case, *or* ◆ adversely affects another party's case, *or* ◆ supports another party's case ... ... but is a document which that party considered would be disproportionate to the issues in the case to permit inspection (*r.31.12(3)*) .

II Disclosure

Before proceedings / By a person not party to proceedings		
	Before proceedings	By a non party
Application (supported by evidence)	Under *SCA 1981 s.33* or *CCA 1984 s.52* (*Sch. 2 - r.16*)	Under *SCA 1981 s.34* or *CCA 1984 s.53* (*Sch.2 - r.17*)
Grounds	a) the respondant is likely to be party to subsequent proceedings, *and* b) the applicant is likely to be a party to those proceedings, *and* c) if proceedings had started the respondant's duty of standard disclosure would extend to the documents, *and* d) disclosure before the start of proceedings is desirable to: i) dispose fairly of the anticipated proceedings, *or* ii) assist in resolving the dispute without proceedings, *or* iii) save costs.	a) the documents are likely to support the case of the applicant or adversely affect the case of another party, *and* b) disclosure is necessary to *either*: i) dispose fairly of the proceedings, *or* ii) save costs.
Order	◆ Must ... • specify the documents or classes of documents for disclosure, *and* • require the respondant to specify those document which are no longer in his control or in respect of which he claims a right or duty to withhold inspection. ◆ May ... • require the respondant to indicate what has happened to documents which he no longer controls, *and* • specify the time and place for disclosure and inspection.	

- 'Standard disclosure' requires a party to disclose only the documents (*r.31.6*):
  - on which he relies, *and*
  - which adversely affect his own case or another party's case or support another party's case, *and*
  - which he is required to disclose by a *PD*.
- Standard disclosure is normal (*PD31: 1.1*) and is ordered unless the court directs otherwise (*r.31.5(1)*).
  - The court may dispense with or limit standard disclosure (*r.31.5(2)*).
  - The parties may agree in writing to dispense with or limit standard disclosure (in which case the agreement should be lodged with the court (*PD31: 1.4*))(*r.31.5(3)*).

Duty of search (*r.31.7*)

- For standard disclosure a party has a duty to make a reasonable search for documents which (*r.31.7(1)*):
  - adversely affect his own case or another party's case or support another party's case, *or*
  - he is required to disclose by a *PD*.
- 'Reasonableness' in ascertained by reference to a number of factors, include (*r.31.7(2)*):
  - the number of the documents,
  - the nature and complexity of the proceedings,
  - the ease and expense of retrieval of any particular document,
  - the significance of any document which is likely to be located as a result of the search.

Procedure for standard disclosure (*r.31.10*)

Parties	➤ Each party must make and serve on every other party a list in practice *Form N265* (*r.31.2, PD31: 3.1*). ◆ The parties may agree in writing to disclose documents without making a list and to disclose without making a disclosing statement (*r.31.8*).
List	➤ The list must: ◆ identify the documents in a convenient order and manner as concisely as possible (*r.31.10(3)*) • Usually this means - listed in date order, numbered consecutively, and consisely described. A large number of documents in a particular category may be listed as such (*PD 31: 3.2*) ◆ indicate documents for which a right or duty to withold inspection is claimed *and* those documents which are no longer in that party's control (*plus* what has happened to those documents) (*r.31.10(4)*). ◆ include a disclosure statement which (*r.31.10(4)-(5)*): • sets out the extent of the search, *and* ■ The statement should state that the belief of the disclosing party that the extent of the search is reasonable in all the circumstances. ■ Attention should be drawn to limitations adopted for proportionality reasons and reasons should should given (eg: expense, difficulty, marginal relevance) (*r.31.7(3)*), *PD 31: 4.2*) • certifies that the party making the disclosure understands the duty to disclose, *and* • certifies that the best of that party's knowledge he has carried out the duty to disclose. ◆ if the person making the statement is a company, firm, association or other organisation (*r.31.10(7)*): • identify the person making the statement (name, address, position (*PD 31: 4.3*)), *and* • explain why that person is considered the appropriate person to the make the statement.

III Inspection

➤ When a document has been disclosed to a party, that party has the right to inspect that document *unless* (*r.31.3*):

a) the document is no longer in the possession of the party who disclosed it, *or*

b) the party disclosing the document has a right or duty to withhold inspection, *or*

c) the party disclosing the document ...

... (which adversely affects his own case or another party's case or supports another party's case) ...

... considers that it would be disproportionate to issues to permit inspection and he stated in his disclosure statement that inspection of the document would not be permitted as to do so would be disproportionate.

➤ A party may inspect a document mentioned in (*r.31.14*):

- a statement of case, a witness statement or a witness summary, *or*
- an affidavit, *or*
- an expert's report (although material instructions on the basis of which the report was prepared need only be available for inspection if the court so orders having reasonable grounds for believing that the statement of instructions is inaccurate or incomplete).

Inspection of witness statements ... or not	
➤ A witness statement which stands as evidence in chief is open to inspection during the course of the trial unless the court otherwise directs (*r.32.13(1)*). ➤ However, a party may apply for a direction that a witness statement should not be open for inspection (*r.32.13(2)*).	
Grounds for the court's refusing inspection	➤ The court is satisfied that the statement (or words or passages in the statement) should not be open to inspection due to (*r.32.13(3)-(4)*): a) the interests of justice, *or* b) the public interest, *or* c) the nature of any expert medical advice in the statement, *or* d) the nature of any confidential information in the statement, *or* e) the need to protect the interests of any child or patient.

➤ A party must give written notice of a wish to inspect a document. The party who disclosed the document must permit inspection not more than 7 days after receipt of this notice (*r.31.15*).

- A party may request a copy and if that party also undertakes to pay reasonable copying costs, the party who made the disclosure must supply a copy not more than 7 days after receiving the request.

➤ If a party accidentally allows inspection of a privileged document, the party who inspected it may use it, or its contents, only with the permission of the court (*r.31.20*).

Privilege

➤ Some documents are recognised by law as 'privileged', they must be disclosed *but* do not have to be available for inspection. The following categories of documents are privileged:

legal professional privilege (items 1–3):

1 **Solicitor-client correspondence,** for the purpose of legal advice.

2 **Solicitor-third party correspondence,** if created after litigation is commenced, *or* if created with a view to starting litigation or to obtain evidence or advice.

3 **Client-third party correspondence,** if the primary purpose at the time of creation was to see if legal advice should be obtained for existing or contemplated litigation.

4 **'Without prejudice' evidence of negotiations** (unless as evidence of a settlement which was reached where the dispute is whether any settlement was reached at all!).

5 **Public policy material,** eg: defence, NSPCC, social work and probation records.

6 **Material incriminating a party to the proceedings** (in UK criminal or penal proceedings).

➤ Secondary evidence of a privileged document is admissible, unless prevented by an injunction (but see 'Professional ethics' in the 'Conduct' section).

➤ Privilege belongs to the client, so the solicitor may not waive it without the client's authority.

N Evidence

I Generally

➤ The court has a general power to control evidence by giving directions as to (*r.32.1*):

- the issues which require evidence, *and*
- the nature of the evidence which the court requires to decide those issues, *and*
- the way in which evidence is to be placed before the court ...

  ... even if this involves excluding evidence which would be otherwise admissible (*r.32.2*).

  - Any fact which needs to be proved by the evidence of a witness is usually proved *either* at trial (by the witnesses' oral evidence given in public) *or* at any other hearing by evidence in writing (*r.32.3*).
    - At a **hearing other than trial**, a party may rely on his statement of case or his application notice provided that the statement or application notice are verified by a statement of truth (*r.32.6*).
  - The court may allow a witness to give evidence through a video link or by other means (*r.32.3*).

➤ Contempt of court proceedings may be brought (by the Attorney General, or with the court's permission) against a person who makes, or causes to be made, a false statement in a document verified by a statement of truth without an honest belief in the statement's truth (*r.32.14*).

Notice to admit or produce documents (*r.32.19*)
◆ A party is deemed to admit the authenticity of a document disclosed to him under *Part 31* (see pp.374-378) unless he serves notice that the wishes the document to be proved at trial.
◆ A notice must be served by the latest date for serving witness statements or within 7 days of disclosure of the document - whichever is later.

Notice to admit facts (*r.32.18*)	
A party may serve notice on another party requiring him to admit facts, or part of the case, specified in the notice	
Service	◆ No later than 21 days before the trial.
Admission	◆ The admission may be used against the party making it only in the proceedings in which the notice to admit is served and only by the party who served the notice. ◆ The court may allow a party to amend or withdraw an admission on such terms as it thinks fit.

II Witnesses (Statements, summaries)

➤ A witness statement is a written statement signed by a person; it contains the evidence which that person would be allowed to give orally (*r.32.4(1)*).

- The court (*r.32.4(2)-(3)*):
  - **will order** a party to serve on the other parties any witness statement on which that party intends to rely on in relation to any issues of fact to be decided at trial, *and*
    - At trial where a witness is called to give oral evidence, a witness statement will stand as a witnesses' evidence in chief unless the court orders otherwise (*r.32.5(2)*).
    - If a witness statement (or summary) is not served within the time limit specified by the court, the witness may not be called to give oral evidence unless the court gives permission (*r.32.10*).
    - If a party who has served a witness statement does not call the witness to give evidence at trial or put the witness statement in as hearsay evidence, any other party may put the witness statement in as hearsay evidence (*r.32.5(5)*).
  - **may direct** the sequence in which statements are served and whether statements are to be filed.
- A witness statement must comply with the relevant *PD* (*r.32.8*).
  - If a statement does not comply with *Part 32* or *PD32*, the court may refuse to admit it as evidence and may refuse to allow costs arising from its preparation) (*PD32: 25.1*).

Witness statements

➤ A witness statement must (*PD32: 17-20*):

- be headed with the name and number of the proceedings and the Court or Division.
- state at the top right hand corner of the first page:
  - the party on whose behalf it is made, *and*
  - the initials and surname of the witness, *and*
  - the number of the statement in relation to that witness, *and*
  - the identifying initials and number of each exhibit referred to, *and*
  - the date the statement was made.
- if practicable, be in the witnesses' own words.
- be expressed in the first person.
- state the full name of the witness, the witnesses' place of residence (or if he is making the statement in a professional or business capacity - the address at which he works, his position and the name of his firm/employer).
- the witness' occupation (or if the witness has none, his description).
- whether the witness is a party to the proceedings or is the employee of such a party.
- indicate which statements are from the witnesses' own knowledge and which are from his information and belief (and any source for such information and belief).
- be verified by a statement of truth: 'I believe that the facts stated in this witness statement are true' (see p.324).

➤ Any exhibit should be verified and identified by the witness.

- If a party is required to serve a witness statement for use at trial but cannot obtain a witness statement, that party may apply to court for permission to serve a witness summary instead of the statement (*r.32.9(1)*).
  - The application is an application without notice.
  - A 'witness summary' is a summary of the evidence (if known) which would be included in a witness statement or (if the evidence is not known) matters about which the party serving the summary wishes to question the witness (*r.32.9(2)*).

Plans, photographs, models, etc (*r.33.5*)

- Where evidence (eg: a plan, a photograph, business records which may be given in evidence under *CEA 1995 s.9*, or a model) is **not**:

  a) contained in a witness statement, affidavit or an expert's report, *or*

  b) to be given orally at trial, *or*

  c) evidence in respect of which a hearsay notice must be given under *r.32.2*, ...

  ... that evidence may only be receivable if the party intending to rely on the evidence gives notice to the other parties (unless the court orders otherwise).

  - Where evidence is to be given as evidence of a fact, notice must be given not later than the last day for serving witness statements, *unless either*
    - the evidence forms part of expert evidence, in which case notice is given when the expert's report is served on the other party, *or*
    - there is not to be a witness statement *or* the evidence is solely to disprove an allegation made in a witness statement, in which case notice is at least 21 days before the hearing the evidence is to be put.
  - If evidence is produced for a reason other than as evidence of fact or expert evidence, the party intending to rely on it must give at notice at least 21 days before the hearing.
- A party must give other parties every opportunity to inspect the evidence and agree its admission without further proof.

III Opinion

- A witness may only testify as to matters observed by him and may not give his *opinion* about those matters.
- Opinion 'evidence' is inadmissible unless it is:

  1 expert opinion (*CEA 1972 s.3(1)*).
  - This is opinion on any relevant matter on which the expert is qualified to give expert evidence.

  2 perception (*CEA 1972 s.3(2)*).
  - The witness conveys relevant facts personally perceived by him. The reason for this relaxation is that it is not always possible to separate facts from inferences.

IV Expert evidence

- See p.387.

V Hearsay

Hearsay - a statutory meaning

➤ Hearsay is 'a statement made by someone *other* than the person *now* giving evidence, intended to prove the truth of the matter stated' whether first hand hearsay (ie: reported directly from a source) or multiple hearsay (coming from a source *via* intermediaries).

Hearsay - a plain English (!) meaning

➤ Hearsay is an assertion, other than one made by a person while giving oral evidence in the proceedings, if the assertion is used to prove the truth of what it asserts.

Hearsay procedure (*CEA 1995*)

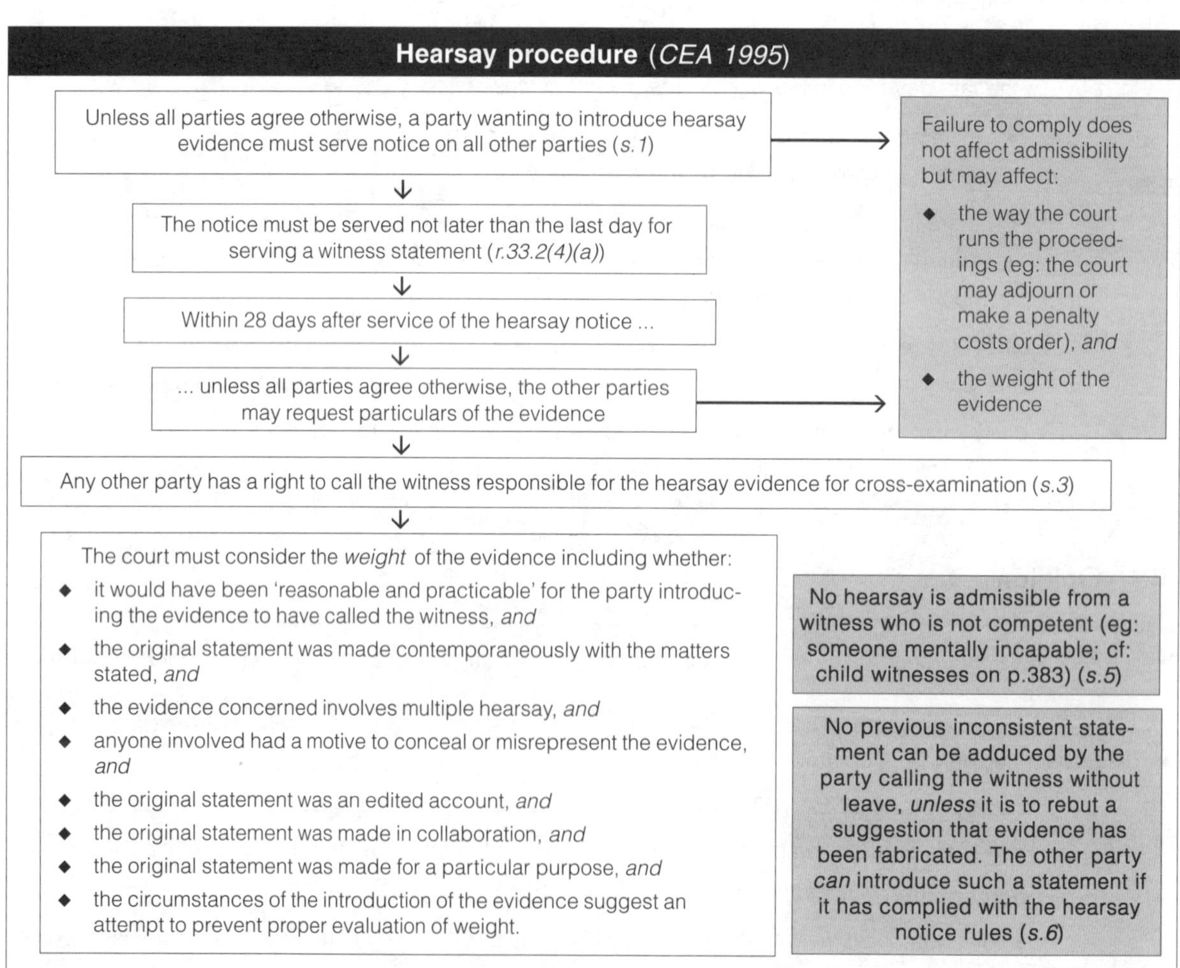

Unless all parties agree otherwise, a party wanting to introduce hearsay evidence must serve notice on all other parties (s.1)
The notice must be served not later than the last day for serving a witness statement (r.33.2(4)(a))
Within 28 days after service of the hearsay notice ...
... unless all parties agree otherwise, the other parties may request particulars of the evidence
Failure to comply does not affect admissibility but may affect:
◆ the way the court runs the proceedings (eg: the court may adjourn or make a penalty costs order), and
◆ the weight of the evidence
Any other party has a right to call the witness responsible for the hearsay evidence for cross-examination (s.3)
The court must consider the weight of the evidence including whether:
◆ it would have been 'reasonable and practicable' for the party introducing the evidence to have called the witness, and
◆ the original statement was made contemporaneously with the matters stated, and
◆ the evidence concerned involves multiple hearsay, and
◆ anyone involved had a motive to conceal or misrepresent the evidence, and
◆ the original statement was an edited account, and
◆ the original statement was made in collaboration, and
◆ the original statement was made for a particular purpose, and
◆ the circumstances of the introduction of the evidence suggest an attempt to prevent proper evaluation of weight.
No hearsay is admissible from a witness who is not competent (eg: someone mentally incapable; cf: child witnesses on p.383) (s.5)
No previous inconsistent statement can be adduced by the party calling the witness without leave, unless it is to rebut a suggestion that evidence has been fabricated. The other party can introduce such a statement if it has complied with the hearsay notice rules (s.6)

Published works

➤ Published works and records are admissible as evidence of the facts contained (*CEA 1995 s.7*).

Contents of a hearsay notice

➤ A hearsay notice must state:

a) identify the hearsay evidence (*r.33.2(3)(a)*), *and*

b) state that the party serving the notice will rely on the hearsay evidence at trial (*r.33.2(3)(b)*), *and*

c) if the witness is not being called to give evidence, gives the reason why the witness will not be called (*r.33.2(3)(c)*).

- If the witness is not being called to give evidence, the party intending to rely on the hearsay evidence must, when he serves the witness statement inform the other parties that the witness is not being called to give evidence and give the reason why the witness is not being called (*r.33.2(3)(c)*).
- If the hearsay is in a document, the party proposing to rely on the hearsay evidence must supply a copy to any party who requests a copy (*r.32.2(4)(b)*).

Cross-examination	Credibility
➤ Any other party may apply to the court for permission to call the maker of statement to be cross-examined on the contents of the statement (*r.33.4(1)*). ◆ An application must be made not more than 14 days after the day on which the notice is served on the applicant (*r.33.4(2)*).	➤ If any other party wishes to call evidence to attach the credibility of the person who made the statement, that party must give notice of this intention to the party who proposes to give hearsay evidence (*r.33.5(1)*). ◆ Notice must be given not more than 14 days after the day on which the hearsay notice was served on the party who wishes to dispute credibility (*r.33.5(2)*).

➤ 1 notice may deal with more than 1 witness.

➤ The duty to give a notice of intention to rely on hearsay evidence does not apply (*r.33.3*):

a) to evidence at hearings other than trials, *or*

b) an affidavit or a witness statement which is to be used at trial but which does not contain hearsay evidence, *or*

c) to a statement which a party to a probate action wishes to put in evidence and which is alleged to have been made by the person whose estate is the subject of the proceedings, *or*

d) where a *PD* excludes the requirement to give such a notice.

Business records

➤ Although hearsay, business records are admissible in evidence (*CEA 1995 s.9(1)*).

◆ To be accepted as a business record, a document must be certified by an officer of the business (*CEA 1995 s.9(2)*).

◆ Computerised statements are also *prima facie* admissible as hearsay (*CEA 1995 s.1-2*).

O Trial preparations

I Making up the trial bundle (*r.39.5, PD39: 3*)

Steps

1 Check through the court's case management directions to see where the trial will be.

2 Check whether any relevant hearings are needed to 'flesh out' existing directions (eg: listing hearings, case management conferences, pre-trial review).

3 The court will consult the parties when it sets a timetable for a trial under (*r.39.4*):

- *r.28.6* (fast track - fixing/confirming the trial date and giving directions), *or*
- *r.29.8* (multi-track - setting a trial timetable and fixing/confirming the trial date or week).

4 The contents of the trial bundle should be agreed where possible.

5 **Not more than 7 days and not less than 3 days before the start of the trial**, the claimant's solicitor files the trial bundle containing copies of (NB: originals should be available at trial):

- the claim form and all statements of case,
- a case summary and/or chronology where appropriate,
- requests for further information and responses to the requests,
- any notices of intention to rely on evidence (eg: photographs) (see p.381) which are *not*:
  - contained in a witness statement, affidavit or experts report, *or*
  - being given orally at trial, *or*
  - hearsay evidence,
- all witness statements being relied on as evidence,
- any witness summaries,
- any medical reports and responses to them,
- any experts' reports and responses to them,
- any order giving directions as to the conduct of the trial,
- any notices of intention to use hearsay evidence (see p.383),
- any other necessary documents.

Trial bundles should be paginated and indexed with a description of each document. If the total number of pages is more than 100, place numbered dividers between groups of documents. The bundle should be contained in a ring binder or lever arch file. Where there is more than 1 bundle, each should be distinguishable (eg: by different colours or letters). If there are numerous bundles, a core bundle should be prepared containing the core documents essential to the proceedings, with references to supplementary documents in the other bundles

6 The parties should also agree where possible that:

- documents contained in the bundle are authentic even if not disclosed, *and*
- documents in the bundle may be treated as evidence of facts stated within even if a hearsay notice has not been served (see p.383).

7 Where it is not possible to agree the contents of the bundle, a summary of the points on which the parties are unable to agree should be included.

8 The party filing the trial bundle should supply identical bundles to all the parties to the proceedings and for the use of the witnesses.

NB: a reading list together with an estimated length of reading time and an estimated length of the hearing signed by all advocates is also required to be lodged.

II Should counsel be instructed?

Steps

1. **A brief - always needed if a barrister is instructed**
2. **A conference may be necessary**
3. **The barrister's fee**

1. A brief - always needed if a barrister is instructed

- A brief is the traditional presentation of the case to the barrister who will appear at the hearing.
- The brief should include:
  - the heading of the action, *and*
  - a list of enclosures being forwarded to counsel (eg: client's statement, witness statements, pleadings, any LSC funding certificate, experts' reports, *relevant* correspondence, pleadings, setting down bundle, trial bundle, counsel's earlier advice, etc).
- It should then:
  - identify the client.
  - set out *both* sides of the case.
  - indicate the solicitor's view, and draw attention to where advice is specifically needed.
  - formally request counsel to carry out the task required.
- The back sheet should be endorsed with:
  - the title of the action.
  - a definition of what the instructions are.
  - counsel's name and that of his chambers.
  - the solicitor's firm's name, address and reference.
  - if relevant, the LSC funding reference number.

Note: the third person is traditionally used in writing to counsel.

2 A conference may be necessary

- This is useful if the facts are complex, or if counsel wishes to assess a client as a witness, or to fully comprehend and assess his injuries.
  - The solicitor should arrange this with the counsel's clerk if it is thought necessary.
- A written opinion may be specifically requested.
  - Costs will not be allowed unless the court decides the need for the conference was reasonable.

3 The barrister's fee

- If LSC funding covers it, the LSC will pay the fee.
- A solicitor negotiates the fee on behalf of a private client. The solicitor is liable to counsel for the fee, so a solicitor should ensure that he has been put in funds by a client before the barrister is instructed.
  - The apperance fee is payable once the brief is delivered, but it is usually waived or reduced if the action settles before the hearing.
  - The fee covers 1 day, unless otherwise agreed. A 'refresher' is due on subsequent days.

III Ensuring attendance of witnesses or taking depositions (*Part 34*)

➤ The solicitor must check the availability of witnesses.

➤ Sometimes witnesses may not attend court voluntarily and it is necessary to compel them to do so by a witness summons.

- **Expert witnesses:** may prefer to be summonsed as the obligation helps break appointments.
- **Police officers:** *must* be summonsed, as they will not otherwise give evidence in a civil matter.

Witness summons (*r.34.2 - 34.7, PD34: 1, 3*)		
Purpose:		A witness summons is a document issued by the court requiring a witness to: ◆ attend court to give evidence, *and/or* ◆ produce documents to the court
Time		➤ General rule: must be served ***at least 7 days*** before the date on which the witness is required to attend. ◆ A court may change this time limit.
Procedure for issue	Steps 1	A witness summons must be in the specified form.
	2	There must be a separate witness summons for each witness.
	3	Obtain the court's permission to issue the summons if summons is to be issued: a) less than 7 days before the date of the trial, *or* b) for a witness to attend court to give evidence or to produce documents on any date except the date fixed for the trial, *or* c) for a witness to attend court to give evidence or to produce documents at any hearing except the trial.
	4	Issue the summons - 2 copies of the witness summons should be filed with the court for sealing. ◆ 1 copy will be kept on the court file. **Note:** A witness summons is issued on the date entered on the summons by the court.
Procedure for service	Steps 1	A witness summons will be served by the court *unless* the issuing party indicates in writing, at the time of issue, that he will serve it himself.
	2	Prepare the 'witness sum' to pay the witness for travelling expenses and loss of time as follows: ◆ the witness's expenses for travelling to court and returning to his home or place of work, *and* ◆ a sum for time during which earnings or benefit are lost (or a lesser sum it may be proved the witness will lose by attending court.
	3	Decide who is to serve the witness summons (see below).
	4a	**Self-service:** 1 Notify the court in writing that self-service will be the method of service. 2 Serve the witness summons and offer the witness the 'witness sum' at the time.
	4b	**Service by the court:** 1 Deposit, in the court office, the 'witness sum' 2 The court will serve the witness summons

Depositions (*r.34.8 - 34.11*)

➤ At times, a party may wish to apply for a witness to be examined *before* a hearing or trial.

- Such a witness is called a 'deponent' and his evidence is called a 'deposition'.
  - The examination is usually conducted as if the witness were giving evidence at a trial.

➤ A deposition may be given in evidence at a hearing or trial *unless* the court orders otherwise.

- However, the court *may* require a deponent to attend the hearing and give evidence orally.

➤ If deposition evidence is to be used, notice must be served at least 21 days before the hearing /trial.

➤ If a deposition is used at trial, it is treated as a witness statement for the purposes of prior inspection.

IV Expert evidence (*Part 35*)

- ➤ **Needed?** Expert evidence is restricted to what is reasonably required to resolve the proceedings (*r.35.1*).
  - ◆ If a claim is on the fast track, the court will not direct an expert to attend a hearing unless it is necessary in the interests of justice (*r.35.2(2)*).
- ➤ **Duty:** An expert has an overriding duty to help the court on the matters within his expertise (*r.35.3*).
- ➤ **Permission:** No party may call an expert or use an expert's report without the court's permission (*r.35.4(1)*).
  - ◆ To apply for permission a party must (*r.35.4(2), 35.13*):
    - identify the field in which he wishes to rely on expert evidence, *and*
    - identify, where practicable, the expert in that field on whose evidence he wishes to rely, *and*
    - disclose the evidence to the other parties.
  - ◆ The court may limit the amount of the expert's fees and expenses that the party who wishes to rely on the expert may recover from any other party (*r.35.4(4)*).
- ➤ **The report:** Expert evidence must be given in a written report unless the court directs otherwise (*r.35.5(1)*).
- ➤ **Questions:** A party may ask an expert written questions about his report.
  - ◆ The answers become part of the report.
  - ◆ Unless the court orders otherwise, or the parties agree, questions:
    - may be put once only, *and*
    - must be put within 28 days of service of the expert's report (and be copied to solicitors), *and*
    - must be for the purpose only of clarification of the report.
  - ◆ Not answering means the evidence may be disregarded and have costs penalties.
  - ◆ The party instructing the expert must pay the fees for the questions (*PD35: 4.3*).
- ➤ **Joint experts:** Where 2 or more parties each wish to submit expert evidence the court may direct that the evidence on that issue is given by 1 joint expert only (*r.35.7*).
  - ◆ Each instructing party must give a copy of its instructions to the other party (*r.35.8*).
  - ◆ The court has a wide discretion to make orders as to the expert's role and his fees(*r.35.8*).
  - ◆ The instructing parties are usually jointly and severally liable for the expert's fees and expenses (*r.35.8*).
- ➤ **Court's discretion:** The court has a wide discretion with regard to experts. It may eg: direct that the experts discuss certain matters between themselves, prepare statements of (non-binding) agreed and non-agreed issues, give the expert directions (particularly if the expert requests them), etc.
- ➤ **Instructions to an expert:** are not privileged against disclosure but the court will not order disclosure of a specific document or allow cross-examination of the expert in court, *unless* it thinks there are reasonable grounds to consider the instructions were inaccurate or incomplete. If the court thinks so, it will allow the cross-examination where it appears to be in the interests of justice to do so (*r.35.10(4), PD35: 3*).

Content of the expert's report (*r.35.10, PD35*)

- ➤ The experts report should be addressed to the court and must contain:
  - ◆ the substance of all material instructions (written *or* oral), on the basis of which the report was written,
  - ◆ details of the expert's qualifications,
  - ◆ details of any literature or other material on which the expert has relied in making the report,
  - ◆ details of who carried out any test or experiment which the expert has used for the report and whether or not the test or experiment has been carried out under the expert's supervision,
  - ◆ the qualifications of the person who carried out any such test or experiment,
  - ◆ (if there is a range of opinion on matters in the report), a summary of it, and reasons for his own opinion,
  - ◆ a summary of the conclusions reached,
  - ◆ At the end: a statement that the expert understands his duty to the court and has complied with it,
  - ◆ A statement of truth (see p.324): ' I believe that the facts I have stated in this report are true and that the opinions I have expressed are correct.'

P The trial

Steps

1 The claimant's side makes the opening speech

- This involves taking the judge through the statements of case and introducing agreed exhibits.
- The judge may dispense with this (particularly in fast track cases - *PD28: 8.2*).

2 The claimant gives evidence

- This is done by oral examination, but examination-in-chief is conducted by using the witness statement exchanged previously, unless the court decides otherwise.
- The sequence of questioning is:
  - examination-in-chief by the claimant's side,
  - cross-examination by the defendant's side,
  - re-examination (on points arising from the cross-examination) by the claimant's side.
- The defendant's case must be put to the claimant during cross-examination.
- Each side should check the admissibility rules (see p.379 et seq).

3 The claimant's side presents evidence

- This is done by oral examination of the witnesses.
- The sequence of questioning is:
  - examination-in-chief by the claimant's side. (This is conducted by using the witness statements exchanged previously, unless the court decides otherwise.)
  - cross-examination by the defendant's side,
  - re-examination (on points arising from the cross-examination) by the claimant's side.
- The defendant's case must be put to the witness.
- Each side should check the admissibility rules (see p.379 et seq).
- If a witness gives consistently unfavourable or adverse answers to the surprise of the claimant, the claimant's side should ask the judge to declare the witness hostile.
  - If the judge does so, previously inconsistent statements can be put to the witness (see *CEA 1995 s.6* and the law on hearsay p.382).

4 The defendant's side makes its opening speech

- The defendant's side may make an opening speech.
- The judge may dispense with this (particularly in fast track cases - *PD28: 8.2*).

cont. 5 **The defendant gives evidence**

- This is done by oral examination, but examination-in-chief is conducted by using the witness statement exchanged previously, unless the court decides otherwise.
- The sequence of questioning is:
  - examination-in-chief by the defendant's side,
  - cross-examination by the claimant's side,
  - re-examination (on points arising from the cross-examination) by the defendant's side.
- The claimant's case should be put to the defendant.
- Each side should check the admissibility rules (see p.379 et seq).

6 **The defendant's side presents the evidence**

- This is done by oral examination of the witnesses.
- The sequence of questioning is:
  - examination-in-chief by the defendant's side. (This is conducted by using the witness statements exchanged previously, unless the court decides otherwise.)
  - cross-examination by the claimant's side,
  - re-examination (on points arising from the cross-examination) by the defendant's side.
- The claimant's case must be put to the witness.
- Each side should check the admissibility rules (see p.379 et seq).
- If a witness gives consistently unfavourable or adverse answers to the surprise of the defendant, the defendant's side should ask the judge to declare the witness hostile.
  - If the judge does so, previously inconsistent statements can be put to the witness (*CEA 1995 s.6* and see the law on hearsay p.382).

7 **The defendant's side's closing speech**

- The defendant may make a closing speech.

8 **The claimant's side's closing speech**

- The claimant may make a closing speech.

9 **Judgment is given and any necessary orders are made**

Are leading questions allowed?		
Examination-in-chief	✗	(except to obtain a denial of the other party's case)
Cross examination	✓	
Re-examination	✗	(except to obtain a denial of the other party's case)

Q Costs

I Basis on which costs are awarded

➤ Costs awarded are a *reasonable* amount in respect of all costs *reasonably* incurred (*r.44.4(1)*).

➤ There are 2 bases on which the Court may assess and award costs (the choice is up to the judge)(*r.44.4(2)*):

1 **Standard basis (most usual) (*r.44.4(2)*)**
- The costs must also be proportionate to the matters in issue.
- Doubts over what is 'reasonable' or 'proportionate' are resolved in favour of the paying party.

2 **Indemnity basis (rare) (*r.44.4(3)*)**
- Doubts over what is 'reasonable' are resolved in favour of the receiving party.

II Duty to notify client of costs orders

➤ Where a party has a solicitor and the party is not present when the order is made, the party's solicitor must notify his client in writing of the costs order *and* why the order was made (*r.44.2*).

- This notification must be no later than 7 days after the solicitor receives notice of the order (*r.44.2*).

III Costs orders and the court's discretion

➤ The court may make an order about costs at any stage in a case (*PD:Costs 8.3(1)*).

➤ The court has discretion as to (*r.44.3(1)*):
- whether costs are payable by one party to another, *and*
- the amount of those costs, *and*
- when costs are to be paid.

Costs may also be agreed between the parties

The court may at any stage in a case order any party to file an estimate of costs and to serve copies on all other parties

➤ If the court makes a costs order (*except* an order for fixed costs) it may either (*r.44.7*):
- make a summary assessment of the costs (see p.393), *or*
- order detailed assessment of the costs by a costs officer (see p.394).

➤ **General rule:** the unsuccessful party is ordered to pay the costs of the successful party (*r.44.3(2)*).

➤ **Not using the general rule:** in deciding what order (if any) to make about costs, a court has regard to all the circumstances, including (*r.44.3(4) - 44.3(5)*):
- **the conduct of all the parties before (especially the extent of any compliance with any pre-action protocol) and during the proceedings, *and***
- whether it was reasonable for a party to raise, pursue or contest a particular allegation or issue, *and*
- whether a claimant who has wholly or partly succeeded in his claim, exaggerated his claim, *and*
- whether a party has succeeded on part of his case, even if he has not been wholly successful, *and*
- any payment into court (or admissible offer to settle) made by a party which is drawn to the court's attention (whether or not made in accordance with *Part 36* (see also pp.358-364)).

If the court decides to make an order about costs ... (*r.44.3, PD:Costs 8.5*)

➤ **General rule:** the unsuccessful party is ordered to pay the costs of the successful party.

- If the factors on the previous page apply, the court may use its discretion to make one of several possible orders, including the following:

Order	Effect	Usual reasoning of court
costs *or* costs in any event	The 'winner' in the costs order is entitled to costs for the relevant part of the proceedings, whatever other costs orders are made in the proceedings	The loser's conduct is unreasonable *or* costs relate to a collateral issue
costs in the case *or* costs in the application	The 'winner' in the costs order, at the end of the proceedings, is entitled to costs for the relevant part of the proceedings	Costs are preliminary to trial and conduct of both parties is reasonable
costs reserved	The decision about costs is deferred to a later occasion. If no later order is made the costs will be costs in the case	It is not yet possible to make a decision on the reasonableness of either party's conduct
Claimant's/ Defendant's costs in the case/ application	◆ If the 'winner' in the costs order is awarded costs at the end of the proceedings, he is entitled to his costs for the relevant part of the proceedings ◆ If any other party is awarded costs at the end of the proceedings, the party in whose favour the final costs order is made is not liable to pay the costs of any other party for the relevant part of the proceedings	Named party's conduct is only considered reasonable if he succeeds later at trial. The loser's conduct is unreasonable
costs thrown away	Where, eg: a judgment or order is set aside, the 'winner' in the costs order is entitled to the costs which have been incurred as a consequence. This includes the costs of: ◆ preparing for + attending any hearing where the judgment/order which has been set aside was made, ◆ preparing for + attending any hearing to set aside the judgment or order in question, ◆ preparing for + attending any hearing at which the court orders an adjournement, ◆ any steps taken to enforce a judgment or order which was later set aside.	The loser's conduct is unreasonable *or* costs relate to a collateral issue
costs of and caused by	Where, eg: a costs order is made on an application to amend a statement of case, the 'winner' in the costs order is entitled to costs of preparing for + attending the hearing and costs of any consequential amendments to his documents	The loser's conduct (which may be reasonable) causes the other party to incur consequential costs
costs here and below	The 'winner' in the costs order is entitled to his costs in respect of the proceedings in the court making the order and also (generally) to costs of the proceedings in any lower court	The 'winner' was correct in having the hearing in a higher court during the proceedings
no order as to costs *or* each party pays its own costs	Each party is to bear his own costs of the relevant part of the proceedings, whatever costs order the court makes at the end of the proceedings	Merits (or lack of merits) of both sides are equal
Costs forthwith	The 'winner' in the costs order, is entitled to costs and to have these assessed immediately.	Costs are unusually heavy or loser's conduct is unreasonable and the court wishes to express disapproval

Possible costs orders (*r.44.3(6)-(8)*)

- pay a proportion of another party's costs
- pay a stated amount in respect of another party's costs
- pay costs from or until a certain date only
- pay costs incurred before proceedings have begun
- pay costs relating to particular steps taken in the proceedings
- pay costs relating only to a distinct part of the proceedings
- pay interest on costs from or until a certain date, including a date before judgment

Where the court has ordered a party to pay costs, it may order an amount to be paid on account before the costs are assessed

Factors the court takes into account in deciding the amount of costs (*r.44.5*)

- the conduct of all the parties, including in particular:
  - conduct before and proceedings, *and*
  - the efforts made, if any, before and during the proceedings in order to try to resolve the dispute.
- the amount or value of any money or property involved.
- the importance of the matter to all the parties.
- the particular complexity of the matter or the difficulty or novelty of the questions raised.
- the skill, effort, specialised knowledge and responsibility involved.
- the time spent on the case.
- the place where, and the circumstances in which, work or any part of it was done.

IV Costs at trial

A. Which type of costs rules apply for costs at trial?

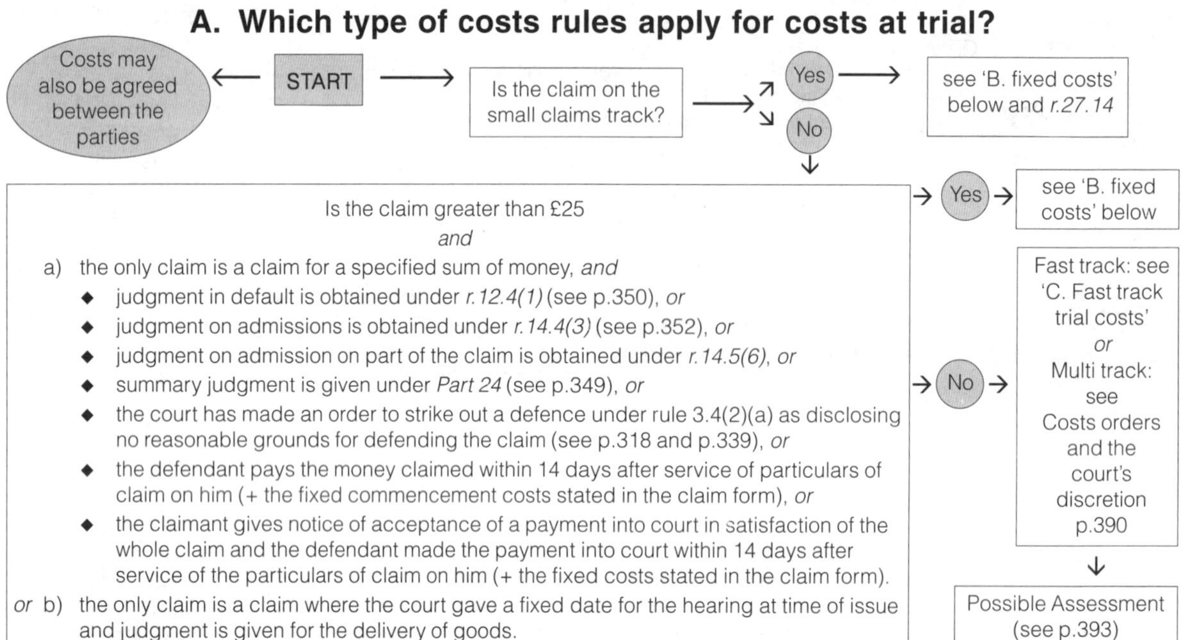

Costs may also be agreed between the parties
START
Is the claim on the small claims track?
Yes
see 'B. fixed costs' below and r.27.14
No
Is the claim greater than £25
and
a) the only claim is a claim for a specified sum of money, and
judgment in default is obtained under r.12.4(1) (see p.350), or
judgment on admissions is obtained under r.14.4(3) (see p.352), or
judgment on admission on part of the claim is obtained under r.14.5(6), or
summary judgment is given under Part 24 (see p.349), or
the court has made an order to strike out a defence under rule 3.4(2)(a) as disclosing no reasonable grounds for defending the claim (see p.318 and p.339), or
the defendant pays the money claimed within 14 days after service of particulars of claim on him (+ the fixed commencement costs stated in the claim form), or
the claimant gives notice of acceptance of a payment into court in satisfaction of the whole claim and the defendant made the payment into court within 14 days after service of the particulars of claim on him (+ the fixed costs stated in the claim form).
or b) the only claim is a claim where the court gave a fixed date for the hearing at time of issue and judgment is given for the delivery of goods.
Yes
see 'B. fixed costs' below
No
Fast track: see 'C. Fast track trial costs'
or
Multi track: see Costs orders and the court's discretion p.390
Possible Assessment (see p.393)

B. Fixed costs (*Part 45*)

➤ The amount of fixed costs (solicitors charges) claimable are:

- fixed commencement costs by reference to Table 1 in *Part 45*. The bands are:
  - the value of the claim exceeds £25 but does not exceed £500
  - the value of the claim exceeds £500 but does not exceed £1,000
  - the value of the claim exceeds £1,000 but does not exceed £5,000 *or* the only claim is for delivery of goods and no value is specified or stated on the claim form
  - the value of the claim exceeds £5,000

and

- certain additional costs for certain types of service of documents, *and*
- the amount claimed, or the value of the goods claimed if specified, in the claim form is to be used for determining the band in the table that applies to the claim, *and*
- fixed costs on judgment entry *but* only if the claimant has claimed fixed commencement costs on the claim form *and* if he is given judgment for certain specified types of claim (set out in Table 2 in *Part 45*).

C. Fast track trial costs (*Part 46*)

➤ **General rule** - this applies *only* where, *at the date of the trial*, the claim is allocated to the fast track: The amount of costs is awarded for an advocate who prepares for and appears at the trial of a claim. Costs are based on value of the claim and are given by the following table:

'Value of claim'	Up to £3,000	More than £3,000 but not more than £10,000	More than £10,000
Costs	£350	£500	£750

➤ The court may also apportion costs to reflect the respective degrees of success on the issues at trial.

1 **Claim is only for the payment of money and claimant gets costs:** 'value of claim' = total amount of the judgment excluding interest, costs and any reduction made for contributory negligence.

2 **Claim is only for the payment of money and defendant gets costs:** 'value of claim' = the amount specified in the claim form (excluding interest and costs), *or*, if no amount is specified, the maximum amount the claimant reasonably expected to recover (see the statement of value in the claim form), *or* more than £10,000, if the claim form says the claimant cannot reasonably say how much this is.

3 **Claim is only for a remedy other than the payment of money:** 'value of claim' = more than £3,000 but not more than £10,000, unless the court orders otherwise.

4 **Claim includes a claim for payment of money *and* for a remedy other than the payment of money:** 'value of claim' = the highest of the values under 1, 2 and 3 above.

Note on counterclaims: If a defendant counterclaim has a higher value than the claim and the claimant succeeds at trial on both the claim *and* counterclaim, 'value of claim' = the value of the defendant's counterclaim.

➤ Under certain circumstances, the court may vary the amounts payable under the general rule.

➤ There are certain special rules where an advocate acts for more than 1 claimant/defendant.

Note on 'additional liability': the court may also make an award in respect of 'additional liability' (*r.46.3(2A)*).

V Assessment

A. General principles

➤ Where the court does not order fixed costs (or no fixed costs are provided for) the amount of costs payable will be assessed by the court. This will be by summary or detailed assessment (*r.44.7*).
- A costs order is decided by a detailed assessment unless the order says otherwise (*PD:Costs 12.2*).

➤ **General rule:** detailed assessment of costs of any proceedings (or any part) should not take place until the conclusion of the proceedings, but the court *may* order them to be assessed immediately (*r.47.1*).

B. Summary assessment

➤ **General rule:** Whenever a court makes an order about costs which does not provide for fixed costs to be paid the court should consider whether to make a summary assessment of costs (*PD:Costs 13.1*). Usually, the court makes a summary assessment (unless there is good reason not to (eg: there are substantial grounds for disputing costs and no time for a summary assessment) (*PD:Costs13.2*)):

a) at the end of a fast track trial, when the order will deal with the costs of the whole claim, *or*

b) at the end of any other hearing which has lasted not more than 1 day, when the order will deal with the costs of the application or matter to which the hearing related.

NB: the general rule is that there is no summary assessment if the court has ordered 'costs in the case'.

➤ **Written statement** (*PD:Costs 13.5*)**:** Each party claiming costs drafts a written costs statement (excluding any additional liability) showing in a schedule: hours claimed, hourly rates, fee earner grade, amount + nature of disbursements (except counsel's fee for appearing at the hearing), solicitor's costs for attending/appearing at the hearing, counsel's fees for the hearing, and VAT - all signed by the party/his solicitor.

➤ **Serving the statement** (*PD:Costs 13.5(4)*)**:** As soon as possible (and in any event not less than 24 hours before the hearing) the statement must be filed and copies served on any party who might pay those costs.

➤ **The hearing:** The court specifies the amount payable separately as base costs and as additional liability (for solicitor's charges, disbursements and allowable VAT) and amounts awarded as Fast Track Trial Costs.

C. Detailed assessment

Steps

1 **Drafting the bill - Receiving party drafts a bill of costs - include (*PD:Costs 4.1-4.4, 4.9, 4.13*):**

- title page containing the full title of the proceedings and the name of the party whose bill it is,
- a description of the document giving the right to assessment and certain background information,
- items of costs claimed under the certain headings,
- summary showing the total costs claimed on each page of the bill,
- schedules of time spent on non-routine attendances,
- certain certificates (eg: LSC certificate and any other relevant certificates).

Note 1: Each item claimed in the bill of costs must be consecutively numbered.

Note 2: The bill of costs must not contain claims for costs or court fees relating solely to the detailed assessment proceedings other than costs claimed for preparing and checking the bill.

2 **Serving the bill - Receiving party serves the bill of costs, notice of commencement and various other documents (*r.47.6-47.8, PD:Costs 32*)**

- This must be done within 3 months of the date of judgment, direction, order, award, right to costs arose (for *Part 36*) etc., otherwise the party may be penalised for the delay.

3 **Disputing the bill? - (*r.47.9, 47.13, 47.14, PD:Costs 40*)**

- Paying party (and any other party) may dispute the bill - this must be done by serving points of dispute within 21 days after the date of service of the notice of commencement, on the receiving party and every other party. The parties may agree to vary this period (*PD:Costs 35.1*).
- Within 21 days after service of the points of dispute, the receiving party may serve a reply.
- Within 3 months of the expiry of the period for starting detailed assessment proceedings, the receiving party must file a request for a detailed hearing. This must be accompanied by a copy/copies of:
  - the notice of commencement; the bill of costs; the document giving the right to detailed assessment; the points of dispute (annotated to show agreed/disputed items and their value); replies served; costs orders made by the court; fee notes + other written evidence served on the paying party; if there is a dispute about the receiving party's liability to pay costs to his solicitors, any written information/letter provided by the solicitor explaining calculation of charges; a statement signed by the receiving party/his solicitor giving contact details of the receiving + paying party and other persons who have served points of dispute and giving a time estimate for the hearing.
- Not less than 7 days before the hearing and not more than 14 days before (*PD:Costs 40.11-12*), the receiving party must file with the court papers supporting the bill: ie: instructions + briefs to counsel (in chronological order); all advices, opinions, drafts in response; reports + opinions of medical and other experts; correspondence files and attendance notes; papers relevant to additional liability.
- The detailed assessment hearing is held.

4 **Default costs certificate - an order to pay the costs to which it relates (*r.47.11-47.12*)**

- The receiving party may file a request for a default costs certificate if he has not been served with any points of dispute or if the 21 days in '3' above has expired.

5 **Interim costs certificate (*r.47.15*)**

- The court may at any time after the receiving party has filed a request for a detailed assessment hearing, issue an interim costs certificate for such sum as it considers appropriate.

6 **Final costs certificate (*r.47.16*)**

- When a completed bill is filed (which must be within 14 days after the end of the detailed assessment hearing) the court will issue a final costs certificate and serve it on the parties. It will include an order to pay the costs to which it relates, unless the court orders otherwise.

7 **Appeal - there are limited rights to appeal (*r.47.20-47.23*)** (see p. 403).

VI Costs in special cases

- ➤ For solicitor and own client costs, see 'Bills' (see p.17).
- ➤ For costs pursuant to a contract, costs payable to non-parties, trustees/PRs, children, patients or litigants in person or costs due to pre-claim disclosure, there are special rules (not dealt with here) (*Part 48*).

VII Assessment of costs of an LSC funded client (*r.47.17, PD44: 21,22*)

- ➤ Summary Assessment:
  - ◆ The court must not make a summary assessment of the costs of a *receiving party* who is an LSC funded client (*PD:Costs13.9*).
  - ◆ The court may make a summary assessment of costs *payable by* an LSC funded client (*PD:Costs13.10*).

The LSC funded client is the... (*r.47.17, PD:**Costs** 21, CLS(CP)R 2000*)

...winner

The costs of the winner's solicitor:

- ◆ there may be a detailed assessment hearing for the winner's 'solicitor and own client costs'

Other Inter partes costs:

- ◆ there may be an order for other inter partes costs to be decided by assessment if not agreed:
  - ● If there is a detailed assessment, a bill of costs may be at 2 rates:
    - i) at the prescribed rate (payable by the LSC), *and*
    - ii) at a 'private individual's rate' (paid by the other side)

Usually, money recoverable through recovery of inter partes costs will pay for the costs of the winner's solicitor. However the LSC may keep:

- ◆ any *inter partes* costs awarded in favour of the winner, *and*
- ◆ any contributions made by the legally helped party, *and*
- ◆ **the statutory charge** (ie: the LSC has the first call on any damages won).

...loser

The costs of the loser's solicitor:

- ◆ the loser's solicitor can claim these costs by filing an LSC schedule for the prescribed rates (and following the '**Summary Assessment**' procedure above if appropriate)

Other Inter partes costs:

Yes: The LSC pays the costs of the winner up to the Cost Protection cap. The LSC funded client must pay any costs (after assessement if necessary) after the benefit of the Cost Protection cap

No: The LSC funded client must pay the costs (after assess-ment if necessary)

Before the LSC can be ordered to pay the whole or any part of the costs incurred by a non-LSC party:

- ◆ the proceedings must be finally decided in favour of the non-funded party, *and*
- ◆ the non-funded party must provide written notice of intention to seek an order against the LSC within 3 months of the costs order, *and*
- ◆ the court must be satisfied that it is 'just and equitable' in the circumstances that costs should be made out of public funds, *and*
- ◆ (in a court of first instance), the proceedings must have been instituted by the LSC funded client and the non-funded party will suffer severe financial hardship unless the order is made

The LSC keeps any contribution paid by the losing LSC funded client

- ➤ Generally, 'Costs Protection' is available to an LSC funded client but not in respect of the following types of funding:
  - ◆ Help at Court, *or*
  - ◆ Litigation Support (but LSC may pay the excess above an insurance payout cap), *or*
  - ◆ Investigative Support, *or*
  - ◆ Legal Help
- ➤ Costs Protection is given by *AJA 1999 s.11*: '**[that] costs cannot exceed the amount it is reasonable for [an LSC funded client] to pay having regard to all the circumstances including the financial resources of all the parties to the proceedings and their conduct in connection with the dispute to which the proceedings relate.**'

Additional Liability (*r.44.3A*) (see also pp.15-16)

- ➤ Additional liability is:
  - ◆ a percentage increase in solicitor's charges, *or*
  - ◆ the litigation insurance premium.
- ➤ Additional liability is assessed (either by summary assessment or detailed assessment) at the end of proceedings (or part of proceedings) to which the funding arrangement relates.

R Enforcing judgments

I	Judgment and orders	IV	Interest on judgment debts
II	Reciprocal enforcement	V	Methods of enforcement (extracting a judgment debt from a debtor)
III	Investigating the debtor's means		

I Judgment and orders (*Part 40*)

1 Form

➤ Every judgment/order must bear: the date on which it is given/made and the court seal (*r.40.2(2)*).

2 Drawing-up and filing

➤ By the court unless *either*:

a) the court orders or permits a party to draw it up *or* dispenses with the need to draw it up, *or*

b) the order is a consent order (*r.40.3(1)*).

◆ If a party draws up an order, that party must file it no later than 7 days after the date on which the order is ordered or permitted to be drawn up so that the court can seal it. *If he does not do so in this period,* any other party may draw it up and file it (*r.40.3(3)*).

3 Service and effect

➤ If a party draws up a judgement/order and the court is to serve it, that party must file a copy to be retained by the court *plus* sufficient copies for service on himself and on the other parties. When the court has sealed the judgement/order it serves a copy on each party (*r.40.4(1)*).

➤ An order which is not made at trial must (unless the court orders otherwise) be served on the applicant, the respondent any other person who the court orders to be served (eg: where a party is acting by a solicitor the party in addition to the solicitor) (*r.40.4(2), 40.5*).

➤ A judgment/order takes effect from the day it is given/made, or any date the court specifies (*r.40.7*).

4 Set aside and correction

➤ Any person (even if not a party) directly affected may apply for set aside or variation (*r.40.9*).

➤ The court may correct accidental slips/omissions; a party may apply for correction without notice (*r.40.12*).

5 Compliance

➤ A party must comply with a judgment/order for the payment of amount of money (including costs) within 14 days of the date of the judgment/order *unless* a) the judgment/order specifies otherwise, b) the *CPR* specify otherwise (eg: *Part 12* (default judgment) and *Part 14* (judgment on admissions)), or c) the court has stayed the proceedings or judgment (*r.40.11*)).

II Reciprocal enforcement (*Sch.1 - r. 71, Sch.2 - r.35*)

➤ **Enforcing a foreign judgment in England and Wales:** Judgments from EU member states and some other European countries *(CJJA 1982*) and certain other countries (*AJA 1920, FJ(ER)A 1933*) may be registered in English courts and enforced. From 1 March 2002, EC Reg. 44/2001 is also relevant.

➤ **Enforcing an English judgment outside the jurisdiction:** English judgments may be registered and enforced elsewhere in the UK (eg: Jersey), in EU member states and in certain other European countries (*CJJA 1982*). There is also provision for reciprocal enforcement of some other foreign judgments (*AJA 1920, FJ(ER)A 1933*). From 1 March 2002, EC Reg. 44/2001 is also relevant.

◆ If a country is not covered, fresh proceedings should be started there.

III Investigating the debtor's means

Investigating and tracing a debtor

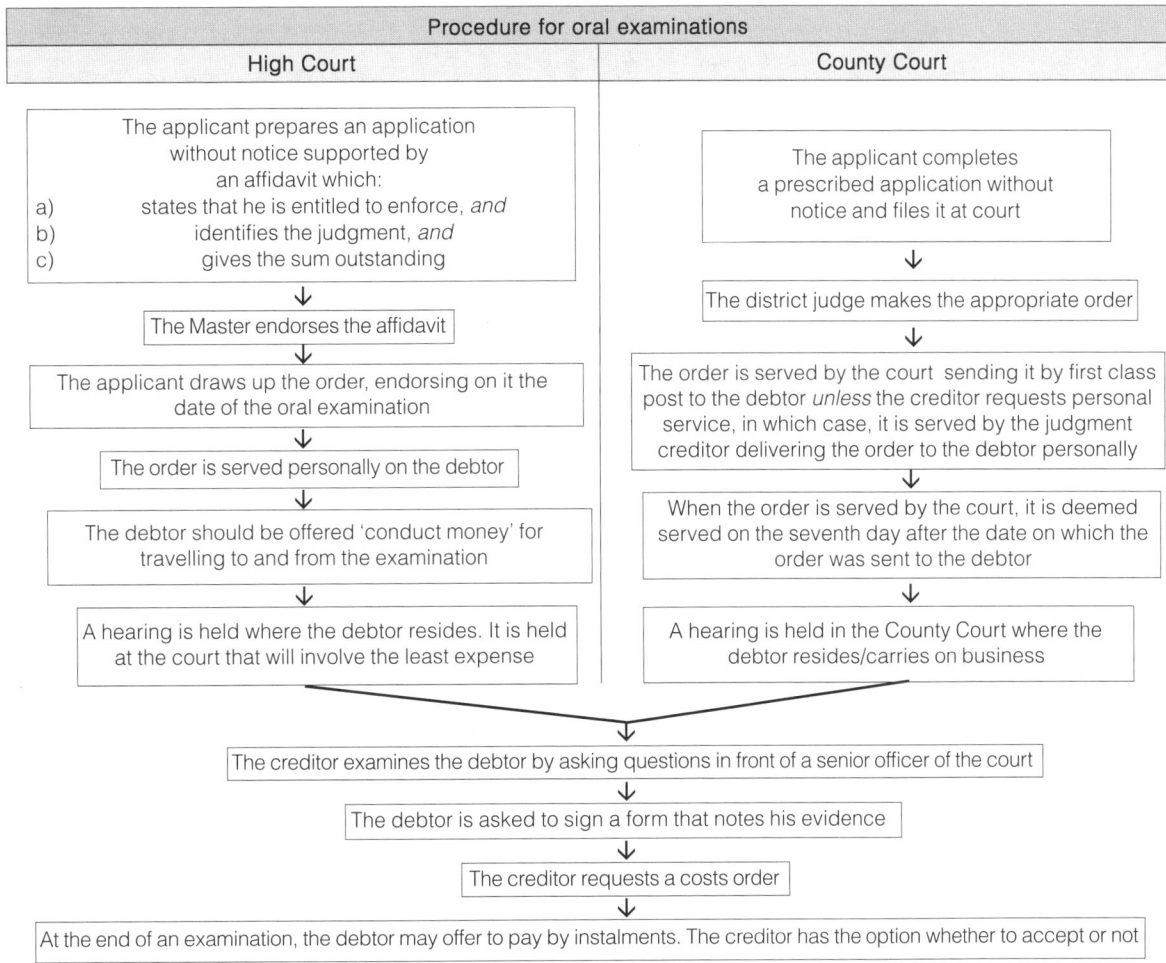

Steps

1 **Use an enquiry agent**

- This is to investigate and trace a debtor (set a cost ceiling to limit the expense).
- ✓ This is relatively fast and may unearth more than an oral examination will.
- ✗ It is more expensive than an oral examination.

2 **Oral examination** (*Sch.1 - r.48.1, Sch.2 - r.25.3*)

- This is an examination of the means of a debtor while he is under oath.

Procedure for oral examinations

High Court

The applicant prepares an application without notice supported by an affidavit which:
a) states that he is entitled to enforce, *and*
b) identifies the judgment, *and*
c) gives the sum outstanding

↓

The Master endorses the affidavit

↓

The applicant draws up the order, endorsing on it the date of the oral examination

↓

The order is served personally on the debtor

↓

The debtor should be offered 'conduct money' for travelling to and from the examination

↓

A hearing is held where the debtor resides. It is held at the court that will involve the least expense

County Court

The applicant completes a prescribed application without notice and files it at court

↓

The district judge makes the appropriate order

↓

The order is served by the court sending it by first class post to the debtor *unless* the creditor requests personal service, in which case, it is served by the judgment creditor delivering the order to the debtor personally

↓

When the order is served by the court, it is deemed served on the seventh day after the date on which the order was sent to the debtor

↓

A hearing is held in the County Court where the debtor resides/carries on business

Both courts

↓

The creditor examines the debtor by asking questions in front of a senior officer of the court

↓

The debtor is asked to sign a form that notes his evidence

↓

The creditor requests a costs order

↓

At the end of an examination, the debtor may offer to pay by instalments. The creditor has the option whether to accept or not

Failure to attend

High Court	County Court
Failure to attend results in an order for committal to prison **Note**: orders for committal to prison, are usually 'suspended' when they are issued for the first time	Failure to attend leads to an adjournment Notice of adjournment is served personally on the debtor and 'conduct money' should be offered Failure to attend the adjourned hearing results in a date being set for a new hearing Failure to attend the new hearing will result in an order for committal to prison

IV Interest on judgment debts (*Judgment Act 1838 s.17*)

➤ Interest (under *JA 1838 s.17* or *CCA 1984 s.74*) runs from the date a judgment is given *unless* the *CPR* or a *PD* provide differently or the court orders otherwise (*r.40.8*).

High Court - Interest on judgment debts

➤ **High Court:** all judgment debts currently carry interest at 8% (see p.310) from the date the judgment is entered until final payment, regardless of whether the sum represents damages or costs.

➤ Where a county court judgment is being enforced in the High Court, the judgment is treated as one of the High Court for enforcement purposes.

County Courts - Interest on judgment debts

➤ **County Court:** (*County Court (Interest on Judgment Debts) Order 1991*) (as amended)

A. Judgments over £5000

a) all judgments over £5,000 carry interest at 8% from the date judgment is entered until final payment.

b) when enforcement proceedings begin, interest ceases to run *unless* the proceedings produce no payment.

- If anything at all is recovered, then the balance of the debt becomes interest-free.

c) An application to enforce interest must be made. This must be done with a certificate setting out:

- the amount of interest claimed, *and*
- the sum on which the interest is claimed, *and*
- the dates to and from which interest has accrued, *and*
- the rate of interest.

NB: If a judgment before trial leaves quantum to be assessed, interest runs from the date of final judgment (*Thomas v. Bunn* [1991] 1 AC 362).

NB: Interest does *not* accrue on instalments (or judgment for deferred sums), until the instalment falls due.

B. Judgments £5000 and under

a) If a debt is a qualifying debt under the *LPCD(I) 1998*, it will attract interest at 8% *on top of the Bank of England's base rate* (ie: the total rate will be much higher than 8%) - see p.310.

V Methods of enforcement

Methods of enforcement	Assets available
1. Bankruptcy (individual) or winding up (company)	Various
2. Execution of the judgment against goods	Goods and chattels
3. Charging order over land	Land
4. Charging order over securities	Securities
5. Attachment of earnings order	Earnings
6. Garnishee proceedings	Money held on the debtor's behalf by others

1. Bankruptcy (individual) or winding up (company)

Steps	
1	If no execution has so far been levied, issue a statutory demand.
2	If execution has been levied but is unsatisfied, see the procedures for bankruptcy/winding up on p.275 et seq

2. Execution against goods
(*HCCJO 1991 Art.8, HCCJ(A)O 1996, Sch.1 - r.45.1,r.46, r.47, Sch.2 - r.26*)

	High Court	County Court
What judgments are enforceable and where?	High Court judgments County Court judgments if £600 or over	County Court judgments under £5,000 (unless proceedings are under *CCA 1984*)
	◆ If a debt is payable by instalments, the claim form can be issued for an instalment or the whole amount	
Procedure	The creditor completes: a) 2 copies of the writ of *fieri facias, and* b) a *praecipe* for a writ of *fieri facias* He sends these to the court office together with the judgment and assessment notice (if costs are involved) NB: If enforcing a county court judgment, the creditor completes a combined certificate of judgment and request for writ of *fieri facias* too	The creditor completes a form of request for a warrant of execution. He files it at the court with a fee
Execution	The court seals the claim form, returns one copy to the creditor who forwards it to the under-sheriff for the county where the debtor resides or carries on his business. The under-sheriff sends it to an officer for execution	The bailiff for the district where the debtor resides or carries on business executes the warrant
	It may not be executed on Sunday, Good Friday or Xmas Day.	

The creditor should tell the officer about all seizable items of which he knows, eg: the type and registration number of a car. The relevant court officer seizes the goods and auctions them off to pay the debt and expenses

Items exempt from seizure (*Law of Distress (Amendment) Act 1888 s.4, AJA 1956 s.37*)

- Goods on hire or hire-purchase
- Tools, books, vehicles and items necessary for the debtor's personal use in his job or business. A vehicle will be seized unless the debtor satisfies the officer that no reasonable alternative transport is possible and that mobility is essential to him
- Clothing, bedding, furniture, provisions and household equipment for the basic domestic needs of the debtor and his family. Microwaves (when a conventional oven is present), a stereo, a TV and video are *not* regarded as being vital for domestic survival!!!

Methods of seizure

- The following are forbidden for the court officer:
  a) forcible entry to premises, *or*
  b) taking goods from the debtor's person.
- 'Walking possession' is a method by which the sheriff or bailiff agrees not to remove items if the debtor agrees not to dispose of them or permit them to be moved. (This gives the debtor an extra chance to meet the claim, or oppose seizure).
- The debtor may apply for suspension of execution. If he succeeds, the writ of *fieri facias* is suspended conditionally on payment by specified instalments.

3. Charging order over land (*Charging Orders Act 1979, Sch.1 - r.50, Sch.2 - r.31*)		
	High Court	County Court
Preliminary matters	◆ Do an index map search to discover if the land is registered. ◆ Search for prior incumbrances and give written notice of the order to prior chargees, to prevent tacking of later advances	
	The court will not make an order if the debtor is up-to-date with instalments	
Which judgments are enforceable and where?	High Court judgments for over £5,000 County Court judgments for over £5,000	All High Court judgments All County Court judgments
Procedure	File at court: a) an affidavit giving: ◆ the name and address of the debtor and of other known creditors, *and* ◆ the amount due, *and* ◆ identification of the land, *and* ◆ verification that the interest is beneficially owned by the debtor b) a draft charging order *nisi.*	
	The district judge considers the application in private and makes a charging order *nisi* if he sees fit	
Register the order *nisi* (if possible)	Register the order with Land Charges Department or HM Land Registry, provided the land is *not* jointly owned. If the land is jointly owned, the order attaches to the debtor's beneficial interest alone, as the debtor's only interest is under a trust, rather than an interest in the land itself. Such an order is not registrable	
Preparation for the hearing for the order absolute	The *nisi* order is endorsed with a hearing date. It is served personally on the debtor, together with a copy of the supporting affidavit at least 7 days before the return day	Same as in the High Court, but service may be personal *or* by post
The hearing for the order absolute	The order absolute is made at the hearing unless the debtor shows cause otherwise. The creditor is granted a charge enforceable by sale	
Enforcement (ie: getting the money)	By sale of the property. This is achieved by fresh proceedings commenced in the Chancery Division	By sale of the property: this is achieved by applying for an order for sale from the County Court only if the debt remaining does *not* exceed £30,000

4. Charging order over securities
The procedure is similar to that for granting an order over land (see above box) but applies to securities instead of land

<table>
<tr><th colspan="2">5. Attachment of earnings order (Attachment of Earnings Act 1971, Sch.2 - r.27)</th></tr>
<tr><th colspan="2">County Court only - High Court proceedings are transferred to the County Court</th></tr>
<tr><td>Conditions</td><td>The debtor is employed (not self-employed or unemployed).
The sum due exceeds £50</td></tr>
<tr><td>Application</td><td>File an application form
↓
The court informs the debtor of the application and asks him to:
◆ pay the sum due, or
◆ file a statement of means form</td></tr>
<tr><td>If the debtor replies</td><td>Steps
1 The court makes a diary entry when the form is returned.
2 The court then fixes repayment according to the following 2 guidelines:
a) 'normal deduction rate' (this is the amount of money to be deducted), and
b) 'protected earnings rate' (this is an amount the debtor must be left with - a 'safety net' for the debtor).
3 The order is served on the debtor and the employer and a copy sent to the creditor. The service is as follows:

The order is served by the court sending it by first class post to the debtor unless the creditor requests personal service, in which case, it is served by the judgment creditor delivering the order to the debtor personally
↓
When the order is served by the court, it is deemed served on the seventh day after the date on which the order was sent to the debtor
↓
Where an order is sent by the court and it is returned undelivered the court sends notice of non-service to the judgment creditor together with a notice saying he may request bailiff service (and a bailiff serves by:
◆ inserting the order, enclosed in an envelope addressed to the debtor through the debtor's letter box, or
◆ deliveringthe order to some person (apparently not less than 16 years old) at the debtor's address, or
◆ delivering the order to the debtor personally)

4 The employer must forward to the court:
a) the deduction, and
b) up to £1 for himself for administrative expenses on each deduction under the order (AtEA 1971 s.7).
5 If either party objects or the court staff consider that the statement of means has insufficient information, a judge hears the matter, but meanwhile the employer complies with the order unless it is varied.
6 If the debtor informs the court of his unemployment or self-employment, the application is dismissed.</td></tr>
<tr><td>If the debtor does not reply</td><td>Steps
1 The court automatically issues an order to produce a statement of means.
2 The bailiff serves this personally on the debtor.
(If the creditor provides the employer's name and address, the court may ask the employer for a statement of earnings).
3 If the debtor does not respond at all, the court automatically issues a 'notice to show cause' which the bailiff serves.
4 Failure to attend a subsequent hearing before a district judge will ultimately lead to committal to prison.</td></tr>
</table>

6. Garnishee proceedings (*Sch.1 - r.49, Sch.2 - r.30*)

	High Court	County Court
Which judgments are enforceable and where?	Judgment for £50 or more	Judgment for £50 or more Apply to the court which passed judgment
Conditions	A third party (the 'garnishee') owes money to the judgment debtor, who in turn owes money to the creditor. The debt *must* belong to the judgment debtor solely and beneficially. The garnishee must be within the jurisdiction of UK courts	
Application	File at court: ◆ an affidavit giving: ● the name and last known address of the debtor, *and* ● details of the date and amount of the judgment, *and* ● the sum outstanding *and* details of the garnishee ◆ a draft garnishee order *nisi* ↓ The district judge considers the application without notice and endorses the hearing date on the order. This is the order *nisi*	
Service of the order	◆ There must be service on the garnishee, at least 15 days before the day fixed for consideration of the order absolute ◆ The garnishee is bound on service to retain money in his possession until the court ruling ◆ There must be ordinary service on the debtor at least 7 days *after* service on the garnishee and at least 7 days before the hearing date	The same rules apply as in the High Court, but service on the garnishee may be by post as per the rulesfor attachment of earnings (p.401) . (A garnishee who admits the debt after service may pay the amount into court, whereupon the application for decree absolute is stayed)
The hearing	The district judge has discretion as to whether to make the order absolute. He will usually do so unless liability is disputed	
Costs	**For a successful application:** costs are retained by the creditor, from the money received from the garnishee in priority to the judgment debt **For a failed application:** the court has discretion as to costs and as to whether to award these against the debtor or the judgment creditor	
Special rules for seeking a garnishee order against deposit taking institutions		
Affidavit	In addition to the details above, the affidavit should state the branch where the account is held and the account number	
Service	Service is to the institution's registered head office *and* to the branch where the account is held	
Hearing	The institution usually complies by a letter sent to the court instead of appearing personally. If the institution claims not to hold any money for the debtor, proceedings are stayed unless the creditor disputes this	
Administration	The institution can deduct up to £30 from the repayment, to cover administrative expenses	

S Appeals

<table>
<tr><th colspan="4">A very simplified table of possible Appeal Courts (Part 52)</th></tr>
<tr><th>Appeal to:</th><th>Appeal from:</th><th>Leave needed?</th><th>Powers on Appeal</th></tr>
<tr><td>Circuit Judge of a county court</td><td>a District Judge of a county court
(r.52.1, PD52: 2A.1)</td><td rowspan="3">Yes
unless the appeal is against:
◆ a committal order, or
◆ a refusal to grant habeus corpus, or
◆ certain actions under CA 1989
(r.52.3)

To obtain leave, an application must be made to:
a) the lower court at the hearing at which the decision was made, or
b) the appeal court
(r.52.3)
Permission is granted if:
◆ the court considers the appeal would have a real prospect of success, or
◆ there is some other compelling reason</td><td rowspan="5">The appeal court has all the powers of the lower court (r.52.10)
eg: to affirm, set aside, vary an order or judgment
eg: to refer any claim or issue for determination by the lower court
eg: to order a new trial/hearing
eg: to make an order for interest payment
eg: to make a costs order
BUT
the appeal is limited to a review of the decision of the lower court unless it is in the interests of justice to hold a rehearing (r.52.11)

Note: for extra provisions on small claims track appeals, see p.369</td></tr>
<tr><td>High Court Judge</td><td>a Master, a District Judge of the High Court, a Circuit Judge
(r.52.1, PD52: 2A.1)</td></tr>
<tr><td>Court of Appeal
(SCA 1981 ss.15-18)</td><td>High Court Judge
(r.52.1, PD52: 2A)
A final decision in the multi-track, irrespective of rank of judge
(PD52: 2A.2)</td></tr>
<tr><td rowspan="2">House of Lords</td><td>Court of Appeal</td><td rowspan="2">Yes
to the Court of Appeal
if refused, apply to the House of Lords</td></tr>
<tr><td>High Court
under the AJA 1969 s.12
'leap-frog' procedure
('Civil Appeals' PD March 2000)</td></tr>
<tr><td rowspan="3">European Court of Justice</td><td>Court of Appeal
(Sch.1 - r.114)</td><td rowspan="3">Yes
Any reference is up to the national court</td><td rowspan="3">The court can make a ruling on any matter in the Treaty of Rome 1957</td></tr>
<tr><td>High Court
(Sch.1 - r.114 and Civil Appeals' PD March 2000)</td></tr>
<tr><td>Crown Court</td></tr>
<tr><td>Costs
a costs judge or a District Judge of the High Court</td><td>Costs
an authorised costs officer on a detailed assessment (but not if LSC funded)
(r.47.20-47.23)</td><td>No</td><td>Costs
power to rehear proceedings and make any order/ directions appropriate</td></tr>
</table>

➤ An appeal is allowed if:

- ◆ a decision of a lower court was:
  - wrong, *or*
  - unjust because of a serious procedural or other irregularity in the proceedings of the lower court.

Note:	Note:	Note:
Judicial review as an 'appeal' against decisions is not dealt with in this table - it is covered by *Part 54*	References to the European Court of Human Rights are not dealt with in this table	Certain specialised jurisdictions (eg: insolvency) are not dealt with in this table

Criminal Litigation

This chapter examines:

Note: The law as set out in this section of the *Legal Practice Companion* applies to adults only unless the text specifically indicates otherwise.

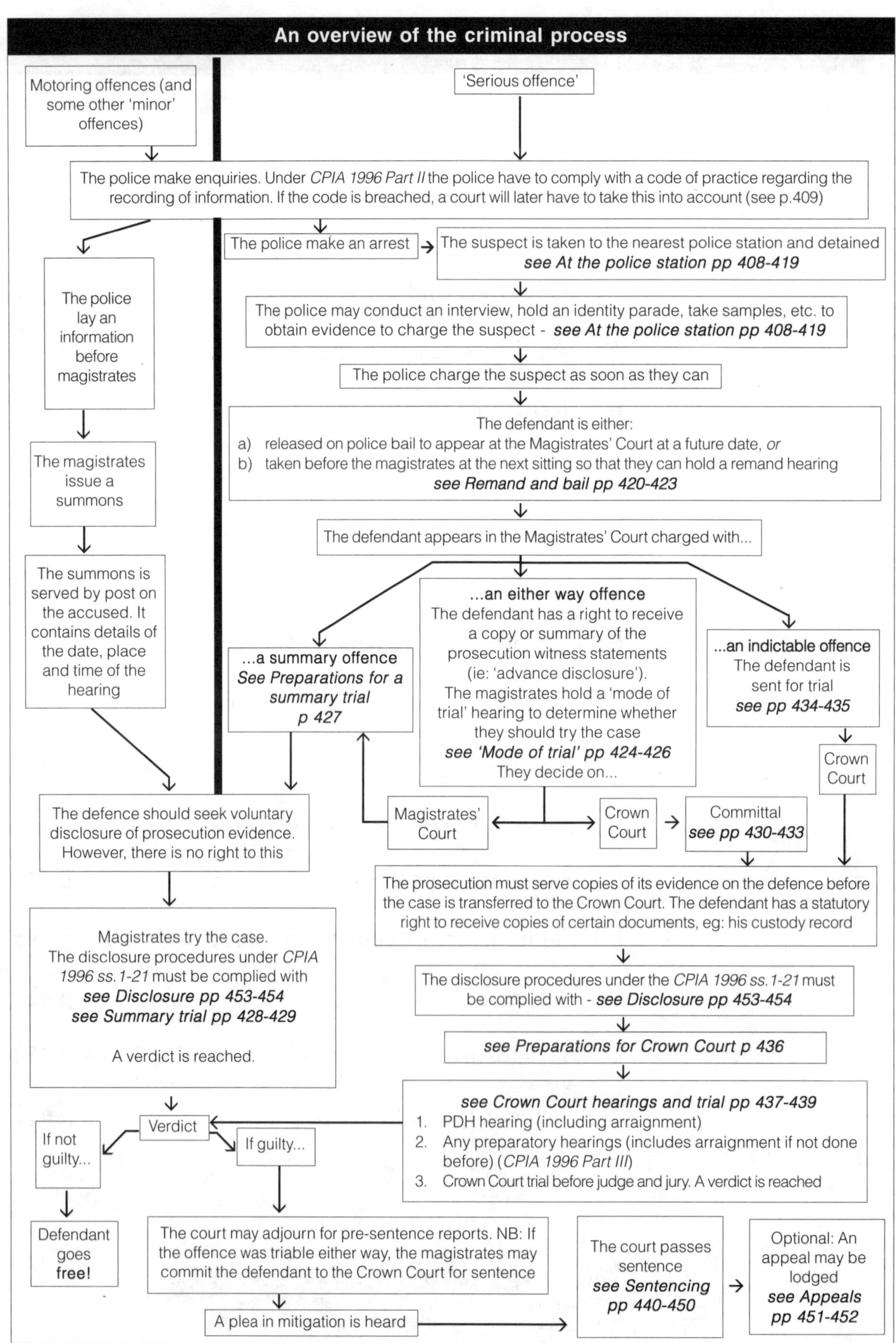
An overview of the criminal process
Motoring offences (and some other 'minor' offences)
'Serious offence'
The police make enquiries. Under CPIA 1996 Part II the police have to comply with a code of practice regarding the recording of information. If the code is breached, a court will later have to take this into account (see p.409)
The police make an arrest
The suspect is taken to the nearest police station and detained see At the police station pp 408-419
The police may conduct an interview, hold an identity parade, take samples, etc. to obtain evidence to charge the suspect - see At the police station pp 408-419
The police charge the suspect as soon as they can
The defendant is either:
a) released on police bail to appear at the Magistrates' Court at a future date, or
b) taken before the magistrates at the next sitting so that they can hold a remand hearing see Remand and bail pp 420-423
The defendant appears in the Magistrates' Court charged with...
The police lay an information before magistrates
The magistrates issue a summons
The summons is served by post on the accused. It contains details of the date, place and time of the hearing
...a summary offence See Preparations for a summary trial p 427
...an either way offence The defendant has a right to receive a copy or summary of the prosecution witness statements (ie: 'advance disclosure'). The magistrates hold a 'mode of trial' hearing to determine whether they should try the case see 'Mode of trial' pp 424-426 They decide on...
...an indictable offence The defendant is sent for trial see pp 434-435
Crown Court
Magistrates' Court
Crown Court
Committal see pp 430-433
The defence should seek voluntary disclosure of prosecution evidence. However, there is no right to this
The prosecution must serve copies of its evidence on the defence before the case is transferred to the Crown Court. The defendant has a statutory right to receive copies of certain documents, eg: his custody record
Magistrates try the case. The disclosure procedures under CPIA 1996 ss. 1-21 must be complied with see Disclosure pp 453-454 see Summary trial pp 428-429
A verdict is reached.
The disclosure procedures under the CPIA 1996 ss. 1-21 must be complied with - see Disclosure pp 453-454
see Preparations for Crown Court p 436
see Crown Court hearings and trial pp 437-439
1. PDH hearing (including arraignment)
2. Any preparatory hearings (includes arraignment if not done before) (CPIA 1996 Part III)
3. Crown Court trial before judge and jury. A verdict is reached
Verdict
If not guilty...
If guilty...
Defendant goes free!
The court may adjourn for pre-sentence reports. NB: If the offence was triable either way, the magistrates may commit the defendant to the Crown Court for sentence
A plea in mitigation is heard
The court passes sentence see Sentencing pp 440-450
Optional: An appeal may be lodged see Appeals pp 451-452

Table of various offences				
Offence	**Power to arrest without warrant? (*PACE s.24*)**	**Type**	**Magistrates' maximum penalty**	**Crown court maximum penalty**
			cf: Mandatory and racially aggravated sentences p.441	
Theft (*TA 1968 s.1*)	✓	Either way	6 months (*TA 1968 s.1(7)*; *s.9(4)*) £5,000 fine (*MCA 1980 s.32*)	7 years (*TA 1968 s.1(7)*) Unlimited fine (*PCCA 1973 s.10*)
Burglary (*TA 1968 s.9*)	✓	Either way Indictment*		10 (14*) years (*TA 1968 s.9(4)*) Unlimited fine (*PCCA 1973 s.10*)
Robbery (*TA 1968 s.8*)	✓	Indictment	Not applicable	Life (*TA 1968 s.8(2)*) Unlimited fine (*PCCA 1973 s.10*)
Harassment, alarm or distress (*POA 1986 s.5*)	✗ ✓ *POA 1986 s.5(4)*	Summary	£1,000 fine (*POA 1986 s.5(6)*)	Not applicable
Fear or provocation of violence (*POA 1986 s.4*)	✗ ✓ *POA 1986 s.4(3)*	Summary	6 months (*POA 1986 s.4(4)*) £5,000 fine (*POA 1986 s.4(4)*)	
Actual bodily harm (*OAPA 1861 s.47*)	✓	Either way	6 months £5,000 fine	5 years (*OAPA 1861 s.47*) Unlimited fine (*PCCA 1973 s.10*)
Collective trespass (*CJPO 1994 s.61*)	✗ ✓ *CJPO s.61(5)*	Summary	3 months £2,500 fine	Not applicable
Careless driving (*RTA 1988 s.3*)	✗	Summary	£2,500 fine Endorsement of licence is obligatory Disqualification is discretionary, otherwise endorse 3-9 points Disqualification until a re-test is discretionary	
Dangerous driving (*RTA 1988 s.2*)	✗	Either way	6 months, £5,000 fine	2 years, unlimited fine
			Disqualification is obligatory Endorsement of offence on licence is obligatory with 3-11 points A re-test before requalifying is obligatory Forfeiture of vehicle is discretionary (*PCCA 1973 s.43*)	
Taking a conveyance (*TA 1968 s.12*)	✓	Summary	6 months, £5,000 fine (*TA 1968 s.12(2)*) Disqualification is discretionary (*RTA 1988 Schedule 2*)	Not applicable
Aggravated vehicle taking (*TA 1968 s.12A*)	✓	Either way Summary if aggravating feature is that damage is worth £5,000 or less	6 months, £5,000 fine	2 years (5 years if death results) Unlimited fine
			and Endorsement on licence is obligatory - endorse 3-11 points Disqualification is obligatory	

Serious arrestable offences (*PACE s.116*)

➤ Whether an offence is a serious arrestable offence can affect how long someone is detained (see p.410), and can give the police extra powers.

➤ An offence which is 'arrestable' (*PACE s.24*) is a 'serious arrestable offence' if:

- the offence is serious as defined in *PACE Schedule 5 Part I*, eg: treason, murder, manslaughter, rape, kidnapping, *or*
- it is on a list of certain statutory offences in *PACE Schedule 5 Part II*, eg: causing an explosion likely to endanger life or property, death by dangerous driving, possession of, or use of, or carrying of firearms with certain intents. *CJPO s.85* has recently added to the *Part II* list certain offences to do with obscene material. This list is varied from time to time, *or*
- the offence led to, or was intended to lead to: a) death, *or* b) serious injury, *or* c) serious financial loss (subjectively from the victim's viewpoint), *or* d) substantial financial gain (from an objective viewpoint).

A At the police station

References in this section are to PACE, unless otherwise stated. References to the Code are to the PACE Codes of Practice, which do not have statutory force, but with which the police must sometimes comply (eg: s.39(1)).

I Criminal investigations - code of practice
II Voluntary attendance
III Arrest
IV Detention before charge
V Interviewing
VI Inferences from silence
VII Identification
VIII Samples in police detention (brief overview)
IX Detention after charge
X Charges
XI Other rights at a police station

Penalty notices

CJPA 2001 ss.1-11 [not yet in force], sets out a discretionary scheme where the police can issue penalty notices on the spot/at a police station for adults for several disorder offences. But where a police officer believes an offence should be dealt with by the courts, all usual powers (eg: arrest) are available. A penalty notice is notice of the opportunity to discharge any liability to conviction of the offence by payment of a fixed penalty. There is no criminal conviction or admission of guilt associated with payment of the penalty, though the alleged offender has the right to opt for trial by a court, and risk conviction. Failure to pay the penalty/opt for trial may lead a fine equal to 1.5 times the penalty amount.

Cautions and Safeguards at the police station

➤ **Cautions**

- Wording: 'You do not have to say anything. But it may harm your defence if you do not mention when questioned something which you later rely on in court. Anything you do say may be given in evidence.' (*C:10*, see pp.412-413)
- A caution *must* be given:
  a) on, or just before, arrest, *and*
  b) on a custody officer authorising detention, *and*
  c) before an interview, *and*
  d) following a break in questioning (*C:10*).

➤ **Safeguards on interview at a police station**

- Rest: for a continuous period of 8 hours in 24 hours, preferably at night (*C:12.2*).
- Drink or drugs: no questioning if the suspect is unable to grasp the significance of the questions, *unless* the superintendent or an officer of higher rank authorises it for the protection of people or property (*C:12.3, Annex C*).
- Interview room: heated, lighted, ventilated; chair for the defendant to sit on (*C:12.4, 12.5*).
- Breaks: at recognised meal times, refreshments every 2 hours (*C:12.7*).
- Identification: a policeman must identify himself by name and rank before interview (*C:12.6*).
- Juveniles (under 17): accompanied by an 'appropriate' adult (a parent/guardian or social worker) for certain situations (*C:1.7*).
- Mentally disordered: accompanied by an 'appropriate' adult (a relative/other responsible person or a special social worker) for certain situations (*C:1.7*).

I Criminal investigations - code of practice

- A code of practice applies for criminal investigations conducted by police officers (*CPIA 1996 s.23(1)*).
- The code provides that there are different functions to be performed by (para 3.1):
  - the investigator,
  - the officer in charge of an investigation,
  - the disclosure officer.

Duty to retain material

- The investigator has a duty to retain material obtained in a criminal investigation which may be relevant to the investigation (para 5.1).

Time to retain material

- All material which may be relevant to an investigation must be retained until a decision is taken whether to institute proceedings against a person for an offence (para 5.6).
- If a criminal investigation results in proceedings being instituted, all material which may be relevant must be retained at least until (para 5.7-5.9):
  - the prosecutor decides not to proceed with the case, *or*
  - the accused is acquitted, *or*
  - the accused is convicted.
    - If the accused is convicted the material must be retained until the later of:
      - the convicted person is released from custody, *or*
      - 6 months from the date of conviction, *or*
      - if an appeal is in progress, the time that the appeal is determined, *or*
      - if the Criminal Cases Review Commission (see p.452) is considering an application:
        - the time it decides not to refer the case to the Court of Appeal,
        - the time that the appeal is determined.

Preparation of schedules (para 6.6 and 7.1)

- The following schedules must be prepared and given to the prosecutor if:
  - the accused is charged, *and*
    - a) the offence is triable only on indictment, *or*
    - b) the offence is triable summarily *and* the accused is considered likely to plead not guilty, *or*
    - c) the offence is triable either way *and*
      - i) it is considered that the offence is likely to be tried on indictment, *or*
      - ii) it is considered that the accused is likely to plead not guilty at a summary trial.

    NB: If, in (b) or (c)(ii) above, it is considered that the accused will plead guilty, and contrary to this, he pleads not guilty, then a schedule must be prepared as soon as practicable.
- Material which may be relevant to an investigation, which the disclosure officer believes will *not* form part of the prosecution case must be listed on a schedule (para 6.2).

Non-sensitive material (para 6.3)	Sensitive material (para 6.4)
Material which the disclosure officer does not believe is sensitive must be listed on a schedule of non-sensitive material	Material which is believed to be sensitive must be: ◆ listed on a schedule of sensitive material, *or* ◆ (in exceptional circumstances) revealed to the prosecution.

II Voluntary attendance

- ➤ The individual may leave at will (*s.29*).
- ➤ If the individual is prevented from leaving at will, he must be informed that he is under arrest (*s.29*).

III Arrest

> *CDA 1998 s.65-66*: a young person may be reprimanded or warned (if this has not happened before) under certain circumstances instead of being arrested. He may be referred to a youth offending team.

- ➤ A suspect should be taken to the police station as soon as possible (*s.30*).
- ➤ The custody officer (at least a sergeant) must decide to:

  a) charge the suspect immediately (*s.37(7)*), *or*

  - ◆ The test is whether:
    - there is sufficient evidence for a successful prosecution, *and*
    - the officer is satisfied that the suspect has said all he wishes about the possible offence (*C:16.1*).

  b) release the suspect (whether on bail or not) without charge (*s.37(7)*), *or*

  c) detain the suspect before charge (only if there are special reasons - see Section IV below).
- ➤ A suspect is treated as arrested if he has returned to a police station to answer to bail (*s.24(7)*).

IV Detention before charge

- ➤ Following arrest
  - ◆ Detention is permitted if the custody officer has reasonable grounds to believe *either* (*s.37(2)*):

    a) that there is insufficient evidence to charge the suspect and detention is necessary to obtain that evidence by questioning, *or*

    b) it is necessary to secure or preserve evidence, or to obtain it by questioning.
- ➤ The police should interview the suspect as soon as possible and decide immediately after an interview whether a charge will be brought - if no charge is brought, release should be immediate (*s.34(2), s.41(7)*).

Detention timetable (before charge) Authority: **c** = custody officer, **i** = inspector, **s** = superintendent, **m** = magistrate

Time	Event	Authority
Monday 1.00 pm	Arrival at the police station. Detention clock begins to run (*s.41(2)(a)(i)*)	
Monday 1.10 pm	Detention is 'authorised' by the custody officer under the grounds in *s.37(2)*	c
Monday 7.10 pm	Latest time for first review of detention - by an inspector. Detention may continue if the original grounds are still valid (*s.40(3)*) NB: The suspect or his solicitor may make representations	i
Tuesday 4.10 am	Latest time for second review; thereafter reviews at 9 hourly intervals (*s.40(3)*)	i
Tuesday 1.00 pm	Charge, or release (*s.41(1)*) *unless* a superintendent has reasonable grounds to believe: a) the grounds in *s.37(2)* still exist, *and*	s
Tuesday 1.00 pm cont.	b) it is a serious arrestable offence, *and* c) the investigation is being conducted diligently and expeditiously NB: This new authorisation is only possible if it is: i) before 24 hours from when the detention clock began to run (*s.42(4)*), *and* ii) after the second review	s
Wednesday 1.00 am	The authority of the superintendent expires. Charge or release *unless* a magistrate grants warrant of further detention (*s.43*)	m
Thursday 1.00 pm	The magistrate's warrant expires. Charge or release *unless* a magistrate grants extension of warrant of further detention (*s.44*)	m
Friday 1.00 pm	Charge or release (*s.44 (3)(b)*) MAXIMUM LIMIT	

V Interviewing

- **An interview is the questioning of a person regarding his involvement or suspected involvement in a criminal offence or offences (for which a caution would need to be given under *C:10.1*).**
- An interview should not be held until the suspect reaches the police station *unless* delay would endanger persons or evidence, alert others, or hinder the recovery of property (*C:11.1*).
- For an interview at a police station, see **Safeguards at the police station**, p.408.
- The suspect must be reminded that he has a right to free legal advice and that the interview can be delayed for this (*C:11.2*), see p.419.
- At the beginning of an interview at a police station, the officer must put to the suspect any significant statement or silence made before the suspect's arrival at the police station, and ask if he would like to confirm, deny, or add anything (*C:11.2A*).
- No oppression may be used by police during questioning (*C:11.3*).
- When police believe that a prosecution should be brought against the suspect, they must ask the suspect if he wishes to say anything further. If he does not, further questioning is forbidden (*C:11.4*).
- A record must be made during an interview (or as soon as practicable after it) (*C:11.5-11.7*).
- Interviewing is forbidden after the suspect has been charged, *unless* it is necessary to (*C:16.5*):
  a) minimise harm to a person or the public, *or*
  b) clarify ambiguity in an answer or statement, *or*
  c) enable the defendant to comment on new information unearthed since he was charged.
- See interviews and other legal rights (p.419) and advice on the qualified right to silence (pp.422-423).

Recording an interview

<table>
<tr><th>Taped interview (aural) (Code E)</th><th>Non-taped interview</th></tr>
<tr><td>➤ Compulsory unless the offence is a purely summary offence
◆ 2 tapes are recorded (E:2)
◆ The master tape is sealed, and signed by the suspect and the interviewing officer (E:2)
◆ A written summary is sent to the defence
◆ The defence has access to the working copy of the tape:
• if the defence agrees, the summary is admissible as evidence
• if the defence objects, a full transcript is made and the seal on the master tape is broken in court</td><td>➤ Summary offences only
◆ An accurate written record must be made (C:11.5)
◆ The record must be made during the interview or as soon as possible after it (C:11.5-11.7)
◆ An interviewee must read and sign the record (C:11.10). Refusals to do so must be recorded. Note: C:11D says that if the suspect agrees, the words are 'I agree that this is a correct record of what was said' and he signs his signature
◆ The interview record will be served on the defence
• If the defence agrees, the record is admissible
• If the defence objects, oral evidence is admissible and the officer may refresh his memory from contemporaneous notes
• Any refusal to sign should be recorded</td></tr>
<tr><th>Taped interview (video)</th><th>Outside the context of an interview</th></tr>
<tr><td>CJPA 2001 s.76 [not yet in force] inserts a new s.60A into PACE to allow visual recording of interviews with suspects, the issuing by the Secretary of State of a code of practice on video recording and enabling him to make an order requiring that certain interviews, in certain police force areas, be videoed in accordance with the code.</td><td>➤ Comments made by the suspect should be:
◆ recorded in writing and signed by the officer concerned, and
◆ shown to the suspect, who should have an opportunity to read, time and sign them - any refusal to sign should be recorded (C:11.13)</td></tr>
<tr><th colspan="2">Written statement under caution</th></tr>
<tr><td colspan="2">This is a prepared statement by the suspect setting out his version of events. It may also be a confession. The rules and the form are set out in Annex D to Code C</td></tr>
</table>

VI Inferences from silence

➤ The *CJPO 1994* cuts down on a suspect's/accused's right to remain silent. The rules are now as follows:

	s.34		s.36	s.37
Situation	a) Before being charged, *and* b) while being questioned under caution by a constable, *and* c) the constable is trying to discover whether, or by whom, an offence has been committed	On a suspect being charged or officially informed he may be prosecuted for an offence	a) On being arrested, *and* b) with an object, substance or mark: i) on his person, *or* ii) in or on his clothing or footwear, *or* iii) in his possession, *or* iv) in any place in which he is, at the time of his arrest, *and* c) the constable reasonably believes that the object, substance or mark has something to do with the suspect participating in a specified offence, *and* d) the constable informs the suspect of his suspicions and asks him to account for the object, substance or mark	a) On being arrested, *and* b) the suspect is at a place where a constable reasonably believes that the person's presence may be to do with participation in an offence, *and* c) the constable reasonably believes that the suspect's presence has something to do with the suspect participating in a specified offence, *and* d) the constable informs the suspect of his suspicions and asks him to account for his presence
Consequences apply if:	a) Suspect fails to mention a fact he might reasonably be expected to mention, *and* b) he later relies on that fact in his defence		Suspect fails or refuses to provide an explanation	Suspect fails or refuses to provide an explanation
Consequences	The court or magistrates can 'draw such inferences as appear proper' from the silence as applied to: 1 a submission of 'no case to answer' in a trial (see p.428 and p.437) 2 determining the guilt or innocence of a defendant at trial NB: Such inferences do *not* decide the matter alone - there must be other factors too (*CJPO 1994 s.38*)			

ss. 34, 36 and 37 will most often apply only to interviews in police stations (because of the general rule prohibiting interviews outside police stations). The usual interview safeguards for police station interviews will, of course, still apply - see pp.408, 410, 417.

Practical advice on silence in light of recent case law

➤ If advising a suspect to stay silent, one should record the reason to avoid 'adverse inferences' at trial (see p.465).

➤ It is wrong to advise clients to answer only some questions but not others, as the *whole* interview will be admissible and the silences will be hard to explain.

➤ The idea that 'an inference can never strengthen the prosecution case but only weaken a defence case once it has been found there is a case to answer' has been eroded by case law:

- ◆ If the defence makes a submission of no case to answer, the prosecution may still respond that the defence has relied on facts not mentioned on an earlier occasion (*Hart & McLean* 1998 6 Archb. News 1). This is significant in:
  - cases where a client has had a 'no comment' interview and then answered questions in a second interview or had several no comment interviews but later hands in a prepared statement when charged. If a solicitor believes there is no case to answer, he should advise the client to stay silent throughout. (Although it might be sensible to make a prepared statement, this should be kept in the solicitor's papers for use only if the judge dismisses the defence submission that there is no case to answer).
  - identification cases where there is going to be a case to answer at any stage because it is critical to raise any alibi at the first possible opportunity and at a time when the police can still check the alibi without the suspect being able to brief the alibi witness (see *R v Taylor* 1999 Crim LR 77).
- ◆ Solicitors and clients should not give reasons for a client staying silent unless they are content for the prosecution to inspect the solicitor's notes of the private consultation which preceded that interview, because the giving of reasons waives legal privilege (*R v Condron* 1997 Crim LR 215 and *R v Bowden* 1999 2 Cr.App.R. 176). This is significant since *CPIA 1996 s. 66* has been in force because a witness summons may now be made against defence solicitors requiring their attendance with their notes at the trial.

Principles from *R v Cowan* [1995] 4 All ER 939

- In normal circumstances, the burden of proof of proving the silence and inferences from it, is on the prosecution.
- The defendant's entitlement to remain silent is his right and choice.
- An inference from a failure to answer questions cannot on its own prove guilt (*CJPO 1994 s.38(3)*)
- A tribunal of fact (eg: the trial court) must first have established a case to answer before drawing a *s.34* inference.
- A tribunal of fact (eg: the trial court) might draw an adverse inference, if despite:
  - any evidence relied on to explain the silence, *or*
  - the absence of any evidence to explain the silence ...

  ... the tribunal concluded that silence could only sensibly be attributed to:
  - the defendant having no answer, *or*
  - the defendant has no answer that would stand up to interrogation.

Advising on silence at police stations

Effect of keeping silent	Risk of damage to client's case (see factors below)	Best advice to a client	
Adverse inferences will be drawn	**Low risk** There is no risk or a minimal risk in terms of possible damage to the client from the interview	Advise the client to answer the questions	
Adverse inferences may or may not be drawn	**Medium risk** The risk from the interview is that the client might not perform well or might come across badly	Advise the client to give a written statement →	see *R v McGarry* (1999 Crim LR 216) and *R v Daniel* (1998 Crim LR 818)
No adverse inferences will be drawn	**High risk** The risk from the interview is that the client will say something damning, possibly because he is frightened, confused or does not understand what is happening	Advise the client not to answer any questions but to remain totally silent or respond 'no comment' to everything that is asked	

Factors to consider in evaluating risk

- whether an early explanation will avoid the suspect being charged at all
- the evidence the police already have - if this is overwhelming, a confession may be advisable to help later in mitigation
- the capacity of a suspect to handle the stresses of an interview (eg: maturity, age and psychological ability to handle the interview)
- the gravity of the offence
- whether the suspect has any prior experience of either questioning or custody

VII Identification

➤ There are identification issues if there is disputed identification evidence (see Disputed identification (Turnbull guidelines) and the warning at trial, p.458).

1 Suspect is not known by police

➤ Evidence of identity is admissible if the witness is taken to the neighbourhood to identify the suspect (*D:2.17*).

➤ Evidence is *in*admissible if the witness is shown a police photograph (because this reveals to the witness that the suspect has a criminal record).

2 Suspect is known by police

➤ There are 5 methods of identification (the first 4 are listed in *D:2.1*):

1 Identification parade.
2 Group identification.
3 Video identification.
4 Confrontation.
5 Court identification.

➤ The suspect is initially offered a parade. If he refuses (*D:2.3*):

- the police may use any of the other methods (*D:2.6*).
- the suspect's refusal is noted **and this may be used in evidence against him at trial.**

1 Identification parade

➤ This is held if *either* (*D:2.3*):
- the suspect disputes an identification, *or*
- the investigating officer considers it would be useful *and* the suspect agrees.

➤ The procedure is set out in *Code D:Annex A* - a summary follows.

➤ It is conducted by a uniformed officer who is an inspector (or higher), and who is unconnected with the investigation (*D:2.2*).

➤ The suspect is told that (*D:2.15*):

a) he has a right to free legal advice, *and*
b) he may have a solicitor or friend present, *and*
c) he or his solicitor may see the first description of the suspect by the witnesses who will attend the parade, *and*
d) he is entitled to refuse, *and* the consequences of refusal (ie: confrontation at trial), *and*
e) he is entitled to know whether the witness has seen any photographs of himself.

➤ 8 persons *in addition* to the suspect take part (*D:8 Annex A*).

➤ Participants must resemble the suspect in height, age, general appearance, position in life (*D:9 Annex A*).

➤ The witness is segregated before and after the parade (*D:12 Annex A*).

➤ The witness must *not* be told if another witness has made an identification (*D:13 Annex A*).

➤ A video recording or colour photograph must be taken of the parade (*D:2.5*).

2 Group identification

- The witness is asked whether he recognises the suspect in an informal group of people (usually a public place) (*D:2.7*).
- The procedure is set out in *Code D Annex E* - a summary follows.
- The suspect must consent, but the police can proceed if necessary without it (*D:2.8*).
- It is conducted in a public place (*D:3 Annex E*).
- It is conducted by a uniformed officer who is an inspector (or higher), and who is unconnected with the investigation (*D:2.2*).
- The suspect is told that:
  a) he or his solicitor may see the first description of the suspect by witnesses who will attend the identification (*D:11 Annex E*), *and*
  b) he may have a solicitor or friend present (but only if he consents to the group identification). (There is no such right if he does not consent.) (*D:34*), *and*
  c) he is entitled to refuse, *and* the consequences of refusal (ie: confrontation at trial), *and*
  d) he is entitled to know whether the witness has seen any photographs of himself (*D:Annex A*).
- The witness must be able to see others whose appearance is broadly similar to that of the suspect (*D:5 Annex E*).
- The witness is segregated before and after the group identification (*D:17 Annex E*).
- The witness must *not* be told if another witness has made an identification (*D:15 Annex E*).
- A video or colour photograph should be taken of the general scene (*D:7 Annex E*).

3 Video identification

- The witness is shown a video tape with several people doing similar things, and asked whether he recognises the suspect.
- The suspect's consent is required, but the police can proceed if necessary without it (*D:2.11*).
- The procedure is set out in *Code D Annex B* - a summary follows.
- It is conducted by a uniformed officer who is an inspector (or higher), and who is unconnected with the investigation (*D:2.2*).
- The suspect is told that (*D:2.15*):
  a) he has a right to free legal advice, *and*
  b) he or his solicitor may see the first description of the suspect by the witnesses who will attend the parade, *and*
  c) he is entitled to refuse, *and* the consequences of refusal (ie: confrontation at trial), *and*
  d) he is entitled to know whether the witness has seen any photographs of himself.
- At least 8 others *in addition* to the suspect are shown on the film (*D:3 Annex B*).
- All the subjects are filmed in the same position, in similar conditions, doing similar things (*D:4 Annex B*).
- Only 1 witness views the film at any one time (*D:10 Annex B*).
- The witness may freeze the film. There is no limit on the number of times he may rerun it (*D:11 Annex B*).
- The witness must *not* be told if another witness has made an identification.

4 Confrontation
➤ A witness is confronted with the suspect and asked if it is the correct person (*Code D: Annex C*).
➤ This is conducted by a uniformed officer who is an inspector (or higher), and who is unconnected with the investigation (*D:2.2*).
➤ Consent is *not* required.
➤ This is used if the alternative methods (above) are impracticable.

5 Court identification
➤ The witness is asked whether he recognises the prisoner in the dock.
➤ Consent is *not* required.
➤ Used as a last resort (its evidential value is limited as the witness is 'identifying' a man in the dock).

VIII Samples in police detention (brief overview)

1 Non-intimate samples in police detention (*s.63*)

- Nails, non-pubic hair, a swab from the mouth (*s.58*) and saliva.
- **When in police detention:** the suspect's consent is *not* needed if one of the following situations apply:
  - a) A superintendent *[lowered to inspector by CJPA 2001 s.80 [not yet in force]]* (or higher officer) authorises the taking of the sample which he can only do if:
    - i) he has reasonable grounds for believing that the suspect has committed a 'recordable offence', *and*
    - ii) the search will tend to confirm or disprove a suspect's involvement.
  - *or* b) i) the suspect has been charged with a recordable offence (or informed that he will be reported for such), *and*
    - ii) - the suspect must not have had an intimate sample taken in relation to the offence being investigated, *or*
      - the suspect must not have had a non-intimate sample taken which has proved unsuitable or insufficient for analysis.
  - *or* c) the suspect has been convicted of a recordable offence.

    NB: this does not apply to anyone convicted before 10th April 1995 unless the conviction was for certain sexual offences.
  - ◆ b and c above also apply if the suspect is not in police detention.
  - ◆ If any of a or b or c are not true then the suspect's consent is needed and must be given in writing (*s.63(2)*).
- *Police have rights to take urine or non-intimate samples to test for drugs, subject to certain safeguards (not dealt with here) (s.63B) [not yet in force].*

2 Intimate samples in police detention (*s.62*)

- Blood, semen, urine, pubic hair, a swab taken from anywhere but the mouth (*s.58*).
- Consent is needed unless the same rules under 1a above (for non-intimate samples) apply.
  - ◆ Refusal means that the jury may draw such inference as they like (*s.62(10)*).

IX Detention after charge

➤ One of the 3 following alternatives applies:

1 **The custody officer *must* release the accused (*s.38(1)*):**

a) unconditionally (this is an unusual occurrence), *or*

b) on police bail.

- Police bail might be conditional upon the accused attending court on a particular date, etc. (*PACE 1984 s.47*) (**This is the most usual and likely occurence.**)

  Note: CDA 1998 s.46 [under pilot test but otherwise not yet generally in force] amends PACE 1984 s.47 so that if a person is bailed to appear before a Magistrates' Court, an early date is set for his first court appearance.

- Other conditions that the police may impose are listed in *BA 1976 s.3A.*
- Conditions may be set to ensure that the accused:

  i) surrenders to custody, *and/or*

  ii) does not commit an offence while on bail, *and/or*

  iii) does not interfere with a witness, or obstruct the course of justice in relation to himself or another.

  NB: The police have a power of arrest if a suspect fails to answer to police bail (*s.46A*).

or 2 **The custody officer *must* keep the accused in police detention if (*CJPO 1994 s.25*):**

➤ ... the suspect is charged with, and has previously been convicted of, one of the following: murder, attempted murder, manslaughter (and has been given a custodial sentence), rape or attempted rape.

➤ He must then be brought before a magistrate as soon as possible (*s.46(1)*).

or 3 **The custody officer *may* keep the accused in police detention if (*s.38(1)*):**

a) his name or address is unascertainable or doubtful, *or*

b) detention is necessary because he has reasonable grounds to believe the suspect will fail to appear at court to answer to bail, *or*

c) (if the suspect is arrested for an imprisonable offence), detention is necessary to prevent the suspect committing an offence, *or*

d) (if the suspect is arrested for a non-imprisonable offence), detention is necessary to protect anyone else from physical injury or damage to property, *or*

e) detention is necessary to prevent interference with the administration of justice or the investigation of offences, *or*

f) detention is necessary for the suspect's own protection.

➤ He must then be brought before a magistrate as soon as possible (*s.46(1)*).

➤ **Note:** 'imprisonable offence' is defined in the *Schedule* to the *BA 1976.*

X Charges

1 Summary offences

- The police must 'lay an information' at a Magistrates' Court within 6 months of the commission of the offence (*MCA 1980 ss.18,127*).
- An 'information' may only concern one offence, otherwise it is void for duplicity (*Magistrates' Courts Rules 1981 rule 12(1)*).
- When an 'information' is laid, the court issues a summons directing the defendant when to appear at court.

2 Indictable offences (including 'either way' offences)

- An indictment must be drawn up.
- It should be drawn up within 28 days of committal, but this time can be extended (*I(P)R 1971 r.5*).

3 Dangerous or careless driving (*RTOA 1988 s.1*)

- If there is no accident as a result of these offences, there can be no conviction for these offences, unless as a preliminary:
  - a) the defendant is warned at the time of the offence that a prosecution is possible, *or*
  - b) a summons is served on the defendant within 14 days, *or*
  - c) within 14 days, a notice of intended prosecution is served on the registered keeper (at the time of the offence) of the vehicle.

4 Summary offence linked with indictable or 'either way' offence: see 'Mode of trial', p.424.

A solicitor's role at the police station

A solicitor should...

- ... go prepared and take:
  - *PACE*, *Codes of Practice*, the Law Society's *Guide to the Conduct of a Solicitor at a Police Station*, copies of the relevant LSC funding application forms.
  - a letter (on headed paper) to be handed to the suspect explaining the solicitor's offer to advise the suspect if he requests it.
  - a standard proforma for taking instructions.
  - a pen and paper.
  - cigarettes (tobacco!), as many people request these.
- ... keep account of passing time with reference to the time limits for detention.
- ... attend any interview at which the client is questioned.
- ... listen to his client, and offer advice calmly; his role is to advise.
- ... ask for the investigating officer; seek details of why a client is detained and evidence against him.
- ... ask, as soon as he arrives at the police station, to see the custody record (the police must agree under *C:2.4)* and ask to speak to the custody officer.
- ... take a contemporaneous note of all that occurs. The solicitor may later be a witness!
- If a relative or friend has requested the solicitor's presence, it is up to the suspect whether or not to see the solicitor.

XI Other rights at a police station

Right to legal advice

Attending the police station voluntarily

- There is an unconditional right to legal representation (*C: Note 1A*).
- There is a right to legal advice in person, in writing, or by telephone, from the suspect's own solicitor (or from a duty solicitor, which is free of charge) (*C: 6.1*).

On arrest (*PACE s.58*)

- This is a right which a suspect has on arrival at the police station, and subsequently whenever he requests it.
- Legal advice from a *particular* solicitor can be delayed for up to 36 hours from the time detention was originally authorised if:

  a) a superintendent, or a higher officer, authorises the delay, *and*

  b) the investigation concerns a serious arrestable offence, and

  c) there are reasonable grounds for believing that this will prevent interference with evidence or people, alert others still at large, or hinder the recovery of property.
- If legal advice is delayed because of a concern that a particular solicitor will pass a message on to someone inappropriate, access to another solicitor on the duty solicitor scheme must be offered (*Code C, Annex B, Paragraph B4*).
- The defendant must be told of an attempt by a solicitor (on the solicitor's arrival) to contact him (*Code C:6.15*).

At interview

- A person who has requested legal advice may not be interviewed (or continue to be interviewed) unless he has received that legal advice, unless *either* (*C:6.6*):

  a) legal advice is barred under *PACE s.58* (see above) *or:*

  b) a superintendent, or a higher officer has reasonable grounds for believing that *either:*
     i) delay will harm persons or property, *or*
     ii) waiting for a solicitor's arrival will unduly delay the investigation (*C:6.6*), *or*

  c) an inspector authorises an interview and *either:*
     i) the nominated solicitor cannot be contacted or will not attend, *and* the defendant refuses the duty solicitor, *or*
     ii) the defendant changes his mind and agrees in writing or on tape (*C:6.6*).
- The solicitor may intervene during the interview (*C:6D*):
  - to clarify or challenge improper questions.
  - to advise the client not to reply.
  - to give further legal advice.
- The interviewer may not exclude a solicitor from the interview unless a superintendent is first consulted and he first speaks to the solicitor.

Reminders of the right to legal advice (*C: 6.5*)

- There is a right to be reminded of the right to legal advice:
  - before the start or recommencement of an interview at a police station.
  - before a review of detention.
  - after a charge if:
    - a police officer wants to draw a suspect's attention to the written or oral statement of another person, *or*
    - if further questions are to be put to a suspect about the offence.
  - before an identification parade or a request for an intimate body sample.

Right to have someone informed of arrival at the police station (*s.56*)

- The right can be delayed for up to 36 hours if:

  a) a superintendent [*lowered to inspector by CJPA 2001 s.74 [not yet in force]*], or higher officer, authorises it, *and*
  b) the investigation concerns a serious arrestable offence, *and*
  c) there are reasonable grounds for believing that this will prevent interference with evidence or people, alert others still at large, or hinder the recovery of property.

B Remand and bail

I Remand generally - in custody or on bail ?
II Bail

I Remand generally - in custody or on bail ?

➤ Remand is considered at every adjournment. It is to ensure the defendant will appear at the next hearing.

➤ The defendant has a right to bail - it is for the prosecution to show why this should not be granted.

<table>
<tr><th colspan="2">Remand</th></tr>
<tr><th>IN CUSTODY</th><th>ON BAIL</th></tr>
<tr><td colspan="2">Remand before conviction or committal for trial (MCA 1980 s.128)</td></tr>
<tr><td>➤ Remand for a maximum of 8 days at a time.
◆ This can be extended for another 8 days at a time if another hearing approves it.
➤ However, custody can be extended for 8 days at a time without the defendant being present, if:
◆ the defendant consents, and
◆ a solicitor is acting, and
◆ there have not been more than 3 consecutive remand hearings in the defendant's absence.
➤ A court can remand a defendant in custody for up to 28 days (MCA 1980 s.128A) if:
◆ it has previously remanded him in custody for the same offence, and
◆ he is in court, and
◆ it can set a date for the next stage of proceedings to occur, so he can be remanded until then.
➤ For a summary offence, the maximum time limit for an adult to be in custody from his first appearance until the start of the summary trial is 56 days (PO(CTL)R 1987 r.4A).
➤ For an either way/indictable offence, the maximum time limits for an adult for cumulative detention are (PO(CTL)R 1987 r.5, POA 1985 s.22, 22B):
◆ for up to 56 days in a Magistrates' Court before a summary trial.
◆ for up to 70 days before committal proceedings.
◆ for up to 112 days in the Crown Court between committal for trial and the start of the trial.
◆ for up to 182 days in the Crown Court between CDA 1998 s.51 sending for trial and the start of the trial (less any period in custody).
● Solicitors should mark the Crown Court file with the period so as to make an application for bail when the period has expired. Bail must then be given.
● If the time limits expire, the proceedings are stayed. Certain types of proceedings can be reinstituted afresh within 3 months.
NB: The defence should not warn the prosecution when the time limits are about to expire.
NB: A court may extend a limit if the prosecution has acted with all due diligence and expedition and there is good and sufficient cause.</td><td>➤ The maximum time limit is unlimited (!) with the defendant's consent.</td></tr>
<tr><td colspan="2">Remand after committal (MCA 1980 s.6(3))</td></tr>
<tr><td>➤ Remand until the case is heard (this can take months), subject to the limits above.</td><td>➤ Remand on conditions set by the court until the case is heard.</td></tr>
<tr><td colspan="2">Remand after conviction, until the next hearing (most probably sentencing) (MCA 1980 s.10(3))</td></tr>
<tr><td>➤ Magistrates' Courts may remand in custody for up to 3 weeks.
➤ The Crown Court may remand until the next hearing, whenever that is.</td><td>➤ Magistrates' Courts can remand on bail for up to 4 weeks.
➤ The Crown Court may remand until the next hearing.</td></tr>
</table>

II Bail

A. Right to bail (*BA 1976 s.4*)

➤ The following have the right to bail:

a) defendants before conviction, *and*

b) defendants after conviction during an adjournment for reports, *and*

c) offenders before magistrates for breaching a community rehabilitation order or community punishment order.

➤ BUT there is *no* right to bail for a defendant before the Crown Court awaiting:

a) sentence, *or*

b) appeal against conviction or sentence.

➤ There is *no* right to bail for someone with a previous conviction for murder, attempted murder, manslaughter, rape or attempted rape and who is now charged with any one of these unless the Court/constable (as applicable) find there to be 'exceptional circumstances' (*BA 1976 4(8), CJPO 1994 s.25*).

B. Procedure for bail hearings

Steps	
1	The prosecution objects to bail (see box overleaf).
2	The defence applies for bail.
3	Evidence is called (rules of evidence do not apply - *Re Moles* [1981] Crim.L.R. 170).
4	The court decides on remand in custody or on bail.
5	The court must give the defendant a note stating whether or not bail will be granted, together with reasons why and a list of any conditions it imposes.

Duty to hear further applications (*MCA 1980 ss.5,10,18* and *SCA 1981 s.81*)

Magistrates' Court	Crown Court
◆ There is a duty on the court to hear further applications for bail if a defendant is still in custody and the right to bail still applies • On a first re-hearing the court hears any argument of fact or law • On subsequent hearings, the court can only hear new arguments	◆ There is a duty on the court to hear further applications for bail if a defendant is still in custody and the right to bail still applies • On a first re-hearing the court hears any argument of fact or law • On subsequent hearings, the court can only hear new arguments ◆ There is a duty to hear further applications from those in custody: • prior to trial, sentence and appeals *and* • when a Magistrates' Court has refused bail after an adjournment *and* a certificate of full argument is presented to the court ▪ Whenever the case has *not* been sent to the Crown Court for trial, sentence or appeal, a certificate of full argument is required from the Magistrates' Court before a bail hearing is possible
Hearing before a High Court judge in chambers (a last resort if neither of the above courts grant bail) (*CJA 1967 s.22*)	
✘ No CDS legal funding is available - this is a civil matter	✘ As a matter of practice, no court will grant bail later if the judge in the High Court refuses it

C. Refusing bail

- The court considers various grounds (see below) in relation to the following 5 factors:
  a) the nature and seriousness of the offence, and the method of dealing with the defendant for it.
  b) character, antecedents (criminal records are admissible here), associations and community ties.
  c) record for previous grants of bail (criminal records are admissible on bail applications).
  d) the strength of evidence against the defendant (except for considering ground **1f** below).
  e) any other relevant factors.
- Strictly speaking, these factors only apply to **1a** and **1b** below, but in practice, they apply to all the grounds.
- The set of grounds that applies depends upon on whether an offence is imprisonable *or* not imprisonable.

1 Imprisonable offences

- Grounds for refusing bail (*BA 1976 Schedule I Part I*)
  a) The court is satisfied that substantial grounds exist to believe that a defendant would (if released):
     - fail to surrender to custody, *and/or*
     - commit another offence, *and/or*
     - interfere with witnesses or obstruct the course of justice.
  b) The offence is an indictable or either way offence *and* the defendant was on bail at the time of the offence.
  c) The defendant's own protection, or if he is young, his welfare.
  d) The defendant is in custody pursuant to a court sentence.
  e) Not enough information has been obtained about the defendant.
  f) The defendant was arrested for absconding or breaking the bail conditions set for *this* offence.
  g) Adjournment for enquiries or a report for which the defendant needs to be kept in custody.

2 Non-imprisonable offences

- Grounds for refusing bail (*BA 1976 Schedule I Part II*)
  a) The defendant's previous conduct on bail suggests he would not surrender.
  b) The defendant's own protection, or if he is young, his welfare.
  c) The defendant is in custody pursuant to a court sentence.
  d) Adjournment for enquiries or a report for which the defendant needs to be kept in custody.

***Drugs** (BA 1976 s.4(9)) [not yet in force]*
➤ *In taking any decisions under 1 or 2 above, the court must consider any misuse of controlled drugs by the defendant.*

Prosecution objections to bail (*B(A)A 1993 s.1(1)*)	
If new evidence comes to light after bail has been granted by a Magistrates' Court for an either way or indictable offence, the prosecution can ask the court to reconsider the decision to grant bail (*BA 1976 s.5B*).	
If a Magistrates' Court does grant bail against prosecution objections to a defendant charged with, or convicted of: ◆ an offence punishable by 5 years' or more imprisonment, *or* ◆ taking a conveyance, *or* ◆ aggravated vehicle taking ... →	... the prosecution can appeal to a Crown Court judge.

D. Bail conditions (*BA 1976 s.3*)

➤ The court may impose conditions to ensure that the defendant:

- surrenders to custody, *and/or*
- does not commit an offence while on bail, *and/or*
- does not interfere with a witness, or obstruct the course of justice in relation to himself or another, *and/or*
- makes himself available for enquiries to be made to assist the court in dealing with him for the offence, *and/or*
- (before the time for him to surrender to custody ie: his next appearance in Court) attends an interview with an authorised legal advisor.

➤ Conditions which the court *may* set include:

- **surety:** the sum depends on a surety's wealth, character, previous convictions, or his proximity to the defendant. The surety pays the money to the court if the defendant defaults on his bail conditions - no money is paid to the court on bail being granted.
- **security:** the defendant surrenders his money, chattels, passport, etc.
- **reporting:** to the police station at specified intervals.
- **curfew:** compulsory attendance between certain times at a certain place.
- **residence:** this may be, for example, in a bail hostel. (If so, the defendant may also be required to comply with bail hostel rules (*BA 1976 s.3(6ZA).*)
- **non-communication with a prosecution witness:** this may involve alternative accommodation for the defendant (possibly in a bail hostel) if a prosecution witness is a relative living in the same house.
- ***electronic monitoring:*** *if a child [not yet in force] (BA 1976 s.3(6ZAA) by CJPA 2001 s.131.)*

➤ Conditions which the court *must* set are:

- if the defendant is accused of murder, a requirement that he be medically examined (unless previous reports of his medical condition are satisfactory) (*BA 1976 s.6A*).

E. Surrender and absconding

1 Surrender

➤ A defendant granted bail must surrender at the time and place appointed (*BA 1976 s.6*).

➤ Failure to surrender is an offence unless there is a 'reasonable' cause - the defendant has the burden of proof (*BA 1976 ss.6(2), 6(3)*). The court may issue a warrant for the defendant's arrest (*BA 1976 s.7(1)-(2)*).

➤ Breach of a bail condition entitles the police to arrest the defendant - the breach is not an offence, but it may provide a ground on which bail can be withdrawn (*BA 1976 s.7*).

- The defendant must be produced before a properly constituted court within 24 hours of arrest (excluding Sundays, Good Friday and Christmas Day - *R v Glen Parva Young Offender Institution ex p G* (1998) 2 CAR 349).

2 Absconding

➤ Magistrates may impose a fine of up to £5,000 and a sentence of up to 3 months (*BA 1976 s.6(7)*).

➤ The Crown Court may impose an unlimited fine and a sentence of up to 1 year (*BA 1976 s.6(7)*).

C Mode of trial on an 'either way' offence

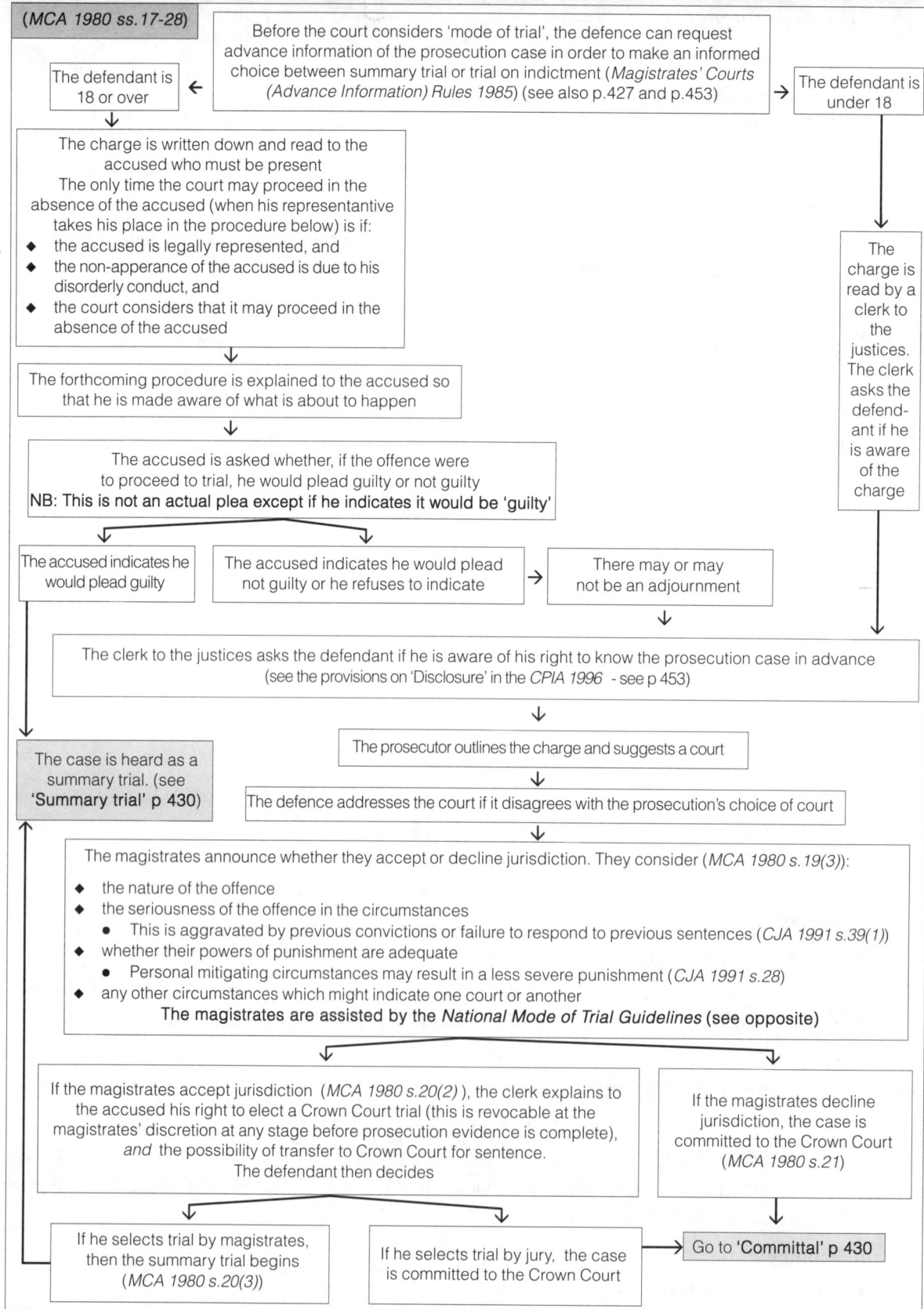

(*MCA 1980 ss.17-28*)

Before the court considers 'mode of trial', the defence can request advance information of the prosecution case in order to make an informed choice between summary trial or trial on indictment (*Magistrates' Courts (Advance Information) Rules 1985*) (see also p.427 and p.453)

← The defendant is 18 or over

→ The defendant is under 18

Defendant 18 or over:

The charge is written down and read to the accused who must be present
The only time the court may proceed in the absence of the accused (when his representantive takes his place in the procedure below) is if:

- the accused is legally represented, and
- the non-apperance of the accused is due to his disorderly conduct, and
- the court considers that it may proceed in the absence of the accused

↓

The forthcoming procedure is explained to the accused so that he is made aware of what is about to happen

↓

The accused is asked whether, if the offence were to proceed to trial, he would plead guilty or not guilty
NB: This is not an actual plea except if he indicates it would be 'guilty'

↓

- The accused indicates he would plead guilty → The case is heard as a summary trial. (see **'Summary trial' p 430**)
- The accused indicates he would plead not guilty or he refuses to indicate → There may or may not be an adjournment ↓

Defendant under 18:

The charge is read by a clerk to the justices. The clerk asks the defend-ant if he is aware of the charge

↓

The clerk to the justices asks the defendant if he is aware of his right to know the prosecution case in advance (see the provisions on 'Disclosure' in the *CPIA 1996* - see p 453)

↓

The prosecutor outlines the charge and suggests a court

↓

The defence addresses the court if it disagrees with the prosecution's choice of court

↓

The magistrates announce whether they accept or decline jurisdiction. They consider (*MCA 1980 s.19(3)*):

- the nature of the offence
- the seriousness of the offence in the circumstances
  - This is aggravated by previous convictions or failure to respond to previous sentences (*CJA 1991 s.39(1)*)
- whether their powers of punishment are adequate
  - Personal mitigating circumstances may result in a less severe punishment (*CJA 1991 s.28*)
- any other circumstances which might indicate one court or another

The magistrates are assisted by the *National Mode of Trial Guidelines* (see opposite)

↓

If the magistrates accept jurisdiction (*MCA 1980 s.20(2)*), the clerk explains to the accused his right to elect a Crown Court trial (this is revocable at the magistrates' discretion at any stage before prosecution evidence is complete), *and* the possibility of transfer to Crown Court for sentence.
The defendant then decides

- If he selects trial by magistrates, then the summary trial begins (*MCA 1980 s.20(3)*) → The case is heard as a summary trial.
- If he selects trial by jury, the case is committed to the Crown Court → Go to **'Committal' p 430**

If the magistrates decline jurisdiction, the case is committed to the Crown Court (*MCA 1980 s.21*)

↓

Go to **'Committal' p 430**

Defendant elects summary trial and subsequently changes his mind before all the prosecution evidence has been heard

The magistrates have discretion to refer the case to the Crown Court (*MCA 1980 s.25*).

National Mode of Trial Guidelines

a) Magistrates should assume that the prosecution version of the facts is correct.
b) If there is a complex question of law or fact, then magistrates should consider transferring the matter to the Crown Court.
c) If more than one defendant is charged, each may select a different court regardless of the choice of the other(s). Advance indication for preference for a particular court by one defendant in such a case is irrelevant at the mode of trial hearing stage - *R. v. Ipswich Justices ex parte Callaghan* 159 J.P. 748.
d) The magistrates must assume there will be a summary trial unless:
   - magistrates' sentencing powers will be insufficient (although they may later change their minds about whatever decision they reach (*R. v. Flax Bourton Magistrates' Court, ex parte Commissioners of Customs & Excise* [1996] The Times, 6th February 1996)), *or*
   - one of the aggravating factors below exists.

List of aggravating factors, per offence, that suggest a summary trial is *not* suitable

1 Burglary
- Dwelling: daytime - house occupied, night-time - house usually occupied, series of offences, soiling, damage, vandalism, professional hallmarks, high value of unrecovered property (greater than £10,000). NB: Violence or the threat of it means it *must* be sent to the Crown Court (*MCA 1980 Sch.I para 28(c)*)
- Non-dwelling: fear or violence caused to anyone lawfully on the premises, professional hallmarks, substantial vandalism, high value of unrecovered property (greater than £10,000)

2 Theft
- Breach of trust by one in authority, committed or disguised in a sophisticated manner, organised gang, vulnerable victim, high value of unrecovered property (greater than £10,000)

3 Assault (*OAPA 1861 ss.20, 47*)
- Weapon likely to cause serious injury, more than minor injury by kicking or head-butting, serious violence to a victim whose work brings him in contact with the public

4 Dangerous driving
- Defendant on alcohol or drugs, grossly excessive speed, racing, prolonged course of such driving, related offences

Summary offences linked to indictable offences which may be tried in the Crown Court

CJA 1988 s.40(1): Defendant accused of...	*CJA 1988 s.41(1)*: Defendant accused of an offence which is...
... common assault, taking a conveyance, driving whilst disqualified, certain types of criminal damage, assaulting a prison custody officer or a secure training centre custody officer *and* a) i) the summary offence is based on the same facts or evidence as the indictable offence, *or* ii) the summary offence is of a similar character to the indictable offence with which the defendant is also charged, *and* b) facts/evidence relating to the offence were disclosed in an examination taken before a justice in the presence of the person charged	a) punishable with imprisonment or involves obligatory or discretionary disqualification from driving, *and* b) it appears to the court that the summary offence arises out of circumstances which are the same as, or connected with, those giving rise to the offence that is triable 'either way'
Subsequent procedure for trial	
The Crown Court must treat the summary offence as an indictable offence, but must deal with the offender as a Magistrates' Court would have done	Evidence for the summary offence is not heard at committal. In the Crown Court the procedure depends on the plea: a) guilty plea: the court sentences for the summary offence with the same powers as a Magistrates' Court b) not-guilty plea: the summary offence is sent to the magistrates for trial

Advice to a client about selecting a court for trial

➤ There are several factors to consider which include the following:

1 Previous conviction?

✗ **Magistrates' Court:** magistrates may be seen as case-hardened, and may already be familiar with a police officer or with the defendant.

✓ **Crown Court:** conviction is thought by some to be less likely in a Crown Court where juries can be seen as sympathetic.

Note: There is no objective proof to support either of these contentions.

2 If there is a question of admissibility of evidence ...

✗ **Magistrates' Court:** magistrates decide matters of fact and law (ie: when giving a verdict, magistrates must attempt to 'forget' evidence which they have heard before holding it to be inadmissible).

✓ **Crown Court:** a Crown Court judge rules on the law, the jury decides matters of fact (ie: the jury is sent out while the judge decides evidential matters, so the jurors never hear evidence unless it is admissible).

3 Questions of cost

✓ **Magistrates' Court:** costs will be lower.

✗ **Crown Court:** costs will be higher.

4 Questions of stress

✓ **Magistrates' Court:** less publicity means less stress.

✗ **Crown Court:** more publicity means more stress.

5 Is the defendant in custody?

✓ **Magistrates' Court:** delay before trial is shorter (usually about 1 month).

✗ **Crown Court:** delay before trial is longer (about 6 months).

6 Sentence

✓ **Magistrates' Court:** sentences are less severe than in the Crown Court (but the defendant may be referred to the Crown Court for sentencing for certain crimes).

✗ **Crown Court:** sentences are more severe than in the Magistrates' Court.

D Preparations for a summary trial

➤ The solicitor should:

- ensure that he has a copy of the custody record (see *Code C:2.4,* p.418).
- ensure, where identification is disputed, that he has a copy of the original description from which the identification was made - see p.414 and note points on p.458.
- obtain a copy of the charge sheet.
- interview the client and take a detailed statement and full instructions as soon as possible.
- interview witnesses: take a proof of evidence signed and dated by the witness.
  - When interviewing a prosecution witness, it is good practice to have an independent party present, and to write to the prosecution to let them know the interview has taken place; this avoids any suspicion of putting pressure on a witness.
  - During an interview, challenge the witness's version of events. (**Note:** 'preparing a witness' for cross-examination is forbidden.)
- visit the area of the alleged offence, and prepare plans if appropriate.
- seek expert evidence: if the client is LSC funded, obtain the LSC's authorisation for the expenditure (cf: p.463 for disclosure of expert evidence).
- write to the prosecution asking for disclosure of the prosecution case.
  - In either way cases, the prosecution provides this before a mode of trial hearing (*Magistrates' Court (Advance Information) Rules 1985 r.4*). The prosecution does not *have* to disclose in purely summary trials, but a solicitor should request it.
  - *CPIA 1996 ss.1-21* and the common law contain the disclosure rules (see p.453). A solicitor should ask the prosecution for voluntary disclosure at this point as the main statutory disclosure will be *after* the plea.
  - details of any evidence the prosecution possesses which is favourable to the defence.
  - a record of any prosecution interviews with the defendant.
  - the names and addresses of witnesses the prosecution will not call.
  - a list of the witnesses interviewed by the police who the prosecution do *not* intend to call.
  - a statement of the defendant's criminal record. (This should be checked for inaccuracies.)
  - details of the criminal records of prosecution witnesses and co-defendants.
- put the prosecution case to the defendant, and note any comments he makes on it.
- decide whether witnesses should attend. (**Note:** where a witness will not need to be cross-examined, a statement submitted under *CJA 1967 s.9* will be sufficient - see pp.462-463.)
- if a witness's presence is desirable, write to him asking for written confirmation that he will turn up at a specified time.
  - If this confirmation is not forthcoming, the solicitor should write to the relevant court officer using the unanswered letter as proof that the witness is unlikely to attend of his own accord. The court officer issues a summons which is served personally on each witness (*MCA 1980 s.97*) or he can summons the releuctant witness to give a deposition (*MCA 1980 s.97A*).
    - The summons should be issued as soon as reasonably practicable, else delay could amount to a refusal to grant the process.

E Summary trial

1 **Joinder**

- Co-defendants tried on one 'information' for the same offence are tried together, unless there is a conflict of interest. The conviction of one does not prevent the acquittal of the other (eg: *Barsted v. Jones* (1964) 124 JP 400).
- Defendants tried on separate 'informations' can be tried together if the defence agrees. But the court always has discretion to consider that as the facts are the same, or that as the offences are similar and related, a joint trial is 'in the interests of justice' (*Chief Constable of Norfolk v. Clayton* [1983] 2 AC 473).

2 **Defect in process**

- If the defence is misled by an error in the 'information', summons or warrant, then it may seek an adjournment to rethink its case. It has no other remedy in these circumstances (*MCA 1980 s.123*).

3 **Procedure**

Steps

1 The charge is read to the defendant (unless summary trial has started straight from a mode of trial hearing where the charge has already been read to the defendant - *CPIA 1996*).

2 The defendant pleads 'guilty' (except if he has already indicated this on a mode of trial hearing (*MCA 1980 s.17(6)*)) or 'not guilty'. He can alter this at any time before sentence.

- If the plea is 'guilty', the court proceeds to sentence (perhaps holding a Newton hearing beforehand, see p.450).

3 The statutory disclosure procedure applies from this point (see p.453) and the disclosure of expert evidence procedure applies too (see p.463).

4 The prosecution makes an opening speech outlining the facts and issues (*MCR 1981 r.13(1)*).

5 The prosecution calls evidence.

6 The legal representative of the defence must tell the court at this point that the defendant will give evidence, else the magistrate will give a 'silence warning' (see p.465) (*CJPO 1994 s.35*).

7 The defence may submit 'no case to answer' (*Practice Direction (Submission of No Case)* [1962] 1 WLR 227) (see p.432 for a discussion of this) if *either*:

- there is no evidence to prove an essential element of the offence, *or*
- the prosecution evidence is so discredited under cross-examination *or* so manifestly unreliable that no reasonable tribunal could convict on it.

- For the effect of 'adverse inferences' on a defendant's decision not to testify, see p.465.
- The prosecution may reply to this submission.
- If the submission is accepted, the case is dismissed, otherwise step 8 applies.

8 The defence may make an opening speech, or may immediately move to calling evidence (*MCR 1981 r.13(2)-13(6)*).

9 If the defence evidence throws up unforeseeable surprises, the prosecution can seek leave to call more evidence.

10 If the defence did *not* make an opening speech, it has the right to address the court last.

11 The magistrates reach a majority verdict and then consider an appropriate sentence and costs.

Points of law at the trial

- ➤ A magistrate's clerk can advise the bench on matters of law, but not of fact.
- ➤ If a point of law is raised at any stage, the other party always has a right to reply.

4 Costs

a) The defendant is acquitted (not LSC funded) (*POA 1985 s.16(1)*).

- ➤ Costs are met from central funds, *unless* the defendant brought suspicion on himself by his own conduct (*POA 1985 s.16(7)*).

b) The defendant is acquitted (he is LSC funded).

- ➤ Costs are not met by central funds, but by the LSC. Any contribution the defendant has made may be refunded (*POA 1985 s.21(4A)*) unless there are exceptional circumstances.

c) The defendant is convicted.

- ➤ Costs must be met by the defendant where the court is satisfied that he has the means and ability to pay (*POA 1985 s.18(1)*). (Costs must be met by the LSC if the offender is an assisted person, but may be subject to a RDCO - see p.13.) The court makes an order for a specified sum *(POA 1985 s.18(3)*).

F Committal and sending for trial

I Committal or sending for trial?

➤ This section governs the next steps in the procedure when an accused is charged with an offence which is an either way offence or triable only on indictment.

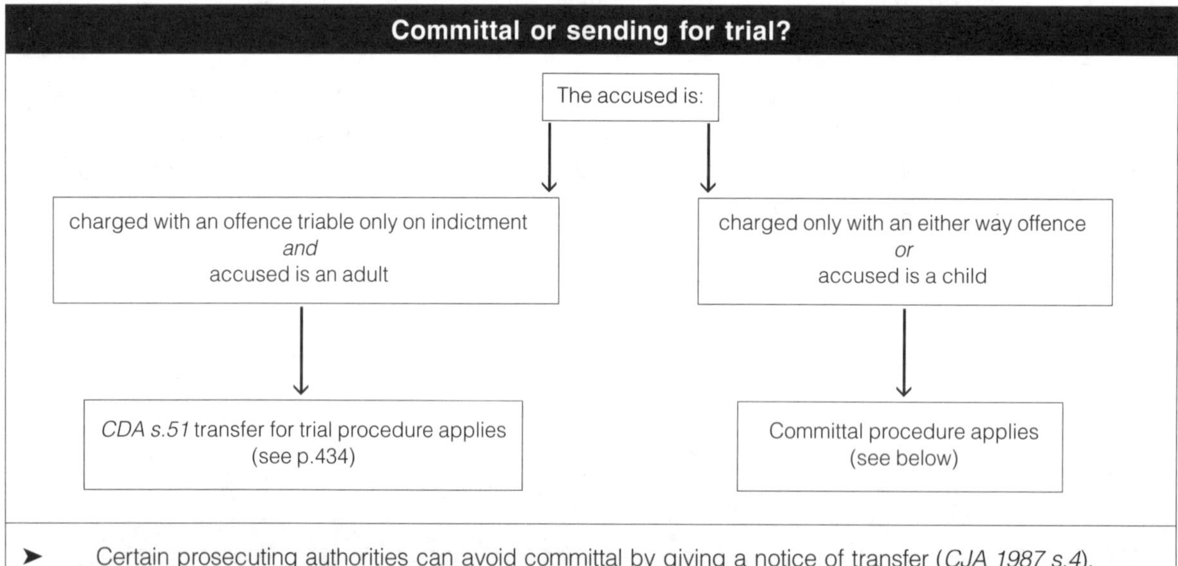
Committal or sending for trial?
The accused is:
charged with an offence triable only on indictment
and
accused is an adult
charged only with an either way offence
or
accused is a child
CDA s.51 transfer for trial procedure applies
(see p.434)
Committal procedure applies
(see below)

➤ Certain prosecuting authorities can avoid committal by giving a notice of transfer (*CJA 1987 s.4*).

- Eg: for offences of a violent/sexual nature where there is a child witness or serious/complex fraud.

II Committal

➤ Committal proceedings are the means by which a Magistrates' Court decides if there is sufficient evidence to send an accused to the Crown Court.

➤ There are 2 types of committal hearing, both in *MCA 1980 s.6* - *s.6(1)* committal and *s.6(2)* committal.

s.6(1) **committal**	***s.6(2)*** **committal**
A committal **with** consideration of evidence	A committal **without** consideration of evidence

Committal procedure

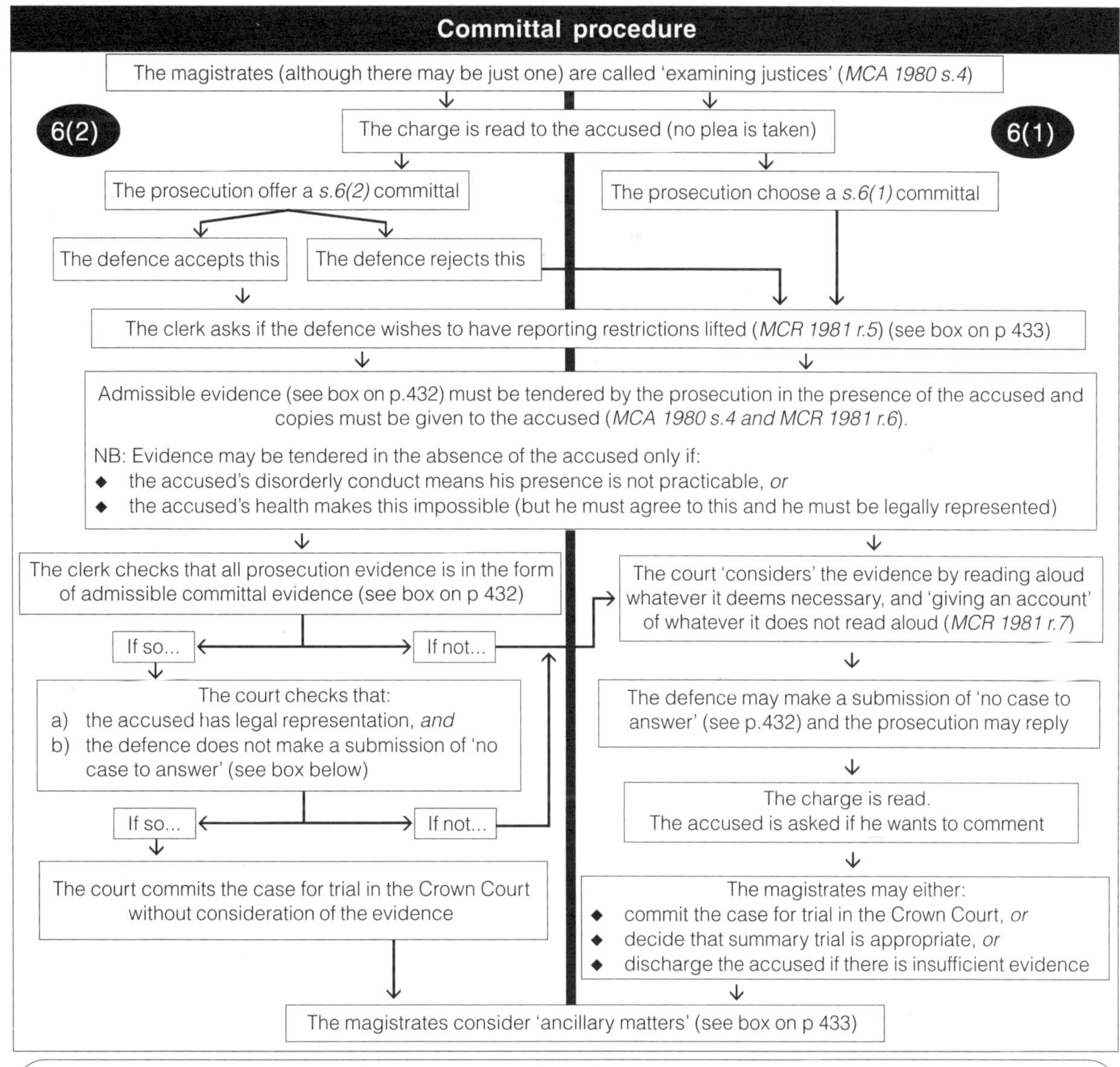

The magistrates (although there may be just one) are called 'examining justices' (*MCA 1980 s.4*)
6(2)
The charge is read to the accused (no plea is taken)
6(1)
The prosecution offer a *s.6(2)* committal
The prosecution choose a *s.6(1)* committal
The defence accepts this
The defence rejects this
The clerk asks if the defence wishes to have reporting restrictions lifted (*MCR 1981 r.5*) (see box on p 433)
Admissible evidence (see box on p.432) must be tendered by the prosecution in the presence of the accused and copies must be given to the accused (*MCA 1980 s.4 and MCR 1981 r.6*).
NB: Evidence may be tendered in the absence of the accused only if:
◆ the accused's disorderly conduct means his presence is not practicable, *or*
◆ the accused's health makes this impossible (but he must agree to this and he must be legally represented)
The clerk checks that all prosecution evidence is in the form of admissible committal evidence (see box on p 432)
If so...
If not...
The court checks that:
a) the accused has legal representation, *and*
b) the defence does not make a submission of 'no case to answer' (see box below)
If so...
If not...
The court commits the case for trial in the Crown Court without consideration of the evidence
The court 'considers' the evidence by reading aloud whatever it deems necessary, and 'giving an account' of whatever it does not read aloud (*MCR 1981 r.7*)
The defence may make a submission of 'no case to answer' (see p.432) and the prosecution may reply
The charge is read.
The accused is asked if he wants to comment
The magistrates may either:
◆ commit the case for trial in the Crown Court, *or*
◆ decide that summary trial is appropriate, *or*
◆ discharge the accused if there is insufficient evidence
The magistrates consider 'ancillary matters' (see box on p 433)

Which committal should be chosen?

- A *s.6(2)* committal is quicker and will usually be preferable.
- A *s.6(2)* committal can only take place if:

a) all evidence tendered by the prosecution at committal is (see p.432 for in-depth definitions):

- in the form of written statements, *or*
- in the form of documents or exhibits referred to in the written statements, *or*
- 6(2) in the form of depositions, *or* 6(2)
- in the form of documents or exhibits referred to in depositions, *or*
- any particular document allowed by statute, *and*

b) the defendant has a solicitor acting for him, *and*

c) the defence do not claim that the prosecution has insufficient evidence.

Prosecution reasons:	Defence reasons:
6(1) identification is at issue - the Attorney General has advised that *s.6(2)* is only suitable if the prosecution, defence and court are satisfied about reliability of identification evidence	◆ to submit no case to answer, *or* 6(1) ◆ to obtain publicity (it may help trace witnesses), *or* ◆ to persuade a court to commit on a lesser charge.

Test for committal to the Crown Court

➤ The test is whether, having heard the case, there is sufficient evidence to put the accused on trial for indictment (ie: if a reasonably minded jury, properly directed, would convict on the evidence provided). If so, then the magistrates will commit the case to the Crown Court for trial.

Test for a submission of 'no case to answer'

➤ *R. v. Galbraith* [1981] 1 WLR 1039 - taken at its highest, could a jury convict on the evidence?
- This 'depends on the view to be taken of a witness's reliability, or other matters ... within the jury's province, and where *one possible view* of the facts is that there is evidence on which the jury could properly convict [and if all these apply, then a submission will fail]'.

➤ *Practice Direction (Submission of No Case)* [1962] 1 WLR 227 (there is doubt if this applies to committal as well as to summary trial) - says that to succeed in the submission, one must show that:
- evidence in support of an essential element of the offence is absent, *or*
- the case is so unreliable that a jury could not possibly convict.

Admissible committal evidence

➤ Admissible committal evidence is evidence that is tendered **by, or on behalf of, the prosecutor**, *and* is:
- **a written statement**, *or*
  - this is a statement that:
    - purports to be signed by the person making it, *and*
    - contains a declaration by that person that:
      - it is true to his best knowledge and belief *and*
      - if tendered in evidence the person would be liable to prosecution if it contained anything he knew to be false or untrue, *and*
    - has been given together with any documents or exhibits it refers to (or copies have been given) (these must be inspectable if copies are not available) to each of the other parties before being tendered by the prosecutor, *and*
    - contains the defendant's age (but only if he is under 18).
- **a deposition**, *or*

  A document is anything in which any information of any description is recorded (*MCA 1980 s.5A(6)*)

  - this is a document that:
    - has been sent to the prosecutor after the *MCA 1980 s.97A(9)* procedure, *and*

      (**NB**: the *MCA 1980 s.97A* procedure is when an evidence statement of has been taken from someone who will not voluntarily give evidence at committal and is made to do so pursuant to a witness summons, or is arrested to do so - see p.427.)
    - has been given together with any documents or exhibits it refers to (or copies have been given) (these must be inspectable if copies are not available) to each of the other parties before the inquiry as 'examining justices' begins.
- **documents or other exhibits referred to in written statements or depositions**, *or*
- **a documentary hearsay statement** (*CJA 1988 ss.23-24* - see p.462), *or*
  - the prosecution must have signed a certificate that there is reasonable cause to believe the evidence may be properly used at trial.
- **any other document allowed by statute**.

Reporting restrictions (*MCA 1980 s.8*)

- The press may report the names of defendants/witnesses, the charge and result of the proceedings.
- The press may not report evidence (to prevent a jury being prejudiced).
- A single defendant may ask that restrictions be lifted (eg: to obtain publicity to help trace witnesses).
  - If a co-defendant requests, restrictions are lifted if it is 'in the interests of justice' (*MCA 1980 s.8(2A)*).

Ancillary matters

1 **Witness summons to ensure witnesses attend the Crown Court trial**

- If the defendant is committed or sent for trial in the Crown Court, the Magistrates' Court must remind the defendant of his right to object (within 14 days) to any statement or deposition being read at trial instead of the witness giving oral evidence (which of course allows cross-examination (*MCR 1981 r.8*)).
  - The general rule, if the defendant does not object, is that all statements of a particular witness forming part of the committal bundle will be read at trial instead of the witness being called to give oral evidence.
- *Criminal Procedure (Attendance of Witnesses) Act 1965 s.2* contains the rules for issue of a witness summons. This is issued to compel any witness with material evidence to attend trial who will not attend voluntarily. Crown Court rules govern the procedure which is very strict.
  - Some of the rules that apply are:
    - if after committal, parties must make an application for a witness summons as soon as reasonably practicable after committal.
    - a detailed affidavit is needed in support.
    - evidence that the evidence sought is likely to be material in the criminal proceedings is needed in support.
    - the court may also make a witness summons of its own motion.
    - a Crown Court judge will punish disobedience of a witness summons as contempt.

2 **LSC funding**

- The defence can apply for an extension of LSC funding to cover a Crown Court trial. It also confirms whether or not the defendant's financial circumstances are altered.

3 **Bail** (*MCA 1980 s.6(3)*)

- Bail is usually extended until trial. If the defendant is in custody, a bail application can be made.

4 **Fix a date for a PDH**

- The magistrates fix a date for a plea and directions hearing (see pp.437-438).

III Sending for trial

➤ An adult before a Magistrates' Court who is charged with an offence triable only on indictment is immediately sent to the Crown Court for trial (*CDA 1998 s.51(1)*).

- The accused is sent for trial (*CDA 1998 s.51*):
  - for the indictable-only offence, *and*
  - for any either way or summary offence with which he is charged which:

    appears to the court to be related to the indictable-only offence, *and*
  - (in the case of a summary offence only), is punishable with imprisonment or involves obligatory or discretionary disqualification from driving.
- Any other adult who is charged jointly with the accused with an either way offence which is related to the indictable-only offence, is also immediately sent to the Crown Court for trial of the either way offence (*CDA 1998 s.51*).
- A child jointly charged with the accused for the indictable offence is, if the court considers it necessary in the interests of justice, sent immediately to the Crown Court for trial (*CDA 1998 s.51*).

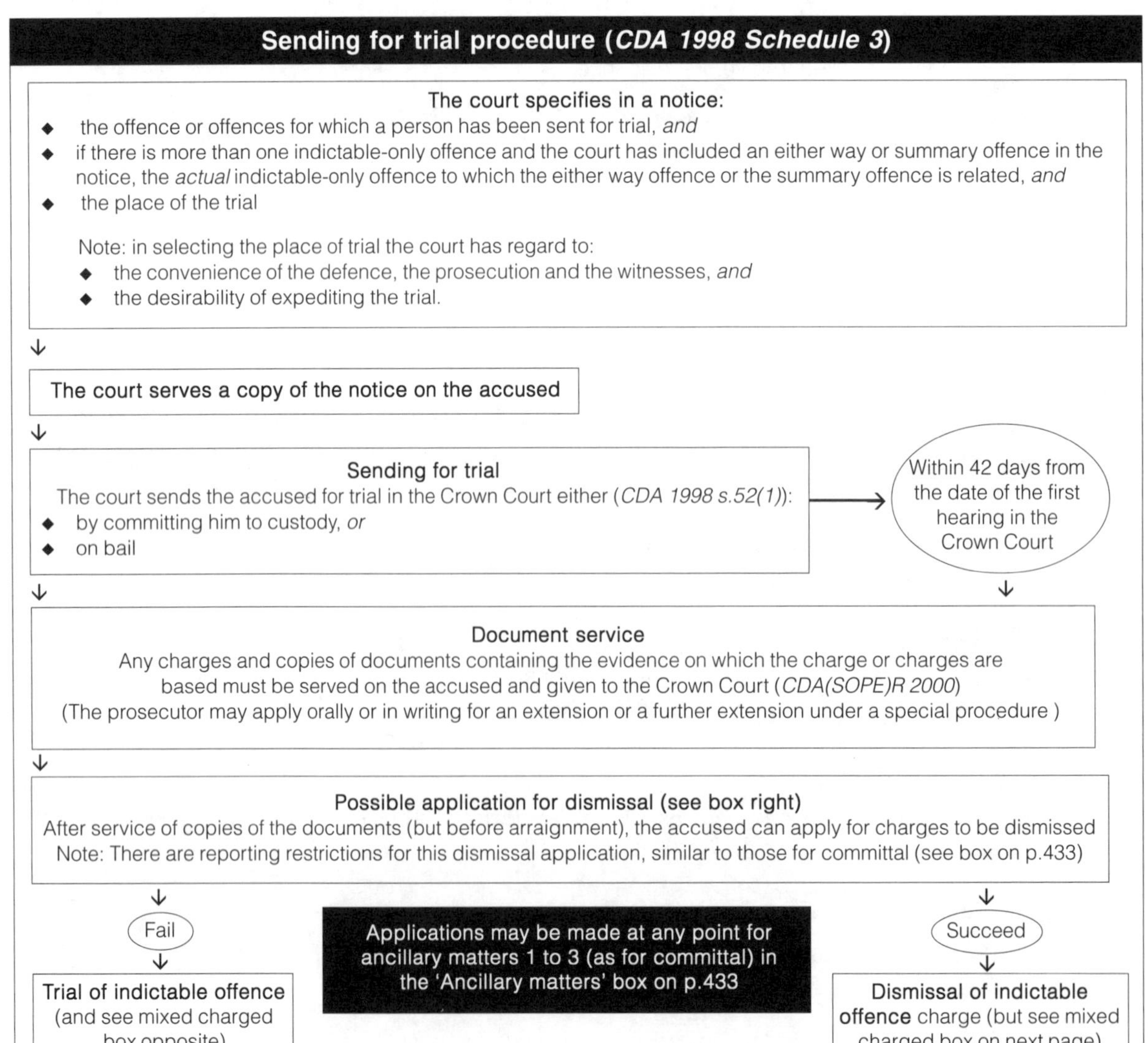

Sending for trial procedure (CDA 1998 Schedule 3)
The court specifies in a notice:
◆ the offence or offences for which a person has been sent for trial, and
◆ if there is more than one indictable-only offence and the court has included an either way or summary offence in the notice, the actual indictable-only offence to which the either way offence or the summary offence is related, and
◆ the place of the trial
Note: in selecting the place of trial the court has regard to:
◆ the convenience of the defence, the prosecution and the witnesses, and
◆ the desirability of expediting the trial.
The court serves a copy of the notice on the accused
Sending for trial
The court sends the accused for trial in the Crown Court either (CDA 1998 s.52(1)):
◆ by committing him to custody, or
◆ on bail
Within 42 days from the date of the first hearing in the Crown Court
Document service
Any charges and copies of documents containing the evidence on which the charge or charges are based must be served on the accused and given to the Crown Court (CDA(SOPE)R 2000)
(The prosecutor may apply orally or in writing for an extension or a further extension under a special procedure)
Possible application for dismissal (see box right)
After service of copies of the documents (but before arraignment), the accused can apply for charges to be dismissed
Note: There are reporting restrictions for this dismissal application, similar to those for committal (see box on p.433)
Fail
Trial of indictable offence (and see mixed charged box opposite)
Applications may be made at any point for ancillary matters 1 to 3 (as for committal) in the 'Ancillary matters' box on p.433
Succeed
Dismissal of indictable offence charge (but see mixed charged box on next page)

MIxed charges (*CDA 1998 Schedule 3 paras.6-7*)

- If the accused is sent to the Crown Court for:
  - an indictable-only offence *and* other either way offences:
    - if the accused succeeds in having the indictable-only offence dismissed, then the Crown Court holds a plea-before venue hearing to ascertain if the either way offence should be tried in the Crown Court or the Magistrates' Court.
      - If the accused pleads guilty, then the court immediately proceeds to sentence.
      - If the accused pleads not guilty, there is a full mode of trial hearing (and the mode of trial guidelines need to be considered) (see p.420).
    - if the accused fails in having the indictable-only offence dismissed, then the Crown Court considers the indictable-only offence and the either way offence.
  - an indictable-only offence *and* other summary offences:
    - if the accused is convicted on the indictable-only offence, the Crown Court considers whether the summary offence is related to any offences triable only on indictment. If they are related, the court states to the person the substance of the summary offence and asks him whether he pleads guilty or not guilty.
      - If the accused pleads guilty, the Crown Court convicts him of the summary offence, but may deal with him for the summary offence only in a manner in which a Magistrates' Court could have dealt with him.
      - If the accused pleads not plead guilty, the powers of the Crown Court cease in respect of the summary offence and the matter goes for trial to the Magistrates' Court.

Application for dismissal of indicatble-only charge

- After service of copies of the documents (but before arraignment), the accused can apply for charges to be dismissed.
- It is possible to obtain the attendance of prosecution witnesses for cross-examination purposes if it is in the interests of justice to do so.

G Preparations for Crown Court hearings and trial

Between committal and trial

1 **Make all relevant preparations as for summary trial (see p.427)** ***and get the committal bundle.***
2 **Apply to the Crown Court or a High Court judge in chambers for bail, if necessary.**
3 **Brief counsel** (see box below for '*Format of a brief to counsel*').
4 **Ensure that the prosecution has turned over all relevant material (following the disclosure procedure - see p.453).**
5 **Ensure that witnesses can attend as planned.**
   ➤ This is achieved by applying for any necessary witness summons (see p.433).
6 **Exchange any expert witness statements with the prosecution as soon as practicable after committal** (*The Crown Court (Advance Notice of Expert Evidence) (Amendment) Rules 1997*) (see p.463)
6 **Take instructions on mitigation.**
7 **Obtain disclosure of materials unused by the prosecution** (a common law right and cf: *R. v. Ward* (1993) 96 Cr.App.Rep. 1).

Format of a brief to counsel

1 **Heading:** case, title, court, relevant LSC funding certificate or fee, case number.
2 **List of enclosures**
   ➤ Eg: LSC representation order, list of previous convictions, bundle of witness statements, comments on witness statements, bail notice, indictment, custody record.
3 **Prosecution allegations**
   ➤ Direct counsel to specific allegations in the witness statements.
   ➤ Define facts which are not in dispute.
4 **Defence allegations**
   ➤ Give a brief statement of the relevant law.
   ➤ Apply the law to the circumstances of the case.
5 **Note any evidential problems**
   ➤ Character: *CEA 1898 s.1(f)(ii)-(iii)* (Note the effect that any 'unspent' convictions may have on the defendant's character (see p.457). Rules for when convictions are spent are in *ROA 1974*).
   ➤ Evidence: admissible as an exception to the rule against hearsay (ie: opinion, *res gestae*, etc).
   ➤ Confessions: point out any grounds for exclusion.
   ➤ Corroboration: note where this is needed, and highlight any suitable evidence, see p.458.
   ➤ Discuss briefly the reasons for and against the defendant testifying, see p.457. State:
   a) why the difficulty is likely to arise, *and*
   b) any consequences which follow.
6 **Mitigation:** give any relevant information.
7 **Request:** 'Would counsel please advise ... and attend court on ... at ...'.

H Crown Court hearings and trial

A. The indictment

- The prosecution is responsible for seeing that an indictment is drafted.
- An indictment is a statement of offences (called 'counts') with which an accused is charged.
  - A 'count' is an individual charge.
  - Each count in an indictment must allege only one offence (*IR 1971 r.4(2)*).
- The indictment must be preferred within 28 days of (*I(P)R 1971 r.5*):
  - the date of committal (if there was a committal), *or*
  - the date on which copies of the documents containing the evidence on which the charge or charges are based are served (if the accused was sent for trial under *CDA 1998 s.51*).
- **Joinder:** Charges for any offences may be joined in the same indictment if the charges are founded on the same facts, or form or are a part of a series of offences of the same, or a similar character (*IR 1971 r.9*).
- 2 or more accused may be joined in one indictment.

B. Procedure

A Plea and Directions Hearing ('PDH') is held (see flowchart on p.438) - this includes arraignment. This also falls into the definition of a pre-trial hearing (see box left below)

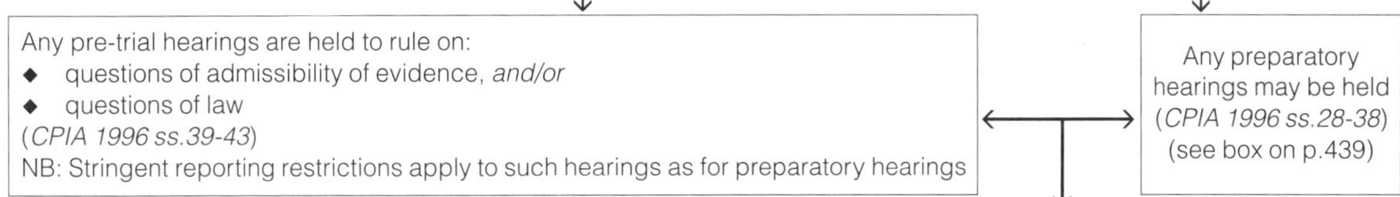

Any pre-trial hearings are held to rule on:
◆ questions of admissibility of evidence, and/or
◆ questions of law
(CPIA 1996 ss.39-43)
NB: Stringent reporting restrictions apply to such hearings as for preparatory hearings
Any preparatory hearings may be held (CPIA 1996 ss.28-38) (see box on p.439)

The trial

Steps	
1	The prosecution makes an opening speech outlining the facts and the issues of the case.
2	The prosecution calls evidence.
3	The legal representative of the defence must tell the court at this point that the defendant will give evidence, else the judge will give a 'silence warning' (see p.465) (*CJPO 1994 s.35*).
4	The defence may submit that there is no case to answer. ◆ The prosecution may reply to this submission. ◆ If the submission is accepted the case is dismissed, otherwise proceed to the next step.
5	If the defence will be producing evidence other than just from the accused, they have a right to an opening speech, otherwise they do not.
6	The defence calls evidence.
7	If defence evidence throws up unforeseeable surprises, the prosecution can seek leave to call more evidence.
8	The prosecution delivers its closing speech to the jury.
9	The defence delivers its closing speech to the jury.
10	The judge sums up and directs the jury as necessary.
11	The jury must deliver a unanimous verdict. ◆ A majority verdict (11:1, 10:2) is acceptable if unanimity is impossible after a reasonable time (minimum of 2 hours) (*Juries Act 1974 s.17(1)*).
12	If the jurors cannot agree on a unanimous or a majority verdict, a retrial may be held. The prosecution have discretion to ask for a retrial.

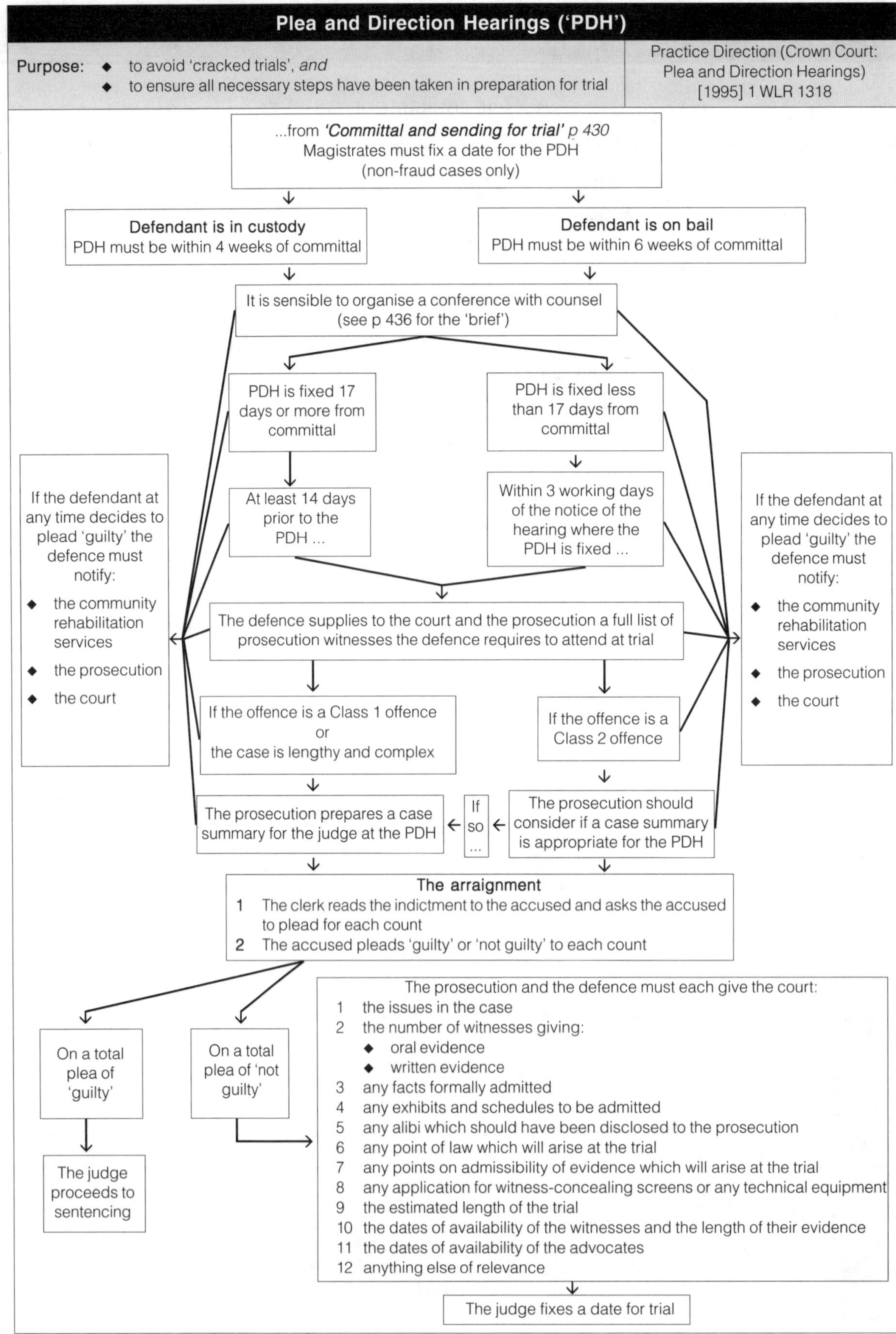
Plea and Direction Hearings ('PDH')
Purpose: to avoid 'cracked trials', and
to ensure all necessary steps have been taken in preparation for trial
Practice Direction (Crown Court: Plea and Direction Hearings) [1995] 1 WLR 1318
...from 'Committal and sending for trial' p 430
Magistrates must fix a date for the PDH
(non-fraud cases only)
Defendant is in custody
PDH must be within 4 weeks of committal
Defendant is on bail
PDH must be within 6 weeks of committal
It is sensible to organise a conference with counsel
(see p 436 for the 'brief')
PDH is fixed 17 days or more from committal
PDH is fixed less than 17 days from committal
At least 14 days prior to the PDH ...
Within 3 working days of the notice of the hearing where the PDH is fixed ...
If the defendant at any time decides to plead 'guilty' the defence must notify:
the community rehabilitation services
the prosecution
the court
The defence supplies to the court and the prosecution a full list of prosecution witnesses the defence requires to attend at trial
If the defendant at any time decides to plead 'guilty' the defence must notify:
the community rehabilitation services
the prosecution
the court
If the offence is a Class 1 offence
or
the case is lengthy and complex
If the offence is a Class 2 offence
The prosecution prepares a case summary for the judge at the PDH
If so ...
The prosecution should consider if a case summary is appropriate for the PDH
The arraignment
1 The clerk reads the indictment to the accused and asks the accused to plead for each count
2 The accused pleads 'guilty' or 'not guilty' to each count
On a total plea of 'guilty'
The judge proceeds to sentencing
On a total plea of 'not guilty'
The prosecution and the defence must each give the court:
1 the issues in the case
2 the number of witnesses giving:
oral evidence
written evidence
3 any facts formally admitted
4 any exhibits and schedules to be admitted
5 any alibi which should have been disclosed to the prosecution
6 any point of law which will arise at the trial
7 any points on admissibility of evidence which will arise at the trial
8 any application for witness-concealing screens or any technical equipment
9 the estimated length of the trial
10 the dates of availability of the witnesses and the length of their evidence
11 the dates of availability of the advocates
12 anything else of relevance
The judge fixes a date for trial

Preparatory hearings (*CPIA 1996 ss.28-38*)

- Any time after committal but before a jury has been sworn, a Crown Court judge may hold a preparatory hearing (in a non-fraud case only), if he decides that a trial will be so complex or so long that there will be a substantial benefit for one of the following purposes:
  - to identify the issues likely to be material to the verdict of the jury.
  - to assist the jury's comprehension of such issues.
  - to expedite proceedings before the jury.
  - to assist the judge in the management of the trial.
- The hearing starts with arraignment (see p.438) (unless it has been done before, eg: at the PDH).
- The powers of the judge at a preparatory hearing are (*s.31*):
  - to rule on the admissibility of evidence.
    - There may be an appeal to the Court of Appeal (only with leave of the judge or the Court of Appeal) (*s.35*). No jury may be sworn until after the appeal is heard.
  - to rule on a question of law.
    - There may be an appeal to the Court of Appeal (only with leave of the judge or the Court of Appeal) (*s.35*). No jury may be sworn until after the appeal is heard.
  - to order the prosecutor to give a written statement of:
    a) the principal facts of the prosecution case, *and/or*
    b) witnesses, *and/or*
    c) exhibits, *and/or*
    d) a proposition of law on which the prosecutor will rely, *and/or*
    e) the consequences of the above.
  - to order, *but only following any order to the prosecution to give a statement,* the defence to give the prosecution and the court a statement of:
    - its defence in general terms and the principal matters in dispute with the prosecution, *and/or*
    - written notice of objections to the prosecution case statement, *and/or*
    - written notice of points of law it might raise, *and/or*
    - written notice of points of admissibility of evidence.
  - to order the prosecution to prepare the case in a form that the jury will understand.
  - to order the prosecution to give a list of documents or matters with which it agrees.
  - to order the prosecution to change its case if there are valid objections raised after the written statement ordered above.
- The judge must warn the accused of the consequences of later departing from the case outlined in the defence statement above (*s.31(8)*).
  - The consequences are that at trial a jury may draw 'adverse inferences' following:
    - the judge's comment on this, *and/or*
    - other parties' comments on this (with leave).

  NB: The judge must point out that the jury must have regard to the extent of departure from the case and any justifications for such departure (*s.34*).

Reporting restrictions (*CPIA 1996 ss.37-38*)

- There is no reporting allowed of the preparatory hearing (or an appeal from it) until after trial unless a judge authorises it. The following details are allowed to be reported however:
  - the identity of the court and the name of the judge.
  - the details of the accused and witnesses.
  - the details of the offence(s).
  - the name of counsel and solicitors.
  - the details of any adjournment.
  - the details of any bail arrangements.
  - the details of whether LSC funded help was granted or not.

I Sentencing powers

NB: All sentences are subject to the statutory limits laid down for particular offences.

I	Custodial sentences	VI	General disqualification from driving
II	Suspended sentences	VII	Motoring penalties
III	Fines	VIII	Ancillary orders
IV	Community sentences	IX	Summary of some youth sentences
V	Discharges		

A court is required to treat a racial element to any crime as an aggravating factor (*PCC(S)A 2000 s.153*)

I Custodial sentences

A. Main principles

1 First custodial sentence

➤ The offender cannot be given a custodial sentence for the first time if he is not legally represented during the sentencing process *unless* (*PCC(S)A 2000 s.83*):
- he was granted a right to representation funded by the LSC as part of the Criminal Defence Service but the right was withdrawn because of his conduct , *or*
- the offender has not applied for such representation despite previous opportunity to do so.

2 Imposition

➤ A custodial sentence can be imposed if ...

a) **... the 'seriousness test' is satisfied (*PCC(S)A 2000 s.79(2)(a)*), *or* ...**
- This test is satisfied if: a 'the offence or the combination of the offence and one or more offences associated with it was so serious that only a...[custodial] sentence can be justified for [it]'.
- Factors that can affect seriousness are:
  - information about the circumstances of the offence (*PCC(S)A 2000 s.81(4)*).
  - previous convictions: 'take into account any previous convictions of the offender or any failure of his to respond to previous sentences' (*PCC(S)A 2000 s.151(1)*).
  - if the offence was committed on bail, the 'court shall treat the fact that it was committed in those circumstances as an aggravating factor' (*PCC(S)A 2000 s.151(2)*).

b) **... the offence was a 'violent' or 'sexual' offence (defined in *PCC(S)A 2000 s.161*) and the public needs protection from serious harm (*PCC(S)A 2000 s.79(2)(b)*).**
- The factors relevant for this are:
  - information about the circumstances of the offence or the offender(*PCC(S)A 2000 s.81(4)*).
  - imprisonment is necessary to protect the public from physical or psychological injury.
  - previous convictions.
  - likelihood of long-term danger.

3 Length (*PCC(S)A 2000 s.80(2)*)

➤ The term should be:

a) 'such term as the court considers is commensurate with the seriousness of the offence or the combination of the offence and one or more offences associated with it', *or*

b) for violent/sexual offences, for 'such longer term as the ... court [considers] necessary to protect the public from the offender' (but not more than the statutory maximum for the offence).

➤ The court must have regard to mitigating/aggravating circumstances and information about the offender (*PCC(S)A 2000 s.81(4)*).

4 **Limits on length**

- Magistrates' Court: maximum 6 months unless an offence presents a lower maximum penalty (*PCC(S)A 2000 s.78*). The minimum is 5 days (*MCA 1980 s.132*).
  - There is a maximum of 12 months for 2 offences triable either way (*MCA 1980 s.133(2)*).
- Crown Court: up to the maximum set by statute for the offence. If none is set then 2 years on indictment (*PCC(S)A 2000 s.77*).
- Time served on remand in custody, is counted as time served as part of sentence *unless* remand was concurrent with an existing term of imprisonment or it is just in all the circumstances not to give effect to this (*PCC(S)A 2000 s.87*).

5 ***Early release under C(S)A 1997 [not yet in force]***

- *A prisoner may be released early on compassionate grounds if there are exceptional circumstances.*
- *If sentence 2 months to 3 years, the prisoner may qualify for early release days for good behaviour.*
- *If a prisoner is sentenced to a term of 3 years or more and the prisoner has served 5/6 of his sentence, the Parole Board may recommend the prisoner for release.*

NB: In certain circumstances, early release may be subject to a release supervision order which is a type of community rehabilitation order subject to certain conditions.

B. Mandatory sentences under (*PCC(S)A 2000 Chapter III*)

1 **Life ((*PCC(S)A 2000 s.109*)**

- If: a) a person is 18 or over at the time of the offence, *and*
  b) a person has previously been convicted of:
    - attempt to, conspiracy to, incitement or solicitation of murder, *or*
    - manslaughter, *or*
    - wounding or grievous bodily harm, *or*
    - rape or attempted rape, *or*
    - certain firearms offences, *or*
    - robbery with a real or imitation firearm, *and*

  c) a person is convicted a second time of any one of the above list (although it does not have to be the same offence second time round),

  then a court must impose a life sentence unless there are exceptional circumstances.
- In such a case, the court will fix a minimum term to reflect the seriousness of the charge before which the Parole Board will not consider when a release on licence might take place.

2 **Minimum 3 years (PCC(S)A 2000 s.111)**

- A convicted burglar must be sentenced to min. 3 years for a third domestic burglary, unless particular circumstances relate to the offence/offender and would make it unjust in all the circumstances.

C. Racially aggravated offences (*CDA 1998*)

- *CDA 1998 ss 28-32* introduces a set of racially aggravated crimes where the maximum penalty is greater where the 'racial' factor is proved. Where it *is* proved, the maximum penalty goes up.
  - Eg: Where it is proved, the maximum custodial penalty (we deal here with indictment convictions only):
    - for grievous or actual bodily harm (*OAP 1861 s.20 and s.47*) goes from 5 to 7 years.
    - for common assault goes from 6 months to 2 years.
    - for criminal damage (*CrDA 1971 s.1(1)*) goes from 10 years to 14 years
    - for certain public order offences (eg: *POA 1986 s.4*) goes from 6 months to 2 years.
    - for certain sections of the *PHA 1997* goes up.

    Note: (*PCC(S)A 2000 s.153*)(see p.440 grey oval), does not apply to these crimes.

    Note: for some of the offences above, if racially motivated, they become arrestable without a warrant.

II Suspended sentences (*PCC(S)A 2000 ss.118-122*)

1 Imposition

- Under certain circumstances a court may suspend a custodial sentence.
- The court must decide to immediately imprison, but due to certain *exceptional* circumstances does not do so (eg: it is not to be used to frighten a small-time offender into behaving himself).
- A suspended sentence may be combined with a fine or compensation order, but not a community sentence.

2 Activation (*PCC(S)A 2000 s.119*)

- The sentence becomes activated on a subsequent conviction for an imprisonable offence within the suspended sentence's 'operational period'.
- A court has discretion not to activate a suspended sentence in full (or at all) if in the circumstances this would be unjust in view of all the circumstances (eg: the new offence is trivial and unconnected with the original offence, *or* the new offence was committed towards the end of the operational period).
- Usually, an activated sentence may run immediately or consecutively with any new term which the court imposes.

Suspended sentencing powers	
Magistrates' Court	Crown Court
➤ Imprisonment term limits are: up to 6 months (unless a particular offence presents a lower maximum penalty) ➤ Imprisonment term limits are: consecutive sentences of up to 1 year in aggregate for 2 or more either way offences (*MCA 1980 s.133(2)*) ➤ The court may suspend the sentence of imprisonment over the same 'operational period' as the Crown Court (*PCC(S)A 2000 s.119*)	➤ Imprisonment term limits are: up to the maximum term set by statute for the offence ➤ The court may suspend, for between 1 and 2 years (called the 'operational period'), a sentence of imprisonment not exceeding 2 years (*PCC(S)A 2000 s.118*)
Note: If a Crown Court has imposed a suspended sentence and an offender is subsequently convicted of an offence in the Magistrates' Court, he should normally be sent to the Crown Court for the activation of the original sentence and the new sentence (*PCC(S)A 2000 s.120*)	

3 Suspended sentence supervision order (*PCC(S)A 2000 s.122*)

- Where a court passes on an offender a suspended sentence of more than 6 months for a single offence, the court may make a suspended sentence supervision order.
  - This is an order placing the offender under the supervision of a supervising officer for the period specified (not to exceed the operational period of the suspended sentence).

III Fines (*PCC(S)A 2000 s.128*)

- Before fixing a sum the court must:
  a) inquire into the offender's financial circumstances (*PCC(S)A 2000 s.128(1)*), *and*
  b) ensure that the penalty reflects the seriousness of the offence (*PCC(S)A 2000 s.128(2)*), *and*
  c) consider the case circumstances, including the state of an offender's finances insofar as they are known, or appear to the court (*PCC(S)A 2000 s.128(3)*).
  - The offender's finances can lead to a reduction or increase in the fine (*PCC(S)A 2000 s.128(4)*).
- If the offender is under 18, the parents are liable to pay the fine (*PCC(S)A 2000 s.137*).

Methods used by the Magistrates' Courts to enforce payment

- The Magistrates' Court may use the following methods to enforce immediate payment of the sum.
- The court:
  a) may order the offender to be searched for money to meet the fine (*MCA 1980 s. 80(1)*),
  b) if the offence is imprisonable, may order detention at a police station until 8 am next day (*MCA 1980 s. 136*),
  c) on conviction (or subsequently), may make a money payment supervision order specifiying terms of payment and placing the offender in someone's care (usually an officer of a local probation board) who should advise and befriend the offender with a view to inducing him to pay and avoid imprisonment. No offender's consent is needed (*MCA 1980 s. 88*),
  d) may issue a warrant of distress to seize and sell the offender's goods to meet the sum (*MCA 1980 s. 76*),
  e) may order the offender's immediate imprisonment.
- If the offender fails to pay the sum within the time allowed, the Magistrates' Court may issue a summons or warrant requiring the offender to appear or issue a warrant to arrest him and bring him before the court to conduct a means inquiry (*MCA 1980 s.83*). The Magistrates' Court may enforce payment by several methods (not detailed here).

IV Community sentences (*PCC(S)A 2000 s.33*)

Note: a community sentence may not be imposed if a sentence is fixed by law (*PCC(S)A 2000 s.34*).

1 Imposition

- The court considers:
  a) whether an offence (or combination of one or more associated offences) is serious enough to warrant a community sentence, *and*
  b) whether particular order(s) are most suitable for a particular defendant, *and*
  c) whether the restrictions on liberty are commensurate with the seriousness of the offence (and any associated offences).
     - Seriousness is ascertained using the same criteria as for imprisonment (see above p.440).
- For certain orders a pre-sentence report is needed (*PCC(S)A 2000 s.36*).
- For crimes against property and minor violence, the court must be satisfied that the offence is too serious for a financial penalty.

2 Breach of a community sentence (*PCC(S)A 2000 various schedules*)

- Magistrates can revoke an order which they imposed.
- The Crown Court alone may revoke the order if it imposed the original sentence.
- Non-compliance penalties: a fine, *or* if non-compliance is wilful and persistent, custody.
- If the defendant re-offends, re-sentencing is possible.

Types of community sentence (*PCC(S)A 2000 s.33*)						
Order	Community rehabilitation	Community punishment	Community punishment and rehabilitation	Curfew	Attendance centre	Drug treatment and testing order
Source	*s.41*	*s.46*	*s.51*	*s.37*	*s.60*	*s.60*
Age	16 or over	16 or over	16 or over	any age	under 21 (25 if for fines)	16 or over
Offender's consent needed?	✗	✗	✗	✗	✗	✗
Descrip-tion	The offender must be under the supervision of an officer of a local probation board and must comply with set requirements	The offender must perform unpaid work	This is a combination of a community rehabilitation order and a community punishment order	This specifes a time and place for a curfew The court appoints someone to monitor the offender	The order specifies a time and place for the offender to partake in a specified activity	The offender must submit to treatment and testing in respect of drugs for a particular time
Period	6 months to 3 years	40 - 240 hours*	1 - 3 years' community rehabilitation. 40 - 100 hours unpaid work	For a period between 2 and 12 hours per day* but: **if aged 16 over over:** up to 6 months **if aged under 16:** up to 3 months	Maximum 3 hours a day up to a different aggregate maximum depending on age (usually 12)	6 months to 3 years
Grounds for, and aims of, the order and restric-tions that the order imposes	The court feels that it is desirable *either* to: a) secure the offender's rehabilitation, *or* b) protect the public from harm, *or* c) prevent the offender committing further offences 'Set requirements' can include: ◆ treatment for drug depend-ency or psychiatric illness, *and* ◆ residence requirements, *and* ◆ supervision, *and* ◆ attendance at a community rehabilitation centre	The offender is convicted of an imprisonable offence, *and* the offender must be a suitable person to do work, *and* there must be work available The aim is to restrict leisure time, and make reparation to the community for the offence	The offender is convicted of an imprisonable offence, *and* the court believes that the order will: a) secure the rehabilita-tion of the offender, *or* b) protect the public from harm, *or* c) prevent further offences being committed	The aim is to prevent the offender reoffending	The offender is convicted of an imprisonable offence The aim is to deprive the offender of leisure This was introduced with 'football hooligans' in mind	The offender is dependant on or has a propensity to misuse drugs *and* this may be susceptible to treatment

Note 1:
The following are also community sentences (p.443):

- a supervision order
- an action plan order

Note 2:
CJCSA 2000 ss46-47 [not yet in force] introduces 2 new community orders:

- *an exclusion order (staying out of an area)*
- *a drug abstinence order (to stay off Class A drugs)*

*If the order is made as a result of persistent non-payment of fines (see p.443) the hourly limits are different (*PCC(S)A 2000 s.59*)

➤ Generally the courts decide on the appropriate community sentence using the following 'rules':
- the offence warrants the punishment
- the order is suitable for the offender
- restrictions on liberty are commensurate with the seriousness of the offence(s)

V Discharges (*PCC(S)A 2000 ss.12-15*)

- A court can issue a discharge if in the circumstances (the nature of the offence, the defendant's character), punishment is inexpedient.
  - **An absolute discharge:** if the offender is morally blameless, but technically guilty.
  - **A conditional discharge:** if the offender has a previously clean record, the offence is trivial, and the publicity and court appearance are sufficient ordeal.
    - A conditional discharge is for up to 3 years only.
    - If the offender commits an offence during this time, he may be re-sentenced for the original offence.

A summary of non-community sentence sentencing provisions		
Penalty	**Imposition**	**Effect**
Custody	➤ Seriousness test ➤ Protect the public from violent/sexual offences	➤ Prison if aged over 21 ➤ If aged under 21, there are other options (see p.448)
Suspended sentence	➤ *Not* for those aged under 21 ➤ When the court has decided to imprison but there are 'exceptional' circumstances	➤ Court has discretion whether to activate the sentence
Fine	➤ Seriousness of the offence ➤ Circumstances of the case	➤ Consider the offender's financial circumstances when deciding to increase or decrease the fine

VI General disqualification from driving

- If a person is convicted of any offence (except those mentioned in the point below), then the Crown Court or a Magistrates' Court may, in addition to, or instead of, dealing with him in any other way, order him to be disqualified from holding or obtaining a driving licence for such period as it thinks fit (*PCC(S)A 2000 s.146(1)*).
- The power to disqualify 'instead of' under *s.146(1)* does not apply to cases where a person is convicted of murder or where the sentence is imposed under (*PCC(S)A 2000 Chapter III*) (automatic life sentence for second serious offence), but the power to disqualify 'in addition to' still applies (*PCC(S)A 2000 s.146(2)*).
- The power is also subject to (*PCC(S)A 2000 s.146(3)*) - disqualification under *s.146* may not be imposed unless the court has been told by the Minister that the power to make such an order is exercisable by that court.

VII Motoring penalties

1 Endorsement

- This is mandatory for i) dangerous driving, ii) aggravated vehicle taking, iii) careless driving.
- Conviction for 2 (or more) offences on the same occasion leads to an endorsement for the offence with the 'higher' number of points allowed. However, the court may wish to exercise its discretion and award more than just the points for the 'higher' offence (*RTOA 1988 ss.28(4)-28(6)*).
- When a court makes an order for obligatory disqualification for 1 offence, it may not at the same time endorse penalty points for another offence committed on the same occasion (*Martin v DPP* [1999] The Times, 30 November 1999).

2 **Disqualification**

a) Obligatory (for at least 1 year): for i) dangerous driving, ii) aggravated vehicle taking.

b) Discretionary (for a period): i) careless driving, ii) taking a conveyance, iii) theft of a motor vehicle.

c) Under the penalty points system (*RTOA 1988 s.35*)

- ➤ If the offender has no previous disqualification of at least 56 days (imposed within 3 years of the commission of the offence now being sentenced), the minimum period of disqualification is 6 months.
  - ◆ If there is one previous disqualification, disqualification is for 1 year.
  - ◆ If there are 2 or more previous disqualifications, disqualification is for a minimum of 2 years.
- ➤ Penalty points are dealt with first.
  - ◆ If there are 12 or more penalty points from:
    - the current conviction (disregarding any order for disqualification for committing the offence) *plus*
    - points previously endorsed for offences within 3 years immediately before the commission of the present offence,

  THEN disqualification is obligatory.
- ➤ Points prior to a previous disqualification are ignored.
- ➤ The court will go on to consider discretionary disqualification if the driver is not automatically disqualified by having 12 points or more.

3 **Avoiding disqualification and endorsement**

a) Avoiding obligatory disqualification or obligatory endorsement

- ➤ A 'special reason' is present.
- ➤ This is a mitigating circumstance (eg: a boomerang thrown across the windscreen).
- ➤ 'Special reasons' are connected with the commission of the offence, but are *not* personal to the offender (*Whittal v. Kirby* [1947] KB 194).
- ➤ A 'special reason' is not anything which could constitute a defence to the charge in law.

b) Avoiding discretionary disqualification

- ➤ *Any* mitigating factor relevant to the offence should be used to avoid discretionary disqualification.
- ➤ The factor may be *either* connected with the circumstances *or* personal to the offender. (For example, an obligatory situation or loss of job is relevant here.)

c) Avoiding disqualification under the points system

- ➤ Disqualification is mandatory unless there are mitigating circumstances.
- ➤ All circumstances are relevant except ((*RTOA 1988 s.35(4)*):
  - i) the triviality of the offence.
  - ii) hardship (unless exceptional).
  - iii) circumstances taken into account to avoid or reduce disqualification under the points system during the last 3 years.

Note: i) a driver can have 7-12 points and escape disqualification.
ii) disqualification wipes a licence clean of all the old points.
iii) if 2 offences are committed simultaneously, both of which carry a point penalty, the court only adds the 'higher' of the penalties to the licence, unless it sees fit to order otherwise.

VIII Ancillary orders

1 **Compensation order** (*PCC(S)A 2000 ss.130-134*)

- The order is for the offender to pay compensation to a victim.
- Generally this order is *not* available for motoring offences (the victim can claim from the offender's insurers) (*PCC(S)A 2000 s.130(6)*).
- Magistrates' limit: £5,000 (*PCC(S)A 2000 s.131*); Crown Court: unlimited.
- The court has the power to make an attachment of earnings order to ensure that the compensation is paid (*CPIA 1996 s.53*).
  - Consent of the offender is required.

2 **Forfeiture order** (*PCC(S)A 2000 s.143*)

- Property in the offender's possession, or control, is forfeit by this order if the property is:
  a) used for committing or facilitating the offence, *or*
  b) intended for use in connection with the offence, *or*
  c) held unlawfully.

3 **Confiscation order** *(CJA 1988 & PCA 1994)*

- An order confiscates the proceeds of crime.
- The prosecution have a right to insist on this order.
- Interest is payable on unpaid orders, with custody in default.
- The prosecution can apply to revalue the offender's crime proceeds for up to 6 years after conviction.
- The court may assume that any of the offender's goods that were obtained or held up to 6 years previously are the proceeds of crime in cases where:
  - the offender has been convicted of 2 or more acquiring offences at one time, *or*
  - the offender has been convicted of 1 acquiring offence on one occasion and another such offence within the previous 6 years.

4 **Restitution order** (*PCC(S)A 2000 ss.148-149*)

- The order is to compensate, or restore to a victim, goods stolen from him.

5 **Costs order** *(POA 1985 s.18)*

- On conviction, 'just and reasonable' costs may be awarded to the prosecution (payable by the offender).
- On acquittal, if the defendant is not LSC funded, the court can order his costs to be paid from central funds. This is usual unless, eg: the acquittal was on a technicality *or* the defendant brought suspicion on himself by his conduct (*POA 1985 s.16, Practice Direction (Crime Costs)* [1991] 1 WLR 498).
- On acquittal, contributions paid by a legally aided defendant may be repaid (subject to the above).

6 **Deferment of sentence** (*PCC(S)A 2000 ss.1-2*)

- Passing a sentence may be deferred for up to 6 months.
- The offender must consent.
- If the offender is convicted during the interval of another offence, he can be sentenced for both offences. The court will have the same powers as on conviction for the original offence.
- The power to defer a sentence is used to assess:
  - the offender's conduct after conviction, *or*
  - any change in the offender's circumstances (marriage, etc).
- The court specifies the conduct it expects, and the sentence it will impose if this is not complied with.

7 **Committal to the Crown Court for sentence** (*PCC(S)A 2000 s.3*)

- ➤ The offender must be aged over 18.
- ➤ The conviction must be for an either way offence *and* when:
  - a) the offence (or a combination of associated offences) is so serious that a punishment greater than that which a Magistrates' Court is authorised to impose, is warranted, *or*
  - b) the offence is a violent or sexual offence, and a custodial sentence is necessary to protect the public from serious harm, *or*
  - c) the offender unexpectedly asks for previous offences to be taken into consideration (rare and usually the result of evidence, unknown at the mode of trial hearing, appearing during the trial.

IX Summary of some youth sentences

➤ No sentence of imprisonment may be passed on an offender under 21 (*PCC(S)A 2000 s.89*).

Some youth sentences

Sentence \ Age	Under 21	20-19	18	17	16	15	14	13	12	Under 12
community sentence	(Under 21 to 16)					see p.444				
detention and training order				(17 to 15)			only if a persistent offender (14 to 12)			only if to protect the public from harm
	half the sentence is a period of training in detention; half is supervision in the community. Imposed where a court could impose imprisonment if the offender was over 21. Orders may be for 4, 6, 8, 10, 12, 18 or 24 months. (*PCC(S)A 2000 s.100*)									
supervision order				places the juvenile under the supervision of a local authority/ social worker / officer of a local probation board. Maximum 3 years. (*PCC(S)A 2000 s.63*)						
action plan order				this requires compliance with an action plan to address offending behaviour. It is imposed if it is desirable either to secure the offender's rehabilitation or to prevent the offender committing further offences. Maximum 3 months. (*PCC(S)A 2000 s.69*)						
reparation order				imposed to allow the offender to make reparation for the offence otherwise than by payment of compensation. Maximum work is 24 hours in aggregate. The consent of the offender is needed (*PCC(S)A 2000 s.73*).						
detention in a young offender institution	if convicted of an offence punishable by imprisonment if he was over 21. **Minimum term:** 21 days. **Maximum term:** the maximum term for the offence (*PCC(S)A 2000 s.97*).				*Note: detention in a young offender's institution is due to be abolished when CJCSA 2000 s.61 is brought into force [not yet in force]*					
detention at Her Majesty's Pleasure				if convicted of murder and was under 18 at the time the offence was committed (*PCC(S)A 2000 s.90*).						
detention under (*PCC(S)A 2000 s.91*)				a) If the offence is punishable with min. 14 years imprisonment *or* b) indecent assault on a woman or man *or*				As age 14-18 and also: c) death by dangerous driving, *or* d) death by careless driving while affected by alcohol		

J Sentencing procedure and mitigation

I Sentencing Advisory Panel

- *CDA 1998 s.80-81* puts a duty on the Court of Appeal to produce sentencing guidelines.
- *CDA 1998 s.80-81* also establishes a Sentencing Advisory Panel to advise the court.

II Preparing a plea in mitigation

Preparing a plea in mitigation

- The defence must present a plea in mitigation for the accused in order to:
  - reduce the severity of sentence, *and/or*
  - persuade that a particular punishment is unsuitable and that some other would aid the offender.
- Preparation:
  1. Make a realistic assessment of the likely penalties.
     - For the Magistrates' Court, consult the Magistrates' Association Guidelines.
  2. If custodial sentence, is the case so serious that only a custodial sentence will suffice? Consider any relevant factors such as (*R v Howells* [1999] 1 All ER 50):
     - any early admissions - particularly with evidence of real remorse,
     - any practical steps taken to address addiction,
     - any youth and immaturity,
     - any good character, especially positive good character,
     - any family responsibilities and/or physical and mental disability,
     - whether it is a first custodial sentence.
  3. For all types of sentence, consider any relevant factors such as:
     - the offender's age and history: youth or old-age may induce sympathy.
     - the circumstances of the offence: provocation, stress, drug dependency.
       - **Note**: voluntary ingestion is *not* good mitigation.
     - the likely effect on the offender of sentence and conviction;
       - **Note:** failure to respond to previous sentences is relevant (*PCC(S)A 2000 s.151(1)*).
     - subsequent behaviour:
       - **remorse**
       - **guilty plea and the time and circumstances of this plea (*PCC(S)A 2000 s.152*)**.
         - There is usually a discount on *custodial* sentences of up to a third.
         - If the evidence is so overwhelming that the defendant has no choice but to plead guilty, there is no discount under *PCC(S)A 2000 s.152 - R. v. Hastings* 1 Cr.App.Rep.(S) 167.
       - **assisting police** - eg: naming others, revealing stolen property, confessing, saving police time.
       - **reparation** - voluntary rectification of damage and motive are important.
- Character witnesses and letters of reference are admissible in a plea for mitigation.

III Newton hearing

- ➤ A Newton hearing comes from *R. v. Newton* (1982) 77 Cr.App.R.13.
- ➤ This is held after a guilty plea. Evidence is heard to ascertain the facts relevant to sentencing, *either*:
  - because the prosecution and defence accounts of the facts differ greatly, *or*
  - to resolve the respective liability of 2 or more defendants.

IV Pre-sentence report *and drug test [drug test not yet in force]*

- ➤ This is compiled by an officer of a local probation board or social worker.
- ➤ It *must* be ordered (if the offender is aged over 18) before:
  - imposing a custodial sentence *unless* the court feels it is unnecessary (*PCC(S)A 2000 s.81*), *or*
  - making a community rehabilitation order with 'requirements' (*PCC(S)A 2000 s.36(4)*) *unless* the court considers it unnecessary (*PCC(S)A 2000 s.36(5)*), *or*
  - making a community punishment order (*PCC(S)A 2000 s.36(4)*) *unless* the court considers it unnecessary (*PCC(S)A 2000 s.36(5)*), *or*
  - making a community punishment and rehabilitation order (*PCC(S)A 2000 s.36(4)*) *unless* the court considers it unnecessary (*PCC(S)A 2000 s.36(5)*).

  NB: There are slightly altered rules for offenders aged under 18 (*PCC(S)A 2000 s.81(3)*)
- ➤ It *may* be ordered before imposing any other sentence, usually when it is anticipated that the accused will plead guilty and he is aged 30 or less.
- ➤ *For offenders over 18, if the court is considering passing a community sentence, it may order a pre-sentence drug test (PCC(S)A 2000 s.36A) [not yet in force].*

V Court proceedings

- ➤ For an offence triable 'either way', if proceedings have been in the Magistrates' Court until now, the court decides if it is appropriate to commit for sentence to the Crown Court (see p.448) (*PCC(S)A 2000 s.3*).
  - This also applies if the defendant pleaded guilty before the mode of trial procedure (*PCC(S)A 2000 s.4*).

Steps

1 The prosecution summarises:
- the nature of the offence.
- the offender's background and previous convictions.
- any other offences of similar or less serious nature to be taken into consideration (admitted by the offender). The offender may not be subsequently charged with these. A compensation order can be made in respect of these offences.
  - The offender signs a 'taking into consideration' form, provided by the police.

2 The pre-sentence report is presented to the court.

3 The defence gives a plea in mitigation.
- ➤ On a driving offence for which disqualification is an issue, 'special reasons' for avoiding disqualification are given by the defendant on oath.

4 The judge passes sentence.

K Appeals

➤ Some main details of 3 different appellate courts are outlined below:

1 **From Magistrates' Court to Crown Court** (*MCA 1980 ss.108-110* and the *Crown Court Rules 1982*)

➤ The defence only can appeal against conviction or sentence.

➤ Conviction:

- if the offender pleaded guilty, there is only a right to appeal against a conviction if the plea was equivocal (ie: a non-genuine plea of guilty) (*MCA 1980 s.108*).
- the Crown Court can remit an equivocal plea to the Magistrates' Court with a direction to enter a plea of 'not guilty'.

➤ Sentence: may be heavier or lighter, provided the magistrates would be empowered to impose it.

➤ Procedure:

Steps	
1	Send a notice of appeal to the magistrates' clerk and the prosecution within 21 days of sentence or conviction. ◆ The Crown Court can grant leave to appeal after this (*Crown Court Rules 1982 r.7(5)*).
2	The appeal is heard by a Crown Court judge *or* a recorder sitting with 2 to 4 magistrates. ◆ If the appeal is against conviction, there is a rehearing following exactly the same process as for a summary trial (*SCA 1981 s.79(3)*). ◆ If the appeal is against sentencing, the prosecution merely outlines the case facts, and the defence makes a plea in mitigation.
3	The court can confirm, reverse or vary the magistrates' decision. It can also remit the matter (with its opinion) to the Magistrates' Court, *or* it may make any order it thinks just, exercising any powers the magistrates might have used (eg: concerning costs and compensation) (*SCA 1981 s.48*).

2 **From Magistrates' Court to Divisional Court** (the QBD of the High Court) **by way of case stated:**

➤ Grounds: the magistrates' decision is wrong in law, or exceeds their authority (*MCA 1980 s.111*).

➤ There is a hearing of legal argument (no evidence is called).

➤ The High Court may reverse, affirm, or amend the decision. It can also remit the matter (with its opinion) to the Magistrates' Court or the Crown Court, or it may make any order it thinks fit, exercising any powers the magistrates might have used (eg: concerning costs and compensation) (*SCA 1981 s.28A*). The High Court may also send the case back for amendment.

3 From Crown Court to the Court of Appeal

- Against conviction or sentence (*CAA 1968 ss.1,2,9,11 and CAA 1995*).
- On a question of law or fact, leave is required.
- The prosecution cannot appeal against acquittal or sentence.
- The Attorney General may, with leave of the Court of Appeal, refer lenient Crown Court sentences to the Court of Appeal for review. The Court of Appeal passes the appropriate sentence in accordance with the Crown Court's powers (*CJA 1988 ss.33-36*).
- If the defendant is acquitted in the Crown Court, the prosecution can appeal on a point of law. The defendant stays acquitted, but the Court of Appeal will nonetheless rule on the point of law.

A summary table of appeals to higher courts

Who appeals	Reason for appeal	Court where the appeal is heard
Appeal from the Magistrates' Court (*MCA 1980 s.108*)		
Defence only	Perverse conviction against the evidence	Crown Court appeal hearing
	Excessive sentence	
Defence *or* Prosecution	*Ultra vires*	Queen's Bench Division of the High Court for judicial review
Prosecution only	Lenient sentence	No right of appeal
	Perverse acquittal against the evidence	
Appeal from the Crown Court (*CAA 1968, CAA 1995*)		
Defence only	Excessive sentence	Court of Appeal
	Conviction unsafe (ie: law or fact)	Court of Appeal, with leave
Defence *or* Prosecution	*Ultra vires*	No provision for judicial review in the High Court
Prosecution only	Lenient sentence	Attorney General can refer the case to the Court of Appeal (Note: in the Magistrates' Court there is no such right)
	Perverse acquittal against the evidence	No right of appeal
	Question of law following acquittal	Court of Appeal The defendant *stays* acquitted, but the court can rule on the point of law anyway

- It should also be noted that the Magistrates' Court has power to hear 'appeals' from itself under certain circumstances (*MCA 1980 s.142 (as amended by ss.26-28 CAA 1995)*). However, this topic is not dealt with in this chapter.
- The *CAA 1995* provides for the Criminal Cases Review Commission ('CCRC') which was set up on 31st March 1997 with powers to refer certain types of cases to appeal.

L Disclosure

All references in this section are to the CPIA 1996.

- ➤ *CPIA 1996 ss.1-21* contains a procedure for advance disclosure of evidence by both sides.
  - Common law rules applying to the prosecution are disapplied (see box below).

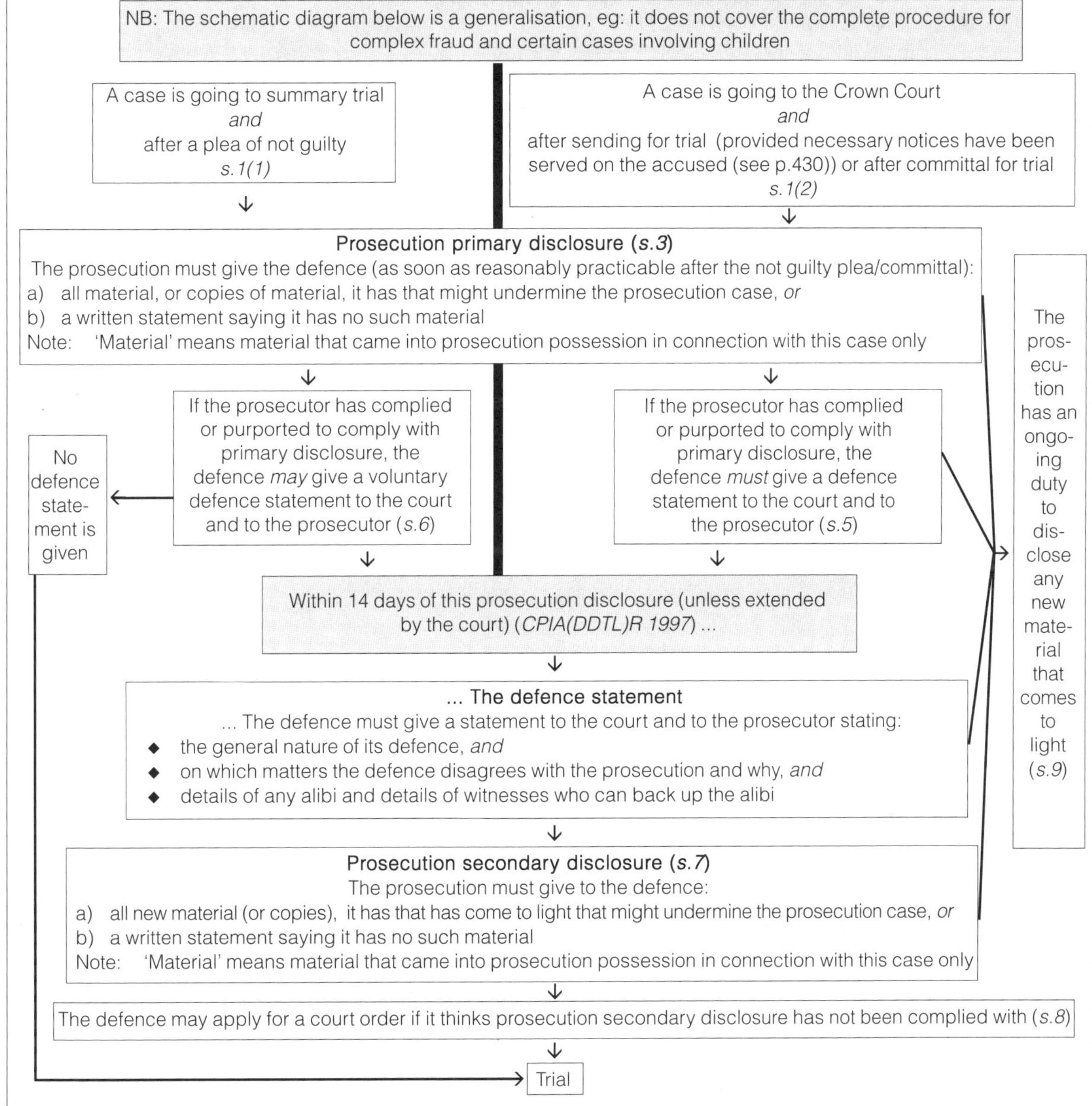

NB: The schematic diagram below is a generalisation, eg: it does not cover the complete procedure for complex fraud and certain cases involving children
A case is going to summary trial *and* after a plea of not guilty *s.1(1)*
A case is going to the Crown Court *and* after sending for trial (provided necessary notices have been served on the accused (see p.430)) or after committal for trial *s.1(2)*
Prosecution primary disclosure (*s.3*)
The prosecution must give the defence (as soon as reasonably practicable after the not guilty plea/committal):
a) all material, or copies of material, it has that might undermine the prosecution case, *or*
b) a written statement saying it has no such material
Note: 'Material' means material that came into prosecution possession in connection with this case only
If the prosecutor has complied or purported to comply with primary disclosure, the defence *may* give a voluntary defence statement to the court and to the prosecutor (*s.6*)
If the prosecutor has complied or purported to comply with primary disclosure, the defence *must* give a defence statement to the court and to the prosecutor (*s.5*)
No defence statement is given
Within 14 days of this prosecution disclosure (unless extended by the court) (*CPIA(DDTL)R 1997*) ...
... The defence statement
... The defence must give a statement to the court and to the prosecutor stating:
◆ the general nature of its defence, *and*
◆ on which matters the defence disagrees with the prosecution and why, *and*
◆ details of any alibi and details of witnesses who can back up the alibi
Prosecution secondary disclosure (*s.7*)
The prosecution must give to the defence:
a) all new material (or copies), it has that has come to light that might undermine the prosecution case, *or*
b) a written statement saying it has no such material
Note: 'Material' means material that came into prosecution possession in connection with this case only
The defence may apply for a court order if it thinks prosecution secondary disclosure has not been complied with (*s.8*)
Trial
The prosecution has an ongoing duty to disclose any new material that comes to light (*s.9*)

Changes to common law rules? (*s.21*)

- ➤ **Summary trial:** for *s.1(1)* disclosure, all common law rules relating to disclosure after the accused has pleaded 'not guilty' are abolished.
- ➤ **Crown Court trial:** for *s.1(2)* disclosure, all common law rules relating to disclosure after the accused has been committed for trial are abolished.
- ➤ **The common law rules of disclosure continue to apply in the period between accusation (charge or summons) and a plea of not guilty/committal - *R v DPP ex parte Lee* [1999] 2 All ER 737.**

Problems with ...

... the defence statement and the final defence

If the defence statement (*s.11*):

- is not given (under *s.5* disclosure), *or*
- is out of time (according to the periods laid down by rules made under *s.12*, *or*
- contains inconsistent defences, *or*
- is different from a defence later put forward at trial, *or*
- does not contain details of an alibi and details of those who will support that alibi, but such evidence is later introduced at trial

At trial (*s.11*):

- the court can comment on this
- any other party can comment on this (with leave)

Note: it must have regard to the degree of any difference between the defence and the defence statement and the justification for any difference

The jury and the court:
may draw adverse inferences as to guilt (but cannot convict solely on this)

... time limits for disclosure

- All prosecution and defence disclosure must occur within time limits set down by the Secretary of State (under *s.12*).
  - These time limits may be set as the Secretary of State sees fit (eg: the 14 day rule for defence disclosure - see previous page).
  - There are various transitional provisions that say that if no regulations are made, the various stages of disclosure must occur 'as soon as practicable' after certain events listed (eg: prosecution disclosure is as soon as reasonably practicable after certain events such as a plea of 'not guilty' or committal for trial) (*s.13*).
- If the prosecutor does not comply with his time limits (*s.10*), then ...
  - ... unless the accused would be denied a fair trial as a result ...
  - ... this is not on its own an abuse of process leading to a stay of proceedings.

... confidentiality

- *ss.17-18* provide that any material disclosed by the prosecutor is confidential.
  - Various new criminal offences are set out for breach of that confidentiality.

Prosecutor will not disclose material 'in the public interest' (*ss.14-16*)

- The prosecutor as a general rule must disclose all material.
- However, the prosecutor may apply to the court for non-disclosure if it would not be 'in the public interest'. The court may grant such an application.
  - **In summary trial**, as long as it is before the verdict, the accused can apply at any time for a review of non-disclosure.
  - **In other cases**, as long as it is before the verdict:
    - the court has a duty to keep any non-disclosure under review, *and*
    - notwithstanding the court's duty, the accused can apply at any time for a court review.
- If:
  - a person claiming to have an interest in the material applies for a review of the non-disclosure, *and*
  - he shows that he was involved in bringing the material to the attention of the prosecutor,

  then he must be heard before any order for non-disclosure is made.
- A third party who has material which has previously been inspected by the prosecution or which is in the possession of the prosecution, may be required to disclose this to the defence.
  - This will be subject to a hearing if necessary on:
    - public interest, *or*
    - confidentiality.

M Evidence at trial

I Evidential proof

A. Burden of proof

➤ **The prosecution** must prove guilt 'beyond reasonable doubt'.

➤ **The defence** has an 'evidential burden' (ie: it must introduce necessary evidence before the court).

- Occasionally, a defence may need to satisfy the court on the balance of probabilities:
  a) insane automatism (*Bratty v. AG for Northern Ireland* [1963] AC 386).
  b) insanity *(Sodeman v. The King* [1936] 2 All ER 1138).
  c) diminished responsibility (*Homicide Act 1957 s.2(2)*).

B. Proof by evidence

➤ **Everything must be proved** *except*:

- facts which are formally admitted by the defence and the prosecution (*CJA 1967 s.10*).
- where judicial notice is taken of a point of fact (eg: dogs bark, they do not quack).
- where judicial notice is taken of a point of law (eg: traffic must stop at a red light).
- circumstantial evidence (rebuttable): where there is an *inference* of fact drawn from *proven* facts.
  - Examples include:
    i) doctrine of recent possession - someone possessing goods illegally came by them illicitly.
    ii) doctrine of continuance - a given state of affairs continues (*R. v. Balloz* (1908) 1 Cr.App.R. 258).

C. Types of evidence

➤ **Oral evidence:** this carries most weight.

➤ **Real evidence:** this consists of objects (eg: weapons).

➤ **Documentary evidence:** this includes recordings and photographs.

- A document must be authenticated by demonstrating in what circumstances it was created.
- A copy is admissible (*CJA 1988 s.27*).

➤ **Written statements and depositions (see p.432):** any that were used at committal may be used at trial, as long as they have been signed by a magistrate.

D. Finding the facts

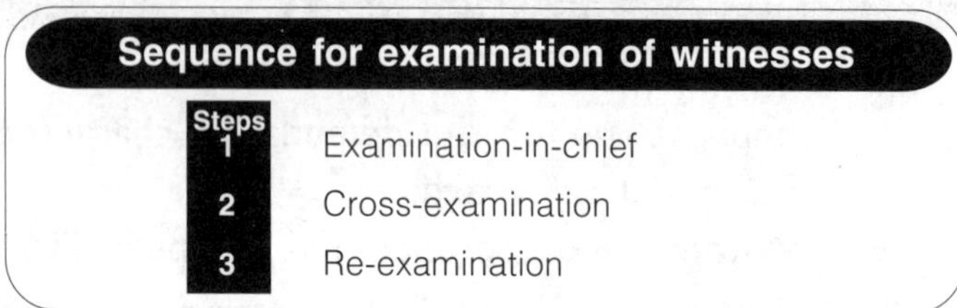
Sequence for examination of witnesses

Steps
1 Examination-in-chief
2 Cross-examination
3 Re-examination

1 Examination-in-chief

- This is where a side calls its own witness and asks questions of that witness.
- A witness may refresh his memory from a contemporaneous document.
- No leading questions are permitted, except to obtain a rebuttal or denial of the opponent's case.
- Even if a witness gives unfavourable answers, the side which called the witness cannot contradict or discredit the witness *unless*:
  - the witness is declared hostile. To achieve this, an application must be made to the judge (*CPA 1865 s.3*)). If this is done:
    - the party calling a witness may cross-examine him and ask leading questions, *and*
    - the witness can be confronted with statements made previously by him which are inconsistent with his testimony. **Note:** These previous inconsistent statements are not admissible as evidence, but they go to the credibility of the witness.

2 Cross-examination

- After a side has called its witness for examination-in-chief, the other side may cross-examine the witness.
- The cross-examiner will seek to:

  a) put his view of the case to a witness, *and*

  b) extract useful information from the witness, *and*

  c) challenge a witness's credibility.

  - The questions must be relevant to the evidence about the offence before the court.
  - A witness's answer is *final* unless the witness:

    i) is biased (*R. v. Shaw* (1888) 16 Cox 503), *or*

    ii) has given evidence which is inconsistent with a previous statement (*CPA 1865 ss.4, 5*), *or*

    - These previous inconsistent statements are not admissible as evidence, but they go to the credibility of the witness.

    iii) has a relevant conviction (*CPA 1865 s.6*), *or*

    iv) has a reputation for untruthfulness (*Toohey v. Metropolitan Police Comm.* [1965] AC 595).

3 Re-examination

- There may now be a re-examination by the other side after the cross-examination on matters brought up during the cross-examination.
- This may be done in an attempt to undo any damage from the cross-examination.

II Implications for the defendant's 'character'

➤ The general rule is that the prosecution may not call evidence about the defendant's character or previous convictions.

- This is a kind of 'shield' that the defendant has *(CEA 1898 s.1(1))*.

➤ There are 3 exceptions to the general rule:

1 **To rebut an assertion of a defendant's good character.**
   - If a defendant testifies and asserts his good character, then the prosecution may call evidence to rebut this.
   - If a defendant does not testify, and the defence makes character an issue, the prosecution can apply for leave to bring evidence of the defendant's bad character.
   - The weight this evidence carries depends on the aspect of character (eg: violence need not imply dishonesty, so evidence of violence might not suggest that a defendant has stolen).

2 **Similar fact evidence** (*CEA 1898 s.1(f)(i)*). See p.461.

3 **If the defendant testifies *and* the defence's conduct at the trial leads to the defendant 'losing his shield'.**
   - If a defendant chooses to give oral evidence, then special rules apply governing what sorts of questions the prosecution can put to him.
   - The general rule is that the prosecution may not cross-examine the defendant on his character (encompassing both reputation and disposition of the defendant) or previous convictions.
   - *CEA 1898 s.1(f)* provides the defendant with a 'shield' against cross-examination in relation to bad character and past misconduct. However, the 'shield' can be lost under a) or b) below:

     a) *CEA 1898 s.1(f)(ii)*
      - Limb 1: a defendant has established (or tried to establish) his own good character.
      - Limb 2: the defence has 'cast imputations' on the character of the prosecution, or a prosecution witness.

     b) *CEA 1898 s.1(f)(iii)*
      - A defendant has given evidence against a co-defendant (ie: a 'cut-throat defence').
   - The court has discretion to prevent *s.1(f)* cross-examination if it would prejudice the defence (*Selvey v. DPP* [1970] AC 304).
   - This discretion does not extend to cross-examination by a co-defendant under *s.1(f)(iii)* (*Murdoch v. Taylor* [1965] AC 547).

➤ Notes:

- 'cast imputations': this bears its ordinary meaning, but does not include an assertion of innocence.
- previous convictions: only go to character. This merits a judicial warning that previous convictions merely show that the defendant's allegations against the prosecution are less likely to be true. The fact of a conviction can be raised, not the evidence for it.
- 'cut-throat' defence: this occurs when a co-defendant can only rebut an implication of his guilt by imputing bad character to the other defendant. Both defendants lose their 'shields'. The defence can seek to avoid this by adopting an alternative argument (eg: the victim suffered harm another way).
- character is indivisible: ie: once some aspects of character emerge (good or bad), they all can be brought up (including previous convictions).

III Evidential safeguards

1 Corroboration

- At common law, one witness is sufficient in all cases.
- By statute, corroboration (ie: independent supporting evidence) is required to convict a defendant of treason (*Treason Act 1795 s.1*), perjury (*Perjury Act 1911 s.13*) and speeding (except if the evidence is from a speed camera). The judge must tell the jury this.
- In other cases, where it is felt that further proof might be needed to support certain evidence, it is within the discretion of the judge to give the jury a corroboration warning - ie: the jury should be warned that further proof is desirable.
- Contents of a corroboration warning:
  - A judge should point out to the jury why evidence is suspect, or identify corroborative evidence and non-corroborative evidence, as a warning that there is a danger in relying on the evidence.
  - Magistrates warn themselves (!) - the defence can remind them in its closing speech.

When is a warning necessary?

When corroboration itself is essential	When a corroboration warning is mandatory	When a corroboration warning is desirable
For charges of: ◆ treason ◆ perjury ◆ speeding	There *used to be* a mandatory warning for the following 2 instances, but this has now been abolished by *CJPO 1994 ss.32-33*. However, a court may still give such a warning even though this is undesirable as it is contrary to the intention of the *CJPO 1994* (*R. v. Makanjuola*; *R. v. Easton*, [1995] 2 Cr. App. R. 469) ◆ An accomplice gives evidence ◆ A victim of an alleged sexual offence gives evidence	◆ A prosecution witness has an interest in giving false evidence (eg: to preserve his own reputation or he bears a grudge) (*R. v. Cheema* [1994] 1 WLR 147) ◆ A defendant tries to incriminate a co-defendant ◆ A witness is shown to be unreliable (eg: a mental patient)

2 Disputed identification (Turnbull guidelines) (*R. v. Turnbull* [1977] QB 224)

- In a case where disputed identification of the defendant is the sole or a substantial issue, there is a danger of wrongful conviction unless the following procedure is complied with:

Steps

1 Evidence of identification is admissible if:
- the evidence is visual *and*
- on at least 2 occasions, the defendant was purported to be seen (eg: at the crime and at an identification parade).

2 The judge or magistrates must consider the soundness of the evidence by contemplating the following 6 factors:

1	the length of observation.	4	conditions.
2	whether the defendant was already known to the witness.	5	distance.
3	how close the witness's description is to the police description.	6	lighting.

3 If the identifying evidence is poor, then the judge or magistrates must order an acquittal.

4 If the evidence is sound, the judge gives the jury a **Turnbull warning.** He must warn the jury (or magistrates must warn themselves!):
- of the dangers of relying on identification evidence, *and*
- to consider factors 1 - 6 above in evaluating the evidence.

IV Witness's competence and compellability

- Competent: a witness is competent if he can lawfully give evidence.
- Compellable: a witness is 'compellable' if he can be required to testify.

Note the YJCEA 1999 s.53 [not yet in force] says:
***anybody** is competent to give evidence except someone who:*
- *cannot understand questions put to him as a witness, and give answers which can be understood, or*
- *is the defendant (as a prosecution witness)*

Note the YJCEA 1999 s.55 [not yet in force] says that the following witnesses may not give sworn evidence:
- *someone who has not yet reached 14 years old, or*
- *someone who has not a sufficient appreciation of:*
  - *a) the solemnity of the occasion, and*
  - *b) the responsibility to tell the truth when taking an oath (although appreciation is assumed unless there is evidence to the contrary)*

1 **Defendant as a prosecution witness**

- *Not* compellable, *not* competent.
- A co-defendant can only be called if he ceases to be a co-defendant either because he:
  - pleads guilty, *or*
  - is tried separately, *or*
  - is acquitted, *or*
  - the Attorney General ends proceedings against him.

2 **Defendant as a defence witness**

- Competent, but *not* compellable (*CEA 1898 s.1*).
- His evidence is admissible against a co-defendant that he implicates.
- If the defendant testifies, he must be called before any other witnesses for the defence (*PACE s.79*).
- If the defendant decides not to testify, this can have adverse consequences, see p.465.
- The judge will comment adversely if the defence raises issues, but gives no evidence in support.
- The prosecution may comment on a defendant's refusal to testify (*CJPO 1994 Schedule10 para 2*).
- A co-accused may comment freely on a defendant's refusal to testify.

3 **Present spouse as a prosecution witness** (*PACE s.80*)

- Competent.
- Compellable only if the defendant is charged with:
  - an assault on the spouse.
  - an assault or sexual offence on a victim aged under 16.

4 **Former spouse as a prosecution witness** (*PACE s.80(5)*)

- Competent and compellable.

5 **Present spouse as a defence witness** (*PACE s.80(2), s.80(4)*)

- Competent and compellable (unless the accused and the spouse are jointly charged).

6 **Child aged under 14** (*CJA 1988 s.33A, CJA 1991 s.52*)

- The child must give unsworn evidence.
- Competent (unless Court thinks the child is incapable of giving intelligent testimony), and compellable.

7 **Co-defendant**

- Whether a co-defendant is competent or compellable to testify against a fellow defendant, and the admissibility of his evidence depends on the co-defendant's plea (see box overleaf).

The co-defendant on a plea of...	
'guilty' (and therefore no longer on trial)	'not guilty'
Competent and compellable	Competent, but *not* compellable
He is like any other witness and any statements made to the police, or a confession, will be inadmissible against the defendant as they will be hearsay	His confession, or statements made to the police, are only admissible against himself. (Evidence not made on oath by the co-defendant is not evidence against the defendant - it is inadmissible and must be disregarded)
A corroboration warning is no longer necessary (*CJPO 1994 s.32*, see p.458)	Some corroboration warning is desirable, see p.458
Cross-examinable on his record	Cross-examination *per s.1(f)(iii)*, see p.457
Note: A defendant is innocent until he *pleads* guilty	Note: A defendant is competent as witness to his own alibi, or to authenticate a document

V Admissibility of evidence

➤ There are 8 primary types of *in*admissible evidence:

1 At common law

- ➤ The common law discretion of a judge to prevent an unfair trial is preserved by *PACE s.82(3).*
- ➤ There is discretion to exclude evidence improperly obtained by the prosecution (*R. v. Sang* [1980] AC 402).
- ➤ Usually the discretion might be applied if the prejudicial effect on the jury of the evidence outweighs its true probative value.
- ➤ However, the discretion is very rarely exercised because as a *matter of law* much improperly obtained evidence is admissible. The following examples are admissible:
  - ◆ evidence from the illegal search of a person (*Kuruma, Son of Kariu v. The Queen* [1955] AC 197).
  - ◆ evidence obtained by an agent provocateur (*R. v. Sang* [1980] AC 402).

2 *PACE s.78*

➤ The court has a general discretion:

a) to exclude evidence, if an admission of the evidence 'would have such an adverse effect on the fairness of the proceedings that the court ought not to admit it' given all the circumstances, including how the evidence was obtained, *and*

b) to prevent cross-examination of a defendant as to his character even if the prosecution are permitted to do this under *CEA 1898 s.1(f)(i)-(ii).* Prejudice must be overwhelming to qualify for exclusion on this ground. This caveat does not apply to *s.1(f)(iii)* (*Selvey v. DPP* [1970] AC 304).

3 Irrelevant evidence

4 **Self-made evidence**

➤ A witness may not support his evidence at trial by introducing a statement he made on a previous occasion.

➤ This is inadmissible *unless* it involves:

a) previous exculpatory statements to the police, *or*

b) statements that come under *res gestae* - 'circumstances of spontaneity or involvement in the event', so there is no possibility of concoction or distortion (see '*res gestae*' on p.463), *or*

c) evidence that rebuts the suggestion that the witness has recently fabricated his testimony.

Admissible self-made evidence

5 **Privileged evidence**

➤ Privileged material is inadmissible and falls within these categories:

a) **legal professional privilege:** (eg: client-solicitor communications, or those with third parties, in contemplation of proceedings (*Parkins v. Hawkshaw* (1817) 2 Stark N.P. 239).

b) **against self-incrimination:** an answer which may lead to a criminal charge for a witness (*R. v. Garbett* (1847) 2 C&K 474, and *Evidence Act 1851 s.3*). However, this does not apply if a defendant elects to testify (*CEA 1898 s.1(e)*).

6 **Public interest immunity**

➤ Evidence that for reasons of public interest is inadmissible.

➤ Such reasons include:

- state interests (*D v. NSPCC* [1978] AC 171).
- details of the prevention, detection and investigation of crime, eg: identity of a police informant, unless this is necessary to prove a defendant's innocence (*R. v. Turner* [1995] 1 WLR 264).

7 **Similar fact evidence**

➤ This is evidence that the defendant has committed offences before, similar to the ones now before the court.

➤ This is inadmissible because:

a) the prejudice created by such evidence outweighs any probative value it may have (*DPP v. Kilbourne* [1973] AC 729), *and*

b) it is irrelevant, since irrespective of the number of similar crimes which have been committed, these crimes cannot connect a person with the crime in front of the court (*R. v. Miller* [1952] 2 All ER 667).

➤ However, if the prosecution can convince the judge/magistrates that in a particular case a) and b) are untrue *and* that the evidence is relevant, the judge/magistrates may rule that the similar fact evidence is admissible.

➤ An accused can *always* introduce similar evidence against a co-accused because the judge has no discretion to exclude it (*R. v. Miller* [1952] 2 All ER 667).

8 Hearsay evidence

➤ Hearsay is a statement made out of court, now being repeated in court, intended to prove the truth of the matter stated out of court.

➤ Hearsay evidence is inadmissible.

➤ The following are *prima facie* hearsay, but admissible anyway as exceptions to the rules of hearsay:

A. Documentary hearsay (*CJA 1988 ss.23-24*).

B. Written statements (usually a statement not in dispute) (*CJA 1967 s.9*).

C. *Res gestae.*

D. Opinion.

E. Confessions (*PACE s.76*).

F. Admissible self-made evidence (see no.4 on previous page).

A. Documentary hearsay - admissible

Witness statements	Business documents
First hand hearsay only (*CJA 1988 s.23*)	First hand and multiple hearsay (*CJA 1988 s.24*)
A statement in a DOCUMENT...	
...and the witness is unable to attend due to...	...and the document was...
a) death, bodily or mental condition, *or* b) not being present in the UK and his attendance is not reasonably practical, *or* c) he is untraceable despite reasonable efforts to find him, *or* d) i) the statement was made to: ◆ a police officer, *or* ◆ another under a duty to investigate offences or charge offenders, *and* ii) the witness is unavailable as he is fearful, *or* because he is being kept out of the way	a) created *or* received by a person in the course of a trade, business, profession, occupation, or office, *and* b) the information was supplied by a person having, or reasonably supposed to have had, personal knowledge of the matter (and each member of the chain between the original witness and the compiler of the document must be under a duty in a) above) NB: A document prepared for criminal proceedings or a criminal investigation is only admissible if either: a) the witness is not present due to: i) death, his bodily or mental condition, *or* ii) not being present in the UK and his attendance is not reasonably practical, *or* iii) he is untraceable despite reasonable efforts to find him *OR* b) i) the statement was made to: ◆ a police officer, *or* ◆ another under a duty to investigate offences or charge offenders, *and* ii) the witness is unavailable as he is fearful, *or* because he is being kept out of the way *OR* c) the maker of the statement cannot be expected to recall the information after such a lapse of time
Excluding hearsay 'in the interests of justice' (*CJA 1988 s.25*)	
➤ The court has discretion to exclude hearsay which would otherwise be admissible under *s.23 or s.24 if* its probative force is outweighed by the prejudice it might cause to a fair trial ➤ Prejudice might be caused because: ◆ a witness may not be cross-examined, *or* ◆ a witness is not liable for perjury if the evidence is fabricated	
When leave of the court is required (*CJA 1988 s.26*)	
If a statement under *s.23 or s.24* has been made for the purpose of criminal proceedings or a criminal investigation, leave of the court is needed to introduce it. Leave will be given if it is 'in the interests of justice'	

B. Written statements - admissible

➤ If:

a) the statement purports to be made by the signatory, *and*

b) there is a declaration that it is true to the best of the witness's knowledge and belief, and it was made in full knowledge of the danger of a prosecution for falsehood, *and*

c) a copy is served before any hearing on all parties *and* none object within 7 days of service,

... **then** these statements are admissible in trials (*CJA 1967 s.9(1)*).

s.9 statement (non-disputed evidence)

C. *Res gestae* (*Ratten v. R.* [1972] AC 378) - admissible

➤ *Res gestae* is:

- a statement by the doer of an act, which is related to the act and is contemporaneous with it.
- a spontaneous statement at the time of an event.
- a statement which was made at the time of an event, and which shows a state of mind, emotion or intention.
- an expression of physical sensation felt at the time.

➤ *Res gestae* is admissible if a judge can disregard the possibility that the statement was concocted or distorted (*R. v. Andrews (Donald)* [1987] AC 281).

➤ A classic example of *res gestae* is a dying declaration (*R. v. Mills* [1995] 3 All ER 865).

D. Opinion - admissible

➤ Opinion is admissible if *either*:

a) a witness recalls his personal perception at the time, *or*

b) the evidence is from an expert witness. The opinion must be pertinent to the expert's expertise.

- If an expert is present, all can see copies of his report.
- If an expert is absent, leave of court is required to admit an expert's report (*CJA 1988 s.30(2)*).

➤ **Magistrates' Court:** advance disclosure of an expert witness's evidence is compulsory (*MC(ANEE) R 1997*).

➤ **Crown Court:** advance disclosure of an expert witness's evidence is compulsory (*PACE s.81* and *Crown Court (Advance Notice of Expert Evidence) Rules 1987*). Leave of the court is needed if the evidence is not disclosed as soon as possible after committal according to *rule 5* of the *Crown Court (Advance Notice of Expert Evidence) Rules 1987*.

E. Confessions - admissible

i) Confessions generally

- A confession is:

  'any statement wholly or partly adverse to the person who made it, whether made to a person in authority or not and whether made in words or otherwise' (*PACE s.82(1)*).

- A part-confession is admissible in total. If there are periods of silence followed by periods of speaking, the whole is admissible.
- A confession implicating a co-defendant is:
  - admissible purely against the confessor.
  - hearsay against a co-defendant (*R. v. Rudd 32 Cr. App.R. 138*).

ii) Excluding confessions

- The following 3 points show ways to attempt to exclude a confession:
  1. *PACE s.76(2)*
     - A confession is inadmissible *unless* the prosecution show 'beyond reasonable doubt' that the confession was not obtained in one of the following two ways:
       - by **oppression** of the person who made it, *or*
       - in consequence of anything said or done which was likely, in the circumstances existing at the time, to render **unreliable** any confession which might be made by him in consequence thereof'.
     - **Oppression:** the Court of Appeal has defined this as the 'exercise of authority or power in a burdensome, harsh or wrongful manner; unjust or cruel treatment of subjects ... the imposition of unjust or unreasonable burdens' (*R. v. Fulling* [1987] QB 426). ('Oppression' includes 'torture, inhuman and degrading treatment and the use or threat of violence' (*PACE s.76(8)*).)
     - **Unreliability:** a breach of a *PACE* Code is, in itself, not sufficient. There must be a causal link between the breach and the unreliability. There is no need for any police misconduct to be shown.
  2. ***PACE s.78*** - see p.460
  3. **At common law** - see p.460

iii) The admission of evidence from an excluded confession

- Factual evidence gained from an excluded confession.
  - Facts are admissible (*PACE s.76(4)(a)*).
- Expression
  - A confession is admissible as evidence that the defendant writes, speaks or expresses himself in a certain way, irrespective of whether the confession itself is excluded (*PACE s.76(4)(b)*).

VI Inferences from silence at trial

➤ The following sections of the *CJPO 1994* can each adversly affect the defendant at trial.

s.35 CJPO 1994

The defendant (of any age) fails to give evidence at trial

Sub-procedure for *s.35*

➤ At the end of the prosecution case, *unless the legal representative of the defendant informs the court that the defendant will give evidence,* the judge will ensure that the defendant knows that inferences may be drawn from his refusal to testify

➤ In the Crown Court this procedure is covered by *Practice Direction (Crown Court: Defendant's Evidence)* [1995] 1 WLR 657.

s.34 CJPO 1994

Situation 1 - questioning before charge

a) The defendant had not yet been charged, *and*
b) was being questioned under caution by a constable, *and*
c) the constable was trying to discover whether, or by whom, an offence had been committed, *and*
d) the defendant failed to mention a fact he might reasonably be expected to mention at the time, *and*
e) **the defendant later (at trial) relies on that fact in his defence**

Situation 2 - questioning at time of charge

a) At the time that the defendant was charged or officially informed he might be prosecuted for an offence, *and*
b) the defendant failed to mention a fact he might reasonably be expected to mention at the time

YJCEA 1999 s.58 says that no inferences from silence are permissable where a defendant had no prior access to legal advice

s.37 CJPO 1994

a) At the time that the defendant was arrested, *and*
b) the defendant was at a place where a constable reasonably believed that the person's presence might be to do with participation in an offence, *and*
c) the constable reasonably believed that the presence of the defendant at that time and place could be attributed to the defendant participating in a specified offence, *and*
d) the constable informed the defendant of his suspicions and asked him to account for his presence, *and*
e) the defendant failed or refused to provide an explanation

s.36 CJPO 1994

a) The defendant was arrested, *and*
b) with an object, substance or mark:
   i) on his person, *or*
   ii) in or on his clothing or footwear, *or*
   iii) in his possession, *or*
   iv) in any place in which he was at the time of his arrest, *and*
c) the constable reasonably believed that the object, substance or mark had something to do with the defendant participating in a specified offence, *and*
d) the constable informed the defendant of his suspicions and asked him to account for the object, substance or mark, *and*
e) the defendant failed or refused to provide an explanation

The right to silence and the inroads into it is one area likely to be of great contention under *HRA 1998*

Consequences of an adverse inference of silence

➤ In the Crown Court, arguments about the admissibility of the defendant's silence when previously being interviewed (ie: any case above apart from *s.35*) take place in the absence of the jury.
- The judge decides on admissibility and the jury decides whether inferences may be drawn.

➤ In the Magistrates' Court, the magistrates decide everything.

➤ The magistrates or jury can 'draw such inferences as appear proper' from the silence as applied to:
1. a submission of 'no case to answer' in a trial (see p.428 and p.437).
2. determining the guilt or innocence of a defendant at trial.

Note: such inferences must *not* decide the matter alone - there must be other factors too (*CJPO 1994 s.38*).

➤ The defence needs to introduce evidence in order to put forward a 'good reason' for the defendant's silence, so as to avoid the 'adverse inferences' from the silence (*R. v. Cowan; Gayle; Ricciardi* [1995] 3 WLR 818 CA).
- This case also shows that *s.35* is not only meant to be invoked in exceptional cases.

Phonelist and Index

Organisation	Telephone
A	
Attorney General	020 7219 3000
B	
Bar Council	020 7242 0082
Baker & McKenzie	020 7919 1000
Benefits Agency	0800 666 555
Blackstone Press Limited	020 8740 2277
British Standards Institution	020 8996 9000
C	
Certificated Bailiffs	
Jefferies & Pennicott	020 8877 1945
Chambers (London sets of high repute)	
(Crime), 3 Raymond Buidlings	020 7831 3833
(Company), Erskine Chambers	020 7242 5532
(Chancery, Commercial), 13 Old Square	020 7242 6105
(Commercial, Employment), 11 King's Bench Walk	020 7583 0610
(Property), Falcon Chambers	020 7353 2484
(Taxation), Gray's Inn Chambers	020 7242 2642
Charity Commission	020 7210 4477
Clifford Chance LLP	020 7600 1000
Companies House	
Birmingham	0121 233 9047
Cardiff	02920 388 588
Edinburgh	0131 535 5800
London	0207 253 9393
Leeds	0113 233 8338
Manchester	0161 236 7500
County Courts	
Central London	0207 917 5000
Ipswich	01473 214 256
Leeds	0113 283 0040
Plymouth	01752 674 808
West London	020 7602 8444
York	01904 629935
Court of Protection	020 7269 7000
Crown Prosecution Service	020 7273 8000
D	
DHL (Couriers)	08457100 300
E	
Employment Appeals Tribunal	020 7273 1041
Enquiry Agents, Process Servers	
Thames Law	01474 702 006
Equal Opportunities Commission	020 8833 9244
European Commission	020 7973 1992
Eurostar	01233 617 575
F	
Financial Services Authority	0845 606 1234
G	
Government Departments of State	
Defence	020 7218 9000
Education and Employment	020 7273 3000
Environment	020 7276 0900
Health	020 7210 4850
Home Office	020 7273 3000
Lord Chancellor	020 7210 8500
Social Security	020 7210 5983
Trade and Industry (DTI)	020 7215 5000
Treasury	020 7270 5000
H	
High Court (London)	
General	020 7936 6000
Clerk of the Lists	020 7936 6021
Family Division, Probate Registry	020 7936 6569
Funds Office	020 7936 6016
Crown Office (for Judicial Review)	020 7936 6653
Masters' Secretaries, Ch. Division	020 7936 6095
Masters' Secretaries, QB Division	020 7936 6474
Winding up petitions	020 7936 7328
Health and Safety Executive	020 7717 6000
HM Customs & Excise	
General	020 7202 4227
VAT Registration	08457 112 114

Organisation	Telephone
HMSO	
Books	020 7873 0011
British Standards Hotline	020 7404 1213
House of Commons	020 7219 4272
House of Lords	020 7219 3000
I	
Inland Revenue	
Capital Taxes Office	0115 974 2400
Financial Intermediaries and Claims Office	0151 472 6000
Technical Division	020 7438 6622
J	
K	
L	
Land Charges Department	01752 635 635
Land Registry, Central London	020 7917 8888
Law Society	020 7242 1222
Legal Aid Commision	020 7813 1000
London Gazette	020 7873 8300
M	
N	
O	
Office of Fair Trading	020 7242 2858
Official Receiver	020 7637 1110
Official Solicitor	020 7911 7127
OYEZ Stationery Group	01908 371 111
P	
Parcelforce	0800 224 446
Prison Department	0208 317 2436
Probation Service (Head Office, SE London)	0208 464 3430
Public Prosecutions, Director of (DPP)	0207 273 3000
Public Record Office	0208 876 3444
Q	
R	
Royal Mail	0845 7 95 09 50
S	
Samaritans	08457909090
Stamp Office (Worthing)	01903 700 222
Stock Exchange	020 7588 2358
T	
Trains	0845 7 48 49 50
U- Z	

Key Number (for telephoning HM Land Registry/Land Charges Department) ....

Account Number (for telephoning Companies House) ....

Account Number (for telephoning the Law Society Library) ....

The organisations selected for inclusion in this directory have been chosen in the belief that readers may find them useful. Neither the authors, nor the publishers have received payment for inclusion. No warranty, representation or assurance is given in relation to any of the organisations listed.

Notes

PRISONER COMPENSATION
ABELL HOUSE
JOHN ISLIP ST
LONDON
SW1P 4LH.

Index

Subject	Page

U

Subject	Page